DESIGN AND STRATEGY
FOR DISTRIBUTED
DATA PROCESSING

A  BOOK

TOP MANAGEMENT
COMPREHENSION
AND COMMITMENT

APPOINTMENT
OF A CORPORATE
DATA STRATEGIST

CORPORATE STRATEGY FOR DATA BASES

Establishment of organizationwide data base standards.

Adoption of organizationwide data description language.

Selection of data base management software

Data dictionary selection and establishment.

Establishment of design procedures.

CORPORATE STRATEGY FOR DISTRIBUTED PROCESSING

Establishment of an organizationwide standard for DDP.

Establishment of areas of control for DDP.

Determination of how data should be distributed and interlinked

Determination of end user methodologies and strategy.

SELECTION OF A
DATA BASE
ADMINISTRATOR

SELECTION OF
DATA BASE INQUIRY
FACILITIES.
QUERY LANGUAGES,
REPORT GENERATORS,
DIALOGUE GENERATORS

END USER
PROGRAMMING
LANGUAGES

TOP DOWN PLANNING

Determination of what subject data bases are needed.

Identification of data structures including files.

Determination of geographical location and data structures.

Mapping data structures against application and processes.

THOROUGH TRAINING
IN DATA ANALYSIS,
CANONICAL SYNTHESIS
& LOGICAL DESIGN

END USER TRAINING

END
USER
QUERIES

ESTABLISHMENT OF A
CONVERSION STRATEGY
TO ALLOW NON-DATA-BASE
SYSTEMS TO COEXIST
UNCHANGED WITH THE
NEW DATA BASE SYSTEMS

ON-LINE
DATA
ENTRY

INITIATION OF
DATA BASE USAGE

SELECTION OF
A SEED PROJECT

PLANNED EDUCATION
AND EXPERIENCE
DISSEMINATION FROM
THE SEED PROJECT

A PLANNED SEQUENCE OF
PROJECTS FOR DATA
BASE EVOLUTION

BOTTOM-UP DESIGN

Data analysis.

Dictionary Building.

Canonical Analysis.

Schema Representation.

Usage path analysis.
Physical design.

Design of
a stable
logical
model of
each subject
data base.

DEVELOPMENT OF
PRODUCTION
SYSTEMS

CREATION OF
SUBJECT DATA BASES

PHYSICAL DESIGN FOR
OPTIMUM PERFORMANCE

ACCURACY
CONTROLS

DATA ENTRY BY
END USER DEPARTMENTS
DATA CAPTURE AT
SOURCE

INFORMATION
QUALITY CONTROLS

SECURITY AND
PRIVACY CONTROLS

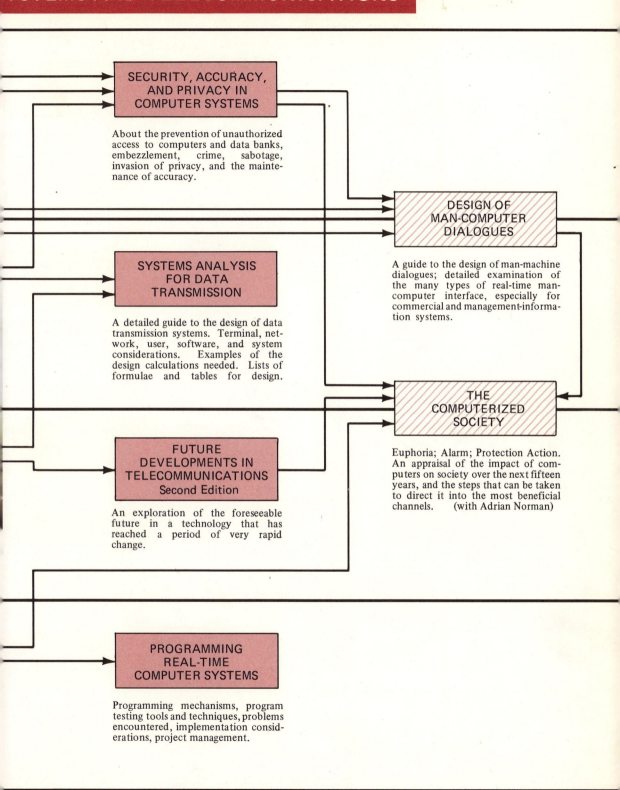

SECURITY, ACCURACY, AND PRIVACY IN COMPUTER SYSTEMS

About the prevention of unauthorized access to computers and data banks, embezzlement, crime, sabotage, invasion of privacy, and the maintenance of accuracy.

DESIGN OF MAN-COMPUTER DIALOGUES

A guide to the design of man-machine dialogues; detailed examination of the many types of real-time man-computer interface, especially for commercial and management-information systems.

SYSTEMS ANALYSIS FOR DATA TRANSMISSION

A detailed guide to the design of data transmission systems. Terminal, network, user, software, and system considerations. Examples of the design calculations needed. Lists of formulae and tables for design.

THE COMPUTERIZED SOCIETY

Euphoria; Alarm; Protection Action. An appraisal of the impact of computers on society over the next fifteen years, and the steps that can be taken to direct it into the most beneficial channels. (with Adrian Norman)

FUTURE DEVELOPMENTS IN TELECOMMUNICATIONS Second Edition

An exploration of the foreseeable future in a technology that has reached a period of very rapid change.

PROGRAMMING REAL-TIME COMPUTER SYSTEMS

Programming mechanisms, program testing tools and techniques, problems encountered, implementation considerations, project management.

CORPORATE STRATEGY
FOR NETWORKS

Establishment of an organizationwide
strategy for networking.

Determination of networking
architecture(s).

Design of a stage-by-stage network
development plan.

DESIRABLE COMPUTER
INDUSTRY DEVELOPMENTS

MORE FLEXIBLE DATA BASE
MANAGEMENT SYSTEMS (RELATIONAL?)

FULLY FLEXIBLE
NETWORK
FACILITIES

STANDARDS FOR DATA
DESCRIPTION

BETTER DATA BASE PERFORMANCE

LAYERED
ARCHITECTURES
FOR DISTRIBUTED
PROCESSING

IMPROVED DATA SEARCHING
CAPABILITIES

NETWORK DESIGN
AND IMPLEMENTATION

DEVELOPMENT OF
A SEARCH ENGINE

EXAMINATION OF
DISTRIBUTED FILE &
DISTRIBUTED INTELLIGENCE
REQUIREMENTS

INDUSTRY STANDARDS
FOR COMPUTER
NETWROKS AND DDP
INTERFACES

DATA BASE MANAGEMENT
SYSTEMS IN HARDWARE

ELECTION OF
ISTRIBUTED DATA
ASE ADMINISTRATOR

HIGHER LEVEL DATA
BASE LANGUAGES

DISTRIBUTED
DATA BASE
MANAGEMENT

SELECTION OF TOOLS
FOR DESIGN OF
DISTRIBUTED DATA

AIDS TO DATA BASE
MONITORING AND TRAINING

DISTRIBUTED END
USER FACILITIES

SELF-OPTIMIZING
DATA BASE
ORGANIZATION

ND USER
ENERATION
F REPORTS

AUTOMATED DESIGN OF
DISTRIBUTED DATA BASE
SYSTEMS

IMPROVED COMMON
CARRIER NETWORKING
FACILITIES

DIRECT END-USER
APPLICATION DEVELOPMENT
DEVELOPMENT

WIDESPREAD END USER
EMPLOYMENT OF
EXISTING DATA BASES

DEVELOPMENT OF
FUNCTIONAL INFORMATION
SYSTEMS

SEPARATION OF
INFORMATION
SYSTEMS AND
PRODUCTION SYSTEMS

LESSENING
OF SCHEDULING
PROBLEMS

DEVELOPMENT OF
DISTRIBUTED FILE
AND DATA BASE
FACILITIES

CORPORATE INFORMATION
SYSTEM NETWORK

DESIGN AND

STRATEGY FOR DISTRIBUTED DATA PROCESSING

JAMES MARTIN

PRENTICE–HALL, INC., Englewood Cliffs, New Jersey 07632

Library of Congress Cataloging in Publication Data

Martin, James, (date)
Design and strategy for distributed data processing.

"A James Martin book."
Includes index.
1. Electronic data processing—Distributed processing.
I. Title.
QA76.9.D5M386   001.64   81-5917
ISBN 0-13-201657-5   AACR2

Design and Strategy
for Distributed Data Processing
James Martin

Editorial/Production Supervision: *Lynn S. Frankel*
Cover Design: *Mark A. Binn*
Jacket Photograph: *Carl Fischer* (*Courtesy of
   Western Electric Company*)
Manufacturing Buyer: *Gordon Osbourne*

Printed in the United States of America

10 9 8 7 6 5 4 3 2 1

PRENTICE-HALL INTERNATIONAL, INC., *London*
PRENTICE-HALL OF AUSTRALIA PTY. LIMITED, *Sydney*
PRENTICE-HALL OF CANADA, LTD., *Toronto*
PRENTICE-HALL OF INDIA PRIVATE LIMITED, *New Delhi*
PRENTICE-HALL OF JAPAN, INC., *Tokyo*
PRENTICE-HALL OF SOUTHEAST ASIA PTE. LTD., *Singapore*
WHITEHALL BOOKS LIMITED, *Wellington, New Zealand*

TO CORINTHIA

CONTENTS

PART **III**   **STRATEGY**

PART **IV**   **DESIGN OF DISTRIBUTED DATA**

PREFACE

The key to success in any enterprise is good design and strategy. This is important for the management of distributed processing. The technology of distributed processing is complex and requires a clear understanding to prevent a formula for chaos.

Distributed processing is *not* a new buzzword designed to increase the attendance at seminars or the sale of books. It has been described as inevitable as the leaves appearing on a tree in spring, and just as useful!

In this book we shall describe a clear strategy for and illustrate the techniques of good design. The benefits of distributed processing are many; the pitfalls are great.

Many factors are contributing to distributed processing and the rate of change is dramatic. Soon it will be necessary for every DP professional including senior management to be fully aware of the technology and how it can be applied. It is essential that management develop a concise strategy which identifies the implementation, if applicable, the choices and commitment for distributed processing. The impact of distributed processing in such areas as office of the future and comparison with centralized processing are discussed.

In the last section of the book, important issues such as security and auditing of distributed processing are reviewed, with recommendations proposed to deal with these sensitive areas.

Distributed processing is here to stay and will change the way hardware and software are implemented. Readers might also be interested in the author's companion book, *Computer Networks and Distributed Processing,* which deals with networks and how to connect machines together.

James Martin

**DESIGN AND STRATEGY
FOR DISTRIBUTED
DATA PROCESSING**

A *James Martin* BOOK

PART **I** POTENTIAL

1 THE REVOLUTIONARY CHANGE
IN DATA PROCESSING
"MIRACLE CHIPS"— TIME MAGAZINE

A revolution is taking place in data processing—again.

Soon after chess-playing machines began to appear in stores, a friend showed me one he had just bought. It was one of several such machines on the market, about the size of a large pocket calculator. It could be set to play at one of six levels of skill. At level 1 it was easy to beat; at level 3 quite difficult; at level 6 it took 24 hours to make each move, blinking its lights menacingly all the while.

Since neither of us could be considered the world's greatest chess player, we decided to tackle the machine jointly. We began after dinner, playing level 3. The machine took about 20 seconds to make each move and longer when we got it worried. In deciding on our moves we took a minute or more debating the alternatives and pointing out dangers to one another. Many hours and half a bottle of Scotch later, the sinister gadget beat us.

The point of this story is that three years previously a game like that would have required one of the world's largest computers. Logic circuitry has been dropping in cost at a phenomenal rate and will continue to do so for the next decade or more. Many programs that require the world's largest computers today will run on small computers three years from now. If there is a large enough market for them, they can be put on sale at low cost, like chess-playing machines.

This breathtaking change in technology is plunging the data-processing community into an era of revolution, in which the methods of the past are no longer necessarily the right methods. From now on all data-processing managers and analysts have to consider the extent to which they will use *distributed data processing*.

Until the mid-1970's most computing was carried out by systems employing a large, centralized computer. The *central processing unit* (CPU) had a diverse collection of relatively simple machines attached to it, some of them connected via telecommunications links. For certain applications networks were built in which large numbers of simple terminals were connected to a central computer system. Sometimes the central computer system had two processors for reasons of reliability, but the processing of each transaction was done by one large computer.

The 1970's brought the era of minicomputers, and later microcomputers. With LSI (large-scale integration) circuits the cost of building a processor dropped steadily until it became clear that one computer system could be comprised of many processors if this were useful. At the same time there was a change in the perception of how computers should be used. The concept of an isolated, factorylike machine room processing batches of data for many users gave way to users wanting their own terminals and processing capability. In some cases the users' local processing machines were connected to a distant, larger machine which maintained a data base and provided extra processing power if needed.

By the mid-1970's requirements for a new type of system architecture had become clear. A new generation must provide a stable foundation for on-line, transaction-driven data-base applications. Unlike architecture designed for batch processing, it must be highly reliable because on-line users become very frustrated if their system has frequent periods of failure. It must meet a diverse range of processing requirements. Furthermore, as technology is changing very rapidly, the architecture must facilitate the introduction of new technology without a major system disruption.

Most important, a very high proportion of people must be able to use the machines. One major study indicated that by 1985, 70% of the U.S. working force would work with computers for at least some portion of their work activity. Most of these people would not have programming skills, nor should we expect them to be able to remember mnemonics or fixed sequences of input, as many of today's operators do.

Computing, then, must change its image. It must be regarded as a communications medium, in the same sense that television, newspapers, telephone directories, and shopping catalogs are communications media. Electronic information systems are a more powerful and flexible communications medium than any of the above, increasingly vital to industry and office work everywhere.

To meet these requirements microcomputers (like the chess-playing machine), minicomputers, and large computers will all play a part. The new and difficult question is, What mix of these will provide the most effective computer resources?

New computer systems are likely to interconnect many processors, large and small. They will often be interconnected over large distances with computer networks. The term *distributed processing* implies multiple processors, usually interconnected by telecommunications.

The main promise of microprocessors and minicomputers is that they will bring computing power to vast numbers of end users. In doing so they compete with the use of terminals connected to traditional data-processing systems. Who wants to use a terminal or time-sharing service to do a job that could be done on one's own pocket calculator? However, in most of its uses a computer does not compete with a pocket calculator. It collects and disseminates information. The question of where the information should be *stored* is as important as where it should be *processed*.

Where and in what form should data be stored? How should the stored data be structured? How should they be accessed? These questions are critical to the overall design of distributed data processing.

Data for such systems can be well designed or badly designed. We will identify the properties of good design. On many working systems the data design has been badly done, and this will have a very damaging effect.

MACHINE COSTS   The major driving force toward distributed processing is the cost of small processors. Until the spread of mini-computers in the early 1970's, a commonly accepted rule was Grosch's Law, which said that the cost per machine instruction executed was inversely proportional to the square of the size of the machine. Economies of scale in computing led to centralization. All work became funnelled into centralized, factorylike data-processing shops.

Grosch's Law came to be questioned in the 1970's. Some suggested that it had become reversed because the cost per instruction on some minicomputers was much lower than on the larger computers, and on microprocessors it was much lower than on minicomputers. This is a somewhat unfair comparison because the large computer has a richer instruction set. It has expensive instructions such as floating-point arithmetic and variable-length data moves. However, most of the processing of commercial transactions can be done on the smaller machine without floating-point arithmetic or other complex instructions.

Suppose that an application program requires only 8-bit arithmetic. The microcomputers on sale for not many dollars from the corner electronics stores can execute it, and the cost per instruction is a thousand times lower than on large computers.

Applications which do not require complex instruction sets can be executed on microcomputers much more cheaply than on large computers. On the other hand, a highly complex application requiring 64-bit floating-point arithmetic and lengthy data moves would be complex and expensive to do on a small computer with a limited instruction set. It would be cheaper if it occupied a small share of a large machine.

Figure 1.1 illustrates this in principle. It shows a simple application becoming more expensive as the machine cost increases but the reverse being true with a complex application.

Many bread-and-butter commercial applications—the preparing of invoices, control of inventory, order processing, and so on—can run satisfactorily on a small machine. Furthermore, the instruction sets of microcomputers are rapidly becoming more elaborate. Already there are 16-bit micros, and before long there will be 32-bit micros. We might say as in the Maurice Chevalier song, "little machines get bigger every day."

The reason for the growth of microcomputers is the use of VLSI (very-large-

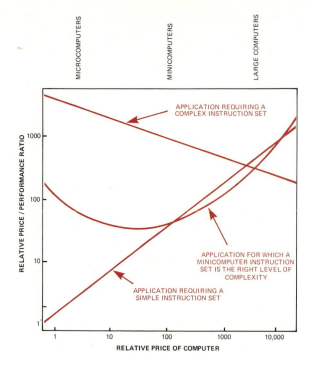

Figure 1.1 Most bread-and-butter commercial applications do not need the instruction set of a large computer; they run much more cheaply on a small computer.

scale integration) circuits which can be mass-produced like newsprint. Not only can small machines be mass-produced, but also their development cycle is much shorter than that of large machines. Therefore they tend to have later technology which is cheaper because the technology is dropping in cost so rapidly. The price/performance ratio on all computers will drop greatly throughout the next ten years, but it will drop much more rapidly on tiny, mass-produced machines than on machines costing hundreds of thousands of dollars.

MICROELECTRONICS   Microcomputers and memory are dropping in cost because the number of components per chip is increasing in microelectronic circuits.

Figure 1.2 shows the increase in the number of electronic components in an integrated circuit. Since the production of the planar transistor in 1959, the number has been doubling every year. The curve in Fig. 1.2 was predicted in 1964 by the director of research at Fairchild Semiconductor, Gordon Moore, and became known as Moore's Law. There are no signs in the research laboratories that this

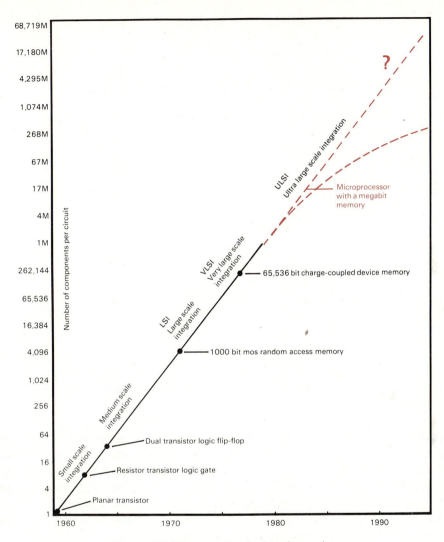

Figure 1.2   The growth of microelectronics.

growth will soon slow, although eventually it must. The technology is far from the fundamental limits imposed by physics. New production techniques will be able to put far more components onto the same surface area, and the surface area of one chip will increase.

The dotted curve in Fig. 1.2 applies Moore's Law to the future. Whether it happens as rapidly as indicated here depends on economics rather than on basic physics. It appears technically possible to climb Moore's curve for at least another 15 years. Individual components will become much smaller as the industry moves from optical etching of chips to electron beam etching (like an electron microscope) and then to X-ray etching. The yield (i.e., proportion of chips without defects) will increase as the industry swings from liquid etching to dry plasma etching and to automated manufacturing under computer control in a controlled atmosphere. As the yield increases, it will be economical to have chips of larger area. Today a silicon wafer about 10 centimeters in diameter is etched and diced into individual chips a few millimeters in diameter. If there were fewer defects, the wafer could be diced into larger chips with the same proportion of defective chips. With very few defects the wafer would not have to be diced; circuitry could be devised to use most of the wafer, automatically circumventing defective portions. In the future, the surface area of chips will increase because there will be fewer defective elements, and the packing density will increase. Integrated wafers with 100 times today's packing density will eventually be made, and chips with 10 times today's area will be made. This gives 1000 times as many components on a chip as today. Computers as complex as an IBM 370, though not as fast as a large 370, will occupy a single chip.

It is likely that before the mid-1980's we will have microcomputers on a chip with 1 million bits of memory.

In addition to conventional semiconductors, magnetic bubble memories and, later, bubble lattice memories will give relatively cheap solid-state storage which does not lose its contents when the electricity is switched off. Microprocessors brought a revolution in the potential application of electronics. We are on the threshold of another revolution: *microfiles*. Today's magnetic bubble products store about 1 million bits per square inch. Future bubble products will store 100 million bits per square inch. Before the end of the 1980's pocket devices may store 10 million bytes.

The potential user population will grow gigantically. A large number of people will have programmable machines with substantial memory. Pocket calculators will have alphanumeric displays so that users can carry out dialogues with programs. This will enormously extend the range and variety of programs that people find useful. Hobby and amateur use of computers will take on innumerable different forms. The home television set in some countries will become a major interactive information medium with schemes like Viewdata [1]. Every store and restaurant will need financial terminals for credit checking, check validation, and possibly electronic fund transfer. Electronic mail will spread. Children of all ages will use electronic teaching facilities. Business people, sales people, scientists, maintenance staff—all will need their terminals and pocket machines.

It will be important that these machines be able to access the data networks of the world cheaply. The main form of access will be via local telephone lines. It is desirable that the user machines be able to plug into the home or office telephone plug, dial a local telephone number and be connected to a data network which gives a cost per message transmitted in keeping with the cost of the technology. Both Viewdata and networks using the international CCITT X.25 Recommendation (described later) promise to make this possible; they also promise a suitably low cost for the small user with a very low traffic volume.

SOFTWARE PATH LENGTH   The impact of microelectronics is spectacular, but in comparing the costs of large and small computers *software* is often a more important factor than hardware.

The operating system of a large computer is very complex, and for each transaction many *software* instructions must be executed in addition to the *application* instructions. The number of software instructions executed for a transaction is referred to as the software *path length*. A typical inexpensive minicomputer handling one transaction at a time and reading and writing file records in a simple, direct fashion often has a software path length of less than 2000 instructions. On a large computer with a virtual operating system and elaborate data-base datacommunications facilities, the path length is often greater than 100,000 or even 200,000 instructions.

The application programs for most commercial jobs execute a fairly small number of instructions per transaction, often less than 1000. The total number of instructions executed per transaction in a large computer can therefore be 50 or more times that in a simple minicomputer.

The user gains many benefits from the complex software of large computers, but the cost in terms of instructions executed is high.

One might ask why the software for big machines is so complex. One reason is the complexity of many transactions sharing the same processor. Another reason is that the software is highly generalized to be suitable for so many different types of processing. Still another reason is that it has to be compatible with so much that has been done in the past; in contrast, software for new, small machines is often cleanly thought out and simple.

There are other advantages of small machines, listed in Box 1.1. Being

BOX 1.1   Increasingly, there are advantages in using small, cheap computers for many applications.

Advantages of Small Computers

- Lower cost per instruction for simple applications (Fig. 1.1)
- Higher availability (longer mean time between failures)
- Simple software support; therefore no sophisticated and expensive software staff needed
- Much lower software path length
- Less training needed

continued

BOX 1.1 *continued*

- Program testing is simpler
- No air conditioning, no false floors, etc.
- Low installation costs
- Finer granularity of growth increments (when multiple machines are used)
- More economical to do a pilot version

Advantages of Large Computers

- More elaborate instruction set (when needed)
- Larger main memory (when needed)
- Can be shared by many uses (when needed)
- Data-base management systems (when needed)
- Powerful software

simpler, they fail less often. The staff they require is less specialized and easier to find. They can be installed simply, with no air conditioning, no false floors, etc. As the load expands, they can be added to in smaller increments.

These advantages have to be traded off against the different advantages of large machines. Often the best systems design uses both large and small machines linked into a distributed configuration.

THE NATURE OF TELEPROCESSING

Formerly the term *teleprocessing* was used to imply the use of telecommunications facilities for accessing processing power. When calculators and minicomputers are cheap, however, what was originally done by terminals and teleprocessing can be done on the local machine. The local machine may itself be connected by telecommunications to other machines, and a transaction may then be processed either on the local machine or on a distant one.

There are two main reasons why a transaction is sent to a distant machine. First, the local machine has *insufficient power;* the transaction may need the number-crunching power of a large machine. Second, the transaction needs *data* which are stored elsewhere. Most commercial transactions—the bread and butter of data processing—do not need much computer power. Today's "intelligent" terminals or controllers to which dumb terminals are connected are sufficient to process them. *Therefore the main reason for teleprocessing in commercial data processing will be to obtain data, not to obtain processing power.* The advent of microprocessors has changed the nature of teleprocessing.

DISTRIBUTED DATA   The location and design of data are particularly important in distributed systems.

Some of the data are used by multiple locations, and often it is desirable to access the data by data-base management systems which permit multiple users to have different views of the same data. Furthermore, the economies of scale in storage systems are different from those in processors. The cost per bit stored on very large storage units is orders of magnitude lower than on small storage units.

There are many problems associated with geographically dispersed data. Among them are integrity problems, ownership problems, and deadlocks which can arise when multiple processors update the same data.

In addition to economies of scale there are powerful reasons for centralizing some data. It may be necessary to provide geographically dispersed users with access to the same up-to-the-minute data, and *data-base* software (which is discussed later) may be used.

SUMMARY   The pattern of future data processing, then, is a proliferation of machines, most of which are connected by telecommunications. Many are small, cheap computers. However, the minicomputers will not *replace* large computers. There remain vital reasons for centralizing some functions and some data. As large machines become increasingly the focal points of distributed-processing data-base networks, much more powerful computers than today's will be needed.

The task of system designers is to decide what distribution of machines will best serve the corporation, what links between them are needed, and where their data will reside. This environment raises fundamental new management questions about who should design and control distributed processing and how corporate management can take advantage of it.

Boxes 1.2 and 1.3 list primary and secondary objectives of distributed systems.

BOX 1.2 Primary objectives of distributed processing

- **Local Autonomy**
  Give local user groups a predetermined degree of local autonomy in computing.

- **Decentralized Operations and Centralized Control**
  Permit decentralized data-processing operations enhanced by centralized services and data bases, with varying degrees of centralized control.

- **End-User Productivity**
  Give end users techniques and languages which provide them the maximum productivity in using computer systems.

- **Application Development by User Groups**
  Provide an infrastructure which enables end-user groups to develop their own applications in an easy, flexible manner, with controls to ensure avoidance of compatibility problems.

- **Appealing Terminal Dialogues**
  Make terminals as easy to use and appealing as possible with powerful dialogue structures taking advantage of distributed intelligence.

- **Access to Remote Resources and Data**
  Enable users of local processors (including very small processors) to employ a rich array of useful resources in different locations, including programs and data.

- **Make Distance Transparent**
  Make the effects of distance as transparent as possible by means of appropriately designed networks.

- **Availability**
  Do not allow failures to be visible to the end user. Maximize the availability of the user's system interface.

- **Privacy and Security**
  Prevent unauthorized access to data and resources. Protect data from failures and catastrophes and from criminals, vandals, incompetents, and persons who might falsely update them.

- **Auditability**
  Ensure that the updating of critical records, especially financial ones, can be fully audited.

- **Accuracy and Consistency**
  Use accuracy controls on all input. Avoid having multiple versions of the same data available to users in different stages of updating.

BOX 1.2 *continued*

- **Ease of Change**
  Recognize that distributed systems will constantly grow and change, and permit this evolution to occur without disruption and expense.

- **Protection of Intellectual Investment**
  Existing programs and logical data structures (representing many man-years) will not have to be redone when changes are made to the system or to other programs.

- **Concealment of Complexities**
  Hide the complexities from the users as completely as possible.

BOX 1.3 Secondary, more technical, objectives needed to achieve the primary objectives

- **Utilization of Minis and Micros**
  Enable microcomputers, minicomputers, and large computers to be interconnected into the *most cost-effective* systems.

- **Data-Base Techniques**
  Use data-base techniques to ensure that the same data can be employed in fully flexible ways by multiple users.

- **Corporation-wide Network**
  Use a network planned on a corporation-wide scale for carrying data, mail, and possibly voice and other traffic.

- **Flexible Network Structure**
  Use a network structure giving high flexibility in adding nodes and circuits, which handles both terminal traffic and computer-to-computer traffic.

- **Standard Line Control**
  Use standard line-control procedures for attaching terminals and for interconnecting computers. Where possible an efficient, bit-oriented protocol such as HDLC should be used.

continued

BOX 1.3 *continued*

- **Standard Network Architectures**

  Use corporate standards for network architectures and interfaces to the network, so that the various machines used can be interconnected at high-level architectural layers.

- **Layered Architectures**

  Employ layered architectures for the interconnection of machines so that new functions can be added or changes made to one layer without changing others.

- **Virtual Terminals**

  Employ virtual terminal, logical units and virtual display space standards so that when terminals or user machines are changed the programs using them do not have to be rewritten.

- **Cryptography**

  Use cryptography where tight security of transmission is needed.

- **Security**

  Use tight security techniques where needed.

- **Auditability**

  Use tools for auditors which make the system easy to audit.

- **High-Level Languages**

  Use high-level languages, especially for end users, to achieve the maximum flexibility of access to data and the maximum productivity of application development.

- **Data Dictionary**

  Use a data dictionary to ensure compatibility of fields, records, and data structures used in distributed storage units.

- **Corporate Strategy**

  Develop a corporation-wide DP strategy which includes three substrategies: distributed data processing, data base, and corporate networks. Develop management structures for implementing the strategies which include the following:

- **Distributed System Administration**

  To ensure that the dispersed systems are interconnectable and work together as well as possible.

BOX 1.3 *continued*

- **Distributed Data Administration**
  To assist distributed-data designers in designing appropriate data structures, to ensure compatibility between the data in separate machines, and to document this with a data dictionary.

- **Corporate Network Administration**
  To ensure that appropriate networks are developed and used on a corporation-wide basis.

REFERENCES

1. James Martin & David Butler, *Viewdata, A Social Revolution?* Prentice-Hall, Inc., Englewood Cliffs, N.J. 1981.

2 THE IMPACT OF DISTRIBUTED PROCESSING ON ORGANIZATIONS

INTRODUCTION   Given Moore's Law (Fig. 1.2), the spread of small computers will continue at a furious pace. If Moore's Law continues to be true for the next ten years, we have a wild decade ahead.

The small machines are a revolutionary challenge to the concept of totally centralized data processing. Distributed processing will spread to every nook and cranny of corporations. It is as inevitable as the budding of trees in spring.

We refer to distributed data processing with the initials DDP. As we will discuss in Chapter 4, DDP can take many different forms. A vital task for corporate management is to decide which of these forms will be most beneficial.

A theme of this book is that, used well, DDP offers great opportunities for better management of organizations. There is no question that it will have a major impact on the running of corporations throughout the 1980's. On the other hand, it is only too easy to make a mess of DDP, and one can see that happening in some organizations. There are major pitfalls in the spread of DDP which need to be avoided. DDP needs to be understood, *designed,* and *managed.* There is a great danger that the distributed machines will spread in an uncontrolled *ad hoc* fashion. The difference between *ad hoc* DDP and *designed* DDP is like that between night and day.

POWER TO END   A major objective of DDP should be to improve and
USERS   expand the way computers are employed by end users.

The term "end user" appears repeatedly throughout this book. By it we mean a person whose work is assisted by using computers, such as an accountant, shop foreman, bank teller, scientist, manager, professional, or head office staff. We do not mean an application programmer because he is not the ultimate beneficiary of computing.

DDP can bring logic, data storage, or computing power to the end-user loca-

16

tion and by doing so can decrease staff, enable work to be done more efficiently, or permit end-user management more authority and responsibility.

The change may be merely a technical one. The end user has better terminals, better data available for use, access to more remote computing resources, or minicomputers which serve user needs better.

Often, however, the change is more fundamental. The user department is drawn into the computing world instead of merely being a passive recipient of its service. The user department may have its own minicomputers or desk-top computers. Some users may learn to program. They may have intelligent terminals or peripheral computers with which they can generate their own reports from a corporate data base and answer questions not anticipated by the systems analysts in the central DP group. They may have facilities to create their own computer applications without being professional programmers (discussed in Chapters 10 and 11). They may learn to specify the data they need for their job and be involved in creating it. User departments may become responsible for entering and maintaining the data they use. In one way or another they take an active part in data processing.

THE END-USER
REBELLION
End users everywhere are becoming more aware of what computing can do for them. This awareness began to spread during the second half of the 1970's. Users began to see terminals obtaining data of different types. For the first time they had a window into the data-processing systems. They began to understand what information was stored. Their imaginations began to tell them how information from the computers could be useful to them.

At the same time general education about computing was growing. Programming was being taught in schools. The business schools had become DP oriented. Hobby computing was spreading like wildfire. The salesmen of minicomputers and desk-top computers were bypassing the DP department and banging on the doors of end users.

Many end-user departments became dissatisfied with the service they were receiving from the central DP organization. They asked for applications and were told there would be a long wait, sometimes years. The applications that were programmed for them often had scheduling problems. They could not gain access to the computer when they wanted it, because of breakdowns, line failures, or more often scheduling. The terminal dialogues they were given were sometimes crude, with poor response times. Sometimes they found the dialogues unusable. Often there was no on-line operation. The users' information came in the form of listings from batch cycles that were often out of date, whereas the minicomputer vendors offered on-line terminals.

Not surprisingly, some of the knowledgeable end users wanted their own machines. For the first time small computers had become sufficiently low in cost that this was practical.

POWER TO THE PEOPLE   Well-designed distributed systems ought to provide a solution to these problems. Computing power will be put in the end-user locations. Sometimes it will be stand-alone minis or desk-top computers. More often the end-user machines ought to be on line to higher-level systems or at least designed in conjunction with higher-level systems because data has to pass between the end-user machines and the higher-level machines. Sometimes the end-user machines will be terminals of larger distant machines but with processing power and possibly storage at the terminal location.

There will be few white collar workers who do not use a terminal when microelectronics has fully pervaded industry and government. Secretaries will use word processing, document storage, and electronic mail equipment. Accountants will be expected to keep up-to-date figures with daily trial balances and control of costs. Production planners will have the information they need available at their screens, and computers can adjust or optimize the production schedule as often as needed. Financial controllers will have the ability to move funds rapidly and use computers to optimize cash management. Research staff or design engineers will have a wide variety of computerized tools, models, and files available to them.

On-line computing power at the user locations will enable users to have faster information and processing. It will enable them to provide faster and more complete service to customers and to transmit quickly to centralized machines data which are important to higher-level management processes. (See Figs. 2.1 and 2.2.)

WORKLOAD   The above applications could all be done without distributed processing, but DDP in its various different forms is likely to make them happen faster, more effectively, and more cheaply.

The backlog of applications requested but not yet implemented is large in most corporations. A recent study of large corporations in the United States showed a *four-year* application backlog on the average. Such a long backlog is extremely frustrating for end users who know that certain applications could improve their efficiency—their bottom line.

The average backlog in 1973 was estimated to be about two years. It has grown larger rather than smaller since then, in spite of the fact that DP departments have been working hard on application development. Why? The reason is that far more applications have been perceived as economical as the cost of computing has dropped, and the dawning awareness of end users has caused them to demand computing resources and data at an increasing rate. The rate will probably continue to increase because we are only at the beginning of the growing awareness and implementation.

The growing backlog indicates that the central DP department is overloaded in its application development capability and that the overload is likely to become worse. This is a serious problem. As computing power continues to drop in cost, far more computing will be used and far more application development needed.

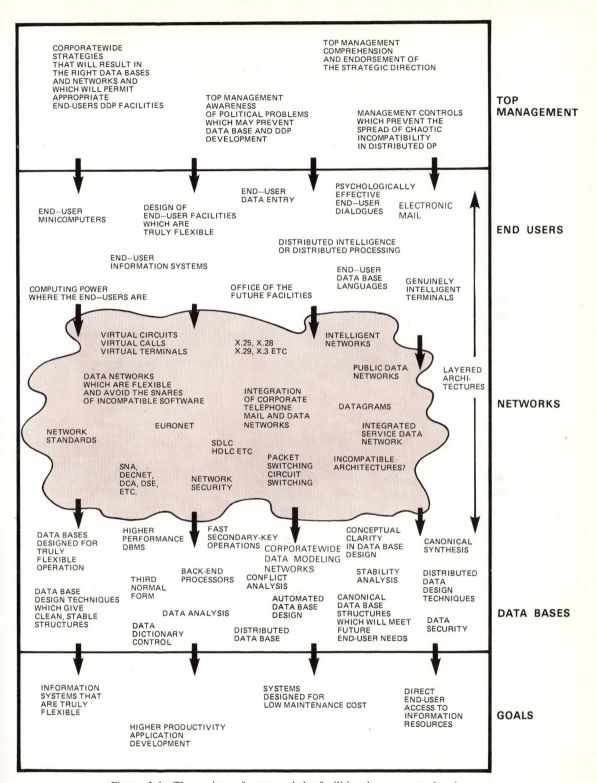

Figure 2.1 The variety of users and the facilities they can now be given.

Figure 2.2 Machines using distributed data processing in the Travelers Insurance Company. Travelers describes its motivation for DDP as follows:

"Our motivation has been to bring computer power to the Field Office level to assist Field personnel with better service to our customers and our Agents, rather than just harnessing out computer capabilities to service Home Office functions.

"As each office attains a high penetration of computer power, we will benefit from timely payment of claims and policy insurance, a computer-prepared complete English-language explanation of benefits, increased accuracy, lower unit cost including a more consistent level of quality service, and perhaps most important, more useful information for both Agents and customers combined with a job enriched environment for Travelers employees.

"Finally, the dramatic transition to Distributed Processing will accommodate the Company's business growth and improved level of quality service without necessitating an increased staff."

Travelers aims to have a terminal penetration ratio (the ratio of visual display terminals to clerks) of 31% [1].

There are two potential solutions to this problem. First, a higher level of *automation* of application development is needed. We have to do something more efficient than programming all applications in today's programming languages, such as COBOL, FORTRAN, and PL/I. Second, the end users must become involved in the development of their own applications.

It is desirable that these two solutions work together. Most end users will never be skilled programmers. In fact, most will never learn to program at all. Therefore it is desirable to supply end users with tools that enable them to generate the information they need from computers *without programming*.

Such tools are now coming into existence in a variety of forms—report generators, general-purpose packages with parameters for selecting what is needed, dialogues for generating dialogues, data-base end-user languages, information retrieval systems, graphics dialogues, flexible application packages. These are discussed in the projected companion book to this, *Software for Distributed Processing* (Prentice-Hall, Inc., Englewood Cliffs, N.J., 1982). Many of these are made practical by the use of distributed systems.

Many of the most effective facilities for allowing end users to create their own applications relate to information already sorted in an appropriate form in on-line files or data bases. The design of the data resources of a corporation are critical to the overall usefulness of DDP.

UNDERSTANDING OF USER REQUIREMENTS

There is another reason for direct user involvement in application development. Only the user departments are likely to have a full understanding of some of the subtleties of complex applications.

The normal method of developing applications has been to ask a system analyst, who is an expert on machines and software, to master an application area such as accounting or production control. Often the analyst has never entered a debit or been on a factory shop floor before. He or she usually manages to make the computer and design process sound complex and mysterious to the users and ends up with almost complete control over the resulting programming, which is done at a distant location. Not surprisingly, this does not always work. The end users are often unhappy with the results. Sometimes they can make the DP department change the programs to be more satisfactory. Sometimes they are told that changes cannot be made quickly because of the application backlog and high cost of change. Often they learn to live with a crude or inappropriate system.

Most of the early uses of computers were fairly simple ones, such as payroll, invoicing, and purchase orders. Today most of the simple applications have been done, and what remains is more complex—production control, portfolio management, plans and budgets, functional management, information systems, etc. The Plans and Budgets Department should be free to change their mind as often as they want about what processing they need. Portfolio managers or persons needing management information change their requirements and need information quickly. Only the end users are likely to know their true requirements on such systems.

This is a strong argument for changing the application development process. Users should have tools which bring *them* into the application design cycle and enable *them* to modify the end results as required.

DATA ENTRY

DDP permits *data entry* to be moved back to the user departments. There are several advantages to this. User departments can be made responsible for their own input data, for the accuracy and completeness of the data, and for the timeliness of the entry. Validation can be done by the machines *as the data are entered;* this is desirable because errors can be corrected immediately, while the source documents are available. The laborious step of key verification following keypunching can be avoided.

It has been observed in many corporations that when user departments are made responsible for entering their own data and for the accuracy of those data, the number of errors drops greatly from when the data were centrally keypunched.

Data entry can often be done by regular clerical staff, who may be performing other duties and who understand what the data mean. Full-time keypunching is a hard function to staff and often has a high turnover.

There are less likely to be backlogs of data entry during peak periods. The peaks can be more easily absorbed by the dispersed user staff.

The machines for data entry may be *on line* to larger computers which file the data and use them to update data bases. On the other hand, they may be stand-alone machines and the data may be delivered manually in disk or cartridge form to the larger centers. More often the data-entry machines will be connectable to the larger centers by means of a *periodic* connection such as a dialed telephone link or a temporary circuit through a data network.

FUTURE CORPORATE COMPUTING

We can draw a picture of the computing facilities of a typical future corporation. There will be one or more large computer centers—in many cases about the same number as there are today but with faster computers. These centers will be interconnected by telecommunications and will be jointly on line to most parts of the corporation. They will perform those computing operations which still benefit from centralization rather than distribution, for example, large number-crunching operations, large-scale print runs or printing needing special equipment, maintenance of files which are by their nature centralized, running old centralized applications which have not yet been converted to distributed form, and (particularly important) *the maintenance of corporate data bases*.

Although there are still large computer centers, there will be a vast proliferation of small computers: microcomputers, minicomputers, programmable terminals, desk-top computers, programmable pocket calculators. Some of the small machines will be permanently linked to the large machines by telecommunications; some will be stand-alone machines; some will be designed for periodic connection to a larger computer by a public telephone line or data network. Some of the small machines may transmit to one another independently of the large machines, and there may be networks for this purpose.

Some of the small machines have data storage. This ranges in size from interchangeable disks small enough to put in a wallet to storage units containing hundreds of millions of characters.

The small machines will be used in entirely different ways by people with entirely different skills. Both the applications and the techniques of usage will vary between wide extremes. The most sophisticated users, such as research personnel and head office staff, will write complex programs and keep their own personal library of programs. Other users will have simpler tools for creating the information they want. Many users will carry out routine data-entry and data-processing functions.

Many of the uses of the small machines will relate to data which are stored on large, centralized data bases. The users will employ these data, extract them into their own machines and manipulate them, and often be responsible for updating them.

FITTING DDP TO THE ORGANIZATIONAL STRUCTURE

Distributed systems can take on all manner of different shapes. The scattered computers and storage can be configured in an infinite number of ways. The question for management is, "What ways would be most beneficial for their organization as a whole?"

Distributed computing can be designed to conform to the existing organizational structure of a corporation. A corporation which is managed hierarchically can have hierarchical control of its data processing. A corporation which gives subsidiaries of factories autonomous control can have autonomous computer centers in these organizations, and the data which flow to the head office can correspond to the degree of corporate management control. User departments can have a degree of authority and responsibility for data processing which is appropriate to the department's position in the corporate structure.

Too often in the past, department heads have used the excuse, "It's not our fault that things are screwed up; the computer did it." And sometimes things remain "screwed up" to a remarkable degree. With DDP the same department head may be made responsible for his or her own computing. The degree of responsibility for DDP is equivalent to the manager's overall responsibility. Computing is no longer a remote, mysterious function over which the manager has no control.

ORGANIZATIONAL CHANGES

While DDP can be adapted to fit the organizational structure, it is vitally important for top management to understand that the organizational structure can be changed to take advantage of the new technology. In some of the most effective uses of DDP this has happened.

Some corporations reorganize themselves every few years to adjust to new business conditions. Using distributed computing to assist in the control and optimization of resources may be an important factor in reorganization, especially with worldwide or geographically dispersed corporations. *The top corporate planners should be asking how data bases, data networks, and distributed systems can affect the way the corporation operates.*

One of the earliest corporations to reorganize its activity with DDP was Fairchild Camera and Instrument. Fairchild has plants for semiconductor manufacture in Korea, Hong Kong, Singapore, and Djakarta and plants for fabrication and testing on both sides of the United States. It has worldwide customers and in 1975 maintained inventories both at these locations and at distribution centers in Australia, South America, and Europe. There was much sending of telex messages around the world to control the inventories and shipments. Inventory managers did not like to be unable to fill orders, and each tended to keep his stock sufficiently high that this did not often happen.

With distributed processing it was possible to have one worldwide inventory, with direct shipping from it to customer locations. This gave substantial global inventory savings, which was important because the semiconductor items in the inventory were rapidly becoming obsolete and dropping in cost. Even if the items had remained of constant value, the cost saving would have been great.

To make this new worldwide organization operate, global logistics were necessary, controlled from the head office location in California. A central data base was set up for worldwide supply and demand. Suitably high-speed data links, the transoceanic ones via satellite, connected the head office data base to interactive distributed minicomputers at the remote sites.

Such a system is designed to *decentralize the functional management processes* which can be handled by local managers and at the same *centralize the strategic management processes* and those operations which benefit from centralization. The local managers had more computing power and tighter instructions. They were made more efficient and more responsive. The strategic management at head office have the world logistics summarized for them. Their computer can assist in making strategic decisions and optimizing the resources and cash flow of the entire corporation.

WHAT SHOULD BE CENTRALIZED?   The advent of DDP throws open the question of what should be centralized and what decentralized. This question applies both at the technical level and at the general management level. At the technical level the designers need to ask which computing functions should be on large central machines and which ones on peripheral machines, and also what data should be stored centrally and what at peripheral locations. We discuss this later.

General management need to understand the principle of putting computer power wherever they want it and having fast data flow between the computers.

They would then ask what are the strategic or decision-making processes which ought to be centralized, and what should reside with functional management groups. What responsibility for computing should be placed with the functional managers? Should the corporation be organized to permit better strategic control, better response to markets, better cash management, different budgetary control, and so on?

RESPONSE TO
MARKETS

In supermarket, department store, and retail chains, distributed processing has been used to provide data processing at the individual store locations. The cash registers are on line to store minicomputers, or they may themselves contain microcomputers. All sales are recorded as they occur. Each store is responsible for its own cash management, inventory control, salesman records, and routine daily functions. But there are some areas in which the head office or centralized management should play a vital role. Certain goods suddenly become high-selling items in certain areas. This may be because of an advertising campaign; television advertising in particular causes sudden peaks. It may be because of fashion, for example, with clothes. It may be sales of a book or record booming, often unexpectedly. Or it may be caused by a spell of hot weather. Central management needs immediate warning of these surges in sales, so that items can be quickly shipped from inventory, purchased, or manufactured. The store computers notify the head office computer quickly of sales, and the head office computer notifies management of any local or countrywide surges. With such a network, head office management can plan the sales logistics countrywide. They may plan advertising in one region at a time so that the peak sales can be better absorbed, and goods can be moved from one area to another to cover abnormal peaks.

DDP thus accomplishes three objectives. It captures data at its source, the cash register. It automates local operations and assists local functional management. And it moves important data to the head office quickly to make possible corporation wide strategic decisions. The overall management organization of the chain may be modified to take advantage of this technology.

CASH MANAGEMENT

Cash management in corporations can be similarly improved by means of data bases, networks, and distributed facilities. A large corporation has very many different bank accounts, loans, and cash reserves. It is desirable that a cash manager or corporate treasurer have an integrated and up-to-date picture of these. Details of all balances, loans, and cash movements should be transmitted to one location daily. These may reside in many different data base records, which need to be assembled to create an overall picture of the cash available.

When the integrated cash summary is produced, a cash manager can decide what loans to pay down, whether to move cash from one location, and what action

BOX 2.1 The types of impact DDP can have on organizations

- End-user departments are given more computing power and better access to data. Processing can be on line with suitably fast response times.

- End-user departments can be made responsible for how they use computing.

- Data entry is moved to user departments, which are made responsible for the accuracy of that data.

- *Functional* information processes can be decentralized while *strategic* information processes are centralized.

- Functional management can be made more efficient and fully responsible for their activities. (No more excuses about how the distant computer fouled up.)

- Strategic management have the corporation wide logistics made available to them at one location.

- Tight strategic control is made possible over inventories, cash management, and functions where central control is beneficial.

- To take advantage of better centralized strategic control and full decentralization of functional process, corporate reorganizations are usually needed.

- The DP department and its relation to other departments is the first candidate for potential restructuring.

- Department managers should be required to become sophisticated in their use of computing now that it is cheaply available to them.

- New data networks may be largely distance-insensitive, so processing can be moved nationwide or worldwide. Worldwide relocation or closing down of functions can result from this.

- Top management involvement is vital, both to seize the new opportunities brought by this technology and to deal with the political problems the DDP causes.

**BOX 2.2 Terms used in different architectures.
The functions of the layers are not exactly
the same in the different architectures.**

NAMES USED BY THE INTERNATIONAL STANDARDS ORGANIZATION	OTHER TERMS USED IN THIS BOOK	TERMS USED BY TELEPHONE COMPANIES FOLLOWING THE CCITT RECOMMENDATION X.25	TERMS USED IN IBM's SNA ARCHITECTURE	TERMS USED IN DEC's DECNET ARCHITECTURE	TERMS USED IN UNIVAC's DCA ARCHITECTURE
LAYER 7 PROCESS CONTROL					
LAYER 6 PRESENTATION CONTROL	SESSION SERVICES SUBSYSTEM		FUNCTION MANAGEMENT	DIALOGUE LAYER	TERMINATION SYSTEM

LAYER 5 SESSION CONTROL					
LAYER 4 TRANSPORT END-TO-END CONTROL	TRANSPORT SUBSYSTEM		TRANSMISSION CONTROL	NETWORK SERVICES PROTOCOL (NSP LAYER)	TRANSPORT NETWORK SYSTEM
LAYER 3 NETWORK CONTROL		LEVEL 3	PATH CONTROL		
LAYER 2 LINK CONTROL	COMMON NETWORK	LEVEL 2	SDLC (SYNCHRONOUS DATA LINK CONTROL)	DDCMP (DIGITAL DATA COMMUNICATIONS MANAGEMENT PROTOCOL)	UDLC (UNIVERSAL DATA LINK CONTROL)
LAYER 1 PHYSICAL CONTROL		LEVEL 1			

BOX 2.3 Names used for different data units

Data Units Interchanged between:	Terms Used in this Book (see Figs. 9.5 and 9.6)	Terms Used by CCITT Recommendations	Terms Used in IBM's SNA Architecture	Terms Used in DEC's DECNET Architecture	Terms Used in UNIVAC's DCA Architecture
Users	User Data; User Messages	User Messages	User Data	User Data	User Data
LAYERS 4 to 7	Session Messages		Basic Information Unit	DAP Message	Port Data Unit
LAYER 3	Packets	Packet	Path Information Unit	NSP Message	Network Data Unit
LAYER 2	Frames	Frame	Basic Link Unit	DDCMP	Frame

BOX 2.4 Advantages and disadvantages of layering

ADVANTAGES OF LAYERED ARCHITECTURES

1. Any given layer can be modified or upgraded without affecting the other layers.
2. Modularization by means of layering simplifies the overall design.
3. Different layers can be assigned to different design teams and different standards committees.
4. Fundamentally different mechanisms may be substituted without affecting more than one layer (e.g., packet switching vs. leased-line concentrators).
5. Different machines may plug in at different layers.
6. The relationships between the different control functions can be better understood when they are split into layers. This is especially true with the control actions which occur sequentially in time from layer to layer.
7. Common lower level services may be shared by different higher-level users.
8. Functions, especially at the lower layers, may be removed from software and built into hardware or microcode.
9. Plug-compatible connections between machines of different manufacturers are made easier to accomplish.

DISADVANTAGES OF LAYERED ARCHITECTURES

1. The total overhead is somewhat higher.
2. The communicating machines may have to use certain functions which they could do without.
3. To make each layer usable by itself, there is some small duplication of function between the layers.
4. As technology changes (e.g., as cryptography and compaction chips become available, or as these functions can be built onto HDLC chips), the functions may not be in the most cost-effective layer.

IN GENERAL, THE ADVANTAGES ARE GREAT, THE DISADVANTAGES SLIGHT.

to take to avoid expensive short-term debts. In order to make the best decisions about loans and short-term funds, a forecast of cash requirements is needed. The information which flows to the central cash manager should therefore have a time dimension, saying what money will be coming in from customers and flowing out to suppliers, contractors, and payrolls at certain estimated times.

Cash management can be particularly complex in multinational corporations where funds can be quickly switched from one currency to another, and there are different national taxation rates and national regulations about currency movement. Worldwide information needs to be passed between the corporate computers. Funds can be moved very quickly between countries now by telex and on the new multinational electronic fund transfer network, SWIFT.

Tight control of cash needs fast movement of financial information. This has become increasingly important with rising inflation, higher interest rates, and turbulent exchange rates. Cash managers often need to make investment decisions early in the day, when yields in the money market are at their peak.

Many corporations are not managing their worldwide cash assets as described here. To reiterate: Distributed processing networks are a new technology offering new opportunities to management, if understood. To take advantage of it may need a top management reorganization of today's methods or corporate structure.

Box 2.1 summarizes the types of impact DDP can have on organizations.

REFERENCE

1. Quotation from the Travellers Insurance Company's house magazine, *Protection,* Hartford, Conn., February 1977.

3 THE CHANGING ROLE OF END USERS

Distributed processing and microelectronics are changing the role of computer end users. In the early days of computing only programmers had an active role in using the machines. With the spread of teleprocessing the number of terminal users grew rapidly, most of them specially trained to use a repetitive dialogue designed for one application. Bank tellers, airline booking agents, and insurance clerks were typical terminal users. There were a much smaller number of terminal users who carried out innovative functions at terminals, such as design work, information retrieval, and sometimes programming.

By the start of the distributed processing era, the number of terminal users was growing very rapidly. End users were beginning to appreciate what valuable information they might obtain from their terminals if only the right system was designed for them. Increasing numbers of terminal users are learning to employ the machines in an innovative fashion. Some end users are learning to program. Programming is taught in schools; hobby computing is spreading furiously; some accountants and managers spend their leisure learning to program pocket calculators.

Figure 3.1 illustrates how the balance may have changed by the not-too-distant time when distributed processing matures. There will be more professional programmers than today, but the relative number of terminal users will be much higher. As the teaching and practice of programming spread, there will eventually be more end users programming (as an adjunct to their main job) than professional programmers. The majority of computer usage, however, will be by untrained, casual users, who learn neither programming nor the use of mnemonics that was required for dumb-terminal dialogues of earlier teleprocessing systems.

A study of computer usage in the United States [1] predicts that the percentage of the working population which will employ computers in their jobs will grow as in Fig. 3.2. Most of these will use terminals in an occasional fashion. Their main training and concern will not be with computers, but the use of terminals will form an indispensible background to their job.

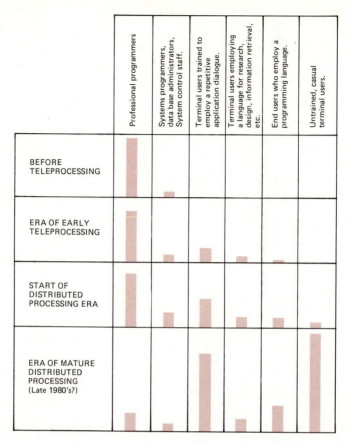

Figure 3.1   Relative number of different types of computer users changing as distributed processing spreads. (The chart does not imply that the
absolute number of programs decrease; on the contrary.)

If the majority of the working force are to use computers, as predicted in Fig.
3.2, then the terminal dialogues have to be far simpler for people to use than most
were in the era of dumb terminals.

The most important reason for DDP is to bring computing to as many end
users as possible. To accomplish this we need to remove the *fear* of computing. It
must be made to seem as simple and natural as possible. This can be achieved only
if the end-user terminal dialogue is elegant, easy to use, and psychologically effective.

A high proportion of the people who ought to be using computer terminals in
the future are afraid of them. They imagine that the device and its dialogue are
complicated and that they will not be able to deal with it correctly. They expect that
it will display things, as it has done in the past, to which they do not know how to
respond. Rather than be made to feel foolish, they try to avoid becoming involved

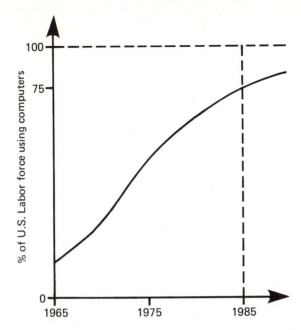

Figure 3.2   Projected involvement in computer usage. (1)

with terminals. Typical programmers and analysts do not anticipate this attitude. They enjoy and experiment with terminals and often fail to comprehend that other people are uncomfortable about them.

Recently in a branch office of a major computer manufacturer a new and impressive terminal facility was demonstrated to me. It would have provided the salesmen with all manner of information of value to them. Unfortunately, none of the salesmen used it, apparently because they felt it was too complicated for them. They were frightened of appearing foolish in the office. If computer salesmen avoid the use of terminals for this reason, how much more so will the general run of potential end users?

A terminal dialogue need not be bewildering. There are always many ways of achieving equivalent results with a terminal. It is desirable to select methods that are appropriate for the users in question. Dialogue techniques that are good for most potential users are quite different from those that are good for programmers and analysts.

Many of the most effective forms of dialogue are economical only if there is a processor close to the terminal. They need a large number of characters displaying quickly, fast response times, and possibly graphics generation. These are too expensive if every bit displayed has to be transmitted over communication lines. With distributed intelligence, or distributed processing, the cost constraint for building psychologically effective dialogues is removed. There is no longer any excuse for bad dialogue structures. One of the great potentials of distributed processing is that end users everywhere can have powerful means of communicating with the DP systems.

THREE TYPES OF   There are three main types of end-user interface:
INTERFACE

1. Fixed, preprogrammed dialogue

With this an end user interacts with an application designed and programmed by someone else. Examples are a bank teller using a terminal to handle customers' requirements or a factory foreman using a terminal to schedule the jobs and enter details of work completed.

2. Programming language

An end user or his staff may create programs, and possibly files, for their own purposes. They may employ a language which is designed for terminal operations, such as APL or BASIC. They may employ a simpler language designed for the non-professional programmers. A variety of these are available, some forming the user interface to particular minicomputer systems. The end users' programs may employ data stored in distant file or data-base systems.

3. Nonpreprogrammed dialogue

With this an end user or his staff obtain results which are not preprogramming for them, but they do not use a formal programming language. They search a data base, use an information retrieval language, generate a new type of report, or perform a calculation on stored data which they specify. They may use a data-base language to interrogate or update a data base. In some cases they may generate a report on a screen which other users, in turn, will fill in.

It was once generally thought that dialogues which achieve such ends had to be similar to programming languages in that the user had to remember mnemonics and fixed sequences of input. More recently a variety of data-base dialogues and report generators have been demonstrated which are natural and easy to use without the skills of a programmer or the training courses needed for mnemonic languages.

These three types of user interface all benefit from distributed computing putting dialogue or language processing at the user's location. They are discussed in the following chapters.

REACTIVE COMPUTING   Microelectronics makes some forms of time sharing obsolete. It is no longer necessary to share a distant computer with many other users and access it by means of a low-bandwidth line. Each user can have substantial computing power *to himself.* The further microelectronics drops in cost, the more this will be true. If users can have substantial computing power at their fingertips at low cost, then system design efforts should be directed to making the person's time on the computer as profitable as possible.

The term *reactive* system has been used (by Alan Kay of the Xerox Palo Alto Research Center [2]) to refer to systems in which a substantial processor has the sole job of catering to a single user. It can afford to do relatively large amounts of processing when the user is doing the simplest of tasks. It can format data on the screen and add text so that it is easy to understand. It can check the user's spelling and flash any items not in the dictionary. It may contain an interpreter or incremental compiler. It can assemble and maintain graphics displays and allow the user to interact with them. It can afford to do extensive processing to figure out what the user wants to say or what information he is trying to obtain, and it can interact with him to deduce or refine his intended input.

As the price/performance ratio of microelectronics drops, a primary concern must be end-user efficiency rather than machine efficiency.

**VARIETIES OF
END USERS**
Society has endless varieties of people, with enormously differing interests and skills. The same is true of computer end users. It is desirable that they should have available a wide variety of techniques for using the computing power which is now spreading to the users. A type of dialogue structure which is good for one user is not necessarily good for another. Some end users will learn to program; most will not. Some end users will learn mnemonics; most will not. Some end users will be happy with simple menu-selection dialogues; others will find these slow and restricting.

We sometimes make the mistake of talking about "end users" as though they were all the same. In fact they could not be more diverse. While DDP gives one class of users terminal dialogues of extreme simplicity, it gives others the capability of using sophisticated languages to manipulate their files. To all these different groups, usability should be the prime consideration of DDP. Value to users is of more concern than machine performance.

REFERENCES

1. T. A. Dolotta, et al., *Data Processing in 1980–1985: A Study of Potential Limitations to Progress,* Wiley-Interscience, 1976.

2. Alan Kay, Xerox Palo Alto Research Center, *Personal Computing,* ACM National Conference, August 1975.

4 THE OFFICE OF THE FUTURE

"Office of the future" is a term which became fashionable in the late 1970's to refer to electronics for automating office administrative functions and providing new types of office services. Box 4.1 lists some of the facilities in question.

Many of the facilities listed in Box 4.1 require the same networks, terminals, and possibly computers as distributed data processing. It makes sense to have the corporate data network serve office administration requirements as well as data processing. The selection of terminals and devices for both then needs to be governed by the same protocol constraints and overall DDP strategy. Substantial cost savings can result from this sharing of resources. Many office terminals should be able to work with both DP systems and office automation applications via the same networking facilities. Corporate DDP strategy should unquestionably include office automation facilities.

OFFICE MANAGEMENT CHANGES More than half of the working force in advanced countries works in offices, and office of the future technology will substantially change what they do.

In the United States the capital expenditure per farm worker is about $35,000. The capital expenditure per blue collar worker is about $25,000. However, the capital expenditure per white collar worker is less than $3,000.

This means, in effect, that mechanization has gone much further in farms and factories than in the office. Now it is the turn of the office. The equipment is coming into existence for massive automation of office work. The last 20 years has brought a continuing rise in productivity in manufacturing. It has increased 90% in the last 10 years. During the same period, office productivity increased only 4%. Until recently there was negligible increase in productivity of secretaries, mailroom personnel, office managers, and administrative office workers.

Office costs have assumed a steadily higher proportion of corporate and

BOX 4.1 Possible types of machines and facilities in the office of the future

1. FACILITIES IN AN EXECUTIVE'S OFFICE

   - Digital telephone with LED display
   - Telephone answering machine
   - Voicegram (speech mail) facility
   - Screen for receiving mail and messages
   - Word-processing terminal in communication with secretary or typing pool
   - Dictation system which permits on-line insertion and change of words
   - Future speech-input word-processing machine
   - Viewdata-like information system
   - Teletext facility (receives data broadcast on a television channel)
   - Video tape player
   - Video tape camera over desk (for complex communication by engineers, scientists, or designers)
   - Video access to local information room
   - Personal computing
   - Executive uses of computer terminal: mail and messages, information retrieval, data-base access, automated diary, automated in-basket work queue, action list, ability to place items on subordinates or other people's work queue, automatic followup, project status tracking, inspection and adjustment of mail types by secretary before it is sent

2. SECRETARIAL OR SERVICE FACILITIES

   Electronic filing and retrieval

   Electronic mail (see next heading)

   Word-processing facilities:

   - Screen for composing, retrieving, merging, and editing text
   - Printer to print the composed document
   - Cursor to assist in inserting items into the text and moving paragraphs
   - Controller for a single machine, or shared logic controller for multiple machines
   - Word wrap (words typed beyond the right margin automatically go on to the next line)

continued

BOX 4.1 *continued*

- Right justification (with the right margin as well as the left aligned, as on the pages of a book)
- Tabs
- Decimal positioning for typing columns of figures correctly aligned
- Multiple type fonts
- Some future word processors will have speech input, especially suitable for executives who do not like to type much

Word processing machines in communication, for example, for a manager to adjust what a secretary has typed. A manager and secretary, or coauthors of a document, might talk by telephone while they inspect and adjust the document on the screen.

Copying machine and collators

Communicating copier. A copying machine which can:

- transmit to distant copiers
- control the accuracy of reception
- receive and print output from a computer
- digitize and transmit documents to computers or electronic filing systems

Intelligent copier. A copying machine which can:

- edit
- merge items onto one sheet
- add corporate logos, signatures, or forms
- shrink or expand the copy
- display input on a screen so that editing functions such as deleting certain items or adding items can be specified
- possibly act as a multifunction communicating copier

Graphics. Automated production of foils, flips charts, or slides.

3. ELECTRONIC MAIL FACILITIES

Output:

- High-speed printer
- Low-speed printer
- Analog facsimile
- Digital facsimile

BOX 4.1 *continued*

- Copying machine
- Screen
- Storage media
- Computer
- Speech

Input:

- Keyboard
- Word-processing machine
- Analog facsimile
- Digital facsimile
- Copying machine
- Speech computer
- Optical scanner

Sorting:

- Slow disk sorter
- Tape sort

Filing:

- Automatic filing for later retrieval
- Automatic Searching

Delivery:

- Immediate
- Scheduled (at a specified time)
- Store and forward when possible
- On demand

Pattern:

- One-to-one
- One-to-many (automatic use of mailing list)
- Broadcast

Priority:

- Immediate

continued

BOX 4.1 *continued*

- When resources are free
- Overnight

Organizational:

- Intercorporate
- Interorganizational
- Intracorporate
- Intraorganizational

Distance:

- Buildingwide
- Citywide
- Nationwide
- Worldwide

Control:

- Automatic labeling with time/date stamp and identification number
- Positive controls to prevent loss or nondelivery
- Auditability

4. FACILITIES FOR BETTER PERSON-TO-PERSON COMMUNICATION

- Facilities for sending, filing, and on-demand receipt of voicegrams
- Facilities for sending, filing, and on-demand receipt of messages
- Terminals or telephones which flash a light when a message is waiting
- "Mailbox" software
- Facsimile to dial conference calls and add on third parties to telephone calls
- Capability to dial conference calls and add on third parties to telephone calls
- Noninteractive still-image transmission, plus telephone
- Interactive freeze-frame video, plus telephone
- Full interactive video, picturephone quality

BOX 4.1 *continued*

- Full interactive video, television quality, possibly with CATV (cable television) wiring in a building or complex
- Interactive video, switchable to higher-resolution still-frame transmission

5. TELECOMMUNICATIONS CHANNELS
  - Telephone
  - Telex
  - TWX
  - Private data network
  - Public X.25 data network
  - Higher-level public data network (Bell's ACS, Videotext)
  - Wideband data circuits like Bell's DDS
  - Wideband network (like Xerox's XTEN)
  - Basic satellite earth station
  - Satellite earth station with variable bandwidth (like SBS)
  - CATV (cable television)
  - Wideband multipoint-addressing cable system (like Ethernet)
  - Radio paging
  - Radio dispatching
  - Citizens' Band radio
  - Packet radio

6. FACILITIES FOR WORKING AT HOME
  - Computer terminal
  - Word-processing machine
  - Telephone-answering machine
  - Dictating facilities, possibly on-line access to a control dictation recording service
  - Telex machines, or ability to connect to the telex network via a terminal used for other purposes
  - Mail and message terminal
  - Executive terminal with work queue (in-basket), action list, diary, and other facilities linked to the main office

continued

BOX 4.1 *continued*

In general, home facilities can provide an extension and continuity of office facilities for secretaries, executives, and professionals. They can also be used for part-time employment of persons who because of children or other reasons cannot work full time.

7. COMMUNICATIONS ROOM:

- Telex
- TWX
- Facsimile
- Other electronic mail machines
- Viewdata
- Hub of data networks
- Control facility for wideband network
- Radio communication, radio paging, dispatching
- Satellite earth station control

8. MEETING ROOM

- Computer terminals
- Projector to display terminal output onto a large screen
- Slide and foil projectors
- Ability to transmit and display slides or foils from a remote location, so that a distant person can make a graphic presentation
- Full interactive freeze-frame video
- Moving video—television or picturephone
- Meeting room with multiple cameras and switching equipment for television or picturephone meetings
- Speakerphone
- Speech teleconferencing so that multiple delegates can hear and be heard remotely
- Facsimile machines
- Video tape, possibly with large-screen playback

9. INFORMATION ROOM

A room where sources of information and information experts are concentrated so that managers can request data they need.

BOX 4.1 *continued*

Communication with managers' offices in the building may be by

- full television
- freeze-frame video
- terminal and telephone
- printer

Information may be displayed from

- terminals
- special wall displays
- slides
- film-chain
- video tape
- color TV camera over desk or on chart board
- facsimile
- video tape
- connections to multiple computer systems

The room may be connected to a corporate library.

10. OPERATIONS ROOM

A room where a set of operations may be controlled, for example, shop floor control, delivery fleet control, control of police resources, cars, and ambulances, a power grid, maintenance operations.

- Special wall displays (manual)
- Special wall displays controlled by computers and data transmission
- Computer terminals with operators able to intercommunicate
- Large screens (such as the NASA Mission Control Center)
- Radio paging
- Radio dispatching
- Computer printouts for backup
- TV links to critical locations

11. MASTER SWITCH

- Computerized PBX (private branch exchange), now called CBX
- CBX which interconnects terminals and telephones

continued

BOX 4.1 *continued*

- CBX which converts machine addresses into dialing commands
- Master switch capable of handling wideband bit streams (up to 64,000 bps; up to 256,000 bps; up to several million bps)
- Interface to computer network or multiple networks

12. BUILDING WIRING

- Radial twisted wire pairs (conventional telephone wiring)
- Radial wire pairs handling a high bit rate
- CATV (cable television) wiring
- Wideband loop like Ethernet
- Optical fiber
- Packet radio
- Plug in the wall for attaching wide variety of terminals and electronic devices

government expenditure. On the average, 50% of the total costs of U.S. corporations are for office work. In banks, insurance companies, and government, 70% to 85% of total costs are office salaries.

The United States is spending $600 billion per year at the time of writing on the salaries (and fringe benefits) of managers, professionals, and secretaries. It spends another $200 billion on support costs. A study by Booz, Allen and Hamilton, Inc., concludes that 20% of these costs could be saved by 1990 with efficient uses of office automation technology. Figure 4.1 illustrates this. The total saving in 1990 is $300 billion. This is a huge figure compared with the total computer industry sales of today ($400 billion in 1979). The office of the future will be one of the largest revenue generators for the computer industry.

Office of the future technology implies a massive redeployment and training of people and an overhaul of management activities everywhere. It requires cultural changes in office procedures which will be resisted in many offices, but which are being grasped enthusiastically by some younger executives and corporations. Whether these changes can be made rapidly enough determines whether the saving will be as great as in Fig. 4.1.

Because of the commonality of the network and some of the equipment, it is often desirable that top data processing management have electronic mail and office automation as part of its responsibilities. This has happened in some corporations, while in others separate management has been responsible for office

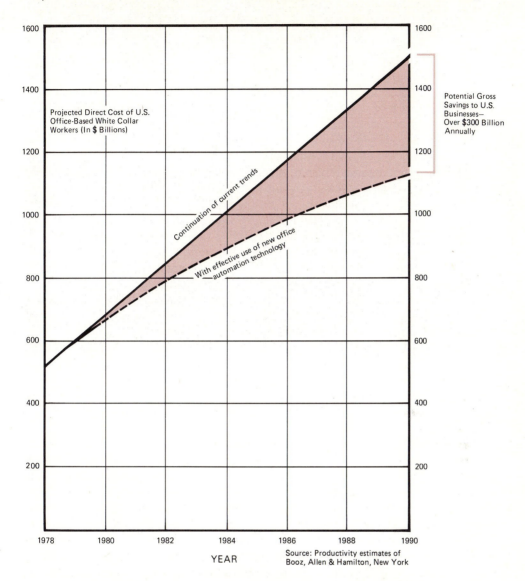

Figure 4.1 With effective use of office automation, it is estimated that $300 billion in office workers costs could be saved by 1990. The potential market for office of the future technology is huge.

automation. In some companies office automation is centrally coordinated, while in others local managers have made their own procurement decisions. In this it exhibits the major problem of DDP: What should be central management and design responsibilities, and what should be decentralized duties?

Office automation technology is often thought of in terms of improving the productivity of secretaries and administrative managers only. Its potential is much greater than that. Surveys have been made by various organizations of how professionals and functional managers spend their time. In many corporations at least a third of their time is spent on chores which do not use their professional or managerial skills. In one government study, Booz, Allen and Hamilton, Inc., discovered that it cost $88 for an employee to fill out a travel request, even for a short car or train trip costing less than $10 [1].

Professionals and executives are more highly paid than administrative personnel, and their effect on the organization is much greater. There is more to be gained from improving the productivity of professionals and managers than improving the productivity of administrative personnel.

If a terminal is placed in the office of a professional or functional manager, he ought to do much more with it than merely administrative functions. He needs access to a variety of information and computing resources. The terminal which he may use for mail or communication with a secretary is also used for information retrieval, data-base access, use of computerized tools, and so on. Managers will call each other on the telephone to talk about information on their screen. The party called will need to be able to access the same data. The screen used for this purpose is the same screen used for administrative functions. Data processing, data networks, and office of the future technology thus tend to merge.

At the time of writing, 78% of U.S. office salaries go to managers and professionals, and only 24% go to clerical workers and secretaries. Figure 4.2 shows the breakdown. The office of the future will benefit the corporation most if it improves the productivity of managers and professionals, rather than clerical staff.

THE PAPERLESS OFFICE

The term *paperless office* is used to refer to an office in which an executive carries out activities without paperwork. He obtains his mail on screen. When he sends mail, he dictates it, possibly by telephone, and then reviews it and changes it on his screen.

A computer manages the executive's paperwork queue—an *electronic in-basket*. In this, unlike an ordinary in-basket, the work may be organized into priority sequence or into different classes of activity. When an item is worked on, the executive can send it to a secretary, to a central word-processing pool, to a subordinate's electronic work queue, or to some other individual for action. Executives' work tends to be constantly interrupted and rapidly switches from one topic to another. The electronic facilities must assist this random-access activity. The executive may want to display a variety of types of information—documents, credit records, production schedules, job status records, business information, or whatever information is relevant. Such information may come from different computers. The means of displaying them should be as simple as possible.

Manual mail reaching the building is converted to electronic form for storage, retrieval, and transmission. It can then be displayed on the office screens. Internal

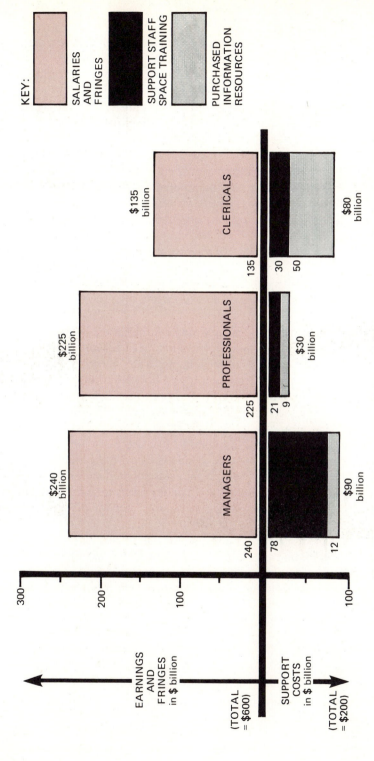

KEY:

SALARIES AND FRINGES

SUPPORT STAFF SPACE TRAINING

PURCHASED INFORMATION RESOURCES

Figure 4.2 The office of the future should not aim solely at clerical staff and secretaries. It can save more money by improving the productivity of managers and professionals. Of the $600 billion the U.S. pays in office salaries, about $465 billion goes to managers and professionals. This figure shows the breakdown. (Source: Booz, Allen and Hamilton)

49

mail sent in electronic form, not on paper. It is only external mail to less automated organizations that has to be printed.

The executive keeps his diary in electronic form. His secretary can see it and update it. A file of reminders or action items is similarly kept.

Operating in this way, a vice-president of a large bank in Chicago decided that a desk was not necessary. He has an elegantly furnished office with no desk. He holds meetings, communicates electronically with other executives, dictates his mail, and carries out a bank executive's "paperwork" without paper. The purpose? Higher executive productivity and better-organized work.

Many managers would like to have an automated diary and reminder list but could not justify the cost. The cost is justifiable only when the terminal is in their office for other reasons. The other reasons usually involve data processing and information retrieval. The office terminal becomes justifiable only when it has a variety of uses. It should not be *solely* a word-processing terminal or mail terminal.

The more terminals and small computers drop in cost, the easier the justification. A 5% improvement in the use of an executive's time pays for a substantial terminal.

The term "paperless society" is used to describe an era when society as a whole replaces its paper with electronic information. Mail becomes electronic. Bills are paid electronically. Paperless offices in separate corporations intercommunicate. The news comes on the television screen in video form, in alphanumeric displays preselected for a home, and in the form of vast news files which can be accessed and searched interactively. Like phrases such as "cashless society" and "checkless society," the term "paperless society" is a gross exaggeration. Printed matter is increasing, not decreasing, in quantity. If it decreases, this will be due to shortage of wood chips, not to abundance of silicon chips. Electronic media will be increasingly valuable, but it would be a social catastrophe if they *replaced* books, newspapers, magazines, and personal letters. Society needs the maximum diversity of media and the freedom to select which medium is best for different forms of communications.

A *completely* paperless office is also undesirable in most situations. The objective is not to do away with paper but to increase productivity, especially the productivity of executives and professionals. Many of these people like to take paper home which they can study at leisure. Paper reports which communicate well need to be designed for them. They should be able to print the contents of a screen for later scrutiny.

WORD PROCESSING   To some authorities the term "office of the future" means mainly word processing.

Word processing has greatly reduced the amount of typing that has to be done by secretaries and typing pools in some organizations.

A legal document can be put together quickly by assembling standard paragraphs with few new paragraphs being typed. Correspondence can be taken from a number of standard letters which need only minor modification. When lengthy documents are reviewed and corrected or added to, the whole document does not need to be manually retyped. The modifications can be entered, and the word processing system will print the results. The printing can be fast so that executives concerned can see the results quickly.

When a document is proofread and then completely retyped, the retyping often introduces new errors. With word processing there is no need to retype what is already correct. A typical typist makes an error every few hundred words and has to do much correction and retyping before a long report is error-free. With word processing the corrections are entered one at a time and a machine prints the result without making new errors.

Ease of change gives more flexibility in making modifications. Some executives and professionals are intimidated by their secretaries so that they dare not make more changes in a report which has already been retyped too often.

The final result can look much smarter. It is typed to fit the pages neatly, with right justification (that is, the ends of the words are aligned on the right-hand side of the page to give a straight right-hand edge as well as a straight left-hand edge, like the printed pages of a book). There are no obvious corrections done with white correction fluid.

Figure 4.3 shows an administrative area with communicating word processing machines.

Most executives and professionals cannot type or do not want to type. They may communicate with a secretary who can look at the same letter or report on a screen and make changes they suggest, using the text-manipulation capabilities of word processing, while they are viewing the document.

SPEECH-INPUT WORD PROCESSING

A technical development now in the research laboratories which will one day make a major difference to the way executives and professionals create documents is a *speech-input* word processor. The machine detects the words which the user speaks. It will often be adjusted to the voice of one specific user. The user sees his words appear on the screen. He will see if the machine misinterprets his words. He will have to spell or type certain words, such as personal names.

Using word processing, he can insert and delete words, shuffle sentences or paragraphs, and obtain previously written items from files. The machine will have a built-in word dictionary, which the user may add to, to aid it in word recognition. Using such devices may be faster than conventional dictation and will enable the user to produce much better text.

Such machines will assume a realistic cost as the cost of microelectronics continues to drop. The world market for such machines is gigantic. They may be the largest single money maker of the office automation revolution. Whether they will be perfected in the next few years or are a decade or two away is not yet certain.

Figure 4.3   An IBM view of an almost paperless administrative area. The IBM 3730 system enables word processing machines to intercommunicate, send mail, queue incoming documents, and communicate with filing systems. At the left is a printer. A high speed line printer can also be used. The machines use the SNA (Systems Network Architecture) protocols for connection to networks.

The same speech-recognition mechanisms will be used to aid the interrogation of data bases and for other interactive computer processes.

OBJECTIVES OF THE EXECUTIVE PAPERLESS OFFICE   Word processing is important in increasing the productivity of secretaries. It has little or no effect on the productivity of managers and professionals, although they can benefit from seeing their letters and reports more quickly. For managers and professionals, other office facilities are needed.

There are three primary objectives in designing an electronic office for an executive or professional:

1. that they spend less time on paperwork

2. that decision-making capability be improved

3. that human communications be improved

Of these only the first can be tangibly measured. With higher-level executives the second two are the most important, and the primary purpose of the first is to give more time for human communications and decision making.

A difficulty in deciding to deploy advanced data-processing resources is the lack of *tangible* justification. The same problem applies to some office administration facilities. It would be difficult to find *tangible* justification for the telephone, for example.

Citibank used the manager's *span of control* as a measure. Office automation, they claimed, should increase the number of people and projects that each manager can handle. Citibank had 40,000 front-line service employees and 8000 managers. The goal of their *advanced technology office* was to allow the size of the front-line staff to grow without increasing the number of managers. This increase in a manager's span of control is a measure of managerial productivity. How effective it is as a measure varies from one organization to another. With some executives, span of control is less important than quality of decision making. Here subjective assessments of the effects of technology are more important than numeric measures.

Another numeric measure is the amount of time a manager spends on paperwork. However, it is difficult to *measure* how managers spend their time because they switch constantly from one activity to another, often with only a brief time spent on one activity before switching. As in nuclear particle physics, attempts at detailed measurement change what is being measured. An analog of the Heisenberg uncertainty principle applies, and there may be more uncertainty about managers than about atoms.

SIX TYPES OF SERVICES

There are six broad categories of advanced technology services that a manager may find valuable in the office:

- Work-queue management
- Information retrieval
- Word processing
- Mail and message services
- Computing services
- Better communications

Box 4.2 lists some of the desirable services in these categories.

WORK-QUEUE MANAGEMENT

The image of a paperless office must have great appeal to those who live in paperwork chaos! All "paperwork" is filed and transmitted by the machines. Jobs to be done are queued for the attention of managers or clerks. No job can be lost. When it has been satisfactorily completed, it is stored in archival files or deleted by its originator.

Each manager has an electronic in-basket. This may be organized into several categories of work. It may be organized by priority, with certain items being marked for urgent attention. The work is organized so that the manager can tackle it whenever he wants, in any order, and can break away from uncompleted items when his many interruptions occur.

BOX 4.2 Services in the paperless executive office

1. WORK-QUEUE MANAGEMENT

- Automated in-basket. "Paperwork" to be done available on the office screen; organized into queues of different types of activity; possibly organized by priority
- Ability to place items on the work queues of subordinates or other persons
- Automated follow-up, to see when tasks have been completed by other persons
- Automated executive diary
- Automated executive action list

2. INFORMATION RETRIEVAL

- Access to information needed when handling the work queue, e.g., customer records, project status reports, budget details
- Access to corporate data-base systems
- Access to information retrieval systems for searching for information
- Access to external information sources
- Access to mail files, document files, transaction archives, possibly using the help of a secretary
- Access to a corporate information center where specialized staff search for information needed by management
- Teletext service (broadcast data)
- Viewdata types of services

3. WORD PROCESSING

- Ability to check and change materials typed by a secretary on the office screen
- Ability to retrieve modules of text for composing semistandard letters, contracts, proposals, and documents
- Telephone communication with a typing pool or secretary, while both parties view and change the same text on the office screen
- Dictation capability, possibly with the capability for on-line insertion and change of dictated words
- Ability for two or more persons to jointly compose flip charts or documents, possibly while in distant offices

BOX 4.2 *continued*

- At some future time, use of speech-input word processing in which words spoken appear on a screen and can be modified

4. MAIL AND MESSAGES

- Ability to receive mail and messages on the office screen (electronic mailbox)
- A flashing light which indicates when mail or messages are waiting to be received; different lights may indicate different levels of urgency
- Ability to send messages, with differing degrees of urgency
- Ability to receive and send speech messages (voicegrams) instead of typed memos. These messages are stored and forwarded. This can save much typing and increase communication.
- Ability in inspecting one's electronic mailbox from remote locations, with appropriate security control

5. COMPUTING

- Personal computing and calculation capability
- Ability to use programs or computer models created for the individual in question. These differ greatly from one type of executive to another.
- Ability to use time-shared computers, carry out data-base processing, generate reports, charts, etc.
- Graphics display capability

6. BETTER PERSONAL COMMUNICATIONS

- Electronic telephone with LED display
- Ability to dial conference calls and add on third parties to existing calls
- Electronic mailbox, message sending, and voicegram facilities
- Telephone and screen communication with other corporate locations, with interactive alphanumeric use of screen
- Still-frame graphics communication capability
- Capability to print remotely the contents of a screen
- Speech-and-video communication (possibly moving video within the building and freeze-frame video to other locations)
- Teleconferencing (possibly freeze-frame)
- Video tape for education
- Video tape for communication

The manager can place jobs in the electronic in-baskets of others—secretaries, subordinates, or other managers. The computers will keep track of such items to ensure that they are responded to.

The manager may be able to find items in the files *himself* from his terminal, or he may use a secretary to assist. The secretary displays requested items on the manager's screen. The terminal dialogs should be easy enough to encourage him to do it himself.

The manager's diary is kept electronically, with himself and his secretary able to fill it in. Similarly, an action list may be maintained with automated insistence that the items be attended to in one way or another. The manager may enter items on other people's action lists, and the system keeps track to ensure that these items are attended to.

WORKING FROM HOME

An executive need not come into his office to manage his work queue. Electronic paperwork could be accessed and handled from any location where a terminal is available, including the executive's home. Suitable networks and security control are necessary for this, just as they are for most aspects of DDP.

Some corporations have employed part-time clerical staff and secretaries at home, using terminals. This enables those who must be at home to care for children to do some work. In cities with a scarcity of clerical staff this can help to fill the shortage. Some professionals work at home, with word-processing machines and personal computing.

The portable terminal gives added flexibility. Some newspaper reporters type, edit, word process and file their copy with a typewriterlike terminal which they carry. An executive device which would greatly extend the value of the automated office is a briefcase which serves as a terminal. It has a flat plasma display in the lid, a flat keyboard, a miniature modem or acoustical coupler for connecting it to telephones, and a built-in microcomputer. With today's miniaturization there could still be plenty of room in the briefcase for papers or sandwiches.

DATA-BASE ACCESS

To assist in handling work the manager has appropriate files and information sources accessible via his screen. A low-level manager may access only a few files specifically related to his job. A high-level manager may be able to access a diversity of information sources.

Data-base technology is maturing and becoming the foundation of data processing in those corporations which have endorsed appropriate techniques of logical data-base planning. High-level data-base languages are now available which make data-base inquiry and report generation easy for non-DP personnel to learn. Data-base access becomes an important facility of office terminals.

A large corporation has many separate data-base (and file) systems. They are becoming connected to networks. The office terminals need to access both local and remote data bases, via networks.

INFORMATION RETRIEVAL

Much of the resources of the electronic office will be concerned with the storage and retrieval of data.

Manual filing cabinets will be replaced and the data filed will become accessible via networks. Unlike the organization of data stored for data processing, filing cabinet organization is fairly simple. Letters are stored in date sequence in electronic equivalents of filing cabinet pockets. The system may provide indices for finding letters and documents, sometimes for finding them in remote locations.

In some systems the indices become highly complex. The data are organized for information retrieval based on the key words and combinations of key words.

There is a great difference in usability between an *on-line* information retrieval system, with which a user can carry out a fast search of the documents, and an *off-line* one or one too slow for effective interactive searching. Many off-line information retrieval systems inundate their users with long listings of abstracts which are often dumped in waste bins without reading. A fast interactive system can be employed by a user when he needs to find information on a particular subject. His search will progress rapidly through the files, rejecting many references as it goes. It will need the speed of a visual display terminal and an inverted file system.

Figure 4.4 shows a typical file structure of an interactive document-searching system. It is the file structure of the IBM STAIRS system [1, 2].

Shown on the right-hand side of Fig. 4.4 is the *document file,* which stores the documents. The documents are numbered by the system. They are subdivided into paragraphs and sentences; the sentences are numbered, and the paragraphs are given codes to indicate the type of paragraph, such as "Title," "Author," "Abstract," "Text," or general categorization.

On the left-hand side of Fig. 4.4 is shown a *word dictionary*. It gives the names of English-language (or other) words which are in the documents. The dictionary can be large and needs a higher-level index. A character-pair matrix is used. For each pair of characters the matrix stores a pointer to the dictionary block containing words beginning with these characters. The characters can be letters, digits, or a special character. The second character can also be a blank. There are thus 37 x 38 = 1406 entries in the matrix. The dictionary contains variable groups or entries, each entry in the group being for a word beginning with the same two characters. (The first two characters are not repeated in the dictionary entries, but they have been left in Fig. 4.4 for ease of reading. Some words in the dictionary may have identical meanings, and these are linked by "synonym" pointers (dotted lines in Fig. 4.4)).

Each entry in the dictionary points to an *occurrence list* giving every occurrence in the document file of the word in question. The occurrence list is headed by fields giving the number of documents containing the word and the total number of occurrences of the word in the entire document file. These numbers are given to the user who is carrying out a search. If they are too large, he may not employ the word

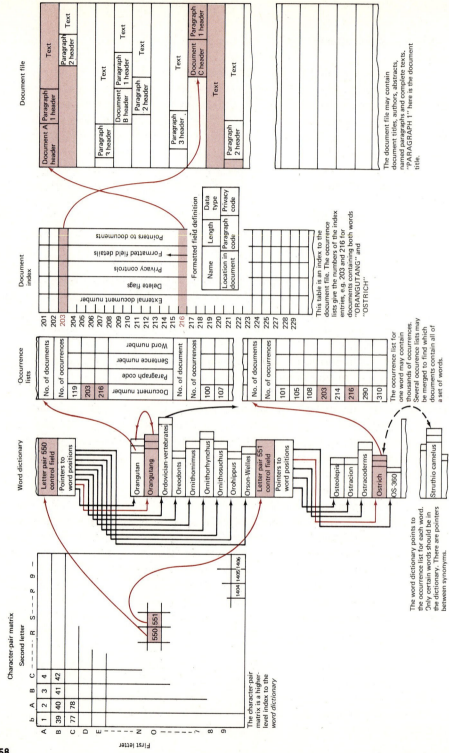

Document file — The document file may contain document titles, authors, abstracts, named paragraphs and complete texts. "PARAGRAPH 1" here is the document title.

Document index — This table is an index to the document file. The occurrence lists give the numbers of the index entries, e.g. 203 and 216 for documents containing both words "ORANGUTANG" and "OSTRICH"

Occurrence lists — The occurrence list for one word may contain thousands of occurrences. Several occurrence lists may be merged to find which documents contain all of a set of words.

Word dictionary — The word dictionary points to the occurrence list for each word. Only certain words should be in the dictionary. There are pointers between synonyms.

Character-pair matrix — The character-pair matrix is a higher-level index to the word dictionary

in question but will attempt to find a more suitable word or words as the basis of his search.

The system gives all documents a unique number which is as compact as possible. It is unrelated to any external number by which the user may refer to the document. The occurence list contains this document number for each occurrence. A search criterion may be *search for all documents containing both of two specified words,* for example, all documents containing the words *computer* and *chess.* The program then obtains from the occurrence list file the numbers of all documents containing the word *computer* and all documents containing the word *chess.* These lists are merged to produce a list of the numbers of documents containing both words.

There are many other possible search criteria. The criteria often specify that two or more words must be adjacent, for example, *nuclear* and *particle* or *data, base, management,* and *system.* For this reason the positions of words in the sentences are recorded in the occurrence list.

The user may attempt to narrow down the search by specifying that more than one sentence contain the key word or words. If the documents are long—say, 30-page reports—then many irrelevant documents could be included in the occurrence list, and so the user may specify that the key words must appear in well-separated sentences.

Particularly important is the *paragraph type.* The user may specify that the key word appear in the title, the abstract, the introduction, or in specially designated paragraphs. Whatever the search criteria, a list of numbers of documents which satisfy them is produced without going further into the files than the occurrence list.

The user is shown how many documents are in the list which results from his search criteria. He may then change his criteria or instruct the machine to display the document titles, authors, abstracts, or text, one screenful at a time.

The internal document numbers form a key to the *document index,* and the document index points to the location in the storage of the document itself. The occurrence list *could* have pointed to the document directly, but such a pointer would contain more bytes than the brief internal document number. Lists containing many thousands, occasionally hundreds of thousands, of document references are merged as part of the search process, so the document references must be as short as possible. For this reason the document index is kept separately.

The document index, in addition to giving the storage address of the document, gives the external document number, deletes flags to indicate whether all or part of the document has been removed from the files, and controls relating to

---

Figure 4.4 An inverted file structure for document retrieval. The marked path shows the answering of the query: "Give me the titles of documents with both the word ORANGUTANG and OSTRICH in the text."

privacy, which can prevent certain users or certain terminals from having access to classified documents.

Specified formatted fields which may contain encoded data can be stored in the document index. These may be inspected in the search operation before the decision is made to retrieve the documents in question.

SUCCESSION OF   The search thus begins with the *dictionary* and may
SEARCH LEVELS   proceed no further until the operator modifies his
search criteria. It continues into the *occurrence* list and again may not proceed further without refinement of the search criteria. It may continue into the *document index,* possibly searching the *formatted fields*. Finally, the documents themselves are inspected. This succession of search levels makes it possible to give the terminal users conversational response times.

A key to success in designing information retrieval operations is to structure this succession of search levels in an appropriate fashion, confining the search, where possible, to sections of the storage which do not require large numbers of time-consuming seeks.

It is very important to control which words are employed in the dictionary. Users of such a system often want to put too many words in the dictionary and to employ words which are too common. If a word is too common, its occurrence list will be very long, and the search operations which merge occurrence lists will be excessively time-consuming. The system can become flooded by the use of inappropriate dictionary entries.

On some STAIRS installations, occurrence lists with nearly 1 million entries for one word have been encountered before the word was pruned from the dictionary.

RETRIEVAL SPEED   Just as data transmitted should be divided into priority
classes (Box 30.2), so data stored should be divided into classes of retrieval speed. Box 4.3 suggests five such classes:

- *Immediate*. Designed for fast computer processing.
- *Fast interactive*. For human retrieval with dialogues needing fast responses.
- *Slow interactive*. For slow retrieval at a terminal.
- *Deferrable*. Retrieval without any urgency so that it can be deferred until appropriate resources are free.
- *Off-line*. Data in archival stores, for example, past mail, paid bills, and old checks. This may be off-line tape or microfilm.

The class of retrieval speed affects both the selection of storage media and the use of transmission. In Part V of this book, Box 30.2 lists priorities of network

**BOX 4.3   Suggested classes of retrieval speed
for electronic filing**

Class 1, Immediate. 0.95 probability of retrieval in 200 milliseconds.

Designed for fast computer processing.

Class 2, Fast interactive. 0.95 probability of retrieval in 2 seconds.

Designed for terminal dialogues needing a fast response time.

Class 3, Slow interactive. 0.95 probability of retrieval in 15 seconds.

Designed for terminal retrieval in which the operator can tolerate a 10- or 15-second wait. This permits slow mass storage units to be used.

Class 4, Deferrable.   0.95 probability of retrieval in 4 hours.

Transmission or access can wait until resources are no longer employed by more urgent traffic.

Class 5, Off-line.

For archival storage of past letters, checks, and old documents, often on microfilm or magnetic tape.

transmission. *Immediate* and *fast interactive* data must be sent at Priority 2 in Box 30.2. Slow interactive data may be sent at Priority 3, and *deferrable* data at Priority 4.

In some systems the interactive searching of indices such as those on the left of Fig. 4.4 happens with fast response times, and then the final retrieval of the documents takes longer. The document may be delivered in a time ranging from a few seconds to a minute, depending on the nature of the storage and transmission facilities and the nature of document encoding (alphanumeric, compressed alphabetic, or digital facsimile).

**MERGING WITH
DATA PROCESSING**   A system which merely handles mail is often not regarded as being in the province of data processing.
However, the same terminals may retrieve documents with a scheme which has substantial computing like that in Figure 4.4. Again, the same terminals may also interrogate computer data bases. There is thus a con-

tinuous spectrum of office terminal usage ranging from simple mail handling to sophisticated data processing.

The same terminal, controller, switching system, and network should handle all of these applications.

MAIL

The 1980's will see major changes in the way mail is sent. It can be sent more cheaply by electronics than by manual methods. It can reach its destination in seconds, and none of it will be lost if the system is well designed.

While electronic mail is dropping in cost, that of manual mail is increasing, and the mail services of the world seem to be steadily deteriorating. The motto of the U.S. Postal Services is chipped in stone over the stately columns of its head office. A *New Yorker* cartoon showed a slightly changed version of the motto as follows: "Neither lethargy, indifference, nor the general collapse of standards will prevent these couriers from eventually delivering some of your mail."

The cost of postage stamps is a small part of the cost of mail. The largest part is the cost of manual operations and the running of the mail room.

Electronic mail can take many different forms. Some of these are listed in Box 4.4. They differ in the numbers of bits required for transmission. A full page of typing takes about 200,000 bits to transmit in facsimile form and about 10,000 bits in *compressed* alphanumeric coding from a computer or terminal controller. An economical form is transmission directly from the computer, terminal, or word-processing machine which originates the document.

Amazingly, 70% of all *first-class* mail in the United States is generated by computers. Much of this is destined for other computers. It is printed, split into separate sheets, fed into envelopes, sent to a mail room, stamped, carried manually to a post office, sorted, delivered to planes and sent to another post office, sorted again, delivered to a mail room, sorted, distributed, and then laboriously keyed for entry into another computer. All this ought to take place electronically.

Much noncomputer mail, including handwritten letters, can also be sent electronically. Once we use electronics, we should ask, What is the best form for a message? Does it need to be written at all?

INSTANT MAIL

Once we are able to have messages delivered almost instantaneously, the way we utilize them changes completely. Instant mail will be fundamentally different from mail delivery by weary letter carriers.

Documents or diagrams can be exchanged by two persons while they are on the telephone to one another. On the other hand, they may not telephone at all; they may converse on a typewriter-like terminal if this costs less than a long-distance telephone call. Callers may prefer sending messages to talking on the telephone when there is difficulty in making telephone contact with busy people.

BOX 4.4   Forms of electronic mail

- Mail originated by secretaries using word-processing machines
- Computer printouts transmitted to remote locations before being printed
- Computer input from on-line machines in remote locations
- Message switching: messages stored and forwarded to terminals which can receive them
- On-demand message switching, in which users can request the system to print or display their message queue when they want it
- Messages sent and received by executives or staff from their office terminals
- Electronic filing: memos and documents sent to and retrieved from electronic filing cabinets
- Voicegrams: messages transmitted and stored in the form of speech, sent and received with a conventional telephone
- Analog facsimile: documents transmitted in analog form between facsimile machines, over telephone circuits
- Digital facsimile: facsimile machines which transmit documents in digital form, so that they can travel over digital networks and be stored in digital machines
- Office copiers transmitting to distant office copiers (a form of digital facsimile)

Some users of data networks have terminals which were installed primarily for sending messages to one another. Communities of users have grown up bound by the ease with which they can interchange messages. As data networks become more widespread, this capability to send a message cheaply to another person's terminal will become more popular. Most offices and many homes will have terminals for sending and receiving messages. Such a terminal could be derived by a cheap addition to an already existing electric typewriter.

Cheap, fast message networks make it possible to hold electronic "meetings" with participants scattered across the world in their offices or homes. The participants send messages in a formal fashion instead of making speeches. Not only are the participants in different towns or different countries; they may not all be attending at the same time. Each has a terminal that logs what the participants have said, giving a serial number to each statement. An attender can wander into his or her office, read what has been contributed during the last few hours, and make a contribution of his own if so inclined.

Users of message networks in the military, in universities with ARPANET, and in corporations have found that such systems change their communications habits. Communication between people takes place where it would not have otherwise. Most people at work check their message files two or three times a day, at times which are convenient to them when they can really pay attention and handle the messages without interruption. Urgent messages ought to flash a light for faster attention.

TELEVISION SET   Some of the facilities in Boxes 4.1 and 4.2 use television
TERMINALS   sets, and some use computer terminals. These may be
                       the same. Some equipment displays both computer
data and video images on a television screen. A word-processing machine or mail display can use a television set, but better resolution is obtained on specially designed equipment. Only a portion of a dense page of type can be displayed at one time on a television set.

Services like Viewdata (such as the British Post Office *Prestel* service) make a potentially vast and diverse amount of information accessible with television [2]. An adapter converts the television set into a terminal, and a dialed telephone connection connects it to a network of data banks. The system has an elegant color dialog structure which enables its users to find the information they want rapidly and easily.

A different form of information service available on television in Europe is *teletext*. Like Viewdata, this is given different names by different organizations which provide it. Unlike Viewdata, the sets pick up data which is *broadcast* along with the television signal. Information such as news, weather forecasts, stock market prices, and sports results are broadcast. The information frames which are of interest are selected with a keyboard using a dialog, in color, something like the Viewdata dialogue. The amount of information which can be broadcast is much less than the amount which can be assessed interactively with Viewdata services. Nevertheless, it could be much greater than today if a whole television channel were used for it. Today the alphanumeric information of teletext is transmitted on the same channel as a normal television program. It is sent in the brief instants when the television scanning spot flies back from the bottom right-hand corner of the screen to the top left-hand corner. This happens 50 times per second (60 in North America). This steady flow of broadcast data is repeated every 10 seconds or so, giving a response time of from 0 to 10 seconds for selecting a requested screen. In this 10 seconds (the time differs from one system to another) several hundred frames of data can be broadcast. Keying a digit into the keyboard selects the next frame to be viewed.

Whereas *teletext* makes hundreds of pages of information viewable, Viewdata makes hundreds of thousands. Figure 4.5 shows Viewdata; Fig. 4.6 shows teletext.

Viewdata systems are in use not only for accessing *public* information sources but also for accessing private sources within one corporation. The information source can be constantly updated.

Figure 4.5 Examples of Prestel Displays.

One of the less-mentioned sales arguments for such services is that some sets can also be used for receiving television. If an executive is watching horse racing on his office set and somebody walks in, he can instantly switch it with the hand-held keyboard to the corporate videotext service!

Video training is rapidly spreading and improving in quality. The author makes courses for executives with Deltak, Inc. on subjects including Office of the future, Distributed Processing Strategy, Corporate Data Base Strategy, and so on. The same television used for information retrieval can be used for training with a video tape or video disk machine.

Video tape is also proving an effective medium for certain types of communication. In some corporations it is used by executives for making speeches to

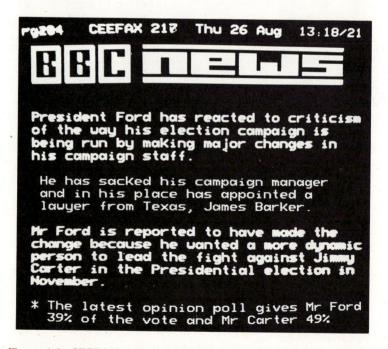

Figure 4.6 CEEFAX screens. A BBC system for enabling television viewers to display frames of broadcast data on their screens. Britain's Independent Television Authority operates a similar system. Screens on television sets in a compatible format can be accessed using a local telephone call to the British Post Office's Prestel system.

employees. In some it is used for recording meetings, presentations, or the views of visiting experts. Some professionals use it for communicating with one another on complex subjects. The author finds it uniquely valuable for the latter purpose.

It is important to stress that communication by video tape does not need an expensive studio. Some corporations have a studio costing $0.5 million or more, but communication which is *effective* for business or professional purposes can be done with an installation costing less than $6000. For professional communication there is no need to photograph faces. All that is needed is a good monitor, a pause control, and a color camera with a zoom lens pointing vertically down at a well-lighted desk.

VIDEO COMMUNICATIONS A particularly valuable office facility is one which enables professionals or executives to communicate more effectively than they do with the telephone.

A few corporations use teleconferencing in which a *television* channel rather than a telephone channel is used for communication. This has not been done much because of its very high cost. Television circuits which are switched, like the telephone, have not existed. Point-to-point television circuits have been difficult to obtain and extremely expensive. The studio facilities at each end of the link have been prohibitively expensive.

Today this situation is changing in some countries for the following reasons:

1. Television channels provided by new communications satellites are dropping to a more reasonable cost.

2. The television bandwidth via satellites need not be allocated full time, as with a point-to-point terrestrial video circuit. It might be used for one video call and then reassigned to other customers in other locations for other purposes.

3. Sophisticated compression algorithms are compressing television with little movement into much smaller digital bit rates.

4. It is becoming generally recognized that *moving* television is not necessary for many communications purposes. Freeze-frame television is adequate. If one frame every 10 seconds is transmitted, this needs 1/300 the bandwidth of moving television This form of communication can be sent over existing digital services such as the Bell System DDS circuits.

5. Expensive television studios or meeting rooms are not needed. A cheap camera and monitor and a brightly lit room suffice. The cost of the transmission equipment is dropping.

6. New common carriers such as XTEN (Xerox) and SBS (IBM, Comsat, Aetna) aim to provide video circuits and equipment for video communications.

7. The cost of the alternative, business travel, is increasing as petroleum increases in costs.

Some types of communication need warm human beings in physical proximity. A good salesman would say that electronics cannot substitute for his physical presence in closing a sale. How much business communication *could* be done by electronics?

There is now substantial experience of video links being used for business purposes. At the time of writing, about 80 of the Fortune 500 corporations of the United States use video links on a small scale. Some of these are full video and some are freeze-frame video.

Based on this experience we can divide human communications into those with a strong *emotional* content and those without. Where there is a strong emotional content, physical face-to-face presence adds something subtle and in some cases is definitely necessary for communication. Where the content of the communication is mainly facts and intellect, electronic video links can work well. The Institute for the Future conducted research on the psychological effects of teleconferencing and concluded that 85% of business travellers' communications requirements could be satisfied with facilities for video conferences and fast facsimile transmission [3].

Certainly, most of the *internal* meetings I participated in at IBM could have been carried out effectively by video conferencing and facsimile. A typical comment on the experience of video communication is that by the President of Dow Chemical on the use of full video links between Dow Head Office and its main plant 1400 miles away. He states that the facility is extremely valuable in making decisions that otherwise would not have been made and that it saves many hours in traveling and much wear and tear on executives. At the same time, it can never completely replace face-to-face discussions. There are some cases when individuals *must* get together in the same location [3].

Perhaps more important than the simple tradeoff between travel and telecommunications cost is the fact that there would be much more person-to-person communication that is lacking today because the parties are geographically separate and cannot constantly be traveling. In many corporate situations this lack of continual communication does much harm. A decision maker often works in isolation when he should have communication with persons in many locations to give him a better understanding.

The Dow link cost $2000 per hour of use. A digital freeze-frame video link working at 56,000 bps could cost less than $100 per hour of use. Executive travel between the two Dow plants takes about 15 hours of a person's time for a one-hour meeting. Its cost is about $500 including the executive's time, but this does not include the wear and tear.

BETTER THAN TELEPHONE COMMUNICATIONS
In order to communicate better than by telephone there is a range of options, and full video is about the most expensive.

At the other end of the cost scale, the parties could send facsimile documents which they then talk about on the telephone.

Similarly, they could display the same computer images on their screens and talk about them.

Some users of office terminals for sending messages have found that that substantially increases their communication effectiveness. The U.S. Army Material Development and Readiness Command used mailbox services developed for ARPANET [4]. The data processing director found that this improved communication to the point where it affected his travel habits. Whereas he has previously visited remote development sites once a month, he began to visit them only once every six months. [5].

In discussing screen images, the conversation would be more flexible if both parties could print to the image and see each other's pointers. A feature of machines designed for such communication could be transmission of the position of a pointer over the same channel that carries speech. Conversation would be more flexible if the parties could each modify the screen contents and see each others' modifications. Modifications could also be transmitted on the telephone channel. A relatively simple extension to word processing machines or computer terminals can thus make them valuable for person-to-person communications.

Again, if full-color television images are used for person-to-person communication, these can be transmitted in times ranging from less than a second to a minute depending upon the bandwidth of the circuit used. If a voice-grade circuit is used, the image can be transmitted in times ranging from seconds to a minute, depending on the type of image and how it is encoded. With these images also, communication would be improved by both parties being able to see each other point to and modify the image. A cheap color camera with a zoom lens pointed down at a desk top would in some ways be preferable to expensive teleconferencing studio facilities. It could be the same camera as that used for making video tapes and the same television set as for obtaining Viewdata services.

TELECONFERENCING   "Teleconferencing" refers to a telecommunications link on which more than two people communicate. It may be a conference call with three or more locations linked. It may be a point-to-point link with several people communicating rather than one person at one or both ends.

A point-to-point link with a meeting can be handled by a *speakerphone* device so that a room full of people can hear and be heard. A multipoint call (conference call) can be set up using the computerized PBXs (Private Branch Exchanges).

When a meeting takes place at one or both ends of a communications link, there is much to be said for having a specially equipped meeting room. A major facility in the office building of the future will be the conference room equipped with visual aids and a computer screen, and also with teleconference facilities.

MEETING ROOM   The office of the future meeting room can range in cost from a shoestring budget to Hollywood opulence. Sometimes its primary purpose seems to be to impress.

It can have one screen or many. The screen(s) can be small or wall-sized. The telecommunications links can be voice-grade, freeze-frame video, or full video. The computer terminals can range from dumb, typewriterlike devices to full graphics.

Equipment can include video tape, access to Viewdata-like services, video circuits in the building or long distance, a facsimile machine, a word-processing machine for modifying and agreeing to memoranda or reports, and terminals with access to a computer network, corporate data bases, or information retrieval facilities.

INFORMATION ROOM   The question of how best to provide information to management, especially top management, is a perennial one in data processing. One solution is the use of an information room from which management's requests for information can be quickly answered. In the room is a staff of information specialists who have the skills needed for locating, retrieving, and, if necessary, processing the information required. These people are professional and have taken some time to learn to do their job well. They have detailed knowledge of the corporate data bases and associated programs, external data banks, information retrieval systems, and other sources. They keep charts and slides of interest to management. They have terminals which access a variety of computer systems. The information room may be adjacent to the corporate library.

When executives or staff have questions, they phone the information room. A helpful information specialist advises them. Sometimes he needs to do research, generate graphics, send messages to other locations, run regression analyses, or write programs.

The link between the information room and the requester's office can be of many different types—telephone, facsimile, computer terminals, freeze-frame video, television.

Inside a head office or building complex, cable television may be appropriate. Some information rooms have a video switch so that a variety of devices can be switched to the requestor's screen—a desk-top camera, a slide projector, a movie projector film-chain, a microfiche viewer, cameras on terminals, or a camera on the information specialist's face.

The information specialist forms a human interface between requests for information and sources of information. As information systems grow more complex and networks access a greater diversity of machines, the need for such specialists will grow. An immensely rich set of information sources are becoming available. The difficulty is in accessing them and separating the wheat from the great quantities of chaff.

OPERATIONS ROOM   Whereas an information room is designed for passive access to data, an operations room is designed to change events actively. A large amount of data is made available in one place where controlling decisions can be made.

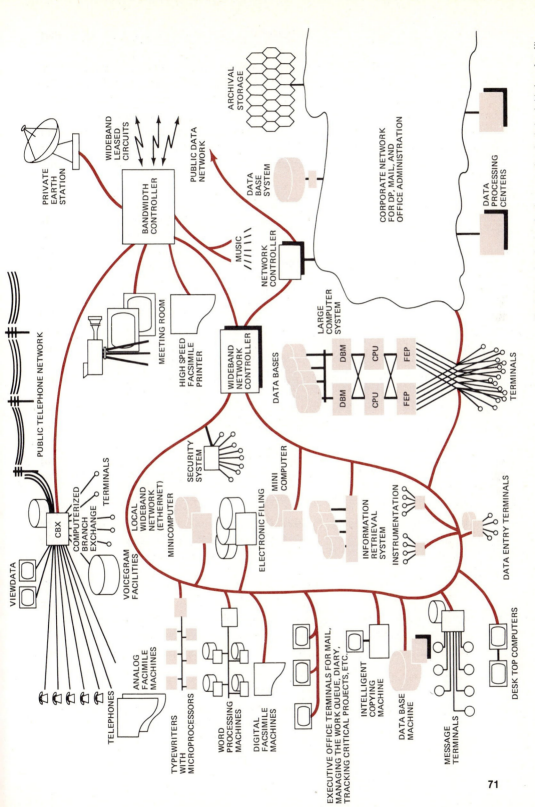

The devices colored red are for data processing, the devices in black are for office administration functions. The two are inextricably intermixed.

Figure 4.7 Office of the future facilities.

71

Spectacular control rooms such as the NASA Mission Control Center or the control rooms of nuclear power stations have long been familiar to the public. The networks and electronic facilities used for other office-of-the-future applications can be applied to control rooms for more common purposes such as controlling activities on the shop floor of a factory or controlling a maintenance force.

Operations rooms range in cost from a room with a blackboard and a few terminals to a showplace with wall screens and a visitor's gallery.

COMMONALITY OF STRUCTURE   The resources we have described affect diverse areas of a corporation, but they have much in common in terms of electronics. They need the same terminals, screens, minicomputers, television, data networks, wideband cables, and so on.

Figure 4.7 illustrates some of the devices and communications links in future offices. The devices colored red are for data processing; those colored black are for office administration or non-DP functions. It will be seen that they are inextricably intermixed.

There should be common management of the *infrastructure* for such equipment. As with distributed processing in general, central management should set corporate standards and provide the networking capability so that diverse machines can be interconnected. Within that framework local management can be responsible for the facilities they procure and for how they use them.

REFERENCES

1. *Computerworld,* May 21, 1979; an article about Harvey Poppel's large-scale study for Booz, Allen and Hamilton, Inc., on the office of the future.

2. James Martin and David Butler, *Viewdata and the Information Society,* Prentice-Hall, Inc., Englewood Cliffs, N.J., 1981.

3. Charles E. Lathey, *Telecommunications Substitution for Travel: An Energy Conservation Potential,* Washington, D.C., Office of Telecommunications Policy, 1975.

4. The U.S. Army Material Development and Readiness Command used *Hermes* for message distribution, file management, and text editing; it is offered by Bolt, Beranek and Newman, Inc., 50 Moulton Avenue, Cambridge, Mass. 02138.

5. "The Automated Office." Part 2. *EDP Analyzer,* October 1978 (Vol. 16, No. 10), Canning Publication, Inc., Vista, Ca.

5 PITFALLS IN DISTRIBUTED PROCESSING

We have indicated that distributed processing is *inevitable,* given the progress of the microelectronics industry. It is a revolutionary change in data processing, happening fast. Its benefits are enormous. Not only is it as inevitable as the leaves coming out in spring; it is potentially as useful—the greening of the computer industry. It will change those end users who are directly affected by it, *and also higher-level management processes* because logistics information about the entire organization can be transmitted to one location. Top management must reassess what functions should be coordinated, integrated, and centralized.

At the same time there are giant pitfalls in DDP. This chapter summarizes some of the pitfalls. Their nature will be discussed more precisely later in the book. This chapter should not be taken negatively, as a condemnation of DDP. The pitfalls can be avoided if the move to DDP is *managed* appropriately.

Some of them require *top* management attention. One of the messages of this book is that *top* management involvement is needed in the strategies for DDP. Prior to the mid-1970's top management could (and usually did) avoid any involvement in data processing. They often felt that it was a technician's job which should be delegated, rather like doing the factory wiring. Now, however, data processing has become too vital to the corporation as a whole. The corporation may be reorganized because of DDP. Worse, if top management is not involved, it is likely that the full advantages will not be achieved because of corporate politics and lack of corporation wide perspective among the groups who install local systems. Optimally designed computer networks and data-base systems often *tend to be counterpolitical,* and the trend to DDP tends to cut across existing empires. There needs to be a top management *strategy* for the implementation of DDP.

Box 5.1 summarizes some of the main pitfalls in distributed processing. Most of the pitfalls listed can be avoided by appropriate design and management.

BOX 5.1 Potential pitfalls in distributed processing

(Note: An equally formidable list could be drawn up of pitfalls of *centralized processing.*) *The objectives of DDP strategy should be to maximize the benefits of DDP while avoiding these pitfalls.*

- LOSS OF MANAGEMENT CONTROL

  DP management loses overall control of data processing as increasing numbers of user groups acquire their own minicomputers. DDP then evolves in a random fashion rather than in a designed and controlled fashion.

- LOSS OF CONTROL OF THE MIS FUNCTION

  Gathering of management information which can strongly effect the organization is made difficult or almost impossible.

- SUBOPTIMIZATION

  Local developers perceive local needs but not the overall data processing required to control the corporation efficiently.

- INCOMPATIBLE DATA

  The same data are represented in different ways in different systems. It is almost impossible to associate these data later to meet higher-level requirements, without rewriting the programs which use the data. This is so expensive that it is not achieved in practice.

- INCOMPATIBLE HARDWARE

  Machines selected by different user groups are incompatible. A floppy disk on one cannot be moved to another; a program on one cannot be run on another; the machines cannot be connected by telecommunications; and so on.

- INCOMPATIBLE SOFTWARE

  Different machines have different software—data link control, network management architectures, session services, data-base management services, etc. Compatible choices of software are necessary to interlink machines, transfer data, and use remote data bases.

- DISTRIBUTED INCOMPETENCE

  Minicomputers are sometimes employed unprofessionally. It is like the bad old days of amateur data processing, without standards, structured techniques, or adequate documentation. Badly thought-out design.

- FAILURE TO USE DATA BASE

  End-user machines often employ on-line files but not data-base management. They fail to take advantage of data-base technology and techniques which improve application development productivity and flexibility.

- EXCESSIVE MAINTENANCE COSTS

  Programs often have to be rewritten because of the reasons above. Unanticipated costs of rewriting programs, performing conversions, redesigning

BOX 5.1 *continued*

data, and restructuring systems may rise to more than 80% of an installation's development work. The high-level manpower thus occupied *should* be in use on new application development. Distributed systems need to be designed for maintenance.

- DUPLICATION OF EFFORT

    The same functions may be programmed many times by different groups. The problem of finding good computer people is multiplied.

- LOW PRODUCTIVITY

    Programming in low-level languages, lack of powerful software, failure to use data base, high maintenance effort, and duplication of programming work on peripheral machines, may lead to low productivity in application development.

- HIGH TOTAL MANPOWER INVOLVEMENT

    User personnel become increasingly absorbed with computing, which becomes like a narcotic; they spend increasing time on it and grow to want more sophisticated facilities. Manpower is often bootlegged from user groups without accounting.

- LACK OF CORPORATE NETWORK DESIGN

    A network is not designed with the ability to interlink the proliferation of small processors as required.

- NO EVOLUTION PLANNING

    The proliferation of small, incompatible systems is extremely difficult to integrate later. Evolution from incompatible decentralized systems to an integrated network and data-base facility is so complex and expensive that in practice it is rarely achieved.

- MIGRATION LOCKOUT

    Major manufacturers' migration paths to better technology cannot be followed.

- LACK OF SECURITY

    Some peripheral systems are often installed with insufficient attention to security. Embezzlement or privacy violation is possible.

- LACK OF FILE BACKUP

    A backup copy of files is often not kept. If a disc is dropped or other damage occurs, the data may be lost.

- LACK OF AUDITABILITY

    Auditors find some distributed systems unauditable. There are inadequate audit trails or records of who used the system or updated files.

continued

BOX 5.1 *continued*

- HIGH REPAIR COSTS

  Repair costs are high on some distributed systems because of many scattered small computers having no pooled repair parts, maintenance staff, or backup.

- CREEPING ESCALATION

  The minicomputers at end-user locations become steadily larger, more complex, and more expensive. Simple end-user systems evolve into complex systems which require more manpower and skill.

- POLITICAL STRIFE

  Many comprehensive DDP plans cut across corporate political structures. At the same time minicomputers give politically competing factions the opportunity to wrest control away from the central DP group.

- INCREASED TELEPHONING

  More telephone calls are made relating to problems with the distributed organization than with a central organization. The increase in telephone costs exceeds the much-acclaimed decrease in data transmission costs.

- UNCONTROLLED TOTAL COSTS

  Total costs often become higher than anticipated or necessary. Total costs would have been lower if centrally controlled. Design techniques for minimizing total system costs are not used.

MANAGEMENT STRATEGY

Minicomputers and other small machines will proliferate, playing a vital role in data processing. Some of them can be completely stand-alone machines, unconnected with any other machine, but most need to exchange data with or be linked to other computers, either now or in the future. Therefore some measure of centralized design and control is needed. How much and what types of central control are desirable vary from one situation to another. Determining this is part of the strategic planning needed for DDP. *The objective of the strategy should be to maximize the benefits of DDP, especially that of making end users participate, while avoiding the pitfalls listed in Box 5.1.*

At the top of the list of pitfalls is the absence of management control. It is only too easy in some corporations for many user departments to obtain incompatible machines. The minicomputer salesmen are persuasive. In some cases the user departments are deliberately breaking away from the central DP authority because they are dissatisfied with the service, scheduling, costs, or rate of application development.

The problem with independent machine acquisition is that the machines have different instruction sets and different telecommunications control. Programs which run on one do not run on another. Diverse machines usually cannot use common computer networks (without expensive modification). The floppy disks and interchangeable storage media on one machine family do not fit onto another. The computer industry which is introducing new machines at such a rapid rate has major problems with compatibility.

In addition, the software is fundamentally incompatible. Various manufacturers have architectures for distributed processing enabling one machine to use and communicate with a distant machine. These architectures are highly complex and different from one manufacturer to another. Data-base management systems are often different from one machine to another. There are great advantages to using such software, but if machines are to cooperate in distributed systems, they need to be carefully selected. The entire distributed configuration needs to be planned.

CENTRALIZED APPLICATIONS   Some applications are best run on a centralized machine, and some data are best stored centrally. We will discuss the characteristics which lead naturally to centralization in Part IV. Some applications are best run decentrally at an end-user location and may be best designed at that location. These decentralized applications often create or use data which are needed or stored elsewhere.

The planning of what applications should be central and what data they need from peripheral systems is critical to the overall design of distributed processing. The concept of centralized *strategic* applications and decentralized *functional* applications discussed in the previous chapter is important. When peripheral groups implement their own minicomputer installations, these may be contrary to the best overall application planning. Local systems may be suboptimized. For example, there might be multiple local inventory control, purchasing, information, or cash management systems when there are major economies in centralized or coordinated systems.

DATA DESIGN   In a peripheral system designed by or for one user department, some of the data employed are used only in that department, but some are also used elsewhere. How much is used elsewhere varies greatly from one set of applications to another. Some literature from minicomputer manufacturers quotes an 80/20 rule: 80% of minicomputer data is used only at the minicomputer location, and 20% is also used elsewhere. In practice the ratio of data in the second category is often much higher. It is common to find installations in which 70% of the data in the minicomputer files is also used elsewhere.

A major danger in distributed development is that the data in different locations are designed by different uncoordinated teams. Each designs their own data with different bits in the fields, different fields in the records, and different associations between records. The same data are represented in many different ways. At a later time it is necessary to use these data in a central system. Extremely expensive conversions are needed in order to accomplish this. The data design should have been coordinated in the first place.

In general, uncontrolled DDP can lead to a proliferation of incompatible machines and data, which do not link together to achieve the broad objectives we discussed in the previous chapter.

LOW-LEVEL SOFTWARE

Minicomputer software is rapidly improving. Nevertheless, many minicomputer installations do not use powerful software such as data-base management systems. Powerful software is (or ought to be) designed to improve the productivity of application development. Productivity with multiple mini installations may then be less than with a powerful central installation. This depends on how the installations are managed. In practice many minicomputer installations with low-level software have achieved results much faster than large installations with sophisticated expensive software. This is often because of the simpler overall operation, avoidance of complex systems programming, and the dedication of the user-group staff.

Peripheral application development can be made easier and more versatile if the peripheral machines are linked to a central data base and the developers are given powerful languages for generating applications which use or update the data.

UNPROFESSIONAL IMPLEMENTATION

The professional programming skills available to user groups are often lower than those in well-managed central installations. This can be overcome by placing skilled programmers with the user groups. Often, however, minicomputer development is unprofessional. Standards are not followed, structured programming is not used, lower-level languages are employed, and the code is repeatedly patched— patches on top of patches on top of patches. The code would be difficult for another programmer to follow. Good comments are not used in the program. The programs are not documented. User-group coders make all the amateurish mistakes that the computer industry as a whole made 20 years ago.

Reorganization, new products, and general business changes bring the need to rewrite the programs, restructure the data, or change the hardware or software. The programs, ill-documented and not designed for change, are difficult to modify. The user groups are finding out what the DP department has long known—that program maintenance is a major headache and should be planned for.

MAINTENANCE

The term ''maintenance'' is used to refer to the adjustment of existing computer programs and facilities; in other words, the term describes conversion efforts, the redesign of data and software, and the rewriting of programs that have already been produced—rewriting the past instead of new application development.

Many computer development staff members spend much of their time on maintenance. When an installation first begins, all of the budget is spent on *new* development. As time passes, the need to change the programs and data grows. A change in one program necessitates a change in a data record, and a change in data record necessitates rewriting all the programs that use that data. A seemingly trivial modification can cause a chain reaction of changes which have to be made, at considerable cost. Figure 5.1 illustrates the rise in maintenance and conversion expenditure.

The manpower spent on maintenance in many installations is 80% of the total development manpower. Skilled staff are rewriting programs, modifying data, and converting files, operating systems, networks, and software. Maintenance can occupy many of the brightest persons in an installation, who ought to be working on new application development.

Systems can be designed to minimize the maintenance cost. This requires complex software, including data-base management systems which derive multiple different user views of data from a given data base, and data-communications software which derives *virtual* circuits.

Uncontrolled distributed processing is likely to make the maintenance problem much worse. There are three reasons for this. First, the random spread of mini-

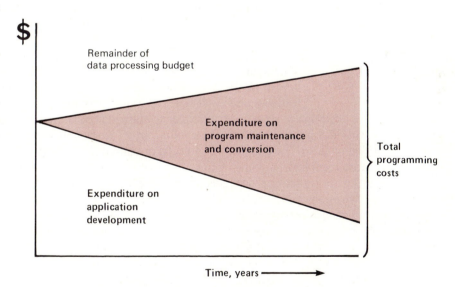

Figure 5.1   New application process is often deferred by the rising cost of modifying existing programs and files. Some corporations now spend more than 80% of their programming budget just keeping current and only 20% forging ahead. A danger of ill-designed distributed processing is that it will increase yet further the effort required for maintenance and conversion.

computers does not give a system designed for maintenance. Software which minimizes maintenance is not used, and the various incompatibilities are likely to make reconfiguration, conversion, and system change expensive. Second, the users design their own data without central coordination. The data design will often have to be changed. Third, the programming is often unprofessional, unstructured, heavily patched, and ill-documented, so changing it is very difficult; it would often be quicker to scrap it and start again.

It is appalling to imagine the needed maintenance effort rising still higher than the right-hand side of Fig. 5.1.

LOW PRODUCTIVITY   There is often substantial duplication of effort when minicomputers are installed by multiple groups to do the same job. The *total* number of programmers in a distributed environment can be much greater than in a central DP group. The numbers are often hidden because labor is bootlegged from various user departments. Clerks, accountants, and laboratory technicians are pressed into service to make the machines yield results. They become fascinated by their new activity but are omitted in any formal manpower accounting.

This, along with the low-level software, unprofessional code, and high maintenance requirements, results in low development productivity.

It is often worth accepting lower total productivity in order to gain a greater end-user involvement in application development.

ESCALATING   While the first applications on a minicomputer may
COMPLEXITY   be easy to install, the addition of further applications leads to greater complexity and rising costs. Minicomputers increase in their main memory requirements and eventually need to use multiprogramming, like larger machines, controlling multiple terminals and job streams. Increasing quantities of data storage must be organized. Data management facilities grow more complex.

User departments sometimes find that these complexities are becoming too much for them. They do not have sufficient skills, and too much time is being consumed. If the user groups eventually ask for help, it may be difficult for the centralized DP group to relate to what they have done. Centralized groups have sometimes recommended scrapping the approach and starting again.

In one DDP installation after another, size and cost of the peripheral machines has risen far beyond what was originally thought reasonable. This history will no doubt repeat itself in many more installations. In some the original intent was to replace a central mainframe with distributed minis, and three years later not only are the minis much bigger than was estimated but the mainframe is still there with its staff.

Creeping escalation of machine cost is common in DDP, and minicomputer manufacturers are unlikely to discourage it. In fact, as with large-computer manufacturers, they like to have a strategy for "growing the customer"—more memory, more disk storage, more and faster machines, and more elaborate software which chews up memory and machine cycles.

It is rare to find a major DDP system on which the peripheral computers did not become much more expensive than when they were proposed.

SECURITY

Computer security is a complex subject that is now well understood [1]. Where appropriate techniques are applied, computer installations can be made appropriately (not absolutely) secure. However, it is rare to find good security in peripheral end-user installations. Tight security requires the professional security management that is found in some centralized installations. This security management can be extended to the periphery of a distributed system.

Once again, we are saying that distributed systems can be fine with good overall control. End-user installations casually implemented may be easy targets for embezzlement or other security breaches.

AUDITABILITY

Auditors claim that some distributed systems are *unauditable*. There is no audit trail with which an auditor can reconstruct the history of who entered what transactions into a terminal or changed what records.

Audit trails or archival information can be stored more economically on a central system because of economies of scale in storage. Audit trails from peripheral machines are often stored on central machines. It is necessary to ensure that the auditors' requirements are met in the initial overall design of a distributed system.

NETWORK INCOMPATIBILITY

In a large corporation it is desirable to have a corporate network. This may be designed as a data network serving multiple computer centers. It is more economical for the internal telephone (voice) data and electronic mail networks to be designed in an integrated fashion. Distributed machines can then be selected or their software designed to plug into this network.

Independently and randomly selected user machines will not all plug into a common network without substantial conversion expense. Often the spread of distributed computers occurs before the network is planned. The two should be planned in an integrated fashion.

PLANNED EVOLUTION   The growth of networks is one form of evolution of distributed facilities. Distributed systems will evolve and interlink in various ways. The more the evolution can be planned for, the better. Unplanned evolution necessitates conversion operations. Sometimes these require the rewriting of so many application programs that, in practice, they are never done. When conversions are too expensive, accountants resist them because they can see no tangible benefit (i.e., new applications) at the end of the conversion. The result may be an inflexible system without the ability to achieve the combination of functional processing and strategic control described in the previous chapter.

Many of the data-processing systems that were built in the 1960's and 1970's were *inflexible*. Management could not obtain the information they wanted from them. The magnetic tape files and carefully scheduled sorting operations held data processing in a straitjacket. The comment was heard in board rooms: "We can't do that—the computer system could not handle it."

The DP community has to learn how to build systems that are powerful but not rigid and inflexible. Spontaneity and flexibility are needed in information systems, and they are the promise held out by terminals, networks, distributed intelligence, and data bases. However, DDP with conversion problems is not going to achieve that promise. A corporation may become filled with incompatible systems using incompatible data—a mess too expensive to straighten out.

Good corporationwide DDP systems are not going to happen overnight. They will be pieced together over many years. Nobody has enough application knowledge to plan exactly how this should be done. *What is needed is a planned infrastructure within which orderly evolution can occur.*

MIGRATION LOCKOUT   Computer technology is evolving very rapidly. This is good news, but it brings the danger of rapid obsolescence. A major computer manufacturer cannot go to its customers and say, "We have built a much better system. To install it you must rewrite a hundred man-years of application code." Instead, the manufacturer plans a "migration path" so that users can convert (relatively) painlessly from today's systems to the next one. Migration paths are planned years ahead by some manufacturers because the time to develop a new computer is often five years. Each machine or software announcement is a step on the path to some perceived future system. Most manufacturers now perceive their future as being in distributed processing. They have architectures and migration paths that will lead to a future of highly distributed cooperating machines—distributed processing data-base networks.

A danger of an *ad hoc* spread of end-user machines or arbitrary network design is that it will lock the users out of a manufacturer's migration path. Organizations have a choice between following a manufacturer's migration path (in whole or part) or adopting a manufacturer-independent posture in the selection of machines and software. Following a well-planned migration path might cause fewer problems in the long run. The choice should be made consciously rather than being forced by arbitrary machine selection.

POLITICAL STRIFE　　　　　Cheap minis, desk-top machines, etc., give user groups the ability to break away from the domination of central DP organizations. At the same time, data networking gives the ability to move to a head office some computing functions previously done in subsidiaries or divisions. The technology makes changes in the power structure possible and often logically or economically preferable. DDP therefore opens up power struggles and political strife in organizations. Some organizations have indulged in these to a spectacular extent. Many major DDP decisions have been made more as a result of organizational politics than the logic of systems design.

Contention between divisions or departments can be valuable for wrenching a DP group out of paths which have become technically obsolete. However, unresolved political strife usually does more harm than good to system development. Very often it prevents the true advantages of data-base and networking technology from being achieved. Sometimes the destructive forces are simply bent on preserving old methods. Infighting which prevents good system design can occur at low levels in an organization, often within a DP department itself.

Once again, strong higher management is needed, perceiving the opportunities and the dangers in DDP, and making sure that it works for the benefit of the organization as a whole.

CONCLUSION　　　　　We can find very good and very bad examples of DDP. The characteristics of the good examples can be summed up in a paragraph.

Processing nodes at end-user locations give a suitable degree of autonomy to the end users. These nodes fit into an overall system designed to give centralized control of those factors where this is beneficial. The interactions between the nodes are kept simple, thus lowering the overall system complexity, but the nodes conform to requirements necessary for networking, data-base operations, and interchange of data. The maximum use is made of software which gives spontaneous access to data, report generation, and higher application development productivity. The system is designed to be auditable and suitably secure.

The key to successful DDP is to design a system structure and management structure which permit suitable cooperation between otherwise autonomous nodes. Careful attention is needed to what should be centralized and what decentralized. A long-range strategy is needed so that the processing and data bases evolve within a strategic framework, avoiding the pitfalls listed in Box 5.1.

REFERENCE

1. James Martin, *Security, Accuracy, and Privacy in Computer Systems,* Prentice-Hall, Inc., Englewood Cliffs, N.J., 1973.

PART II

**FORMS OF DISTRIBUTED
PROCESSING**

6 WHAT IS DISTRIBUTED PROCESSING?

INTRODUCTION   Distributed processing has been defined in widely differing ways by different authorities. There is probably no definition on which all authorities would agree, because the word is used with different meanings.

DEFINITIONS   Some of the definitions are as follows:

"Putting computer resources where the people are" [1]

"An organizational structure for data processing with centralized capability, processing at least part of an application in a decentralized way" [2]

"A series of data-processing nodes interconnected by telecommunications to each other and to a host which is used to provide control of the whole network" [3]

"The philosophy of physically dividing up an organization's computing resources so that they are geographically and organizationally as close to the application as possible" [4]

"We have three criteria by which to define distributed processing. First, the system should possess two or more geographically separated processors. Second, the processors should be linked. Third, the processors should serve a single organizational entity" [5]

"Replacement of a large centralized DP facility with separate small computers which are not necessarily connected by telecommunications. Their selection and use is entirely the responsibility of local management" [6]

"A distributed processing system is one in which applications programs and/or data reside in separate interlinked processing nodes and are designed in an integrated and tightly controlled fashion" [7]

A divergence of opinion is apparent in these definitions. Some authorities say that distributed processing must have a central machine; others not; some insist that distributed processing implies the deliberate avoidance of centralized facilities. Some say that the processors must be interlinked, others not. Some say that the entire distributed system must have a central integrated design; others say that local managers are responsible for their own system.

We will list some of the characteristics that various authorities have associated with distributed processing. The only characteristic that all definitions would agree upon is that there are multiple processors. Other characteristics are as follows:

- *The processors are linked by telecommunications or other channels.* (In some cases they are not linked or are linked by tapes or disks that are manually delivered.)

- *The processors are geographically separate.* (In some cases they are in the same room.)

- *Peripheral processors are subordinate to a higher-level central machine.* (There may be no higher level of central machine, but instead a mesh or ring-structured network or machines of equal status.)

- *The separate processors run application programs.* (They may not; peripheral processors may contain distributed functions, such as editing, which do not themselves process a transaction.)

- *Data are distributed as well as processing power.* (They may not be.)

- *The processors serve one organizational entity.* (Processors in different organizational entities may be interlinked.)

- *The application programs in the separate machines are designed in a coordinated fashion.* (They may not be. The system may be designed to allow users to program whatever they require and take responsibility for it.)

- *Data in separate machines are designed in a coordinated fashion.* (They may not be; users may be free to design their own data.)

- *Standards of various types apply to the different processors.* (Some distributed processing systems have virtually no standards.)

- *A network architecture is used for interconnecting separate processors.* (It may not be.)

- *The distributed system should not be visible to the user. He should not know whether he is being served by a local or a remote machine.* (Often not true.)

It is perhaps not surprising that the term has different meanings to different persons, because processors can be connected in many ways for many purposes.

At one extreme of the range of definitions, the term is used to describe multiple processors in one location linked to form a new computer architecture. They may be identical processors sharing the transaction stream, or they may be specialized processors each carrying out a different function. The processors may be linked by a bus inside one cover. They may be in separate covers and linked by channels.

In the more common use of the term, the processors are linked by telecommunications.

TYPES OF   In theory an architecture for processors linked by tele-
CONNECTION   communications could be similar to an architecture for
processors linked by channels in a machine room or
processors linked by a bus. The only difference is the channel capacity. The architecture with slow channels could be a subset of that with fast channels. In practice, today, the architectures for machines linked by telecommunications are substantially different from those for machines linked by machine room buses or channels. It is worth questioning whether this need be so.

For the moment let us observe that some of the differences in definitions of distributed processing relate to the different ways processors are interconnected. The types of interconnection are summarized in Box 6.1.

There is a very wide range of possible communication speeds—from 100 to 10^9 bits per second. The highest speeds have been used only for internal machine buses, but there are now on the market optical fiber cables which can transmit data at

BOX 6.1   Types of connection between processors.
The different types are used in different forms
of distributed processing.

TYPE OF CONNECTION	TYPICAL SPEED (bits per second)
• Bus	Up to 10^9
• Machine room channel	10^7–10^8
• Local wideband network (CATV, Ethernet, etc.	10^6–10^7
• Nationwide (or multinational) data network (ARPANET, Corporate datagram networks, X.25 networks, DDS, etc.)	10^3–10^5
• Leased telephone line	100–9600
• Periodic dialed telephone connection (or virtual call)	100–9600
• No electronic connection. Tapes or disks transported manually.	10^3–10^5

speeds of up to 10^9 bits per second between machines. These can be used with a building or complex of buildings.

For transmission between locations, common carrier (telephone administration) channels are used. These are often voice-grade lines transmitting at speeds up to 9600 bits per second. In some countries wideband links (such as AT&T's DDS) are in common use at typical speeds of 56,000 bits per second. Faster telecommunications channels are becoming available from networks such as XTEN and SBS in the United States.

Because common carrier links are usually 1000 times slower than links within a machine room or building complex, the functions distributed over them are likely to remain different from those distributed within a machine room or building.

The next generation of communications satellite systems may change the distribution of function because they will transmit brief bursts of data almost as fast as the buses or channels in a machine room [8]. However, there will be a propagation delay of about 270 milliseconds—the time it takes light to travel to the satellite and back—and this will inhibit some types of function distribution. It could make sense to put devices such as mass storage (library) subsystems or printer subsystems at the other end of satellite links designed to transmit large bursts of data at high speed.

SCATTERED PROCESSORS

Another extreme in the range of definitions employs the term "distributed processing" to mean the use in scattered locations of minicomputers or even microcomputers which are not connected by telecommunications. In the mid-1970's much publicity was given to this use of the term by Citibank in New York, and minicomputer marketing teams enthusiastically followed suit. Citibank swung from a highly centralized use of large machines to a completely decentralized approach in which individual local managers were made responsible for the selection, programming and operation of their own small systems. In many corporations unconnected minicomputers in user departments have sprung up like mushrooms.

To use the same term for scattered, unconnected minicomputers as for a planned and integrated distributed system is confusing. It would be better to call the former "scattered" or "fragmented" processing, but these words do not have the fashionable appeal of the term "distributed" processing.

DISTRIBUTIVE PROCESSING

Some corporations use the term *distributive processing* to mean a *system in which peripheral small processors are subordinate to one or more central processors. The peripheral machines are linked to the center by telecommunications, and the entire complex is designed in a coordinated fashion.* This terminology creates a useful distinction but is not universally accepted.

DELIVERY TRUCK   Small computers could be associated in an integrated design without the use of telecommunications. Rather than employing a periodic dialed telephone connection to transfer data between the computers, the data could be transported manually. Use of a delivery truck or taxi to carry tapes or disks between computers is a form of communication which would be cheaper than data transmission and have a much higher bandwidth. The systems connected in this way could follow the best principles of integrated design, common data structures, and coordinated management which we discuss later.

This form of distribution is much advocated in countries where telecommunications are expensive or of poor quality.

NONINTEGRATED DISTRIBUTION   The term *distributed processing* is often used to describe linked computers which have little in common. They are implemented by different managements, contain different application programs, and store data which follow no common design. They send transactions to one another, or the users of one system employ programs in another.

Some authorities claim that this ought not to be called distributed processing. They define the term to imply integrated design of the data that the separate machines use and possibly of their programs also. In common use, however, the term often describes computers in user departments having little relation to the higher-level machines they are linked to, or networks of systems each designed independently. One of the much-advocated reasons for distributed processing is to allow users to "do their own thing."

Whether the design of connected systems is integrated or not, the software required for their connection may be the same. "Distributed processing" hardware or software is sold regardless of whether the system design is integrated or nonintegrated, good or bad.

DISTRIBUTED INTELLIGENCE vs. DISTRIBUTED PROCESSING   In some distributed systems, *functions* are distributed but not the capability to process entire transactions fully. These systems employ intelligent terminals or intelligent controllers in which processors are used for functions such as message editing, screen formating, data collection, dialogue with terminal operators, security, or message compaction or concentration. They do not complete the processing of entire transactions.

We will refer to this distribution as *function distribution*. It is sometimes called *distributed intelligence*. It should be contrasted with *processing distribution,* in which the machines at user locations process transactions completely and occasionally pass transactions or data to other machines. The term *systems distribution* is also used to indicate complete distributed systems which are interconnected.

Large computers often have small, subordinate processors linked to them. The subordinate machines may be entirely different from, and incompatible with, the higher machines. In a function-distribution environment, close cooperation between the subordinate-level and higher-level machines is vital. Overall system standards are necessary to govern what functions are distributed and exactly how the lower and higher machines form part of a common system architecture with appropriately integrated control mechanisms and software.

Most manufacturers use the term "distributed processing" to describe and to market intelligent terminals which do not completely process a transaction. We will employ the term *function distribution* for that. In some cases the same intelligent terminal or terminal controller may perform either function distribution or processing distribution.

There are thus various levels of capability that can be distributed.

- *Distributed logic* in computer architecture (e.g., units for error detection, cryptography, Fourier transform, data link control, associative search).

- *Distributed intelligence.* Small processors at terminal locations which carry out functions such as editing, validity checking, handling screen formats, communications concentrators, etc.

- *Distributive processing.* Processors at terminal locations which can completely process some transactions but are subordinate to a higher-level computer.

- *Integrated systems.* Data processing systems which are each self-sufficient but which are part of a larger integrated design.

- *Nonintegrated systems.* Computer systems of entirely independent design which are interconnected by a computer network.

Figure 6.1 indicates how these processing entities can be linked by the different forms of communications.

HORIZONTAL vs. VERTICAL DISTRIBUTION

Whether we are talking about distribution in the machine room or computer networks, we can distinguish between horizontal and vertical distribution.

By *vertical distribution* we mean that there is a hierarchy of processors, as in Fig. 6.2. The transaction may enter and leave the computer system at the lowest level. The lowest level may be able to process the transaction or may execute certain functions and pass it up to the next level. Some, or all, transactions eventually reach the highest level, which will probably have access to on-line files or a data base.

The machine at the top of a hierarchy might be a computer system in its own right, performing its own type of processing on its own transactions. However, the data it uses are passed to it from lower-level systems. The machine at the top might

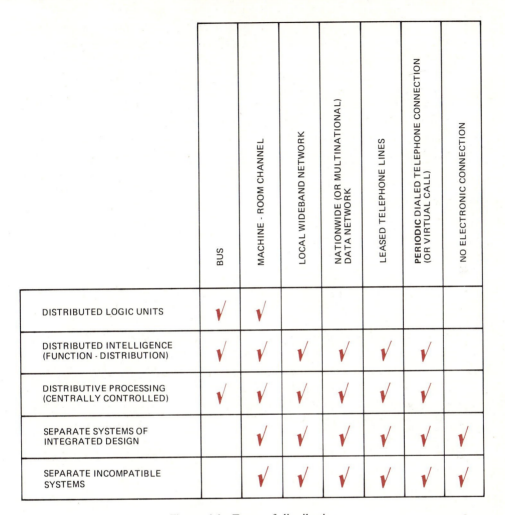

	BUS	MACHINE - ROOM CHANNEL	LOCAL WIDEBAND NETWORK	NATIONWIDE (OR MULTINATIONAL) DATA NETWORK	LEASED TELEPHONE LINES	PERIODIC DIALED TELEPHONE CONNECTION (OR VIRTUAL CALL)	NO ELECTRONIC CONNECTION
DISTRIBUTED LOGIC UNITS	√	√					
DISTRIBUTED INTELLIGENCE (FUNCTION - DISTRIBUTION)	√	√	√	√	√	√	
DISTRIBUTIVE PROCESSING (CENTRALLY CONTROLLED)	√	√	√	√	√	√	
SEPARATE SYSTEMS OF INTEGRATED DESIGN		√	√	√	√	√	√
SEPARATE INCOMPATIBLE SYSTEMS		√	√	√	√	√	√

Figure 6.1   Types of distribution.

be a head-office system which receives data from factory, branch, warehouse, and other systems.

By *horizontal distribution* we imply that the distributed processors do not differ in rank. They are of equal status—peers—and we refer to *peer-coupled* systems. A transaction may use only one processor, although there are multiple processors available. On some peer-coupled systems a transaction may pass from one system to another, causing different sets of files to be updated.

Figure 6.3 illustrates horizontal distribution. The top diagram shows multiple processors connected to a bus constituting the architecture of a computer. The second diagram shows multiple processors connected to a loop, perhaps spanning

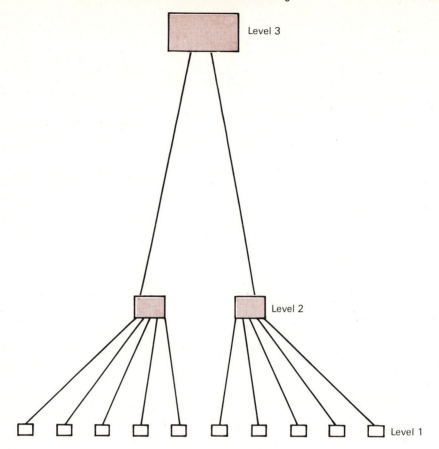

Figure 6.2   Vertical distribution.

several buildings in a factory complex, university campus, or shopping center, but in some systems being comprised of long common-carrier connections. The third and fourth diagrams show horizontal computer networks in which a user may access one of many machines.

HOMOGENEOUS vs. We may further distinguish between homogeneous and
HETEROGENEOUS heterogeneous systems.
SYSTEMS   By *homogeneous* we mean that each of the processors (for example, in Fig. 6.3) is similar. A minicomputer system may employ multiple identical minicomputers, either in one location or geographically scattered. Homogeneous distributed computer architecture employs multiple identical processors operating in parallel, as in the ILIAC IV or CDC Cyber systems.

By *heterogeneous* we mean that the interconnected processors are dissimilar.

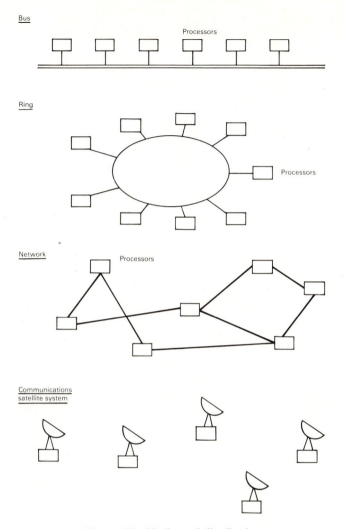

Figure 6.3   Horizontal distribution.

Different processors, capable of executing entirely different functions, are interconnected. Sometimes they are entirely different and incompatible machines set up by different administrations. A user of the network may be able to access any (or most) of them. He therefore has available a rich diversity of computing power.

COOPERATIVE
OPERATION?
In some networks the user has available a choice of computer systems, but he normally employs only one computer at a time. The computers are programmed independently, each to perform its own functions.

In other networks the computers are programmed to cooperate with one another to solve a common set of problems. This is often the case in a vertical system; the lower-level machines are programmed to pass work to the higher-level machines. It is sometimes true also in a horizontal system. The processing of one transaction may begin on one machine and pass to another. The different computers perform different functions or maintain different files. The transaction processing passes from one machine to another to update the appropriate files. The machines may be minicomputers in the same location or computers scattered across the world on a network.

COMBINATIONS   Many configurations are neither purely vertical nor purely horizontal, neither entirely homogeneous nor entirely heterogeneous. Instead, they are combinations of these. Function distribution and processing distribution will be combined in one configuration.

Figure 6.4 shows a horizontal and vertical association of machines. It contains both function distribution and vertically distributed systems.

Figure 6.5 shows some typical shapes of systems:

1. *A centralized configuration.* Peripheral machines are connected to a central computer. This is the most common shape of distributed system.

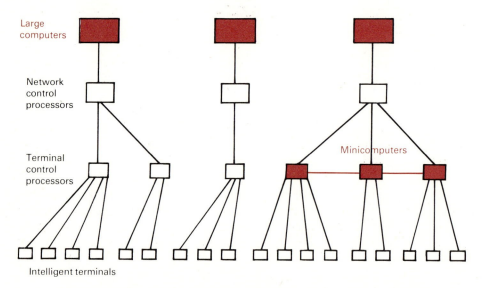

Large
computers

Network
control
processors

Terminal
control
processors

Minicomputers

Intelligent terminals

Figure 6.4 Some networks contain both vertical and horizontal combinations of processors; and both function-distribution and distributed system aspects. The shaded machines are processors capable of processing entire transactions.

1 CENTRALIZED CONFIGURATION

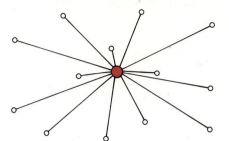

4 HORIZONTAL (PEER–COUPLED) CONFIGURATION

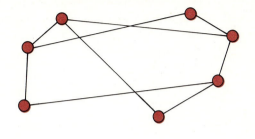

2 BICENTRAL CONFIGURATION
(Higher security than a centralized system)

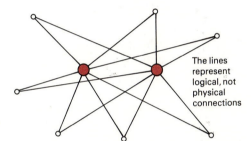

The lines
represent
logical, not
physical
connections

MULTILEVEL CONFIGURATIONS:
5 HORIZONTAL–VERTICAL

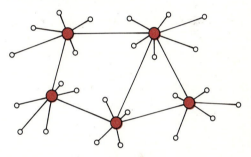

3 MULTICENTERED CONFIGURATION
(Different activities in different centers)

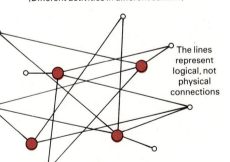

The lines
represent
logical, not
physical
connections

6 VERTICAL–VERTICAL

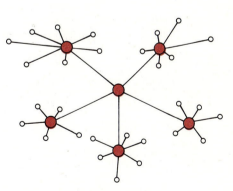

Figure 6.5 Configurations of distributed systems.

2. *A bicentral configuration.* Two centers are used instead of one, often to give higher security in case one center is destroyed.

3. *A multicentered configuration.* The peripheral machines can connect to multiple central machines, which carry out different activities.

4. *A peer-coupled configuration.* Any machine can connect to any other. A purely horizontal network.

5. *A vertical-horizontal configuration.* Higher-level machines are horizontally connected; lower-level machines connect vertically to their higher-level machine.

6. *A vertical-vertical configuration.* Two levels of vertical connection.

DISTRIBUTED DATA   A particularly important consideration in the planning and design of distributed processing is where the data should be located. They could be either centralized or distributed. The constraints which apply to the locating of data are different from those which apply to locating processors. In many systems the structure and usage of the data determine what is practical in the distribution of processors.

Data can be stored in two types of ways: as straightforward data files or as data bases. A file is data-designed to serve a particular application or related group of applications. A programmer's view of a file is similar to the file which is physically stored. A data base is an application-independent collection of data from which many different programmers' records can be derived by software. There are major advantages in employing data-base software, but the software is complex and usually operates today on data stored at one location. Therefore distributed data are often in the form of *files* rather than of a *data base,* although multiple data-base systems may be interconnected.

Much of the literature on distributed systems uses the term "data base" when it is really referring merely to on-line files. The same is true in the marketing publications of some minicomputer vendors. It is important to distinguish between the two because the design considerations for them are quite different.

We discuss distributed files and data bases later in the book.

PROCESSING, DATA,   In general, there are three aspects of data processing
AND CONTROL   that may or may not be distributed: *processing, data,*
                          and *control.* The arguments relating to the three are different. There may be arguments for centralizing some of the *data* and distributing others. These are different from the arguments relating to the distribution of *processing.* A system may have much of its processing geographically scattered, and yet the overall *control* of the system may reside centrally.

In some computer networks the control mechanisms are mostly centralized. In others they are mostly distributed. Where purely centralized control exists, loss of the center puts the entire network out of action. With distributed control, if any portion of a network is destroyed, the rest will continue to function. A centralized system may have its reliability enhanced by having more than one center or more than one computer capable of control at the center.

Both centralized and distributed control are found in nature, often in combination. A city has largely distributed control. Some functions are centralized in the City Hall, but the city would go on working if the City Hall were destroyed. Some packet-switching computer networks would go on functioning if any single portion were destroyed even though a few management functions are centralized. The human body has vital centralized functions. It can tolerate much damage, but not the destruction of the brain or heart. Some computer networks are equally dependent on certain critical components. As networks assume increasingly vital purposes, fault-tolerant control mechanisms will become more important.

INTERNAL DESIGN   The term "distributed processing" is sometimes used to refer to forms of computer architecture in which one mainframe or minicomputer system is composed of multiple processors. The cost of microcomputers is such that they will perform many tasks in future computer systems. Some minicomputers will be built out of many microcomputers.

The system in Fig. 6.6 has both vertical and horizontal combinations of processors. For reliability it is designed with redundancy of critical processors such as the back-end (data base) and front-end (communications) processors. The transactions load may be shared by several main processors. The architecture is designed so that as technology or requirements change, new processors can be added.

The I/O bus in Fig. 6.6 may transmit between 10 and 50 million bits per second. Transmission at this speed can take place over relatively inexpensive coaxial cables and optical fiber cables for distances of several miles. The devices connected by the I/O bus in Fig. 6.6 could therefore be anywhere in a building or in nearby buildings connected by such a cable.

Technologies such as Ethernet [9] permit many devices to share a high-speed local cable. The wideband cabling of buildings will become very important to the future of local-area distributed processing.

HEXAGON DIAGRAM   To illustrate the different types of system at a glance we will use a hexagon diagram, shown in Fig. 6.7.

Red shading at the inside represents centralization of a resource. Red shading at the outside represents distribution. The degree of shading could indicate the extent to which the resource is complete, of full function, or large in extent. The diagram relates to six aspects of systems which may be either centralized or distributed:

1. Application processing

2. Files

3. Data bases

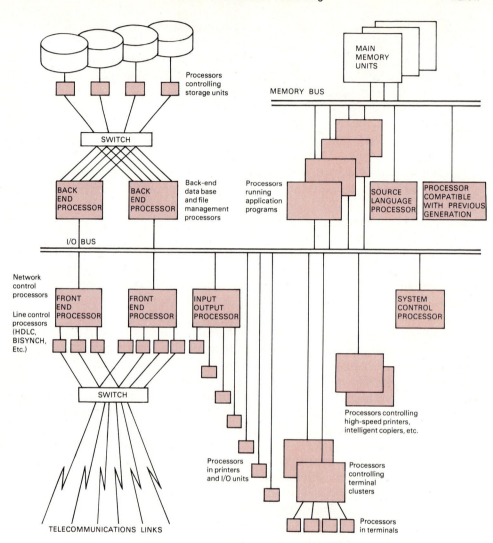

Figure 6.6 Future mainframe and minicomputer systems will be composed of multiple processors, many of them microprocessors. The I/O bus on this diagram could be a wideband coaxial or optical fiber telecommunications channel spanning many offices or nearby buildings.

4. Input/output

5. Network control

6. Intelligence (i.e., function distribution)

A red line between the inner and outer parts of the diagram indicates integrated design. For example, distributed and centralized data have the same fields, records, or data-base structures; application programs can be executed on central or

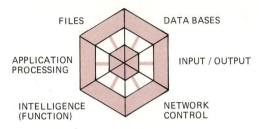

FILES

DATA BASES

APPLICATION
PROCESSING

INPUT / OUTPUT

INTELLIGENCE
(FUNCTION)

NETWORK
CONTROL

Figure 6.7 A hexagon diagram used to indicate different types of distributed systems at a glance. Shading on the inside means a centralized resource. A red line between the inside and the outside means integration of design.

peripheral machines; network control mechanisms use an integrated architecture.

Figure 6.8 shows some examples. The top diagram in Fig. 6.8 is for a system which does not employ any distribution of function or processing. It is a conventional system with files and dumb terminals.

The second diagram shows a data-base communications system with intelligent terminals. The terminals (or their controller) have the logic to assist the operators with data entry or dialogue, but they do not process complete transactions. The application processing and the data base it uses are centralized. The functions performed by the intelligent terminals are tightly linked to the application design.

The third diagram is for a system with files, not a data base. The data are distributed, and so are the application programs. The distributed and centralized programs and data are designed in a coordinated fashion. Control of the network is distributed, and all of the machines use an integrated network architecture (discussed in Part V).

The fourth diagram represents a system without an integrated network architecture, but with an integrated design of the distributed files, programs and intelligent terminals. The system has a central data base which may contain the data elements and subschemas (Part IV) which are on the distributed files. In some corporations this has been a successful, workable approach to distributed processing.

The design integration of the third and fourth diagrams is missing in the fifth and sixth. The fifth diagram represents scattered processing units, with files and terminals. There is no network control and no data base. This may represent the much-advocated situation of users with their own minicomputers "doing their own thing" without central coordination or management.

The sixth diagram represents a computer network which facilitates the sharing of resources, and with decentralized network control, like ARPANET or CYCLADES [9]. The separate systems connected to the network are separately designed and managed.

The seventh diagram represents a corporate computer network, again completely decentralized, with network software which interlinks computers, and which may be similar to that used in the sixth diagram. Now the data are planned in an integrated fashion. There is a data-administrator function serving the corporation as a whole.

There are an almost infinite number of possible configurations of distributed systems. In the future it will be desirable that software for distributed systems

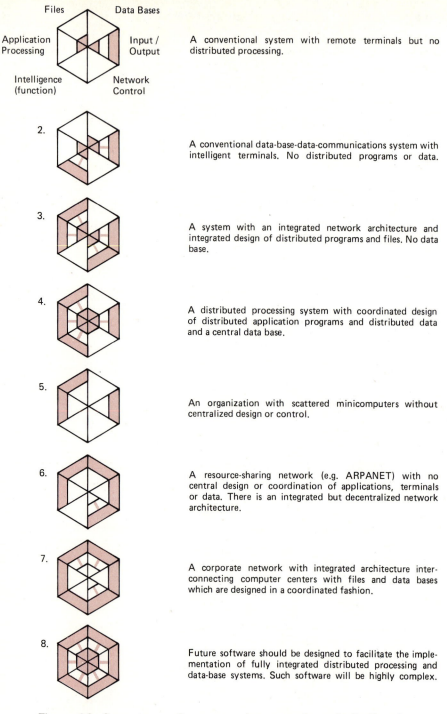

Files   Data Bases

Application Processing   Input / Output

Intelligence (function)   Network Control

A conventional system with remote terminals but no distributed processing.

2. A conventional data-base-data-communications system with intelligent terminals. No distributed programs or data.

3. A system with an integrated network architecture and integrated design of distributed programs and files. No data base.

4. A distributed processing system with coordinated design of distributed application programs and distributed data and a central data base.

5. An organization with scattered minicomputers without centralized design or control.

6. A resource-sharing network (e.g. ARPANET) with no central design or coordination of applications, terminals or data. There is an integrated but decentralized network architecture.

7. A corporate network with integrated architecture interconnecting computer centers with files and data bases which are designed in a coordinated fashion.

8. Future software should be designed to facilitate the implementation of fully integrated distributed processing and data-base systems. Such software will be highly complex.

Figure 6.8 Some types of systems using networks and distributed facilities.

enable corporations to employ any configuration that may be useful. The software will eventually satisfy all the possibilities in the eighth diagram.

DEFINITIONS   To summarize, here are some working definitions of distributed facilities.

Distributed Processing

Computer system configurations with more than one processor.

There are an almost infinite number of possible configurations of such systems. Different authorities add different constraints to limit the extreme generality of the above statement. Among the more common and useful constraints are the following:

- Processors are in different locations.
- The processors are interlinked by telecommunications.
- The configuration serves one organization.
- The configuration has a specific set of objectives.
- The configuration is planned and designed in an integrated fashion.

Any of these constraints, especially the last one, is violated by some systems which are described by their instigators as "distributed processing" systems.

Distributed Data-Processing System

A system for handling data within an organization which employs more than one geographically separate processor. Usually the processors are linked by tele-communications.

Distributed Intelligence

The use of processors in terminals, controllers, or peripheral machines to execute functions which are not the complete processing of a transaction.

Function Distribution

The same as the above definition of distributed intelligence. It may be contrasted with *processing distribution* (below).

Processing Distribution

The use of remote processors which perform the complete processing of a transaction.

Sometimes identical machines are used for *function distribution* in some systems and *processing distribution* in others.

Distributive Processing

This term describes a system in which peripheral small processors can completely process a transaction but are subordinate to one or more central processors. The peripheral machines are linked to the center, and the entire complex is designed in a coordinated fashion. The system may be designed so that the distributive machines cannot be programmed at the peripheral locations. Programs are centrally prepared and down-line loaded into the peripheral machines.

Integrated Distributed System

A distributed system designed in a coordinated fashion so that the separate components employ commonality of data fields, data structures, programs, and protocols, wherever this can improve the effectiveness or future evolution of the system.

There are widely varying degrees to which a distributed system can be integrated in its design.

Nonintegrated Distributed Systems

A system interlinking processing and storage subsystems designed by different teams without coordination.

REFERENCES

1. H. Donaldson, *Distributed Processing Systems,* State of the Art Report on Distributed Processing, published by Infotech International, London, 1977.

2. A. Diebold, *State of the Art in Distributed Processing,* Research Program Report, New York, 1976.

3. Burton S. Goldberg, IBM Vice-President, in *SCD News,* October 1978, IBM Systems Communication Division, Raleigh, N.C.

4. Infotech International *Report on Distributed Processing,* Volume 1, London, 1977.

5. David Butler, Butler Cox and Partners, Ltd., London, 1977.

6. Definitions from Citibank, New York, 1977.

7. Definition from IBM, 1978.

8. *The SBS Digital Communications Satellite System,* Satellite Business Systems, 8003 Westpark Drive, McLean, Virginia 22101.

9. Ethernet, ARPANET, and Cyclades are described in the companion book to this, *Computer Networks and Distributed Processing,* by James Martin, Prentice-Hall, Inc., Englewood Cliffs, N.J., 1981.

7 FUNCTION DISTRIBUTION

"Yes," said Piglet, "Rabbit has Brain."
There was a long silence.
"I suppose," said Pooh, "that's why he never understands anything."

—A. A. Milne, *The House at Pooh Corner*

The nodes of a distributed system may be data-processing systems in their own right. They process and file the local data and communicate occasionally or often with other data-processing systems. In some distributed systems, however, the nodes are not self-sufficient systems. They contain processors which perform a function subservient to a higher-level, distant computer. We speak of *intelligent terminals, intelligent controllers,* or *intelligent concentrators.*

As indicated in Chapter 6, we distinguish this subservient use of distributed processors from the use of distributed, self-sufficient data-processing systems with the term *distributed intelligence,* or *function distribution.*

Distributed intelligence implies a vertical distribution of function in which all or most transactions have to be transmitted, possibly in a modified form, to a higher-level computer system, or possibly to a network of higher-level computer systems.

The centralized teleprocessing system of 1970 employed simple terminals and carried out almost all of its functions in the central computer. As microprocessors dropped in cost, functions were increasingly moved out of the central computer. First, system control and housekeeping functions were moved out, then functions such as data collection, editing, and dialogue with terminal operators, and finally many of the application programs themselves.

Figure 7.1 shows places where intelligence could reside in a vertical distributed intelligence system:

1. In the host computer, B

2. In a line control unit or "front-end" network control computer, C

Many functions are necessary to control a terminal network. If the host computer performs all the operations itself, it will be constantly interrupting its main processing, and many machine cycles will be needed for line control. Some of the line control functions may be performed by a separate line control unit. In some systems, all of them are performed by a separate and specialized computer.

The proportion of functions performed by a line control unit, by the host computer hardware, and by its software varies widely from system to system. Some application programs such as accuracy checking and message logging, could be performed by the subsystem computer.

A major advantage of using a front-end network-control computer is that when the host computer has a software crash or brief failure, the network can remain operational. Restart and recovery of the network without errors or lost transactions is a tedious and often time-consuming operation, and if it happens often, it can be very frustrating to the end users.

3. In the mid-network nodes, D and E

The mid-network nodes or concentrators may take a variety of different forms. They may be relatively simple machines with unchangeable logic. They may have wired-in logic, part or all of which can be changed by an engineer. They may be microprogrammed. Or they may be stored-program computers, sometimes designed solely for concentration or routing, but sometimes also capable of other operations and equipped with files, high-speed printers, and other input-output equipment.

The term may refer to the nodes of a public data network. The nodes of AT&T's ACS network, for example, may contain customers' data or programs.

4. In the terminal control unit, F

Terminal control units also differ widely in complexity, ranging from simple hardwired devices to stored-program computers with much software. They may control one terminal or many. They may be programmed to interact with the terminal operator to provide a psychologically effective dialogue in which only an essential kernel is transmitted to or from the host computer. They may generate curves on a graphics terminal or interact with the operator's use of a light pen. They

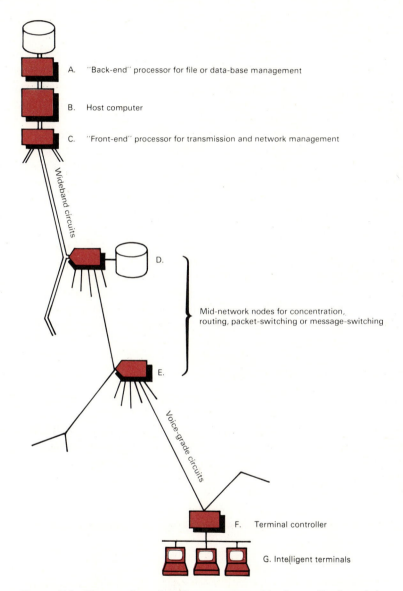

A. "Back-end" processor for file or data-base management

B. Host computer

C. "Front-end" processor for transmission and network management

Wideband circuits

D.

Mid-network nodes for concentration, routing, packet-switching or message-switching

E.

Voice-grade circuits

F. Terminal controller

G. Intelligent terminals

Figure 7.1 Places where intelligence can reside in a distributed intelligence network.

are often the main component in carrying out the assortment of distributed-intelligence functions which this chapter will list.

5. In the terminal, G

"Intelligent terminals" are becoming more intelligent. Their processing functions range from single operations, such as accumulating totals in a system which handles financial transactions, to dialogues with operators involving much programming. Some intelligent terminals do substantial editing of input and output data. Some terminals perform important *security* functions.

Where several terminals share a control unit, F, such functions are probably better performed in the control unit, leaving the terminal a simple, inexpensive mechanism in which the main design concern may be tailoring the keyboard and other operator mechanisms to the applications in question.

6. In a "back-end" file or data-base management
processor, A

File or data-base operations may be handled by a "back-end" processor. This can carry out the specialized functions of data-base management or file-searching operations. It can prevent interference between separate transactions updating the same data. It can be designed to give a high level of data security protection.

"Back-end" processors, where they exist today, are normally cable-connected to their local host computer. They could, especially when high bandwidth networks or communications satellite facilities are available, be remote from the host computers which use them.

**CHOICE OF
FUNCTION LOCATION** The designer, faced with different locations in which he could place functions, may choose his configuration with objectives such as the following:

1. Minimum total system cost

There is often a tradeoff between distributed function cost and telecommunications cost.

2. High reliability

The value attached to system availability will vary from one system to another. The systems analyst must evaluate how much extra money is worth spending on duplexing, alternate routing, and distributed processing to achieve high availability. On some systems reliability is vital. A supermarket must be able to keep its cash registers going when a communication line or distant host computer fails.

3. Security

In some systems distributed function is vital for system security (as we discuss later).

4. Psychologically effective dialogue with terminal users

Distributed intelligence is used to make the dialogue fast, effective, and error-free.

5. Complexity

Excessive complexity should be avoided. The problems multiply roughly as the square of the complexity.

6. Software cost

Some means of distributing intelligence throughout a network incur a high programming expenditure. The use of stored-program peripheral machines may inflate the cost.

7. Flexibility and expandibility

It is necessary to choose hardware and software techniques that can easily be changed and expanded later, especially because telecommunications and networking technology is changing so fast. Some approaches make this step difficult.

REASONS FOR FUNCTION DISTRIBUTION

Box 7.1 lists the main reasons for function distribution. They fall into three categories:

1. Reasons associated with the host

Many machine instructions are needed to handle all the telecommunications functions. The load on a central machine could be too great if it had to handle all these functions. A single computer operates in a largely *serial* fashion, executing one instruction at a time. It seems generally desirable to introduce parallelism into computing so that the circuits execute many operations simultaneously. This is the case when machine functions are distributed to many small machines.

2. Reasons associated with the network

There are many possible mechanisms which can be used to make the network function efficiently. We will discuss them later in the book. They are used to lower the overall cost of transmission and increase its reliability. The network configuration is likely to change substantially on most systems, both because of application

BOX 7.1 Reasons for function distribution

1. PSYCHOLOGICALLY EFFECTIVE DIALOGUES

   - LOCAL INTERACTION

     Much of the dialogue interaction takes place locally rather than being transmitted, and hence it can be designed without concern for transmission constraints.

   - LOCAL PANEL STORAGE

     Panels or graphics displayed as part of the dialogue can be stored locally.

   - SPEED

     Local responses are fast. Time delays, which are so frustrating in many terminal dialogues, can be largely avoided. The delays that do occur when host response is needed can be absorbed into the dialogue structure.

2. REDUCTION OF TELECOMMUNICATIONS COSTS

   - REDUCTION OF NUMBER OF MESSAGES

     In many dialogues the number of messages transmitted to and fro can be reduced by an order of magnitude because dialogue is carried on within the terminal or local controller.

   - REDUCTION OF MESSAGE SIZE

     Messages for some applications can be much shortened because repetitive information is stored locally and only variable information is transmitted.

   - REDUCTION OF NUMBER OF LINE TURNAROUNDS

     Because the number of messages is reduced, and because a terminal cluster controller or concentrator can combine many small messages into one block for transmission.

   - BULK TRANSMISSION

     Non-time-critical items can be collected and stored for later batch transmission over a switched connection.

   - DATA COMPACTION

     There are various ways of compressing data so that fewer bits have to be transmitted. This effectively increases the transmission speed.

   - MINIMUM COST ROUTING

     The machine establishing a link could attempt first to set up a minimum-cost connection, e.g., a corporate tie-line network. If these are busy, it could try progressively more expensive connections (e.g., WATS, Direct Distance Dialing).

BOX 7.1 *continued*

- CONTROLLER NETWORK ACCESS

  Terminal users may be prevented from making expensive, unauthorized calls.

3. AVAILABILITY

   - LOCAL AUTONOMY

     A local operation can continue, possibly in a fallback mode (using a minimal set of functions) when the location is cut off from the host computer by a circuit, network, or host failure. On certain systems this is vital.

   - AUTOMATIC DIAL BACKUP

     A machine may be able to dial a connection if a leased circuit fails.

   - AUTOMATIC ALTERNATE ROUTING

     A machine may be able to use an alternate leased circuit or network path when a network failure occurs.

   - AUTOMATIC LOAD BALANCING

     A machine may be able to dial an extra circuit or use a different computer to handle high-traffic peaks.

4. LESS LOAD ON HOST

   - PARALLEL OPERATIONS

     The parallel operation of many small processors relieves the host computer of much of its work load, and lessens the degree of multiprogramming. In some systems this is vital because the host is overburdened with data-base operations.

   - PERMITS LARGE NUMBERS OF TERMINALS

     Some systems require so many terminals that it is impossible to connect them directly to a host computer. Distributed control and operations make the system possible.

5. FAST RESPONSE TIMES

   - PROCESS MECHANISMS

     Local controllers can read instruments rapidly and give a rapid response to process control mechanisms when necessary.

   - HUMAN MECHANISMS

     Fast reaction is possible to human actions such as the use of a plastic card or the drawing of a curve with a light pen.

continued

BOX 7.1   *continued*

- DIALOGUE RESPONSE TIMES

    Dialogues requiring fast response times (such as multiple menu selection) can be handled by local controllers.

6. RELIABILITY AND INTEGRITY
    - DATA VALIDATION

        Data can be checked when it is entered. Field checks. Batch totals. An attempt is made to correct the errors before transmitting them.

    - CONTROL PROCEDURES

        Control procedures (including use of serial numbers) can be used to recover from errors or failures and ensure that no messages are lost or double processed.

7. TRANSACTION BUFFERING
    - ABSORPTION OF PEAKS

        Peaks too great to be transmitted or processed can be buffered in the peripheral storage for later transmission.

    - MESSAGE STORAGE

        Messages which a terminal is not ready to accept can be stored until it is ready (as in message-switching systems).

8. SIGN-ON
    - GENERATION OF PROCEDURES

        Difficult or complex procedures for signing on to networks and remote machines can be made to appear as simple dialogues.

9. HANDLING PEAKS
    - PEAK BUFFERING

        When there is a temporary overload, traffic may be stored at peripheral machines until the system can handle it. This avoids the need to build a system with the capacity to handle extreme peaks.

    - PRIORITIZATION

        Certain transaction types may have lower priority. During peaks these are held at the peripheral machine while the high-priority items are transmitted and processed.

BOX 7.1 *continued*

10. APPLICATION TAILORING

- ### DATA-ENTRY TERMINALS

  Many inexpensive data-entry terminals (for example, on a factory shop floor) can be connected to a local controller which gathers data for later transmission.

- ### INSTRUMENTATION

  Local controllers scan or control instruments, gathering the result for transmission to a host computer.

11. MORE ATTRACTIVE OUTPUT

- ### LOCAL EDITING

  Editing of output received at terminals can lay out the data attractively for printers or screen displays. Repetitive headings, lines, or text, and page numbers can be added locally. Multiple editing formats can be stored locally.

12. SECURITY

- ### CRYPTOGRAPHY

  Cryptography on some systems gives a high measure of protection from wiretapping, tampering with magnetic-stripe plastic cards, etc. Cryptography is vital on certain electronic fund transfer systems.

- ### ACCESS CONTROL

  Security controls can prevent calls from unauthorized sources from being accepted and prevent terminals from contacting unauthorized machines.

13. NETWORK INDEPENDENCE

- ### NETWORK TRANSPARENCY

  Programmers of machines using networks should not be concerned with details of how the network functions. They should simply pass messages to the network interface and receive messages from it.

- ### NETWORK EVOLUTION

  As networks grow and evolve and as different networks are merged, programs in machines using the networks should not have to be rewritten.

- ### NEW NETWORKS

  Network technology is changing fast. As applications are switched to new types of networks (e.g., DDS, value-added networks, Datadial, satellite

continued

BOX 7.1 *continued*

networks), the programs in the using machines should not have to be rewritten.

14. TERMINAL INDEPENDENCE

- NEW TERMINALS

Terminal design is changing fast. If a new terminal is substituted, the old programs should not have to be rewritten. Software in terminal controllers may make the new terminals appear like the old.

- VIRTUAL TERMINAL FEATURES

Application programs may be written without a detailed knowledge of the terminal that they will use. For example, the screen size or print-line size may not be known. The programmers use specified constraints on output and the distributed-intelligence mechanisms map their output to the device in question.

15. STATISTICS

The peripheral machines collect statistics about response times and network performance which are important in monitoring and evolving the network.

development and increasing traffic, and because of changes in networking technology, which are now coming at a fast and furious rate. Function distribution may be used to isolate the changing network from other parts of the system so that the other parts do not have to be modified as the network changes. The term *network transparency* is used to imply that, whatever changes occur in the network, they are transparent to the users.

Mechanisms relating to the network may reside in any of the locations indicated in Fig. 7.1. A terminal, or a controller for a cluster of terminals, may have mechanisms intended to minimize the transmission cost. A front-end communications processor may relieve the host of all network functions and maintain network operations without loss of data if the host or its software fails. Intelligence may also reside in mid-network nodes such as packet-switching devices, concentrators, or intelligent exchanges. The phrase "intelligent network" is increasingly used to imply that the network itself employs computers to achieve its function in an efficient, dependable manner.

3. Reasons associated with the end user

Probably the most important of the three categories is that associated with the end user. The dialogue that takes place between the terminal and its operator on many systems built prior to the era of distributed intelligence is crude. It is often difficult for the person to learn, and clumsy and frustrating in operation. The person is forced to learn mnemonics and to remember specific sequences in which items must be entered. The response times are often inappropriate. The majority of the end users who should be employing terminals are unable to make the machines work, and generally discount the possibility of ever using them because they perceive them as being difficult—designed for technicians, programmers, or specially trained and dedicated staff. One psychologist describes many of these user-terminal interfaces as "unfit for human consumption."

In the past there has been a good reason for the crudity of terminal dialogues. The terminals had no intelligence. Every character typed and displayed had to be transmitted over the network. The network often used leased voice lines serving many terminals, and to minimize the network cost the numbers of characters transmitted were kept low. The response times were often higher than was psychologically appropriate.

With intelligent terminals or controllers the dialogue processing can take place in the local machine. Most of the characters are not transmitted over the telephone lines. The only characters transmitted are those which take essential information to the central computer and carry back essential information to the terminal. These characters will often be only a small fraction of the total characters typed and displayed in a psychologically effective dialogue.

DEGREES OF PERIPHERAL CAPABILITY   Various degrees of capability of a peripheral machine are listed in Box 7.2. The list may be used for categorizing the various machines on the market. Degree 0 relates to dumb terminals. Degrees 1 to 5 are levels of function distribution. Degrees 6 to 12 are levels of processing distribution.

BOX 7.2   Degrees of capability in a peripheral machine

DEGREE

0.   A nonintelligent terminal.

1.   An intelligent terminal capable of emulating a nonintelligent (Degree 0) terminal.

2.   A terminal capable of storing screen formats.

3.   A terminal capable of editing and formating data sent to it so that it displays or prints them attractively, capable of editing data entered into a format, and of validating input transactions.

continued

BOX 7.2 *continued*

4.   A terminal capable of carrying out a dialogue with an operator and transmitting the results.

5.   A device which can store and forward transactions, e.g., store input batches while they are completed and checked, or store output messages until the operator can receive them. (A device which has functions similar to a Bell ACS (Advanced Communications Service) node.)

6.   A device which can process and store data with application programs which are down-line loaded from a host.

7.   A device which can load, compile, and run its own programs without assistance from the host.

8.   A device which can operate host programs such that these programs can be run either in the host or the peripheral device.

9.   A device which can run programs which access remote data bases in one host.

10.   A device which can run multiple simultaneous programs, some employing data in remote data bases.

11.   A device with its own data-base management system.

12.   A device with full distributed data-base capability.

**DISTRIBUTED
INTELLIGENCE
FROM COMMON
CARRIERS**

The mid-network nodes of Fig. 7.1 could be part of a private corporate network or part of a public network. They represent the situation where a network is an entity in its own right, and many diverse machines can use that network.

Many of the distributed-intelligence features listed in Box 5.1 could be provided by a common carrier rather than by an intelligent terminal or terminal controller. This is the intent of AT&T's Advanced Communications Service, ACS. Figure 7.2 shows the nodes of ACS which reside at telephone company offices. They provide both processing power and storage. The programs in the nodes which give the distributed intelligence capability can be written either by the telephone company or by its customers. The nodes are interconnected by a packet-switching network, as shown in Fig. 7.3.

The intelligence in the ACS nodes can be used for such functions as

• Editing and performing validation checks on input

• Storing data while they are being entered for transmission in a batch

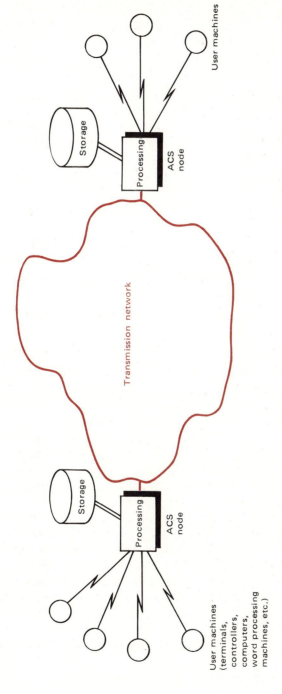

Figure 7.2 A logical view of ACS as seen by the users. What can the processing and storage be used for?

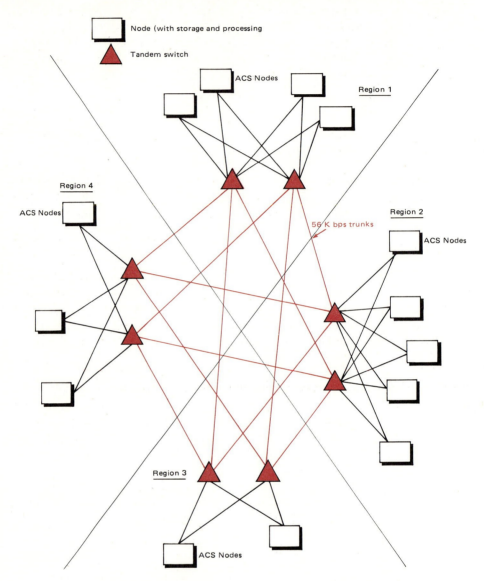

Figure 7.3 The ACS trunking network. Two disjoint points between each node containing not more than two tandem switches.

- Taking batch counts and totals
- Assembling audit records
- Storing formats and displaying them on a terminal screen to guide data input
- Displaying menus on a terminal screen so that the operator can select an item from the menu

- Carrying out a dialogue to assist the operator in performing some action. For example, in a dialogue consisting of a succession of commands and responses, the commands may be sent to the terminal by the ACS node. Similarly with a succession of menus or panels to be filled in

- Assisting the operator in signing on to a distant computer and application

- Storing output messages to be delivered to a terminal

- Queuing messages until an operator requests to read his queue

- Editing and expanding an output message to display it attractively or print it suitably positioned on preprinted stationery

Many services are possible from the computers and storage of ACS. All manner of different uses of this distributed intelligence will grow up as customers program their own requirements in it. As good programs come into use, they will probably be sold to other users, and AT&T will expand its own range of ACS software. This might be regarded as *distributed-intelligence time sharing,* and as with time sharing, all manner of innovative uses of it will emerge.

Will it be cheaper to have such functions in the common carrier network or residing in intelligent terminals or terminal controllers? Sometimes in one; sometimes in the other. It is desirable that competition in the marketplace should select the most cost-effective technique. There will always be much use of isolated dumb terminals, and these can be given intelligence by a common carrier network node.

EASE OF USE   Much of the future growth of the computer industry is dependent on making the machines easy to use and understand for the masses of people in all walks of life who employ them. Distributed intelligence in its various forms can play a vital part in this.

8 HIERARCHICAL DISTRIBUTED SYSTEMS

In the previous chapter we used the constraint that the peripheral machines were not self-sufficient except when isolated from their host by a telecommunications or other failure. We refer to this as *function distribution*. The processing *power* needed to carry out a substantial set of distributed functions is such that the peripheral machines are indeed powerful enough to be self-sufficient.

In this chapter we discuss systems in which the peripheral processors keep their own data and can be self-sufficient but are connected to higher-level systems, i.e., *processing distribution*.

There is not necessarily a sharp boundaryline between *function distribution* and *processing distribution*. In some cases there has tended to be growth from function distribution to processing distribution, more and more power being demanded in the peripheral machines. In other cases the peripheral machines started as stand-alone minicomputers and became linked into a higher-level system.

CRITERIA FOR TELEPROCESSING

The application programming steps for most (but not all) commercial transactions do not require a large computer. Small, inexpensive, mass-produced processors such as those discussed in the previous chapter could usually handle the whole transaction. They would handle it with a *much* smaller software path length than a large computer. Usually the difference in software path length offsets any of the (now weakened) arguments about economies of scale.

In some cases there are good reasons for storing the *data* which a transaction requires *centrally*. In other cases the data also can be kept in storage attached to the local machine. We discuss the centralization of data in Chapters 17, 18, and 21.

As we commented earlier, criteria for whether a transaction is transmitted could be:

120

1. It needs the power of a large computer.

2. It needs data which are stored centrally.

If one of these criteria does not apply, then the transaction is processed locally. Most commercial transactions and many scientific calculations do not need the power of a large computer. There are exceptions, such as simulations and complex models. Many of these exceptions would not use teleprocessing anyway. But the second criterion, centralized data, is important to some, but not all, data. Consequently data-base and data-communications techniques became closely related and computer manufacturers produced *data-base data-communications (DBDC)* software.

EXAMPLES OF HIERARCHICAL CONFIGURATIONS

Systems in which some of the processing takes place on a central system and some on local systems close to the end user are known as hierarchical configurations. Some examples are as follows:

1. *Insurance.* The branches of an insurance company each have their own processor with a printer, card reader, and terminals. This processor handles most of the computing requirements of the branch. Details of the insurance contracts made are sent to a head office computer for risk analysis and actuarial calculations. The entry and assessment of claims —sometimes an elaborate procedure—is done on-line on the local machine, and the results are sent to head office. The head office management has up-to-the-minute information on the company's financial position and exposure and can adjust the quotations given by the salesman accordingly.

2. *A chain store.* Each store in a chain has a minicomputer which records sales and handles inventory control and accounts receivable. It prints sales slips (receipts) for customers at the time of sale. Salesmen and office personnel can use terminals to display pricing, inventory, and accounts receivable information and customer statements. The store management can display salesmen performance information and goods aging and other analysis reports (Fig. 8.1).

    The store systems transmit inventory and sales information to the head office system. At night they receive inventory change information. The fast receipt of inventory and sales information enables the head office system to keep the inventory of the entire organization at a minimum. The store systems run unattended. Any program changes are transmitted to the systems from the head office computer.

3. *Production control.* Various different production departments in a factory complex each have a minicomputer. Work station terminals on the shop floor are connected to the minicomputer, and the workers enter details of the operations they perform. The task of scheduling the operations so as to make the best utilization of workers and machines is done by the minicomputer. The shop foreman displays these operations schedules and often makes changes to them because of local problems and priorities. He frequently makes a change and instructs the machine to reperform its scheduling program.

    Details of the work to be done are made up by a higher-level computer which

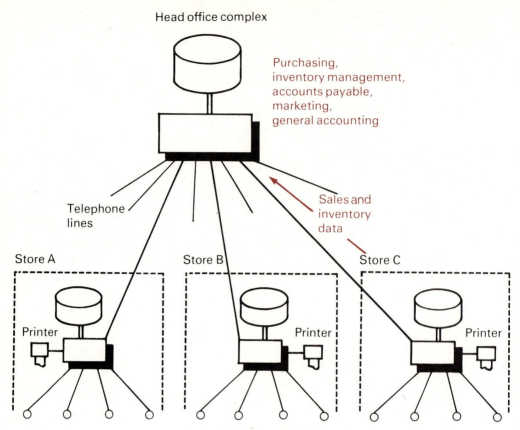

Head office complex

Purchasing,
inventory management,
accounts payable,
marketing,
general accounting

Telephone
lines

Sales and
inventory
data

Store A

Store B

Store C

Printer

Printer

Printer

Point-of-sale terminals, and terminals for staff and management

Figure 8.1 A hierarchical configuration in a chain store. Each store has a stand-along minicomputer system, with files and terminals, which handles the store operations. It transmits sales and inventory summaries to the head office where nationwide planning is done. Any program changes in the store computers are made and tested at the head office and transmitted to the store computer.

receives information about sales and delivery dates, and performs a breakdown on the parts that must be manufactured to file the orders. The central computer passes its job requirements to the shop floor minicomputers and receives status reports from them.

PROCESS CONTROL   Hierarchies of processors were common in process control applications before they were used in commercial data processing. Many instruments taking readings in an industrial or chemical process are connected to a small, reliable computer which scans the readings, looking for exceptions or analyzing trends. The same computer may automatically control part of the operation, setting switches, operating relays, regulating temperatures, adjusting values, and so on.

Response time must be fast on some process control applications. A local minicomputer is used to ensure fast response. Increasingly today, tiny, cheap microprocessors are being employed in instruments and control mechanisms. Many such devices may be attached to a minicomputer which stores data relating to the process being controlled.

A higher-level computer may be concerned with planning the operations, optimization, providing information for management control, or general data processing. Figure 8.2 shows a configuration in a steel mill, with different processors

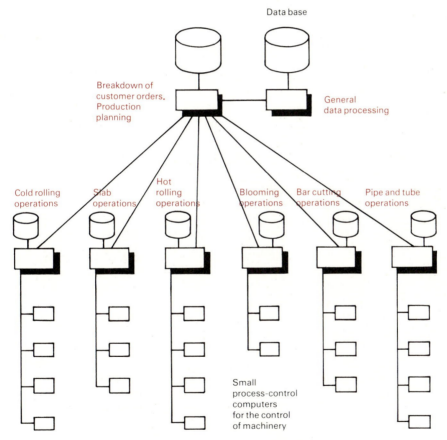

Figure 8.2 A hierarchy of computers in a steel mill which integrate the process control in several plant areas, and production planning. The system gives higher productivity of plant operations and permits immediate response to customer orders.

each having their own two-level process-control system, and these systems being linked to a higher production planning system.

In hospitals, the elaborate patient instrumentation used in intensive care wards is monitored and controlled on small, local, highly reliable computers. These in turn are linked to higher level machines which can perform complex analyses, provide information to nurse stations, record patient histories, and so on.

CASUALLY COUPLED?   In some configurations the design of the peripheral systems is largely independent of the design of the higher-level systems. In others the periphery and the center are so closely related that they are really separate components of the same system.

An example of a *casually coupled* configuration is a corporate head-office *information system* which derives its data from separate systems, separately installed in different corporate departments. These systems transmit data at the end of the day to the control system, where it is edited, reformated, and filed in a different manner from that in the peripheral systems, to serve a different purpose. The installers of the peripheral systems designed them for their own needs and were largely unaware of the needs of the central system.

An example of a closely coupled design is a banking system in which all customer data are stored by a central computer. (This does not apply to all banks. Some have loosely distributed systems.) A small computer in each branch, or group of branches, serves the processing needs of that branch, providing the tellers and the officers with the information they need at terminals. Customer data are also stored in the branch computers, largely in case of a failure of the central system or the telecommunications link to it. The peripheral files are strictly subsets of the central file. The programs developed for the peripheral computers are compiled on the central computer and loaded from it into the peripheral computers. Changes in the peripheral programs are made centrally and transmitted. Account balancing requires tight cooperation of the peripheral and central machines.

MULTIPLE LEVELS   Vertically distributed configurations may contain more than two levels of processor. In some there may be as many as four levels (Fig. 8.3).

The lowest level may consist of intelligent terminals for data entry, or microprocessors in a factory, scanning instruments.

The next level may be a computer in a sales region assembling and storing data that relate to that region, or a computer in a factory assembling the data from the microprocessors and being used for production planning.

The third level is a conventional large computer system in the divisional head office, performing many types of data processing and maintaining large data bases for routine operations. This computer center receives data from the lower systems and sends instructions to them.

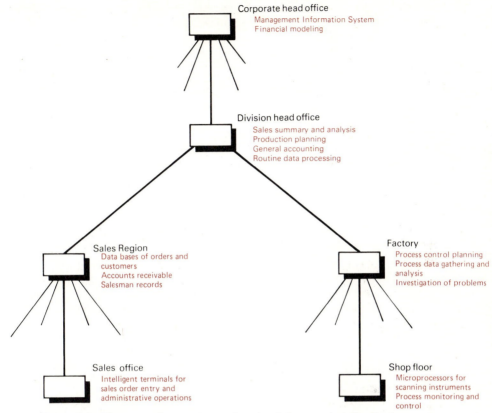

Figure 8.3 There may be as many as four levels in a vertical distribution of applications.

The highest level is a corporate management information system, with data structured differently from that in the systems for routine operations. This system may be designed to assist various types of high-management decision making. It may run complex corporate financial models or elaborate programs to assist in optimizing certain corporate operations, for example, scheduling a tanker fleet. It receives summary data from other, lower, systems.

REASONS FOR HIERARCHIES   Reasons for using hierarchical systems are summarized in Box 8.1. The set of reasons should include those in Box 7.1 on function distribution.

An important group of reasons on some configurations is related to data—where they are kept and how they are maintained. We discuss this later in the book.

Also of great importance are arguments relating to human, political, and organizational reasons, rather than technical reasons.

BOX 8.1   Technical reasons for using hierarchical distributed processing

(Note that there are also human, political, and organizational reasons, which are discussed in Chapter 13.)

- COST

    Total system cost may be lower. There is less data transmission, and many functions are moved from the host.

- CAPACITY

    The host may not be able to handle the workload without distribution. Distribution permits many functions to be performed in parallel.

- AVAILABILITY

    Fault-tolerant design can be used. Critical applications continue when there has been a host or telecommunications failure. The small peripheral processors may be substitutable. In some systems (e.g., a supermarket system or hospital patient monitoring) high reliability is vital.

- RESPONSE TIME

    Local responses to critical functions can be fast; no telecommunications delay; no scheduling problems; instruments are scanned and controlled by a local device.

- USER INTERFACE

    A better user interface can be employed, e.g., better terminal dialogue, when the user interacts with a local machine, better graphics or screen design, more responses, faster response time.

- SIMPLICITY

    Separation of the peripheral functions can give a simpler, more modular system design.

BOX 8.1 *continued*

- MORE FUNCTIONS

  More system functions are often found because of ease of implementing them on the peripheral machines. Salary savings often result from increased peripheral functions.

- SEPARATE DATA ORGANIZATIONS

  The data on the higher-level system may be differently organized from those on the peripheral systems (e.g., corporate management information organized for spontaneous searching vs. local, detailed, operational data tightly organized for one application.

See also Box 7.1 on distributed intelligence and function distribution.

9 HORIZONTAL DISTRIBUTED SYSTEMS

In the previous chapter we discussed vertically distributed systems. In this chapter we discuss horizontal distribution.

Some software, control mechanisms, and systems architectures are primarily oriented to vertical distribution, and some are primarily for peer-coupled systems. A transmission subsystem which merely transmits data between computers *could* be designed to serve a horizontal or vertical configuration equally well. The differences are more important in the higher-level mechanisms such as file management, or data-base management, intelligent terminal control, data compression, editing, man-machine dialogues, recovery, restart and so on.

In reality, major differences are found in the transmission subsystems as well. A transmission subsystem designed for vertical distribution can have simpler flow control and routing control mechanisms, and hence simpler recovery procedures. It may use elaborate concentrators or other devices for maximizing network utilization and may employ some of the function distribution features listed in Box 7.1.

PATTERNS OF WORK   Because of the mechanisms built into software or systems architecture, designers sometimes try to make all configurations vertical, or all configurations horizontal. This can result in excessive overhead, system inflexibility, or clumsy control. Whether or not a configuration *should* be vertical, or horizontal, or both, depends on the *patterns of work* the configuration must accomplish and the *patterns of data usage*.

A conical diagram is sometimes drawn to reflect the units of work or the data used at different levels in a corporation (Fig. 9.1). At the lower levels there tend to be many relatively simple, repetitive jobs. At the top there tend to be few complex jobs. At the bottom there tend to be many data used in simple, repetitive ways. At the top all the detail used at the low levels is not needed; instead, summary data are

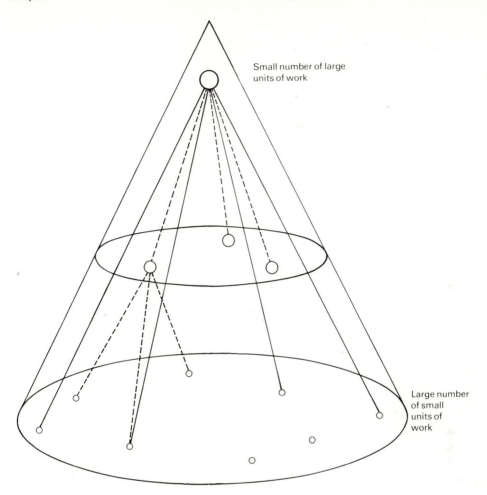

Figure 9.1 Vertical communication.

needed which are used in complex, unpredictable ways. In between there may be tasks of intermediate complexity.

In designing a distributed system we are concerned with such questions as:

- Where are the units of processing work required?
- How large are these units? What size of processing machine do they need?
- Are the units independent, or does one depend on the results of another?
- What stored data do the work units employ?
- Do they share common data, or are the data independent?
- What transactions must pass between one unit and another? What are the patterns of transaction flow?

● Must transactions pass between the units of work immediately, or is a delay acceptable? What is the cost of delay?

The answers to these questions differ from one organization to another. The patterns of work are different. The patterns of information flow between work units are different. Different types of corporations tend, therefore, to have their own natural shapes for distributed processing. What is best for an airline is not necessarily best for an insurance company. Often firms in the same industry are different because of differing corporate structures and management patterns.

In Fig. 9.1 the circles represent the work units in an organization. The nature of the work units may be such that they can be independent and have no need to know what other units are doing. They may be stand-alone units having no communication with any other unit, possibly performed in stand-alone minicomputers. On the other hand, they may need to share common data which reside centrally. In this case there are vertical links to a common data store. They may be multiple such data stores which themselves pass information to a higher system. On the other hand, the work units at one level may be such that they need to pass information to other units at the same level. This situation may lead naturally to horizontal communication (the red lines in Fig. 9.1); but it could also, if necessary, be handled vertically with a centralized processor relaying transactions between the units.

Some configurations serve multiple separate organizations. Each organization may have any of the forms of communication of Fig. 9.1. Between them, however, data may be passed horizontally (Fig. 9.2.) Figure 9.2 shows horizontal communication between the *top* units in each organization. It may be between lower level units also.

EXAMPLES

1. An airline reservation system requires a common pool of data on seat availability. Geographically scattered work units use, and may update, the data in this pool. Each of them needs data which are up to date second by second. These data need to be kept centrally. The bulkiest data are those relating to passengers. A passenger may telephone the airline in cities far apart, and when he does so the agent to whom he talks must be able to access his data. In order to find the data it is easier to keep them centrally also.

2. A car rental firm may permit its customers to pick up a car at one location and leave it at another. When the car is picked up, a computer terminal prepares the contract. When the car is left, a terminal is used to check the contract and calculate the bill. If a minicomputer at each location performed these functions, horizontal communication would be needed between the destination location and the location where the car was picked up. However, some centralized work is also needed because it is necessary to keep track of the company's cars and ensure that they are distributed appropriately for each day's crop of customers. Credit and other details about regular customers may also be stored centrally.

   The shape of the work therefore indicates both vertical and horizontal distribution. However, because the centralized (vertical) links are needed, the customer contracts may also be stored centrally and the same links used to access them. The rental offices may then use intelligent terminals rather than complete minicomputers.

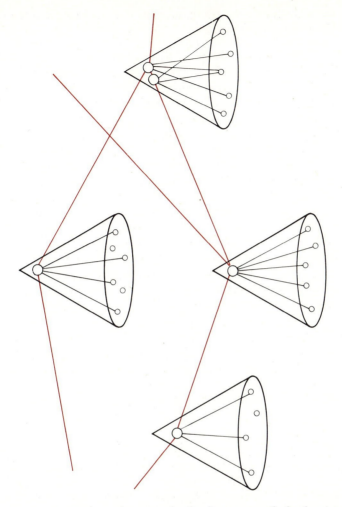

Figure 9.2   Horizontal communication between vertical subsystems.

3. Insurance companies have offices in different locations. They keep details about customers and their policies. An office does not normally need to share these data with another office or pass transactions to it. The offices could therefore use stand-alone machines. Customers in different locations may have different requirements. For example, in the United States different states have different insurance regulations and tax laws. Thus the different machines may be programmed somewhat differently. The insurance company head office, however, needs to know enough details of all customer policies to enable it to evaluate the company's cash flow and risks and to perform actuarial calculations which enable it to control the company's financial exposure. Enough data for this purpose are therefore passed upwards to the head office. This vertical communication does not need to be real-time, as in the case of an airline reservation system. The data can be transmitted in periodic batches.

Although the shape of the work in an insurance company is appropriate for processing distribution, that does not necessarily mean that most processing will be distributed. There are various arguments for centralization, which we discuss in Chapter 13, among them economies of scale when storing the vast files of insurance companies, and use of data-base software. A distributed-intelligence rather than a distributed-system configuration is used in some insurance companies.

4. A group of banks each handle their own customers with their own data processing system. However, a customer in one bank can make monetary transfers to customers in other banks. A network is set up by the banks to perform such transfers electronically. The money is moved very rapidly and hence is available for use or interest-gathering by banks for a longer period. The use of this "float" more than pays for the network. In this example we have a peer-coupled configuration with a need for horizontal transfer between the work units.

DEGREE OF HOMOGENEITY

We may classify horizontal configurations according to the degree of homogeneity of the systems which communicate. This affects the design, the choice of software and network techniques, and often the overall management.

Figure 9.3 shows three factors involved in the degree of homogeneity: machines, applications, and the organizations served. At one extreme we have identical machines running the same application programs in the same corporation. In other words, the processing load has been split between several identical computers. At the other extreme we have incompatible machines running entirely different programs in different organizations, but nevertheless interconnected by a network. One of the best known examples of this is the ARPA network shown in Fig. 9.4.

NONCOOPERATIVE SYSTEMS

We may subdivide configurations into those composed of *cooperative* and *noncooperative* systems. A noncooperative configuration consists of computer systems installed independently by different authorities with no common agency controlling their design but linked by a shared computer network.

The ARPA network (ARPANET) interlinks computer systems in many different universities, and some research organizations, mostly in the United States. It was developed with ARPA funds (Advanced Research Projects Agency of the U.S. Department of Defense) to explore the use of packet switching for providing a *resource-sharing* network. The organizations which are interlinked have incompatible computer systems with a wide variety of different facilities. It was intended that a terminal user at one of these locations should be able to employ the resources of systems either at his own location or at any other location on the network. The network should be reliable enough and have a fast enough response time to appear "transparent," so that it makes almost no difference to the user whether he is using a local or a remote machine. The resources interconnected by the network are very

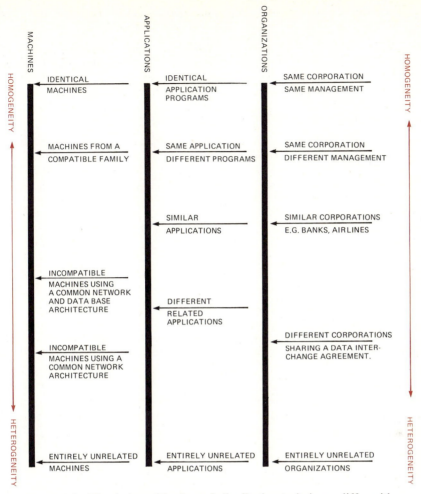

MACHINES APPLICATIONS ORGANIZATIONS

HOMOGENEITY

IDENTICAL MACHINES — IDENTICAL APPLICATION PROGRAMS — SAME CORPORATION SAME MANAGEMENT

MACHINES FROM A COMPATIBLE FAMILY — SAME APPLICATION DIFFERENT PROGRAMS — SAME CORPORATION DIFFERENT MANAGEMENT

SIMILAR APPLICATIONS — SIMILAR CORPORATIONS E.G. BANKS, AIRLINES

INCOMPATIBLE MACHINES USING A COMMON NETWORK AND DATA BASE ARCHITECTURE — DIFFERENT RELATED APPLICATIONS

INCOMPATIBLE MACHINES USING A COMMON NETWORK ARCHITECTURE — DIFFERENT CORPORATIONS SHARING A DATA INTER-CHANGE AGREEMENT.

HETEROGENEITY

ENTIRELY UNRELATED MACHINES — ENTIRELY UNRELATED APPLICATIONS — ENTIRELY UNRELATED ORGANIZATIONS

Figure 9.3 The design of horizontal distribution techniques differ with the degree of homogeneity of the interconnected systems.

expensive in total, and the additional utilization of them which results from the networking more than pays for the cost of the network.

Noncooperative systems exist in corporate and government environments as well. Different data-processing systems for different purposes have been set up by different groups who do not talk to one another. In some cases the end users could benefit by gaining access to more than one of these systems. In other cases it is desirable to pass information from one system to another. Large corporations and government entities could benefit from a network interlinking their computers. However, there may be insufficient traffic to justify the type of network that ARPA built. Simpler links or public facilities may be used.

Because the cost and ease of networking will improve greatly in the future, some corporations have attempted to impose on their diverse systems groups certain standards which will eventually make interconnection of the systems more practical

A logical map of ARPANET in 1972 showing the various incompatible computers that it interconnected:

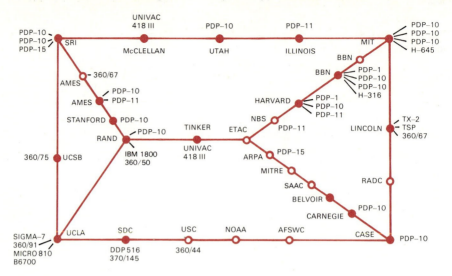

A physical map of ARPANET two years later. ARPANET continued to grow and change and was the pioneering system that paved the way for horizontal heterogenous networks.

(a)

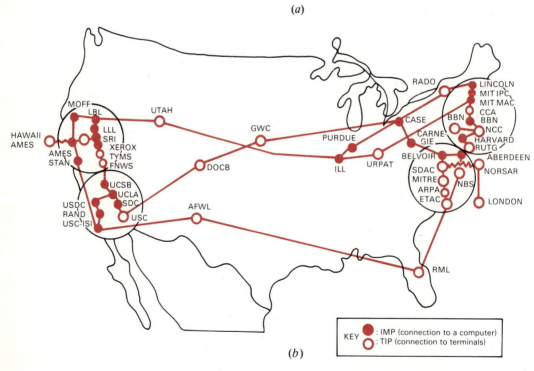

(b)

Figure 9.4 (*a*) A logical map of ARPANET in 1972 showing various incompatible computers that it interconnected; (*b*) A physical map of ARPANET which continued to grow and change and was the pioneering system that paved the way for horizontal heterogeneous networks.

or more valuable. Among the types of standards imposed or attempted have been the following:

1. Standardization of transaction formats

2. Standardization of line-control discipline

3. Use of compatible computers (one large corporation decreed that all minicomputers should be DEC machines, possibly anticipating future use of DEC's network architecture)

4. Standardization of data field formats and use of an organizationwide data dictionary

5. Standardization of record or segment formats

6. Use of a common data-description language (e.g., CODASYL DDL, or IBM's DL/I)

7. Use of common data-base management software

8. Use of a common networking architecture

Standards are an important part of a corporate strategy for DDP.

COOPERATING SYSTEMS

Cooperating systems are designed to achieve a common purpose, serve a single organization, or interchange data in a manner agreed upon.

We can subdivide cooperating systems into those in which the separate systems are used by the same *organization* and those in which *separate corporations* are interlinked.

Networks which interlink separate corporations are found today in certain industries. In the future they may become common in most industries to bypass the labor-intensive steps of mailing, sorting, and key-entering orders, invoices, and other documents which pass from a computer in one organization to a computer in another.

Industries with intercorporate computer networks today include banking and airlines. Most major airlines have reservation systems in which terminals over a wide geographic area are connected to a central computer. Worldwide airlines have worldwide networks. Many booking requests cannot be fulfilled completely by the airlines to which they were made. The airline might have no seats available, or the journey may necessitate flights on more than one carrier. Booking messages therefore must be passed from the computer in one airline to the computer in another, and often the response is passed back swiftly enough to inform the booking agent who initiated the request at his terminal. In order to achieve this linking of separate systems, all participating airlines must agree to a rigorously defined format for the messages passing between airlines. This format is standardized by an industry association, ATA in the United States and IATA internationally. To operate the interlinking network, the airlines set up independent nonprofit organizations, ARINC (Aeronautical Radio, Incorporated) in the United States and SITA (*Société Internationale de Télécommunications Aéronautique*) internationally. The separate airlines must send ATA-format or IATA-format messages using the SITA or

ARINC protocols. These networks began as networks for sending low-speed off-line teleprinter messages. As the need arose, they were upgraded to handle fast-response messages between computers as well as conventional teleprinter traffic. Figure 9.5 shows the computer-to-computer network of SITA.

Figure 9.6 shows another international network designed to connect bank computers for moving money and messages almost instantaneously between the banks. As in the case of the airlines, the bank computers are differently programmed, incompatible machines, set up by widely different corporations in different countries. Like the airlines, the banks must send rigorously formated messages and observe precise network protocols. In this case a very high level of security must be built into the cooperative procedures because sums exceeding $1 million are transmitted between the computers.

Like the airlines, the banks set up a nonprofit corporation to design and operate the network, SWIFT (Society for Worldwide Interbank Financial Transactions). SWIFT is wholly owned by the participating banks. The banks finance the system and are charged for its use on a per-message basis plus a fixed connection charge and an annual charge based on traffic volumes. The banks which use the network range from very small banks to ones with more than 2000 branches.

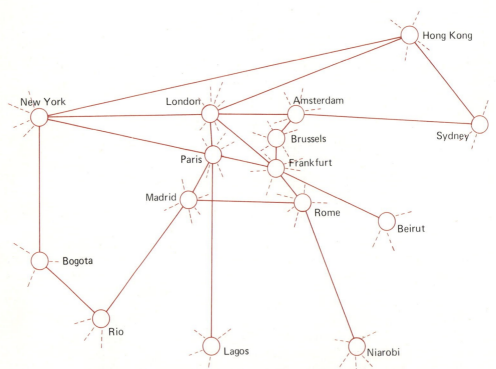

Figure 9.5 The SITA networks present and proposed trunks. Many smaller, lower level, centers are connected to those shown.

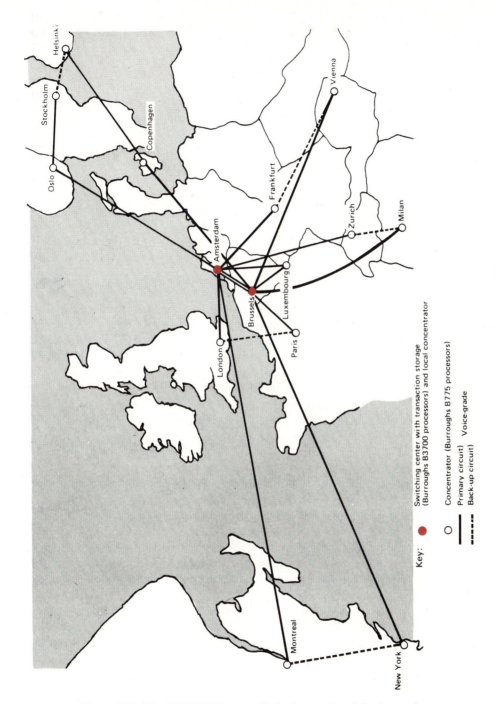

Key:

● Switching center with transaction storage
(Burroughs B3700 processors) and local concentrator

○ Concentrator (Burroughs B775 processors)

—— Primary circuit)   Voice-grade
- - - Back-up circuit)

Figure 9.6 The S.W.I.F.T. network for international fund transfer.

137

Both SITA and SWIFT are designed for large traffic volumes. In the early 1980's SWIFT will handle 100 million transactions per year and SITA several hundred million.

SYSTEMS UNDER Much of the use of distributed computing is within one
ONE MANAGEMENT corporation under one management. This could result
in a compatible configuration using a common net-
working architecture. Often, however, the systems to be linked were installed separately in separate locations without any thought about eventual interconnection. The files or data bases are incompatible; the same data field is formatted differently in different systems; programs cannot be moved from one computer to another without rewriting; where teleprocessing is used, the terminals are incompatible and even the line-control procedures are different, so that the terminals cannot be changed without a major upheaval in the systems they are connected to.

In this environment a major reprogramming and redesign effort is needed before networking becomes of much value, and often this effort is too expensive.

It is necessary that systems in different functional areas of a corporation be developed by different groups. Corporate data processing is much too complex for one group to develop more than a portion of it. The current trend to decentralization is resulting in more and more autonomous groups carrying out application development. This is a valuable trend because it results in more people being involved in application development, and in the development being done locally where the application problems are understood.

In order to make computer networking of value, it is desirable that the *interfaces* between these separately developed systems be rigorously defined and adhered to. *If the interfaces are preserved, each development group can work autonomously.*

Consider a small corporation that divides its data processing up into six functional areas: sales, engineering, production, stores and purchasing, accounting, and planning. The applications within these six areas are shown in Fig. 9.7.

With distributed processing the six areas could be handled by separate computer systems, as shown in Fig. 9.8. The data which pass between the systems are shown. Each line relates to one type of transaction, and there may be large quantities of such transactions passing between the computers. Some of these transactions need to pass in real time. Others could be saved for batch transmission.

In an earlier era many of the transactions in Fig. 9.8 passed between the functional areas in the form of paper documents. Division of labor in distributed computing sometimes copies the division of labor of earlier manual systems. What one clerk used to pass to another clerk, one small processor may pass to another processor.

A chain store organization in the United States designed a system with seven large minicomputers interconnected in a ring so that each can pass information to

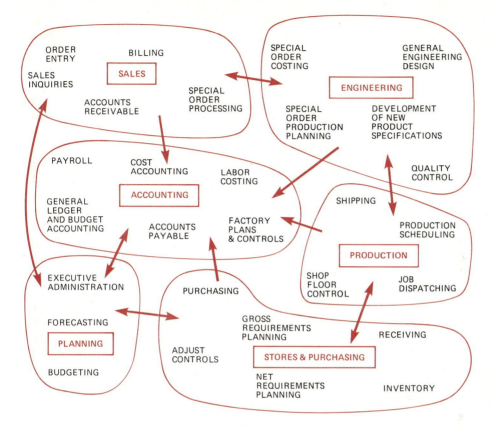

Figure 9.7

any other (Fig. 9.9). The seven computers operate in different functional areas, forming self-contained systems, as follows:

1. A marketing system

2. A purchasing system

3. An accounts payable system

4. A general accounting system

5. A personnel system

6. A communications controller which is connected to a minicomputer in each of the stores (discussed in the previous chapter)

7. A control system for monitoring and operating the configuration, dealing with failures, and so on

Each of the seven systems has up to 40 terminals, several printers, a tape drive

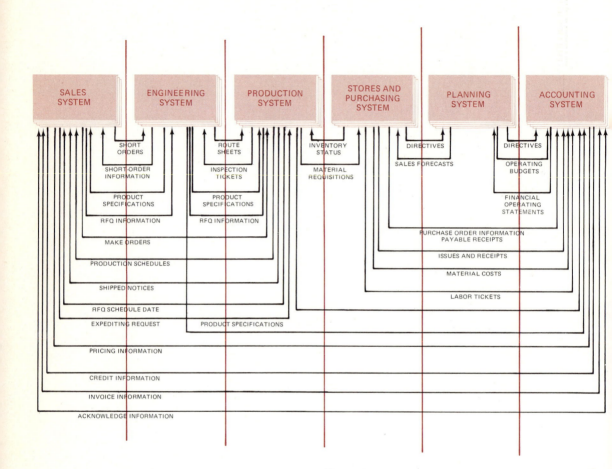

SALES SYSTEM

ENGINEERING SYSTEM

PRODUCTION SYSTEM

STORES AND PURCHASING SYSTEM

PLANNING SYSTEM

ACCOUNTING SYSTEM

SHORT ORDERS

ROUTE SHEETS

INVENTORY STATUS

DIRECTIVES

DIRECTIVES

SHORT-ORDER INFORMATION

INSPECTION TICKETS

MATERIAL REQUISITIONS

SALES FORECASTS

OPERATING BUDGETS

PRODUCT SPECIFICATIONS

PRODUCT SPECIFICATIONS

FINANCIAL OPERATING STATEMENTS

RFQ INFORMATION

RFQ INFORMATION

PURCHASE ORDER INFORMATION PAYABLE RECEIPTS

MAKE ORDERS

ISSUES AND RECEIPTS

PRODUCTION SCHEDULES

MATERIAL COSTS

SHIPPED NOTICES

LABOR TICKETS

RFQ SCHEDULE DATE

EXPEDITING REQUEST

PRODUCT SPECIFICATIONS

PRICING INFORMATION

CREDIT INFORMATION

INVOICE INFORMATION

ACKNOWLEDGE INFORMATION

Figure 9.8

for transaction logging and backup, a fast fixed-head disk for program overlaying, and several hundred million bytes of disk storage for data.

The division of labor between the systems is the same as that between the departments in the head office. Each department, in effect, has its own independent computer and maintains its own data. Data passing from one department to another are transmitted immediately on the ring.

If one of the computers fails, some of its critical functions may be taken over by another computer on the ring. The control system will detect the malfunction because it fails to receive a signal which it expects repetitively from each system. It notifies the operating personnel, who may temporarily move data files to a different

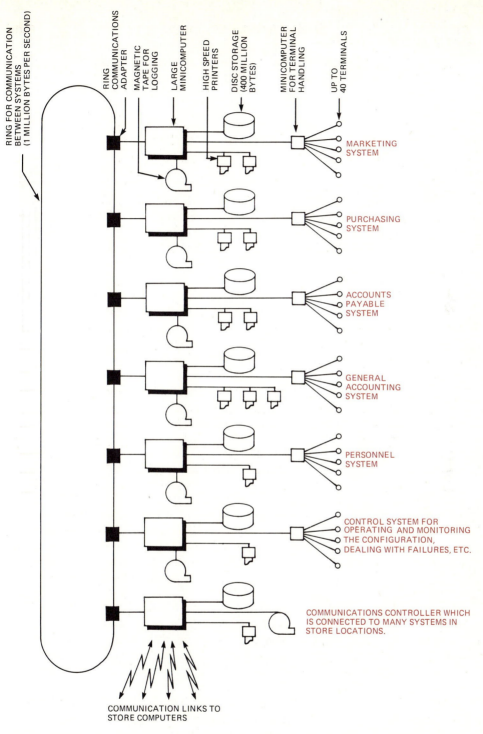

RING FOR COMMUNICATION BETWEEN SYSTEMS (1 MILLION BYTES PER SECOND)

RING COMMUNICATIONS ADAPTER

MAGNETIC TAPE FOR LOGGING

LARGE MINICOMPUTER

HIGH SPEED PRINTERS

DISC STORAGE (400 MILLION BYTES)

MINICOMPUTER FOR TERMINAL HANDLING

UP TO 40 TERMINALS

MARKETING SYSTEM

PURCHASING SYSTEM

ACCOUNTS PAYABLE SYSTEM

GENERAL ACCOUNTING SYSTEM

PERSONNEL SYSTEM

CONTROL SYSTEM FOR OPERATING AND MONITORING THE CONFIGURATION, DEALING WITH FAILURES, ETC.

COMMUNICATIONS CONTROLLER WHICH IS CONNECTED TO MANY SYSTEMS IN STORE LOCATIONS.

COMMUNICATION LINKS TO STORE COMPUTERS

Figure 9.9 Horizontal distribution in one building. Multiple systems handling different applications connected by a ring.

system. The control system will transmit a revised copy of the data map to each of the systems so that transactions are sent to the new location.

SMALLER FRAGMENTATION   On some minicomputer systems the fragmentation of work between processors is finer than that in Figs. 9.8 and 9.9. If the processors are small and inexpensive, they may handle only one application at a time. Each application in Fig. 9.7 rather than each functional area may have a minicomputer to itself. As some of them are not on-line or real-time applications, they wait their turn for a processor just as they would have done in the old days of second-generation computers.

On some banking systems the processor handling checking accounts is different from the one handling savings accounts. When a customer moves money from a checking to a savings account, a transaction must pass from one processor to the other.

Figure 9.10 shows three sets of files for a banking operation: customer information records, checking records, and savings records. In a centralized configuration all three files reside in the storage accessible by one computer. In a distributed configuration the three files could be on separate computers and processing would proceed as in the bottom half of Fig. 9.10. When work is decomposed into basic fragments, each fragment can be relatively simple. In total, however, there is more application programming in the bottom half of Fig. 9.10 than the top half, because the transfers between computers have to be programmed and there are additional logging operations for recovery purposes and protection against data loss.

SPLIT WORK   The computers in Figs. 9.8, 9.9, and 9.10 are all performing different work. In some configurations the minicomputers perform *identical* work and the work load is split between them.

The Bank of America uses a set of minicomputer modules in two computer centers, as shown in Fig. 9.11. Many of the modules perform identical work. Direct file organization is used, and the software is simple compared with that on large computers; the transaction *path lengths* are much shorter. The total number of machine instructions executed is far lower than if the same work were done on a large computer with a typical operating system and associated software. In this example the traffic volume is so high that a typical large computer in each computer center could not handle it when the system was designed. Multiple large computers would have been needed at a cost much higher than the minicomputer configuration.

GEOGRAPHICAL DISPERSION   The systems in Fig. 9.9 are all in one building. In Fig. 9.11 the transactions are sent to one of two computer centers for processing. Horizontally distributed systems could be *either in one location or geographically dispersed*. The property of being

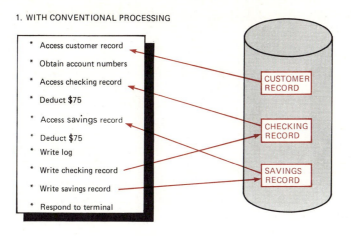

1. WITH CONVENTIONAL PROCESSING

* Access customer record
* Obtain account numbers
* Access checking record
* Deduct $75
* Access savings record
* Deduct $75
* Write log
* Write checking record
* Write savings record
* Respond to terminal

CUSTOMER RECORD

CHECKING RECORD

SAVINGS RECORD

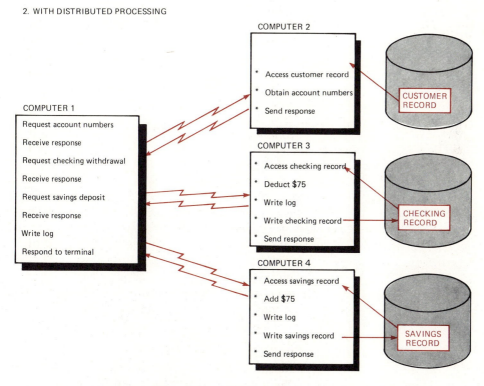

2. WITH DISTRIBUTED PROCESSING

COMPUTER 1

Request account numbers
Receive response
Request checking withdrawal
Receive response
Request savings deposit
Receive response
Write log
Respond to terminal

COMPUTER 2

* Access customer record
* Obtain account numbers
* Send response

CUSTOMER RECORD

COMPUTER 3

* Access checking record
* Deduct $75
* Write log
* Write checking record
* Send response

CHECKING RECORD

COMPUTER 4

* Access savings record
* Add $75
* Write log
* Write savings record
* Send response

SAVINGS RECORD

Figure 9.10 An illustration of distributed processing in which a single transaction uses data in three separate systems.

143

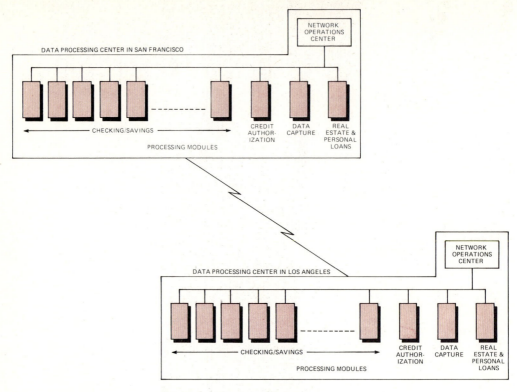

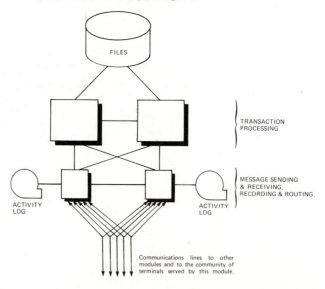

Figure 9.11 Horizontal distribution in two centers of the Bank of America, making possible the handling of a very high transaction volume.

geographically scattered may make little difference to the system organization, with the exception of that portion which relates to data transmission.

A system might be developed with the philosophy that its modules are initially in one location, but they are designed so that they can be dispersed at a later time. A system like that in Fig. 9.11 might eventually have its modules geographically scattered.

It is interesting to note, however, that many of the systems which have components distributed in one location today could not have these components geographically dispersed at an acceptable cost because of today's telecommunications links. The traffic volume between the modules is too high, or the speeds of telephone lines are too low. It is likely that distributed systems will flourish when we have better facilities for data transmission. Both new common-carrier data networks and new communications satellites offer the promise of the transmission capability needed.

SOFTWARE　　　　　　As changing costs take the computer industry increas-
PORTABILITY　　　　　ingly toward distributed processing, one highly desir-
　　　　　　　　　　　able characteristic is portability of programs. Programs
should be capable of being moved from one processor to another and gaining access to distributed instead of centralized data. There are arguments for, and against, distributed processing, and there are many possible distributed configurations. It is desirable that manufacturers' product lines should permit the flexibility to change configurations without creating the need to rewrite programs.

CONSTRAINTS　　　　　Distributed processing, it will be seen, gives the capabil-
　　　　　　　　　　　ity to form systems of an endless variety of shapes. Not
all of the possible shapes are desirable. There are arguments against the scattering of processing in certain types of systems. There are constraints on where the data should be located when multiple locations access it, for example. Later chapters will discuss the constraints and describe methodologies for designing distributed systems. Box 9.1 lists the reasons for horizontal computer networks.

BOX 9.1　Reasons for horizontal computer networks

(Some of these reasons apply to vertical configurations as well.)

- RESOURCE SHARING

  Expensive or unique resources can be shared by a large community of users, as on ARPANET.

continued

BOX 9.1 *continued*

- DIVERSITY

  Users have access to many different computers, programs, and data banks.

- TRANSACTION INTERCHANGE

  Transactions are passed from one system to another or from one corporation to another, e.g., financial transactions passed between banks on SWIFT, airline reservations or messages passed between computers in separate airlines as on SITA.

- SEPARATE SYSTEMS LINKED

  Separate, previously existing systems are linked so that one can use another's data or programs or so that users can access all of them.

- LOCAL AUTONOMY

  Local, autonomous minicomputer systems are favored, with their own files, and some transactions need data which reside on the file of a separate system.

- FUNCTIONAL SEPARATION

  Instead of one computer center performing all types of work, separate centers specialize in different types. For example, one does large-scale scientific computation. One does information retrieval. One has a data base for certain classes of application. One does mass printing and mailing.

- TRANSMISSION COST

  Separate systems share a common transport network designed to minimize the combined data (and possible voice) transmission cost.

- RELIABILITY AND SECURITY

  When one system fails, others can process transactions. If one system is destroyed, its files can be reconstructed on another.

- LOAD SHARING

  Unpredictable peaks of work on one machine can be off-loaded to other machines.

- ENCOURAGEMENT OF DEVELOPMENT

  A corporate network can permit small data-processing groups to develop applications.

PART **III** STRATEGY

10 STRATEGIES FOR DISTRIBUTED DATA PROCESSING

There is no doubt that distributed processing is part of the mainstream evolution of data-processing technology. Used correctly, it can bring enormous benefits. Used badly, however, it can be a formula for chaos.

This section of this book is concerned with the strategy for distributed data processing. How can we maximize the benefits and avoid the pitfalls?

The objective of the strategy should be to establish a framework within which distributed processing can grow rapidly, with maximum end-user involvement, with high productivity of application development, and without the pitfalls listed in Box 5.1.

Some of the early teleprocessing systems, management information systems, data-base systems and computer networks were disasters. Corporationwide distributed processing makes possible even more costly disasters. To avoid them and gain the benefits, informed planning is needed.

STRATEGY HEXAGON   There are different aspects of the management of systems which can be centralized or distributed. The main ones are:

- *The setting of standards*

- *The selection of architectures,* including the selection of a computer network architecture such as SNA, DECNET, or CCITT X.25, the selection of data-base approaches such as CODASYL or DL/I, the decision to use files or data-base systems and how they are interconnected

- *The selection of hardware and software.* This selection may have to conform to the higher-level architectural decisions.

- *Usage decisions:* the selection of projects; feasibility studies
- *The design of data:* data-base administration; record design; data dictionary control
- *Application development:* design, programming and maintenance

In Chapter 6 we used a six-sided diagram to illustrate the different ways in which *hardware* can be centralized and decentralized (Fig. 6.7). We will now use a different hexagon diagram to show the different ways distributed data processing is managed. The above six aspects of management are represented by the six sides of the diagrams in Fig. 10.1. For each side an arrow pointing inwards means decision, design, and action by a central DP group. An arrow pointing outwards means decision, design, and action by decentralized group, usually a user group. An arrow pointing in both directions represents close cooperation between the central authority and the user groups. Two arrows, one in each direction, means a mixture of centralized and decentralized operation.

Diagram 1 in Fig. 10.1 represents totally centralized design and management. This was common before the era of distributed data processing. Many DP executives have tried to retain similar control as systems have become partially distributed.

Diagram 2 represents the opposite extreme, much publicized as "distributed data processing" by some corporations which have done it. The user managements are free to "do their own thing," unfettered by central architecture. The user groups create their own standards, if any, and determine their own projects and requirements. They select their own minicomputers and software.

Diagram 3 gives the user groups almost the same freedom as Diagram 2 but makes them follow standards laid down by a central authority.

In Diagram 4 the user groups carrying out their own implementation conform not only to central standards but also to a centrally determined architecture. They may be constrained to use a centrally developed computer network, SNA or DECNET machines, certain classes of data-base management system, and so on.

Diagram 5 represents close cooperation between the user groups and the central DP group. They work together to select hardware and software, determine what projects to implement, and work jointly on their design and development. Programmers and systems analysts from the central group may be placed with the user groups. The central group determines standards and architecture. Particularly important for future growth, there is central coordination of the design of data, probably with a centrally controlled data dictionary and data-base administration function.

In the sixth diagram of Fig. 10.1 the users are free to select their own projects and do their own application development, but they do so within a tightly controlled framework. The central group determines standards and architecture, has a data-base administration function and data dictionary which applies to all data stored in the distributed systems, and works with the user groups in hardware and software selection.

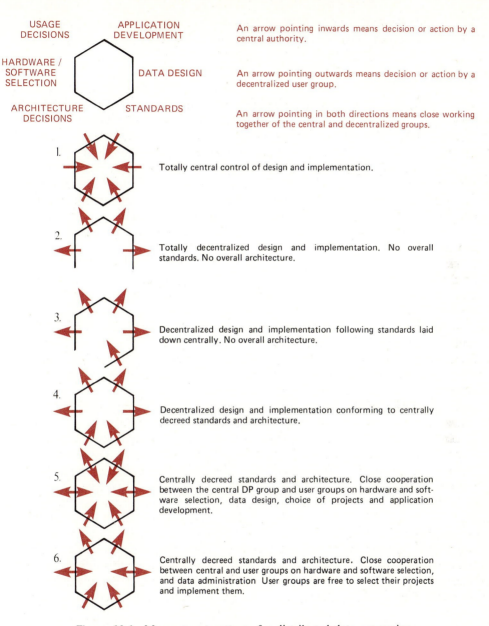

USAGE
DECISIONS

APPLICATION
DEVELOPMENT

HARDWARE /
SOFTWARE
SELECTION

DATA DESIGN

ARCHITECTURE
DECISIONS

STANDARDS

An arrow pointing inwards means decision or action by a central authority.

An arrow pointing outwards means decision or action by a decentralized user group.

An arrow pointing in both directions means close working together of the central and decentralized groups.

1. Totally central control of design and implementation.

2. Totally decentralized design and implementation. No overall standards. No overall architecture.

3. Decentralized design and implementation following standards laid down centrally. No overall architecture.

4. Decentralized design and implementation conforming to centrally decreed standards and architecture.

5. Centrally decreed standards and architecture. Close cooperation between the central DP group and user groups on hardware and software selection, data design, choice of projects and application development.

6. Centrally decreed standards and architecture. Close cooperation between central and user groups on hardware and software selection, and data administration User groups are free to select their projects and implement them.

Figure 10.1 Management patterns for distributed data processing.

MANAGEMENT STYLES   The hexagon diagram which is best for one organization may be different from that which is best for another. Organizations differ greatly in their management style and structure.

However, some management patterns for distributed processing are more likely to bring success than others.

Perhaps the greatest danger of distributed processing and minicomputers is that *incompatible* systems will spread at a rapid rate through an organization. They cannot easily be hooked together at a later time. They use incompatible data fields and records. Although some of these data are vital for higher-level management functions, they cannot be used without redesigning the peripheral systems, which is prohibitively expensive.

PITFALLS   The objective of the strategy and design process should be to gain the advantages of DDP while avoiding these pitfalls that were discussed in Chapter 5 (Box 5.1).

MANAGEMENT   Badly managed decentralized or distributed computing
CONTROL   can become expensive and may prevent a corporation from building the integrated control systems that it needs to keep ahead of competition.

To avoid the potential pitfalls it is important that distributed data processing be *managed,* and well managed. It should be directed by a central authority which understands how to avoid the pitfalls and maximize the advantages. One of the most important advantages is harnessing the creativity, knowledge, initiative, and hard work of the end-user groups.

The following management pattern runs the risk of all the pitfalls listed in Box 5.1:

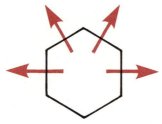

On the other hand, totally centralized control fails to harness the capability of the end users:

This strategy on the part of the DP department tends to be that in which the maximum end-user rebellion has occurred.

Standards are important for controlling the development in a professional manner. Architectural decisions will facilitate the interlinking of the distributed systems to meet higher-level corporate requirements. Together these form a foundation for distributed systems, which is why they are at the bottom of the hexagon. At a minimum, centralized control might relate merely to network architectures and standards:

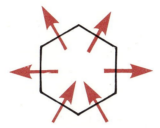

Of particular importance are the data structures. Some data used by the local systems will be transmitted to other systems. Much of them may be relevant to the needs of higher management. The design of data should therefore be centrally coordinated. A central data administration team may assist the local groups in their design of data, at the same time ensuring compatibility. The following diagram adds this characteristic:

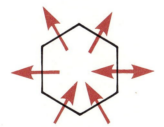

The central group may be concerned with hardware and software purchasing. Some measure of uniformity in the peripheral computers has the following advantages:

- Programs can be transferred from one peripheral computer to another.
- Control software does not have to be developed separately for each machine.
- Compatibility can be achieved in data-base operations.
- Compatibility can be achieved in networking.
- Total costs of repair may be lower.
- Standards may be more uniform and effective.
- Staff can be more easily transferred from one system to another.
- Bulk buying discounts may be available.

In some companies the central group discusses the purchase of hardware and software with the peripheral groups. In others it controls these purchases, telling user groups what they will employ:

These diagrams show the peripheral groups selecting the projects that are implemented and being responsible for their implementation. It often makes sense for some of the projects to be centrally coordinated. The same application code may be developed for multiple user groups, or applications created by one user group may be usable by others. A mixture of independent and centrally coordinated program development is often desirable.

Some top DP executives think that the following management pattern is ideal:

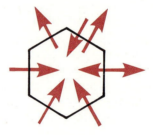

If well managed, this can give the user groups the following advantages:

- They are free to decide how they use the computers.
- They can develop their programs or decide how they use report generators, data-base query and update facilities, and so on. They are given professional help in complex matters such as the selection of hardware and software, architecture, and the design of data structures. They can employ corporate networks and data bases. Their data are compatible with data stored centrally, so that they can both employ and transmit to the central facilities when desirable.

In some cases it is sensible for the users to decide how computers will be used. For other applications a central DP authority should perform feasibility studies and usage decisions. The DDP strategy can permit both, and this is often the optimum form of hexagon diagram:

Because this is the strategy that will often bring the most benefits in DDP, we have used this diagram on the jacket of this book. Although rules are employed to enhance interchange between systems, there should be no inhibition of the user groups' initiative and creativity. User groups can be made responsible for how they use data processing and how it effects their overall efficiency and profitability.

MULTIPLE PATTERNS   In a large organization multiple management patterns often exist, sometimes in conflict with one another. These sometimes reflect separate divisional management or separate subsidiaries. Sometimes they reflect the realities of the corporate politics.

Figure 10.2 illustrates this. The head office DP organization has a data-base administration team labeled ① and is recommending a network architecture labeled ①. The marketing division and its regional subsidiaries conform to the central data coordination and the network architecture. The factory cooperates with the data coordination but not the network architecture, because its computers are incompatible with it. The laboratory is a world unto itself, conforming with nothing from the head office DP group. A subsidiary company also goes its own way, having its own network architecture, labeled ④, and its own data administration, labeled ②.

The regional marketing offices have programs, labeled △2, developed by the marketing division DP group, not the head office DP group. Similarly, the subsidiary plant has programs, labeled △3, developed in the subsidiary company head office, not the main head office. The subsidiary distribution chain has computer staff who select their own hardware and develop their own programs with standards, architecture, and data from the subsidiary head office, not the main head office.

Across some parts of the hexagons there are two arrows, indicating a mixture of facilities, some conforming to central plan and some not.

Part of the strategy design process should be to determine what parts of the organization can be covered with one strategy, i.e., one hexagon diagram. In some corporations central DP management has sufficient control for one hexagon diagram to be relevant to the entire corporation. In others there is little relationship between the data processing in separate divisions, or different subsidiaries. For example, ITT has largely autonomous subsidiaries. There is no point in having a com-

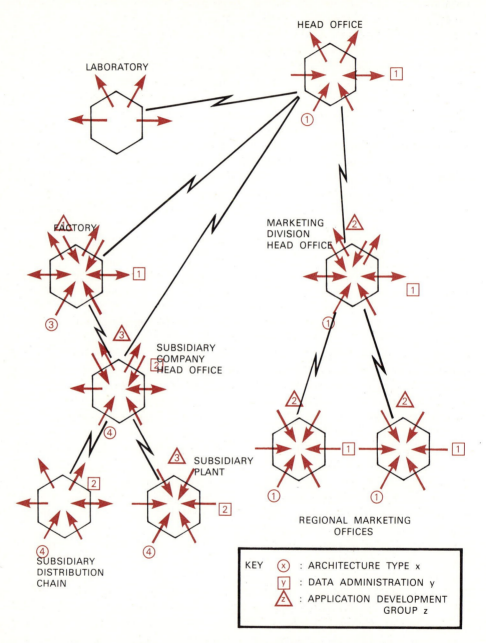

HEAD OFFICE

LABORATORY

FACTORY

MARKETING
DIVISION
HEAD OFFICE

SUBSIDIARY
COMPANY
HEAD OFFICE

SUBSIDIARY
PLANT

SUBSIDIARY
DISTRIBUTION
CHAIN

REGIONAL MARKETING
OFFICES

KEY (x) : ARCHITECTURE TYPE x
     [y] : DATA ADMINISTRATION y
     △z : APPLICATION DEVELOPMENT
          GROUP z

Figure 10.2 Multiple management patterns often exist within one corporation.

mon DDP architecture or strategy for a separately managed bread-making sub-sidiary, a car rental firm, and a telecommunications manufacturer, even though they are within the same corporation. The Travellers Insurance Company is of such a structure that one hexagon diagram can describe the DDP strategy of the whole corporation. The Aetna Insurance Company, covering the same geographical area, has three largely autonomous, separately managed divisions with almost no data in common. Only at the very top of the company do their data-processing re-quirements need to converge. Three separate strategies and hexagon diagrams are appropriate, although the three divisions may want to share a common network, and this should be indicated on their version of Fig. 10.2.

In some corporations, like IBM, the management style is such that head office DP edicts or architecture can apply worldwide. In others no central group has this authority or could reasonably be expected to have because of a more fragmented management structure. This needs to be reflected in the planning of the hexagon diagram.

Figure 10.3 shows a strategy diagram for a corporation with three autonomous divisions.

THE DESIGN   The implementation of distributed data processing
PROCESS   takes one of two forms: *designed* or *ad hoc*. In *ad hoc*
                         systems user groups "do their own thing," hoping
for no external interference. Sometimes they comment that the separate systems might be interconnected at some later time and that this will be all right because computer network software can do anything—like ARPANET. They are wrong.

Designed systems need to begin with a corporate strategy. What will the management pattern be? And how will it be translated into a working form of distributed data processing?

Figure 10.4 suggests components of a corporate DDP strategy, leading to the overall design of a framework within which DDP can grow. The strategy requires a broad view of what should be centralized and decentralized, and what management patterns will be used for controlling the activities. The hexagon diagrams need to be converted into an organization structure with definitions of authority and respon-sibility. Centralization and decentralization is discussed in more detail later.

The DP or DDP strategy should start with a top management view of where the corporation is going and how its direction might be changed by networks, data-base usage, microcomputers, and DDP. Figure 10.4 suggests creating a scenario of what the technology will look like five years in the future. The question should be asked: How might this technology change the corporation? Some markets have ended abruptly or been curtailed because of electronic technology. More often markets have opened up for new products and services. More surely, networks and DDP are likely to lead to management reorganizations as described in Chapter 2.

Figure 10.4 suggests a five-year look ahead. Some corporations use a longer strategy time-frame (e.g., seven years) and some shorter. Five years seems to the

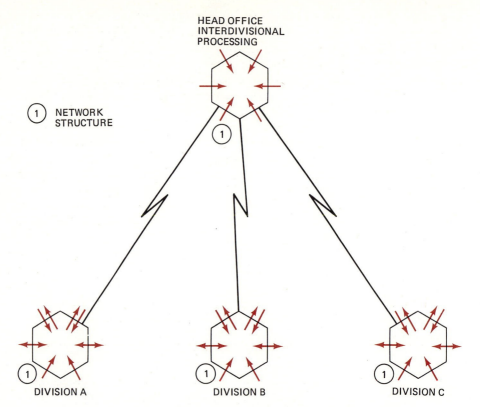

Figure 10.3   A strategy diagram for a corporation with three autonomous divisions. They have almost no data in common. Only at the very top of the company do their data-processing requirements need to converge to achieve overall financial control. However, for reasons of economy, they do share a common network.

author to be realistic for forecasting broad technology trends and for planning the directions of DDP. It is possible to take actions today that will *lock an organization out* of the distributed systems that would be most beneficial. For example, creating convoluted, centralized data structures and much application code using them can make future distribution prohibitively expensive because of the cost of reprogramming. For reasons such as this it is vital to take tomorrow's technology into consideration, not merely today's.

   In the DATA PROCESSING STRATEGY slice of Fig. 10.4 there are three blocks. They relate to DDP, file and data-base strategy, and network strategy. The file and data-base strategy is discussed at the end of Part IV and the network strategy in Part V. These blocks are expanded in Figs. 25.10 and 35.4, respectively.

   A strategy is needed for file and data-base operations. Data are a vitally important resource for managing a corporation, and in a DP environment, data must

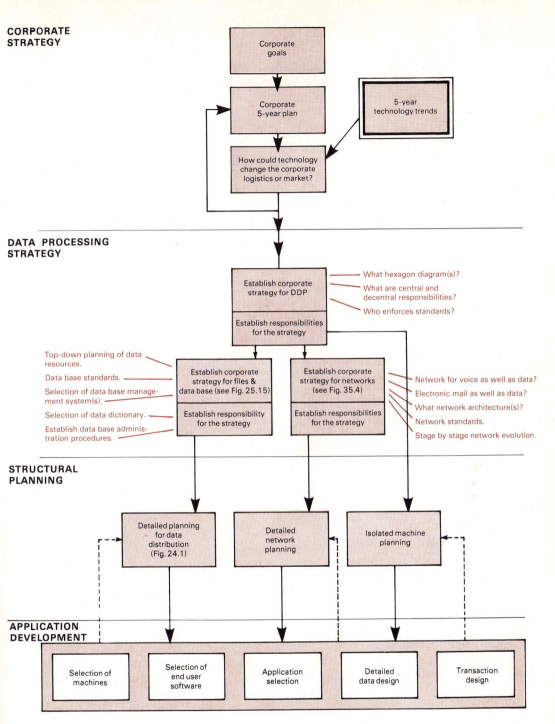

CORPORATE STRATEGY

Corporate goals

Corporate 5-year plan

5-year technology trends

How could technology change the corporate logistics or market?

DATA PROCESSING STRATEGY

Establish corporate strategy for DDP

Establish responsibilities for the strategy

What hexagon diagram(s)?

What are central and decentral responsibilities?

Who enforces standards?

Top-down planning of data resources.

Data base standards.

Selection of data base management system(s).

Selection of data dictionary.

Establish data base administration procedures.

Establish corporate strategy for files & data base (see Fig. 25.15)

Establish responsibility for the strategy

Establish corporate strategy for networks (see Fig. 35.4)

Establish responsibilities for the strategy

Network for voice as well as data?

Electronic mail as well as data?

What network architecture(s)?

Network standards.

Stage by stage network evolution.

STRUCTURAL PLANNING

Detailed planning for data distribution (Fig. 24.1)

Detailed network planning

Isolated machine planning

APPLICATION DEVELOPMENT

Selection of machines

Selection of end user software

Application selection

Detailed data design

Transaction design

Figure 10.4 Strategy and planning for DDP.

159

be carefully controlled because of the incompatibilities which so quickly arise. There is a world of difference between a data-base environment with appropriate software and well-structured design of data, and an uncontrolled collection of files created for different applications by programmers and analysts at different locations. Data design is discussed in Part IV.

Similarly, a network strategy is needed. Without it, it will become difficult and expensive to hook the different machines together. Network design and DDP software are discussed in Part V.

Different data-base management systems are incompatible, with a few exceptions. A data schema which works on one does not work on another. The cost of data conversion is very high because it necessitates so much program rewriting—so much in practice that it has often been avoided or abandoned. Similarly, much of the network software for distributed processing is incompatible. Incompatible machines cannot be hooked together without the users writing their own software, which often causes problems and locks them out of the manufacturers' evolution to better technology. Avoidance of incompatibility problems needs a corporationwide knowledge of where compatibility is needed and where not.

STRUCTURAL PLANNING

The slice labeled STRUCTURAL PLANNING in Fig. 10.4 goes into more detail. It is concerned with detailed planning for data distribution, detailed network planning, and plans for isolated machines—the stand-alone minicomputers which are separate from the networks, architectures, and data structures of DDP.

Planning for data distribution is discussed in Part IV and expanded in Fig. 24.1. *Detailed network planning* is illustrated in Fig. 35.4 and discussed along with the software for DDP networks in Part V.

A particularly important part of the bottom slice of the diagram is the *selection of end-user software*. This software ought to give users the maximum capability in deriving the information they need from the system and creating applications. Much of this can be done without the use of conventional programming. This is discussed in the companion book, *Software for Distributed Processing*. A deliberate effort is needed as part of the strategy to identify that end-user software which gives the highest user productivity, making the systems as easy to use as possible.

TOP-DOWN OR BOTTOM-UP DESIGN

In most DDP environments, neither top-down nor bottom-up design works by itself. Complete top-down design is usually unworkable because no design team can anticipate or comprehend all the ways the end users will want to employ the system (although such teams have sometimes made claims to the contrary). Bottom-up design by itself does not work because it results in multiple fragments which cannot be joined together (also contradicted by fragment designers and vendors of small computers). What is needed is a combination of the two.

Top-down design is done to create an overall architecture or framework into which the user modules can fit. User modules are created with bottom-up design but so that they fit into the planned framework which specifies the interfaces between the modules and thus work together when necessary. Top-down planning should also plan those application types which need centralized control, such as perhaps centralized purchasing, management information, and corporationwide logistics. Top-down design needs to specify such items as the following:

- The network architecture(s) used for distributed processing
- The line-control protocol used for transmission between the modules
- The message headers and techniques for controlling messages, where this is not part of a common DDP architecture (Chapter 33)
- The data-base architecture used
- The techniques for recovering from failures
- The techniques for security and auditability

As part of an evolving relationship between the top-down team and the user teams, the following should be specified:

- The data fields used, defined in a data dictionary
- Data groupings—records, segments, data-base subschemas
- The field structure of messages
- Data which are to be sent to central systems for central applications, management information, strategic control, etc.

A FRAMEWORK FOR GROWTH

The design of DDP is not something that can be done at one time by one group. It is something that will evolve over many years in a corporation. An almost infinite number of combinations of centralization and distribution are possible. Different applications and the needs of different locations will have to be considered at different times.

What is needed therefore is *not an all-embracing, grandiose plan but a framework which will permit step-by-step growth, each step being suitably small. The separate steps should fit into an overall framework so as to have whatever degree of compatibility and interconnectability is beneficial to the corporation as a whole, now and in the future.*

While the implementations span many years, the strategic plan (the second slice of Fig. 10.4) needs to be created at one time. The strategy will be modified over the years as new perceptions become clear and new facilities become available, but the management patterns, architectures, and controls need to be set before the *ad hoc* implementations get out of hand.

The decisions indicated in Fig. 10.4 and the expanded diagrams in Figs. 25.10 and 35.4 often plunge an organization into bitter political strife. They change the empires of DP executives and affect the way user executives manage and are judged. The exponentially growing power of microelectronics will change the jobs of many people and upset the practices with which many managers are comfortable.

Observing the structures of DDP in organizations, one can conclude time and time again that they come into existence more as a result of politics than of technical design. The strong individual or skilled politician wins. Too often the politics results in fragmented rather than coordinated systems or overcentralized systems with frustrated end users.

A corporate network ought to span divisions and subsidiaries which are separately managed, in many cases. Similarly, some of the same *data* are used in separately managed empires. Given the vital importance of computing and information in corporate management, it is essential that *top management* understand, broadly, the issues involved. Top management alone can set up the high-level management structures and directives that are necessary to make distributed data processing as beneficial as it should be.

Prior to the mid-1970's it was reasonable for top management to regard computing as a job which could safely be delegated to technical management. Now, with distributed processing, corporationwide networks, and data-base systems, that will not suffice. Top management understanding is needed to prevent the spread of harmful incompatibility or of systems which are too inflexible to serve rapidly changing needs. Top management direction is needed for establishing multidivisional networks, data bases, and systems which assist with high-level decision making and control.

11 CONTROL OF COMPLEXITY

A move to distributed processing can enormously increase the complexity of a system, or it can decrease it, depending on the design. Good design should decrease the complexity.

As systems grow in size, they grow in complexity. The number of interactions and hence the complexity grow disproportionately to the size.

It is sometimes the custom at a dinner party that when the wine is poured each person should clink glasses with each other. If there are 3 people, there will be 3 clinks; with 4 people, 6 clinks. With a dozen people the number is beginning to get out of hand, and with 46 people more than 1000 clinks are needed. People would spend all their time clinking rather than drinking.

If every module of a system interacts with every other, the number of interactions grows at approximately the square of the number of modules ($N(N-1)/2$ interactions for N modules). It has been observed that as systems grow, they become more complex and harder to manage, the complexity and cost following roughly a square law.

However, as systems grow, there are economies of scale. Over a certain range these economies of scale may be substantial, keeping far ahead of the increasing complexity. Economies of scale do not go on indefinitely as size rises. Beyond a certain size, diminishing returns set in, as shown in Fig. 11.1. Further growth becomes difficult because it pushes the upper limits of a technology, or because there are limited resources. Early this century motor cars became faster at an exponential rate, becoming more valuable. After a point, further increases in speed were of little or no value because of higher accident rates, expense of building fast roads, and increased petroleum consumption.

There are limits to growth with high-speed computers. Above a certain speed circuitry becomes expensive and heat dissipation from the circuits becomes a severe technical problem which is costly to solve. Above a certain scale of operation paging becomes excessive, the computer center building expensive, and operation staff

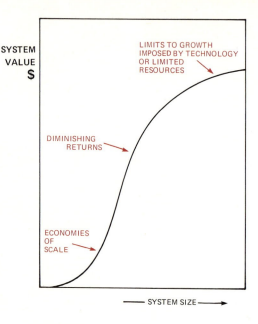

Figure 11.1 Economies of scale in systems usually exist up to a certain size above which there are diminishing returns.

costs far more than the machine. As size increases, system value grows more slowly, as in Fig. 11.1.

The technology of computers is still changing rapidly, so the scales on Fig. 11.1 are changing with time. Also as size increases, complexity grows. The operating system becomes more elaborate. Interactions between programs using the same data become complex, and so the cost of changing the programs grows disproportionately. The number of software instructions (not application code) for executing one transaction grows until it reaches figures as high as 100,000. One could say that, like the guests at the dinner party mentioned above, the software spends nearly all its time clinking rather than drinking.

The growing system cost is added to the plot of system value in Fig. 11.2. Over a certain range the *value* greatly exceeds the cost, but not when the system becomes too big.

The broad shape of the curves in Fig. 11.2 applies to systems of widely differing types. Systems and organizations tend to grow, if uncontrolled, until cost exceeds value. Big government schemes often provide little value for taxpayers' money. Some big cities have become unworkable without massive external finance. The biggest ocean liners have become dinosaurs. Some big DP departments are sluggish and unresponsive to users' needs.

When organizations grow too large, they become bureaucratic. One might define bureaucracy as *a situation in which when the rules come into conflict with common sense the rules are followed rather than reason about the objectives*. This happens time and again in big government and big corporations. It is sometimes sad to observe a fine, fast-growing corporation, where sweet reason once prevailed,

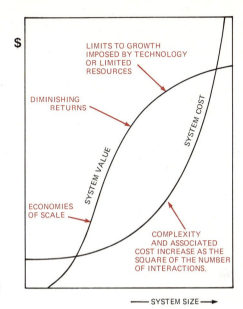

Figure 11.2 Systems tend to grow until the cost of complexity becomes too great.

slowly rigidifying so that bureaucracy spreads like cancer. Large DP organizations can also become bureaucratic.

Bureaucracy of a sort can exist in software too. For example, large operating systems are so complicated that they are very difficult to change. Routines which were designed for batch operations and small main memory tended to be preserved when new technology brought interactive operations and large main memory. Centralized networking control tended to be preserved with highly distributed networks.

The author was recently involved with a system which was running out of processing power as the transaction volume increased to about 30 transactions per second. An average transaction used about 8000 instructions of object application code. However, the computer was the fastest of a manufacturer's product line. It executed almost 4 million instructions per second. 30 x 8000 is only 240,000 instructions per second. Where were all the rest going? Software! This system, like the 46 dinner guests, spent its time clinking rather than drinking.

The answer to going too far up the curves of Fig. 11.2 is to lessen the degree of centralization and give autonomy to small groups with project and financial responsibility. Small groups can be highly motivated and can be at the locations where the user problems are. Today's technology permits them to have their own computer, much lower on the curves of Fig. 11.2. To lower the total complexity, the interfaces between the autonomous groups must be simple and precisely defined. There should be as few interfaces between the autonomous groups as possible.

If there are negligible economies of scale in the execution of machine instructions, then it is generally desirable that processing be done as close to the end user as possible. An exception to this occurs when data are kept at a location other than that of the end user, which may be necessary for a variety of reasons, discussed later.

A principle of distributed processing ought to be that each processing node should be as self-contained as possible, and logical connections to distant nodes should be minimized.

The developers of a distributed module should be made responsible for that module, and hence have autonomy in the creation of the module. One of the objectives of top management introducing DDP in some corporations has been to *make user management responsible* for their own use of computers. They can then no longer place the blame for problems on a distant machine which they do not control. Autonomy and responsibility go hand in hand.

Usually the local developers would like to have as little interference as possible from outside sources. They *want* autonomy. The dependencies between modules should be eliminated, or at least minimized, because they cause on-going arguments, bugs, and the need to rewrite programs. Dependencies can be minimized by making the development groups autonomous and creating simple, formal interfaces between groups.

The local user groups should be made responsible for the profitability and return on investment of their computer usage. They will then be concerned with performance and bug-free operation. They will take steps to protect themselves from failure. They will avoid exotic and unprofitable uses of computers and will control the excesses of systems staff who want systems and software which are intellectually interesting rather than simple and profitable.

An objective of the design of distributed processing should be to maximize the autonomy of the individual units and minimize the interdependence between them.

A type of interdependence which is particularly undesirable is that in which one user group, changing its plans or programs, causes another user group to have to change *its*. Each user group wants minimum coupling to other user groups. In the words of George Washington it wants "no foreign entanglements."

It is usually not possible to avoid *all* foreign entaglements. Often it will be necessary for the small groups to use data which are designed elsewhere or designed in conjunction with a central data administrator. Sometimes it will be necessary for them to use data which are *stored* elsewhere. The groups are thus not completely autonomous, but they should be as autonomous as is reasonable within a normally specified framework. After all, none of us is *completely* autonomous; we have to pay taxes and obey the police.

The project leaders should be responsible for the way they use computers. When data have to be designed by an external data administrator, project leaders should regard this individual as a professional from whom they acquire services. It is like employing an architect to design a house which both meets the user's needs and at the same time conforms to government regulations.

The autonomous groups thus work within a set of rules established by a central authority, these rules being necessary for communication. They work together with a central service to design data and possibly to select machines. They are free to choose their own projects and organize their own application development.

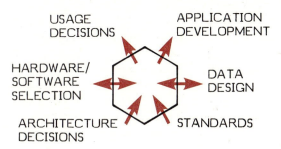

They may choose to write their own programs, use external consultants or software houses, or employ a service within their own corporation which develops programs for multiple user groups.

If the users employ data already stored in a remote data base, they should be making a conscious decision to use a precisely specified service for which there may be a charge. The same is true with use of remote programs such as a time-sharing service.

A central DP group may make application programs available for user groups to employ. If the user groups are to be truly autonomous and responsible for their own computing, they should be free to decide whether they employ these programs or not.

In some organizations the user groups are given only partial freedom. They are directed by a higher authority to use application programs which are centrally developed or transferred from other user locations.

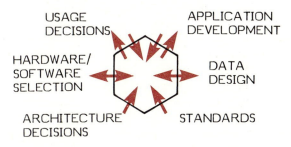

In some cases it is necessary that they use programs provided to them to transmit specified data to a central information system.

MINIMIZATION OF INTERFACES　　Minimization of interfaces, especially those spanning distant machines, is important for reducing the overall complexity. A vertical configuration is apt to give fewer foreign entanglements than a horizontal one. Figure 11.3 illustrates this. The lines represent interfaces between application modules. The top diagram has far more interfaces than the bottom one, and they are in more complex patterns. In the bottom diagram each peripheral node is connected to only one other node, and that is likely to have professional DP staff who have defined and documented the interface well. If one lower node has an interface with another lower node, it is via a central file. In a horizontal configuration each node could be connected to many others, and they might be less professionally managed with less well documented interfaces. Horizontal interfaces are often more likely to change unpredictably.

Figure 11.3 shows one central node. There are often several central nodes, each less complex in itself than a totally centralized system would be. Figure 11.4 illustrates this. There are the same number of lines in Fig. 11.4 and in Fig. 11.3.

Figure 11.5 is similar to Fig. 11.4 except that *logically similar* nodes are con-

A set of logical nodes, horizontally connected :

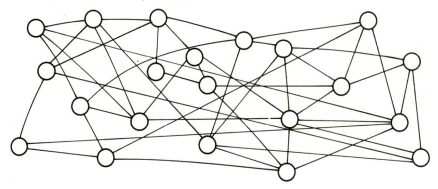

The same set of logical nodes, vertically connected :

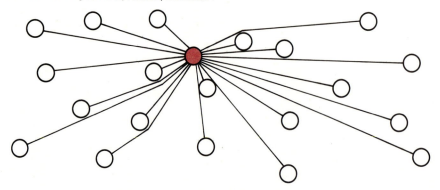

Figure 11.3 A vertical configuration often has fewer interfaces than a horizontal configuration. They are usually better controlled and documented.

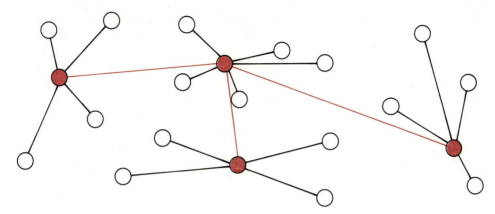

Figure 11.4 The same logical nodes as in Fig. 11.3, interconnected with multiple centers. There are the same number of lines on this diagram as on the bottom one of Fig. 11.3.

nected to the centers instead of *geographically* close nodes. The association of logically similar nodes can lessen the complexity, and *long-distance teleprocessing is not necessarily more complex than short-distance teleprocessing.* The physical structure of a computer network can be quite separate from the logical structure of the interconnection between logical nodes. Figure 11.5 has the same number of interfaces as the bottom diagram of Fig. 11.3.

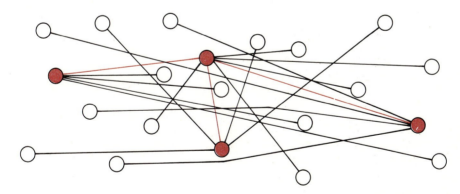

Figure 11.5 A configuration similar to that in 11.4 except that *logically similar* nodes are connected to the red centers instead of geographically close nodes. Increasing the application specialization of the upper nodes can lessen the overall complexity. The circles in this diagram are in the same position as the bottom of diagram 11.3. Although this diagram looks more complicated there are in fact the same number of lines as in the bottom of Fig. 11.3 (i.e., the same number of interfaces).

APPLICATION GROUPS   In most corporations today the best use of data processing entails a mixture of centralized development and operation, and decentralized development and operation by user groups.

The decision about whether to decentralize, or what aspects to decentralize, should be made separately for different applications. Applications can usually be considered in groups, closely related so that the same arguments apply to them. These *application groups* form the modules to which we refer in this chapter. The application groups should be selected to be as self-contained as is reasonable, use a small number of record types, and have as little interaction as possible with other application groups, especially ones executed at a distance.

We discuss the division of data processing into such modules in Part IV.

GOOD AND BAD DDP   Distributed processing can either increase overall system complexity or decrease it. Good DDP design is that which decreases it.

Some DDP systems become excessively convoluted. The software becomes extremely complicated. There are complex interactions between distant data-base systems. Complicated design can push the overall system too far up the curves in Fig. 11.2. Compartmental design uses multiple systems simply interconnected, each on an optimum part of the curves of Fig. 11.2. For some minicomputers or subsystems the optimum may occur at small system sizes.

Box 11.1 summarizes characteristics of good and bad design in DDP. Aspects of this will be discussed later in the book.

It must be emphasized that good design consists of separate autonomous nodes, each appearing to be simple to its users (the complexities being hidden under the covers, and these nodes connected by a standard, flexible network, which also

BOX 11.1

GOOD DDP DESIGN	BAD DDP DESIGN
• Overall system complexity is decreased.	• Overall system complexity is increased.
• Interfaces between subsystems are simple and small in number.	• Complex, convoluted patterns of interaction exist between subsystems.
• End-user processors are autonomous to a substantial degree.	• End-user processors have complex relationships with distant processors.

BOX 11.1 *continued*

- The distributed processors all conform to a common system's interfaces and standards.

- The distributed processors give the end users powerful facilities for access to data, report generation, and application development.

- End users have autonomy in application development where this is useful.

- A common high-level network architecture which is reliable and flexible is used (Part V).

- Application development productivity is a dominant design concern.

- The peripheral processors are easy to use and need no elaborate system skills.

- The design of data is centrally coordinated, except where data are usable by only one location.

- Careful attention is paid to database design, location, and use (Part IV).

- Stable logical data-base design is used, employing third normal form and canonical structures (Chapter 25).

- Data dictionary control of data in all locations is used.

- Careful attention is paid to system-wide security.

- Facilities for system auditing are carefully designed. (See Box 37.2.)

- An effective balance is designed between what ought to be centralized and what ought to be decentralized.

- The distributed processors are selected by different groups without central coordination.

- The distributed processors have to be programmed in low-level languages.

- Only centralized application development is permitted.

- Random low-level teleprocessing links or a rigid, clumsy network architecture are used.

- Only conventional programming is used for application development.

- The peripheral processors need systems programmers or highly trained operators.

- Incompatible versions of the same data are used at different locations.

- Data-base management systems are not used.

- Casual logical record design is used without canonical synthesis.

- No data dictionary is used, or it applies only to a centralized location.

- Security is neglected at the peripheral nodes.

- The system is unauditable. (See Box 37.1.)

- Restrictive centralization, or uncoordinated implementation by user departments.

appears to be simple (the complexities again being hidden under the covers). The pattern of transmission between the nodes is simple. The nodes plug together and cooperate because the interfaces between them and the data that are shared between them are centrally planned.

The system may be compared to an airline. The jet planes are each complex but reliable; most of their complexities are hidden under the covers. The captain of each jet is completely in command of that plane, but nevertheless there is a rigorous overall plan with timetables, flight plans, crew schedules, maintenance activity, and so on. More than one type of plane is used but they are members of a fleet planned for optimum corporationwide operation.

An image of autonomous nodes in tight but simple cooperation should be contrasted with three bad images.

In the first, distributed processing is like a plateful of spaghetti with a higgledy-piggledy jumble of interrelations between the processors. Because of the convoluted interactions, the system eventually becomes unwieldy and difficult to change. The complexity leads to rigidity and high maintenance costs.

In the second, each user group "does its own thing" with its own computer. The incompatible pieces cannot be fitted together. When the need arises to transfer data from one machine to another and for users in one place to use processes and data in other places, excessive conversion and software writing activity are needed, so most multisite applications are avoided. Data processing loses much of its potential value.

The third bad image uses no DDP. Instead all processing is centralized with conventional terminals in user locations. The activities at the DP center grow increasingly complex. An application backlog of years builds up. Users cannot obtain the new applications they need. The scheduling of jobs becomes complex, and when it is changed, some users' response times plunge. The DP staff become so enmeshed in the complexities of the center that they do not respond to the concerns and needs of the growing body of would-be users.

The task of data processing now is to build a clean, workable distributed infrastructure that serves the corporation in a highly responsive, cost-effective manner.

12 PROBLEMS OF INCOMPATIBILITY

Earlier we commented that a danger in distributed or decentralized processing is the spread of incompatibility, which will prevent the interlinking of systems to meet higher-level goals. The problems takes several different forms:

- The machines may be difficult to interconnect by telecommunications because they use different line-control procedures.

- Computer network architectures of different manufacturers are fundamentally incompatible.

- Even if compatibility can be achieved in the transport network, fundamental incompatibility exists between manufacturers' software external to the transport network.

- Different types of data-base software are incompatible (even without considering distributed data bases).

- File structures are expensive (sometimes prohibitively so) to *convert* to other file structures or to data-base structures.

- Technology is evolving rapidly, and migration to better technology may be difficult in a distributed environment unless planned for.

- Even if all the software is compatible, severe problems may arise from incompatible data fields and data structures due to inadequate data administration in an organization.

LINE CONTROL   To transmit data to one another, machines must have a common line-control discipline. Unfortunately, there are many line-control disciplines: start-stop, binary synchronous, DEC's DDCMP, IBM's SDLC, and many more. A machine using one of these cannot communicate with a machine using a different one.

Major attempts at standardization have been made, and perhaps the most important of the different standards is the International Standards Organization's HDLC (Higher-level Data Link Control). This is an efficient line-control discipline, ideally suited to distributed processing. The communicating machines need a small amount of logic to execute its procedures.

Unfortunately, many machines do not use HDLC. There are many with old line-control procedures, and some manufactures have a line-control procedure of their own. To make matters worse, several variations are permitted in the HDLC standard. This is like having electrical outlets of several permissible shapes. Some HDLC machines cannot plug into other HDLC machines.

Organizations using DDP need a central directive saying what line-control procedure will be used. This directive may restrict the choice of machines.

**COMPUTER
NETWORKS**
A line-control standard relates merely to the physical links between two machines. In computer networks, data, like a posted parcel, often travel on a journey involving multiple physical links. The end user does not want to know about the journey; he merely wants to hand a packet to the "post office" and be sure it is delivered. However, the packet must have the right address, stamps, return address, customs declaration, and so on. A standard is needed for this. How a user sends data over a *virtual circuit* is discussed in Part V.

Prior to the mid-1970's common carriers defined mainly the *physical* interface for their users—modems and electrical connections for data machines to physically connect to the circuit. Users connected their machines to switched public telephone or telegraph circuits or to leased lines of varying bandwidth. In 1975 the first *value-added* common carriers came into operation in the United States.

Telenet and proposed packet-switching networks in other countries specified a link control and packet interface for their customers. They defined protocols that would provide their customers with switched and permanent *virtual* circuits, rather than the physical circuits of conventional tariffs.

It became clear that different carriers were proposing different end-user protocols. This would be harmful because users would like to have machines, and manufacturers would like to make machines, which can connect to the networks of many (ideally, all) common carriers. Consequently in 1976 there was great activity in the international standards organization for telecommunications, the CCITT, to agree upon a single user protocol for virtual circuit networks. This resulted in the CCITT X.25 Recommendation. It will have a far-reaching effect on the future design of networks, user machines, and software.

X.25 seems to be the most likely *lingua franca* for computer networks, and its use will probably become widespread. However, at the time of writing most of the network software of major manufacturers is entirely different from it and incompatible.

The ARPA network demonstrated that a large number of incompatible computers can be interconnected with a common packet-switching network. To accomplish this, interfacing software which makes the various computers use the network protocols has to be written. In the future such a network may use CCITT X.25 protocols. The interfacing of many incompatible machines to such a network may be expensive, but it can be done.

Incompatibilities in the transport network can be solved, albeit expensively in some cases. The problems become worse when we discuss the software external to the transport network.

ARCHITECTURES   Major computer manufacturers perceived in the mid-1970's that a large part of their future market was to come from distributed data processing. A wide range of machines would be hooked together into all manner of configurations. To accomplish this certain compatibility is needed between the machines and software. Therefore "architectures" for distributed systems were devised.

An architecture defines protocols, formats, and standards to which different machines and software packages must conform, in order to achieve a given goal. When these products are created, they will then be compatible, capable of being interlinked or of sharing data, programs, or resources which already exist.

Architectural standards are important for both the customers and the manufacturer. For customers they provide the ability to change the system and be flexible in their configurations. They should permit portability of programs. They should permit the advantages of function distribution and processing distribution (discussed in Part II), which need precise cooperation between distant intelligent machines. They should permit corporate computer networks to be built. For manufacturers they should permit the mass production of building blocks (hardware or software) which can be used in diverse machines. The building-block approach lowers cost and lessens compatibility problems. Architectural definitions are important for the development laboratories because they give freedom to create new machines which will be compatible with the architecture and hence can become components of distributed systems.

INCOMPATIBILITY   While the early network architectures facilitate in-
BETWEEN   terconnectability between the machines *of one manu-*
MANUFACTURERS   *facturer,* they make it very difficult to interconnect machines of different manufacturers. The reason for this is that the protocols used by the machines are highly complex and completely different from one manufacturer to another. It is relatively easy to hook a dumb terminal from one manufacturer to a computer from another. However, it would be extremely difficult to hook a DECNET machine from the Digital Equipment Corporation to an SNA machine from IBM. To do so would require a very complex

protocol conversion module, and even if it were accomplished, it would not be possible to obtain the full facilities of either because they provide different facilities. Both DECNET and SNA are evolving sufficiently rapidly that the attempt to build a bridge between them might be defeated before it began.

Some of the large manufacturers perceive little advantage in providing compatibility with foreign architectures. They would rather have all the machines in a system be from their own product line. Customers may be ill-advised to mix machines from incompatible architectures, as this, even if accomplished correctly, could lead to endless problems and would probably lock the customer out of future developments of the rapidly evolving architectures.

Architectures for distributed processing and computer networks are being designed mainly by three types of organizations:

1. Computer manufacturers

2. Common carriers and telecommunication administrations

3. Standards organizations creating interfaces such as CCITT Recommendation X.25

The architectures of some major computer manufacturers are incompatible with the architectures of common carriers. The manufacturer transport network often is entirely different from X.25. Worse still, the transport networks of some common carriers are incompatible with each other. There is not much resemblance between Bell's TNS, Bell's ACS, fast-connect circuit-switching networks (implemented in several countries), France's Transpac, Germany's EDS, SBS's network, Viewdata, and so on.

The computer manufacturers and their customers can bypass these networks, if so desired, and build their own networks with basic telephone, wideband, or data circuits. Most computer networks and distributed systems are built that way today. With concentrators, cluster controllers, and switching machines, efficient and economical networks can be built from traditional leased or switched lines. They do not necessarily need the common carriers to provide virtual circuits.

There exists a competitive situation over who will provide the transport subsystem nodes and interface equipment—the computer manufacturer or the common carrier.

The view of some telephone company executives is that, since *they* provide the private branch exchanges and telephone handsets, they should also provide the front-end network controllers, the concentrators, switches, and terminals. This market represents a *vast* future revenue. Some authorities perceive the rapid development of X.25 by the telephone administrations who control the CCITT as a major step towards wresting this market from the computer manufacturers.

It is possible that in the future telephone administrations of those countries without common carrier competition may set the cost of leased lines sufficiently high to swing this market in their favor.

SESSION SERVICES INCOMPATIBILITY

There is hope that the transport network incompatibilities will be solved by building bridges to some common protocol such as X.25. Protocol conversion will become one of the functions of distributed intelligence. The problem is more severe at the higher levels of software, the session services, because of the wide-ranging collection of functions that are possible.

It is likely that some, but not all, of the session service functions will become standardized. It may be a long time before such standards are agreed upon, and by then major manufacturers will have spent much money on developing software that uses techniques which are incompatible. We explore this theme in Part V.

As an example, the Digital Equipment Corporation's DECNET software permits programmers to write GET or PUT and similar macroinstructions in their programs when they are referring to a distant file, just as they would when using a file in the system running the program. The programmer need not know where the file resides. It could be in Paris or Rio. He refers to it symbolically in his program. This facility simplifies the application programming for distributed systems, but it only works when all of the machines involved use DECNET software.

In general, the software for distributed processing can make the effects of distance transparent to the programmer. To do so requires complex protocols and software which is exactly compatible in the communicating machines.

This exact compatibility exists between machines of the same manufacturer, but not in general between machines of different manufacturers.

DATA-BASE INCOMPATIBILITY

In data-base systems the logical structure of the data is important for application development. Unfortunately, the same data are structured differently in many data-base management systems. Data-base management systems of different types are incompatible in that if data are transferred from one to another, the programs which use that data have to be rewritten.

The CODASYL organization attempted to standardize data-base management by specifying languages for describing and using the data. However, several of the most widely used data-base systems are fundamentally different from the CODASYL approach, including IBM data-base systems using the DL/I language, TOTAL, ADABAS, SYSTEM 2000, relational data bases, and most of the data-base systems created by the minicomputer vendors. Only a fraction of data bases *installed* follow the CODASYL specification fully.

It is possible to have distributed computing with incompatible data-base software in the different machines, but it would be highly inconvenient because programs could not be interchanged between the machines without being rewritten. In some cases records also would have to be restructured when passed from one machine to another.

As DDP evolves, the advantages of using data bases in mulitple locations will grow, and data-base compatibility will become increasingly important. Increasingly, one machine will need to process data stored in data-base form in another machine.

CONVERSION

It is expensive to convert data from one form to another because many programs which use them have to be rewritten. The larger the amount of application code, the greater the rewrite burden. As time goes on, the cost of converting data tends to increase because more programs use those data.

Many data-processing centers have large quantities of *files,* and it has been seen as worthwhile to convert these to *data bases* to achieve easier and more flexible application development. However, the conversion task has proved to be so lengthy and expensive that it has never been accomplished. Often it is stopped by accountants who can see the many man-years involved with no new applications resulting. The author has seen many attempts to convert from complex file systems to data-base operation but can find only trivial cases of it being completed successfully. We may conclude that it will be difficult to accomplish in the future as well. The sooner an organization builds the data base it needs, the better. If it goes too far with the *file* development, it may have great difficulty crossing the bridge to data-base operation.

In the long run an early commitment to data base, and a strategy which requires the data bases in an organization to be compatible, will pay off.

SHARED DATA

Even if compatible software and hardware are used throughout an organization, crippling incompatibilities can arise through uncoordinated design of data. Compatible data are more important than compatible software in some organizations.

If each application design group is left to its own devices, it will design its own data fields and structures. The same field will be different in different parts of the organization. In most DDP environments there is much exchange of data and use of remote data. This requires not only that the same field should have the same design in different places but also that record structures or data-base groupings of fields (records, segments, tuples) should be the same where possible.

The conversion task that results from the spread of incompatible data can be immense. Some organizations have tried to clean up the data they designed earlier and realized that for years they will have to live with the problems of incompatible data because it is too expensive to rewrite all the programs necessary to make them compatible.

The evolution of DDP requires central coordination of data design, with the organizationwide use of a data dictionary.

Not all machines can use data bases. Small computers and intelligent terminals often employ on-line files. Frequently it is desirable that these files be related to a distant data base. Their structure should be derivable from the data base either for obtaining data from it or updating it. In other words, they should be a sub-schema of the data base—one of the many logical data structures that can be derived from it for use by programmers.

This needs careful planning of the data used throughout the distributed system, rather than *ad hoc* growth of incompatible data structures.

MIGRATION   The technology of computing is changing very rapidly. Cost is dropping; machine structures are changing; new architectures are appearing. Corporations will need to move to the new systems because they are more cost-effective and enable computing to be used in new areas. However, they will not want to rewrite old programs because there are too many, and any available programmers are needed for new applications development.

Long-established computer manufacturers understand this problem and plan to introduce new technology without a major need to rewrite old programs. They plan long-range *migration* paths for their customers. Facilities in a new operating system may be leading the way to future hardware changes. A software architecture is planned to accommodate future machines.

A manufacturer can plan a migration path to distributed facilities so that they can be installed without too much disruption. Well-planned migration will become increasingly important as the software for DDP becomes increasingly complex. However, there is likely to be no migration path from one manufacturer's equip-ment to another's, and no way in which migration can occur from an *ad hoc* collec-tion of distributed machines to an established system.

Architectures like DEC's DECNET and IBM's SNA are part of a lengthy migration path into the future. They are highly complex (SNA more so than most), and architectures of different manufacturers are likely to be noninterconnectable except at a lower level.

At IBM it is common for the details of an architecture not to be made fully public, partly because of legal constraints. The computer industry and customers see the current software and hardware products, but not necessarily the details of the long-range plan.

The implementation of a major manufacturer's network architecture can become very intricate because there are so many different products, such as operating systems, data-base management systems, and control programs which the networking software must employ. Incorporation of, and compatibility with, these software products is highly complicated. To make matters worse, there are multiple versions of the different products installed, most of which have to work with the networking facilities. A major computer manufacturer therefore has a far more complex implementation task than, say, a common carrier implementing an X.25 network.

The architecture itself is a moving target. Ideas about what a network ar-chitecture should do are evolving rapidly and are likely to go on evolving for many years, especially in areas external to the transport subsystem. The products which the architecture should serve are changing quickly, and the capability of the hardware is fast improving. Communication links will change, for example, with the increasing use of satellites and with virtual circuit tariffs. Furthermore, pragmatic constraints, which provide feedback to the architects arise in the implementation of the architecture. This causes continuous review of detailed points in the architecture.

Nevertheless, the creation of long-range network architectures is a great step forward, and much of the future of the computer industry will evolve within the framework of these architectural concepts.

A corporation planning DDP has to decide what value it places on future migration. Following the path planned for it by one manufacturer has major advantages but may tend to lock the corporation into that manufacturer. Using multiple manufacturers leaves more options open for the future but may result in expensive or even crippling incompatibilities.

It is important that the alternatives be carefully thought out and planned. In too many organizations distribution of processing is happening almost by accident.

13 CENTRALIZATION vs. DECENTRALIZATION

The argument about centralization vs. decentralization, head office control vs. local control, one large machine vs. many small machines, has been raging in data-processing circles since the early 1960's. As the argument involves strongly felt political issues as well as technical ones, it will probably continue for decades more.

The argument assumed a different flavor with the spread of minicomputers and distributed processing. First, economies of scale became a much less powerful argument for centralization. In some cases it is now cheaper to have a collection of minicomputers than a large, central machine. Second, distributed processing created a third alternative between complete centralization and complete decentralization. Many local computers could be used, but all could be linked to a central computer. The work could be split between the local machines and the center in a variety of possible ways. The linkage could encourage some measure of compatibility between the local machines. Some functions, by their nature, are best performed locally. Therefore, *the best of both worlds can be achieved by a judicious mixture of centralized and distributed functions.*

Arguments about what should be centralized and what distributed apply to walks of life other than computing. How much authority should a head office have in controlling local operations? What functions in society should be state-controlled and what left to private enterprise? Are small autonomous units better than large centralized units? Would village communities with wideband communication trunks be better than large metropolises?

In many cases a mixture of central and decentral facilities are needed. Central processes should be those benefiting from economies of scale, bulk processing, far-flung logistics, and centralized planning. Decentral processes should be those benefiting from local initiative, drive, knowledge of the local situation, and local authority and control.

A pragmatic balance is needed between what should be centralized and what distributed. Many aspects of that balance change when there are cheap computers

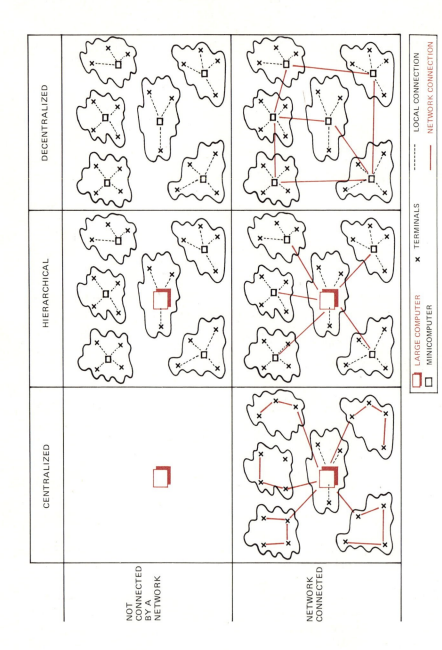

Figure 13.1 Approaches to centralization and decentralization.

and cheap, fast communications links between the peripheral and central locations, like the corporate data networks which are now emerging.

In this chapter we discuss the arguments for and against centralization. However, data transmission provides us with more than the two simple alternatives. Figure 13.1 shows the possibilities. Without a network the possibilities in the top row exist:

1. One centralized computer

2. A centralized computer and unconnected minicomputers

3. Multiple computers with no centralization

With a network, the possibilities in the bottom row exist:

1. A centralized system with terminals in many parts of the organization

2. A hierarchical system in which both processing and data may be hierarchically distributed

3. A peer-coupled network, like those discussed in Chapter 9

TYPES OF ARGUMENTS There are several types of arguments relating to centralization:

1. Total cost (discussed in Chapter 14)

2. Technical arguments other than cost

3. Arguments relating to application development

4. Arguments relating to which applications should be centralized and which decentralized

5. Arguments involving corporate politics, the behavior of people, or the impact on the human side of the enterprise. Box 13.1 summarizes these arguments.

**TECHNICAL
ARGUMENTS** We have discussed various technical arguments relating to centralization and distribution in the previous chapters. Some of them are listed in Boxes 8.1, 17.1, and 21.1.

A major reason for using centralization has been that much advanced software requires a centralized system, or possibly several centralized systems which are interconnected. This is particularly true of data-base management systems and hence of the report generator and interrogation facilities which are designed to employ data bases and which give the promise of much easier and more flexible creation of applications. Advanced data-base and dialogue software are intended to create the valuable trends shown in Fig. 13.2. Now, however, data-base management systems and other powerful software are appearing on relatively small machines. A major concern is whether peripheral installations can afford the skilled staff needed to run them.

BOX 13.1 Arguments for centralization and for decentralization

Arguments for Centralization	Arguments for Decentralization
1. COST ARGUMENTS	
PROCESSOR COSTS	
• Economies of scale may make a centralized system cheaper.	• Minicomputers have become inexpensive.
	• Because of a short development cycle, minicomputers often employ more up-to-date technology than large computers.
	• The cost per instruction is often much cheaper on minicomputers than on mainframes and chapter on micros than on minis. This is partly because the small machines have a simpler instruction set. (e.g., no floating-point arithmetic). But much transaction processing does not need a rich instruction set.
STORAGE COSTS	
• There are major economies of scale in storage costs. The cost per bit is *much* lower with large storage units.	• Centralized data may result in major telecommunications costs in order to access them.
• Distributed data may result in multiple copies of the same data being stored.	
TELECOMMUNICATIONS COSTS	
	• Decentralization can lower transmission costs because of local processing, fewer messages transmitted, local dialogue processing, local data storage, compaction of transmitted messages.
RESOURCE SHARING	
• Resource sharing permits the use of better resources for a given cost.	• Resource sharing may be an argument for specialized resources in dispersed locations rather than complete centralization.

BOX 13.1 *continued*

SOFTWARE PATH LENGTH

- Minicomputers have a much shorter software path length; hence more of the raw computer power is used for application programs.

INSTALLATION COSTS

- Most minicomputers need no air conditioning, false floors, or special building facilities. Most minicomputers do not need highly trained operators and staff to run the installation.

ESCALATION

- In many distributed installations the size and cost of the distributed minicomputers have steadily risen to levels far exceeding the original estimates.

COSTS OF REPAIR

- In some distributed installations the cost of repair and maintenance engineering of the multiple minicomputers has been very high.

MANPOWER COSTS

- Multiple decentral systems can result in a major duplication of programming effort.
- Total manpower costs may be lower on a central system. Often it is difficult to add up the full cost of user-group development because persons in various noncomputing job categories participate.

OVERVIEW COST PLANNING

- Central planning can reflect the overall corporate information economics and needs, minimizing the total costs.

continued

BOX 13.1 *continued*

2. TECHNICAL ARGUMENTS (other than cost)

DIALOGUE

- Processing power close to the user permits economical use of psychologically effective dialogue. (This could be done with a centralized system with intelligent terminals.)

AVAILABILITY

- Local systems are unaffected by telecommunications failures and large-machine software crashes. Minicomputers, being simple, are generally highly reliable. On some applications this high availability is vital.

- Job scheduling difficulties on centralized system mean that the computing facility is not always available to the user department when it needs it. This is sometimes highly frustrating.

RESPONSE TIME

- Local systems have faster response times, because of smaller workloads and no need for data transmission. Fast responses are important in some types of terminal dialogue.

DATA

- Data employed by geographically dispersed users need centralized maintenance.

- Multiple copies should not be permitted of data which are updated in real time.

- There are major advantages to having a data base rather than separate

- Data structures are simpler when designed for local needs only.

- Some data are used at one location only. They may be entered, maintained, and possibly designed by the users at that location.

BOX 13.1 *continued*

files (see Box 21.1), and appropriate distributed data-base management systems do not yet exist.

- Decentralized, nonstandardized data make it extremely difficult to associate the data in a later management information system.

- Centralization may be needed when the data as a whole are to be searched or when inverted files or secondary indices are to be used.

- The data may be too bulky to store on peripheral storage units.

- Data-search, secondary-key, or inverted-list operations may be better run on a user department machine where they cannot interfere with performance of a central machine, and the user is responsible for costs.

SECURITY

- Tight, professional design of security and privacy controls is possible on a centralized system. On locally implemented small systems, security is often very sloppy. Bicentral systems may be preferable for catastrophe protection.

- If a breach of security occurs on a peripheral computer, the harm may be restricted to a local area. On a centralized system the harm may be more damaging.

- Local responsibility for security of local data.

DATA ENTRY

- Users can be responsible for their own on-line data entry. They are responsible for its accuracy and timeliness. (This is true with distributed data entry or centralized system).

WORKLOAD

- The volume of work in most corporations is too great for centralized (nondistributed) systems.

CHANGE

- Software facilities are designed to facilitate change. E.g., data-base management systems.

- Fewer people or programs are involved with a local system; hence change is less complicated.

BOX 13.1 *continued*

- Centralized control avoids the proliferation of incompatible systems, which are extremely difficult to integrate later.

- On many systems without central data administration, 80% of the manpower becomes involved in maintenance.

- Centralized systems or centrally planned systems are more likely to be designed for maintenance.

- Migration from incompatible decentralized systems to an integrated system or distributed network is so complex and expensive that in practice it is rarely achieved.

SOFTWARE

- A large, centralized system permits powerful software to be used—languages, data base management, virtual storage or virtual machines to facilitate application programming, program generators, data-base interrogation and maintenance facilities. These should give the desirable trends shown in Fig. 13.3. (However, minicomputer software is rapidly catching up.)

- Many application software packages are available for large systems.

- The software path lengths of the large machines have become great. Because of this their throughput and response time are often poor. The cost per transaction is relatively high.

- Minicomputer software is often simple, avoiding the jargon and system-generation difficulties of large-machine software.

- Highly specialized system programmers are usually not needed.

APPLICATION PROGRAMS

- Application programming is easier because of higher-level languages, virtual storage, data-base management, and other software.

- Large systems have aids for conversion, change, and maintenance.

- Application program requirements are simpler because they meet the needs of only one location, not all locations.

- Faster application development because user groups can do it themselves.

BOX 13.1 *continued*

- Data-base interrogation facilities, report generators, etc., may bypass some of the need for programming.

- A centralized professional group is more likely to write structured programs that are well documented.

- Change is easier because it involves one small user group, not many.

- Application programs are better tailored to local needs when developed locally.

MANAGEMENT INFORMATION

- A centralized computer makes data available for a management information system, where it may become of great value. Much of the value of the data may be lost if they are in incompatible local files.

TIME SCALE

- The bad effects of decentralization often do not appear until late; these are incompatible data, difficulty of reprogramming, migration problems, after-the-fact connection to a network, difficulties of growth to provide head office management information.

- Minicomputer systems can be implemented quickly.

- End users sometimes have to wait years before the centralized group responds to their needs.

3. APPLICATION DEVELOPMENT ARGUMENTS

SKILLS

- A central group can have skilled DP management and professional systems analysts and programmers who are skilled in structured design, planning for change, etc.

- A certain critical mass of computing is needed to afford special talents like those of a good data-base administrator.

- Comprehending the real end-user problems is difficult, especially with complex applications. End users themselves are uniquely able to understand their own changing requirements and should be as involved in application development as possible.

continued

BOX 13.1 *continued*

- User groups may not yet have the sophistication to handle their own data processing.

- Centralized DP specialists understand sophisticated techniques such as operations research methods.

PLANNING

- The system can be designed with a knowledge of the overall corporate needs and the overall information economies.

- Multiple decentral application developments without coordinated control and data design will result in a Tower of Babel.

- Local groups are close to the real end-user problems, and can adapt the system to them. The central group is too far away to acquire a detailed knowledge of local problems.

- Local computing needs can be locally justified and prioritized.

- There may be more application innovation from the user groups than from a centralized group.

REACTIVITY

- User groups with their own computer facilities can handle their own needs promptly. A centralized group often takes a long time, sometimes years to react to their application needs and changes. User groups often perceive the central DP organization as lethargic and unresponsive.

APPLICATION BACKLOG

- Many corporations have a large backlog of applications waiting to be implemented. The central DP group is overwhelmed with work, much of which is related to system changes—operation system conversion, a switch to a data-base system, migration, conversion. The user

BOX 13.1 *continued*

groups have to wait a long time unless they can do their local application development.

MANPOWER

- Centralized development requires fewer programmers.

- Multiple decentralized systems can result in a major duplication of programming effort.

- Applications which may run identically in multiple locations should be developed once, centrally.

- Involvement of end-user groups in their own system design and programming results in far more persons involved in the total application development.

- The control group is usually insufficiently staffed to respond to all end users' needs.

- End-user work on their own application development may eventually be seen as the only way to make full use of the proliferation of inexpensive computing devices.

APPLICATION CHARACTERISTICS

Applications such as the following should run on a centralized system:

- Applications needing centralized files or data bases.

- Applications needing a large computer.

- Applications which benefit from economies of scale and so should not be distributed (e.g., bulk purchasing).

- Applications involving corporation-wide logistics.

Applications such as the following may be run on local systems:

- Applications involving only one user group.

- Applications where the initiative comes from the local user group.

- Applications for which user management should be *responsible*.

- Applications which should be developed by the user group because of local subtleties and users' frequent need for change.

4. POLITICAL ARGUMENTS

AUTHORITY

- The existing DP department wishes to retain control of all computing.

- End-user groups want local autonomy in computing.

continued

BOX 13.1 *continued*

- DP is designed to reflect the corporate management hierarchy.

- Local managers resent centralized control.

- The corporate head office wants to force local responsibility.

POWER

- Centralized data and facilities can give more power to top management or head office staff.

- Local management wants to avoid higher management having too much information too soon.

- Strike action by a small group of computer personnel could be highly damaging with a centralized system. Decentralization avoids putting too much power into a few hands.

- Complete centralization of data may make probing by external authorities or government too easy.

BUREAUCRACY

- A centralized DP organization growing too large becomes entangled in its own management procedures and is often slow to move and change.

- Increasing size leads to increasingly formal structures which tend to be inflexible.

- DP management tend to protect their organization with complex arguments which external management cannot understand.

COSTS

- Total costs, including salaries, are likely to be lower.

- Centrally planned costs can reflect the overall corporate information economics.

- User groups control and justify their own data-processing expenditures.

- User groups sometimes find costs from a central DP group difficult to comprehend, especially conversion, migration, and software development costs for which they cannot see the need.

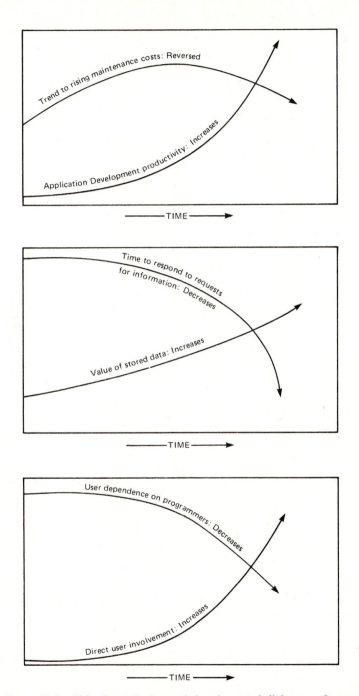

Figure 13.2 Objectives of advanced data base and dialogue software.

Centralized data bases can be used with certain categories of distributed processing, as we have discussed. Hence a designer may select a combination of centralization and distribution that gives the advantages of both.

Often the bad effects of decentralized systems do not appear until several years after they are first installed. At first decentralized minicomputers are attractive because they are easy to install and applications can be brought into operation more quickly than with a centralized system. Later the burden of changing the minicomputer programs becomes apparent. There may be more programmers in total than with a centralized approach and usually less discipline in program structuring. Program documentation is often neglected almost completely in the rush to make the machines work, and often the original persons trained as programmers in the end-user departments leave because they see faster advancement and higher pay in professional data processing. They often have undocumented, unstructured, heavily patched programs written in a low-level language. In typical commercial minicomputer installations which are a few years old, 80% of the manpower is spent changing or rewriting past programs [1].

As data processing develops, some of the data in the local minicomputers are needed elsewhere, often at higher levels in the corporation. They are valuable for the higher levels of management control. However, the files were designed locally by user groups who did not communicate, and consequently the same type of data exists with different representations in different locations. It would be very expensive to change them because so many programs would have to be rewritten. The compatibility problems discussed in the previous chapter become damaging. Management therefore loses many of the advantages that a better planned approach would have.

The spread of minicomputers for commercial DP without central control and standards can produce a Tower of Babel, whereas minicomputer installations conforming to a DDP strategy can be innovative and can have many advantages such as access to remote data and programs.

Migration from disjoint, incompatible systems to a distributed processing network, or from incompatible data-base management systems to compatible ones, is so complex and expensive that in practice it is rarely accomplished. Networking in these circumstances is often never achieved satisfactorily, or else it becomes an inadequate patchwork of incompatible pieces which is expensive to maintain and makes application development extremely difficult.

DISTRIBUTED COMPROMISE   As shown in Box 13.1, there are good, powerful arguments on both sides.

The objective of DDP ought to be to achieve the advantages of both centralization and decentralization by building a system that combines local autonomy with centralized standards and facilities. Some applications are centralized and some decentralized. It is suggested that the reader go through the arguments in Box 13.1 and evaluate to what extent it is possible to achieve the benefits of both sides by use of a distributed configuration and a mixture of centralized and decentralized management.

Figure 13.3 lists characteristics of a DDP system designed to achieve the best of both worlds.

HUMAN
CONSIDERATIONS
The human arguments for or against centralization are often more important than the technical arguments. They are becoming increasingly important because as computing spreads and drops in cost, more managers in the corporate structure are becoming directly involved with it.

In the early 1970's few persons took an interest in the future directions of the data processing department. Now, with distributed processing, most managers in some corporations perceive that they can influence how computers are used and that, indeed, they must if they are to have the support they need in the time frame they need it. Data processing no longer has a minor influence on a corporation; it has become its heartbeat, and data communications the arteries.

In a period of two years in the mid-1970's, as distributed processing was beginning to spread, half of all top data-processing executives in the United States were replaced, and 70% of them were replaced by executives without a data processing background. In today's corporations, computing is too important to be left to the computer experts.

From the mid-1960's to the mid-1970's there was a trend in most corporations towards centralization of data processing. Most authorities believed in Grosch's Law.

At least as important as the technology cost was the cost and scarcity of competent computer professionals. Centralized facilities with large machines and the latest software attracted good professionals, and there was enough work to employ them economically.

Operating systems permitted greater degrees of multiprogramming and then virtual operation so that many unconstrained application programs could share the same large computer. Centralization led to software complexity, and this complexity encouraged centralized facilities where experts could commune.

During this period teleprocessing changed from pioneering to bread-and-butter technology. This further encouraged the consolidation of separate systems. As networks grew, their operation and software also became complex, requiring skilled expertise.

In the 1970's data-base systems grew up, encouraging the sharing of common pools of data by many different applications. Data-base technology gives the very real advantages discussed in Chapter 21, but it usually requires some degree of centralization, because of the sharing of data and because software for true distributed data bases is not yet available. The design of efficient, stable, broadly useful data bases is an expert job and again encouraged the centralized gathering of talent. The tape and disk libraries became large, needing specialized staff to maintain them,

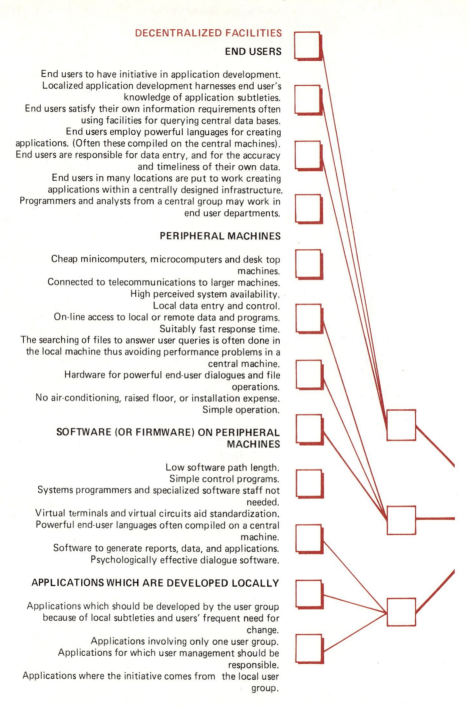

DECENTRALIZED FACILITIES

END USERS

End users to have initiative in application development.
Localized application development harnesses end user's
knowledge of application subtleties.
End users satisfy their own information requirements often
using facilities for querying central data bases.
End users employ powerful languages for creating
applications. (Often these compiled on the central machines).
End users are responsible for data entry, and for the accuracy
and timeliness of their own data.
End users in many locations are put to work creating
applications within a centrally designed infrastructure.
Programmers and analysts from a central group may work in
end user departments.

PERIPHERAL MACHINES

Cheap minicomputers, microcomputers and desk top
machines.
Connected to telecommunications to larger machines.
High perceived system availability.
Local data entry and control.
On-line access to local or remote data and programs.
Suitably fast response time.
The searching of files to answer user queries is often done in
the local machine thus avoiding performance problems in a
central machine.
Hardware for powerful end-user dialogues and file
operations.
No air-conditioning, raised floor, or installation expense.
Simple operation.

SOFTWARE (OR FIRMWARE) ON PERIPHERAL MACHINES

Low software path length.
Simple control programs.
Systems programmers and specialized software staff not
needed.
Virtual terminals and virtual circuits aid standardization.
Powerful end-user languages often compiled on a central
machine.
Software to generate reports, data, and applications.
Psychologically effective dialogue software.

APPLICATIONS WHICH ARE DEVELOPED LOCALLY

Applications which should be developed by the user group
because of local subtleties and users' frequent need for
change.
Applications involving only one user group.
Applications for which user management should be
responsible.
Applications where the initiative comes from the local user
group.

Figure 13.3 The mix of centralized and decentralized facilities should be
designed so as to take advantage of the best characteristics of both.

196

CENTRALIZED FACILITIES
CENTRALIZED MANAGEMENT CONTROL

Central design of the distributed system infrastructure.
Central network design and administration.
Central setting of standards.
Central administration of data bases and peripheral files to ensure compatibility.
Central security administration.
Monitoring of usage of the network, data bases and central systems.
Billing end users for use of facilities which they do not own.

PEOPLE

Staff with specialized skills: systems programmers, software experts, data design, structural programming, structured analysis, operations research.
Training given to end user staffs when needed.
Work backlog on central DP group is lessened by the large number of end users creating their own data, reports, and applications.

CENTRALIZED MACHINES AND SOFTWARE

Full-function data base management systems hardware and software.
Centralized shared storage of data which needs it.
Information retrieval software.
Economies of scale in large storage.
Large computer power for applications which need it.
Powerful compilers.
Virtual storage; virtual machines.
Central program maintenance and control.
Tight security.

CENTRALIZED APPLICATIONS

Applications with corporatewide applicability. (e.g. payroll, personnel administration).
Applications needing centralized files or data base (e.g. airline reservations).
Applications which benefit from centralized economies of scale (e.g. bulk purchasing).
Applications involving corporatewide logistics (e.g. cash management, corporatewide inventory control, airline crew scheduling, management information systems).
Applications needing a large computer (e.g. modeling, simulation, answering 'What if ?' questions).

mount them on the machines, and ensure that data could not be lost, stolen, erased, or damaged.

DECENTRALIZATION SCENARIO　　　Many corporations with centralized DP facilities found that the spread of terminals brought increasing strains on the DP department, sometimes culminating in a partial breakdown of relations with the user groups. A common scenario has been as follows:

The quantities of data stored on-line grow by leaps and bounds. Terminals become installed in most departments of a corporation, and many types of management begin to perceive what data are available. The terminals provide windows into the vast data warehouses. Management steadily begins to realize how they could put these invaluable data to use. They realize that they *must* put them to use because the same data are visible to *their* management. The potential value of the data, if used well, is great.

At first the user departments employ the data in simple ways. They replace their lengthy listings of data with the ability to make simple inquiries at a terminal. Steadily user perception grows of how data could be processed to enable the user to do a better job. The more the system does for the users, the more they understand its potentials and the more they demand. Increasingly powerful systems are used to handle increasingly complex applications. Computer-assisted decision making spreads, with top management demanding of their subordinates, "The data are there; why don't you use them?" Increasingly, the computer has the potential of driving the day-to-day tactical aspects of the business.

As the on-line windows into the data bases spread among end users, a new pressure builds on data-processing managers. Instead of having to sell applications to the user departments, users are demanding new types of processing from the system. In order to accommodate more on-line data-base applications, elaborate hardware and software conversions are needed, often necessitating the rewriting of old batch programs.

A large backlog of applications awaiting development builds up. The end-user departments are told that there will be a long wait before they can have what they are asking for. Often the wait would be years. Sometimes the request is turned down indefinitely because the work load of the data-processing department is too high.

Economic pressures related to the national economy sometimes make the situation worse. Often the DP department has its staff or budget cut back at the time it needs extra staff. Accountants perceive this as a way to improve immediate cash flow. The same pressures make user departments need to increase productivity and employ new computer applications.

The software complexity of the centralized systems is beyond the comprehension of the end users. They do not understand why so much time is being spent in conversion, migration, installing new operating systems, new data-base software, and the like. They often have difficulty understanding what the DP staff are talking about. The DP staff seem like an exclusive club, a priesthood, talking in incomprehensible terms, not appreciating the end-user problems, and often not responding to their needs.

At the same time, minicomputers are becoming cheap. They appear simple and easy to use, and their salesmen find ways to help with the programming needed.

Some machines have report generators or application packages which make installation quick and easy. This form of decentralization spreads rapidly, bypassing the DP department. In scientific as well as commercial operations it makes sense to the end users—small systems for small applications. Users become proud of owning their own computer with which they can do what they want. The small systems become status symbols, and the users are glad to be free of the battles with the centralized DP group.

Some DP managers lament the erosion of their empire. Some force their computer salesmen to stay out of the user departments, but this does not keep the minicomputer salesmen out. Some DP managers welcome the users having their own machines because it lessens the pressure on their own strained resources. They regard the total user demands as impossible to meet. In some cases there is a major breakdown in relations between the DP department and the user departments.

User departments learn how to use minicomputers directly. Many are prepared to allocate staff to set up local systems. Some personnel learn to program or to use report generators. They become less bother to the harassed DP manager.

Later the DP department has its new software running; its computers have more memory and more power; its new data-base system can merge the data of users in different departments and derive major information-system advantages. Unfortunately, the user departments are reluctant to give up their systems or their control. They enjoy their new-found autonomy. Their systems are growing and now using multiprogramming.

The user departments will not accept new development costs for a takeover by the central system. In some cases duplicate costs are incurred as both the local and central systems continue to grow. There are duplications of inputs and differences in outputs. The same data are used by both systems in incompatible forms. There is now open hostility between the user departments and the centralized authority, both expanding and both looking at the same areas to justify their costs.

LOCAL AUTONOMY   There are both good and bad aspects to this scenario. The good aspects stem from local autonomy. The end users become responsible for their own operations. They can produce information they need more quickly and foresee their computing requirements more clearly. They understand their own local problems better than a centralized group ever could. They can adjust their applications and make changes easily because a change affects only their own programs and data, not hundreds of others as it might on a centralized system. They become enthusiastic about their own local computing and usually handle it well. They destroy the myth of the DP priesthood, that only the centralized, highly paid professionals can make computers work.

Young employees, often without college degrees, discover to their surprise that they can create programs. This is more fun than administrative paperwork. The user groups begin to understand data processing, at least in its simpler forms.

The managers of the user departments think more creatively about what their machine could do for them.

Programs work well when they control their own destinies.

MANPOWER   The most serious constraint slowing down the effective use of computers is shortage of manpower. Most corporations have a large application backlog today, and the bottleneck is going to become even more constraining because the number of computers, especially minicomputers, available to humanity is growing at a very rapid rate. The power of computers is growing, and the number of machines being manufactured is growing. The growth rates are higher with minicomputers than with large computers and higher with microcomputers than with minicomputers.

A study by the SHARE computer users' association on *Data Processing in 1980-1985* [2] concludes that the total number of MIPS of conventional computing power available (i.e., not including microcomputers and desk minicomputers) will increase by a factor of 400 between 1975 and 1985. Programmer productivity during the same ten years will slightly more than double. Even assuming that these estimates are very approximate, we are faced with the question, How are the world's computers going to be programmed? If the computer industry does not find a satisfactory answer to this question, it may be badly harmed by the rapidly falling cost of electronics. It seems unlikely that the answer can come from centralized DP groups programming in the computer languages which they use today.

Faced with the prospect of more MIPS than programmers for them, we should welcome the sight of the end users rolling up their sleeves to put the machines to work. This is an inevitable and very important trend in the computer industry. We will argue not about *whether* the end users should go to work on the machines, but about *how* they should do so.

FRAGMENTATION AND INCOMPATIBILITY   Undesirable aspects of the above decentralization scenario have already been described in Chapters 5 and 12. There may be substantial duplication of effort among end-user groups. While the first applications may be easy to install, the addition of further applications leads to greater complexity and escalation of costs. The programs are not designed for maintenance, and the systems are not designed for security. Most serious of all, in some cases, the corporation becomes filled with incompatible systems using incompatible data. Some of the data are needed beyond the user department responsible for it. They are needed in certain other departments and are invaluable in the overall management and control of the corporation. The data are in scattered, incompatible files (not data bases) and are not available for corporate decision making.

This spread of incompatible files has occurred in many organizations—in some, long before the days of minicomputers. It is a Herculean task to clean up the mess, to obtain some measure of compatibility in the data—the data-processing equivalent of the Augean stables. In some corporations the struggle for standardization of data goes on for years, and often standardization is never really achieved.

THE BEST OF BOTH WORLDS Distributed processing, appropriately managed, can give the best of both worlds.

The user departments still have their own small processors, now connected to larger machines in other parts of the corporation. The users can develop their own programs and now may have powerful compilers, report generators, and other software on a central system, to help them. While most of their programs use the local machine, they are not restricted to using only that. They can develop applications which sometimes need the power of a large, remote machine, or data which are maintained centrally.

Most important, the *data* which are kept and maintained can be planned with the needs of the corporation as a whole in mind. Some of the data, for example, customer ship-to addresses, may be of value only to the user department; other data are likely to be used centrally or in other departments. Data may therefore be divided into those items which can be left to the discretion of the user department and those which must be centrally planned.

Centralized standardization can be welcomed by decentralized groups *if it has the appearance of being a service to them,* as in the case of a corporate data dictionary.

The advantages of *data-base,* as opposed to *file,* operation are very significant. Data bases will be the foundation of much data processing in the 1980's. The computers in some user departments are too small to have a data-base management system today, but their data can conform to the structure used in a remote data base to which they are connected. The files of the decentralized machines are structured as *subschemas* of the centralized data base. The local machines can then transmit their records to, and obtain records from, the data-base machine. This implies that the design of the data cannot go on in isolation at the user locations. A data administrator needs to coordinate the design, as we will describe in Part IV. This data administrator should persuade the user departments that his job is to help them in the difficult task of designing the data.

The user departments will be free to derive files for which they perceive the need, from the data bases which exist elsewhere.

In one broadcasting company a staff group plans the scheduling of television studies and other expensive resources. This job has become steadily more hectic, especially at the end of each month when the plans and budgets for the next month must be determined. For two or three days at this time people in the department are found working late at night. The studio managers have been extremely frustrated at the inability of the DP department to respond to their needs quickly enough. Some persons in the scheduling group became enthusiastic about the APL language. They saw how APL models could be used in the operations and succeeded in conveying their enthusiasm to their colleagues. The organization used a centralized data-base system which derived much data from a distributed hierarchy of smaller machines. Unfortunately, the data-base system had no APL interface. The scheduling group therefore built a bridge with which files for their own use were derived from the data base whenever they needed them. They were then free to manipulate these files and use them in whatever programs they created. The decision-making capability improved and the average utilization of the studios and resources increased.

Distributed processing can thus facilitate local autonomy, initiative, and responsibility, without obliterating the advantages of centralized data planning and data-base software. The user departments are freed from most of the frustrations of being tied to an overburdened DP department. They can achieve much quicker implementation of their requirements and tailor them exactly to their needs. They can quickly modify their programs to adjust to local situations. The rigidities of centralized scheduling are avoided. The user departments have control of most of their data-processing costs. They understand them, as they did not with the centralized system. The centralized authorities, on the other hand, have not lost the ability to manage overall systems growth in the corporation.

There is a delicate balance between the degree of local autonomy and the degree of centralized control. Box 13.2 suggests a breakdown of local and central responsibilities. Some such breakdown should be agreed upon and formalized; it is likely to differ from one corporation to another.

The numbers of people involved in application development can increase greatly. The head of the data-processing department may view this increase as an expansion of his own responsibility and sphere of control.

In modern corporations and government the potential of the average human being is greatly underutilized. Most are capable of exercising much more imagination and creativity in their work than they do. The spread of distributed processing should be made a challenge to the initiative of white collar workers everywhere. Many will respond to the challenge, especially the young who have not yet had their thought patterns frozen into administrative drudgery.

REFERENCES

1. Datapro report of minicomputers.

2. SILT report of SHARE on *Data Processing in 1980–1985*, SHARE, Inc., 25 Broadway, Suite 750, New York, N.Y. 10004, 1975.

BOX 13.2   A possible division of centralized and decentralized responsibilities

CENTRALIZED RESPONSIBILITIES

- Definition of central and local responsibilities.
- Choice of network standards.
- Choice of corporation wide data-description language.
- Choice of data-base software.
- Data-base administration services, including the coordinated design of the data.
- Maintenance of a corporate data dictionary.
- Selection and design of applications to serve multiple locations.
- Selection of applications to be transferred between locations.
- Review of documentation of applications transferred between locations.
- Guidance on modularization needed to facilitate application transfer.
- Technical consulting services.
- System security design and administration.
- Design of system auditing controls and facilities.

DECENTRALIZED RESPONSIBILITIES

- Local application development.
- Design of locally used files.
- Design of subschemas which relate to a central or remote data base in conjunction with a central data-base administrator.
- Selection of equipment within the constraints of corporate recommendations.
- Development and documentation of applications intended for transfer to other locations.
- Modification of applications received from other locations.
- Liaison with centralized authorities on schema development and standardization of data items.
- Liaison with other locations on applications developed for common use.

14 COST AND BENEFIT ANALYSIS

Management usually require financial evaluation of alternative approaches in DP. It is desirable to contrast in dollars the costs and benefits of centralized and different distributed approaches.

Most distributed systems are neither totally centralized nor totally decentralized. It is possible to plot a chart showing the cost of differing degrees of offloading or difference of distribution. Sometimes the curve of total system cost has a minimum somewhere between the totally centralized approach and the totally decentralized approach, as shown in the left-hand side of Fig. 14.1.

More often the curve of total cost as plotted in Fig. 14.1 is bowed upwards rather than downwards, as in the right-hand chart. This might suggest either total centralization or total decentralization. However, the previous chapter and particularly Fig. 13.2 indicated that the best approach is often a judicious combination of centralization and decentralization.

Partially distributed systems often come out best when dollar values are assigned to the benefits.

PHASED PLANNING In some corporations the moves into distributed systems have been planned as a series of phases. They are sometimes designed to avoid major changes in the DP budget. Figure 14.2 illustrates this. The eight phases shown are *not necessarily intended to be introduced sequentially.*

For some electronic mail (Phase 7) and some personal computing (Phase 8) may be introduced before the distribution of data bases (Phase 6). However, the eight phases provide a means of comparing the costs and regulating the expenditure as more terminals, peripheral computers, and applications are added.

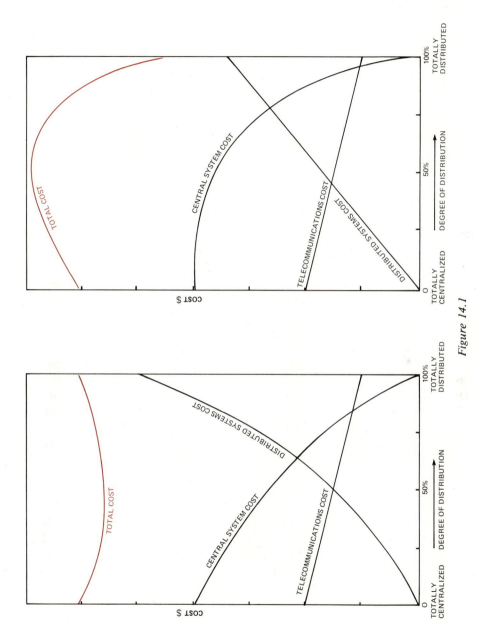

Figure 14.1

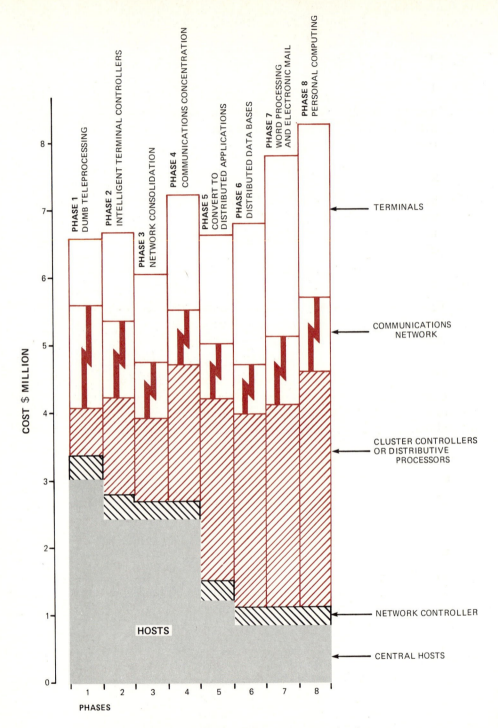

Figure 14.2 An 8-phase plan for distributed system development.

The eight phases are as follows:

Phase 1

The existing system with simple dumb-terminal teleprocessing. This serves as a base line for comparing costs. If its architecture were not changed, the costs would rise substantially as new applications and more terminals were added.

Phase 2

The introduction of intelligent terminal controllers. This reduces the cost of the communications network and makes possible improved application development, including data entry in the end-user departments and better terminal dialogues.

Phase 3

Network consolidation. Several separate networks exist, and this phase combines them into one. Even though terminals are added at more locations, there is a substantial saving.

Phase 4

Computers are installed in remote locations, originally to act as concentrators but in a later phase to contain distributed applications and files. The total cost is increased, but the hardware is in place for distribution which will reduce the control host expenditure. The central hosts remain until most of Phase 5 is working.

Phase 5

Phase 5 distributes many applications and permits a major reduction in the hosts at the central site.

Phase 6

Phase 6 distributes some of the data bases and increases the number of terminals. It introduces powerful end-user languages so now the stage is set for a high level of end-user involvement in developing their own applications and generating the information they need.

Phase 7

Phase 7 ties in word-processing machines and provides a facility for sending mail electronically. The $1 million increase in cost replaces $1.5 million of manual internal mail. The increase in network capacity gives more communications capability for the terminals and distributed machines.

Phase 8

Phase 8 provides personal computing resources, from the same terminals that are used for mail and other applications. Documents and personal files are now stored on the distributed machines. The components of the "office of the future" are coming together.

COSTS OF PEOPLE   Figures 14.1 and 14.2 show only the costs of the machines and telecommunications. There are many other cost factors which need to be considered. Often the largest of these is costs involved with people.

Figure 14.3 shows a comparison of costs taken from a manufacturer's proposal. The diagram compares costs for a centralized teleprocessing system with simple terminals and a hierarchical configuration with terminals connected to a programmed controller with disk storage. The salary costs in this case are those of ter-

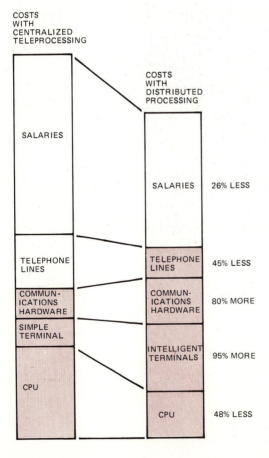

Figure 14.3 Change in costs resulting from the move from a centralized system to a distributive system. This example, taken from a manufacturer's proposal, shows an increase in machine costs but a decrease in the total cost.

minal operators. They are reduced because of increased productivity due to lower response times, a faster dialogue, and various support functions. Although the manufacturer's charges increase, the total costs are lower.

Often salary savings of operators or DP personnel are lower than those of other personnel affected by the system.

Figure 14.4 shows a comparison of the cost of internal mail in a corporation and the cost of the same mail sent electronically. This chart is plotted from figures in a top management computer network strategy document. Often when discussing the costs of electronic mail one hears them compared with the cost of postage stamps. It will be seen on the left-hand side of Fig. 14.4 that the postage stamp costs are small compared with the personnel costs—mainly the costs of running the mail room.

As hardware costs continue to drop, the costs of software, program development, and maintenance will often be more significant than hardware costs.

The costs in Fig. 14.5 are for a system which assists in processing orders from

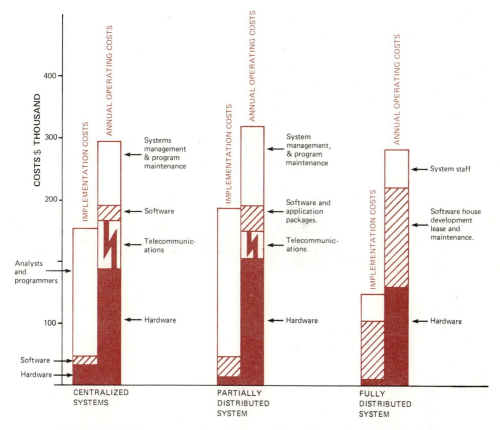

Figure 14.4   Three approaches for an order handling system. See Fig. 14.5 and 14.6 for the benefits.

	CENTRALIZED SYSTEM			PARTIALLY DISTRIBUTED SYSTEM			FULLY DISTRIBUTED SYSTEM		
	ESTIMATE	PROBABILITY	PRODUCT	ESTIMATE	PROBABILITY	PRODUCT	ESTIMATE	PROBABILITY	PRODUCT
SAVINGS									
Replacement of existing system	289,304	1	289,304	289,304	1	289,304	289,304	1	289,304
Less mail	8,510	1	8,510	8,510	1	8,510	8,510	1	8,510
Saving of staff and overheads									
Order clerks	38,000	.8	30,400	68,000	.8	54,500	68,000	.8	54,400
Invoicing clerks	50,000	.8	40,000	70,000	.8	56,000	50,000	.8	40,000
Stores clerks	21,000	1	21,000	50,000	.8	40,000	20,000	.5	10,000
Inventory saving	89,000	.6	53,400	89,000	.8	71,200	40,000	.5	20,000
Fewer lost sales	15,000	.8	12,000	30,000	.8	24,000	15,000	.6	9,000
Few bad debts	10,000	.8	8,000	15,000	.8	12,000	10,000	.8	8,000
INTANGIBLE BENEFITS.									
Fewer errors	50,000	.5	25,000	50,000	.5	25,000	50,000	.5	25,000
Better customer service	80,000	.4	32,000	80,000	.4	32,000	80,000	.2	16,000
TOTAL :			519,614			612,414			480,214

Figure 14.5 Estimates of benefits resulting from the three system approaches in Fig. 16.4. These are charted in Fig. 14.6.

customers and shipping the goods they order from inventory. The orders are received at and the goods shipped from 12 locations.

A batch-processing system was replaced with an on-line system, and three possibilities were considered: a centralized system with conventional dumb terminals, a fully distributed system with minicomputers at each of the twelve locations, and a partially distributed system with minicomputers at the twelve locations on-line to a central system. The latter is the most expensive in hardware costs, as shown in Fig. 14.5. When telecommunications, software, system development, and management are included, it is still the most expensive but not so far ahead of the others. Nevertheless, it would not be selected unless its benefits substantially exceed those of the other approaches. As is often the case, they do.

Figure 14.5 lists the benefits assessed for the three possible systems, and Fig. 14.7 charts them.

The configurations with peripheral computers facilitate data entry at the end-user locations, with tight on-line integrity checks. This is expected to reduce the data entry errors (see Fig. 14.6).

The partially distributed approach has the advantage that, if an order cannot be filled from the local inventory, it can be immediately passed on to the central location for handling from the central plant warehouse. This makes the consequences of running out of stock at a local site less severe. The local inventories can be smaller, giving an overall inventory saving of 15%. This also saves storage management costs. It saves clerical costs because less staff is required in dealing with out-of-stock situations and following up back orders. It gives fewer unfilled orders and hence better customer service, and fewer lost sales.

Bad debts are reduced by use of credit control with the on-line access to up-to-date account status records, at the time an order is accepted.

The fully distributed version would not give access to central customer or product data bases. These are too large to be held on the peripheral machines. Customer account and order history records facilitate quick resolution of customer queries and give better customer service.

Figure 14.7 summarizes the costs and benefits of the three approaches. It will be seen that the partially distributed version gives the largest difference between benefits and costs.

BENEFITS   The benefits of DDP, apart from possibly lower hardware and telecommunications costs, fall into three categories:

- Cost savings
- Future cost avoidance
- Intangibles

Box 14.1 lists potential benefits in these three categories.

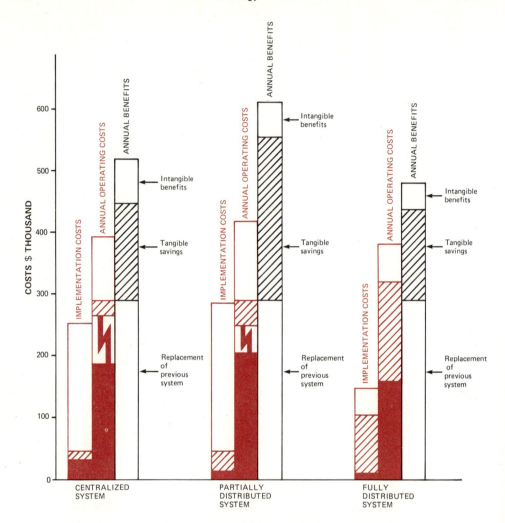

Figure 14.6 Estimated benefits from Fig. 14.5 added to the cost chart of Fig. 14.4.

Most items in the first category—saving of existing costs—can be measured and have a relatively high probability of realization. Most items in the second category—future cost avoidance—can have a cash figure associated with them if certain assumptions are made about the future growth of the business. Because of the uncertainty of these assumptions there is a lower probability of realization than for items in the first category.

Benefits in the third category—intangibles—are often potentially the largest and they are difficult or impossible to quantify. When an accountant demands to see only quantifiable savings, ask him how he justifies his telephone. The company

	YEAR						6 YEAR TOTAL
	1	2	3	4	5	6	
ESTIMATED COSTS							
Equipment rental and maintenance	128,000	141,000	150,000	160,000	169,000	178,000	
Additional DP staff (& overheads)	36,000	72,000	80,000	82,000	84,000	86,000	
Application analysis	97,000						
Data base design	15,000						
Application programming	179,000	84,000					
Program maintenance		10,000	17,000	22,000	27,000	32,000	
File conversion	84,000						
Other conversion costs	67,000						
Site Preparation	53,000						
Forms and supplies	11,000	21,000	24,000	26,000	28,000	30,000	
Miscellaneous one time costs	45,000						
Miscellaneous operating costs	5,000	10,000	15,000	15,000	15,000	15,000	
TOTAL	720,000	338,000	286,000	305,000	323,000	341,000	2,313,000
ESTIMATED SAVINGS							
Reduction in staff (& overheads)		340,000	360,000	388,000	416,000	440,000	
Office rental savings		15,000	17,000	19,000	21,000		
Sale of central site equipment	85,000	45,000					
Elimination of rental equipment		13,000	15,000	16,000	17,000	18,000	
Reduction in central site software		23,000	27,000	30,000	33,000	36,000	
Miscellaneous savings		10,000	15,000	25,000	19,000	14,000	
TOTAL	85,000	431,000	432,000	476,000	504,000	529,000	2,457,000
Net savings (losses) before Federal Income Taxes.	(635,000)	93,000	146,000	171,000	181,000	188,000	144,000

Figure 14.7   Illustration of costs and benefits of a distributed system.

telephone bill can only be justified intangibly. Some of the intangibles can have cash figures associated with them, for example, reduction of error handling, fewer bad debts, fewer lost orders, closer control of credit, and so on. Some have savings of clerical staff associated with them, such as automatic transfer of out-of-stock orders to another location. Some, such as improved human communications, are almost impossible to assign cash values to. Sometimes the largest intangibles are factors like restructuring the business, changing management structures, and new business opportunities.

Of the three categories of items, intangibles usually have the lowest probability of realization.

RISK BENEFIT ANALYSIS   To factor the risks into the cost-benefit calculation, the dollar figures may be multiplied by the probability of their being realized.

A saving which is regarded as certain may be multiplied by 1. A saving which is thought to have an 80% chance of realization is multiplied by 0.8, and so on. Some of the more questionable intangibles, if a cash value can be attached to them at all, may be multiplied by a low probability figure. Figure 14.6 illustrates the use of probability estimates.

Similarly, certain costs might be multiplied by a probability figure. Most costs

BOX 14.1 Possible example of benefits of distributed processing other than possible reduction in hardware and telecommunications costs.

POSSIBLE COST SAVING

Fewer employees, salaries, overheads associated with employees, and fringe benefits.
Less office space. Fewer offices.
Reduction in repairs, maintenance, insurance, tax, utilities.
Reduction in central site software costs and systems programming.
Reduction in mail and mailroom costs.
Reduction in outside processing costs.
Reduction in other equipment, sale of equipment.
Lower inventory carrying costs. Fewer inventory sites.

POSSIBLE FUTURE COST AVOIDANCE

Avoiding future increases in any of the above costs as the business volume grows.
Less future requirements.
Reduction in future software and application program maintenance costs.
Investment saving by faster application development.

POSSIBLE INTANGIBLE BENEFITS (potentially the largest benefits)

Better information for decision-making.
Better communications.
Increased productivity.
Better or faster customer service.
New business opportunities.
Management restructuring.
Better business guidelines.
Tighter local management decision making.
Higher morale.
Faster decisions.
Better dialogues, ease of use, user-friendly terminals.
Fewer errors.
Local responsibility for users' own data accuracy and security.

BOX 14.1 *continued*

Faster application development.
End user involvement in the application development process.
Better control of order acceptance.
Fewer lost sales.
Fewer bad debts.
Earlier satisfaction of back orders.
Increased customer loyalty.
More effective use of management's time.
Faster handling of situations.
Greater use of mathematical techniques.
Spreads computer use to more end users.
End-user employment of graphics techniques.
Improved scheduling.
Improved production control.
Closer control of expenses.
Closer control of investment.
Closer control of credit.
Closer control of benefits.
Better quality of control.
Fewer out-of-stock situations.
Fewer schedule disruptions.
Better planning.
Improved promotional efforts.
More effective employment of resources.
More timely management reports.

are only too certain, but there may be a small probability of cost overruns, extra salaries, delayed schedules, additional hardware, and so on. These might be evaluated and their dollar value multiplied by an assessed probability of their happening.

Sometimes the analyst is at a loss what probability figure to assign to benefits. In this case he might divide them into *high, medium,* and *low* probability of realization and use the following figures:

	High	Medium	Low
For Cost Savings:	1	0.75	0.5
For Future Cost Avoidance:	0.8	0.55	0.3
For Intangibles:	0.7	0.45	0.2

FINANCIAL EVALUATION METHODS

Several methods are in use for summarizing the cost and benefit figures:

1. Cost and benefit comparison

In the simplest method the total cost and the total benefit figure are listed for each projected year of operation and the difference is calculated.

2. Breakeven analysis

In this common method the time taken to pay back the investment is calculated. If an item cost $20,000 to purchase and generated $5,000 per year income, the payback period would be 4 years. Ongoing costs may be compared with ongoing benefits to calculate a payback period.

3. Rate of return

The cash inflows as represented by benefits are compared with the total cash expenditure to calculate a rate of return on investment.

4. Discounted cash flow

The problem with all of the above methods is that they do not take into consideration the changing value of money with time. A thousand dollars spent in five years is worth less than a thousand dollars spent now. A thousand-dollar benefit today is worth more than a thousand-dollar benefit in the future. The greater the investment rate and inflation rate, the more important it is to take this into consideration.

Discounted cash flow takes the changing value of money into consideration by means of a *discount factor*. This factor takes in consideration the cost of money—the rate charged when money is borrowed or the rate earned when money is invested.

Suppose that the rate is i. In other words, one dollar invested today will be worth $1 + i$ dollars in one year. The rate is $(100.i)\%$. Today's dollar can be regarded as being worth $1/(1 + i)^n$ dollars in n years.

If the rate is 12.5%, today's dollar will be worth 88.889 cents next year, 79.012 cents in two years, 70.233 cents in three years, and $\$1/1.125^n$ in n years.

A retirement pension of $10,000 from a corporation for retirement in 20 years will be worth only $948.

Discounted cash flow lists the total cost and total benefits for each year and calculates the differences, as in the *cost and benefit comparison* method above. It then reduces the net amount for future years by multiplying it by $1/(1 + i)^n$. The total for all of the years in question may be added. This total is referred to as the *total discounted cash flow*.

216

If a cost item in year n is C_n, and the probability of its occurrence is PC_n, then the total costs for year n can be calculated as the sum of the values of $C_n PC_n$:

$$\Sigma\ C_n PC_n$$

Similarly, if a benefit in year n is B_n and the probability of its realization is PB_n, then the total for year n can be calculated as the sum of the values of $B_n PB_n$:

$$\Sigma\ B_n PB_n$$

The nondiscounted cash flow for year n is

$$B_n PB_n\ -\ C_n PC_n$$

The discounted cash flow for year n is

$$\frac{B_n PB_n\ -\ C_n PC_n}{(1\ +\ i)^n}$$

The total discounted cash flow for N years is

$$\sum_{n\ =\ 1}^{N}\ \frac{B_n PB_n\ -\ C_n PC_n}{(1\ +\ i)^n}$$

DISCOUNT OR NOT?   Many proposals for DP systems do not use discounted cash flow. The proposal looks more impressive if *non-discounted* cash flow is used because most of the expenditure is at the front and the benefits come later.

With some distributed systems the benefits may come earlier than with a centralized system. In this case, when comparing a centralized approach with a distributed approach, *discounted* cash flow will tend to favor the distributed approach (rightly so).

Sometimes DP planners compare costs and benefits without adjusting for the time value of money and find to their surprise that their figures are challenged, and sometimes their justification destroyed, by accountants. Figure 14.8 shows a DP assessment of the costs and benefits of moving to a distributed system for a marketing organization. The total figure at the bottom right indicates a net saving of $144,000. Justification enough, it was thought. However, the accountants in this case applied a discounted cash flow analysis. The discount rate used was 12.5% and the justification vanished.

In fact, there was an excellent justification for the system in question, but it is not revealed in Fig. 14.8. The system would provide better control of customer orders, resulting in fewer errors and lower acceptance of bad orders. This alone

Year (n)	1	2	3	4	5	6	TOTALS
Net savings (losses) from Fig. 14.7 before Federal Income Taxes.	(635,000)	93,000	146,000	171,000	181,000	188,000	144,000
Net savings (losses) after Federal Income Taxes at 48%	(330,200)	48,360	75,920	88,920	94,120	97,760	74,880
Discount Rate $(1/1.125^n)$	·88,889	·79012	·70233	·62430	·55493	·49327	
Discounted net savings (losses)	(293,511)	38,210	53,321	55,513	52,230	48,222	(46,015)

Figure 14.8 An accountant applying discounted cash flow to the figures of Fig. 14.7 turns the apparent profit of $144,000 before taxes to a loss of $46,015 after taxes.

would justify the system, but it would also give better service to customers and reduce branch office personnel. It can absorb an increase in sales volume without an increase in administrative costs. The analysts made a near-fatal mistake in not showing future cost avoidance or intangibles.

The feasibility study for electronic mail from which Fig. 14.4 was plotted also uses simple cost comparisons rather than discounted cash flow. Discounting would drastically reduce (but not eliminate) the apparent justification. However, the corporation in question is growing fairly rapidly and an electronic mail system would be able to absorb this growth without much extra cost. The future growth is not projected in the feasibility study and, as in most cases, would greatly strengthen it.

15 DISTRIBUTION AND POLITICS

INTERDEPARTMENTAL RIVALRY

Antony Jay, in his book *Management and Machiavelli* [43], compares corporate department heads to the barons of medieval England. Like other countries, England was frequently torn by interbaronial rivalries and jealousies even when there were great dangers threatening or great opportunities beckoning from overseas. The internal strife, says Jay, should be no surprise to those familiar with large corporations. Few employees of large corporations would be so naive as to say, "After all, we're part of the same company, aren't we? Why can't we all work together instead of wasting our time on these internal wrangles?" The employees understand the strength of the interbaronial rivalries. The barons, when permitted, would build superbly strong castles. Periodically the kings used to find it necessary to knock down some of the castles.

Many organizations foster a high level of competitiveness between departments and between managers. In many ways this is healthy. It keeps managers on their toes and helps to ensure that they make the best possible demands on their management. However, in such an environment managers tend to build walls around their domains to protect them from other departments, and they tend to be secretive about information.

The DDP fortress has been largely impregnable. The barons have regarded it with annoyance and forced resignation. Now at last it is attackable. The barons want their own data-processing and information sources.

In Jay's analogy, the bricks and mortar that corporate barons build their castles with are often *withheld information* and *unreferred decisions*.

The relationship between managers and departments is far more complex than the organization chart would indicate, and the information which passes between them is not governed by straightforward rules. This is especially so in old or large corporations where managers have long since learned that in order to survive, or be promoted, certain modes of political behaviour are necessary and care is needed in handling most types of information. Executives in bureaucratic organizations have a long and successful education in how to protect themselves and their departments. Computerized information systems threaten to wreck the carefully cultivated patterns.

In many organizations the education in bureaucratic survival teaches managers to hide or manipulate certain information. It teaches rivalry and mistrust. Elaborate coverups become a way of life. Much information is prevented from reaching other departments or higher levels of management, and much communication of information is deliberately delayed, distorted, or funneled through certain channels. The image of a corporate "information system," making information freely available to higher management, is a cause for alarm. Just as computerized inventory systems revealed the chaotic state of the stores, so network data-base systems may reveal to top management how much has been hidden from them.

The designer of a distributed information system steps into this environment. He wants to make the data kept by different departments compatible and organize a free and efficient flow of data. The same data items go to work for different departments. Interdepartment withholding of data has no place in the designer's scheme for maximizing the value of the data. In his view the maximum cooperation is needed. He sees corporate politics as a barrier to efficient systems design, which has to be overcome. In some corporations the barons, who are divided on everything else, have united on the fact that the information system designer is a menace. Fortunately for them, he needs a long time to bring his plans to fruition, and he may be unlikely to survive that long.

The primary difficulty in the design of DDP is that the overall designs which are most appealing to a systems engineer tend to be counterpolitical.

Top executives who want such systems must be prepared to wield power over the barons.

THINKERS AND THUMPERS

The majority of decision makers in corporations tend to be at one or the other end of a scale; they tend to be organizers—men of action with little contemplation— or to be creative men with little organizing ability. One colleague who works with the military refers to them as "thinkers" and "thumpers." The thinker may be found in the operations research department or on the corporate planning staff. Sometimes he is the brain behind many aspects of the computer systems. He is bored with routine administration and cannot organize anything. His secretary has to organize him. However, his ideas are often brilliant and his knowledge formidable. Sometimes he has a keen vision of the future and how the corporation must change over the years ahead.

The thumper, on the other hand, may never have had an idea in his life, but he can give orders and make sure they are obeyed. He can make a department shipshape and efficient and can motivate people to work well. He can see that accounts and documentation are kept efficiently. When persons or organizations fail to perform well, he thumps the table. His world is one of routine. Often he has little respect for the intellectual. To him the thinker is a necessary evil, and perhaps not even all that necessary. The thumper finds no satisfaction in contemplation of things that *could* be done or methods that *could* be used.

The thumpers form the backbones of corporations because of the vast amount of routine work which has to be done. Put in charge of a department the thinker would be a catastrophe, and the thumper knows it. On the other hand, the thumper is incapable of questioning the need for his own department. He will perpetuate it, make it grow, and fight with other departments for the resources he wants. He has little idea about future directions if they are different from the present. He steers the course he has been given, or if he is not given a course, he charges straight ahead. If there is disaster ahead, he will run straight into it.

Now, with the spread of computing, the thumper fears that his world may be eroded. His actions can be monitored on a terminal. He is receiving detailed instructions from computers. The thinker is building an APL model of the planning process. What on earth is APL? He fears that the thinker may try to tell him how to thump.

A psychological need of the thumper is his feeling of wielding power. Computerized decision making tends to deemphasize the use of personal power. A decision is implemented because it is the computed optimum, not because it is so-and-so's decision. Many managers fear that computerization will reduce their ability to give orders simply because the computers have been given power. The thumper has become familiar with "shaking the place up," "turning the joint around," "rattling the cage," "tightening the screw." His magical ability to obtain results has often resulted from the sloppiness of current practices or the lack of adequate measurements or data. The more the operation comes under the tight surveillance of on-line distributed systems, the less the scope for the aggressive manager to produce dramatic improvements.

Increasingly what is needed as computer-related methods spread is an effective combination of thumper and thinker. The person who can organize and motivate people will always be essential, but in an increasing number of situations he will have to understand the capabilities of the computer and carry on terminal dialogues. Few people are pure thinker or pure thumper. Most thumpers have some ability to think, and most thinkers have some ability to thump. However, the person who does both well is rare. Most people tend to be primarily one or the other.

What makes the grafting of the two species especially important is that the thinker and the thumper have serious difficulties in communicating with one another. The thinkers need to be led by other thinkers and have little respect for the leadership of the thumpers. The thumpers need equally strong thumpers to control them. The person who is primarily thumper has an emotional horror of the invasion of his domain by the management scientists and data-base designers. He usually has to make a show of embracing them, but they should not be deluded by the smile with which they are received. They are in hostile territory. They need their wits about them if they are to survive.

THE WAR OF THE PRINTOUTS

Increasingly in corporations, computer printouts are being used as weapons of politics. For the person skilled in using them they can be very effective. When a difficult moment comes in a meeting or sales situation he says, "Let me show you something" and with a sense of high drama produces a massive printout. The printout cannot be argued with because it comes from a computer, and is suitably obscure to the opposition. There is no good means of counteracting it except perhaps another printout.

The unexpected producing of a printout is a means of establishing a case, leading the opposition into a trap, or drawing the discussion away from a problem area. It is an irresistible means of changing the subject at a difficult moment.

The executive skilled with printouts does not want a display terminal except to select and prepare what should be printed. He takes the printouts home, studies them and marks them to prepare his case. He may want adjustments made in what is printed. When he wields his printout, he does not want the opposition to be able to counterattack with some other action on a terminal.

As his skill improves at using printouts both to get his own way and to manage and comprehend better, he increasingly wants control of his own computing resources. He does not want to be dependent on and restricted by a central DP department.

A thumper caught in the war of the printouts may happily embrace, for a time, the expert who can give him his own armaments. He has no interest in data dictionaries, network architectures, standardized interfaces, or other such aspects of DDP design, but he may join forces with a systems analyst who acts as a weapons supplier. He will be very reluctant to have his information transmitted to other computers which may be in enemy hands or to have his data merged into a shared data base. He may be eager to extract information from other people's data bases or from centralized systems, provided that his own data can be locked and information withheld for a rainy day when it might be needed.

TOO RAPID INFORMATION TRANSFER

With a powerful information system, information can pass very rapidly up the chain of command. In the Vietnam war the American field commanders reportedly expressed much concern at certain times because the Pentagon and even the President were becoming involved in decisions which should have been theirs. With some corporate systems higher management similarly becomes involved and may not know all the facts. Data which should have been the concern of a department manager have been seen by *his* manager first. The data are collected at their source, are processed in real time, and are then available at the display screens of the system.

The department manager does not have the time buffer that he had before, during which he could chew over the situation, find out the reasons for anything that was wrong, put it right, think up excuses, devise policy suggestions, or hide the facts. In other systems a manager's performance has been analyzed by his boss using the computer, and the first view he has seen of the analysis figures was when he was called into the boss's office to justify them.

A shop floor foreman was responsible for scheduling the sequence of work under his control. He knew everything that was taking place in his area, and people outside his area knew only what the foreman chose to tell them. With computers, each worker enters details of the status of his operations into a work station terminal. Such information passes immediately to a computer which correlates it and plans the job schedule. The foreman has lost part of his control. When management wants to argue about the scheduling of a certain job, they go first to the computer terminals or information room staff, and not to the foreman.

Similarly arguments apply from the top to the bottom of a computerized corporation. Managers, who have been used to retaining control over information about the work they are responsible for, lose the ability to withhold, delay, or manipulate the information. It passes into the all-too-accessible data bases far too quickly.

FEAR OF FUTURE POTENTIAL

In many cases it is not so much what a computer can do today that causes the fear of computers but the potential, vividly expressed but not yet accomplished fear of what a real-time information system will eventually do. There will be nowhere to hide. A manager's mistakes will be highly visible. Decisions which are less than optimal, or tricks necessary for making his forecasts and budgets into self-fulfilling prophecies, may be confronted with all manner of interference. When he exceeds his quota, or is well within his budget, he cannot save some of the excess for next time. He may have much more difficulty in setting a budget or quota which he knows he can meet because he now has to argue with staffs who have access to the information system. He had many little secrets which he could use in times of difficulty, and he fears that an all-pervading data base might prevent use of these, making everything too precise and too open. Managers who have relied on hiding the full facts in order to increase their chances of political survival fear that a computerized information system will pull the rug out from under them.

Having their own minicomputer with appropriate privacy locks may be perceived as a way for them to attempt to retain control. The data entry devices are attached to *their* computer, and they pass on what information they want.

FEAR OF PERSONAL INADEQUACY

Most people feel nervous about the nature of their jobs being changed, but often a new job demands the same types of abilities as the old and they feel reasonably sure that it will only be a matter of time before they have mastered it. A machine tool operator can learn to operate a new machine tool even if it uses a high level of automation. A scientist can learn a new field of research and will probably enjoy doing so. But a manager confronted with the spread of computerized decision making often feels decidedly apprehensive because he simply cannot understand what the operations research staff is talking about. Nobody has explained "integer programming" or "regression analysis" to him; he has forgotten all but the simplest of his mathematics; he simply does not know how to judge the validity of the output of a computer model. He once went to a one-day course on management science, but he cannot relate what was said to his own job and doubts whether he will ever understand. He may not even want to understand. When he talks to the accountants or lawyers, his management skill enables him to extract the essence from what they are saying, ask the right questions, and make judgments about the value of their advice. Not so with the operations research staff. He tries to ask the right questions but somehow seems to receive responses which are both condescending and as difficult to make judgments about as the pronouncements which triggered the questions.

NEW SKILLS

A high-level manager once asked the author to sit in on a meeting, as a personal favor, in which the senior OR man was going to present the conclusions of a year's work. The manager pleaded, "I know I won't be able to understand what the hell he's talking about. I'd like you to listen to it and explain to me whether it makes sense and how far it would be sensible to go with it." The bearded OR man came in with flip charts. He spent the first half hour explaining in child-like terms how one function of the corporation operated. The manager listened with tactful patience, suppressing his growing irritation at being told information which he thought everybody knew. The OR man then switched his presentation to a mathematical analysis of the operations. His charts had partially unlabeled axes, his symbols were inadequately explained, and the purpose of his mathematics was not made clear. Only a person already familiar with the techniques in question could have followed what he was saying. The lecture ended with no clear proposal for action, and the manager said, "Well, what do you want us to do?" This triggered another burst of unclear mathematics which was cut short after ten minutes by the manager saying he did not understand and the OR man reverting to the child's guide to how the company operates.

It was difficult to be sure whether the OR man had subconscious motives for being obscure, but there was virtually no chance at the end of the afternoon that the manager could have made a confident decision about how best to proceed. He appealed for help afterwards: "It's always like that. Did you understand what he was talking about? . . . Why can't he give a straightforward answer to my questions?"

It is not surprising that such managers produce an irrational reaction to rational systems. On the surface their reaction may be annoyance that the management scientist cannot express his views more clearly, but beneath the surface there is a fear of making decisions with the basis for the decisions unclearly understood.

Worse—much worse—there is a horror that the management skills they have so arduously acquired may be inadequate in a world of computers and mathematics.

To some extent the executives in a highly computerized corporation have needed skills and talents different from those required before computers. The type of person best suited to decision making with computers has often not risen through the ranks of conventional management. Conventional managers are often skilled at using intuition for judging situations and make much use of past experience, but experimentation with computer models or dialogue with an information system is foreign to both their temperament and their intellect. Distributed processing and cheap personal computing is bringing the computer within range of *all* managers. New managers should now be expected to learn to use computers early in their careers and steadily improve their familiarity and skills with them. To do this they will often need a substantial amount of help from the systems analysts.

POWER AND   In some areas a major effect of computers is likely to be
FREEDOM   that they can automate those parts of jobs which were
                   easy for people but cannot touch the parts which were
difficult. Where this is true they increase the overall difficulty people have in doing their work. This is seen in many walks of life in the steady spread of complexity that the modern world is bringing. Paradoxically, it is not necessarily bad for the individual concerned. His job may become more difficult, but it also becomes more interesting, more stimulating, and more fulfilling. The easy parts of his job were the dull parts, and it is now possible to dream of a world in which dull jobs are done by machines and interesting jobs are done by humans. Unfortunately, we are some way from this world as yet.

A less fortunate aspect of computerization occurs where it is possible to automate those parts of a job that give one a feeling of power, achievement, or responsibility.

It is interesting to reflect on the reasons people in corporations seek power. No doubt some of them do it for the sheer enjoyment of exercising power. Except in a few extreme cases, however, this is probably not the main reason. Some want power in order to achieve objectives they believe in. Probably the major reason, however, stems from the need for freedom. The more power they have, the freer they are to take the actions they want—the freer they are to control their environment. Freedom of action is a basic need of capable people. How many of the younger capable employees in a corporation do you hear saying that they want to be their own boss? They would like to leave the organization and work for themselves, or they want to be left free to see a job through in their own way. It has become a cliché of youth that they want to "do their own thing." They are asking for freedom.

Centralized computers and data bases can decrease the freedom of action of junior or middle management, and for some this can be exceedingly frustrating. Information is collected in real time, and computers are involved in decision making.

The data-base system can centralize many of the important decisions. Many decisions are taken out of the hands of the local managers. If a local manager wants to alter a plan, he may not be able to do so. He may make a request for a change and have a new plan given him by the computer. Central computer systems sometimes create an unattractive environment for the local decision maker.

On the other hand, *distributed* systems can increase the freedom of action of lower management if the managers in question can come to grips with making their local computers manipulate the information they need. The local manager in a distributed environment will "do his own thing," using his own computer, within a minimal set of rules determined by higher-level management. He will know how his efforts are measured and judged.

Chris Argyris, Professor of Administrative Sciences at Yale, has studied the effects of computers on middle management [44] and concludes that they can be similar to the effects of job specialization on lower-level employees.

> A young man can start working on an assembly line with a rather high degree of commitment. But he learns very soon that if he maintained that commitment, he could go mad. So he begins to withdraw psychologically. And as he withdraws certain things begin to happen: He no longer cares about the quality of the work as he used to; he also begins to see himself as a less responsible human being.

Confronted with computers making the decisions, Argyris claims, many middle managers also lose much of the commitment.

> Daily goals are defined for [the manager], the actions to achieve those goals are specified; his level of aspiration is determined for him; and his performance is evaluated by a system *over which he has no influence.*
>
> These conditions may lead managers to perform as expected. However, they will also lead to a sense of psychological failure. Those managers who aspire toward challenging work with self-responsibility will be frustrated; those who prefer less challenge will be satisfied. The former may leave, fight, or psychologically withdraw: the latter stay and also withdraw. In short the manager, because of information systems, will experience frustrations that his employees once experienced when quality control engineers first designed their work and monitored their performance.
>
> Middle managers feel increasingly hemmed in. In psychological language, they will experience a great restriction of their space of free movement, resulting in feelings of lack of choice, pressure, psychological failure. These feelings in turn can lead to increasing feelings of helplessness and decreasing feelings of responsibility. Result: a tendency to withdraw or to become dependent upon those who created or approved the restriction of space of free movement.

GOOD AND BAD DESIGN

With this view we should return to our comments on good and bad distributed system design.

Good design creates nodes which are largely autonomous. They operate within a set of objectives set centrally and rules which are necessary for interconnection. The interactions between the nodes are neither excessively complicated nor restrictive.

The lower-level managers have objectives set for them. They have an appropriate degree of power and freedom in meeting those objectives. This includes the freedom to utilize and devise computer applications and to develop their information sources.

Rather than having no scope for initiative, as Argyris describes, they should have authority and responsibility for the local systems they employ. The danger of very cheap minicomputers is that demands on local management initiative may become too great rather than nonexistent.

MANAGEMENT STYLE   Many managers believe in the natural superiority of their own methods. They have their own style of managing, and if any technique comes along which is incompatible with that style, it will be largely ignored. Often the style of managing is cultivated by the corporation. It is a corporate style rather than an individual style, but the individual, in order to succeed, has assimilated the style completely.

If the general manager says, "I will not have a boob-tube in my office," then the systems analyst may have no hope of persuading any of top management to have a terminal. If certain types of decisions are made by committees, it may be next to impossible to have them made by computer models. Management may have unshakable faith in its own intuitive decisions. This is their style, and woe betide any computer specialist who challenges it.

It can be extremely frustrating, and indeed baffling, for a management scientist to find that after working for five years on a financial model of the corporation, management ignores it and continues to make financial decisions in the same intuitive way. This has happened and will go on happening because many top managers, especially older ones, have unshakable faith in their own style of decision making (usually borne out by past success).

Distributed systems can allow a substantial degree of variance in management styles. To a greater extent than with centralized computing managers can run their own department in their own way.

The job of the systems analyst in this environment becomes twofold. First, he should assimilate himself as completely as possible into the local environment. He should live there and be the *confidant* of the key local manager. He should understand that manager's style and how best he can make use of distributed systems. He should be part of the local environment rather than a visitor from head office. Second, he must make sure that the rules which are necessary for tying together a distributed system are obeyed.

One of the most attractive features of DDP is that it can adapt to fit the management styles and organization structure.

MATRIX MANAGEMENT   The question arises: Who should the person who runs the local computing facilities report to?

In most cases he should report to the local *user* management. They are the management who must ultimately judge the usefulness and value of the computing facilities. They need the closest cooperation with whoever creates these facilities and designs their applications, dialogues, and printouts. User management should talk to them on a daily basis when necessary about the printouts they want and the problems they foresee. To create the most effective facilities user management and their computer staff need to be very close. User management must feel that *their* computer staff are on *their* side in the political arguments we have described. The barons will demand unerring loyalty from their own DP staff.

This creates a conflict. We stress for many different reasons in different chapters of this book that DDP needs *overall* management and design. It must not be an *ad hoc* collection of minicomputers strung together arbitrarily. The pitfalls of *ad hoc* DDP are many (Box 5.1) and severe.

The local DP management must also report to central DP management, as shown in Fig. 15.1. This situation of having two bosses is known as *matrix* management. It happens elsewhere and can cause problems.

Certain characteristics are necessary in order to make the situation in Fig. 15.1 work. First, the primary loyalty of the local DP management must be clearly spelled out. It is shown by the solid arrows in the figure. The barons must have no doubt about who their local DP manager *really* works for, who judges him, and who can fire him.

Second, the characteristics of the dotted line reporting must be spelled out in detail. These include conforming to corporate standards, architectures, overall system design and distributed data administration, appropriate documentation, attendance at meetings, memberships on committees, and so on.

Third, the dotted line reporting should not be expected to work fully unless there is a higher-level authority to enforce it. Both the barons and the central DP

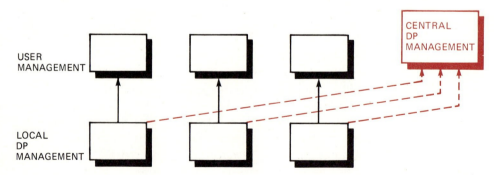

Figure 15.1 Lines of reporting: Matrix management. Certain characteristics are necessary to make this work.

228

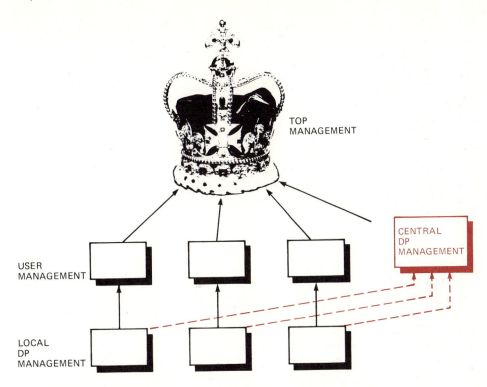

TOP
MANAGEMENT

CENTRAL
DP
MANAGEMENT

USER
MANAGEMENT

LOCAL
DP
MANAGEMENT

Figure 15.2   To make matrix management work, top management comprehension and support of the DDP strategy is vital.

management must report to the king. If the barons violate the rules set by the central DP management, the latter must appeal to the king, who has the ultimate
authority over the barons (Fig. 15.2).

    To make DDP work, then, *top management* comprehension and support are
vital.

16 THE BUREAUCRATIC IMPERATIVE

Time and time again, when one examines those corporations where a *strong* decision has been made about distributed processing, one finds that it has been more a political decision than a technical one. Sometimes it is a decision for widespread fragmentation of DP; sometimes for *distributive* processing with totally central control; sometimes for forging data networks, office automation, and the telephone network into one empire. But usually there is a "tough guy" who has got his way politically.

More often distribution has happened by default. The barons, as described in the last chapter, obtain their own computers. The central DP department ignores this or protests about it but is extremely slow to recognize that it complements its own service. What is occurring is the intrinsic development of DDP without the company recognizing it. DDP developed by default has the problems we described in Box 5.1.

LOSS OF EMPIRE   Not least of the political emotions is the fear of DP executives that they might lose their empire. Winston Churchill once said, "I will not preside over the dissolution of the British Empire"; some DP managers feel no less strongly about the spread of minicomputers. They will fight fiercely to prevent the Plans and Budgets Department from losing its colonial status.

The technology of the near future will lead inexorably to decolonization. User departments will have their own computer, just as they have their own copying machine, because it will not cost much more. They may or may not do their own application development, but the trend to DDP will inevitably lessen the *proportion* of application development done in a centralized DP shop.

MONKS DON'T DISSOLVE MONASTERIES
As data processing moves from the head office to end user locations, the central DP organization might prove remarkably resiliant.

History is filled with examples of organizations growing in size when in fact their function was diminishing. Northcote Parkinson points out that from 1914 to 1928 the number of capital ships in the British Navy decreased from 62 to 20 but at the same time the number of Admiralty officials increased from 2000 to 3569 [1].

BRITISH ADMIRALTY STATISTICS

Year	Number of capital ships in commission	Dockyard officials and clerks	Admiralty officials
1914	62	3249	2000
1928	20	4558	3569

The country where this book was written introduced a Department of Organization and Management to examine government inefficiencies. Within a few years this department became bigger than most of the departments it was policing.

Particularly relevant to DDP is the size of the British Colonial Office during the years when it was losing its colonies:

BRITISH COLONIAL OFFICE STATISTICS

Year	1935	1939	1943	1947	1954
Number of Colonial Office officials	372	450	817	1139	1661

It seems a safe bet that, as many centralized DP departments lose their colonies, they will likewise grow in size. The desire to reduce the central DP department will not usually come from within that department. Monks don't dissolve monasteries.

THE BUREAUCRATIC IMPERATIVE
The debate about centralization vs. decentralization is as relevant to society as it is to computing. We are in an age of big bureaucracies.

Big bureaucracies tend to grow. The size of the system is considered an important source of status and power to the managers who run it, and they usually attempt to foster growth of their organization. They prefer to multiply their subordinates rather than multiply their rivals. Once an organization has become sufficiently complex, it becomes difficult to do without it or replace it with a different one. There is therefore a ratchet effect. Steps downward in size do not occur; steps upward occur by offering the constituency more services.

Richard Goodwin, writing in the *New Yorker,* described the resistance of bureaucracies to structural changes:

> The passion for size, reach and growth is the soul of bureaucracy. Within government, the fiercest battles are waged not over principals and ideas but over jurisdiction—control of old and new programs. Radically new pronouncements and policies are often digested with equanimity, but at the slightest hint of a threat to the existing structure, the entire bureaucratic mechanism mobilizes for defense. Almost invariably, the threat is defeated or simply dissolves in fatigue, confusion, and the inevitable diversion of executive energies.

Some top executives shake their heads in despair at the prospect of attacking the DP department again. It seems as firmly dug in as HEW.

As bureaucracy or system size grows, it becomes increasingly complex, specialized, and difficult to understand. Its user community feels increasingly alienated from it, incapable of influencing it. Elliot Richardson, a seasoned bureaucrat, writes in his book *The Creative Balance* [2]:

> Unless we can succeed in [managing complexity] we shall lose our power to make intelligent—or at least deliberate—choices. We shall no longer be self-governing. We shall instead be forced to surrender more and more to an expert elite. We may hope that it is a benevolent elite. But even if it is not we shall be dependent on it anyway. Rather than participating in the process of choice, we shall be accepting the choices made for us.

We will not argue here about whether the DP center is "benevolent." We could argue about whether it is *efficient* and substitute in the above quotation: "We may hope that it is an *efficient* elite. But even if it is not we shall be dependent on it anyway."

PROBLEMS OF SCALE   When human organizations grow too large, they tend to become bureaucratic and inflexible. They interact with their users in a rigid fashion.

Duane S. Elgin of the Stamford Research Institute has studied the growth of human organizations and what he considers to be the limits to growth in their management [3]. He divides their growth into four stages, described in Box 16.1.

In the early stages there are economies of scale. The value of the organization grows more rapidly than its size or cost, as in the portion of Fig. 16.1 labeled *Spring.* A DP organization is likely to improve its effectiveness as it builds up to a

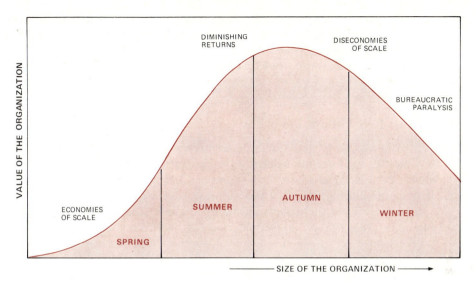

Figure 16.1 Stages of growth of organizations.

certain size and acquires the skills that are needed for efficiency. The slope of Fig. 16.1 increases with increasing organization size.

In the *Summer* of Fig. 16.1 the value of the organization still grows as its size increases, but there are diminishing returns. The curve reaches a point of inflexion after which the slope begins to decrease. The organization is now becoming large and complex. Dealing with the complexity requires increasing overhead costs. The number of interactions between separate decisions and processes would grow approximately as the square of the size of the organization if these decisions and processes were not channeled into more formal structures.

Creative administrators design the channels and procedures for making the growing organization workable. The formality, growing of necessity, brings greater rigidity, greater job specialization, and narrower channels. The enthusiastic inventors and entrepreneurs of the first phase have to be reined in. Standards, regulations, and more paperwork are necessary.

How quickly an organization reaches the top of the hill in Fig. 16.1 varies greatly with the nature of the organization. The top will be reached in organizations of smaller sizes when those organizations are, by their nature, *fast growing, complex* in the number and diversity of elements, *interdependent* in that there is tightness of coupling between the elements and have *complex relations with the outside world.* All of these conditions apply strongly to a DP organization. They supply weekly to many government organizations, and hence these bureaucracies can grow to large sizes and establish rigid patterns before the *Autumn* of Fig. 16.1.

By the *Autumn* the organization is highly preoccupied with its own internal workings. A much smaller proportion of its effort is concerned with the needs of its

BOX 16.1 Four stages of growth of human organizations (From an SRI study by Duane S. Elgin and fellow researchers on the *Limits to the Management of Large, Complex Systems* [3].)

Stage I: High Growth/Era of Faith

The relative level of systems comprehension is high, and the scale, complexity, and interdependence of the bureaucracies are low. There is a strong faith in the efficacy of shared values and goals. There is a belief that these values are part of the natural order and that basic to this system's destiny is the natural unfolding of these values. This is also a period of great vitality, innovation, and energy as economic and socio-political entrepreneurs are the agents of creative expression of this social order. The social leaders have considerable legitimacy, and the high performance of the system speaks of unbounded potentials.

Stage II: Greatest Efficiency/Era of Reason

The relative level of systems comprehension is moderate, and the scale, complexity, and interdependence of the bureaucracies have increased substantially relative to the earlier period. The systems have become sufficiently complicated that their effective functioning is not simply a matter of faith but requires the efforts of a brain trust. Creative, intellectual advisors bring rationality and order into the operations of the systems and become an integral part of leadership.

The level of alienation increases, but this seemingly reflects a consequence of higher geographic and occupational mobility. Rather than a pathological condition, this era seems healthy in comparison to the parochialism of the preceding era. The level of systems performance is still increasing, but the bursts of vitality of Stage I have been replaced by a more methodical planning and implementation process. The costs of coordination and control are beginning to mount but can be kept within tolerable limits by the judicious use of rules and regulations to rationalize, standardize, and simplify operations.

Stage III: Severe Diseconomies/Era of Skepticism

The relative level of systems comprehension is low and dropping rapidly as large, barely comprehensible bureaucracies have grown into largely incomprehensible supersystems. As leaders disavow their responsibility for error and maximize the visibility of their own increasingly modest achievements, the system's constituency becomes increasingly

BOX 16.1 *continued*

disillusioned, apathetic, and cynical. Both faith in the basic soundness of the system and trust in rationality to solve the mounting problems are virtually exhausted.

Leaders are more tolerated than given active support and legitimacy—there seems little alternative than to cynically acquiesce to those leaders who say that they alone have adequate information to truly understand what is happening. Yet, the declining levels of systems performance, the crisis atmosphere that pervades the management of the system, the growing numbers of disturbing events, and the loss of allegiance to basic values create a situation in which consensus falls to very low levels. Decision makers are increasingly unable to cope with complex problems that demand superhuman abilities. Costs and problems of coordination and control are mounting rapidly, and the benefit to the constituency seems to be declining with equal rapidity; consequently, people are less willing to support the actions of the bureaucracy.

The bureaucracy is becoming increasingly rigid, distant, and dysfunctional and yet insists that its constituency conform to its increasingly rationalized and standardized procedures when interacting with the system—thereby reinforcing the apparent inhumanity of the system and further reducing the system's legitimacy. Further, the rigidity of the system engenders a loss of resilience and, coupled with growing perturbations (many of which arise from the counterintuitive and unexpected consequences of ill-considered policy actions), the system seems increasingly vulnerable to disruption.

Stage IV: Systems Crisis/Era of Despair, Then . . . . ?

The relative level of systems comprehension is minimal. The systems are on the verge of chaos and collapse. There is a rapid turnover of leaders, prevailing ideology, and policy solutions—yet nothing seems to work. Every attempt at creating order (short of a highly authoritarian structure) seems overwhelmed by growing levels of disorder. The level of systems cohesion is very low, which, in turn, exacerbates the problem of system's leaders who govern virtually without support.

The rigidified bureaucracy is made somewhat more resilient by the rapid turnover of personnel and policy, but the vulnerability of the system is so high and mounting crises are of such seriousness that whatever additional resiliency has been added to the system is quickly depleted in a grinding, downward spiral into bureaucratic confusion and chaos. The situation becomes simply intolerable and untenable.

users, customers, or public. The comment is made in some venerable universities: "This would be a great place if only we didn't have students!" This bureaucracy solidifies. Since human diversity adds greatly to an organization's complexity a necessary means of coping with complexity is to formalize the human interactions and reduce their diversity. This tends to dehumanize the organization. It becomes less comprehensible to its user, less friendly, more difficult to deal with, often impossible to deal with in nonstandard ways. Try writing a letter to the president of a large credit card company, for example. From 1966 to 1975 the U.S. government spent a fortune on welfare, HEW (Health, Education and Welfare) growing until its budget was greater than the total *national* budget of all but two countries. A Harris poll showed that during the same years the proportion of the public answering "People running the country really don't care what happens to me" rose from 33% to 63%. At the same time health costs skyrocketed and educational test scores dived."

Elgin's SRI study concluded that many government bureaucracies are beginning to exceed our capacity to comprehend, manage, and control them [3].

As Autumn gives way to Winter, the organization is in the grip of bureaucratic paralysis. Few things work as they should. The costs are growing. The value is decreasing. The organization is big, complex, and powerful. Its users are cynical and despair of it. But nobody knows how to get rid of it. It spends much effort protecting itself. Its primary motivation is now to preserve it's own existence.

DISTRIBUTE BEFORE AUTUMN The solution to the problem represented by Fig. 16.1 seems clear. The organization must never be allowed to reach the Autumn of its years. Before that happens it must be split into self-governing fragments that are close to the end users and their problems.

However, it is usually very difficult to break up a large organization. In DP, many programs may have to be rewritten; a centralized data base may have to be restructured. This is often too expensive to be practical.

What is the solution?

The solution is to *plan* for distribution before it becomes vital.

Figure 16.2 illustrates this. The organization should never be allowed to reach the top of the curve. An appropriate time to distribute is at the point of inflexion when the slope of the curve starts to decrease and value starts to grow more slowly. In practice it would be difficult to measure this point, and there are many separate arguments for distribution discussed elsewhere in this book. It is important, however, to design the organization so that later distribution will be practical. In the early stages care is necessary not to take actions or adopt designs that will preclude later distribution. A data base, for example, can be designed in such a convoluted way that it will be nearly impossible to distribute it later on. The early development of data entry at end-user locations will make later distribution easier.

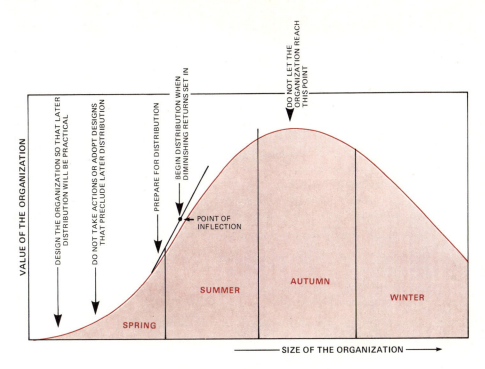

Figure 16.2 If the stages of growth are as in Fig. 16.1 then plan for distribution to take place before diminishing returns set in.

The avoidance of nonstandard teleprocessing will help. Modularization is desirable anyway; do it with future distribution in mind.

　　If the DP strategy says clearly that distribution is coming one day, DP executives will be less likely to build impregnable empires which are designed to prevent distribution at all costs. In many cases the human obstacles to distribution become worse than the technical ones. What is needed is enlightened government which plans to make its colonies self-governing one day and plans an infrastructure that will make this efficient.

　　Many DP organizations (and just about all social organizations) have been planned without any such thought. It is then that revolution may occur. The colonies may try to take matters into their own hands. Distribution by revolution is much less efficient than planned distribution.

　　It is, of course, much easier to plan the distribution of a corporate DP department than to achieve in political reality the distribution of HEW, HUD, the British Post Office, Canada, or most public-sector bureaucracies. Nevertheless, as vast government departments slide into the Winter of Fig. 16.1, one cannot help but feel that eventual fragmentation is the only answer—either geographical distribution or fragmentation into competing entities.

　　As in DP, the critical question is, What is the most creative balance between centralization and decentralization? Human factors tend to make organizations grow too large and corrective forces need to be applied, preferably with prior planning.

Box 16.2 lists some of the problems of a DP organization growing too large. They are problems which restructuring as in Fig. 16.2 will largely solve.

BOX 16.2   Problems of a DP organization growing too large

- Disproportionate growth of the costs of coordination and control.

- Declining overall effectiveness because of increasing complexity.

- Increasing size leads to increasingly formal structures needed to manage the organization.

- Increasingly formal structures lead to rigidity, reluctance to change, and a narrowing span of diversity of innovation.

- Complexity causes internal interactions to grow geometrically.

- It becomes increasingly difficult for an executive to take corrective action or make changes.

- DP staff spends increasing efforts on problems internal to the DP department rather than external to it.

- Increasing dependence on software experts and professionals who are isolated from the end users.

- High number of system crashes and disturbing events due to increasing complexity.

- DP executives frantically trying to keep their noses above water, racing from one problem to the next.

- Political pressures and problems cause emphasis on short-term actions when long-term design and structuring are needed.

- Diminishing end-user ability to influence the directions of computing.

- Diminishing outside participation in DP decision making.

- End users increasingly perceiving the DP department as a priesthood with which only limited communication is possible.

- Increasing feeling of user management that they cannot influence DP and that DP, not themselves, is responsible for what goes wrong. A feeling that they cannot effectively argue with DP when customer statements or orders are fouled up.

BOX 16.2 *continued*

- Increasing job scheduling problems.

- Diminishing comprehension by user departments of the changes that are levied.

- DP users become increasingly critical, disillusioned, and cynical.

- Growing difficulty in measuring the DP organization's true value and return on expenditure. There are no reliable measures of performance.

- DP management protect their organization with complex arguments which external management cannot understand.

- A wrong decision has increasingly far-reaching implications as the interconnected web of systems interactions grows.

- As the complexity of the interactions grows, the likelihood of a failure or narrow decision causing unexpected or counterintuitive side effects becomes greater.

- The corporate vulnerability to a major DP fire, sabotage, or loss of a group of key staff increases.

Often, however, the larger the DP group becomes, the less likely it is to fragment itself as in Fig. 16.2. The power structure wants to retain control.

Top management needs to perceive what is needed and to create the appropriate new structure.

If a central DP organization has the form shown in Fig. 16.2, a question arises: Should the central coordinating DP entity do any application development of its own?

There are usually many central applications to be maintained and many new applications which ought to be centrally developed because they serve multiple departments or serve the corporation as a whole. However, the central coordinating entity could be separate from the central DP application group. The central application group could be one of the lower DP management boxes in Fig. 16.2. The advantage of this is that the group responsible for DDP strategy, design, networks, data administration, and so on, can concentrate on that without being entangled in application problems. The coordinating group is a smaller group, possibly more effective, and possibly more likely to develop an appropriate relationship with top management (Fig. 16.2), whose involvement is so important.

The coordinating group, building the desirable infrastructure, ought to be responsible for the corporation's telecommunications and office of the future systems as well as data processing. So it will be a powerful, vitally important group.

Top management must ensure that the group has the authority and power it needs. In some corporations the peripheral DP groups can take almost no notice of the central DP organization.

REFERENCES

1. C. Northcote Parkinson, *Parkinson's Law,* Houghton Mifflin Co., Boston, 1957; Ballantine Books (paperback), New York, 1964.

2. Elliot Richardson, *The Creative Balance,* Holt, Rinehart & Winston, New York, 1976.

3. Duane S. Elgin, *Limits to the Management of Large, Complex Systems.* Project 4676 prepared for the U.S. National Science Foundation by SRI, Inc., Menlo Park, Ca. 94025, 1977.

PART **IV** DESIGN OF DISTRIBUTED DATA

17 DISTRIBUTED DATA

The question of which configurations make sense in distributed processing is determined to a major extent by what data are used and whether the data should be distributed.

Data, distributed or otherwise, can be kept in one of two forms: in a data base or in a collection of files. We will discuss the difference in Chapter 21 because it can have a major impact on the distribution decisions. The arguments in the chapters prior to Chapter 21 relate to either form.

CATEGORIES OF
DATA DISTRIBUTION

There are a number of types of ways in which data can be distributed and used. Figure 17.1 shows types of data system configuration. The diagrams apply either to file systems or to data base systems, or in some cases to combinations of the two.

The top two diagrams show systems in which the data are centralized. Where multiple hosts are used, these might be either local to the data or remote from it.

The next two diagrams show hierarchical data systems. In the first, labeled *dependent* hierarchical data, the data in the lower-level machines are closely related to those in the higher-level machine. They are often a subset of the higher-level data used for local application. The master copy of the data may be kept by the higher-level machine. When a change is made to the data in the lower machine, this change must be passed up to the higher machine—sometimes immediately, sometimes later in an updating cycle.

In other systems the lower machines may store some of the data that are in the higher machine and also have some which are its own and which are never passed upwards. The lower machines, for example, might keep addresses of and general information about customers. These bulky data are never needed by the higher-level system. However, the higher-level system might store customer numbers, names,

243

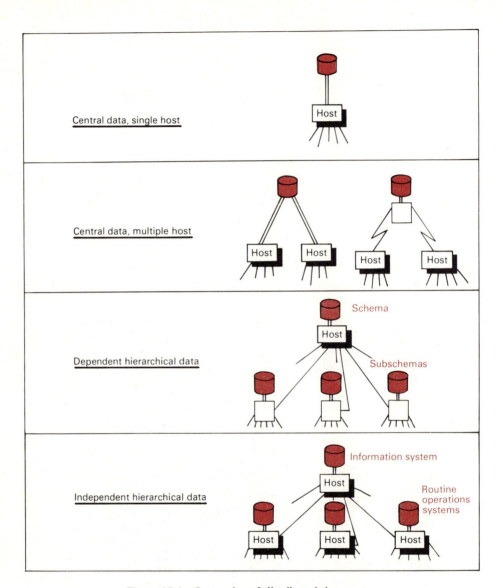

Figure 17.1 Categories of distributed data systems.

credit information, and details of orders. These are also stored by the lower machines, and any modifications to them must be passed upwards.

In the diagram labeled *independent* hierarchical data, all of the processors are independent, self-sufficient data-processing systems. The structure of data in the lower-level machines is probably different from that in the higher-level machine. A

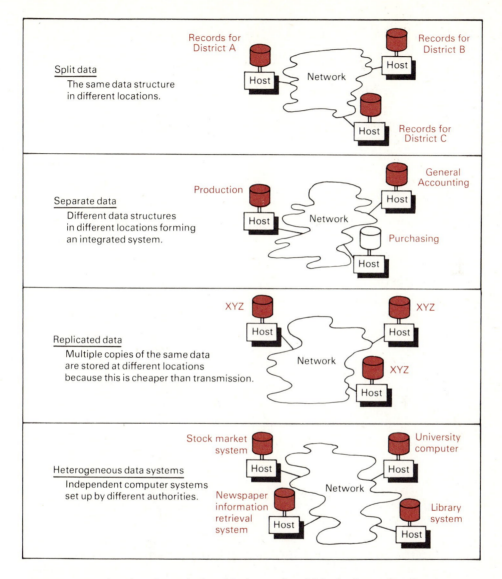

Split data
The same data structure in different locations.

Records for District A
Records for District B
Host
Network
Host
Host
Records for District C

Separate data
Different data structures in different locations forming an integrated system.

Production
General Accounting
Host
Network
Host
Purchasing
Host

Replicated data
Multiple copies of the same data are stored at different locations because this is cheaper than transmission.

XYZ
XYZ
Host
Host
Network
XYZ
Host

Heterogeneous data systems
Independent computer systems set up by different authorities.

Stock market system
University computer
Host
Network
Host
Newspaper information retrieval system
Library system
Host
Host

common example of such a relationship is one in which the lower-level systems are designed for routine repetitive operations such as order entry, production control, inventory, and so on. The high-level machine is an *information system,* possibly at a head office location, designed to answer spontaneous queries from management, planning staff, forecasters, product or strategy designers, etc. All of the data in the higher-level machine may be culled from the lower-level machines, but the data are summarized, edited, and reorganized with secondary indices or other means of searching it to answer spontaneous queries [1].

The next diagram shows a *split data* system. Here there are multiple data systems containing identical data *structures* and formats (but not identical data). The system in District A keeps District A data, that in B keeps B data, and so on. Most of the transactions processed require the data in the system which handles them, but occasionally a transaction originating in one district needs the data in another district. Either the transaction or the data must be transmitted over the network. Some organizations have installed many minicomputers, each with similar split-data files and a network interconnecting them.

We distinguish between a *split-data* and a *separate-data* system. In the former the application programs and data structures are similar in the different systems. The machines are planned and programmed by a common group. In the separate-data configuration the interconnected systems contain different data and different programs and are probably installed by different teams. Nevertheless, they serve the same corporation or government body. One of the computers might be able to request data from another. An end-user terminal might be connectable to all systems.

In the configuration shown, one of the systems handles *production,* another *purchasing,* and the third *general accounting.* These systems are in different locations. The production system, which might be in a factory, creates purchasing requisitions, and these are transmitted to the purchasing system. Both the purchasing and the production system generate data which must be passed to the general accounting system.

Figure 17.2 shows a working example of a separate-data system installed with large computers, and Fig. 17.3 shows one installed with minicomputers. In the former, the computer systems are 300 miles apart, each have their own development staff, and are both connected to terminals throughout North America. The terminals exist in all locations of a large marketing organization. A transaction is relayed to the system it needs by means of the communications concentrators. The two hosts have a link connecting them so that one may use data in the other when necessary. The minicomputer system is more truly "distributed." Here each store has its own minicomputer and data files. These minicomputers communicate with the central *purchasing, marketing,* and *general accounting* systems.

The next diagram in Fig. 17.1 shows replicated data. Identical copies of the data are stored in geographically separate locations, because this duplicate storage avoids the need for high-volume transmission between the systems and is cheaper. Such an organization only makes sense if the volume of updates of the data is low.

An example would be a public data service such as the British Post Office *Prestel* system (originally called *Viewdata*). This makes data available on home or office television sets linked by telephone lines to the system. Multiple copies of the same data will be stored on relatively small local systems. This data will be updated from a central system. Another example is a multinational corporation using data to which inquiries are made in many countries. It is cheaper to store replicated copies in different countries than to handle the inquiries with an international data network.

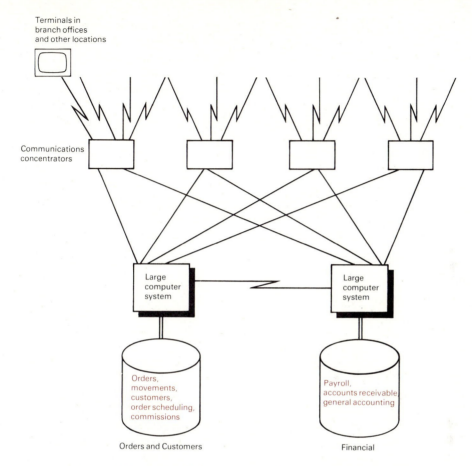

Figure 17.2   An installed example of a large separate-data system.

The last diagram in Fig. 17.1 shows heterogenous data systems—independent computer systems set up by different authorities for different purposes, and interconnected by a general-purpose computer network like ARPANET or the public packet-switching networks. Each computer keeps its own data, and there is no commonality or relationship between the different forms of data organization. A user can access any computer on the network, but he must know the details of how that particular computer's data are organized.

COMBINATIONS   Figure 17.1 illustrates different forms of data distribution which give different problems. Many configurations contain mixtures of these forms. Figure 17.4 shows a typical corporate configuration containing most of them.

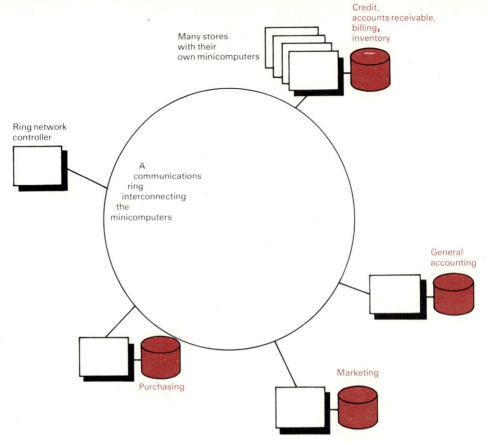

Figure 17.3 A ring network of minicomputers forming both a *separate data* and *split data* system.

SPLITTING CRITERIA Data can be divided within a distributed system according to the following criteria:

1. Geography

2. Type of data

3. Type of usage

1. Geographical division

It may make sense to divide the data geographically when they both originate and are used in given geographical areas. This can result in the various forms of distributed files discussed above. Distribution may or may not increase the total system cost.

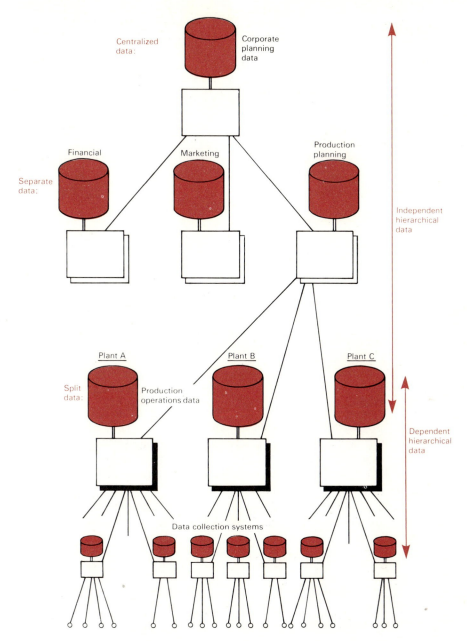

Figure 17.4 The categories of data distribution in Fig. 17.1 are *often combined in one system.*

Reasons for simple geographical *splitting,* as in the fifth diagram of Fig. 17.1, could be as follows:

1. To reduce the total system cost

2. To increase system availability as perceived by the end user. It can protect the user, to some extent, from line failures.

3. To increase the accessibility of the data. Centralized storages can handle a vast quantity of data, but the largest storage units cannot handle a high rate of accesses. A higher rate of accesses can be handled (at a higher cost) with multiple smaller storage units which may or may not be geographically scattered.

4. To give faster response times

5. To permit local users to maintain control over their own data

None of these reasons may be particularly good ones as better networks and better storage hardware come into existence. The disadvantages of splitting the data may be:

1. Substantial increase in total system cost

2. It becomes complex and time consuming to search or process the data as a whole

3. Security procedures may be better and safer at a central location

4. Incompatible data may proliferate, making later integration very difficult

2. Division by type of data

In a large organization, computer systems perform different sets of functions. They may be entirely independent systems. Increasingly, however, telecommunications links are found between them, or one terminal may have access to multiple systems. The data are divided by data type. The advantages of this type of division can be:

1. Local implementation and control are desirable. The head office cannot run the factory data system, because it is too remote from the factory problems.

2. Simplicity: To put all applications on one machine can be highly complex. It is often easier to implement smaller systems.

3. Politics: Local management wants control of its own data processing.

4. Security: The system in Fig. 17.2 was split in case fire or bombs destroyed one computer center. The data could be reconstructed at the other center from log tapes and file dump tapes. Processing vital to the corporation could then continue.

Perhaps the major danger of separate data systems arises when the data are designed in incompatible ways. As we have discussed, many corporations, government departments, and military organizations have a staggering proliferation of incompatible data and a growing need to merge data or develop applications which use data from separate systems. It becomes a Herculean task to clean up the mess, and in most cases the desirable conversion or migration is never performed.

3. Division by type of usage

The distinction is sometimes made between an *operations* or *production* system and an *information* system. An *operations* system is designed for a precisely predefined and limited set of operations. The exact nature and approximate volume of the transactions that will be handled is known when the data structures are designed. In an *information* system the nature of the queries is not known in detail. The data structures are designed to handle spontaneous queries which may differ widely in their nature and may require the data to be searched in various ways.

The Internal Revenue Service, for example, has systems for handling queries and operations relating to individual tax accounts. Such operations are relatively straightforward and entirely preplanned. The IRS also needs an *information system* which will answer *ad hoc* questions for senators and social planners, such as "What percentage of taxpayers with more than three dependents are in a net income bracket less than $6000?" or "What percentage of short-term capital gains taxes from individuals arose from the sale of land?" or "For persons in a gross income bracket between $5000 and $6000 and paying less than 10% of their income in taxes, list the three largest categories of deductions. Repeat this for larger income brackets going up in steps of $1000." Such questions cannot be anticipated in detail, but it may be necessary to answer them fairly quickly. Figure 17.5 shows a configuration with multiple operations systems, possibly handling entirely different applications, passing information to a centralized information system.

Information systems are now becoming more common in corporations as well as government.

In an information system, because the types of queries are not anticipated, lengthy searches through the files may be necessary when the query is made. In an operations system, lengthy searches can generally be avoided because the information is stored in the form in which it is needed.

The two types of systems use data bases which are differently structured, both logically and physically.

Examples of operations systems are

- A banking system with terminals for tellers
- A factory shop floor system
- An airline reservation system
- A sales order entry and inquiry system
- A credit-checking system
- An air traffic control system
- A police emergency system

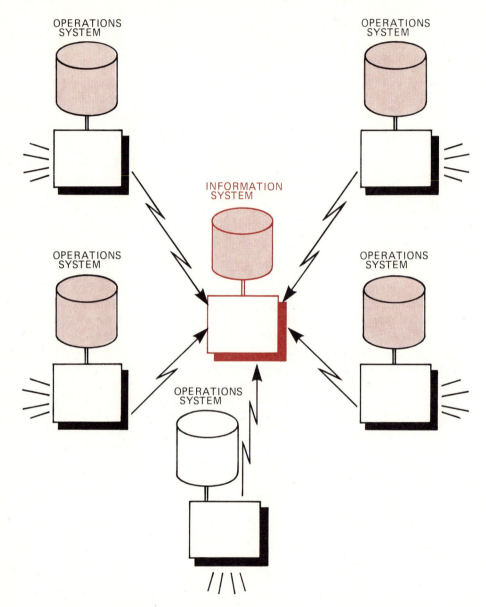

Figure 17.5 Multiple operations systems feeding an information system. The operations systems may be similar (e.g. IRS) or entirely dissimilar (e.g., factory, sales, engineering).

Examples of information systems are

- A library information retrieval system
- A marketing management information system
- A system for searching a litigation data base
- A personnel search data base
- A police detective information system

There are far more operations systems than information systems installed. The cost justification for an operations system is more likely to be *tangible* than that for an information system. Although it is difficult to quantify on an accountant's forms, the value of a good information system is sometimes higher than that of an operations system using the same data, because it enables management to make better decisions. Some information systems have not been of high value. What makes the difference is understanding how information can change a user's job, and this understanding usually must come from *the user*.

MULTIPLE COPIES OF DATA   If processors in more than one location need to use the same data, it is possible that they could each keep their own replicated copy. There are several possible advantages to having more than one copy. First, there is less transmitting of data. The reduction in communication costs may be greater than the increase in storage and possibly processing costs. Some distributed systems have many copies of certain data, one in each location. Second, if one copy is damaged, a duplicate copy exists. Third, system availability as perceived by the end users may be enhanced. Fourth, response time to end users may be improved.

The main disadvantage in having more than one copy, apart from storage cost, is that updating and file reorganization have to be done multiple times. If the data are never updated, this presents no difficulties. The system designer would be concerned mainly with cost: Is it cheaper to have multiple copies or to use telecommunications to access one common copy?

The more frequent the updates, the more the tradeoffs swing away from having replicated data.

PROBLEMS WITH DISTRIBUTED DATA   Distributed data can have a number of problems associated with them. We will describe these problems here and discuss solutions to them later in the book. The problems are such that it is often desirable not to have unconstrained distribution and replication of data.

The problems are as follows:

1. *Interference between updating transactions.* Two transactions may be updating the same data item on a remote storage unit and can interfere with one another, giving incorrect data. This can be prevented by appropriate locks or protocols.

2. *Inconsistent reads.* With more than one copy of data, and sometimes with only one copy of distributed data, inconsistent information can be obtained when reading the data. Sometimes, as a result of timing problems, the data read can be invalid. This can also be prevented with appropriate locks or protocols.

3. *Deadly embrace.* The locking of distributed data to prevent update interference could cause deadlocks unless appropriate (fairly complex) protocols are used.

4. *Protocol overhead.* Unless carefully thought out, the protocols to prevent invalid updates, inconsistent reads, and deadly embrace situations can incur excessive overhead, especially when multiple replicated copies of data are used.

5. *Recovery.* Recovery after failure needs to be controlled so that updates are not accidentally lost or double-processed.

6. *Recovery of multiple copies.* When multiple copies of data exist, they may be in different states of update after a period of failure. They have to be brought back to the same state—resynchronized—but it may be complex to do this while real-time transactions are being processed.

7. *Auditing.* It is difficult on some distributed systems to find out who did what to the data. Appropriate design for auditability is needed.

8. *Security and privacy protection.* Security controls and privacy protection are sometimes poor on distributed systems and need to be built into the basic design.

UPDATE
INTERFERENCE
On any storage system in which records are updated by multiple transactions simultaneously, there is a potential interference problem. Consider two transactions A and B, both of which should add an amount to a given field. The following sequence would result in the field being updated erroneously:

1. A reads the value in the field, x_0.

2. B reads the value in the field, x_0.

3. A updates the value, making it $x_0 + x_A$ and writes it in the storage.

4. B updates the value, making it $x_0 + x_B$, and writes it in the storage.

The final result should have been $x_0 + x_A + x_B$; however, B has overwritten A's update, making it $x_0 + x_B$.

To prevent this type of error, storage management systems usually have a mechanism which permits a transaction to *lock* the record between reading it and writing it so that no other transaction can slip in and cause an erroneous update. It is relatively simple for commands which update a single record, but more complex for commands which cause data to be searched with multiple records updated.

Unfortunately, if the data module which locks the data is remote from the processors which use it, the lock has to remain in force while the read data are transmitted and the updated data are transmitted back. With a high update rate such locks impose an excessive overhead. An alternative method of preventing invalid updates uses transaction timestamps and is discussed in Chapter 20.

When an operation reads two or more records in a distributed environment, it is possible that the data could be in inconsistent states of update. On occasion this can result in invalid data being read. This problem and a solution to it are also discussed in Chapter 20.

DEADLY EMBRACE

A situation which is more difficult to control occurs when the updating process requires two records. Record Y is read, but cannot be updated until record Z is read. Record Y must be locked during the updating process. We therefore have the following sequence of events:

Transaction A: 1. locks record Y.

2. reads record Y.

3. reads record Z.

4. updates record Y.

5. unlocks record Y.

A situation referred to as a *deadly embrace* can occur if another transaction locks record Z and cannot release until it has read record Y. The program for transaction B is as follows:

Transaction B: 1. locks record Z.

2. reads record Z.

3. reads record Y.

4. updates record Z.

5. unlocks record Y.

The two transactions form a deadly embrace as follows:

Transaction A locks record Y.

Transaction A reads record Y.

Transaction B locks record Z.

Transaction B reads record Z.

Transaction A tries to read record Z, but it is locked.

Transaction B tries to read record Y, but it is locked.

Both wait for the records they want to become unlocked, but neither is programmed to release the record it has locked.

Deadlock!

A deadly embrace could apply to whole files. For example, suppose process 1 is using file A and needs file B, but process 2 is using file B and needs file A.

A file or data-base management system must be designed to recognize and correct a deadly embrace situation. When this occurs with distributed data, it is more complex. In the above example, records Y and Z may be in different geographical locations. More complex still, the deadly embrace may relate to more than two transactions, for example:

Transaction A locks record X until it has read Y.

Transaction B locks record Y until it has read Z.

Transaction C locks record Z until it has read X.

Figure 17.6 illustrates these deadly embrace situations.

There are two ways to deal with a deadly embrace problem: First, back out of it when it does happen, and second, prevent it happening at all.

To deal with a deadly embrace the software must detect that a transaction is hung up, and have a means of temporarily terminating one of the programs that is causing the deadlock. It must back out of the activities on the terminated program without affecting the integrity of the stored data. This backing out and the subsequent restart of the program should be done automatically and be transparent to the program itself. To accomplish this the application programs require *synchronization points*. The system saves the transactions following a synchronization point until the program makes a *commitment,* i.e., the data are correctly updated. The system will back out of the deadlocked program to its synchronization point, pause long enough for the other deadlocked transactions to finish, and then restart the program.

This backing out of a deadly embrace can be clumsy and complex in a distributed environment. It is perhaps better to prevent it from happening at all. This can be achieved by timestamping the transactions and ensuring that their data operations are performed in timestamp sequence. This, in effect, is an alternative to locking the data; it is discussed in Chapter 20.

PROBLEMS WITH
DUPLICATE REAL-TIME
COPIES

When the data must be updated in real time, the use of multiple copies presents problems. It would be easy if failures never occurred. In reality there can be many different types of failure, and the system must recover from all of them without losing or harming data.

Suppose that for a period of time one copy of a file is not updated because of failure. The failure is corrected, and now the file must be updated, using either a log

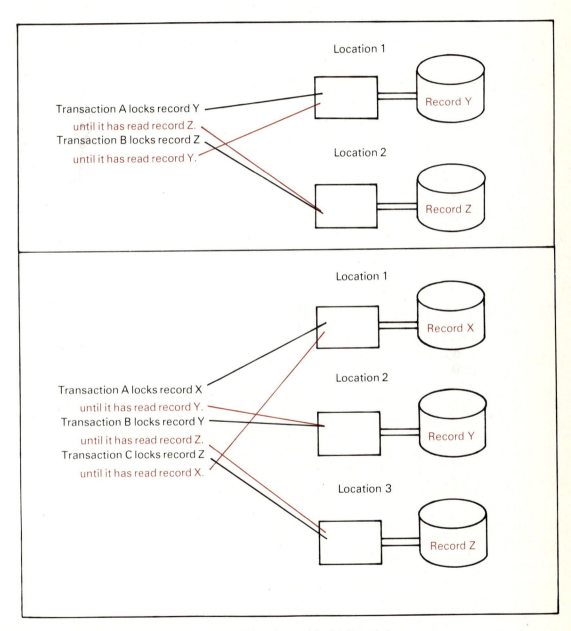

Figure 17.6 Deadly embrace situations with distributed data.

of transactions or the other copies. However, while it is being updated, new transactions are arriving and themselves causing updates. Complex control mechanisms are needed to manage this process of recovery from failure. To make matters worse, there may be another failure during the recovery period.

The situation would be still more complex if different actions are taken when records are updated in a different sequence. There may be restrictions on updating such as a balance that cannot fall below zero, or an overbooking limit that cannot exceed a certain value. Certain values reached in the updating process may trigger exception programs.

SYNCHRONOUS UPDATE CONSTRAINT   Most data network software does not handle real-time updating of multiple data copies satisfactorily when failures occur. Because of this a realistic constraint is suggested for the design of distributed data.

Duplicate copies of the same data should not be used if both (or all) copies have a substantial update rate and the separate versions need to be in real-time synchronization.

Duplicate copies can be used if:

1. They are not updated, or

2. They are updated off-line, or

3. They are updated with single transactions and each transaction is processed to completion with appropriate controls before the processing of the next transaction begins, or

4. The separate copies are not kept in synchronization; one might be updated several hours later than another.

Software has been created for some systems that permits a high level of distribution of replicated data [2]. However, for most of today's commercial data processing, instead of attempting to keep multiple copies in real-time synchronization, it is easier to keep one copy with communications links to it, as in teleprocessing systems prior to the era of distributed processing.

The use of distributed copies of the same data is discussed in Chapters 19 and 20.

REFERENCES

1. James Martin, *Computer Data-Base Organization,* Second Edition, Prentice-Hall, Inc., Englewood Cliffs, N.J., 1977, contains details of techniques for information searching.

2. For example, in the Computer Corporation of America's SDD-1 (System for Distributed Data Base): J. B. Rothnie and N. Goodman, "An Overview of the

Preliminary Design of SDD-1: A System for Distributed Databases,'' 1977 Berkeley Workshop on Distributed Data Management and Computer Networks, Lawrence Berkeley Laboratory, University of California, Berkeley, May 1977. (Also available from Computer Corporation of America, 575 Technology Square, Cambridge, Mass. 02139, as Technical Report No. CCA-77-04.)

18 THE LOCATION OF DATA

One of the most important technical considerations in the design of distributed processing is where the data are located. The arguments about distribution of data are different from those about distribution of processing. Indeed, on some systems the distribution of processing is determined by where the designer decides to locate the data.

This chapter summarizes the considerations which affect the location of data.

COST

First let us comment on costs. The cost per instruction on a microprocessor is much less than that on a large computer, but a similar cost ratio does not apply to storage. There are still substantial economies of scale in storage hardware.

Figure 18.1 illustrates this. Storage of 10 megabytes is an order of magnitude more expensive per byte than storage of a thousand megabytes. There are factors other than the cost per byte stored. Figure 18.1 does not show access times, and the mass-storage devices have much longer access times than the disk units.

The vertical scale of Fig. 18.1 is a long log scale ranging from below $10 to above $1000 per megabyte. The entire curve will drop as technology continues to improve. The part of the curve for small storage units is likely to drop rather faster than the part for large storage units, but major economies of scale will remain.

Figure 18.2 is an estimate of how storage costs will change by the mid 1980's. By then many thousands of bytes will be available in pocket calculators, many millions of bytes of bubble memory in personal desk-top machines, many billions of bytes on disk storage systems, and trillions of bytes in mass-storage (library) units.

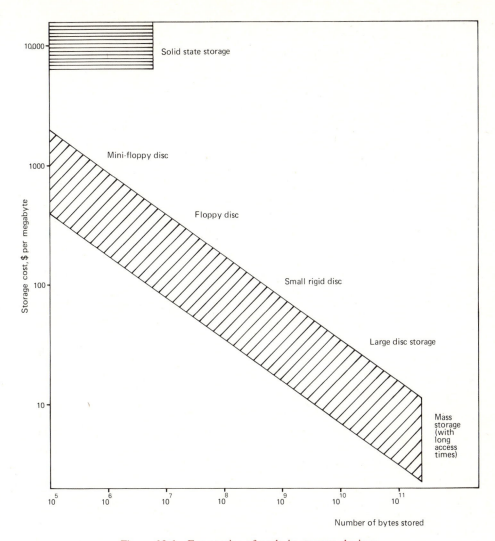

Figure 18.1   Economies of scale in storage devices.

TRADEOFF WITH   In some systems a balance is struck between transmit-
DATA TRANSMISSION   ting data and storing them in peripheral units. When
                        only the cost is considered, we can ask what the trade-
off is between multiple storage units and transmission to one central unit.

In North America, transmission is relatively efficient and cheap. This is a factor for centralization. In parts of the world where transmission is expensive and apt
to break down, this is a factor for decentralization.

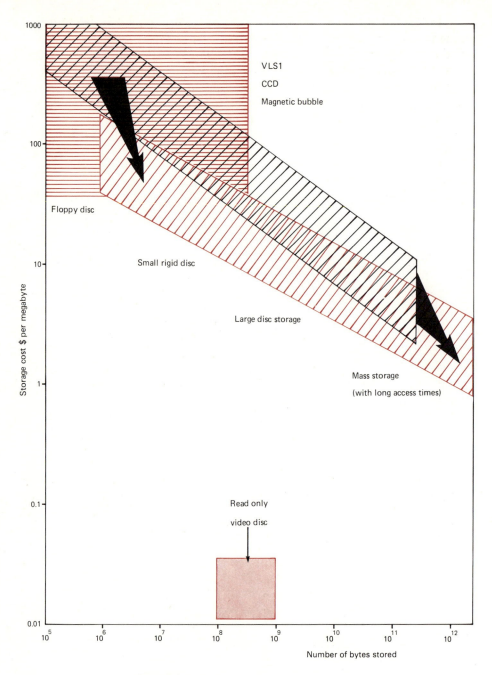

Figure 18.2 Future change in storage costs.

In North America the cost of storing a few million bytes for a week is similar to the cost of transmitting it one thousand miles on fully utilized leased lines. In some European countries it is similar to the cost of transmitting it one hundred miles. Thus if data are to be accessed more than once a week, it would be cheaper to store them locally than to transmit them.

Transmission over public circuits or leased lines of low utilization is more expensive, and the breakeven volume falls (Fig. 18.3). Storage is then cheaper than transmission for all but the smallest amounts of data. This is an economic argument for distributed data.

How much would be stored and how much transmitted varies greatly with the nature of the application. Sometimes the size of transmitted messages is small compared with the size of the data employed. Sometimes data are stored locally until a

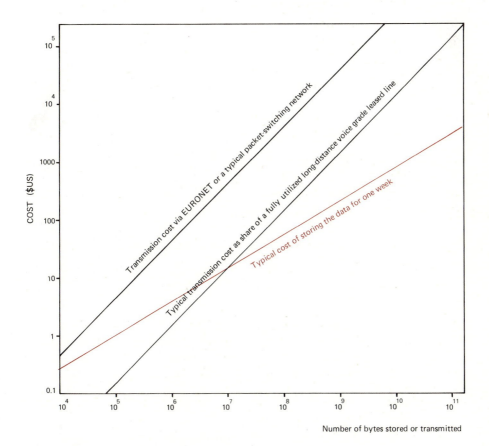

Number of bytes stored or transmitted

Figure 18.3 Relative costs of transmission and storage. The trade-off varies greatly with different types of transmission and usage.

batch of transactions can be sent at once, thus saving transmission costs. They may be stored until there are cheap night telephone rates or until corporate voice circuits are switched over to data at night. The systems designer can estimate the relative costs of centralizing and distributing the storage. Transmission costs and other costs vary greatly, and the tradeoff needs to be evaluated independently for each system.

Over the next ten years transmission costs will not fall as rapidly as storage costs. The *technology* of telecommunications is rapidly falling in cost, but the benefits are not being passed on fully to the user except where lively competition exists between common carriers. Some European countries have experienced rapidly *rising* telecommunications costs from their government telephone administrations, even though the technology costs are dropping rapidly.

Competition, where it is permitted, affects mainly long-distance links, not local links. In the United States the cost of long-distance links has fallen substantially since the early 1970's. Long-distance data transmission links will continue to fall in cost and increase in capacity because of packet-switching networks, improved design of satellite systems (e.g., SBS [1]) competing with new terrestrial facilities (e.g., Bell's L5 carrier, Data Under Voice, Bell's DDS, the specialized carriers, Xerox's XTEN network, digital microwave, and eventually optical fiber systems [2]). At the same time as these transmission improvements, there are revolutionary improvements in switching (packet-switching, computerized circuit switching) and techniques which will make the new data networks accessible at low cost by small users [3].

Because of the fall in cost of long-distance circuits, the price of transmission in some countries is tending to become independent of distance, over a certain range. A 3000-mile link may cost little more than a 300-mile link. If a terminal has to be connected to a remote storage system, there is not much difference in cost between transmitting to distributed storage one hundred miles away and to centralized storage one thousand miles away. In Fig. 18.4 the middle configuration may be less expensive than the top one. It has fewer storage systems (decreasing the cost) and about the same number of point-to-point links. The bottom configuration may be cheaper than the middle one where distributed intelligence can lower the communication costs.

In some types of systems, terminals are much more *clustered* than in Fig. 18.4. Factories or large offices may be interconnected, with many terminals in each. In this case the data they use may be stored locally in a factory or office system. Again the data used by many terminals in a city may be stored at that city, and different city systems then linked.

In general the drop in both storage costs and long-distance communication costs will give the designer more freedom to choose where he locates the data. Increasingly he will make this choice on a basis *other* than merely storage hardware cost, as indicated below.

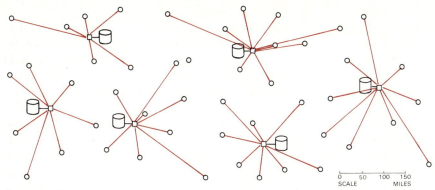

Where communication costs do not vary greatly with distance, the above configuration is likely to be more expensive than that below, because of economies of scale in storage units.

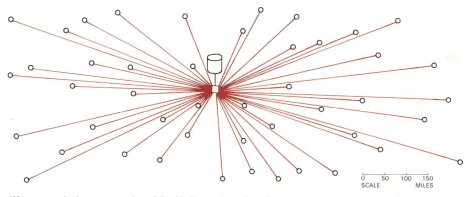

Where communication costs vary substantially with distance, the configuration below will reduce the cost.

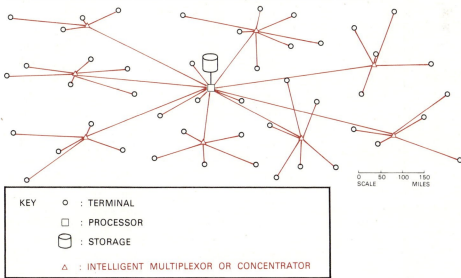

KEY	○	: TERMINAL
	□	: PROCESSOR
	⬡	: STORAGE
	△	: INTELLIGENT MULTIPLEXOR OR CONCENTRATOR

Figure 18.4

REASONS FOR DECENTRALIZING DATA

If the technology cost permits, it often makes sense to store the data *where they are used*.

It has been shown repeatedly that when user departments regard files of data as "our data" and have full responsibility for data entry and accuracy, the integrity of the data is higher. In many installations data entry and storage have reverted from being a central DP function to a function under full control of the using department, and the accuracy of the data has improved greatly.

There are properties inherent in certain data which lead naturally to decentralization, and properties in other data which lead naturally to centralization. Boxes 18.1 and 18.2 list these.

The main property favoring decentralization is that the data are used at one peripheral location and are rarely or never used at other locations. Much of the information in a branch office (for example, client addresses) is of no use anywhere but that branch office. However, other information generated in a branch office is needed elsewhere (for example, customer orders which are needed in manufacturing plants, sales figures which are needed for central purchasing, or insurance company policy figures which are needed for actuarial calculations in the head office).

Another property of data that leads naturally to distribution is that the files are simple and are used only by one or a few applications. There is no need for the complexities of data-base operations.

BOX 18.1   Properties inherent in certain data which lead naturally to decentralization.

1. The data are used at one peripheral location; they are rarely or never used at other locations. To transmit such data for storage may be unnecessarily complex and expensive.
2. The accuracy, privacy and security of the data is a local responsibility.
3. The files are simple and are used by one or a few applications. Hence there would be little or no advantage in employing data base software.
4. The update rate is too high for a single centralized storage system.
5. Peripheral files are searched or manipulated with an end-user language which implicitly results in inverted list or secondary key operations. Too many end user operations of this type can play havoc with the performance of a central system. They may be better located in a peripheral system with end users responsible for their usage and costs.

BOX 18.2 Properties inherent in certain data which lead naturally to centralization.

1. Data is used by centralized applications such as a corporate-wide payroll, purchasing, or general accounting.
2. Users in all areas need access to the same data and need the current up-to-the-minute version. The data are frequently updated. Data may be centralized to avoid the problems of real time synchronization of multiple copies with a high update level.
3. Users of the data travel among many separate locations, and it is cheaper to centralize their data than to provide a switched data network.
4. The data as a whole will be searched. They are part of an **information system** which will provide answers to spontaneous queries from users, many of which can only be answered by examining many records. Searching data which is geographically scattered is extremely time consuming. The software and hardware for efficient searching require the data to be in one location. Secondary indices may be used and the indexing software refers only to data in one storage system.
5. The data structures are designed to serve multiple applications and to be used with data base software giving the advantages discussed in Chapter 21. For reasons of efficiency and complexity this software operates today on centralized rather than geographically scattered data.
6. A high level of security is to be maintained over the data. The protection procedures may be expensive, possibly involving a well guarded, secure vault, and tight control of authorized users. The data are better guarded if they are in one location, with external backup copies, than if they are scattered.
   Catastrophe protection is often an argument for bicentral systems rather than for single centralized storage.
7. The data are too bulky to be stored on inexpensive peripheral storage units. The economies of scale of centralized bulk storage are desirable.
8. To make systems auditable, details are sometimes kept of what transactions updated certain data. It may be cheaper, and more secure, to dump these in a large centralized archival storage unit.

Another reason for storage of a certain body of data in a user department is that users search it or employ it in an "information system" mode. This may require secondary indices, inverted files, or data structures different from those in the central machine. The time taken to search such data to handle user queries may be substantial, and it is better done in the end user's own minicomputer. There, it does not play havoc with the performance of the central machine, and central machine scheduling does not interfere with the users' employment of their own data. The user department is in charge of how much time it uses in information system searches.

There is much to be said for getting end-user information system activities out of a production-oriented mainframe and leaving the users free to employ the data in their own way.

**REASONS FOR
CENTRALIZING DATA**   Box 18.2 lists properties of data which lead naturally to centralization.

On many systems data exist which are of both types: naturally centralized and naturally kept locally. Much of the information in a branch office (for example, client addresses) is of use anywhere but that branch office. However, other information generated in that branch office is needed in centralized information or control systems or centralized applications such as purchasing or production control.

A property of data which argues strongly for centralization is that the data are being constantly updated and referred to by multiple users in different geographical locations. The users need to have an up-to-the-minute picture of the data as a whole, and the data are being modified by users in different locations. One copy of the data is therefore kept in one place. This is done on reservation systems for airlines, hotels, and rented cars. It is done on inventory control systems, military early warning systems, credit checking systems, and so on.

Data to which many inquiries are made could be distributed if the data are updated only infrequently, if the data given to the inquirers can be a few hours old rather than up-to-the-second, or, possibly, if the updates come from only one source. In a national information service, such as Prestel [4] (formerly Viewdata), in which a wide variety of encyclopedic information is made available on television sets, the data can be replicated in many locations. If there are a large number of references to it, this will save transmission costs. The data are updated infrequently from a central source. A stock market system giving the current stock prices and other information could employ multiple replicated copies of the same data. The updates are frequent but come from a single source.

Figure 18.5 tabulates different usage and update patterns and indicates where these patterns would be better served with centralized data.

If a user always employs terminals at the same location, it might be possible to store the data of interest to him at that location. If users move geographically, then

		USERS			
		USERS ARE IN ONE LOCATION		USERS ARE GEOGRAPHICALLY DISPERSED	
UPDATES		UP-TO-THE-SECOND INFORMATION REQUIRED	INFORMATION PROVIDED CAN BE HOURS OLD	UP-TO-THE-SECOND INFORMATION REQUIRED	INFORMATION PROVIDED CAN BE HOURS OLD
INFREQUENT UPDATES	UPDATES FROM ONE SOURCE	ONE LOCATION		DATA CAN BE DISPERSED WITH UPDATES DISTRIBUTED VIA A NETWORK	
	UPDATES FROM GEOGRAPHICALLY DISPERSED SOURCES	DATA IS CENTRALIZED AT THE LOCATION OF THE USERS		DATA IS CENTRALIZED OR DISPERSED WITH UPDATES DISTRIBUTED VIA A NETWORK	DATA CAN BE DISPERSED WITH UPDATES DISTRIBUTED BY BATCH TRANSMISSION
FREQUENT UPDATES	UPDATES FROM ONE SOURCE	ONE LOCATION			
	UPDATES FROM GEOGRAPHICALLY DISPERSED SOURCES	DATA IS CENTRALIZED AT THE LOCATION OF THE USERS		DATA IS CENTRALIZED	DATA IS CENTRALIZED OR DISPERSED WITH UPDATES DISTRIBUTED BY BATCH TRANSMISSION

Figure 18.5 The pattern of usage and updates may determine whether data is centralized or dispersed. A high rate of updates from dispersed sources and differently dispersed users needing up-to-the-second data, is an argument for centralization.

either the data must be centralized or a means of switching must be employed to connect a user to the system which contains data relevant to him. In a bank with many branches customer records might be stored at the branch which holds their account. A major advantage of banking automation, however, is that customers can use *any* branch. Many banking systems with distributed intelligence therefore have centralized customer record storage. Customer transactions may be stored locally and transmitted to the center at appropriate intervals. Possibly only balances and account restrictions will be stored centrally, as this would be enough to serve most of a customer's demands when he is in a branch other than his own. It is likely that only a small fraction of all customer visits are to branches other than their home branch, so a switching mechanism might route non-home-branch transactions to the home-branch computer when necessary.

Different patterns of use often exist in the same system. Because of this, some data in the same system may be centralized and some decentralized.

In an airline reservation system the majority (often 90%) of the messages are for information about flights and seat availability. This is a small fraction of the total data and could easily be stored at the terminal location. Other data, particularly passenger booking records, occupy much more space. Bookings for a specific flight would all go to one location where that flight is controlled. This location might be a central computer, but not necessarily; different flights might be controlled by distributed computers close to where the most bookings for the flights originate (especially on worldwide airlines). The computer which controls the flight would send messages to the terminal computers when the booking level on the flight became critical. It would keep the seat availability records of the terminal computers up to date. This form of operation would have various advantages over a fully centralized system: low telecommunications costs, low response times, better reliability. It is interesting to note that it is closer to the way airlines operated before the introduction of today's centralized reservation systems.

OTHER REASONS FOR CENTRALIZED DATA   Other properties of data that favor centralization are listed in Box 18.2.

One is bulk. The data occupy a sufficiently large volume that the economies of scale of large storage units are desirable.

Another is security. Highly professional security is needed for certain data. These are usually a small proportion of all the data in a corporation. Their protection procedures may involve a fireproof, bombproof, intruderproof vault, possibly with the storage unit inside it accessible via coaxial cable. Guards are used at the secure location, as is a security officer who is responsible for tightly, programmed controls on access to the data [5]. A corporation may have more than one secure storage location. Catastrophe protection is often an argument for *bicentral* systems.

There is a strong argument for centralization when the data have to be searched as whole. Secondary key operations may have to be performed in order to answer certain types of user questions. The data organization may be part of an *information* system which will provide answers to spontaneous queries from users, many of which can only be answered by examining many records. Excellent software is available for these types of operations, but it requires the data in question to be in one machine. Searching or secondary key operations on geographically scattered data would be very time-consuming and inefficient. To improve the performance of information systems, hardware is likely to become available to assist in associative or secondary key operations. Again this will require the data to be in one machine. The one machine could be centralized as in Fig. 18.5, or peripheral as with small, functional information systems.

Only a small proportion of the data in an organization needs searching or secondary key operations. This will often be transmitted from distributed systems to specialized information systems.

DATA BASE   A powerful reason for centralizing data today is to be able to use data-base management rather than file storage. Chapter 21 discusses the advantages of data-base operations. If data-base technology is used correctly, it should lead to higher-level of automation of application development and much greater flexibility in adapting systems to the changing needs of users.

Software which performs functions well enough to obtain the full advantage of data-base operation has often required larger computers. Data-base systems have therefore been centralized or multicentered. In the future, as minicomputers grow in power, data-base operations will be performed on machines of lower cost and will spread to more end-user locations. A major marketing need of minicomputer manufacturers is the automation of application development that will be derived from data-base systems. Data-base systems obtain results by interlinking many types of record (segment). To be effective, the right types of record must be gathered together in one system.

REFERENCES

1. Further information is available from Satellite Business Systems, McLean, Va. 22101.

2. Explained in James Martin, *Future Developments in Telecommunications,* Second Edition, Prentice-Hall, Inc., Englewood Cliffs, N.J., 1977.

3. Explained in James Martin, *Computer Networks and Distributed Processing,* Technology Insight Foundation, Inc., Weston, Conn., 1978.

4. Further information on Prestel is available from the British Post Office, London, England.

5. James Martin, *Security, Accuracy, and Privacy in Computer Systems,* Prentice-Hall, Inc., Englewood Cliffs, N.J., 1974.

19 MULTIPLE COPIES OF DATA

Many distributed systems have two copies or multiple copies of the same data. When this is so, care is needed in planning the updates and the recovery from failures. Restart and recovery can present problems if the data are being continuously updated. This chapter and the next discuss the control of duplicate or multiple copies of data, and they indicate that there are circumstances when multiple copies should be avoided.

Box 19.1 summarizes the reasons for having more than one distributed copy of the same data.

TWO PHILOSOPHIES   As with other aspects of distributed systems, there are two types of design approaches: centralized and decentralized.

The normal and most easily controllable approach is to have a single, secure *master copy* of the data. The other replicated copies are regarded as secondary to the master copy. The system is designed so that if the master copy is destroyed, it can be reconstructed. Different data each have a single master copy, but these could be stored in different locations.

The other approach is for data to be stored in multiple nodes, no one of which is of higher status than the others. The updates go to every copy. Often they cannot be updated simultaneously, so the protocols are designed so that the system converges to a state in which every copy is the same. No one copy is designated a "master" copy.

The latter, *horizontal* approach needs elaborate, carefully thought out protocols to deal with the various failures, update interference, and deadlock conditions that can occur. Most available software for distributed systems does not contain such protocols but relies instead on a master copy approach.

This chapter discusses the master copy approach. The following chapter discusses horizontal, freely distributed data.

BOX 19.1   Reasons for multiple distributed copies of data

A system may be designed with more than one copy of the same data in different locations for any of the following reasons:

1. Transmission costs

   It may be cheaper to have replicated copies than to transmit data over long distances.

2. Response time

   Access to local, rather than remote, data may significantly improve the response time.

3. Availability

   Access to local data or to alternate copies of data may significantly increase the availability of the data.

4. Security

   Two or more copies may be used in case one copy is destroyed. (The term "survivability" is used in the military to imply that data are still accessible after multiple copies of them have been destroyed.)

5. Data organization

   The same data may be organized differently in different machines, for example, in a production system and information system.

6. Conversion expense

   Old existing files may be preserved after data bases or distributed systems are implemented because of the cost and time of converting their programs to work with the new data structures.

   Problems arise in controlling the integrity of multiple copies when the data fall into certain classes. See Box 19.2.

MASTER COPY UPDATING   When a master copy of data is used, it may or may not be updated in real time. Two approaches are practical:

1. • All transactions immediately update the master.
   • The master issues new copies of changed records to other processors periodically.
2. • Transactions update a nonmaster file.

- All transactions are saved for periodic updating of the master.
- When the master is updated, new copies of changed records are sent to other processors which use them.

After a failure of part of the system, resynchronization is achieved by issuing new copies of any changed records in the master to the processors which keep them. If the master itself fails, then copies of transactions must be kept until it recovers so that it can be updated, and then in turn issue copies of the changed records to other processors which keep them.

In practice it is more reasonable to keep two copies than many copies of data which are frequently updated. This is commonly done on hierarchical systems. When the volume of changes is not too great, a central system sometimes broadcasts copies of master data to multiple local processors.

CONFIGURATIONS

There are various possible configurations in which two or more copies of the same data may be arranged. Figure 19.1 illustrates these. In each there is one (and only one) master copy of the data. The procedures for restart, recovery, and maintenance of integrity differ with the different configurations. The diagrams in Fig. 19.1 should be regarded as *logical* configurations; they could be implemented with a diversity of physical configurations. The diagrams avoid showing the network or other details of the links among the data.

UPDATE RESPONSIBILITY

It is desirable that one processor should be responsible for each item of data at any time. This responsibility includes the time when the data item is moving between nodes. The processor in question is responsible for updating the data and for security, accuracy, and privacy of the data.

The processor which is responsible for updating the data is not necessarily the one which stores the master copy of the data. The top row in Fig. 19.1 illustrates situations with two copies of the same data.

In the first diagram the updating is done by the central machine, which also maintains the master copy of the data. The peripheral machines contain the same data (or some of them) but do not update them. Users of the peripheral machines may display the data, make inquiries, search the data, use report generators, employ the data in programs, and use information system software with secondary indices, inverted lists, etc. This activity can have fast response times and high availability, can avoid interfering with the central machine, and in general can have the advantages we have listed for decentralized activities.

When the data are updated, copies of the updates will be sent to the peripheral machines. This may be done in real time if up-to-the-second data are needed.

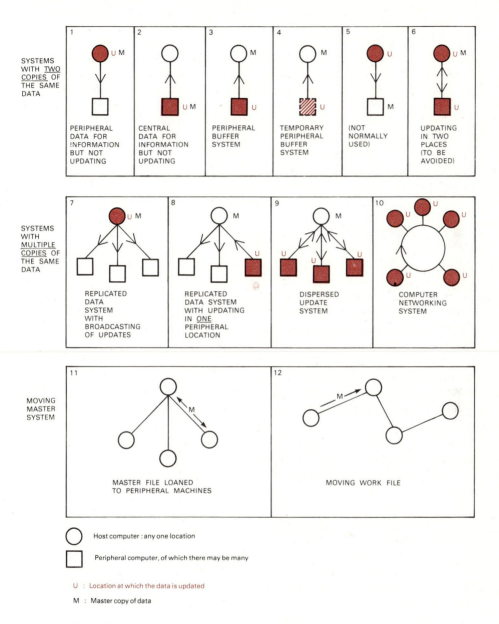

SYSTEMS WITH TWO COPIES OF THE SAME DATA

1 | U M — PERIPHERAL DATA FOR INFORMATION BUT NOT UPDATING

2 | U M — CENTRAL DATA FOR INFORMATION BUT NOT UPDATING

3 | M / U — PERIPHERAL BUFFER SYSTEM

4 | M / U — TEMPORARY PERIPHERAL BUFFER SYSTEM

5 | U / M — (NOT NORMALLY USED)

6 | U M / U — UPDATING IN TWO PLACES (TO BE AVOIDED)

SYSTEMS WITH MULTIPLE COPIES OF THE SAME DATA

7 | U M — REPLICATED DATA SYSTEM WITH BROADCASTING OF UPDATES

8 | M / U — REPLICATED DATA SYSTEM WITH UPDATING IN ONE PERIPHERAL LOCATION

9 | M / U U U — DISPERSED UPDATE SYSTEM

10 | U U U U U U — COMPUTER NETWORKING SYSTEM

MOVING MASTER SYSTEM

11 | M — MASTER FILE LOANED TO PERIPHERAL MACHINES

12 | M — MOVING WORK FILE

○ Host computer : any one location

□ Peripheral computer, of which there may be many

U : Location at which the data is updated

M : Master copy of data

Figure 19.1 Configurations with two or more copies of the *same* data.

275

Usually there is not this urgency, and the updates may be sent to the peripheral machines in batches or at night.

PERIPHERAL MASTERS   The second diagram in Fig. 19.1 is the converse of the first. The peripheral machines keep the master copies and are responsible for updating and integrity of the data. User departments may have been given full responsibility for their own data. The data (in whole or part) also reside with the central machine, where they are used for other purposes—for centralized applications or as part of a management information system. Updates to data are sent to the center in real time or, more likely, in batches or at night.

SEPARATION OF UPDATE AND MASTER RESPONSIBILITY   Diagram 3 in Fig. 19.1 represents the case where the update responsibility is in a different machine from the master copy. Records are created, updated, and stored in machines at user locations. The data are relayed to a central machine which maintains the master copy.

An example would be an insurance system in which local offices are responsible for their own data entry about customers, policies, and claims. They maintain their own files, but the data are also sent to head office for storage and for use in different applications.

In some cases the peripheral machine does substantial processing; in others it does little more than buffer the data after data entry. The configuration might be referred to as a *peripheral buffer system*. Diagram 4 in Fig. 19.1 represents a system in which the files reside only temporarily in the peripheral storage—*a temporary peripheral buffer system*. The data are entered and checked at a user location and then shipped, possibly at night, to the center.

For completeness, the fifth diagram shows the master copy being stored peripherally but updated centrally. This is unlikely to be done in practice.

UPDATES IN TWO PLACES   Diagram 5 in Fig. 19.1 shows the same data being updated both at the central machine and at the local machine. This double updating introduces a number of problems which make data integrity difficult to achieve. We will discuss them shortly and will comment that for most commercial data processing *it is best to avoid configurations where the data items are updated in more than one place.*

MORE THAN TWO COPIES   When *more than two* copies of the same data exist, it is generally desirable that the master copy should reside on a central machine.

Diagram 7 in Fig. 19.1 shows a *replicated data system*. The same data exist in many locations where they can be used but not updated. Updates take place at one location only. The multiple copies may be in different end-user locations, different geographical locations, or different countries. The use of multiple copies improves response time and availability and lowers telecommunications costs. Users or local computer centers may be permitted to do anything they want with their copy of the data but are prevented from gaining access to the central master copy. If they need to update or change the master data, they send a message to the central computer requesting the change, and the central computer controls all updates.

Diagram 8 is a variant on Diagram 7 which is less likely to be used. Here a peripheral location updates the data. Possibly different peripheral locations are responsible for different data. The changes are sent to the location keeping the master copy. When this is updated, the changes are transmitted to all peripheral copies.

MULTIPLE UPDATE LOCATIONS   There are systems in which the same data are stored in many locations and the updates originate in many locations. It is difficult and complex to control the correctness of the updating unless *the updates are applied to a single copy of the data,* which usually resides with a central machine and is the master copy, as in Diagram 9. This means that a common location is in fact doing the updating (as in Diagram 7), but the peripheral locations request the updates. The results of the updates are then distributed to the peripheral machines.

Diagram 10 shows multiple computers attached to a network. Certain data items may be contained in each of them, and each of them is required to update certain data. This is a complex situation. It can be handled with complex distributed storage protocols as indicated in the following chapter. Most commercial software is not designed to operate in a free-for-all distributed data environment. Instead *one machine* must tightly control each type of data. This is similar to the centralized configuration of Diagram 9, except that now different types of data have their master copies on different types of machines.

Each machine in Diagram 10 might control *different* data. This is the case with an airline booking system in which the reservation computers of different airlines are connected to a common network. The booking of one journey may involve two or more airlines. Booking requests therefore have to be sent from one airline computer to another. But each controls the booking of its own set of seats. To lessen the traffic flow the controlling computer for a flight may allow the others to book up to a certain number of seats without first asking permission of the controlling computer. Details of the booking (or cancellation) are then sent to the controlling computer. When the flight is close to being fully booked, the computer controlling that flight changes the rules and every seat booked must be done by means of a request to the controlling computer.

The point is that *to achieve data integrity one machine must control the up-*

dating even though the data reside, and the requests to change those data originate, in multiple machines.

MOVING MASTERS   A further complication arises when the master copy and responsibility for updating it moves from one machine to another.

In Diagram 11 in Fig. 19.1, a host may lend a data item to a local processor for a time. During that time it relinquishes the authority to update that data item. It may flag the data item to indicate this. The local machine assumes responsibility for the borrowed data item. When the local machine has finished, it returns control to the central machine and deletes or flags the data item in its own store.

When the local machine has responsibility for updating the item, inquiries about the item may be handled by the central machine as in Diagram 2. The local machine therefore sends details of updates it makes to the central machine.

An example is an organization which maintains a pool of large machinery such as bulldozers and excavators. The machinery is assigned to units which keep their own records and minicomputers. When one unit has finished with a bulldozer, it may be assigned to a different unit. Maintenance records for the bulldozers are complex and need to be updated by the unit which has the bulldozer. The records are transferred with the bulldozer, but a copy of these records is kept at the central location.

Diagram 12 relates to a system in which a file is passed from one computer to another. Data items are updated in a dependent fashion by a succession of machines.

An example is taken from a Swedish report [1]. It describes a system which supports government enforcement of ecology legislation. A company might ask for permission to build a pipeline. The data are forwarded to a municipality, and a "timer request" is stored to ensure a reaction if the municipality is late in answering. Eventually the data are returned and permission refused. The company appeals to the county, which then has the data transmitted to *its* computer. The government process continues, in the words of the report, *"ad libidum"* until finally the data reposes in the vast archives of a large computer.

STATIC AND   There are two characteristics of data that we should
DYNAMIC DATA   add to the diagrams, which affect the control procedures. First, data may be static or dynamic. By *static* we mean unchanging or only slowly changing. No data are completely unchanging, but some, like customer names and addresses, may change very infrequently. These data present little problem in controlling integrity.

In Fig. 19.1 we used arrows to show the flow of updated data items to the other copies of data. We will now use a single arrow to indicate a very low rate of updates, in other words, static data; we will use two arrows to mean dynamic data with a fairly low rate of update; and three arrows to mean dynamic data with a high update rate. Thus:

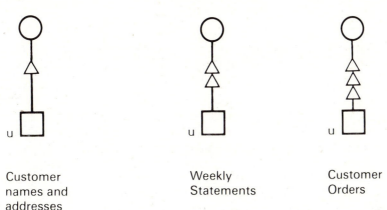

Customer
names and
addresses

Weekly
Statements

Customer
Orders

**REAL TIME AND
NONREAL TIME**

Some data need to be kept current, up to the second. It is more difficult to maintain integrity with real-time data than with data which can be brought up to date periodically.

When updates need to be transmitted to the duplicate copies of data *immediately,* we will write "R" (for *real-time*) by the update arrow. When updates can be deferred for a time and sent in a batch, we will write "B" (for *batch*) by the arrow. Thus:

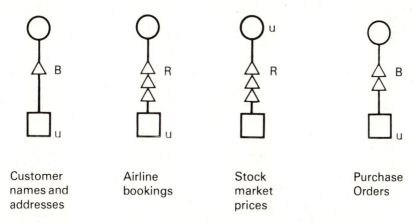

Customer
names and
addresses

Airline
bookings

Stock
market
prices

Purchase
Orders

**MULTIPLE DATA
PATTERNS**

One system often has more than one pattern of data. The logical diagrams we have drawn provide a useful way to summarize the multiple data patterns. Figure 19.2 illustrates this. The top diagram in Fig. 19.2 illustrates an insurance company, for example, which has local office files. The master copies of most of the files are kept at the head office. The bulky storage of customer names, addresses, and

AN INSURANCE COMPANY WITH DISTRICT OFFICE PROCESSORS

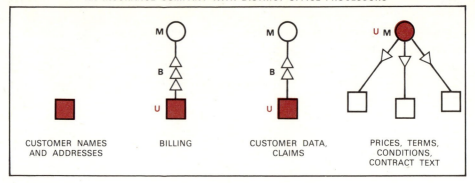

| CUSTOMER NAMES AND ADDRESSES | BILLING | CUSTOMER DATA, CLAIMS | PRICES, TERMS, CONDITIONS, CONTRACT TEXT |

A BANK WITH PROCESSORS IN THE BRANCHES

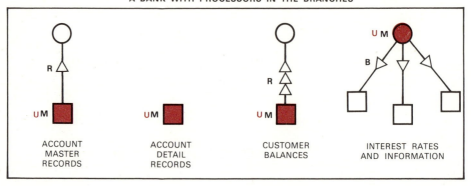

| ACCOUNT MASTER RECORDS | ACCOUNT DETAIL RECORDS | CUSTOMER BALANCES | INTEREST RATES AND INFORMATION |

A RETAIL STORE CHAIN WITH PROCESSORS IN THE STORES

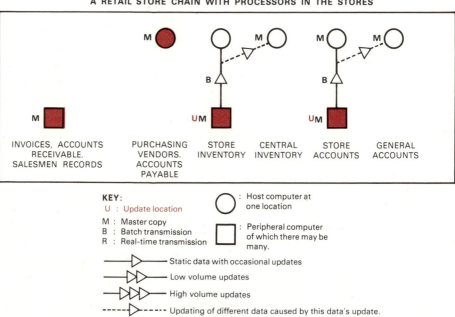

| INVOICES, ACCOUNTS RECEIVABLE. SALESMEN RECORDS | PURCHASING VENDORS. ACCOUNTS PAYABLE | STORE INVENTORY | CENTRAL INVENTORY | STORE ACCOUNTS | GENERAL ACCOUNTS |

KEY:
U : Update location
M : Master copy
B : Batch transmission
R : Real-time transmission

◯ : Host computer at one location

▢ : Peripheral computer of which there may be many.

▷ Static data with occasional updates
▷▷ Low volume updates
▷▷▷ High volume updates
------▷------ Updating of different data caused by this data's update.

Figure 19.2 Diagrams showing the logical distribution of data.

details is done entirely at the local offices (so backup and recovery for these is local responsibility). Billing records are created at the local office and transmitted to the head office in batches. Details of claims and those details of customers required by the head office are entered and stored at the local offices and transmitted intermittently to the head office. Insurance prices, terms, conditions, and text of contracts are created at the head office and transmitted periodically for storage in the local files.

The second diagram shows a bank and the third diagram a retail store, with distributed data.

DESTRUCTION OF THE MASTER

Catastrophic destruction of the master copy of data should be planned for. It might be destroyed by fire, flooding, accident (possibly by dropping a disk pack), or by malice or sabotage. It must be possible to reconstruct the data. To do so a copy of it is stored periodically in a location distant from the master copy. Transactions which update the master copy must also be stored. These can then be used to reconstruct the master copy.

In systems with a central master copy the data stored in peripheral machines may be designed for reconstruction of the master. In systems with peripheral masters these will be reconstructed from the data at the center. At certain points in time, sometimes at night, the nonmaster data will be made identical to the master. This time is sometimes referred to as the *synchronization point*. Between synchronization points the updates will be logged so that if the master is destroyed, it can be reconstructed.

Security of distributed data is discussed further in Chapter 36.

CLASSES OF UPDATES

With certain types of data there is little or no concern about integrity problems caused by having multiple copies. This is because the data are rarely updated, the updates are not time-critical, or the updates are simple—simply replacing one customer address with another, for example. With other data the updates have to be carefully and tightly controlled.

Box 19.2 lists five classes of data, graded according to the complexity of the updates. The techniques for controlling updates, the recovery procedures, and the desirability of replicating data differ from one data class to another.

Class 0 contains data which do not change or which are added to or replaced very infrequently. Much of the world's data are in this class—the books in libraries, street names and towns, historical data, encyclopedic information, much of the data that would be made available on a public information retrieval system. They can be replicated with impunity on many nodes of a system if that lowers the overall cost of obtaining adequate user facilities.

Class 1 contains data which are updated by simply replacing certain values or adding new records. If a transmission line or machine fails, the update can be sim-

BOX 19.2   Five classes of data

Different update and recovery techniques may be applied with the different classes.

CLASS 0: UNCHANGING DATA

> Data which are never or only infrequently changed.

> EXAMPLES: Town names and streets, technical report abstracts, encyclopedic information, historical information.

CLASS 1: DATA WHICH ARE UPDATED BY SIMPLE RE-PLACEMENT

> Data with simple updates of such a nature that *if they are performed twice, no harm is done.* Or data which are upgraded by adding new and separate records.

> EXAMPLES: Customer names and addresses, airline timetables, price lists, stock market prices and ratios, statistical data, personnel data.

CLASS 2: DATA WITH INDEPENDENT, NONREPEATABLE UP-DATES

> Data with updates which *cannot be applied twice* but which are *independent of any other updates.* The updates can take place at any time (within limits).

> EXAMPLE: Bank account balance (which is allowed to become negative in the system). The update adds to or subtracts from the amount. The update is nonrepeatable because a bank account must not have the same transaction applied to it twice. If the update is delayed (but not lost), data integrity is not harmed.

> CONTROL TECHNIQUE: The update transactions may have serial numbers to ensure that no transaction is lost or double-processed.

ply reapplied. Data can be moved from a master copy to copies in use elsewhere with no synchronization problems. Changing a detail in the data (for example, changing a customer's address, changing a person's identification number, or changing stock market prices or airline timetables) involves no calculation or logic. It is relatively straightforward to replicate this class of data.

   Class 2 is somewhat more complicated to control because the updates cannot

BOX 19.2 *continued*

CLASS 3: DATA WITH TIME-CRITICAL UPDATES

If this type of update is reapplied at a different time (e.g., after a restart), its effect may not be the same. Its effect is tied to other events or other updates which occur independently. If the updates occur in an incorrect sequence, the resulting data may be invalid.

EXAMPLES: A booking on a flight. An account balance with multiple sources of update where different action is taken when the account falls below zero or below preset levels.

CONTROL TECHNIQUE: Timestamps may be used (as described in Chapter 20) to ensure that transactions are not processing an invalid sequence. Serial numbers may be needed as well as timestamps to prevent loss or double processing of transactions on recovery.

CLASS 4: DATA FOR WHICH AN UPDATE MAY TRIGGER AN ACTION IN A DIFFERENT MACHINE

When the data are updated, this may trigger the updating of different data or other actions in a different machine. Those actions are not easily reversable.

EXAMPLE: An inventory balance with automatic reordering done in a different machine when the balance falls below certain levels.

Data in different machines are read in order to answer user queries; if they are not in a consistent state of update, invalid information is produced.

CONTROL TECHNIQUES: Global timestamps to control processing sequence (described in Chapter 20). Commitment control: ensuring integrity before committing results to processes which are difficult to reverse.

be applied twice. However, it can be applied at any time (within limits) and is independent of any other updates. An example would be a bank account transaction or an addition or subtraction to an amount (which is allowed to become negative). The update is nonrepeatable because a bank account must not have the same transaction added to it twice. The update can take place at any time (within a day or two).

Transactions which update Class 2 data are commonly given serial numbers, and these are used to ensure that no transaction is lost or updates the data twice. To achieve integrity control the serial numbers may be written on the data records.

Class 3 is less common but is more difficult to control if there are two or more copies. If a transaction is reapplied at a different time (e.g., after a restart), its effect may not be the same. If transactions are applied in a different sequence, there may be different results. A transaction is related to other events which occur independently. Examples are booking systems, inventory control systems where different actions are taken at different stock levels, or accounts where the balance cannot fall below zero.

If there are two copies, they may be in different states of update when a failure occurs. Later, when recovery occurs, the update cannot be simply reapplied. Complex action which varies from one application to another is needed to restore data integrity.

Where two (or more) copies of data exist, the updating logic should be applied to only one copy. The other should be made current by transmitting an image of the first after updating.

Class 4 updates are even worse. A failure may occur such that a data item in one machine is updated and an associated data item in a different machine is not. Complex action may be needed to restore data integrity, but while this is being done, another failure might occur.

Because of the complexity of recovery from all possible types of failures, it is often best to avoid Class 4 updates. When a transaction causes multiple data to be updated, these data should be in the same machine, and data management software which has appropriate restart recovery controls should be used.

MULTIPLE REAL-TIME COPIES   As indicated earlier, there are problems in trying to keep the same data in two machines up to date *in real time*. When a failure occurs, this may result in one copy continuing to be updated and the other not. The two copies diverge. After the failure is corrected, the nonupdated copy must be brought up to date. To do this, either the transactions or the after-images of the updated data are logged. The log is used for restoring the failed copy. With Class 3 or 4 updates, after-images rather than transactions should be used.

While the failed copy is being updated, transactions are still arriving. These, or the after-images of data updated by them, must also be logged until finally the two copies of data are identical again.

Unfortunately, while this resynchronization process is going on, there may be another failure. Programs for resynchronizing the real-time copies when multiple failures occur must be highly complex if they are to be fail-safe.

The complexity is such that in most cases it is usually better to avoid multiple copies of the same data with every copy being updated in real time. An alternative is to have only one copy, with data transmission links to it, as in most teleprocessing systems before the advent of distributed processing.

If only one copy of data is updated in real-time and the others are updated at periodic intervals, the synchronization problems are avoided.

How up-to-date do the copies of data have to be? There is a continuous scale ranging from real-time updating to updates which are made at infrequent intervals. A duplicate copy may be updated by a batch of updates every day, every hour, or every five minutes. Only in a few cases is there a need for duplicate copies to be *immediately* up to date.

A system for giving stock market information with the configuration of Diagram 7 in Fig. 19.1 might cycle through the stocks in sequence, transmitting to the peripheral machines all that have changed.

A distributed banking system might have a file of customer records in each branch and details of all customer balances also stored in the head office, so that any branch can inquire about the balance of a customer of another branch. Each time a balance changes, the new balance is sent to the head office machine. If the updating of the head office balance fails to be completed, the data items are logged for a later attempt. The head office machine should continuously monitor its communication with the branch machines. When any such communication fails, the head office machine flags this so that a branch inquiring a customer's balance is warned that it may not be up to date. The bank in this case might limit the cashing of a check to not more than, say, $500.

As a general rule in most commercial data processing the need for real-time synchronization of two copies of large files should be avoided, unless the data are fairly static. A few systems *do* use replicated copies of real-time data. Elaborate control mechanisms have been written for this purpose. Nevertheless, it is best avoided in most commercial data processing with today's software.

SOFTWARE FUNCTIONS
Some software for distributed systems has a function which automatically controls the updates of duplicated data. It automatically generates transactions from a central computer to peripheral machines, or vice versa, controls them with serial numbers, and ensures that both copies of the data are the same. When a failure occurs, the software handles the restart and recovery in such a way that integrity is restored.

This is a valuable feature to have. It is one of the reasons for using a family of machines with compatible software. The work of writing equivalent restart and integrity control functions may take several man-years and cost over $100,000. Nevertheless, many distributed configurations do not have such software functions. If a peripheral machine from one manufacturer is connected to a central machine from another, restart and recovery may be a critical concern, and the programs for controlling it have to be designed and written.

SUMMARY   There are two approaches to distributed duplicate data: a master copy approach and an approach with elaborate protocols which cause multiple distributed copies to converge safely to a common state. The latter is discussed in the next chapter. For the master copy approach the following recommendations apply. They are appropriate for most commercial data-processing systems:

1. One machine alone should have the responsibility for updates, integrity control, and security of updating.

2. One machine should maintain a master copy of the data, and there should be careful planning of how the master will be reconstructed if it is destroyed.

3. The need for real-time synchronization of two copies of large files should be avoided, unless the data are fairly static.

4. Good restart-recovery software exists for many central mainframes but is often lacking in peripheral processors. The need to develop elaborate restart-recovery software in peripheral processors should generally be avoided by users of these machines.

5. In view of the above point a reasonable ambition is often to avoid *Class 3* and especially *Class 4* updates in peripheral processors.

6. A major factor in the selection of equipment for distributed processing should be the restart and recovery capabilities and preservation of data integrity after failures.

REFERENCE

1. *Distributed Systems Architecture,* IBM Nordic Education Center, Stockholm, August 1978.

20 CONFLICT ANALYSIS

In the previous chapter we stressed that for most commercial data-processing systems, constraints should be placed on the replication of data—at least for data of Classes 2, 3 and 4. For certain types of systems a more general distribution and replication of data is desirable, but in such cases the protocols (rules) for updating the data must be rigorously thought out and built into software.

The types of objectives which give the requirement for *freely* distributed data are as follows:

1. A highly distributed user community, possibly worldwide, who share data.

2. Low cost. Data replication is cheaper than long-distance transmission for the traffic volumes in question. This argument is stronger for worldwide systems or for countries which do not have low-cost data networks.

3. A need for high availability. The data remain available when one or more copies of it are inaccessible or long-distance transmission links are down.

4. The military need for survivability. Data remain available after destruction of multiple system nodes.

5. Fast response time. Access to local data is faster than access to distant, highly shared data.

6. Tunability. Data can be moved to different nodes as usage patterns change. Data heavily used in one geographic region can be stored near that region.

7. Traffic volumes are too high for a single storage system (especially with very large storage).

DATA INTEGRITY   The above objectives can be met without severe data integrity problems if only Class 0 and Class 1 data are stored (Box 19.1). A Viewdata system or information system with high-volume usage is best implemented with many nodes on which data are replicated. Changes to data may be made at one or more designated nodes and distributed from these to the replicated copies. If part of the system fails temporarily, the updating may be delayed on some nodes. If a node at which changes are entered is disabled, they may be entered at another of the designated nodes.

A distributed data system with Class 2, 3, and 4 data, in which updates can be made at various nodes, needs much more careful control. A high level of data redundancy introduces severe problems in performing the updates in a consistent manner. There is good reason to solve these problems because data redundancy plays a key role in achieving the above objectives. Reliability and survivability are enhanced by having multiple copies of data. Efficiency is enhanced because data accessed by widely separated user communities can be stored near those communities.

Such a system can grow flexibly and accommodate large increases in traffic volume without degrading response times, by the adding of further storage units, and more replicated copies of frequently used data.

GUARANTEEING CONSISTENCY

With replicated data, a READ operation is simpler than a WRITE. The READ operation can read any copy of the data. The WRITE operation must update *all* copies of the data it refers to.

The distributed system must maintain consistency of all copies of data. It must organize recovery after a copy of the data has been down for a period. Furthermore, it must prevent one update operation from interfering with another. To do this with a high update rate and not incur excessive system overheads requires tight and rather complex protocols.

A processor, processing a transaction, can retrieve the data it requires from more than one place. The different copies of data should therefore all be up to date; when an update is made, it should be applied immediately to all copies of that data. It is not practical to update all copies *exactly* simultaneously. The system should be designed so that they *converge* quickly to a consistent state. If one copy is inaccessible for a period due to a failure, then a recovery action should follow, bringing it up to date as quickly as possible.

As we discussed in Chapter 17, two transactions attempting to update the same data at the same time can interfere with one another and write invalid data. Similarly, a READ could occur while data are in the process of being updated and could give invalid results. These problems are solved on many centralized data systems by *locking* the data while a transaction is updating them, to prevent any other transaction from interfering.

In general, noninterference requires the property of *serializability* (or *serial reproducibility*) [1, 2]. This means that if instead of being interleaved the same transactions were run serially, one after another, each one being run to completion, the results would be the same.

To summarize, there are two important properties of a system with replicated, distributed data [3]:

Property 1: Convergence

All physical copies of a logical data item converge to the same value. If updates were stopped, then after some period of time all copies of the same data would have the same value.

Property 2: Serializability

The interleaved operation of the system is equivalent to one in which the transactions are run to completion, one at a time, serially. (Note that there could be many possible sets of serial operations, and with Class 3 updates they might give different results. The property of serializability requires that *one* such serial operation be equivalent to the interleaved operation which actually takes place.)

LOCKS We discussed the *locking* of data while updating it in Chapter 17. Update locks are used on most data-base management systems.

In a distributed data system with a high level of updates, locking the data can cause substantial performance degradation. The node processing a transaction is often distant from the node containing the data. The data have to be locked for the time taken to *transmit* the data to the processing node, prepare the update, *transmit* the update back to the data node, and write the new data. Because the transmission times are lengthy, the data are locked for a *much* longer time than with a centralized system at one location.

To make matters worse, the system may have several (perhaps many) copies of the data in different nodes. Each has to be locked during the updating process.

A variety of locking schemes have been devised for distributed data systems [3, 4, 5]. Some require a *primary* site for updating [4]. Some avoid any site having primary authority. All involve substantial transmission overhead if *all* data being updated have to be locked *and* there is a high update rate. Probably the best way to lower the overhead is to structure the updating protocols so as to avoid time-consuming locks whenever possible. We will describe a technique which does this used on SDD-1 (System for Distributed Data bases) of the Computer Corporation of America [6, 7].

CONFLICT ANALYSIS In order to avoid the high overhead of locking *every* transaction (or enforcing some type of conflict avoidance protocol on *every* transaction) it is desirable to analyze which transaction could interfere with which.

Transactions can be grouped into *classes* based on which node executes the transaction and what data the transaction uses. Potential conflicts between the classes can then be analyzed.

There are two major types of conflict, *update conflicts* and *read conflicts*.

With the former, separate transactions trying to update the same data interfere with one another, producing invalid data. With read conflicts a transaction reads data while changes are being made to it and obtains wrong results.

The protocols for avoiding read conflicts are less severe than those for avoiding update conflicts. Many classes of transaction have no potential conflict with other classes, and so burdensome protocols should not be used with them.

Conflict analysis is a technique for analyzing what conflicts could occur in a system, so that appropriate protocols can be applied. With distributed systems it can be difficult to know what potential conflicts exist unless a formal method of examining them is used. This chapter describes such a method and discusses appropriate protocols for controlling conflicts.

To achieve both consistency and serializability with freely distributed data, techniques can be used which employ *timestamps*.

The timestamps used must each be unique within the entire distributed system. To give globally unique timestamps two characteristics are needed:

1. After a clock has been read, it cannot be read again until it has been incremented.

2. The number of the node originating the timestamp is used as the lower-order bits of each timestamp.

A 40-bit timestamp gives a resolution of a fraction of a millisecond, with the possibility of several thousand system nodes.

It is not necessary to synchronize exactly the clocks on all system nodes. A technique for achieving approximate synchronization is for each node to push ahead its clock time if it ever receives a message with a timestamp in the future of its own clock time. This simple technique gives sufficient synchronization for the control of distributed systems.

When the system is started up, a message may be sent to all nodes telling them to set their clocks to a given time of day. Their timestamps may then be used to assist auditors.

The processing nodes place timestamps on all transactions. These timestamps are recorded on the data that are written by those transactions. Every updatable record (or possibly every data item) that is stored many times and each physical copy carries the timestamp of the messages which last updated it.

LOSSES OF TRANSACTION

In order to minimize the overhead involved in locking transactions, Bernstein et al. [3] propose that a database administrator should divide the transactions into *classes*.

A given *class* originates at one given processing node and is defined in terms of the logical set of data it reads and the logical set of data it writes. There may be many transaction types in one class, providing they are processed at the same node and use the same logical read-set and write-set of data. These sets of data are defined by the data-base administrator and may be large or small.

The processing of one class of data may or may not interfere with the processing of another class. In most cases there will be no interference. If there is potential for interference, then tighter protocols are used. They vary substantially in their overhead. The choice of protocol depends on the possible interaction between classes, as described below.

PIPELINING   For the transactions *within one class* there is a simple rule to ensure serializability:

For any particular data-storage node and class of transaction, the messages from that class arrive and are handled in timestamp order.

This is referred to as *pipelining*. The reader might think of a pipeline from the processing node for a given class to each data node it uses (Fig. 20.1). Messages pass down the pipeline in timestamp sequence. Consequently no two transactions in the same class are interleaved. There is no problem with interference between any two transactions in the same class because they are pipelined.

The red tubes in Figs. 20.1 to 20.5 represent logical transmission links over which this pipelining rule is enforced.

INTERFERENCE   The problems set in when transactions from two of the above pipelines meet at one of the data nodes and access the same data (Fig. 20.2). They can then become interleaved. Locks or some control mechanism are needed to prevent one transaction from interfering with another.

For example, a quantity field in data *y* (Fig. 20.2) reads 100. Processor 1 updates it, adding 200, and Processor 2 updates it, adding 300. The final value should be 600, but in fact the transactions interfere as described in Chapter 17:

1. READ message from Processor 1 reads the value 100.

2. READ message from Processor 2 reads the value 100.

3. Processor 1 adds 200 and sends a WRITE message: 300.

4. Processor 2 adds 300 and sends a WRITE message: 400.

The two processes have interfered, giving an incorrect final value of 400, not 600.

Where such interference between classes is possible, some set of rules must be used to prevent it. The messages going to a data node may contain not only their timestamp but also a code indicating which classes of transactions they can interfere with. If a READ message in class *j* arrives at a data node and indicates that it can interfere with class *k*, then class *k* transactions must be protected from it.

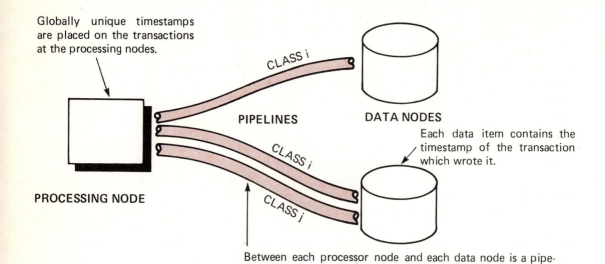

Globally unique timestamps are placed on the transactions at the processing nodes.

CLASS i

PIPELINES

DATA NODES

Each data item contains the timestamp of the transaction which wrote it.

CLASS i

CLASS j

PROCESSING NODE

Between each processor node and each data node is a pipeline for each class of transaction. The transactions in the pipeline are maintained in timestamp sequence.

Figure 20.1 Pipelining. The red tubes in this and the following four figures represent logical transmission links over which the pipeline rule is enforced.

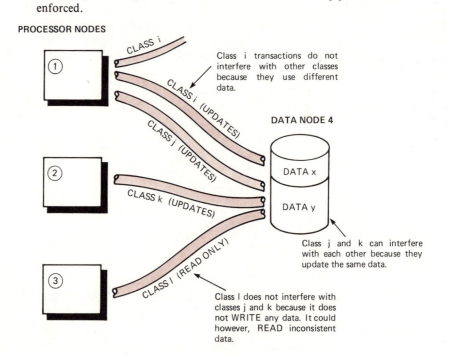

PROCESSOR NODES

CLASS i

Class i transactions do not interfere with other classes because they use different data.

CLASS i (UPDATES)

CLASS j (UPDATES)

DATA NODE 4

① ② ③

CLASS k (UPDATES)

DATA x

DATA y

CLASS l (READ ONLY)

Class j and k can interfere with each other because they update the same data.

Class l does not interfere with classes j and k because it does not WRITE any data. It could however, READ inconsistent data.

Figure 20.2 Interference between classes.

PREVENTING INTERFERENCE

A data node cannot process a class i READ message with timestamp until it is sure that all WRITE messages of class j with a timestamp prior to it have been processed.

How does it know that all class *j* WRITE messages have been processed? The class pipelining rule aids in this. All class *j* transactions come down the class *j* pipeline to this data node in *sequence*. The data node can therefore wait until it receives a class *j* message with a timestamp greater than *t*. At this point it processes the class *j* message with timestamp *t*. Only when it completes this does it process the class *k* message.

In other words, if there can be interference between class j and k at a data node, that node ensures that class j and k transactions are processed in timestamp sequence (Fig. 20.3).

There is a problem with this. When the class *i* message is received, the data node might have to wait a long time before it receives a class *j* message. How can it be sure that there is not a delayed message in the class *j* pipeline? It might be a long time before the class *j* processor happens to send another transaction, and the class *i* message cannot be kept waiting for long.

To solve this problem, a flow of timing messages is needed in each pipeline. Each processor sends a timing message down each pipeline at intervals if there are no data messages. The timing message specifies the class of transactions and a timestamp. It is semantically equivalent to a write message which does not write any data. After it has been sent, no message with an earlier timestamp can be sent. How frequently these messages are sent depends on the response time that is engineered into the system. A waiting processor or a data module may send a request to a processing node asking for such a timing message to be sent.

Let us look again at the above example of Processors 1 and 2 updating the quantity field which reads 100. With the protocol we have outlined the updating proceeds as follows:

1. Processor 1 sends a READ message with timestamp t_1. This is a class *j* message and it indicates a possible conflict with class *k* (Fig. 20.3). It cannot be processed immediately, because no class *k* message has yet been received with a timestamp later than t_1.

2. Processor 2 sends a READ message with timestamp t_2. This is a class *k* message which indicates a possible conflict with class *j*.

   If $t_2 > t_1$, this indicates that no write messages earlier than t_1 will be received through the class *k* pipeline and therefore the class *j* READ from processor 1 with timestamp t_1 can be handled.

   Conversely if $t_2 < t_1$, the class *k* READ with timestamp t_2 can be handled.

   Let us suppose that the latter case applies. The READ from processor 2 with timestamp t_2 is handled.

3. Processor 2 receives the result and sends a WRITE message to update the quantity to 400. The WRITE carries timestamp t_2. As $t_2 < t_1$, the request from processor 1 still waits.

4. Processor 2 sends a timing message with timestamp t_3 (possibly as a result of a request

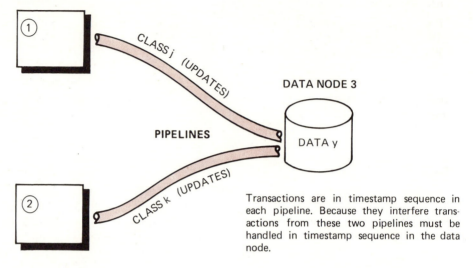

PROCESSOR NODE

CLASS j (UPDATES)

DATA NODE 3

PIPELINES

DATA y

CLASS k (UPDATES)

Transactions are in timestamp sequence in each pipeline. Because they interfere transactions from these two pipelines must be handled in timestamp sequence in the data node.

Figure 20.3 Sequencing transactions from multiple pipelines.

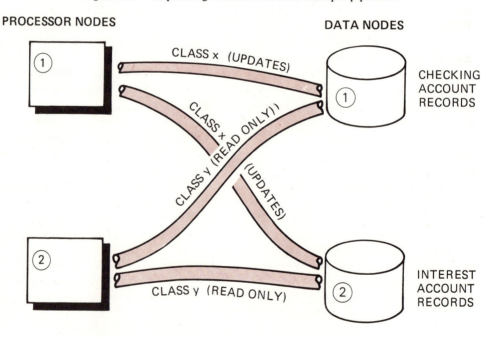

PROCESSOR NODES

DATA NODES

CLASS x (UPDATES)

CHECKING ACCOUNT RECORDS

CLASS x (READ ONLY)

CLASS y (READ ONLY))

(UPDATES)

CLASS y (READ ONLY)

INTEREST ACCOUNT RECORDS

Figure 20.4 Inconsistent information can be read unless appropriate protocols are used.

from in impatient processor 1). Since $t_3 > t_1$, the READ transaction from processor 1 is released and executed.

5. Processor 1 receives the result and sends a WRITE message to update the quantity to 600. The quantity record had a timestamp of t_2 on it after step 3 above. Since $t_1 > t_2$, the t WRITE can be handled and the timestamp t is written on the data item.

This use of timestamps achieves the necessary property of *serializability*. The interleaved operation achieves the same results as if each transaction were run to completion by itself, serially.

DEADLOCKS

Figure 17.7 illustrated a *deadlock* or *deadly embrace* situation in a distributed data system. The use of timestamps avoids cyclic dependencies being created among transactions waiting for resources. They avoid a situation where A is waiting for B while B is waiting for A. Hence such an algorithm is free of intersite deadlocks.

READING INCONSISTENT DATA

So far we have discussed preventing damage to data by updates which interfere with each other. Another problem of distributed data, which perhaps is slightly less serious, is the reading of data in an inconsistent fashion.

Suppose that a terminal user enters a query and to answer it requires data from two data modules. Normally the data in the two modules would be consistent, but at this time one or both of them are in process of being updated. The user sees the results of a half-complete update, and this may be quite invalid.

A protocol is needed to prevent the reading of inconsistent data. This protocol need not be as strong, or cause as much system degradation, as the protocol for preventing update interference.

Imagine, for example, a banking system in which a customer instructs that when the balance in his checking account exceeds a certain amount, the excess amount is automatically placed in an interest-bearing account. (This privilege is enjoyed by bank customers in some countries and not others.) When the customer makes an inquiry he wants to know how much money he has available to spend. The computer must look at the balances in both accounts and add them. Now, suppose that the checking and interest accounts are maintained on different machines in a distributed system (perhaps a system like the Bank of America system in Fig. 9.11.)

In Fig. 20.4 the checking account is held in data node 1 and the interest-bearing account is in data node 2. While Processor 1 is moving $1000 from the checking account into the interest account, the customer makes an inquiry on Processor 2. The events take place as follows, leaving the customer with the alarming view that the bank has lost $1000 of his money:

1. Processor 1 reads the checking account balance from data node 1.

2. Processor 1 sends WRITE messages to both data nodes 1 and 2, making the balance of the checking account $1000 less and the balance of the interest account $1000 more.

3. Data node 1 has processed the WRITE, but data node 2 has not done so when information is obtained for a customer query in Processor 2.

4. Processor 2 sends READ messages to both data nodes 1 and 2. These are answered, and Processor 2 adds the balances, giving the customer a result which is $1000 lower than it should be.

5. Data module 2 completes the WRITE, and the data on the two nodes are consistent again.

Timestamps can again help in avoiding this type of inconsistent read.

Let us suppose that the transactions which move money from one account to another are class x and the inquiry messages are class y, as shown in Fig. 20.4.

The inquiry messages carry a timestamp and an indication that they must check for consistency of class x messages. (Class x messages, on the other hand, do not need to worry about class y.) A class y READ cannot be answered until the system has ensured that there are no more outstanding WRITE messages of class x with a timestamp earlier than that on the class y message. (Also if any class x WRITE messages with a *future* timestamp have been processed, the class y message must be rejected and a new version of it sent.)

Again to ensure that there are no outstanding WRITE messages, timing messages or NULL WRITES would be sent sufficiently frequently in each WRITE pipeline.

The protocol which prevents update conflicts (Fig. 20.3) would also prevent inconsistent reads. Where pipelines intersect with possible conflict, the transactions from these pipelines are processed in timestamp sequence. However a *weaker* protocol would also suffice, and a weaker protocol incurs less system overhead and delay. The protocol could be weaker in two respects. First, the class x messages do not need to look out for class y messages. Second, *any* time within a range can be used for ensuring consistency. It does not need to be exactly the time of the class y operation. What is required is consistent information, not up-to-the-millisecond information.

INCONSISTENT DATA
IN ONE NODE
In the above case the data which alarm the bank customer are drawn from *two* nodes. It is also possible to alarm a customer with data read from one node. Data in one node can be in an inconsistent state for a brief period because they are being updated by separate processors.

Figure 20.5 illustrates this. Consider the following events:

1. A transaction (class i) in processor 1 updates data item x and sends a copy of the update to data node 3. The update does not yet arrive in data node 3.

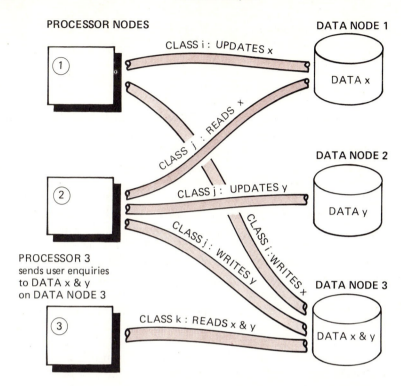

Figure 20.5 Data is one node (DATA NODE 3) may be inconsistent briefly if written by distributed processors. A protocol is needed to prevent class k inquiries receiving inconsistent x and y values.

2. A transaction (class *j*) in processor 2 reads the new data item *x* and as a result of this updates data item *y* in data node 2. It sends to data node 3 a copy which does arrive and is processed.

3. An inquiry (class *k*) in processor 3 reads both data item *x* and data item *y*. However, data item *y* is dependent on the updated version of data item *x*, which has not yet been written in data node 3. *Processor 3 obtains inconsistent data.*

4. The version of data item *x* from processor 1 now arrives and is written in data node 3, removing the brief inconsistency, but too late for processor 3's inquiry.

The class *k* transaction intersects with the class *i* and class *j* transactions (at data node 3). To ensure that it reads consistent data a time should be selected, t_0, and the data node 3 should ensure that in the class *i* and class *j* pipelines to that node all WRITE messages up to but not ahead of that time have been processed. This timing consistency should be guaranteed before the class *k* READ is processed. *Any* time t_0 would do to ensure consistency.

Because *any* time t_0 can be used, *data node 3 can select the time* it uses. It may select the time of the most recent WRITE message in class i or j, then wait until the other of these two pipelines catches up. This will incur somewhat less delay than using the time of the class k READ message.

CONFLICT GRAPHS   In an environment where data are distributed and replicated for performance reasons, there is a danger that some classes of transactions might interfere with one another; other classes are free from this concern.

Bernstein et al. [3] use a diagram called a *conflict graph* to indicate the potential conflicts. There are three types of points on the conflict graph, as shown in Fig. 20.6: An EXECUTE point, a READ point, and a WRITE point.

For any one *class* of transaction there is one EXECUTE point. The EXECUTE point may be connected to one or more READ points above it, indicating the processing of READ messages, and to one or more WRITE points below it, indicating the processing of WRITE messages. The numbers on the graph indicate which physical nodes execute the transaction and store the data in question. The same physical node may appear many times on one graph because it is used by different classes of transaction.

The transaction class in Fig. 20.6 writes replicated data onto four storage nodes. When the processor which executes this transaction class reads data, it always reads them from storage node 2. There are therefore four WRITE points but only one READ point in the graph.

A conflict graph may illustrate many data classes and draws lines between them to indicate interactions between the classes. The classes are drawn in red in Fig. 20.7 to 20.15, and the interactions between them are drawn in black.

A read-write interaction between classes is drawn as a *diagonal connection*. In Fig. 20.7 class j transactions READ data which are written on data node 2 by class i transactions.

There is sometimes more than one diagonal connection between classes.

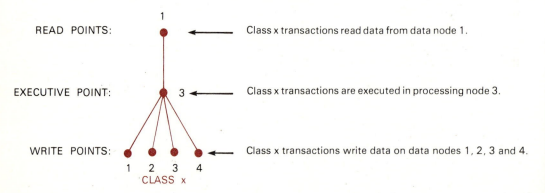

Figure 20.6   The drawing of a transaction class in a conflict graph.

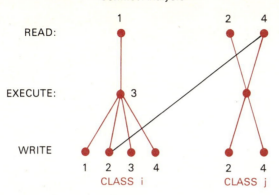

Figure 20.7   The black diagonal connection indicated that class j reads the same data at data node 2 as class j writes. The data which class j reads at data node 4 is different data from that which class i writes and there, no diagonal connection is drawn between these.

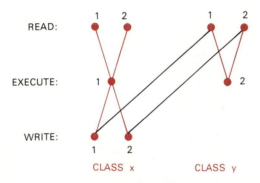

Figure 20.8   A conflict graph of the situation in Fig. 20.6. The two diagonal connections between class y and class x constitute a cycle. A protocol may be necessary to prevent class y reading inconsistent data.

Figure 20.8 shows two Class *y* transactions READ data which are written on data nodes 1 and 2 by class *x* transactions.

   A *horizontal connection* is drawn between the EXECUTE points of two classes if there is a write-write interaction (in other words, if both classes WRITE the same data item). Figure 20.9 shows this.

   The graph should contain all classes and all possible interactions between classes. It will be used to indicate what conflicts exist and what protocols are needed for controlling the interactions.

CYCLES IN THE   If it is possible to follow lines continuously in a cycle in
CONFLICT GRAPH   the conflict graph, this can indicate that special precau-
                           tions have to be taken to prevent separate classes of
transactions from interfering with one another.

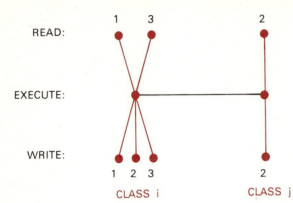

READ:

EXECUTE:

WRITE:

CLASS i   CLASS j

Figure 20.9 A horizontal connection is drawn between classes when they WRITE the same data.

In Fig. 20.7 the diagonal connection between the classes does not produce a cycle. In Fig. 20.8 there are two diagonal connections, and these do constitute a cycle. There are also cycles in Figs. 20.10 and 20.15.

Figure 20.10 represents the situation in Fig. 20.3 where two classes of transactions update the same data. The two diagonal connections create a cycle. This cycle occurs with data which are not replicated. A similar cycle could occur if the two transaction classes executed on only one computer.

Figure 20.11 is a conflict graph of the situation in Fig. 20.2. Class *j* and *k* have the same pattern of conflict as in Fig. 20.10. In addition, class *L* tries to read data updated by Classes *j* and *k*, and this creates another cycle. If the conflict between classes *j* and *k* is removed by a protocol which enforces timestamp sequencing of the class *j* and *k* updates, then there is no longer a problem with class *L* reading inconsistent data. In effect classes *j* and *k* then behave as though they were one class. If the diagonal connections between classes *j* and *k* were removed, there would be no cycle with class *L*.

In a system with many transaction classes the conflict graph can contain multiple cycles.

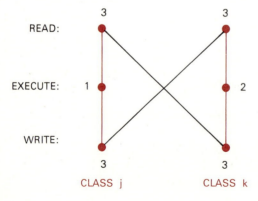

READ:

EXECUTE:

WRITE:

CLASS j   CLASS k

Figure 20.10 An update conflict (shown in Fig. 20.3). The cycle indicates that both class j (run on professor 1) and class k (run on professor 2) update the same data.

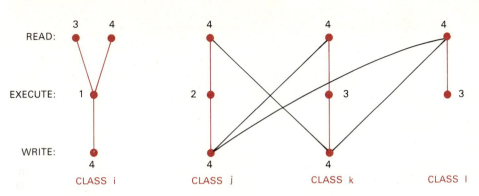

Figure 20.11   A conflict graph of the situation in Fig. 20.2. There is an update conflict between class j and class k, and a read conflict between class l and classes j and k.

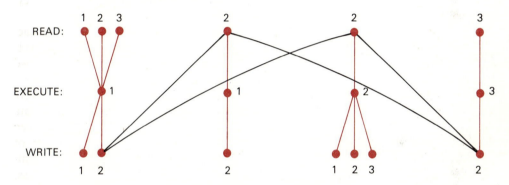

Figure 20.12   A safe cycle-safe because it does not include any *red* lines (lines within one class).

TYPES OF SITUATION

From the conflict graph we can identify the following types of situation:

1. No cycle

Where no cycle exists between classes, this means that no special protocol is needed other than the class pipelining rule which keeps all transactions of one class to one data node in sequence. Transactions from different classes can be interleaved with impunity. The class pipelining rule is sufficient to guarantee serializability. With Fig. 20.7, for example, no special protocol is needed for controlling the interactions between the classes. With Fig. 20.8 the cycle indicates that there can be interference between the classes.

2. Safe cycles

A cycle which does not contain a red line (a line drawn within one class) is a safe cycle. It does not indicate a danger of invalid data. Such a cycle may be composed entirely of diagonal connections (as in Fig. 20.12) or horizontal connections.

3. WRITE cycles

A WRITE cycle is one in which invalid information could be written if appropriate protocols are not used. Class i transactions are in this danger if a cycle exists containing one of the following subpaths:

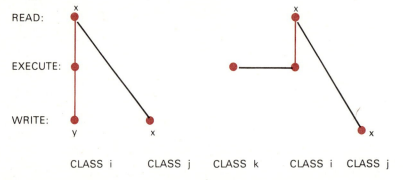

In this case every transaction in class i must be run with a protocol with respect to class j which prevents the two classes from interfering. This may be done by ensuring that the transactions from the classes i and j which intersect at data node x in the above diagram are processed strictly in timestamp sequence.

Most WRITE cycles involve two classes, as in Fig. 20.10. Some involve more than two, as in Fig. 20.13. In Fig. 20.13, class x transactions must be synchronized with class y at data node 1, class y must be synchronized with class z at data node 2, and class z must be synchronized with class x at data node 3.

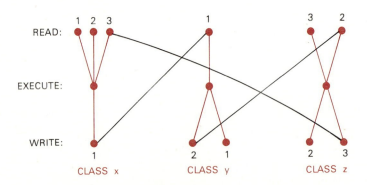

Figure 20.13   A WRITE cycle involving three classes.

4. READ cycles

A READ cycle is one in which inconsistent information may be read (but not written) if appropriate protocols are not used. The protocols needed to prevent READ inconsistencies are somewhat weaker and need less overhead than those for preventing invalid WRITE operations. Furthermore, not all types of READ transactions need to be protected in this way. Inconsistencies in the timing of updates do not matter when reading certain types of data.

There are two types of READ cycles.

The one which is somewhat easier to control involves data which are all read from the same data node. It can be identified by a cycle which contains the following subpath:

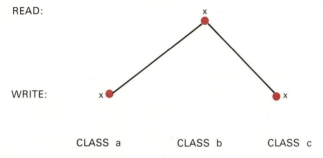

Transactions obtaining data from the class *b* node above may need a protocol which ensures that the data are read at a moment of consistent update timing. The data node may select *any* time (within limits) and ensure that all updates of the data are completed up to that time and no updates in the future of that time have been processed.

Figures 20.5 and 20.14 show situations with this type of WRITE cycle.

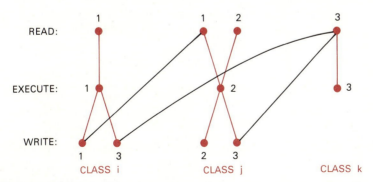

Figure 20.14 A conflict graph of the situation in Fig. 20.5. A read cycle exists from which class k transaction needs protection. If class k is removed (and the diagonal links to it) no cycle remains. There is no conflict between classes i and j.

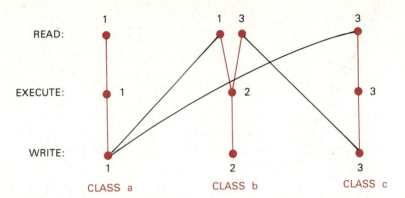

Figure 20.15 A READ cycle in which class b needs protection from reading inconsistent data which is on two separate data nodes.

In the second type of READ cycle the class to be protected reads the data in question from two or more data nodes, as with class *y* in Figs. 20.4, 20.8, and 20.15. The class needing READ protection can be identified by a cycle which contains one of the following subpaths:

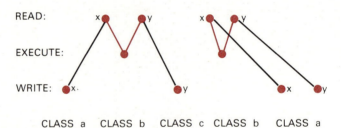

Class *b* transactions obtaining data from nodes *x* and *y* may need a protocol which ensures that the data are read at a moment of consistent update timing. Again, *any* time may be used, but now it needs to be assigned by the class *b* EXECUTE node because there is more than one data node. Again, the protocol must ensure that all updates of the data are completed up to that time and no updates in the future of that time have been processed.

The above comments about types of cycles and the protocols needed with them are formally proved in Bernstein et al. [3].

CONFLICT PREVENTION   The objective of conflict analysis is to determine what potential conflicts exist so that appropriate protocols can be used. We have identified four situations:

1. No conflict. No protocol needed other than class pipelining.

2. Update conflict. Data need to be protected during updating.

3. Read conflict with one data node. When two or more records are read in one data node, the timing needs to be such as to avoid obtaining inconsistent data.

4. Read conflict with more than one data node. The same as the previous case except that the data in question are read from multiple nodes, which makes conflict avoidance somewhat more difficult.

When a transaction is received by the processor which executes it, that processor will determine what data must be read and written and to what class the transaction belongs. If the potential conflicts have been preanalyzed, the processor may then do a table lookup to determine what form of protection is needed. Sometimes there is one potential conflict, sometimes none, and sometimes many because the class participates in multiple cycles. A READ or WRITE message to a data node may then carry a code saying what classes that transaction needs protection from and what protocols should be used.

The protocols we have described are implemented on a system developed by the Computer Corporation of America called SDD–1 (System for Distributed Data bases) [6, 7]. SDD–1 was designed to support data bases distributed worldwide over many sites and connected to communication channels of varying capacity and delay. It is a prototype for a naval command-and-control system with some data bases on land and some on ships [6].

AVOIDANCE OF COMPLEXITY

As will be seen, carefully thought out protocols are needed to support distributed data with Class 2, 3, and 4 updates. Protocols equivalent to those we have described do not exist in much of the software for distributed systems. Because of this and because of the complexity in general, caution is recommended in the design of distributed data. In commercial systems it is often better to have a single master copy approach with updates being carefully controlled as described in the previous chapter.

The techniques described here for controlling distributed data rely upon a prior analysis of the transaction classes and class conflicts. On some systems it is desirable to process *spontaneous* transactions, often generated by high-level end-user languages. In such systems another question arises. Can such transactions be *automatically* assigned to a class which has been defined and analyzed? In some cases, yes. But on some systems there may be many cases of transactions which do not fit into the preanalyzed classes. These should probably be read-only transactions because of the difficulty of controlling updates. Updates should be planned by the data-base administrator. With spontaneous read-only transactions, will conflict controls be applied? A further protocol could be devised for controlling spontaneous transactions [3], or the end user could be restricted to reading data for which there is no danger of inconsistency.

As we commented earlier, distributed systems can be designed in such a way that they greatly increase overall system complexity or greatly reduce it by splitting it into simply controllable modules. Freely distributed data bring the need for complex protocols and tend to increase the overall system's complexity. It is appropriate for certain types of systems, including military command-and-control systems. For most commercial purposes an objective of distributed data design should be to simplify the transaction handling on peripheral systems, to produce largely self-contained modules which have simple interactions with other modules. This objective requires constraint in the replication and distribution of data.

REFERENCES

1. K. P. Eswaran, J. N. Gray, R. A. Lorie, and I. L. Traiger, "The Notions of Consistency and Predicate Locks in a Database System," *Communications of the ACM,* Vol. 19, No. 11, November 1976.

2. J. N. Gray, R. A. Lorie, G. R. Putzolu, and I. L. Traiger, *Granularity of Locks and Degress of Consistency in a Shared Database,* Report from IBM Research Laboratory, San Jose, Ca., 1975.

3. P. A. Bernstein, J. B. Rothnie, D. W. Shipman, and N. Goodman, *The Concurrency Control Mechanism of SDD-1: A System for Distributed Databases (The General Case),* Technical Report No. CCA-77-09, Computer Corporation of America, 575 Technology Square, Cambridge, Mass. 02139, 1979.

4. P. A. Alsberg and J. D. Day, *A Principle for Resilient Sharing of Distributed Resources,* Report from the Center for Advanced Computation, University of Illinois, Urbana, 1976. (Also accepted for proceedings of the Second International Conference on Software Engineering.)

5. R. H. Thomas, *A Solution to the Update Problem for Multiple Copy Databases Which Uses Distributed Control,* BBN Report No. 3340, July 1975.

6. Computer Corporation of America, *A Distributed Database Management System for Command and Control Applications: Semi-Annual Technical Report,* Technical Report No. CCA-77-10, Computer Corporation of America, 575 Technology Square, Cambridge, Mass. 02139.

7. J. B. Rothnie and N. Goodman, *An Overview of the Preliminary Design of SDD-1: A System for Distributed Databases,* 1977 Berkeley Workshop of Distributed Data Management and Computer Networks, Lawrence Berkeley Laboratory, University of California, Berkeley, May 1977. (Also available from Computer Corporation of America, 575 Technology Square, Cambridge, Mass. 02139, as Technical Report No. CCA-77-04.)

21 DATA-BASE MANAGEMENT

There is a fundamental difference between storing data in a *data-base* system and storing it in files. This chapter explains the difference and the rationale of data bases. It is important that this be clearly understood before we discuss distributed data bases. Readers familiar with data base management may omit this chapter.

A *file* is usually designed for one application or a closely related group of applications. It is often designed by one programmer for his own needs. *A data base is a collection of interrelated data which are independent of application programs and which can serve many applications, present and future. A well-designed data base represents the inherent properties of the data* [1] *rather than just the properties required for a specific application. A common and controlled approach is used in adding new data and modifying and retrieving existing data.*

In non-data-base processing, one or more files of records are often kept for each application. The intention of a data base is to allow the same collection of data to serve as many applications as is useful. Hence, a data base is often conceived of as the repository of information needed for running certain functions in a corporation, factory, university, or government department. Such a data base permits not only the retrieval of data but also the continuous modification of data needed for the control of operations. It may be possible to "search" the data base to obtain answers to queries or information for planning purposes. The collection of data may serve many departments, often cutting across political boundaries.

The reader should note that the term *data base* is often misused. File systems with no data independence are sometimes called data-base systems because it sounds better. The term is deliberately misapplied in some sales literature and naively misapplied by the ill-informed. The term *distributed data base* is often used to describe what is really a distributed *file* system.

The Digital Equipment Corporation (DEC) uses the terms *data base* and *Data-Base* in their literature, the former referring to file systems, usually on-line, and the latter referring to data stored with a Data-Base Management System (such as IDMS).

In this book *data base* refers *only* to data stored with a data-base management system, and hence having the properties in the above definition.

The intention of *data-base* technology is that it should make the development of new applications fast and flexible. High-level languages, report generators, and dialogue generators, all using the data base, should facilitate the rapid production of new applications. It should be possible to modify applications quickly and easily. On most *file* systems, especially on-line file systems with stored data, it is surprisingly difficult to make modifications. The enormous cost of seemingly trivial changes has held back application development seriously. This cost has resulted from the need when one program is changed to rewrite other programs, to restructure and convert data, and to deal with the many bugs introduced by the changes. One small change results in a chain reaction of changes to other programs. One of the most important objectives of data-base management is that one programmer's view of the data can be changed without affecting the other programs already operating. Over the years the number of application programs grow in an organization until eventually it would be unthinkable to rewrite a substantial proportion of them. Hence the growing importance of storing data in the form of a data base rather than in separate files.

A major task for most corporations over the ten years ahead is to decide what data bases they need, where they are best located, what data should be stored in them, and how they should be organized. The amount of data stored will increase drastically, and the ways the data are organized will be fundamentally changed to increase their usefulness. Data bases will become the foundation stone of much corporate data processing.

MULTIPLE USAGE OF DATA

Figure 21.1 illustrates the way data are organized for computers which do not use data-base techniques.

There are many files of records, some on tape and some on direct-access media such as disk. The records contain fields, shown as circles in Fig. 21.1. When a program is written for a new application or a variation of an old application, there may be a file which contains the required set of fields. Often, however, there is not, and a new file has to be created. Suppose that a new user request needs a file with fields A, F, and H. These fields do not appear together in the existing files in Fig. 21.1. Other files must be sorted and merged to obtain the new file, but this will not be straightforward if the existing files do not have the required sets of keys. There may not be an H field for every pair of A and F fields.

Figure 21.2 shows the concept of a data base. The fields are pooled to form a data base with software that can extract any combinations of fields that a programmer wishes. In reality the fields are usually not stored entirely in isolation, as suggested by the drawing in Fig. 21.2, but in groups of related fields sometimes called

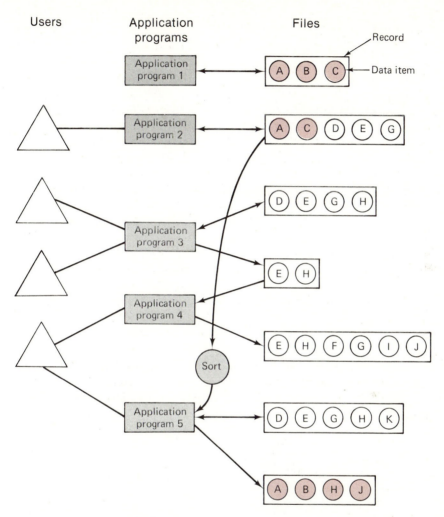

Figure 21.1 A system without a data base: redundancy and inflexibility.
[Imagine 1000 such files.]

records, sometimes *segments.* The software may be able to extract segments and combine them to form the records that an application program uses.

Another important feature shown in Fig. 21.2, at the bottom right, is the data-base interrogation software. This enables some users of the data to interact directly with the data base without application programs having to be written. Instead, the user fills in a form expressing a data request or employs a language which is part of the interrogation software.

Figure 21.2 suggests that a corporation's data are stored in a large reservoir in which the users can go fishing. Although this figure forms a useful way to explain

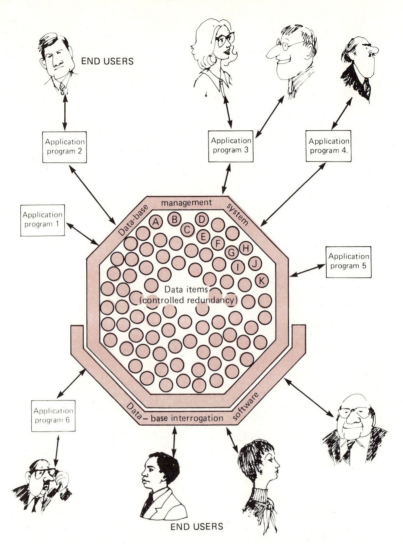

Figure 21.2 The system of Fig. 21.1 with a data base: more responsive
and lower development costs. (Caution: This diagram presents a dangerously naive view.)

data-base concepts to management, it is nevertheless a naive view of a data base—in
some cases dangerously naive. The fields inside the octagon of Fig. 21.2 have to be
organized in such a way that they can be found and accessed with sufficient speed.
The organizing introduces many complexities into data-base design.

The "reservoir" concept of management information systems, or other information systems, is much easier to conceive than to implement. It is a complex and

lengthy operation to build up such data bases, and with current hardware it is expensive to search them sufficiently quickly to give real-time answers to unanticipated queries.

However, the striving for flexibility is vital. Increasingly, management wants a fast reaction to new requests. As management realizes the potential value of the data that are stored, their requests will be an increasing plague to the data-processing manager. Nonetheless, they must and should be readily answered, with minimum disruption.

In many corporations, systems (of accounts, organization, methods, responsibilities, and procedures) have been more of a hindrance to change than physical plant and unamortized capital investments. For some, retraining the whole labor force would be easier than changing the system. Quite frequently the computer has contributed to the inflexibility by dressing hallowed procedures in a rigid electronic framework. The computer has been hailed as one of the most versatile and flexible machines ever built, but in many corporations, because of the difficulty and cost of changing the programs and files, it becomes a straitjacket which precludes change and even constrains corporate policy. Application modifications are often avoided because change is too difficult for the computer system.

One of the most difficult tricks that we have to learn is how to introduce automation without introducing rigidity. The computer industry is only now beginning to glimpse how that can be done. Data-base techniques are an important part of the answer.

CHANGE AND   A data base is intended to make data independent of
MAINTENANCE COST   the programs that use them. Old application programs
                         do not have to be rewritten when changes are made to
data structures, data layout, or the physical devices on which data are stored. The data can be easily reorganized or their structure added to.

This independence of data is essential if data are to become a general-purpose corporate resource. In the past data structures have been devised by a programmer for his own use. He writes a program to create a file of data. Usually when another programmer needs the data for another purpose it is not structured in the way he wants, so he creates another file. Hence the duplication in Fig. 21.1.

Data independence is one of the most important differences between the way data are organized in data bases and the way they are organized in the file systems of computers that do not use data-base management software. The programmers can each have their own logical data structure, as shown in Fig. 21.3, and can program in blissful ignorance of how the data are really organized. When the data organization is changed, *the old programs still work*.

A data base in an organization is no more a *static* entity than are the contents of the organization's filing cabinets. The details of data stored, and the way they are used, change continuously. If a computer system attempts to impose an un-

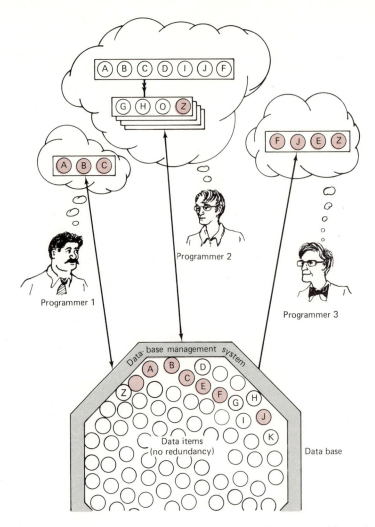

Figure 21.3 The programmers can live in blissful ignorance of how the data are really stored.

changeable file structure on an organization, it is doomed to the types of pressure that will result in most of the programming efforts being spent on modifying existing programs rather than developing new applications.

Figure 5.1 illustrated how the proportion of application development hours spent on new applications has fallen steadily. The reason is that the effort to maintain or modify the existing programs becomes greater and greater. It is often thought by systems analysts and data-processing managers that existing programs which work well can be left alone. In reality, however, the data which they create or use are needed for other applications and almost always needed in a slightly different form. New data-item types are added. New record types are needed with data-item types from several previous records. The data must be indexed in a different way. The physical layout of data is improved. Data bases for different applications are merged, and so forth.

In summary, one of the most important characteristics of data bases is that they will constantly need to change and grow. Dynamic restructuring of the data base must be possible as new types of data and new applications are added. The restructuring should be possible without having to rewrite the application programs, and in general it should cause as little upheaval as possible.

The total number of man-years that a corporation has invested in application programs grows steadily. The programmers are long since gone, and it is too late to complain that their documentation is inadequate. The greater the number of programs, the more horrifying the thought of having to convert them or their data.

The ease with which data structures can be changed will have a major effect on the rate at which data-processing applications can be developed in a corporation.

It is often easy for a systems analyst to imagine that the data structure he has designed for an application represents its ultimate content and usage. He leaves some spare characters in the records and thinks that these will accommodate any change that will occur. Consequently he ties his data to a physical organization which is efficient for that particular structure. *Time and time again he is proven wrong.* The requirements change in unforeseen ways. The data structures have to be modified, and consequently many application programs have to be rewritten and debugged. The larger an installation's base of application programs, the more expensive is this process.

As we commented earlier, in some installations at the time of writing 80% of the programming budget is being spent on maintaining or modifying past programs and data; only 20% is being used for new application programming. This ratio is extremely inhibiting to the development of data processing in the organization. It is desirable to write today's programs in such a way that the same ratio will not apply five years hence. If we continue to write programs without data independence, the maintenance difficulties will grow worse as the numbers of programs grow, until the impact cripples the ability to take advantage of the new hardware and techniques that are now under development. (See Fig. 21.4.)

The decade ahead is likely to be an era of great invention in the techniques for storing and organizing data, and many of the new techniques will be highly complex. The greater the rate of introduction of new techniques or modified data organizations, the greater is the need to protect the application programs and programmers from them. This is one of the main reasons why we need *data-base* systems rather than merely *file* systems without the data independence.

Now, with distributed systems, we have a new requirement which is a variation on the same theme. If the data themselves are *distributed,* existing programs should not have to be rewritten. In other words we want the data-base system itself to be distributed.

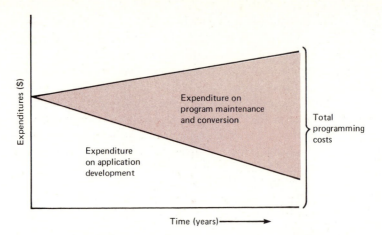

Figure 21.4   New application progress is often deferred by the rising cost
of modifying existing programs and files. Some corporations now spend
more than 80% of their programming budget just keeping current and only
20% forging ahead. A danger of ill-designed distributed processing is that
it will increase yet further the effort for maintenance and conversion.

**LOGICAL AND
PHYSICAL DATA
INDEPENDENCE**

There are two levels of data independence in the better
base software. We call these *logical* and *physical* data
independence.

    Logical data independence means that the overall
logical structure of the data may be changed without changing the application programs. (The changes must not, of course, remove any of the data the application
programs use.)

    Physical data independence means that the physical layout and organization
of the data may be changed without changing either the overall logical structure of
the data or the application programs.

    Figure 21.5 illustrates the concept of logical and physical independence. At
the center of Fig. 21.5 is the overall logical structure of the data, sometimes referred
to as the *global* logical view of the data. It is the data-base administrator's view.
This view is often entirely different from the physical structure of the data, shown
at the bottom of the figure. The application programmer's views—the application
program files—are shown at the top of the figure. These three views of the data are
separate. The application programmer may, for example, view the files as a set of
master records with subordinate detail records. The data administrator views the
data base as a whole, but still in a logical form. The physical organization is concerned with the indices, pointers, chains, and other means of physically locating
records, with the overflow areas and techniques used for inserting new records and
deleting records, and with physical layout and compaction techniques.

    The data-base software will convert the application programmer's view of the

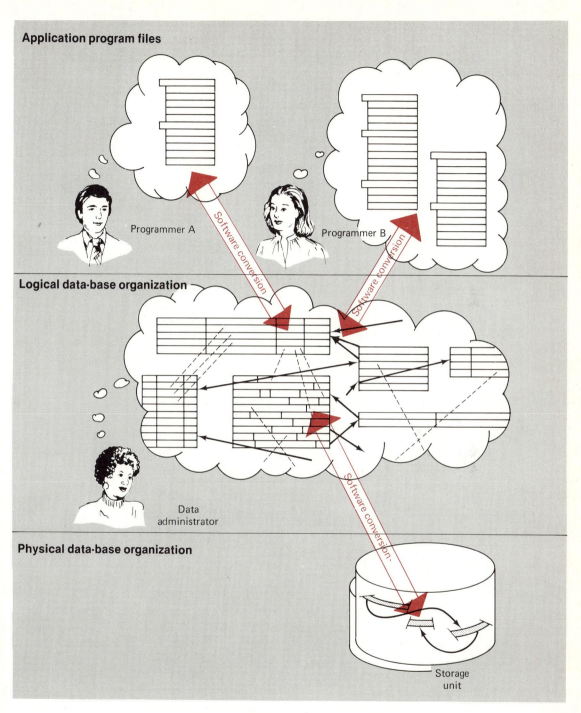

Application program files

Programmer A

Programmer B

Logical data-base organization

Software conversion

Software conversion

Software conversion

Data
administrator

Physical data-base organization

Storage
unit

Figure 21.5   Separate views of the data.

data into the overall logical view and will then map the overall logical view into the physical representation.

The purpose of the separation of views shown in Fig. 21.5 is to permit the maximum freedom to change the data structures without having to rehash much of the earlier work on the data base. Figure 21.6 lists a number of changes that are common on a data-base system and indicates whether they can be accomplished without restructuring the physical storage organization, the global logical view of the data, or the application programs other than the one which initiated the change. The crosses in the columns of Fig. 21.6 represent an objective of contemporary data-base software design.

Figure 21.7 illustrates physical data independence, and Fig. 21.8 illustrates logical data independence.

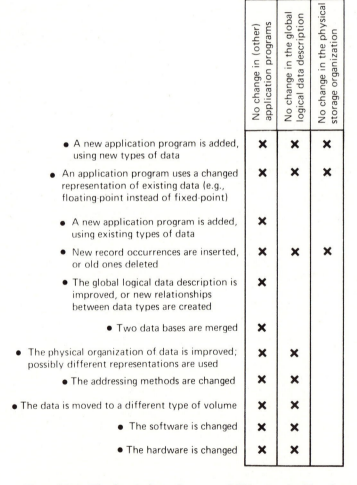

	No change in (other) application programs	No change in the global logical data description	No change in the physical storage organization
• A new application program is added, using new types of data	✗	✗	✗
• An application program uses a changed representation of existing data (e.g., floating-point instead of fixed-point)	✗	✗	✗
• A new application program is added, using existing types of data	✗		
• New record occurrences are inserted, or old ones deleted	✗	✗	✗
• The global logical data description is improved, or new relationships between data types are created	✗		
• Two data bases are merged	✗		
• The physical organization of data is improved; possibly different representations are used	✗	✗	
• The addressing methods are changed	✗	✗	
• The data is moved to a different type of volume	✗	✗	
• The software is changed	✗	✗	
• The hardware is changed	✗	✗	

Figure 21.6   The data independence capabilities required in advance data-base systems.

Application program files

Programmer A

Programmer B

Global logical organization

The software should sever the physical data organization from the logical data descriptions as completely as possible so that the physical data organization can be tuned or totally changed without necessitating any rewriting of the logical data descriptions on application programs.

Data administrator

Physical organization

Storage unit

Figure 21.7 Physical data independence.

317

Data independence is critical to future development. A data base and its applications should be regarded as something which is constantly changing and improving. It will change for two reasons. First, the storage hardware and organization will change. The research establishments are full of new storage devices and access methods. As new applications are added, it will be necessary to change the storage, reorganize, improve performance, and tune the system. *Physical* data independence makes this possible without playing havoc with the logical data base and application programs (Fig. 21.7).

Second, the applications will change. No commercial organization is static. Change is a way of life. It is important that when a programmer changes his data requirements, he should not effect the multitude of other programs which use that data. *Logical* data independence makes this possible (Fig. 21.8).

SCHEMAS AND
SUBSCHEMAS

The overall logical view of a data base is referred to as a *schema* (the center data structure in Fig. 21.6). The programmer's view is referred to as a *subschema* (the lower structures in Fig. 21.4).

Many subschemas can be derived from one schema. A programmer may specify a subschema, and then, when his program issues a data-base *read* which refers to it, the data are extracted from the data base and presented to the program in the subschema format by the data-base management system.

The subschema is sometimes referred to as a *local view* or LVIEW. One subschema may serve several application programs and may be defined separately from the application programs. The term *submodel* is also used for subschema.

The American National Standards Association ANSI X3 SPARC study group on data-base systems published an interim report in 1975 referring to the overall logical view (schema) as a *conceptual schema,* and the programmer's view or end user's view (subschema) as an *external schema.*

Table 21.1 shows the various terms that are used. We will use the words *schema* and *subschema.*

Table 21.1 Alternate terms which describe the views of data.
This book uses the words **subschema, schema,**
and **physical data** as these are simple clear terms.

	ANSI X3 SPARC	CODASYL	IBM's DL/I	OTHER TERMS
Programmer's view:	External schema	Subschema	PSB (Program specification Block)	Submodel; LVIEW (Local view)
Overall logical view:	Conceptual schema	Schema	Logical DBB (Data Base Description)	Model; Entity set Entity record
Physical view:	Internal schema	Physical data	Physical DBD (Data Base Description)	

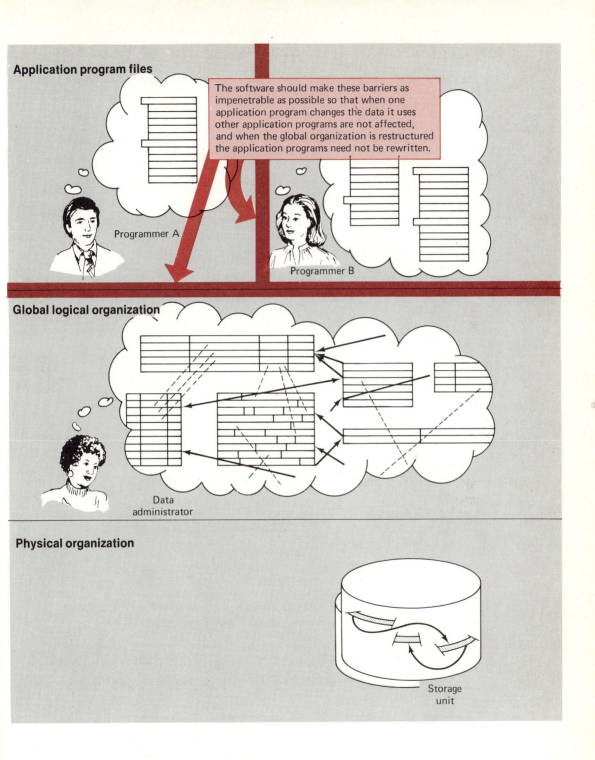

The software should make these barriers as impenetrable as possible so that when one application program changes the data it uses other application programs are not affected, and when the global organization is restructured the application programs need not be rewritten.

Application program files

Programmer A

Programmer B

Global logical organization

Data administrator

Physical organization

Storage unit

Figure 21.8 Logical data independence.

SUMMARY   Box 21.1 summarizes the advantages of data-base management over the simpler *file* management.

BOX 21.1 Advantages of a data-base system over a file system

(We assume a good quality data-base management system, a good data dictionary, and good dialogue software for interrogating, searching, maintaining, and generating reports from the data base.)

- THE DATA CAN HAVE MULTIPLE USES

    Different users who perceive the same data differently can employ them in different ways.

- INTELLECTUAL INVESTMENT IS PROTECTED

    - One program can be changed without affecting the others.

    - The logical data-base structure can be added to or improved without affecting previously existing programs.

    - The physical layout and structure of data can be changed without affecting the programs or the logical structure.

    - The storage hardware can be changed without affecting the logical data base or programs.

    - The data bases can be merged without the programs having to be rewritten.

    - In future distributed data-base systems, the data or program execution may be moved to a different location without program rewriting.

- CLARITY

    Users can easily know and understand what data are available to them.

- EASE OF USE

    Users can gain access to data in a simple fashion. Complexity is hidden from the users by the data-base management system.

- FLEXIBLE USAGE

    The data can be used or searched in flexible ways with different access paths.

- UNANTICIPATED REQUESTS FOR DATA CAN BE HANDLED QUICKLY

    Spontaneous requests for data can be handled by data-base interrogation languages without having to write programs (a time-consuming bottleneck).

BOX 21.1 *continued*

- AVOIDANCE OF APPLICATION PROGRAMMING

  It should be a goal that most application programming be avoided by using report generators, dialogue program generators, and data-base interrogation and maintenance software. This alternative to programming may eventually prove to be the most important reason for using data bases.

- LESS DATA PROLIFERATION

  New application needs may be met with existing data rather than by creating new files, thus avoiding the excessive data proliferation in today's tape libraries.

- BETTER CONTROLS

  Data-base management systems in some cases have better controls than file management systems for security, privacy, accuracy, and reliability.

- ACCURACY AND CONSISTENCY

  Accuracy controls will be used. The system will avoid having multiple versions of the same data item available to users in different stages of updating.

- PRIVACY

  Unauthorized access to the data will be prevented. The same data may be restricted in different ways from different uses.

- PROTECTION FROM LOSS OR DAMAGE

  Data will be protected from failures and catastrophes, and from criminals, vandals, incompetents, and persons who might falsely update them.

- AVAILABILITY

  Data are quickly available to users at almost all times when they need them.

- TUNABILITY

  The data base should be tunable, to improve performance without affecting application programs. This is important when usage patterns change greatly, as they often do. In future systems physical data organization may be automatically adjusted according to usage.

REFERENCES

1. James Martin, *Computer Data-Base Organization,* Second Edition, Prentice-Hall, Inc., Englewood Cliffs, N.J., 1977 (Chapter 15 on canonical data structures).

2. The data-base concepts summarized in this chapter are discussed more fully in the author's data-base books, listed on the front endpapers.

22   DISTRIBUTED DATA BASES

Data-base management software is highly complex and in most cases today is designed to exist in a single computer or computer complex. There is much talk about distributed data-base systems; however, in reality so far most systems with geographically scattered data are *distributed file systems* rather than *distributed data-base systems*. Some configurations use more than one data-base system with separate data structures, but still each data-base system resides in one location.

Data-base technology has tended to encourage centralized configurations so far. Distributed intelligence and vertical distributed processing are sometimes used with centralized data bases. Horizontal networks sometimes link disjoint (usually noncooperative) data bases which are themselves centralized.

Distributed data bases could, in theory, have their data distributed in any of the types of configurations shown in Fig. 17.1. In order to be a *data base* rather than a *file* system we need the schemas and subschemas discussed in the previous chapter. The questions arise: Where are they located? And where is the mapping between them performed?

LOGICAL RECORDS   In a conventional data-base system, a programmer or user refers to a *logical* record or logical file. The data-base management system derives this record from the physical records. The same is true in a distributed data-base system, but now the data might be in a distant location and the system has to find them.

The system may be more efficient if certain data are stored in duplicate in two or more locations. The user (ideally) does not want to know where the data are stored. He merely refers to a *logical* record and expects it to be provided. The distribution and networking should be completely invisible to him.

PERIPHERAL SUBSCHEMAS

There are several different forms of distributed data base. They are illustrated in Fig. 22.1.

In the first diagram in Fig. 22.1, the peripheral machine can run programs but does not have a data base. A program refers to records and files with commands such as GET, GET NEXT, PUT, UPDATE, INSERT, and DELETE. These commands may refer to *remote* data. With distributed data-base software they refer to *logical* records or files which are derived by a remote data-base management system as in Fig. 22.2.

The central data base may be shared by many peripheral machines with different programs. The currency controls in a conventional data base need to be extended to the distributed environment to make sure that one program's updating of a record cannot interfere with that of a program in another machine. This, as discussed in Chapter 20, can be complex.

DATA-BASE SYSTEMS IN COMMUNICATION

The second diagram in Fig. 21.1 shows the application program in question in a machine which itself has a data-base management system. (Let us use the initials DBMS for short.) If the program refers to a logical record which is not in the domain of that DBMS, the system makes contact with another DBMS which does have the requested data. A protocol (set of rules) exists for transferring either a single record or a file between the DBMS's. If data in one machine at a time are *read* only, the procedure is relatively straightforward. If the data are updated, then careful controls are needed to prevent conflicts and deadlocks, as discussed in Chapter 20.

In this multiple DBMS environment, each DBMS needs to be able to find the location of logical records which it does not itself store. It might have a directory of all logical records in the multi-DBMS system, so that it can send the request on to the appropriate machine. Alternatively, it may send the request to a separate directory machine which assists in establishing the communications path.

REMOTE DATA STORAGE

The third diagram in Fig. 22.1 shows another form of distributed data base. Here the physical data may be stored remotely from the data-base management system. This is illustrated in Fig. 22.3.

There are several reasons why remote data storage can be of value:

1. *Security.* The data may be stored in a highly secure vault far from the data-processing center, perhaps in a location such as Iron Mountain in New York State (where many corporations store data needing high security in a disused mine which has been adapted for this purpose).

2. *Audits and archives.* Data relating to transactions may be dumped into remote storages to form archives or a tamperproof audit trail.

3. *Economy of scale.* It may be cheaper to store the data on a portion of a mass storage

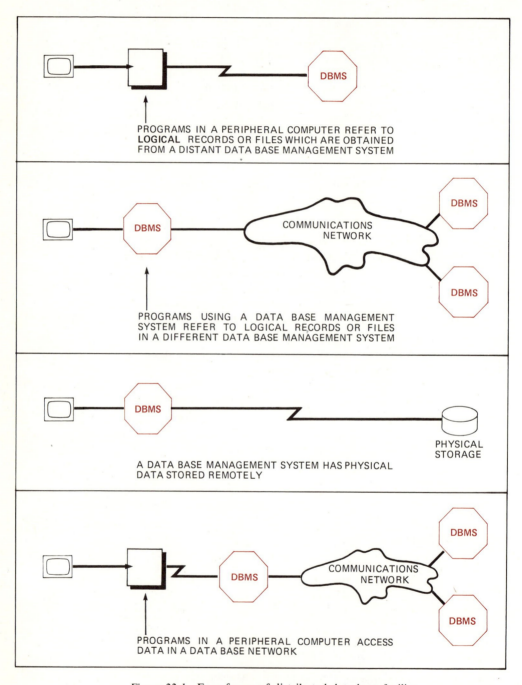

PROGRAMS IN A PERIPHERAL COMPUTER REFER TO
LOGICAL RECORDS OR FILES WHICH ARE OBTAINED
FROM A DISTANT DATA BASE MANAGEMENT SYSTEM

DBMS

COMMUNICATIONS
NETWORK

DBMS

DBMS

PROGRAMS USING A DATA BASE MANAGEMENT
SYSTEM REFER TO LOGICAL RECORDS OR FILES
IN A DIFFERENT DATA BASE MANAGEMENT SYSTEM

DBMS

PHYSICAL
STORAGE

A DATA BASE MANAGEMENT SYSTEM HAS PHYSICAL
DATA STORED REMOTELY

DBMS

COMMUNICATIONS
NETWORK

DBMS

DBMS

PROGRAMS IN A PERIPHERAL COMPUTER ACCESS
DATA IN A DATA BASE NETWORK

Figure 22.1   Four forms of distributed data base facility.

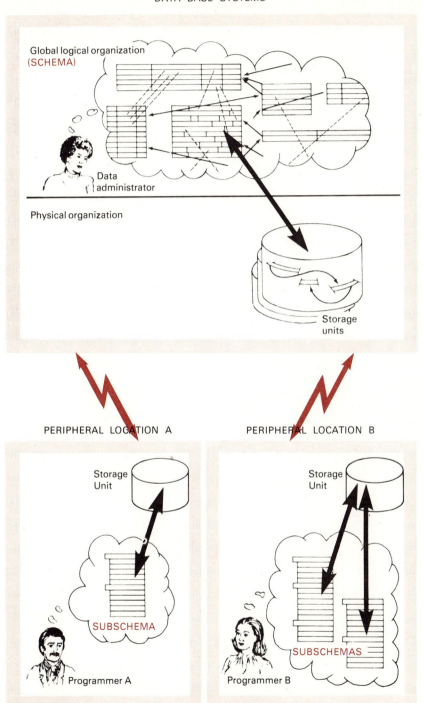

Figure 22.2 A hierarchical distributed data base.

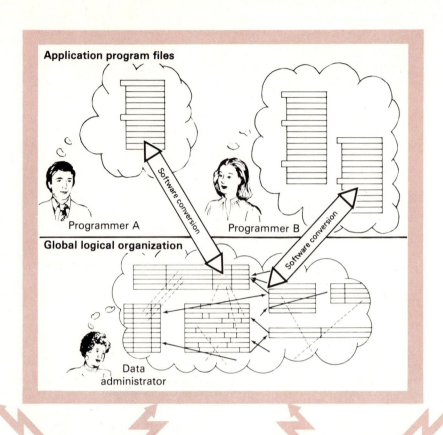

Application program files

Programmer A

Software conversion

Programmer B

Software conversion

Global logical organization

Data administrator

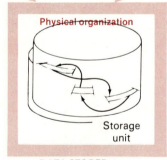

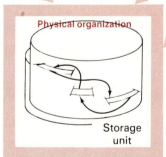

Physical organization

Storage unit

Physical organization

Storage unit

DATA STORED
REMOTELY IN
SECURE LOCATION
AND POSSIBLY
SHARED BY
MULTIPLE SYSTEMS

Figure 22.3 Remote storage of the physical data.

system. The cost per bit is much lower on large storage devices, and if the networking costs are low enough, this could give cost savings, especially for infrequently used data.

4. *Data sharing.* The same physical data may be used by many systems. They may be data which are *read* and not *written* by users. They may be written by users if appropriate controls are possible. With many types of data updating, the conflicts described in Chapter 20 do not occur.

5. *Information retrieval.* Massive quantities of data are kept in some information retrieval systems. For example, copies of all available technical reports in certain subject areas, or all documents relevant to an antitrust case. In the future, copies of newspapers, magazines, trade literature, financial reports, and so on, will be stored ready for transmission to any computer which can use them. The using computers may operate an information retrieval system which permits users to search for information on subjects of interest to them. Such systems are likely to be economic only if they do not *each* have to store such large quantities of data.

The fourth diagram in Fig. 22.1 shows another variation on the theme. A logical record is requested by a small computer, one too small to have a DBMS. The request goes to its parent DBMS computer or to the nearest *host* on a distributed data-base network. The DBMS then finds the data that were requested, possibly from another DBMS.

COMPLEXITY   Some advocates of distributed data bases have claimed
                          simplicity and ease of implementation as advantages of
the distributed approach. The individual data bases are smaller, localized, and hence simpler than a large, centralized data base. While this is true, the software is likely to be very complicated unless many of the principles of data base are ignored. It is likely that such software will gradually come into existence, giving logical, physical, and geographical data independence. The software (and firmware) will, it is hoped, hide most of the complexities from the users and to some extent from the application and data-base designers.

HOW ARE THE   A system whose data are scattered geographically must
DATA LOCATED?   have some means of determining where any required
                          piece of data is stored. As with other aspects of distributed data bases, finding the location of data can range from being a very simple operation to a highly complex one.

A simple method is for the user to specify the location of the data when he makes a request to use them. His transaction may then be transmitted to a computer at the location of the data, or alternatively the data may be transmitted to a location where they can be processed—possibly the location where the transaction originates.

A slightly more complicated approach is for the user to specify information about the data from which their location can be simply determined. In a large bank with multiple data centers, for example, a customer may indicate which branch he banks with, and this information determines where his account records are stored.

In some hierarchical configurations, the data are always stored either at the peripheral location or at the central location. The program in the computer at the peripheral location determines whether it needs to pass the request on to the central computer or not.

Locating the data becomes more complex in horizontal distribution when the user does not know where the data are located. The system must contain some form of catalog or directory, like a telephone directory, which permits the data to be found. The directory may exist in one particular computer in the network, the request for data being passed to this computer and the location of the data established. Alternatively, every computer in such a network may have a complete directory, listing each file in the network and indicating where it is physically located. Disadvantages of having a directory in every computer are, first, the storage space required for such directories and, second, the work of keeping them all up to date. In addition, the local computers may not be so well equipped for searching the directories rapidly as a specialized or larger computer. The directory may be replicated in regional computers, but not in the small, peripheral machines. In other words, in Fig. 9.2 each computer at the top of the cones may keep a copy of the directory.

In many systems, most of the transactions received by a local computer relate to the data kept at that location, whereas a few transactions are for data in other locations. In this case the computers may each have a directory of their own data only and may pass the request on to another computer if it relates to data they do not have.

The directory problem is a distributed data problem on a small scale. Should the data in the directories be replicated for efficiency reasons? Probably. To what extent should they be replicated? How are the replicated copies updated and maintained in a consistent state?

The directory may be treated just like any other data by the system or may be given special treatment for improved efficiency and safety. System design is simplified if the directory is treated *like any other data*. Like other data, it can be fragmented or replicated. There is one aspect in which the directory data cannot be treated identically to user data. The system must know where the directory itself is stored. There must be a starting point from which directory information can be found. Information about where the directory, or fragments of it, are stored must be at every node.

TRANSMISSION OF
DATA OR FILES?
When a transaction is processed by a computer which does not have the data it requires, there are two possibilities:

1. Move the data to the processing computer.
2. Move the transaction and process it where the data are.

Which method is used is affected by the machines and their software and by what would have to be transmitted and how frequently. It is expensive to move large amounts of data too often, and it is slow. It is often cheaper and faster to move the transaction.

Sometimes processing a transaction requires data in multiple locations. Complex decisions may then be necessary about how the process should be broken up and where the pieces should be implemented.

LOCAL AND GLOBAL DATA MANAGERS   It is desirable that the software for distributed database management should employ *existing* data-base management systems. A conventional DBMS should operate either in a single-DBMS environment or in a distributed DBMS environment. If the latter, another piece of software should be added which tackles the problems associated with distribution—directory, network interface, conflict avoidance, etc.

Figure 22.4 illustrates this. Each location has a *local data manager* and a *network data manager*. The network data manager is sometimes given the name *global data manager*.

The local data manager manages data at its own location and has no awareness of data at other locations or of any issues related to data distribution. It can be a conventional, single-site DBMS. It could also be a *file* (as opposed to *data-base*) management system.

The network data manager cannot itself access the data. It relies on the local data manager to read and write the data. It handles all data-distribution issues. It examines access requests and uses a directory to determine which local data manager can handle them. It initiates the transmission of data and data requests and receives transmitted data. It uses protocols such as those described in Chapter 20 to prevent invalid updates, inconsistent reads, and deadly embrace situations. If multiple copies of data exist, it ensures that all copies are updated and that when a read is requested a copy giving the best access efficiency is used.

It is possible that the local data managers could be different DBMS's which do not use compatible data-base languages. Each network data manager is equipped to make calls on its local data manager in the language of that local system.

INTEGRATED GLOBAL MANAGER   The network data manager may be quite separate from the DBMS's which it interlinks, or it may be integrated into their architecture. No doubt the software (and firmware) of major manufacturers will eventually include integrated network data managers.

The CODASYL committee has proposed an extension to its DBMS architecture which adds the software layer shown in Fig. 22.5, called NDBMS, Network

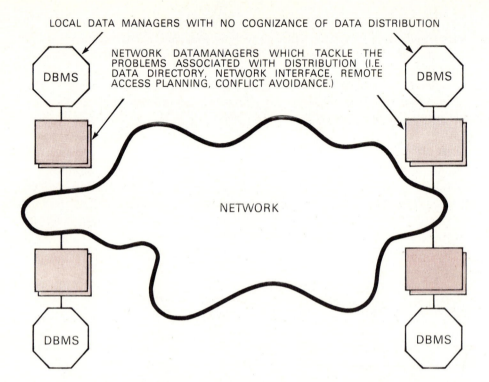

LOCAL DATA MANAGERS WITH NO COGNIZANCE OF DATA DISTRIBUTION

NETWORK DATAMANAGERS WHICH TACKLE THE PROBLEMS ASSOCIATED WITH DISTRIBUTION (I.E. DATA DIRECTORY, NETWORK INTERFACE, REMOTE ACCESS PLANNING, CONFLICT AVOIDANCE.)

DBMS

DBMS

NETWORK

DBMS

DBMS

Figure 22.4 Conventional single site data base management systems may be used in distributed data base environment by using an additional *network datamanager* component which manages the distribution. Here the network and DBMS software may previously exist; a network datamanager is added to interconnect them.

Data Base Management System [1, 2]. The NDBMS does the network data management functions. The DBMS manages the local data and has no cognizance of any other data nodes. The NDBMS functions might be integrated with those of the DBMS, they might be in a disjoint software unit, or they might be in a separate machine; that is a packaging decision.

The NDBMS functions include the following:

1. Intercept a user request and determine which nodes to send it to for processing. The majority of user requests should use local data and not require the NDBS. These may go to the local DBMS directly or be passed to it by the NDBMS.

2. Access the network directory (which may possibly be remote) for the above purpose.

3. If the target data are on multiple nodes, coordinate the use of these nodes.

4. Manage the communication between its node and DBMS's in other nodes.

5. If the data bases are heterogeneous, provide the necessary translation.

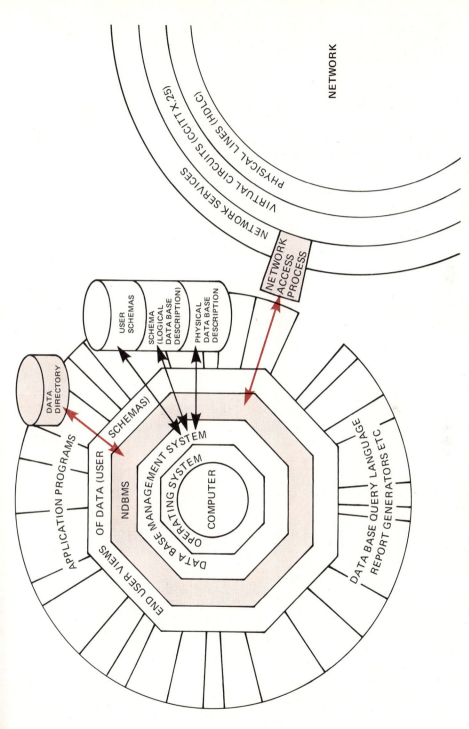

Figure 22.5 The CODASYL architecture for distributed data base adds the components shown in red to conventional DBMS and network architectures. The NDBMS, Network Data Base Management System manages all accesses to remote data.

331

The task of the NDBMS is extension of the task of the DBMS in locating data. When a request for data is made, the DBMS must determine on what disks and what pages the data reside. The NDBMS must determine at what node the data reside.

Efficiency of operation of the DBMS depends on clustering onto the same page data which are referenced together. Efficiency in a distributed system depends on clustering at the same node data which are referenced together and ensuring as much as possible that they are at the same node as the user.

In the distributed environment envisioned by the CODASYL committee, there would be three types of nodes, as shown in Fig. 22.6:

1. A user node without a data base, for example, a minicomputer or intelligent terminal

2. A conventional data-base system without the NDBMS or any cognizance of data distribution

3. A full-function distributed data-base node with the NDBMS

Bachman [2], giving an ANSI (American National Standards Institute) reaction to the CODASYL proposals, stated that this was too narrow a view. A distributed system should permit cooperating user work stations and *file* management work stations as well as data-base work stations.

SSD.1   The Computer Corporation of America claims to have built the world's first working distributed data-base system [3, 4]. This is SDD.1 (System for Distributed Data Bases), which has an architectural stucture designed to permit new data-base sites to be added worldwide, giving a large and freely evolving configuration.

SDD.1 employs ARPANET (Fig. 9.4) as its communications network and could employ the world's X.25 packet-switching networks. The work was supported by the Defense Advanced Research Project Agency of the U.S. Department of Defense. SDD.1 was designed for naval command and control applications, but the techniques and protocols it uses are applicable to distributed data bases in general. The team have analyzed the directory problem [4], the conflict problem [5], and the efficiency problem [6] of distributed data-base systems and have implemented elegant solutions to these problems.

SDD.1 is designed to permit a large amount of replication of data. This is desirable for lessening the transmission done by a potentially worldwide system and for increasing availability and survivability of the information resource, especially when under military attack.

Like other distributed data-base systems, SDD.1 uses a local data manager and a separate network data manager. The local data manager has the functions of a conventional single-site DBMS and has no cognizance of distribution problems. The network data manager does not access the data itself but determines the access

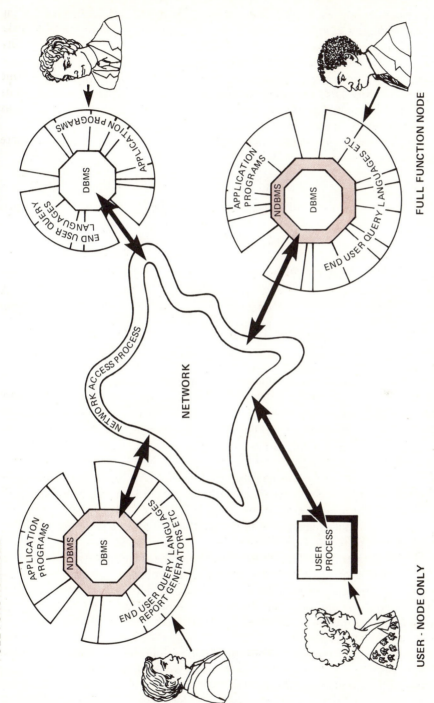

FULL FUNCTION NODE

DBMS - ONLY NODE

FULL FUNCTION NODE

USER - NODE ONLY

Figure 22.6 User and data at different types of nodes in a CODASYL distributed data environment.

333

strategy for handling each distributed data operation efficiently. It requests the local data managers at any site to perform local processing and/or move portions of data from one site to another.

Figure 22.7 illustrates SDD.1. The local data manager is called the DM (data-module). The network data manager is called the TM (transaction module). One TM and up to three DMs can reside at each site. Each TM maintains a global data directory and is capable of planning an access strategy relating to the entire network. The control is completely distributed. Any node can fail, and the system will continue to function. New nodes can be added freely. Many queries involve data in multiple nodes.

RELATIONAL DATA BASES

Any DBMS must have a *logical* description of the data it manages. This description ought to describe the *logical* properties of the data and not include any properties of the machines, physical storage techniques, or physical access methods. During the 1970's a diverse collection of techniques for logical description of data came into use. The most common were the CODASYL technique [7] using interconnected sets, a set being a two-level tree structure; Syncom's TOTAL using multilevel trees connected by external pointers [8]; and IBM's DL/I using multilevel trees incorporating pointer segments [9]. Data-base enthusiasts began to advocate the use of a different technique which was simpler and yielded to precise mathematical formulation—*relational data bases* [10].

Relational data structures consist of multiple two-dimensional matrices of fields. Each matrix is called a relation. There are no tree structures, CODASYL sets, or pointers to pointers to pointers. By grouping together appropriate combinations of fields, any data structures, no matter how complex, can be represented as relations. In order to do this some fields exist redundantly in the *logical* data description.

The mathematics of relational algebra describes how relations can be joined or subdivided to produce new relations and thus create the logical records which a programmer wants or an end user perceives [11].

The network data manager in distributed data-base systems must be able to find out where different fragments of data are stored. It may bring together fragments of data from different nodes and combine them in various ways. The complex problems of a distributed data base can probably be best solved if the description of the data perceived by the network data managers is *relational*. User requests for data operations can be put into terms of what relations must be retrieved and how they may be joined or subdivided. The distributed data directories refer to relations and precisely defined fragments of relations. For efficiency reasons, fragments of one relation may be stored at multiple locations. The concurrency controls and controls for preventing conflicts similarly relate to relations.

The definition of complex data operations in terms of relations can be simpler or more precise than when data structures are used which are not two-dimensional

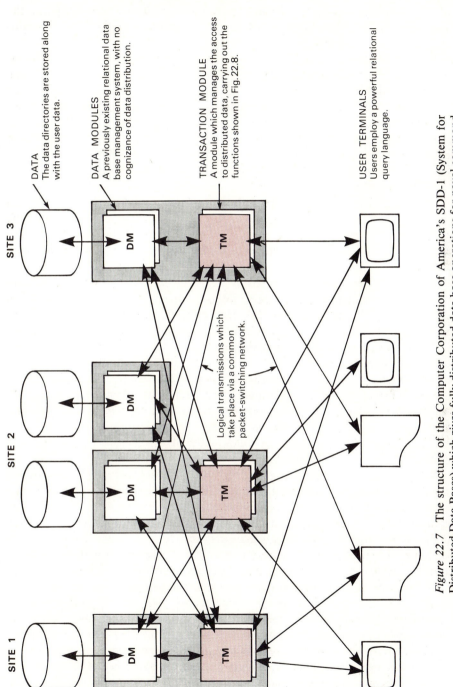

DATA
The data directories are stored along with the user data.

DATA MODULES
A previously existing relational data base management system, with no cognizance of data distribution.

TRANSACTION MODULE
A module which manages the access to distributed data, carrying out the functions shown in Fig. 22.8.

USER TERMINALS
Users employ a powerful relational query language.

Logical transmissions which take place via a common packet-switching network.

SITE 3

SITE 2

SITE 1

DM

TM

Figure 22.7 The structure of the Computer Corporation of America's SDD-1 (System for Distributed Data Bases) which gives fully distributed data base operations for naval command and control applications (4).

335

as with most of the DBMS's which date back to the 1970's. These more complex data structures do not yield so easily to precise mathematical description and manipulation.

Because of this the Computer Corporation of America based its SDD.1 architecture on relational data structures, employing an existing relational DBMS called Datacomputer.

The chunks of data which are stored at the nodes of SDD.1 and referred to by the distribution mechanisms are portions of relations called *fragments*. Each fragment is a rectangular subset of a relation. It may be a vertical subset composed of specified fields (columns) of the relation (i.e., a *projection* of the relation [10]). It may be a horizontal subset defined by one or more expressions such as

$$\text{Value of field } A \leq x$$

$$\text{Value of field } K = y$$

$$\text{Value of field } D > z$$

The SDD.1 fragments are formed by first splitting a relation horizontally (if necessary) and then splitting it vertically, i.e., selecting certain fields. The horizontal slice may be only one tuple (record). The resulting fragments must include the primary key of the data, the unique identifier of each tuple.

A given fragment is either *completely* present or completely absent at a given data module. Any fragment may be stored redundantly at more than one data module. The data directory is itself a relation which tells where all of the fragments are stored. *It* can also be fragmented and stored redundantly at any node. This gives complete flexibility in directory management. Every node has a means to *locate* the directory.

Figure 22.8 shows the major modules of the SDD.1 transaction module and how they use the relational data bases [4].

Requests for data operations are received in an end-user language. The requests are passed to determine what files and fields are required. The data directory is used to determine that these are available and that the end user is authorized to access them. The system then determines what operations on logical relations are needed. The relations are stored as fragments, and different fragments may be in different machines. The needed operations on relations are therefore translated into operations on the stored fragments. The fragments may be replicated on multiple sites, and the operation may require multiple fragments so there can be many alternative means of carrying out the required operation. The *access planner* determines the optimum method. It finds out from the directory which sites store the fragments. A cost estimator module attempts to determine how much data would have to be moved. Often transmission is minimized by carrying out operations on data before transmission at the site where they are stored. The cost estimator obtains statistics about the size of data in an attempt to evaluate how much will be transmitted after these operations.

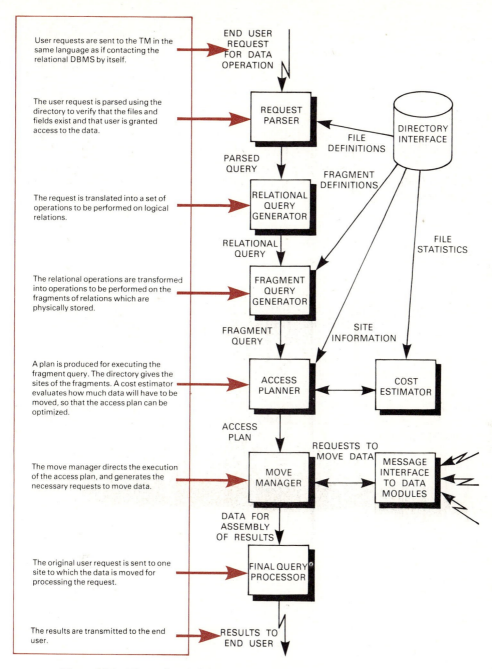

User requests are sent to the TM in the same language as if contacting the relational DBMS by itself.

END USER REQUEST FOR DATA OPERATION

The user request is parsed using the directory to verify that the files and fields exist and that user is granted access to the data.

REQUEST PARSER

DIRECTORY INTERFACE

FILE DEFINITIONS

PARSED QUERY

FRAGMENT DEFINITIONS

The request is translated into a set of operations to be performed on logical relations.

RELATIONAL QUERY GENERATOR

RELATIONAL QUERY

FILE STATISTICS

The relational operations are transformed into operations to be performed on the fragments of relations which are physically stored.

FRAGMENT QUERY GENERATOR

FRAGMENT QUERY

SITE INFORMATION

A plan is produced for executing the fragment query. The directory gives the sites of the fragments. A cost estimator evaluates how much data will have to be moved, so that the access plan can be optimized.

ACCESS PLANNER

COST ESTIMATOR

ACCESS PLAN

REQUESTS TO MOVE DATA

The move manager directs the execution of the access plan, and generates the necessary requests to move data.

MOVE MANAGER

MESSAGE INTERFACE TO DATA MODULES

DATA FOR ASSEMBLY OF RESULTS

The original user request is sent to one site to which the data is moved for processing the request.

FINAL QUERY PROCESSOR

The results are transmitted to the end user.

RESULTS TO END USER

Figure 22.8   The actions of the network data management (TM) portion of the SDD-1 system illustrated in Fig. 22.7. (4)

337

The *move manager* directs the execution of the access plan and generates the necessary requests to move data. For efficiency reasons, the final processing of the data may take place at a different site from that where the above operations are performed. The access planner selects this site, and the results are then transmitted to the end user.

MULTISITE QUERY PROCESSING   A distributed data-base system may deal with information requests all of which involve the data at *one site only*. Alternatively it may, like SDD.1, handle requests requiring data from multiple sites to be joined or searched. The latter results in far more complex operations and access planning.

If data from multiple sites are *joined,* then bulk transmission may be needed from one site to another. It is desirable to determine at which site to do the join operation in order to minimize the transmission, or in general at which site to process the data in order to minimize transmission.

Most commercial systems can be designed so that queries or data operations do not require files from multiple sites to be joined or searched. The locations of data (including replicating the data) can be planned so that bulk transmissions are avoided except for activities such as data entry, restart-recovery, and batch transmission at night. Queries may require single records to be transmitted from more than one site, but they can avoid any bulk transmission.

Figure 22.9 shows a use of SDD.1 in a naval command-and-control environment. A query is processed which asks for *details of ships which have a readiness rating of C1 and which carry torpedoes with a range of 20 miles or more*. To answer this query five logical files (relations) are needed. They are located at four separate sites [12]. The files are:

Site 1: SHIPWEPSDIR.

For each weapon ths file indicates which classes of ship carry it.

Site 1: SHIPCLASDIR.

For each class of ship this file gives the ships which are in it.

Site 2: READY.

For each readiness rating this file indicates which ships are in it.

Site 3: SHIP.

This file gives details of each ship.

Site 4: WEPSCHAAR.

This file gives the characteristics of every type of weapon.
The data bases contain much other information about the ships (including

QUERY: LIST DETAILS OF ALL U.S. SHIPS WITH A READINESS RATING OF C1
          AND TORPEDOES WITH A RANGE OF 20 MILES OR MORE.

To answer this query needs five files (relations) in four different locations.
Thus:

PRIMARY KEY: **WEAPONS**
Can answer queries such as "What classes of
ship carry a given weapon?"

PRIMARY KEY: **READINESS RATING**
Can answer queries such as "What ships have
a given readiness rating?"

PRIMARY KEY: **CLASS**
Can answer questions such as "What ships are
in a given class?"

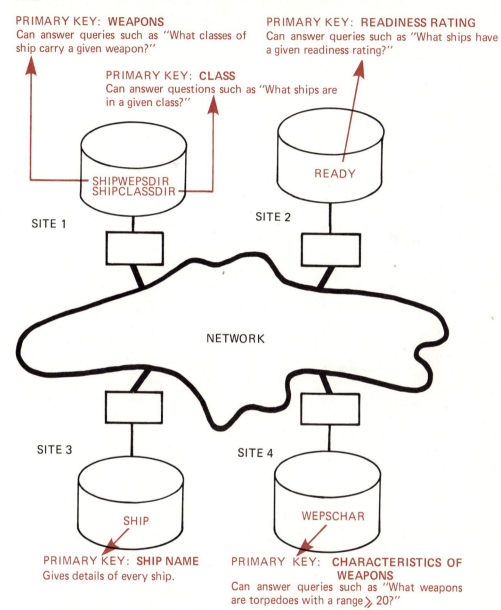

Figure 22.9 An example of a query which needs data from multiple locations. (12).

foreign ships), their positions, crew, weapons, activity, equipment, casualties, and so on.

The above query reaches site 1. The transaction module at that site must check the query and determine what relations (or fragments) are needed to answer it. Several different access and processing sequences could be used. The transaction module must select an efficient one.

Figure 22.10 illustrates the actions needed to process the query.

1. The query reaches site 1.

2. The transaction module at site 1 determines what steps are required to answer the query (as shown in Fig. 22.8).

3. Site 1 sends an instruction to site 2 instructing it to select from the READY file all U.S. ships with a readiness rating of C1 and transmit this list to site 3.

4. Site 1 sends an instruction to site 4 to use the WEPSCHAP file to select weapons which are torpedoes with a range of 20 miles and transmit this list to site 1.

   These requested actions can take place in sites 2 and 4 *simultaneously*. Actions needed for handling complex queries can often take place in parallel.

5. Site 4 sends the list of weapons to site 1. The movement of data is shown in Fig. 22.10 as thick red lines.

6. Site 1 uses the SHIPWEPSDIR file to determine what classes of ships have the requisite weapons.

7. Site 1 uses the SHIPCLASDIR file to determine what U.S. ships are in these classes.

8. Site 2 sends a list of ships with the requisite readiness rating to site 3.

9. Site 1 sends a list of ships with the requisite weapons to site 3.

10. Site 1 instructs site 3 to select all ships which are on both of the above lists, obtain their details from the SHIP file, and transmit the results.

11. Site 3 transmits the results to the end user.

REQUIREMENTS FOR MULTISITE QUERIES How much more complex is this than answering the query if all of the data are in one machine? Let us assume that relational date bases exist and have an end-user language capable of dealing with this type of query in one machine. Let us also assume that a network architecture exists that is capable of moving data from one node to another. These main problems have to be solved in order to handle multisite queries like that above.

First, there is the data directory problem discussed earlier.

Second, there is the problem of avoiding conflicts and deadlocks, discussed in Chapter 20.

Third, the node which plans the accessing operations must be able to do so in an optimal, or at least efficient, fashion. It must decide at which nodes it would be best to do the processing. This is important because there is a vast difference in the

NDBMS or the SDD.1 transaction module, such software needs a global data directory to enable it to find the requested data. There may be one global datamanager or, better, a distributed network of them. A function of this facility is to form an interface to otherwise incompatible DBMS systems.

A major purpose of such network datamanagers is to make use of the data which already exist on-line in corporations without the excessive costs of converting today's systems into compatible distributed systems. A secondary objective is to enhance security, because all data flow between sites would have to go through the network datamanager and be subject to control.

At the time of writing such network datamanagers are being custom-built in some large corporations. The expense of writing this software is high, but not as high as an attempt to convert the existing systems.

While the incompatibility problem is important to solve, many commercial systems can avoid some of the difficulties of distributed data bases. They may avoid unconstrained *replication* of data, as on SDD.1, and the complexities it introduces. They may avoid multisite queries of the type illustrated in Fig. 22.10.

PRIMARY AND
SECONDARY
KEY OPERATIONS

We can divide data-base accesses into those that employ only a *primary key* and those that employ searching or secondary key operations. (A primary key identifies one and only one record; a secondary key is the basis of a search or sort operation and as such identifies zero, one, or many records.) Distributed data operations are much simpler than that in Fig. 22.10 if all accesses to remote data are for single records accessed by their primary key. This can be relativley easy to do even if the records reside on different types of DBMS, provided that these DBMS's have appropriate interfaces to a common network.

Although a substantial restriction, this scheme can be appropriate for many commercial situations. Often a functional information system has been built for management or professional staff. Data are drawn from other systems and summarized in the information system with appropriate secondary keys and searching mechanisms (Figs. 17.5 and 17.6). If it has been well thought out, the information system itself should answer many of its users' queries, but sometimes the user wants more detail. He wants the original data rather than the summary data. He would like to inspect a customer's account, an employee's personnel file, or a machine tool record. He would like these queries to be answered via a network. They are, however, primary-key queries. The more complex secondary-key queries are answerable from his own information system without any distributed operations.

A network datamanager may provide the link between a local information system and a distributed data-base network. Like the transaction module of SDD.1, it provides a user interface, but its distributed data operations are much less complex. Network datamanager modules may link the users to *file* systems as well as *data-base* systems, as shown in Fig. 22.11.

A network may have more than one network datamanager connected to dif-

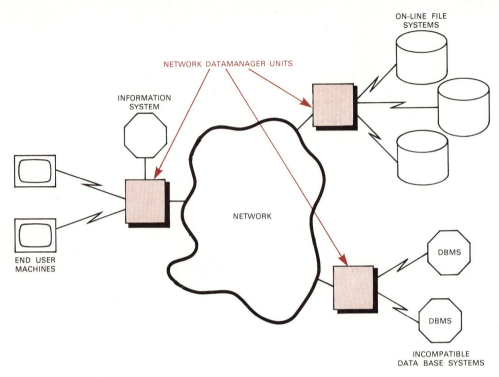

Figure 22.11 A network datamanager facility designed to give access to various, installed, incompatible data resources.

ferent systems. Some may employ the facilities of the local machines' data-base management systems. Some may be connected to local machines which have no data-base management, and so they provide some of the features of a data-base management system themselves.

One way of building a highly flexible network between incompatible data bases would be for a network datamanager to convert all of the data-base structures to a relational form. Relational operations like those of SDD.1 could then be employed.

STANDARDS   The software and hardware product lines of major manufacturers are likely to evolve so that they can support the various forms of distributed data base illustrated in Fig. 22.1. In IBM, for example, separate IMS systems can be linked together, and IMS is linked to SNA, which enables peripheral processors to access a data base. The capabilities of IMS and SNA or their replacements will steadily grow. In other manufacturers, CODASYL systems are being extended and interlinked for distributed use. In the minicomputer manufacturers, both network architectures and data-base management systems are being implemented on steadily cheaper computers. A major capability will emerge for interlinking data bases of the same minicomputer.

Much distributed data-base software, then, will operate with machines from one manufacturer that are tightly integrated in their design. It is very important that international standards be developed for interconnecting data bases of different manufacturers over networks that are truly multinational. Much work is going on to create such standards in CODASYL, ANSI (American National Standards Organization), and ISO (International Standards Organization) and various other organizations. However, there are grounds for pessimism that *incompatibility* between different manufacturers' systems (and even within one manufacturer) will be a major problem for data-processing managers for years to come.

KEEP IT SIMPLE   The computer industry does not yet have software which can do everything that might one day be desirable with distributed data bases. For the time being, the rule for systems analysts with such systems ought to be "Keep it simple." To do all that may be theoretically advantageous is exceedingly complicated.

REFERENCES

1. The CODASYL Systems Committee, *Distributed Data Base Technology—An interim report of the CODASYL systems committee,* Proc. NCC 1978, AFIPS Press, Montvale, N.J.

2. C. W. Bachman, *Commentary on the CODASYL systems committee's interim report on distributed data base technology,* Proc. NCC 1978, AFIPS Press, Montvale, N.J.

3. J. B. Rothnie and N. Goodman, *An Overview of the Preliminary Design of SDD.1: A System for Distributed Data Bases.* Computer Corporation of America Technical Report CCA–77–04, Cambridge, Mass. 02139, 1977.

4. *A Distributed Data Base Management System for Command and Control Applications: Semi-Annual Technical Report 3,* Computer Corporation of America Technical Report CCA–78–10, Cambridge, Mass. 02139, 1978.

5. P. A. Berstein, J. B. Rothnie, D. W. Shipman, and N. Goodman, *The SDD–1 Redundant Update Algorithm (The General Case),* Technical Report in progress, Computer Corporation of America, 575 Technology Square, Cambridge, Mass. 02139.

6. E. Wong, *Retrieving Dispersed Data from SDD–1: A System for Distributed Databases,* 1977 Berkeley Workshop on Distributed Data Management and Computer Networks, Lawrence Berkeley Laboratory, University of California,

Berkeley, May 1977. (Also available from Computer Corporation of America, 575 Technology Square, Cambridge Mass. 02139, as Technical Report No. CCA–77–03.)

7. National Bureau of Standards Handbook *CODASYL Data Description Language Journal of Development,* U.S. Department of Commerce, National Bureau of Standards, Washington, D.C., 1978.

    For an overall description of the CODASYL approach see James Martin, *Computer Data-Base Organization,* Second Edition, Chapter 11, Prentice-Hall, Inc., Englewood Cliffs, N.J., 1977.

8. Information manuals on TOTAL available from CINCOM, Inc., 2300 Montana Avenue, Cincinnati, Ohio 45211.

9. *Information Management System/Virtual Storage (IMS/VS), General Information Manual GH20–1260,* IBM, White Plains, N.Y., 1979.

    For an overall description of IBM IMS and DL/I approach, see James Martin, *Computer Data-Base Organization,* Second Edition, Chapter 12, Prentice-Hall, Inc., Englewood Cliffs, N.J., 1977.

10. For an overall description of relational data bases, see James Martin, *Computer Data-Base Organization,* Second Edition, Chapter 13, Prentice-Hall, Inc., Englewood Cliffs, N.J., 1977.

11. Various papers by E. F. Codd describe relational languages, including *A Data Base Sublanguage Founded on the Relation Calculus,* Proc. ACM-SIGFIDET Workshop on Data Description, Access and Control, 1971. ACM (Association for Computing Machinery), New York, London, and Amsterdam, 1972.

12. This example is based on a video tape describing SSD–1, available from Computer Corporation of America, Cambridge, Mass. 02139, 1979.

23 DISTRIBUTED APPLICATION CONFIGURATION: A QUALITATIVE METHOD

In the design of distributed processing we need to decide where the various application programs should run. In this chapter we discuss a qualitative approach on this question, and in the next we discuss a quantitative approach.

LOGICAL APPLICATION GROUPS   Applications can usually be considered in groups, closely related so that the same arguments apply to them. These application groups form the modules to which we refer in this chapter. The application groups should be selected to be as self-contained as is reasonable, use a small group of record types, and have as little interaction as possible with other application groups, especially ones executed at a distance.

Application groups relate to activities such as

Order entry

Credit checking

Local inventory control

Invoicing

Accounts receivable

Cash analysis

Salesman information

Shop floor routing

Engineering functions

LOGICAL END-USER NODES   The designer may begin by determining the *logical end-user nodes*.

To do this we list the end-user categories and the locations at which they exist. Thus:

Warehouse staff, Bridgeport

Warehouse staff, Los Angeles

Order clerks, New York

Order clerks, Chicago

Order clerks, Los Angeles

For each end-user category we list the application groups which they employ. Thus:

Warehouse staff, Bridgeport

   Receiving

   Materials stores control

   Product stores control

   Shipping

This gives a set of logical application nodes. Some of these nodes (for example, the control of parameters in an automatic process) may not be associated with a person.

For each of the logical end-user nodes centralized processing or processing at the end-user location may be used.

FACTOR TABLES   Multiple factors are involved in the decision whether to centralize or distribute an application group. A design technique first used at the Sloan School, MIT [1], employs a table for each application group, listing the pros and cons. The arguments for centralized or decentralized *development* are different from those for *operations* and those for *management*. The columns in Fig. 23.1 relate to different aspects of these. The rows in Fig. 23.1 relate to factors to consider in the choice of centralization and decentralization.

For any application group there are likely to be conflicting factors. The *factor table* gives the capability to see these at a glance.

Different organizations may choose the factors which they think are relevant in different ways. Figures 23.2 and 23.3 show two examples.

Figure 23.2 is for a bank with many branches. The factor table relates to the decision on how to automate the handling of customer checking accounts. The letters in red indicate the factors which were considered dominant. One of the most important was that a customer would be able to walk into a branch in any location and obtain the service he requires. This factor is a strong argument for centralized files (or data base) with information about the customer's account. The importance of control and auditability was also an argument for centralization, though a lesser one. The other factors in Fig. 23.2 argue for decentralized files and decentralized processing. Particularly important were the need for high availability and high protection from catastrophes such as fire or bombs. Making the system available at all times argues for storage at user locations, avoiding the dependence on telephone lines, but with telephone line backup to a central system in case of a local failure. Catastrophe protection argues for *not* having *one* centralized facility.

High accuracy needed on input argues for peripheral input editing and checking. The large network with fast responses argues for peripheral intelligence for data communications.

In practice the bank designed a system with mixed centralization and decentralization. Catastrophe protection argued that there should be two centers, not one. Transaction processing was handled peripherally but could also be handled centrally in the event of a failure. The design team would have liked to store enough information about *every* customer to handle his essential requirements at any branch. The storage at the peripheral machines was not large enough, so the team stored critical information about *every customer in a geographical region* at each branch of that region. When a customer strays into a branch outside his region, he has to be served by the central system. When in his own region his enquiries can be handled if the central system is inaccessible. In addition, a small number of inquiries are from foreign regions.

The factors in Fig. 23.2 all argue for application development by the central DP group, and this was done.

Figure 23.3 shows a factor table used in another organization for the development of a customer credit-scoring system [1]. The factors considered to be dominant are shown in the table in red:

- Critical application for the user groups requesting it
- Integration with other files and application groups
- Large memory required intermittently
- Reliable and responsive control DP group

The first of these factors was a reason for decentralization because of the investment the subunits had in the success of the system. The other three were reasons for centralization. The application relied heavily on an existing customer data base and involved a complex scoring algorithm. It would have been expensive to duplicate the data base in decentralized minicomputers.

A centralized system was eventually used, with centralized development. The dominant reason was the excellent reputation of the central DP group. The subunits had confidence that their previous experience with this group would hold true again.

Where user groups have succeeded in wrenching control away from a central DP group, they have often done so because of DP's unresponsiveness, poor service, poor scheduling, or low availability of the central facilities.

The system configuration that is finally chosen often depends not on one application group but on many. The decision may be made with a set of factor tables

Figure 23.1

KEY:
- C : STRONG REASON FOR CENTRALIZATION
- c : WEAK REASON FOR CENTRALIZATION
- D : STRONG REASON FOR DECENTRALIZATION
- d : WEAK REASON FOR DECENTRALIZATION
- DC : COOPERATION BETWEEN CENTRAL & LOCAL GROUPS

	SYSTEM DEVELOPMENT				SYSTEM OPERATIONS					MANAGEMENT CONTROL	STRATEGIC PLANNING
	APPLICATION SELECTION	APPLICATION DEVELOPMENT	DESIGN OF DATA	HARDWARE/ SOFTWARE SELECTION	INPUT & EDITING	PROCESSING	FUNCTION DISTRIBUTION	FILE	DATA-BASE		
Application location is in a different country from DP center.	D	D	D		D	D	D	D	D	D	
Fast response time is important.					D	D	D	D	D	D	
High availability is important.					D	D	D	d			
There is a large application backlog.		d	d	d	d	d		d			
Application is already implemented centrally.		C				C		C	C		
Application is entrepreneurial in nature.	D	D	D	d	d	d		d	C	d	
Application is highly sensitive and critical for the subunit.	D	D	D	D	D	D		D			
High subunit management involvement.	D	D	D	D		D		D			
Need to make subunit management responsible for the application.	D	D	D	D	D	D		D	D	D	
Application security is vital to the entire corporation.						C		C	C	D	
Large memory or large CPU facilities needed intermittently.						C		C	C	d	
Local staff skilled and intelligent in general.	d	d	d		d	d				d	
Local staff skilled with computers.	C	C	C	C				C	C	d	
Local staff unskilled.	C	C	C	c				C	C	C	
Central group reliable and responsive.	C	C								C	c
Central group overworked or unresponsive.	D	D	D	d		d				C	

350

KEY:

- C : STRONG REASON FOR CENTRALIZATION
- c : WEAK REASON FOR CENTRALIZATION
- D : STRONG REASON FOR DECENTRALIZATION
- d : WEAK REASON FOR DECENTRALIZATION
- DC : COOPERATION BETWEEN CENTRAL & LOCAL GROUPS

	SYSTEM DEVELOPMENT				SYSTEM OPERATIONS					MANAGEMENT CONTROL	STRATEGIC PLANNING
	APPLICATION SELECTION	APPLICATION DEVELOPMENT	DESIGN OF DATA	HARDWARE/ SOFTWARE SELECTION	INPUT & EDITING	PROCESSING	FUNCTION DISTRIBUTION	FILE	DATA-BASE		
Needs data which are stored centrally.			DC		D	D		C	C		
Most data can be stored locally.			DC	d	D	D		D			
Needs data base (as opposed to file) management.			DC						C	DC	C
Data are integrated with those of other locations.			DC						C	DC	C
Generates data needed by central management.	d	d	DC		d	d		d		d	
Application is simple.	d	d									
Application requires much computer expertise.	C	C	c	c							
Application requires much local knowledge.	D	D	d	d							
Application rarely changes.	c	c	c								
Application changes frequently due to local factors.	D	D	D	D							
Application changes frequently due to non-local factors.	C	C	C	C			C				
Application is unique to one location.	D	D	D	D							
Application is replicated in many locations.	C	C	C	C							
Application affects central corporate management.	c	DC	DC	c						c	C
Local subunits are highly similar.	c	c	c	c							
Local subunits are diverse in structure.	d	d	d	d							
Application location is a long distance from DP center.	d	d	d	d	d	d	d	d		d	c

Figure 23.1 (continued)

351

	SYSTEM DEVELOPMENT				SYSTEM OPERATIONS						
	APPLICATION SELECTION	APPLICATION DEVELOPMENT	DESIGN OF DATA	HARDWARE/ SOFTWARE SELECTION	INPUT & EDITING	PROCESSING	FUNCTION DISTRIBUTION	FILE	DATA-BASE	MANAGEMENT CONTROL	STRATEGIC PLANNING
Customer account data may be needed by any branch								C	c	c	c
Application identical at many bank branches	c	C	C	C							
Branches are highly similar	c	C	C	C							
Application does not require much local knowledge.	c	c	c	c							
Application rarely changes											
Some branches are far apart							D				
Fairly quick response time needed					d	d	d	d			
System should be available at all times					D	D	d	D			
Off-line terminal operations are desirable					d	d		d			
Many operators must be trained using the terminal					d	d		d			
Auditability is very important		c	c			c			c	c	
High catastrophe protection is vital						D			D	d	
High accuracy is needed (input validation)					D	d				c	
Local groups have no DP skills	c	c	c	c						c	
Central DP group is reliable and responsive	c	c	c	c							

Figure 23.2 A factor table applied to customer transactions in a bank with many branches. The items marked in capitals were considered dominant in the choice.

like Fig. 23.2 or Fig. 23.3. In some cases the set of tables indicates that certain application groups ought to be run on separate computers, sometimes network-connected computers and sometimes stand-alone machines. The banking system in Fig. 23.2, for example, chose to run several applications, such as the processing of travellers checks, on small, free-standing computers.

	SYSTEMS DEVELOPMENT	SYSTEMS OPERATIONS
APPLICATION GROUP		
Critical application for subunit	d	D
Operation control application needing high availability		d
High degree of DP expertise required	c	
Sophisticated processing	c	
Adaptability to rapid change is needed	d	
Integration with other files and application groups	C	C
Large memory required, intermittently		C
SUBUNIT		
Specialized task		d
Rapid change environment		d
Good management talent available	d	
Resident DP expertise in subunit	d	d
ENVIRONMENT		
Organization currently centralized	c	c
DP currently centralized	c	c
DP group are reliable and responsive	C	C

Figure 23.3   Factor Table for a Consumer Credit Scoring Application
(Redrawn from (1)). The items in capitals were considered dominant.

CASE STUDY   Figures 23.4 to 23.11 relate to a case study. This study
is based on two real manufacturing corporations. It has
been considerably simplified for purposes of this discussion.

Figure 23.4 shows a set of application groups used in running a manufacturing
corporation. The corporation has employed largely centralized batch processing
with dumb terminals in sales offices and some other locations. It now wants to raise
the level of automation to achieve better sales and production efficiency, and to
reduce staff. Distributed data processing is under consideration.

The corporation has three factories, many sales offices, a development
laboratory which serves the whole organization, and a head office. It has traditionally been divided into six functional areas as shown in Fig. 23.5. The documents
which flow between these functional areas are formally defined (whether computer
records or manual documents).

Some of the applications are carried out continuously, on-line; some are daily
batch runs and some less frequent, as shown in Fig. 23.4. The corporation wants to
put more of its operations on-line, improve DP's flexibility and responsiveness, im-

Figure 23.4 Application groups in a manufacturing organization. How should distributed processing be applied to these?

prove data accuracy, and provide more effective information sources for management decision making.

There are a number of data transfers between the corporation and the outside world, as shown in Fig. 23.6. A larger number of data transfers occurs internally between the separate applications, as shown in Fig. 23.7. It is desirable to use distributed processing so that it reduces rather than worsens the complexity of Fig. 23.7.

Some of the application groups in Fig. 23.7 are closely associated and employ the same data. For example, *billing* and *accounts receivable, receiving* and *accounts payable, gross requirements planning* and *net requirements planning* (of parts and materials, *shop floor control* and *job dispatching*. Closely related application groups which share the same data should be part of the same subsystem to lessen the transfers of data between subsystems.

Factor tables might be used with each of the application groups in Fig. 24.4 to determine the preferred location for

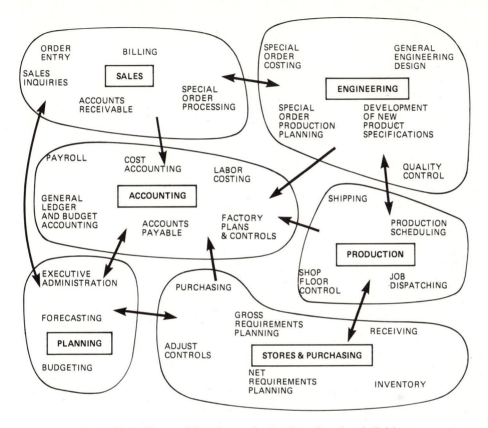

Figure 23.5 The traditional organization into functional divisions.

1. Its processing

2. The data it uses

3. The application development

LOCATION OF PROCESSING MODULES

Small processors are recommended at the branch offices to handle the simpler functions: *order entry, billing, accounts receivable,* and simple *sales inquiries.* More elaborate functions such as complex sales inquires or handling special orders are not processed by the small branch office machines but in factory or head office machines where the requisite data base exist.

Sometimes closely related applications have end users at different locations.

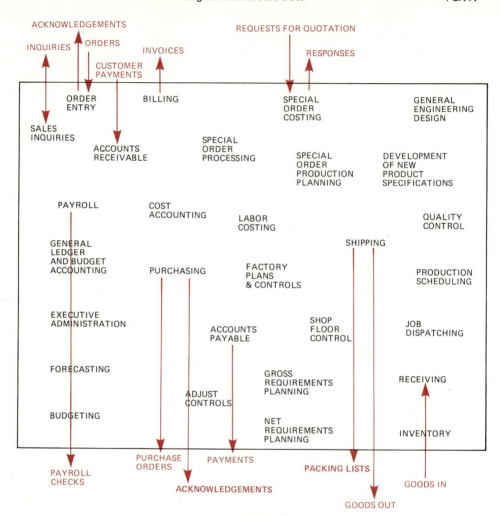

Figure 23.6 Transfers of data between the application groups of Fig. 23.6 and the outside world.

For example, *shipping* and *billing* are at different locations in Fig. 23.8. So are *purchasing* and *accounts payable*. This may be an argument for executing one of the applications away from its end-user location, or it may be better to execute the applications at separate locations, close to the end users, but employing the same data. For example, *shipping* may be done in the factory computer with the factory data base, while *billing* may be done in the branch office along with *accounts receivable* because the branch office controls both of these.

Purchasing has always been done by a head office group who have detailed

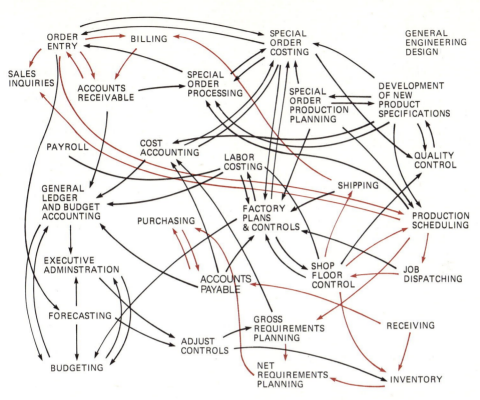

Figure 23.7   Internal transfers of data between the application groups of Fig. 23.4. If distributed processing is used the configuration should be chosen to give a small rather than large number of transfers between modules.

knowledge of suppliers and who can obtain larger discounts by bulk buying. The decision of what to purchase, and when, comes from the factories after *net requirements* planning. *Receiving* and *accounts payable* are done in the factories but are closely linked to *purchasing*. The data used in factory, head office, and branch applications are closely related and need coordinated planning.

The only application group in Fig. 23.8 which is unrelated to any other is that labeled *general engineering design*. This is a collection of applications run by engineers for their own purposes. They want them to be run on a laboratory computer to avoid the scheduling problems experienced with time-sharing on the distant head office machine.

Job dispatching and *shop floor control* are essential to controlling the minute-by-minute production processes in the factories. To avoid problems with large computer scheduling or software crashes these two critical applications are run on a separate small computer, with backup on the main factory computer. They use files

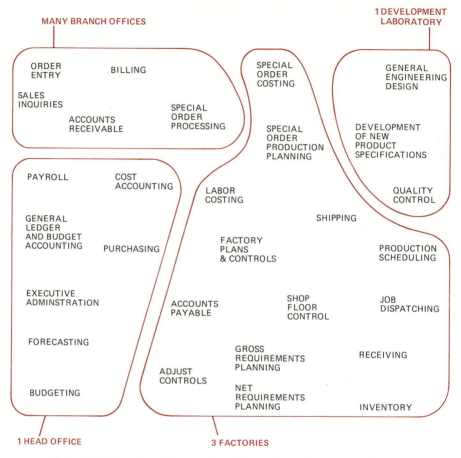

Figure 23.8 Locations of the users of the application groups in Fig. 23.4

rather than data bases, but the files are closely related to the *production scheduling* data base.

Factory plans and controls is run by a skilled group of end users who prepare the monthly budgets and plans for the factory. This is a complex activity which greatly affects the efficiency and profitability of the factory. The group usually works substantial overtime to finish the plans and budgets prior to the start of a month. In one factory the group used much computing to run modules, simulation, and detailed "What if?" calculations. This group found the factory data base invaluable, but the members needed their own files derived from the data base, which they would be free to modify when they needed. They were given their own small computer, on-line to the factory data-base system. It could read but not change the data base and created its own files from the data base. These files could then be modified for "What if" calculations. This form of operation was successful because a highly skilled group of users were devising their own form of computing.

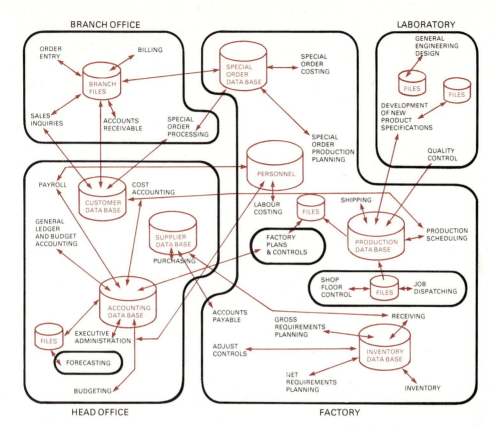

Figure 23.9   The areas on this diagram, and all areas within areas, are separate computers, all interlinked. To control the overall complexity the interfaces between these computers are precisely defined and maintained, and are relatively simple. A key to success is the coordinated design of the data (both data bases and files).

Head office management tries to establish the same methods of planning in the other two factories.

The head office also had a skilled user group "doing its own thing" with the *forecasting* application. Many different models and techniques were used by the forecasting department, which eventually found the use of graphics very valuable in creating an interface between the forecasting programs and the management who used the results. User management at a graphics terminal could challenge the assumptions behind the forecasts and see how the resulting curves and figures varied when the assumptions were modified. To do this the forecasting department wanted its own computer with fast-response graphics capability.

Figure 23.9 shows the resulting collection of processors, files, and data bases. It is a vertical configuration of processors with the exception of the laboratory system. It is redrawn in Fig. 23.10.

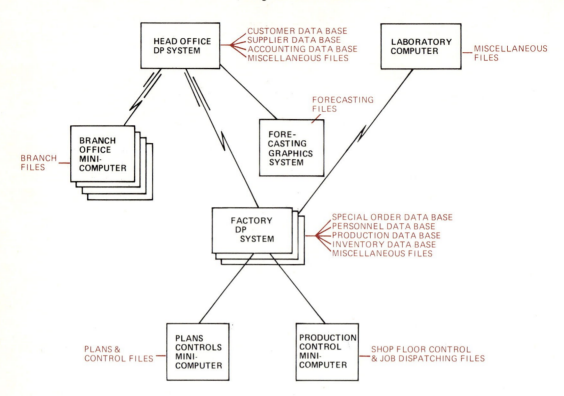

Figure 23.10 The configuration of processors shown in Fig. 23.9.

WHERE DESIGNED?   Factor tables should be summarized to indicate where the system development should be done.

The branch office systems are replicated in many such offices and therefore need to be developed centrally.

The laboratory systems are unique and in general need to be developed by engineers involved, with assistance from programmers.

A head office DP department develops all of the head office applications with the exception of *forecasting*. A set of head office data bases is employed widely in the development, as part of the corporate data-base strategy.

Forecasting is done by a group of skilled staff whose use of computers is highly specialized and growing rapidly. They develop their own programs and files, using the corporate data structures where possible. They are developing an extensive graphics capability.

Each of the factories has its own DP group. The factories are all different and can share applications to only a limited extent. Applications which *are* shared are

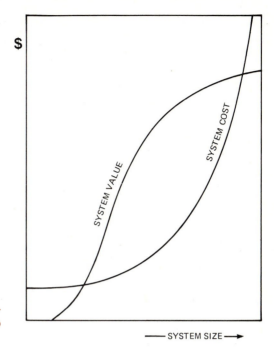

Figure 23.11 Systems tend to grow until the cost of complexity becomes too great.

receiving, accounts payable, and *shipping.* These are identical in the three factories and related to applications elsewhere. They are therefore developed centrally for installation by the factory DP groups. Much of the factory data processsing is complex and apt to change and needs an intimate understanding of the local problems. It is therefore best developed by the factory groups.

The necessity to understand complex end-user situations effectively dominates the way the factory DP groups are organized. Project teams deal with related clusters of applications, working closely with the users in question. One such cluster is *gross* and *net requirements planning* for parts and materials. Another is *production scheduling, shop floor control,* and *job dispatching.* The applications concerned with special orders form another cluster, but here *special order processing* is a branch office application. It is therefore developed in head office in close liaison with the factory teams.

Factory plans and controls, which is the most complex of all the application groups, is critical because of its direct effect on profitability. In one factory the end users began to handle this development themselves, as discussed above. This was highly successful, and head office tried to initiate the same type of end-user control of this computing in the other factories.

Figure 23.12 maps the primary application design responsibilities.

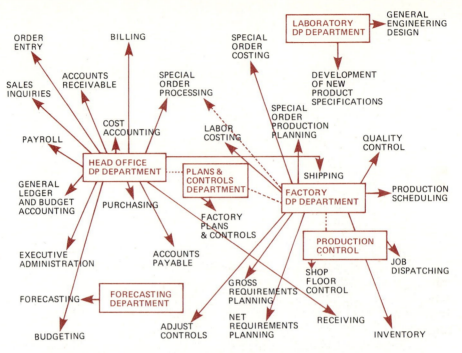

Figure 23.12 Primary responsibilities for the design and development of the application groups.

SUMMARY

The configuration in Fig. 23.10 avoids the excessive complexity at the top of the curves in Fig. 23.11. It gains many of the advantages of distribution that we have discussed while retaining those advantages of centralization that are worthwhile. Some of the more complex applications are handled by skilled, autonomous end-user groups with programming assistance. Central development is used where this is beneficial. A key to success is good design of data files and data bases and coordination of the data structures throughout the corporations.

REFERENCES

1. J. F. Rockart, C. V. Bullen, and J. L. Levantor, *Centralization v Decentralization of Information Systems: A Preliminary Model for Decision Making,* Center for Information Systems Research, Sloan School, M.I.T., Cambridge, Mass.

24 DISTRIBUTED APPLICATION CONFIGURATION: A QUANTITATIVE METHOD

The previous chapter took a *qualitative* approach to distributed application design. Now we will take a *quantitative* approach. The quantitative approach is useful, but it must be emphasized that important factors in the decision of how to distribute are nonnumeric. The design of distributed systems cannot be completely reduced to an algorithm.

The quantitative approach attempts to arrange the locations of processing and data in such a way that the traffic and interaction between nodes is low. The applications and data are arranged into groups such that each group has a high level of autonomy and a low level of interdependence with other groups.

The procedure we will describe is illustrated in Fig. 24.1.

It begins, as in the previous chapter, with the identification of end-user locations and the application groups which the various end users employ. Again, most of the end users will be associated with humans such as order clerks and shop floor foremen; but some, such as automatic processes, will not.

LOGICAL DATA NETWORK

To carry out their processing the end users (human or otherwise) need data. In some cases the data are associated *exclusively* with the end user. In other cases data are employed by more than one end user.

We can draw a diagram showing each end-user node, with separate nodes drawn for any data which are shared, as shown in Fig. 24.2. We will refer to this as a logical data network.

With some types of data a node in Fig. 24.2 can refer to a logical record or group of data items. In other cases individual data items (fields) have to be shown. In many cases the data node can refer to a logical data-base structure.

In some cases the data node can refer to a *type* of record or *type* of data. In other cases it must refer to an occurrence or category of occurrences. For example,

A procedure for designing the data distribution

1. Establish end use locations and applications.
2. Determine what data the end uses require.
3. Determine what data can be replicated.
4. Draw or tabulate a logical data structure network (Fig. 24.2).
5. Examine possible strategies for locating the data (with the help of Boxes 18.1, 18.2, and 24.2, and the technique in Fig. 23.1).
6. Draw or tabulate a geographical data structure network (Fig. 24.4).
7. Examine practical constraints on data structure locations (Box. 24.1).
8. Determine what transactions and application programs are to be used.
9. Draw or tabulate an application program map (Fig. 24.5).
10. Classify the programs (Fig. 24.6).
11. Analyze the distribution of programs (Fig. 24.7).
12. Analyze the transaction flow (Fig. 24.8).
13. Determine what data structures are to be used (files and data bases).
14. Adjust the data structures distribution if improvements can be made.

Figure 24.1 A procedure for designing the data distribution.

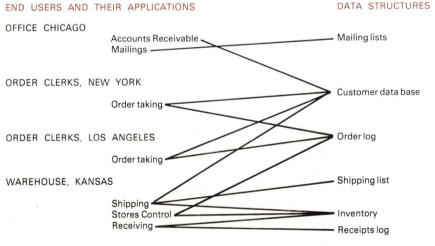

Figure 24.2 A logical data structure network.

users at different branch offices may each refer to a different customer set—the same *type* of data but different customers.

In the first preliminary designs a drawing like that in Fig. 24.2 is useful. In detailed designs it rapidly becomes too complicated to be drawn easily in the form of Fig. 24.2. Instead, it can be represented in tabular form. Data dictionary software may be used or adapted for this purpose. The table should show not only data which are shared between user nodes but also data which reside *exclusively* with a user node.

The logical network in Fig. 24.2 will bear little resemblance to the physical network that is eventually designed. The question that confronts us is, "How do we convert the logical network into an efficient physical design?"

DATA STRUCTURES

The data used by the applications are organized into *data structures*. These can be of various types. Step 3 in Fig. 24.1 is to determine what data structures are used.

A data structure can be either a file or a data base (explained in Chapter 21). Either of these can be on-line. In the postulated configuration, the *peripheral* machines might use files rather than data bases because the machines are not big enough to use a data-base management system.

If a data item is used, the data structure will often encompass multiple records which are joined with whatever linkages the DBMS uses. In a CODASYL data base there may be several interlinked CODASYL *sets*. In a DL/I data base (the data-structuring language used in IBM's IMS) there may be several physical data bases interlinked with logical child and logical parent pointers. A large data-base system usually contains multiple *disjoint* data bases of these types—in other words, multiple collections of interlinked data with no linkages spanning the separate collections.

Some corporations use the term *data bank* to refer to a collection of interlinked data. The term is sometimes used, for example, to refer to a group of interlinked physical data bases in IMS. It is not a generally accepted use of the term, so we will employ the term *data structure*.

A data structure can range from being very simple to very complex. At one extreme it could be a single data item (field) type. At the other it could be an interconnected data-base structure such as that shown in Fig. 24.3. Figure 24.3 represents a typical complex data-base structure in an IMS installation.

One typical example of a factory with good data-base usage employs 45 *physical* IMS data bases. These are grouped into 17 *data structures*. Of the 17, eight contain more than one physical data base. The most complicated data structure interlinks ten physical data bases, two of which are very small. A similar breakdown of complexity is found with other types of data-base software. For example, if the above example had been implemented with a CODASYL data base, it might have had many *sets* interconnected into the same 17 data structures.

Diagrams such as Fig. 24.2 need to refer to *data* structures rather than merely

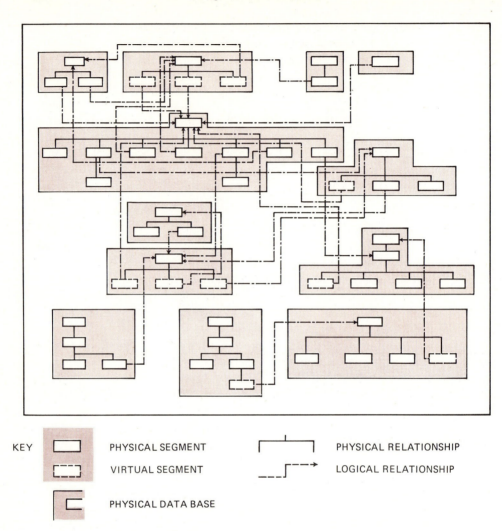

KEY

PHYSICAL SEGMENT   PHYSICAL RELATIONSHIP

VIRTUAL SEGMENT   LOGICAL RELATIONSHIP

PHYSICAL DATA BASE

Figure 24.3   A typical DL/1 data base with 12 physical data bases. Multiple disjoint data bases like this exist in one data base system. This may form one *data structure*. A smaller data structure may be derived from it.

files or records. To make this clear we will refer to this type of diagram from now on as a *logical data structure network*.

RESTRICTIONS ON DATA STRUCTURE CHOICE

Step 4 of the procedure in Fig. 24.1 is to draw a *logical data structure network*. In so doing, the designer must decide which ought to be data base and which *file* structures. This will depend on many factors: the size of

BOX 24.1 Possible restrictions on the choice of data structure or location of data structures

- The machine in question does not have a data-base management system.
- The data-base management system in use has restrictions on the data structure it permits.
- The data are already structured for previous applications, and conversion would be too expensive.
- A peripheral or small machine has limited storage capacity.
- A peripheral machine has limited buffer capacities. (One, for example, cannot handle records longer than 240 bytes.)
- A peripheral machine has a limited number of buffers. (One has six buffers, for example.) This means that applications which use and possibly compare data from many files would become inefficient and complicated to program.
- A peripheral machine location has limited security.
- Integrity controls on the data must be planned.
- Fallback must be provided during a period of machine failure.
- The data must be reconstructible if accidentally lost.
- Restart procedures must be designed so that data updates can be lost or double-processed.

the machines, the manufacturer, the designer's attitude to data-base techniques, and his perception of the advantages and added costs of DBMS. In particular it will relate to what files, data bases, and application programs *already exist* and need to be incorporated into the design.

There are various practical constraints on data structures that can be used. Some possible restrictions are listed in Box 24.1. Some machines, especially peripheral machines, and software place restrictions on record sizes, file sizes, and the use of data-base management. The need to have adequate security, data integrity, and fallback procedures also affects the design.

GEOGRAPHICAL DATA STRUCTURE NETWORK The next step is to postulate where the data structures might be located physically. Step 5 suggests examining the arguments which relate to this discussed in previous chapters and summarized in Boxes 18.1, 18.2, and 13.2 and Figs. 13.4 and 23.1.

Step 6 is to draw (or tabulate) a *geographical data structure network*. Figure 24.2 can be redrawn as shown in Fig. 24.4. Although we use the rather grand term "geographical," the separated data structures might be quite close, possibly in the same building.

In an earlier era the data and applications of Fig. 24.2 would all have been centralized. The configuration postulated in Fig. 24.4. has a minicomputer or intelligent terminal system at each order clerk location and a minicomputer at the

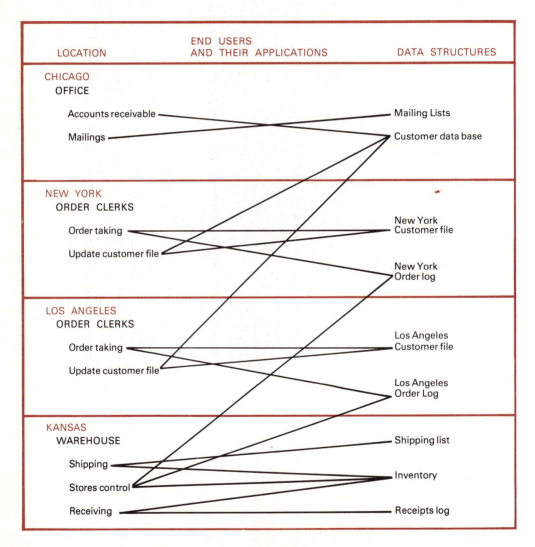

Figure 24.4 A geographical data structure network. The logical data structure network of Fig. 8.2 with data structures to users locations.

warehouse location. The central computer could be smaller (or additional applications could be put on the same machine).

Enough information from the customer data base has been placed at the order clerks' locations to ensure that they can control data integrity in the order-taking process without needing to refer to a central location.

The examination of practical constraints on data positioning, including fallback, security, and restart (Step 7), may cause an adjustment of the postulated physical data structure network.

PROGRAM/DATA STRUCTURE GRAPH

The next step is to examine the application programs. One application may involve multiple transactions with different application programs to process them. The designer (in Step 8) determines what transactions are used and what application programs are required to handle them.

A graph may then be drawn showing which data structure each program uses. Sometimes this is similar in its shape to the geographical data structure graph. Sometimes it is very different because one application uses several transactions and multiple programs, and some programs may *reside in a different geographical node from that of the application they serve.* With completely centralized teleprocessing, most application programs are geographically distant from the end-user application nodes, which are at terminal locations.

Figure 24.5 shows an application program map. Once again, on a complex system it is much larger than in Fig. 24.5 and might be better represented in tabular form.

CLASSES OF PROGRAMS

To examine the effect of the application distribution we will divide the application programs into three classes, shown in Fig. 24.6.

A *Class 0* program has both the application it serves and all the data it uses in its own location.

A *Class 1* program is in a different location from the application it serves, but it is at the same location as all the data it uses. This is the case with conventional teleprocessing.

Class 2 is in the same location as the application it serves, but some or all of the data it uses are in a different location. This is the case with processing distribution or function distribution using remote data.

In rare instances *Class 3* programs are found which are distant from both their application and some of the data they use. These might be similar to Class 2 programs, separated from their application so as to be close to their data, but not all of the data are at the same location.

Class 0 is the most desirable of these types of programs, and Class 3 is generally to be avoided. Class 1 is common with centralized systems.

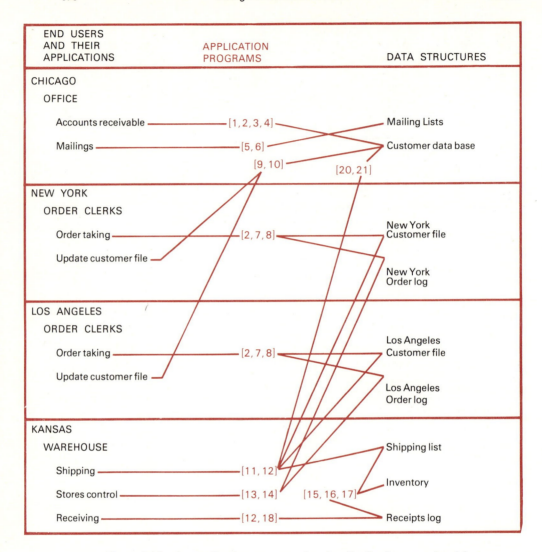

Figure 24.5 An application program for the distribution postulated in Fig. 26.6.

To avoid interactions between modules, the geographical data structure network (Fig. 24.4) should be adjusted so as to maximize the proportion of Class 0 programs as possible.

The designer might draw a table such as that in Fig. 24.7, showing the number of programs in each class.

Programs not in Class 0 must be handled either by the use of data transmission or by replicating the data structures in question to make the program Class 0.

	Application Node	Data Structure
Class 0 program:	Same location	Same location
Class 1 program:	Different location	
Class 2 program:	Same location	Some or all are in a different location
Class 3 program:	Different location	

Figure 24.6

Classes of program

	CLASS 0 (Local application, Local data)	CLASS 1 (Remote application, Local data)	CLASS 2 (Local application, Remote data)
CHICAGO			
Accounts Receivable	4		
Mailings	2		
NEW YORK			
Order taking	3		
Update customer file		2	
♦LOS ANGELES			
Order taking	3		
Update customer file		2	
KANSAS			
Shipping			2
Stores control	3		2
Receiving	2		
TOTALS	17	4	4

Figure 24.7 A count of the number of programs of each class in Fig. 26.5.

371

Factors which favor replicating the data are:

- The transaction volume is high.

- The data size is low.

- The data are updated infrequently.

- The updates are simple, so that the integrity and restart problems discussed in Chapter 19 are easily avoided.

- The replicated data structure is simple (although it might be derived from a complex data base).

- An additional factor in less developed countries is that data communications give problems.

The designer may calculate the cost of replicating (storage cost) and not replicating (transmission cost).

Figure 24.8 illustrates this, showing whether the traffic is batch or on-line. The worst in Fig. 24.8 is the on-line use of the customer data base by the shipping application. The designer should focus on this. Can it be reduced by putting customer data at the warehouse location?

The designer is concerned not merely with the numbers of programs, as in Fig. 24.7, but also with the frequency of their use, the amount of traffic that results from the interactions. He may focus on the programs which are not Class 0 and calculate the mean amount of data traffic per day that is associated with them.

Reconfiguring the data structures can often substantially reduce the volume of heavier traffic types, especially when the application map is complex.

DIVIDING AN EXISTING DATA BASE
In many corporations a large, centralized data base exists which might benefit from distribution. In such a case the documentation of the data structures is likely to be good. The design team can postulate moving some of the data structures and analyze the effect.

The utility outputs of the DBMS give the programs, data structures, transactions types, and sometimes the volume of transactions. An application program map of a nondistributed system can be drawn from this and converted into a map for a distributed system. Figure 24.9 shows the typical complexity of a corporate data-base system which may be a candidate for distribution.

In the results of such an analysis, distribution often appears attractive in principle. Unfortunately, it would often require a major conversion and reprogramming effort, and so DP management usually decide to let well enough alone. In the future, distributed technology will gain strength, and it is desirable that software for data bases and peripheral computers should make distribution easy when analysis shows that it is desirable.

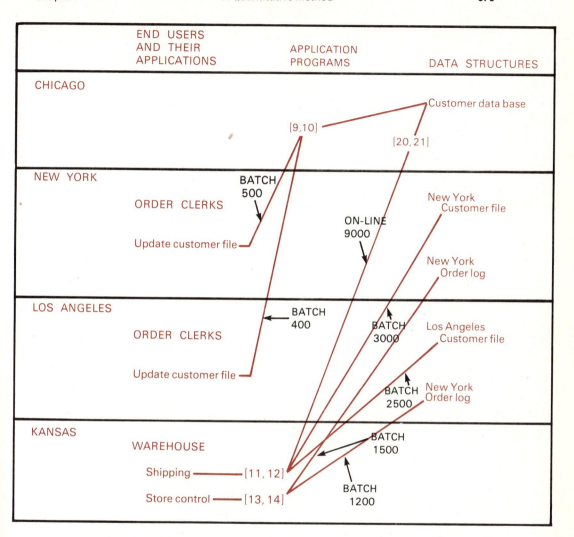

Figure 24.8 The non-Class 0 programs are marked to show the class of traffic and mean volume per day.

While we wait for better software, today's data-base administrators should be encouraged to design their data structures with possible future distribution in mind. They might analyze and adjust postulated distributed data structures, as described in this chapter, and then compromise on a version of such structures which can be handled by the DBMS of their choice.

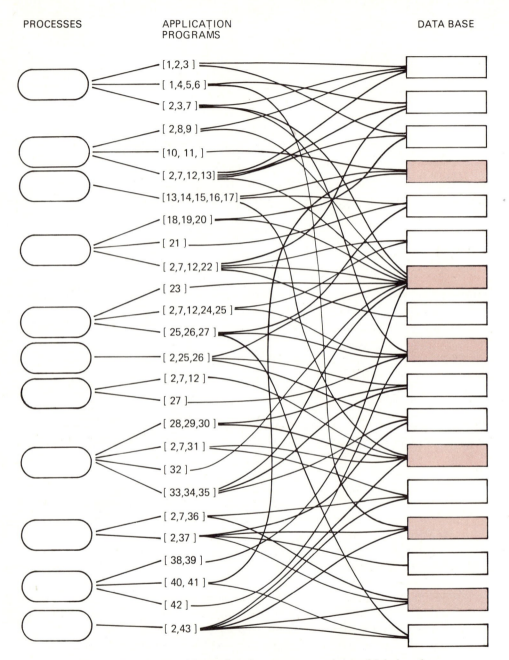

PROCESSES

APPLICATION
PROGRAMS

DATA BASE

[1,2,3]

[1,4,5,6]

[2,3,7]

[2,8,9]

[10, 11,]

[2,7,12,13]

[13,14,15,16,17]

[18,19,20]

[21]

[2,7,12,22]

[23]

[2,7,12,24,25]

[25,26,27]

[2,25,26]

[2,7,12]

[27]

[28,29,30]

[2,7,31]

[32]

[33,34,35]

[2,7,36]

[2,37]

[38,39]

[40, 41]

[42]

[2,43]

Figure 24.9 A typical large data base system serving multiple locations.
Each of the shaded rectangles is a structure involving multiple sets or
physical data bases possibly as complex as that in Fig. 26.3. How should
this be distributed?

25 STRATEGY AND MANAGEMENT FOR DISTRIBUTED DATA

Now that we have discussed various aspects of the distribution of data, let us return to the subject of corporate strategy and overall management of the data resources.

Figure 25.1, excerpted from Fig. 10.4, shows strategy and planning for DDP. In this chapter we expand upon the blocks relating to data.

The centralization, decentralization, and in general the geographical siting of data need to be designed in a coordinated fashion.

DATA ADMINISTRATION In data-base installations a *data administration* function is established to coordinate the design of the data. In a distributed environment this function needs to be extended to all locations where data are stored.

Good data base requires advanced training. To give such training to subordinate groups would be too expensive and would divert their attention from their assigned tasks, complicating and delaying the implementation.

Just as one group of specialists in a corporation is responsible for all purchasing or all shipping, so one group should be responsible for the custody and organization of data. Individual departments do not do their own purchasing, shipping, or data-base design.

As we commented in Chapter 10, a complex corporation may have multiple autonomous divisions or subsidiaries. It may require multiple hexagons of the type drawn in Chapter 10, shown here as Figs. 25.2 and 25.3. Unrelated data planning may be done for each autonomous division, subsidiary, or for each hexagon in such diagrams. On the other hand, hexagons which are separate for some other reason, such as use of different manufacturer's architectures, may employ common dictionary control of data, or logical modeling of data, or data administration in general.

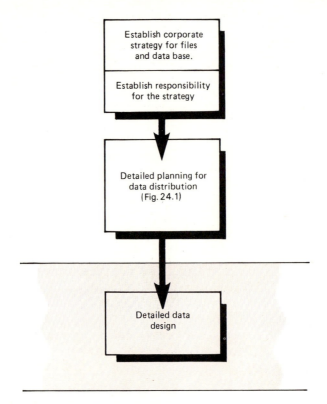

Figure 25.1 Strategy and planning of data resources.

LEVELS OF PLANNING   There are several different aspects to creating and controlling the data resources in a corporation. These aspects need widely differing talents and are carried out at different management levels.

At the highest level is the strategic planning of the data resources of a corporation. We refer to the person who does this top-level planning as the *data strategist*. He is ultimately responsible for what files, data bases, and information resources exist. His staff may set data-base policy and standards, evaluate and select software, determine what design tools are used, and maintain a corporationwide inventory of data resources and a data dictionary.

Very important to long-range success with data-base systems is the logical modeling of the data used. We will refer to the person who does the logical modeling as the *data administrator*. He works closely and sensitively with the end users and systems analysts to find out what data they want to use. Jointly they agree to the definitions of data used and record them in a data dictionary. The data administrator synthesizes the separate views of data into a logical data-base model. He holds meetings with end-user representatives to validate the model and ensure that it

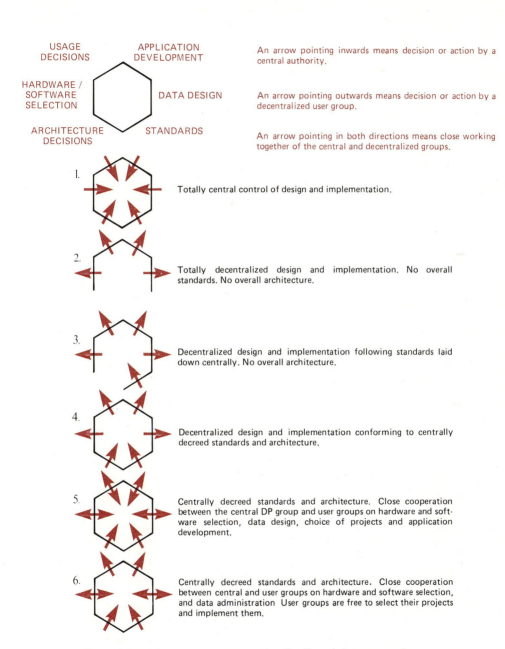

USAGE DECISIONS   APPLICATION DEVELOPMENT

HARDWARE / SOFTWARE SELECTION   DATA DESIGN

ARCHITECTURE DECISIONS   STANDARDS

An arrow pointing inwards means decision or action by a central authority.

An arrow pointing outwards means decision or action by a decentralized user group.

An arrow pointing in both directions means close working together of the central and decentralized groups.

1. Totally central control of design and implementation.

2. Totally decentralized design and implementation. No overall standards. No overall architecture.

3. Decentralized design and implementation following standards laid down centrally. No overall architecture.

4. Decentralized design and implementation conforming to centrally decreed standards and architecture.

5. Centrally decreed standards and architecture. Close cooperation between the central DP group and user groups on hardware and software selection, data design, choice of projects and application development.

6. Centrally decreed standards and architecture. Close cooperation between central and user groups on hardware and software selection, and data administration User groups are free to select their projects and implement them.

Figure 25.2 Management patterns for distributed data processing.

377

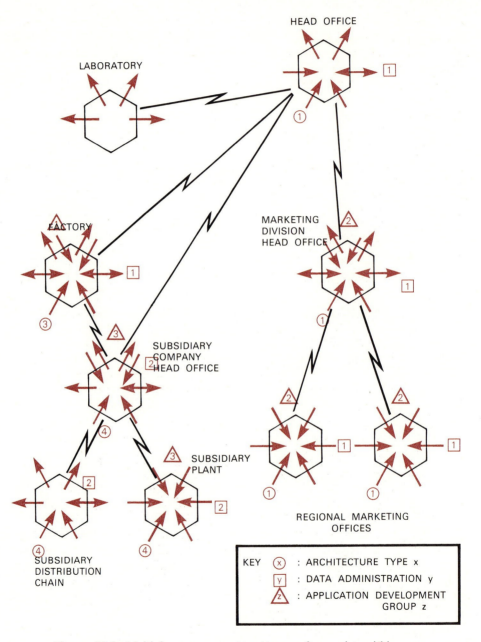

LABORATORY

HEAD OFFICE

FACTORY

MARKETING
DIVISION
HEAD OFFICE

SUBSIDIARY
COMPANY
HEAD OFFICE

SUBSIDIARY
PLANT

REGIONAL MARKETING
OFFICES

SUBSIDIARY
DISTRIBUTION
CHAIN

KEY (x) : ARCHITECTURE TYPE x

  y   : DATA ADMINISTRATION y

  z   : APPLICATION DEVELOPMENT
         GROUP z

Figure 25.3 Multiple management patterns often exist within one organization.

meets their needs. End users usually have concerns about the data-base environment, which the data administrator deals with.

Data models are designed to represent the inherent properties of the data needed in the corporation rather than the narrower groupings of fields perceived by one programmer, user, or distributed file designer. The models are created by analyzing the data needs of end users and of the corporation as a whole. User views are synthesized into a third-normal-form [1] canonical data structure [2], designed to be as stable as possible. This is a complex iterative process, and a tool is needed to automate and document it so that the resulting data structure can be validated and easily modified [3]. Figure 25.4 shows a canonical model of data used in an oil company.

At the level closest to the machine is the person who designs the data bases used by that machine, their schemas, the subschemas derived from them, and the physical structure of the data. We will refer to this person as the *data-base designer*. The term *data-base administrator* is sometimes used. The data-base designer is concerned with physical data-base design, machine performance, and techniques for recovery and maintenance of integrity.

In small installations the data-base designer is also the data administrator. That is, the same person does the data analysis, logical modeling, and physical data-base design.

DATA DISTRIBUTION ADMINISTRATOR   The three types of jobs described above are used in a nondistributed data environment. When data are distributed, there are some new design and control questions:

- Where should the data be located?
- How should integrity be maintained with synchronized copies of the data?
- What conflicts could occur (Chapter 20) and how are they avoided?
- Who designs the data?
- Who enforces compatibility of data structure between different locations?

We will assume that an individual is responsible for these concerns and refer to this individual as the *data distribution administrator*. This may be a separate function. It may be an extension of the data administrator's function.

In a large organization there may be several data administrators for different portions of the data. Data distribution administration may need to span these. It needs the authority to enforce its decisions in multiple locations, so it may be a high-level function. It may report to the top-level corporate DP management or be a function of the top-level data strategy group.

The conventional data administration function will design the logical models

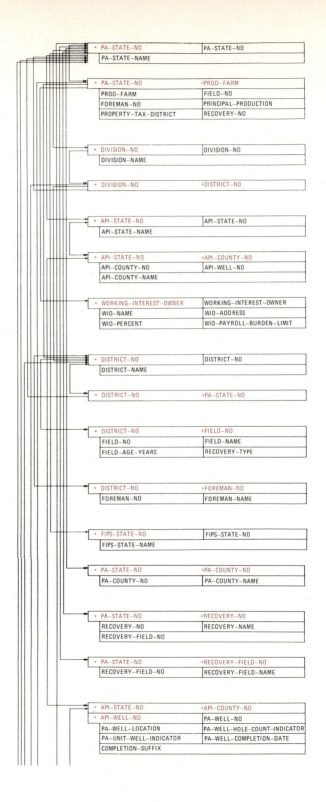

* PA—STATE—NO	PA—STATE—NO
PA—STATE—NAME	

* PA—STATE—NO	+PROD—FARM
PROD—FARM	FIELD—NO
FOREMAN—NO	PRINCIPAL—PRODUCTION
PROPERTY—TAX—DISTRICT	RECOVERY—NO

* DIVISION—NO	DIVISION—NO
DIVISION—NAME	

* DIVISION—NO	+DISTRICT—NO

* API-STATE—NO	API-STATE—NO
API-STATE—NAME	

* API-STATE—NO	+API—COUNTY—NO
API—COUNTY—NO	API—WELL—NO
API—COUNTY—NAME	

* WORKING—INTEREST—OWNER	WORKING—INTEREST—OWNER
WIO—NAME	WIO—ADDRESS
WIO—PERCENT	WIO—PAYROLL—BURDEN—LIMIT

* DISTRICT—NO	DISTRICT—NO
DISTRICT—NAME	

* DISTRICT—NO	+PA—STATE—NO

* DISTRICT—NO	+FIELD—NO
FIELD—NO	FIELD—NAME
FIELD—AGE—YEARS	RECOVERY—TYPE

* DISTRICT—NO	+FOREMAN—NO
FOREMAN—NO	FOREMAN—NAME

* FIPS—STATE—NO	FIPS—STATE—NO
FIPS—STATE—NAME	

* PA—STATE—NO	+PA—COUNTY—NO
PA—COUNTY—NO	PA—COUNTY—NAME

* PA—STATE—NO	+RECOVERY—NO
RECOVERY—NO	RECOVERY—NAME
RECOVERY—FIELD—NO	

* PA—STATE—NO	+RECOVERY—FIELD—NO
RECOVERY—FIELD—NO	RECOVERY—FIELD—NAME

* API-STATE—NO	+API—COUNTY—NO
* API—WELL—NO	PA—WELL—NO
PA—WELL—LOCATION	PA—WELL—HOLE—COUNT—INDICATOR
PA—UNIT—WELL—INDICATOR	PA—WELL—COMPLETION—DATE
COMPLETION—SUFFIX	

380

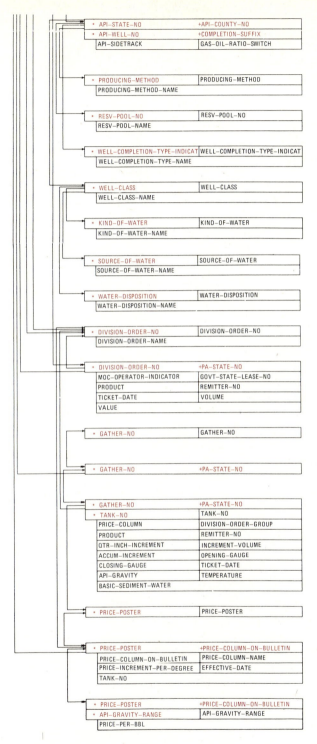

API—STATE—NO	+API—COUNTY—NO
API—WELL—NO	+COMPLETION—SUFFIX
API—SIDETRACK	GAS—OIL—RATIO—SWITCH

| PRODUCING—METHOD | PRODUCING—METHOD |
| PRODUCING—METHOD—NAME | |

| RESV—POOL—NO | RESV—POOL—NO |
| RESV—POOL—NAME | |

| WELL—COMPLETION—TYPE—INDICAT | WELL—COMPLETION—TYPE—INDICAT |
| WELL—COMPLETION—TYPE—NAME | |

| WELL—CLASS | WELL—CLASS |
| WELL—CLASS—NAME | |

| KIND—OF—WATER | KIND—OF—WATER |
| KIND—OF—WATER—NAME | |

| SOURCE—OF—WATER | SOURCE—OF—WATER |
| SOURCE—OF—WATER—NAME | |

| WATER—DISPOSITION | WATER—DISPOSITION |
| WATER—DISPOSITION—NAME | |

| DIVISION—ORDER—NO | DIVISION—ORDER—NO |
| DIVISION—ORDER—NAME | |

DIVISION—ORDER—NO	+PA—STATE—NO
MOC—OPERATOR—INDICATOR	GOVT—STATE—LEASE—NO
PRODUCT	REMITTER—NO
TICKET—DATE	VOLUME
VALUE	

| GATHER—NO | GATHER—NO |

| GATHER—NO | +PA—STATE—NO |

GATHER—NO	+PA—STATE—NO
TANK—NO	TANK—NO
PRICE—COLUMN	DIVISION—ORDER—GROUP
PRODUCT	REMITTER—NO
QTR—INCH—INCREMENT	INCREMENT—VOLUME
ACCUM—INCREMENT	OPENING—GAUGE
CLOSING—GAUGE	TICKET—DATE
API—GRAVITY	TEMPERATURE
BASIC—SEDIMENT—WATER	

| PRICE—POSTER | PRICE—POSTER |

PRICE—POSTER	+PRICE—COLUMN—ON—BULLETIN
PRICE—COLUMN—ON—BULLETIN	PRICE—COLUMN—NAME
PRICE—INCREMENT—PER—DEGREE	EFFECTIVE—DATE
TANK—NO	

PRICE—POSTER	+PRICE—COLUMN—ON—BULLETIN
API—GRAVITY—RANGE	API—GRAVITY—RANGE
PRICE—PER—BBL	

Figure 25.4   A canonical model of data used in an oil company produced
by the DATA DESIGNER synthesis tool.

of the data used, and the data distribution administrator will ensure that they inter-link appropriately between separate sites.

BREAKDOWN OF RESPONSIBILITIES   Figure 25.5 shows a suggested breakdown of responsibilities.

The *data-base designer* is perceived as being a skilled technician concerned with the data bases at one location and the subschemas which are derived from them. Some of these subschemas may be used as *file* structures in peripheral machines connected to that location.

The data-base designer needs to have a close relation with the *data administrator* who models the data, and with the *data distribution administrator* if this is a different person. The data-base designer is concerned with performance and for performance reasons may occasionally want to deviate from the data administrator's structure. He may sometimes find it desirable to split a data structure into two structures which run on different machines.

Most corporations will continue to have independent *files* (as opposed to data bases) for some applications. The use of files rather than data bases may be one of the concerns or decisions of the top-level data strategist. Where independent files are used, a systems analyst may design and control them in the conventional way.

The most common reason for using files is that they already exist, often in large quantities, and the reprogramming needed to convert them to data base is too expensive at the present time. New data bases must then coexist with the old files. This is a concern for the data administrator who must ensure that there are suitable bridges, where needed, for data to pass from one to the other. This may affect his logical model design.

The *data strategist* is seen as creating the organizationwide strategy for the use of data. He must form a clear view of the corporation's future information requirements and must steer the evolution of data facilities so that the requirements become realizable. A set of data bases is needed which provide for the most rapid, high-productivity application development, using higher-level data-base languages where possible, and which provide the information systems needed by all levels of management.

If possible within the organization management structure, the data strategist should be responsible for the selection of what types of data-base management system are used (CODASYL, DL/1, Relational, etc.) so that the logical data descriptions of different systems can be compatible. In some organizations the top data-base management has created standards for data-base design, such as the use of *third normal form* [1] or *canonical data structures* [2]. This should be done and should be linked to design tools which enforce the best form of logical data modeling.

Figure 25.5   Suggested responsibilities for data design for distributed data processing.

	USER GROUP	PROGRAMMER AND SYSTEMS ANALYST	DATA BASE DESIGNER	DATA ADMINISTRATOR	DATA DISTRIBUTION ADMINISTRATOR	TOP LEVEL DATA STRATEGIST	AUDITOR	SECURITY OFFICER
TOP LEVEL DATA STATEGY								
Planning corporatewide file and data base strategy				C		PRIME		
Planning what corporate data resources are needed.						PRIME		
Planning responsibilities and job descriptions.						PRIME		
Determining data base standards and design techniques.						PRIME		
Data base software evaluation and selection.			C	C	C	PRIME		
Selection of a data dictionary and modelling tool				C		PRIME		
Control of corporatewide dictionary maintenance				P		PRIME		
DATA ADMINISTRATION								
Data analysis.	P	P		PRIME				
Field definition and design.	P	P		PRIME				
Logical model design.			P	PRIME				
Stability analysis.	C	C		PRIME				
Logical model validation.	P	P		PRIME			P	P
Planning what subject data bases are to exsist.				PRIME	P	P		
DATA DISTRIBUTION ADMINISTRATION.								
Data distribution analysis.				P	PRIME			
Deciding what data structures should reside at what locations.				P	PRIME	P		
Distributed recovery/integrity planning.					PRIME		P	
Conflict analysis.					PRIME		P	
Enforcement of compatibility of data structure between different locations.				P	PRIME	P		
DATA BASE DESIGN								
Design of schemes used in one data base system.			PRIME	P				
Physical data base design for that system			PRIME	C				
Integrity/recovery planning for that system.			PRIME				P	
Performance analysis.			PRIME					
Subschema file design (including subschema files at peripheral locations)	C	P	PRIME	P			P	
Planning the data base's compatibility with existing files.			PRIME	P				
INDEPENDENT FILE DESIGN								
Design of files which do not use data base systems.	C	PRIME				P		
AUDITING & SECURITY								
Audibility design.	C	C	C	P	P	P	PRIME	P
Security stategy and design.	C	C	P	P	P	P	P	PRIME

Key PRIME=PRIME RESPONSIBILITY
  P ⚌ PARTICIPATING RESPONSIBILITY.
  C ⚌ CONSULTING WHEN NECESSARY

The data strategist should ensure that a common data dictionary is used throughout the organization. In a large corporation the task of trying to clean up and unify the definitions of data used goes on for years. The data administrators are very much involved in this.

The data-base administrator's responsibilities in Fig. 25.5 are the same as in a nondistributed environment or in an environment with simple peripheral storage devices connected remotely to a central data-base system. In an organization with multiple host computers, each with a data base, there will be multiple data base administrators each with their own sphere of activity. This sphere may include peripheral remote storage units. The *distributed data administrator* acts as a bridge between the separate data-base administrators.

Files (as opposed to data bases) fall into two categories: those which are derived from data bases and those which are completely independent. The data-base designer may handle the design of the former in the same way that he handles local subschemas. Independent files may be designed by the programmers or analysts who employ them.

INDEPENDENT FILES   In an organization committed to data base, independent (non-data-base) files may be permitted to exist for the following reasons.

First, they exist on peripheral machines too small to have data-base software.

Second, they are cheaper and apply to an environment which is static and simple so that the data-base advantages listed in Box 22.1 do not apply.

Third, an adequate level of performance would be difficult to obtain with a data-base management system because the transaction volume is so high, the files are so large, or the level of volatility (rate of creation of new records and destruction of old ones) is so great.

Fourth (and in practice this is often the most important), files already exist and many application programs employ them. The cost and man-years needed to convert these files to data-base form is too great.

Peripheral machines often store data which are associated with a distant data base. The peripheral machines usually do not have a powerful enough processor to perform data-base management themselves. Therefore a compromise may be used in which the peripheral locations physically store data in a form corresponding to a *subschema* of the centralized data base. This is illustrated in Fig. 25.6. There may be much sharing of the *central* data base by different applications and different programmers with different data views. However, each peripheral file is related to one application or a set of applications, small enough for the programmers to have no difficulty sharing the peripheral files.

Synchronizing the peripheral files with the central data base may be done by having only one master copy, as discussed in Chapter 19.

Figure 25.6   A hierarchical distributed data base.

CENTRALIZED
DATA BASE SYSTEMS

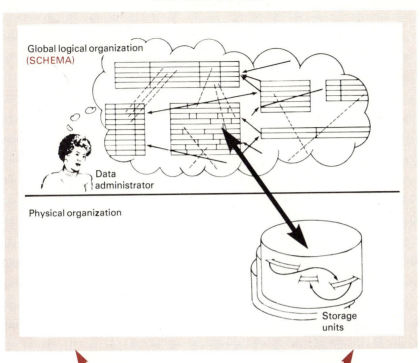

Global logical organization
(SCHEMA)

Data administrator

Physical organization

Storage units

PERIPHERAL LOCATION A

PERIPHERAL LOCATION B

Storage Unit

SUBSCHEMA

Programmer A

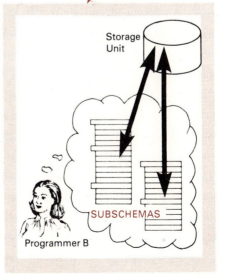

Storage Unit

SUBSCHEMAS

Programmer B

385

THREE FORMS OF **HIERARCHICAL DATA**   There are three possible ways to build a hierarchical data base system, illustrated in Fig. 25.7.

In the top diagram the peripheral groups design their own files independently, ignoring the structure of the centralized data base.

In the second diagram the peripheral files correspond to subschemas of the central data base, as in Fig. 25.6. This is perhaps the simplest form of distributed data base. A data-base administrator must be in control of both the central and perhiperal data design.

In the third diagram the peripheral computers have their own data base and a data-base management system which can map between the subschemas and the schemas, and between the schemas and physical data structure. The peripheral and central schemas may or may not be related.

Figure 25.7 relates to a hierarchical system; and the same three relationships between data systems could also be found on a mesh-structured network or horizontal configuration.

Using the middle type of relationship in Fig. 25.7, the lower-level machines might be able to contact more than one higher-level data-base system. The lower-level files may then correspond to subschemas from more than one data base.

In the bottom type of relationship shown in Fig. 25.7 there may be multiple data-base systems with the same schema, or they may be entirely different.

In many systems the middle diagram of Fig. 25.7 will be the most advantageous. It extends the flexibility and advantages of data-base operations outwards to peripheral machines. Too often the data in peripheral machines are designed independently by teams "doing their own thing," when they could easily have been designed as data-base subschemas.

SECURITY AND **AUDITABILITY**   The strategy for auditability and security is centrally planned in some organizations. Only a small proportion of the data in most organizations needs very tight security control. Many transactions do not need tight audit control. A central authority should decide which data need a high measure of protection and what constraints this places on the design of distributed systems.

Figure 25.5 suggests that the primary responsibility for the security and auditability of data should reside with a professional security officer and auditor, respectively. The data strategist may work with these people. Most of the above cast need to participate in making a system secure and auditable.

The main point to observe here is that both security and auditability are usually inadequate when left to distributed groups. Peripherally stored data are often inadequately protected from accident, catastrophe, snooping, embezzlement, sabotage, or the acts of incompetent employees. Peripheral systems are often unauditable, as discussed in Chapter 37. Security and auditing are complex subjects because there are so many ways that security can be violated. They need highly pro-

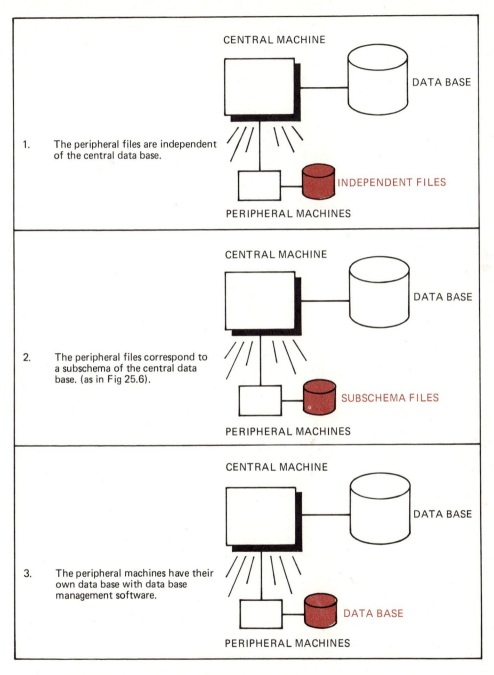

CENTRAL MACHINE

DATA BASE

1. The peripheral files are independent of the central data base.

INDEPENDENT FILES

PERIPHERAL MACHINES

CENTRAL MACHINE

DATA BASE

2. The peripheral files correspond to a subschema of the central data base. (as in Fig 25.6).

SUBSCHEMA FILES

PERIPHERAL MACHINES

CENTRAL MACHINE

DATA BASE

3. The peripheral machines have their own data base with data base management software.

DATA BASE

PERIPHERAL MACHINES

Figure 25.7   Three types of hierarchical configuration which use a data base.

fessional design. This usually means design by central authorities. However, this should not constrain the use of distributed systems in areas which are not sensitive.

DATA DICTIONARY   A data dictionary is desirable in all data-base installations. In a *distributed* data environment, whether files or data base, it is vital.

A data dictionary is a tool (normally computerized, though a few installations use manual index cards) which lists all fields that are used, their definitions, how and where they are used, and who is responsible for them. In a distributed environment the dictionary ought to be on-line so that the same definitions are available to all locations.

All fields in all locations are in the dictionary. The dictionary helps to enforce agreement on the definition of each field and its bit structure. It helps to avoid having different fields in different places with the same name (homonyms) and the same field having different names in different places (synonyms). In some cases the same field *does* have different names for historical reasons, and the dictionary informs its users of these aliases. The dictionary is a vital tool for the data administrator's work of ensuring compatibility in the distributed data.

The dictionary tells how fields are arranged into groups and records and how records are linked into data-base structures. It indicates where data reside geographically and what data are replicated. It indicates which programs read the data and which update it. It should indicate who owns the data, who are responsible for their accuracy, who update them, and who can read them.

The dictionary user can request a variety of reports from it. A designer at one location can ask to see where else his data are used. A data administrator faced with the prospect of changing a certain field can ask what programs use that field. Figure 25.8 shows some typical data dictionary reports [3]. A programmer starts off with well-documented data.

A good data dictionary should automatically generate program source language descriptions of the data, for example, the Data Division statements of COBOL, the data descriptions of PL/I, or the data descriptions of a data-base language such as MARK IV. It should generate the control blocks and parameters required by DBMS programs, for example, the PSBs of DL/I, the DBGENs, DCBs, format buffers, etc., of IDMS, ADABAS, SYSTEM 2000, TOTAL and so on. This automatic generation of data for programs ensures that the programmer cannot ignore data definition standards. It helps the programmer avoid inaccuracies and alleviates some of his documentation tasks. Figure 25.9 illustrates automatically generated source code.

Figure 25.8   Typical example of data dictionary output. Dictionaries need to be expanded to encompass multiple systems in a distributed environment. (5).

```
                          WHAT USES DEPARTMENT.

ITEM DEPARTMENT IS USED BY
    GROUP    EMPLOYEE-RECORD
    GROUP    HISTORY-RECORD
    GROUP    TRANSACTION-RECORD
    GROUP    HISTORY-REPORT-RECORD
    GROUP    REPORT-RECORD

GROUP EMPLOYEE-RECORD IS USED BY
    FILE     EMPLOYEE-MASTER

GROUP HISTORY-RECORD IS USED BY
    FILE     EMPLOYEE-HISTORY-MASTER

GROUP TRANSACTION-RECORD IS USED BY
    FILE     EMPLOYEE-TRANSACTIONS-SORTED
    FILE     EMPLOYEE-TRANSACTIONS

GROUP HISTORY-REPORT-RECORD IS USED BY
    FILE     EMPLOYEE-HISTORY-LIST

GROUP REPORT-RECORD IS USED BY
    FILE     EMPLOYEE-LIST

FILE EMPLOYEE-MASTER IS USED BY
    PROGRAM EMPLOYEE-HISTORY-REPORT
    PROGRAM EMPLOYEE-MASTER-UPDATE
    PROGRAM EMPLOYEE-REPORT

FILE EMPLOYEE-HISTORY-MASTER IS USED BY
    PROGRAM EMPLOYEE-HISTORY-REPORT
    PROGRAM EMPLOYEE-HISTORY-UPDATE

FILE EMPLOYEE-TRANSACTIONS-SORTED IS USED BY
    PROGRAM EMPLOYEE-HISTORY-UPDATE
    PROGRAM EMPLOYEE-MASTER-UPDATE
    PROGRAM EMPLOYEE-VET

FILE EMPLOYEE-TRANSACTIONS IS USED BY
    PROGRAM EMPLOYEE-VET

FILE EMPLOYEE-HISTORY-LIST IS USED BY
    PROGRAM EMPLOYEE-HISTORY-REPORT

FILE EMPLOYEE-LIST USED BY
    PROGRAM EMPLOYEE-REPORT
```

```
PROGRAM EMPLOYEE-HISTORY-REPORT IS USED BY
    SYSTEM MAINTAIN-EMPLOYEE-HISTORY

PROGRAM EMPLOYEE-MASTER-UPDATE IS USED BY
    SYSTEM MAINTAIN-EMPLOYEE-DATA

PROGRAM EMPLOYEE-REPORT IS USED BY
    SYSTEM MAINTAIN-EMPLOYEE-DATA

PROGRAM EMPLOYEE-HISTORY-UPDATE IS USED BY
    SYSTEM MAINTAIN-EMPLOYEE-HISTORY

PROGRAM EMPLOYEE-VET IS USED BY
    SYSTEM MAINTAIN-EMPLOYEE-DATA

SYSTEM MAINTAIN-EMPLOYEE-HISTORY-IS USED BY NO MEMBERS

SYSTEM MAINTAIN-EMPLOYEE-DATA IS USED BY NO MEMBERS
```

```
                 WHICH ITEMS CONSTITUTE MAINTAIN-EMPLOYEE-DATA.

THE FOLLOWING CONSTITUTE SYSTEM MAINTAIN-EMPLOYEE-DATA
    ITEMS          ACTION-CODE
                   DEPARTMENT
                   EMPLOYEE-NUMBER
                   NAME
                   TYPE
                   ADDRESS
                   JOB-STATUS
                   JOB-TITLE
                   SALARY
                   TAX-CODE
                   DEDUCT-CODE
                   SOCIAL-SECURITY-NUMBER
                   FILLER00002

                 WHICH FILES USE DEPARTMENT.

THE FOLLOWING USE ITEM DEPARTMENT
    FILES          EMPLOYEE-MASTER
                   EMPLOYEE-HISTORY-MASTER
                   EMPLOYEE-HISTORY-LIST
                   EMPLOYEE-LIST
                   EMPLOYEE-TRANSACTIONS
                   EMPLOYEE-TRANSACTIONS-SORTED

                 WHICH PROGRAMS USE DEPARTMENT.

THE FOLLOWING USE ITEM DEPARTMENT
    PROGRAMS       CALCULATE-GROSS-EARNINGS
                   EMPLOYEE-HISTORY-REPORT
                   EMPLOYEE-MASTER-UPDATE
                   EMPLOYEE-REPORT
                   EMPLOYEE-HISTORY-UPDATE
                   EMPLOYEE-VET

                 WHAT FORMS 'COBOL'.

THE FOLLOWING ARE CATALOGUED UNDER ALL THE SPECIFIED ENTRIES

    PROGRAM EMPLOYEE-HISTORY-REPORT
    PROGRAM EMPLOYEE-HISTORY-UPDATE
    PROGRAM EMPLOYEE-MASTER-UPDATE
    PROGRAM EMPLOYEE-REPORT
    PROGRAM EMPLOYEE-VET
    SYSTEM MAINTAIN-EMPLOYEE-DATA
    SYSTEM MAINTAIN-EMPLOYEE-HISTORY
    SYSTEM MAINTAIN-EMPLOYEE-PAY
    PROGRAM PAY-PROCESS
```

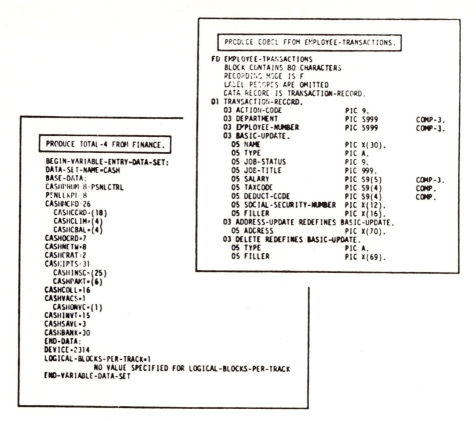

Figure 25.9 Typical *source language* generation by a data dictionary. Source language for the DBMS user facility MARK IV, and for a COBOL program, generated by MSP's DATAMANAGER.

SUBJECT DATA   In a data base the data relating to many different entities can be combined into one structure. Because of practical considerations in implementation, not *all* of the data types in the corporation are combined into the same shared structure. Instead the data are divided into disjoint data structures serving a given area. Some of these are complex like that in Fig. 24.3.

To obtain the maximum future benefits, the separate data bases should be related to business *subjects* rather than to conventional computer *applications*. For example, there should be a *product* data base rather than separate *order entry, quality control,* and *product inventory* data bases. Many applications may then use the same data base. The development of new applications relating to that data base becomes easier than if application-oriented data bases had been built.

Typical *subjects* for which data bases are built in a corporation are:

- Products
- Customers
- Parts
- Vendors
- Orders
- Accounts
- Personnel
- Documents
- Engineering descriptions

Some applications use more than one such data base, as in Fig. 25.10.

Using *subject* data bases rather than *application* data bases makes the eventual number of data bases far lower. A corporation builds up a very large number of applications but does not have a large number of operational *subjects*. If *files* are designed for specific applications, the number of files grows almost as rapidly as the number of applications and results in the great proliferation of redundant data found in a typical tape library today. Application-oriented data bases can also proliferate rapidly. With the use of *subject* data bases, however, the number of applications grows much faster than the number of data bases, as shown in Fig. 25.11. Eventually most new applications can be implemented rapidly because the data are available and the software provides tools to manipulate it. Indeed many of the corporations that have successfully installed subject-oriented data bases have found that the curve in Fig. 25.11 grows so rapidly that they run out of power on a centralized machine. In some cases they have run out of power on their manufacturer's most powerful processing unit—an argument for having distributed machines.

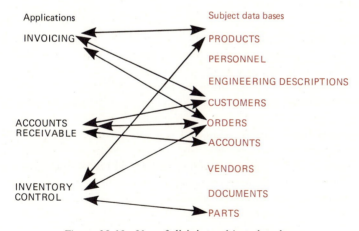

Figure 25.10   Use of disjoint *subject data bases*.

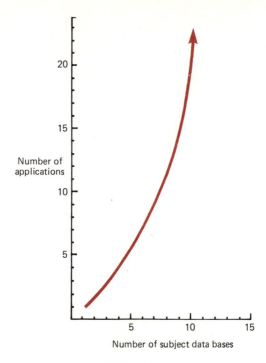

Number of
applications

Number of subject data bases

Figure 25.11

This dilemma of inadequate computer power will become worse in giant corporations because the combination of application and software usage of machine instructions per second is growing much faster than the development of higher-speed machines.

There are several ways out of the dilemma that do not involve sacrificing the genuinely valuable functions of the data-base management system. One is to place the disjoint subject data bases in different machines. In other words, use a horizontally distributed data-base system. Figure 25.12 illustrates this approach. The data bases in Fig. 25.12 are grouped so as to minimize the traffic between systems. Moreover, certain data bases may require a different type of structure from others. The PRODUCT and PARTS data bases, for example, may use structures appropriate for bill-of-materials applications. Those data bases needing a high level of security may be grouped together on a system using special security precautions. In Fig. 25.9 the PERSONNEL, PAYROLL, and ACCOUNTS data bases need a high level of privacy control and are grouped on the same system.

The data bases, shown in Fig. 25.12 as though they are part of the same installation, could also be remote, connected to a computer network. An application needing subject data bases in more than one location would cause messages to be transmitted between the locations. If suitable software existed the application pro-

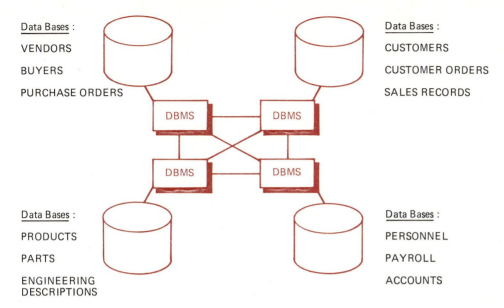

Data Bases :

VENDORS

BUYERS

PURCHASE ORDERS

Data Bases :

CUSTOMERS

CUSTOMER ORDERS

SALES RECORDS

Data Bases :

PRODUCTS

PARTS

ENGINEERING
DESCRIPTIONS

Data Bases :

PERSONNEL

PAYROLL

ACCOUNTS

Figure 25.12 Groups of subject data bases in separate machines. The machines may be in the same building or far apart on a network.

gram would simply make a data-base *call* and the data in question would be retrieved or updated via the network. The programmer need not know where it resides. However, distributed data-base software of this power would be very complex and would have to deal with the various failure and conflict conditions that can occur (as described in Chapter 20).

TWO APPROACHES   Subject data bases provide a development methodology
TO DEVELOPMENT   for data processing that is different from conventional
                      development and in many cases much better.

Conventional development starts with a systems analyst deciding what functions should be programmed. He determines the input, processing, and output and decides what data should be stored for that application. If a data base is in use, the data-base administrator then synthesizes many such analyst views of data into a data-base structure [2]. We will refer to this as an *application data base*. It is a byproduct of specific application design.

The other approach is to ask what data could be stored relating to a given *subject*. What data should be stored about customers? What data should be stored about suppliers? And so on. All of the data types that are relevant for a given subject are synthesized into a *subject data base* structure with records in third normal form [1]. Applications are then built on top of the data base, and the designer asks two different questions: How is the data base updated? And how are the reports and information that end users need created form the data base? The data bases become the foundation stone on which applications are built, rather than stored data being an afterthought or adjunct to the input-process-output method of application developmnent.

Higher-level data-base languages become critical to the productivity of application development, and if they are powerful, new applications can be developed very quickly. The end users ought to be able to generate the listings, reports, and queries they need spontaneously. The applications analyst and programmer cease to be a bottleneck for many applications.

Data-base software is improving at a rapid rate. More important, data-base management systems are being built into hardware [4]. *Back end* data-base machines are coming into use, so that host computers are relieved of the excessive software load of data-base operations. In summary, data-base operation is becoming more efficient and cheaper and is descending to small computers. Increasingly, as this happens, data base will become the foundation stone of future application development.

A corporation will have not one data base but a vast number. These data bases need to be planned, and this is the job of the top-level data planner in the corporation (the data strategist, as we have called him). He needs to ask, What subject data bases or other data resources does this corporation need?

If he answered that question for today's technology, he might perhaps conclude that the data bases would be highly centralized, especially if they are to be compatible with data structures that already exist. If he answered the question assuming the technology of five years hence, the answer would probably be different and would include a high degree of distribution. Unfortunately, it is extremely expensive to move from the convoluted structures of many of today's centralized data bases to a distributed alternative. The conversion costs are so high that many organizations are effectively locked into their centralized structures. They can *add* distributed resources but will not extensively tear apart the centralized data structures that exist. It is for reasons such as this that the strategy diagram of Fig. 10.4 stresses the assessment of long-range technology trends. The data strategist should be cautious about allowing highly convoluted, centralized data structures to be built. Instead he should take a long-range view of the technology, do the type of planning indicated in Chapters 23 and 24, and then ask, How do we get from here to there? What succession of practical steps will lead to the data infrastructure needed for the computerized corporation of the future?

INFORMATION SYSTEMS AND PRODUCTION SYSTEMS

There is a strong argument for making *information system data bases* reside in a different machine from *production system data bases*.

In the 1970's most data were accessed by means of a *primary key* such as Customer Number, Job Number, or Passenger Name and Flight. Increasingly *search keys,* also called *secondary keys,* came into use so that data could be accessed by more than one key. For example, jobs could be accessed by specifying which customer they were for, as well as by Job Number. Data bases could be queried to answer questions such as "List all surgical patients under 30 in the last year who have gone into coma."

The more we employ higher-level data-base language, the more secondary key operations, as opposed to pirmary key operations, will be initiated.

However, secondary key operations can give performance problems. Many records may have to be searched by means of a secondary index or other mechanism. Because of this the response time on some systems is poor for queries involving secondary key actions. Response time, and often availability of systems as perceived by the terminal user, is affected by the job scheduling. Where many different types of activities take place on the same machine, scheduling becomes complex. Changes in schedules are made frequently, and these sometimes affect the end user adversely. With complex queries (and sometimes less complex ones) he can perceive a sudden drop in response time from, say, 3 seconds to 30 seconds or sometimes much longer. This is extremely frustrating for the user.

This is a problem both with large computers and with minicomputers. The terminal user response time on a minicomputer can suddenly go to pieces when the machine is doing compilations, sorts, etc.

Conversely, the data-processing manager is often concerned that much high-level data-base query usage will play havoc with the performance of the system's other activities.

This, again, is a problem of too much complexity in a single machine. The solution is to remove some of the activity into separate, cheap machines. In particular, the data structures for a high level of secondary key usage should usually not be mixed up with the data structures for production runs.

Although it may contain much of the same data, the information system should often be separate from the production system and use a separate collection of data. The reasons for the two collections of data being separate and disjoint are as follows:

1. The physical data structures used for information systems are such that it is difficult or excessively time-consuming to keep the data up to date. Production systems, on the other hand, have simpler data structures which can be designed for fast updating.

2. More serious, it is very difficult to insert new data and delete old data from the information system data base except by lengthy off-line operations. Production systems have data structures into which records can easily be inserted and from which records can easily be deleted.

3. Production systems usually have to contain the latest transactions. However, it usually does not matter if an information system gives information which is 24 hours or more out of date.

4. Production systems may handle a high throughput of transactions, so that file structures permitting rapid access are necessary to cope with the volume. Information systems containing the same data usually handle a relatively small number of queries.

5. The information system may contain summary information or digested information without all the details that are in the production system.

6. End users employing an information system may want freedom from the constraints placed on machine usage by the management of a high-volume, production-oriented system.

7. Powerful languages for end-user information systems are becoming available, but management of the production system does not want end users to have free access to the production data with these languages. They prefer the end users to have their own files where they can do no harm.

8. Job scheduling is complex on systems handling widely different types of transactions and jobs. Changes in the scheduling or in the job mix can play havoc with response times. A flood of queries using secondary key operations will interfere with the production runs and their deadlines.

9. DP managers responsible for production runs are reluctant to give end users too much freedom to use high-level data-base languages because they may adversely affect performance or even damage the data.

10. End users need their own information systems to tune and adjust, to meet their own varying information needs. They should keep their own data in their own information systems.

For these reasons a production system and an information system which relate to the same data sometimes store their data in separate data bases. The production system is updated in real time. Often there is on-line data entry at end-user locations. The information system is updated off-line, possibly each night, with files prepared by the production system. The production system files may have a high ratio of new records being inserted and old ones deleted, but this volatility can be accommodated with reasonable ease. The information system is not concerned with real-time insertions and deletions, because new records are inserted off-line.

Figure 25.10 illustrates this approach. For example, the system on the left might be a sales order entry system with terminals in branch sales offices. Its files are updated in real time, and many modifications to the data have to be made in real time. New items must be inserted into the files as they arise. The files are all structured and manipulated on the basis of primary keys such as PART-NUMBER and CUSTOMER-NUMBER. Although the files are volatile, a fairly straightforward technique can be devised for handling insertions and deletions.

The system on the right on Fig. 25.13 is designed to provide information to management and its staff. For example, it might answer questions such as "How have the sales of the model 88 in the eastern region to public utilities been affected by the introduction of the new compensation plan? To answer a diverse set of such questions spontaneously the system uses special index or pointer structures (often in software but preferably built into hardware or microcode). Inserting new records with these structures is complicated and time-consuming because the secondary indices or pointer structures must be updated. It is therefore done off-line when the terminals are not in use. The data for the off-line updating is transmitted by the

PRODUCTION SYSTEM

- Complete data

- Updated continuously

- Data accessed
  by primary keys.

- Simple primary-key inquiries

- Insertions and deletions are
  straightforward but must be
  handled in real-time.

- Complex operating system

- Often on-line data entry.

- High volume of transactions.

- Complex scheduling of work.

- Main design criterion: **EFFICIENCY OF HIGH
  VOLUME PROCESSING**

INFORMATION SYSTEM

- Summary data

- Updated periodically

- Data structured so that
  they can be searched using
  multiple secondary keys.

- Psychologically powerful
  end-user language

- Insertions and deletions are
  complex because of the secondary
  keys, but are handled off-line in
  periodic nightly maintenance runs.

- Simple control program

- Off-line updates

- Low volume of transactions.

- Scheduling problems avoided.

- Main design criterion: **EASE OF USE AND VALUE
  TO END USERS**

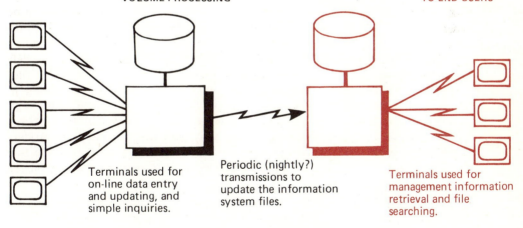

Terminals used for
on-line data entry
and updating, and
simple inquiries.

Periodic (nightly?)
transmissions to
update the information
system files.

Terminals used for
management information
retrieval and file
searching.

Figure 25.13   Information systems are separate from production systems
even though they contain much of the same data, because the characteristics of their data structure and usage are fundamentally different.

system on the left-hand side of Fig. 25.13. If this technique were not used, the volatility would be very difficult to handle.

The production system handles a high volume of transactions. A major design criterion is to maximize the efficiency of high-volume processing. Data and system structures are selected with this objective. The information system handles a very low volume of transactions compared to the production system. The design criterion is therefore not to optimize machine efficiency but to optimize the ease of use and value to the end users.

If the details of the type of information sought are not known prior to its being requested, then a special capability is required in the system: the ability to generate quickly a program that will respond to the request. For example, a file may contain details of all branch office expenditure, and an executive may ask, Which branch offices have had the largest expenditures for entertaining customers? A program must be generated quickly which can search the files to produce a precise answer to this question. The executive might go on to ask, How does this expenditure correlate with their sales performance? This question could be answered precisely using correlation analysis, or it could be answered in a simpler way which would probably suffice, by listing performance figures alongside branch office entertainment expenses, in sequence of decreasing peformance. In either case the *data exist but the question is new,* so a new program must be generated rapidly to answer the question. The program might be generated quickly by means of a database interrogation language.

Until the late 1970's, information systems tended to be centralized systems. As minicomputers become more powerful, it became practical to have information systems in user departments, sometimes with very small computers such as the Microdata *Reality* system.

In many cases the data stored in the information system are much smaller than those in the production system—only summary data. Therefore a small minicomputer is appropriate. In other cases the information system storage must be very large because historical or archival data are kept.

There will be inquiries into the production system as well as the information system, but they will be mostly *primary key* inquiries, often requesting a degree of detail that does not exist in the information system. It may be desirable that the end-user terminal connected to the information system also be linked to the production system of Fig. 25.13, or possibly to many systems via a network, so that managers or users can inspect detailed records of customers, bank statements, orders, and so on, when they need to.

The production system has a complex operating system, and the scheduling of jobs on it is complex. The information system may have a simple operating system or control program which handles the low volume of queries in a first-come-first-served fashion.

The main design concern with the production system is *efficiency* of high-volume operations. With the information system there is little concern with machine efficiency. The main design concerns are *effectiveness, ease of use,* and *value to end users.*

SELF-SUFFICIENT MODULES   In general what we should be striving for with distributed data is modules which are largely self-sufficient, which serve the particular user community they are designed for, and which are not excessively complex. The interactions between the separate modules should be relativley simple and easily auditable. Some of the modules will be production systems, some information systems, and some combinations of these when the volume of complex queries is low.

What is to be avoided is excessively convoluted systems with complex interactions, systems with job scheduling so complex or tight that a change in schedules or work mix plays havoc with some users, systems where the complex data structures impose inflexibility of usage, and systems with excessively entangled problems of distribution.

A system in which the answering of queries can trigger complex multilocation searches or complex movement of data between machines is to be avoided. The distributed data-base query in Figs. 22.9 and 22.10 is an impressive demonstration of distributed data-base software, but for most commercial systems it should be regarded as *bad design of data resources*. It is unnecessarily complex. The data in question should be located in one machine (and in a military system replicated in multiple machines, for survivability reasons).

Systems which trigger complex patterns of data conflicts are to be avoided.

To repeat the comment made earlier (it probably requires frequent repetition): *Good design of distributed processing reduces overall system complexity; bad design increases it.*

THE DATA STRATEGY   The task of the *data strategist* should relate to information systems, subject data bases, files, and conversion problems and to changing the application development methodology so that conventional programming is replaced by the use of higher-level data-base languages wherever possible.

What subject data bases are required in the organization? What information systems? There may be small, functional information systems built with minicomputers such as the Microdata Reality system, and large information retrieval systems built with software such as IBM's STAIRS.

Figure 25.14 shows a data-base plan that was put together in a large bank [5]. This plan calls for 21 data bases. With these 21 data bases most of the applications of the bank can be built over a period of years. This plan was for a centralized system. A distributed system plan should identify the locations of the data structures and indicate which are independent files, subschema files, subject data bases,

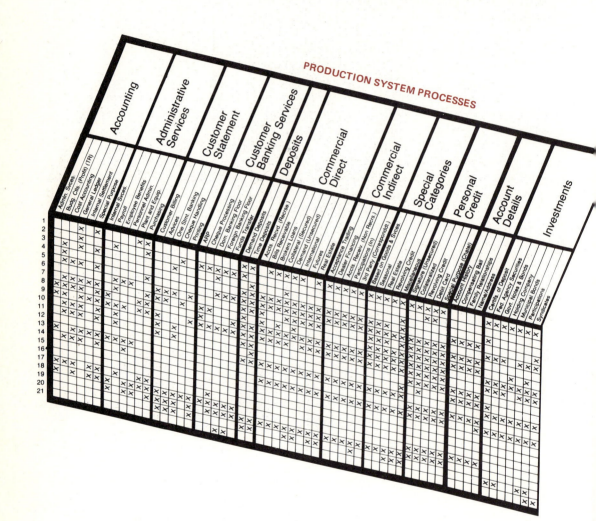

PRODUCTION SYSTEM PROCESSES

400

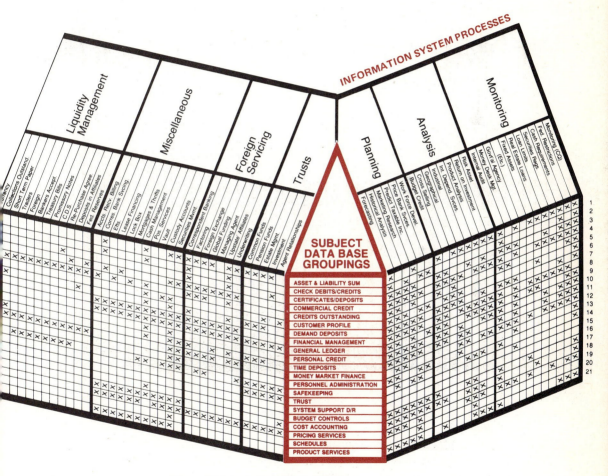

Figure 25.14 A large bank DB plan.

and application data bases. On the left are production system processes—the standard banking processes. On the right are information system processes for decision-making support. For information systems with high-volume secondary key usage, it may be economical to create separate data bases.

Figure 25.15 suggests the steps in forming a corporate data strategy. This is an expansion of the strategy diagram of Fig. 10.4. The black central portion of Fig. 25.15 illustrates top-down planning of the data resources. The red blocks at the left center illustrate the bottom-up design of individual data bases within the plan. Details of bottom-up data-base design are beyond our scope here and are discussed in other books by the author. The term *canonical synthesis* refers to a technique for taking many user views of data or separate views of data that ought to go into a subject data base, and merging these into a minimal structure designed to be as stable as possible [2]. It is a recommended bottom-up technique for data-base design.

A BRIDGE TO THE OLD WORLD

A crucial decision is: Which existing file structures will be allowed to remain in non-data-base form? The question is often asked: Should we convert our file systems to the more modern world of data base? Often the best decision is *not* to convert them. If they are part of a production system which *works well and is stable,* it may be better left alone. The manpower needed for conversion is better employed on new application development. On the other hand, if they are constantly having to be modified and thus causing high maintenance costs, they should be changed to data-base form.

In planning data resources it is often unwise to assume that files will be converted easily to data-base form. This has frequently proved so expensive that the conversion has never been completed. It is safer instead to assume that the files and their application programs will continue to exist, and plan a bridge that links the old *file* world to the new *data-base* world.

Figure 25.16 shows such a bridge. At the top is the output file from an existing application program. The data in it must update the data base, and a simple utility program is written for this. The old file records become a "user view" or subschema which must be represented in the data base. Possibly some of the field formats must be adjusted by the utility program in order to accomplish this. There may be items on the file which would not have appeared in the data base if it had been designed by itself, but they must now be there for compatibility reasons.

The data base is updated by new programs, and from the updated version the old files are derived. The bottom part of Fig. 25.16 shows this being done by another utility program. This conversion program is needed every time the old application programs are used. It may be in effect a high speed dump which creates batch files to be run once a week or so. It may create on-line files for terminal usage. This bridge must be one of the first data-base programs to be tested, to ensure that the old application programs continue to run.

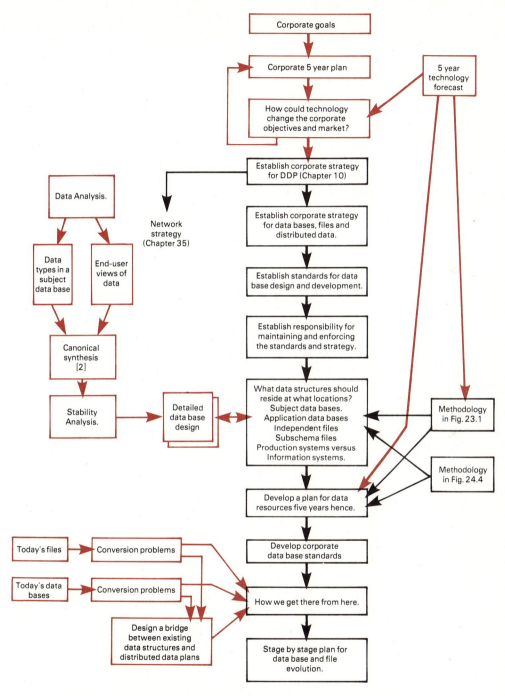

Figure 25.15   Strategy and planning for distributed data resources.

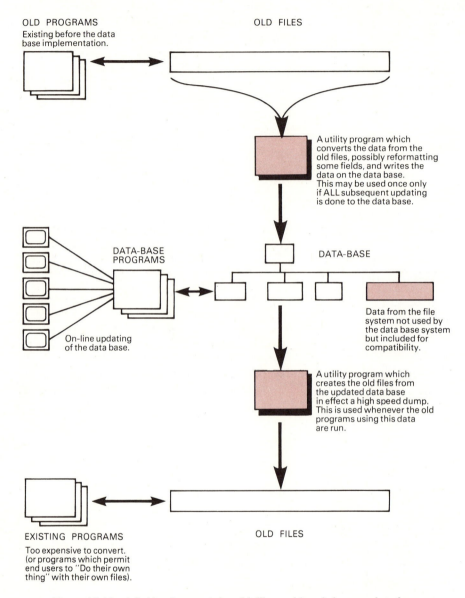

OLD PROGRAMS
Existing before the data
base implementation.

OLD FILES

A utility program which
converts the data from the
old files, possibly reformatting
some fields, and writes the
data on the data base.
This may be used once only
if ALL subsequent updating
is done to the data base.

DATA-BASE
PROGRAMS

DATA-BASE

Data from the file
system not used by
the data base system
but included for
compatibility.

On-line updating
of the data base.

A utility program which
creates the old files from
the updated data base
in effect a high speed dump.
This is used whenever the old
programs using this data
are run.

EXISTING PROGRAMS

Too expensive to convert.
(or programs which permit
end users to "Do their own
thing" with their own files).

OLD FILES

Figure 25.16 A bridge between the old file world and the new data base world.

In many cases an input to a data-base system must also be used to create input to a separate file system, possibly on a different machine. Such input should be entered into the system only once, and a necessary function of the data-base system is to create the required input for other operations.

A similar bridge may be used for creating files which end users manipulate in their own way. This use of separate files keeps the end users out of the data base. Similarly, a disjoint end-user data base may be created for manipulation by a language such as Query-by-Example.

HOW DO WE GET THERE FROM HERE The five-year look ahead in the planning process will usually suggest data resources and data distribution substantially different from the present. The strategy must decide what steps, standards, and guidelines will lead the organization, one stage at a time, to the desirable future sructures. The strategy must take into consideration conversion problems and the bridges to the past.

Working towards a planned goal will, in the long run, be much more beneficial than *ad hoc* application development and distribution. That goal will probably look very different if future technology is considered (as in Fig. 25.15) rather than today's technology.

REFERENCES

1. Explained in James Martin, *Computer Data-Base Organization,* Second Edition, Chapter 14, Prentice-Hall, Inc., Englewood Cliffs, N.J., 1977. Original paper: E. F. Codd, ''Further Normalization of the Data Base Relational Model,'' Courant Computer Science Symposia 6, *Data Base Systems,* ed. R. Rustin, Prentice-Hall, Inc., Englewood Cliffs, N.J., 1972.

2. Explained in James Martin, *Computer Data-Base Organization,* Second Edition, Chapter 15, Prentice-Hall, Inc., Englewood Cliffs, N.J., 1977.

3. Examples of the use of MSP's DATAMANAGER. *DATAMANAGER Fact Book,* MSP, London/Lexington, Mass., 1979.

4. The first example of a major commercial DBMS built into hardware and microcode is that in IBM's minicomputer, System 38.

5. The author is indebted to Ms. Francis Chu for this illustration, which is part of her design for Chemical Bank, New York.

KEY

P = Participating responsibility

C = Consulting when necessary

	User Group	Programmer and Systems Analyst	Local Data-Base Adminis- trator	Distributed Data Adminis- trator	Top-Level Data Strategist
Planning what corporate data resources are needed	C	P	P	P	Primary responsi- bility
Planning data-base strategy standards and responsibility		C	P	P	Primary responsi- bility
Planning what subject data bases are to exist	C	P	P	P	Primary responsi- bility
Deciding what data structures are to exist at what locations	C	P	P	P	Primary responsi- bility
Selection of DBMS software		C	P	P	Primary responsi- bility
Data dictionary selection		C	P	Primary responsi- bility	P
Data dictionary maintenance	C	C	P	Primary responsi- bility	P
Field design and definition	C	P	P	Primary responsi- bility	P
Coordination of distributed data structures	C	P	P	Primary responsi- bility	P
Logical data-base design at one location	C	P	Primary responsi- bility	P	P
Physical data-base design at one location		C	Primary responsi- bility	C	C
Subschema file design (including subschema at peripheral locations)	C	P	Primary responsi- bility	P	C
Independent file design	C	Primary responsi- bility			P

406

	User Group	Programmer and Systems Analyst	Local Data-Base Adminis-trator	Distributed Data Adminis-trator	Top-Level Data Strategist
Planning data-base compatibility with files at that location	C	P	Primary responsi-bility	P	P
Auditability design	C	P	P	P	Primary* responsi-bility
Security design	C	P	P	P	Primary* responsi-bility

* In conjunction with auditors and security administrators.

PART **V** **SOFTWARE AND NETWORK STRATEGY**

26   SOFTWARE AND STRATEGY

The software for distributed processing varies enormously in its complexity, depending on how automatic the facilities are and how transparent the effects of distance are made.

Ideally, one would like the user processes to communicate as automatically as possible, but this is often not possible because of incompatibilities between DDP software architectures. The incompatibilities need to be a major concern of corporationwide DDP strategy. This strategy may determine at what *level* categories or zones of machines are to be interlinked. We describe the concept of *levels* of interconnection in this and the following chapters.

COMPLEXITY In a fully transparent system the programmer would refer to all the facilities he uses by a symbolic name and would not need to know where they reside or on precisely what type of machine. In a data-base environment he would refer to the *logical* file or record which he perceives, and this would be created for him from the physical collection of data, which may or may not be distributed. Ideally he should perceive no difference between a file environment and a data-base environment. The transmission path would be set up automatically, bypassing any failures. Wherever possible, report generators or data-base interrogation facilities would be used to avoid the need for programming in conventional languages. The automatic generation of application code would be used wherever possible.

Such software would be highly complex even if failures never occurred. However, a characteristic of the distributed environment is that a very wide range of different types of failures will occur, and the system must recover from them, automatically if possible, without losing or damaging the data.

Such a software environment is *exceedingly* complex. It is made far more complex for the major computer manufacturers by the fact that many of the machines, operating systems, and software packages that must be hooked together in a distributed system already exist and to a large extent are incompatible. When they were devised, there was no conception that they would eventually be interlinked into distributed systems. Large manufacturers have the task of adapting a most formidable array of operating systems, data-base systems, access methods, teleprocessing systems, and languages, so that they can be interlinked in a distributed fashion. Worse, they have to enable their customers' old programs and files to keep running. Most of such manufacturers' products had their roots in the world of batch processing, which needed fundamentally different mechanisms from the interactive communications environment which now confronts us.

A large operating system contains over 5 million lines of code and represents an investment of over $50 million of development effort. It can be modified only slowly and cautiously because of the highly complex effect of errors. A seemingly trivial change often triggers a long chain reaction of changes elsewhere.

Data-base management systems are less complex than operating systems but are rapidly growing in complexity as they incorporate more of the functions which users and data-base committees demand.

Bugs in a data-base management system can be disastrous for the users, sometimes causing data to be lost, damaged, or inaccessible. Therefore, like operating systems, they can be modified only slowly and cautiously and need extremely thorough testing.

Large corporations have a vast number of working application programs. These often represent a programming investment five or ten times greater than the cost of the hardware used. They cannot be abandoned or quickly modified. It is vital to the managers of such installations that these programs continue to run, and they will only consider changes in hardware and software which permit this. Large manufacturers therefore plan an evolutionary change rather than a revolutionary change in mainframe architecture and software. They plan a *migration* path that will permit their customers to use new equipment, operating systems, data-base management, and so on, while keeping their existing programs running.

Meanwhile, intelligent terminals, minicomputers, and distributed processing hardware and software are reaching the marketplace at a fast and furious pace. A main concern of the long-established manufacturers and their customers is to make thie new world coexist with the old.

CLEAN START There is no question that incompatibility with existing products is enormously impeding new architecture development. The large, established customer base of the mainframe manufacturers is a godsend to the marketeers but a millstone around the necks of the developers.

Because of this millstone there is much to be said for adopting a dual strategy and developing two ranges of machines. One is compatible with the past to whatever extent is necessary to preserve the application program investment. The other starts with a clean sheet of drawing paper. The developers are asked to forget completely about the past. Instead, they should consider what we know today about end-user needs, networking, no-fail architectures, data-base machines, office-of-the-future needs, and application development without programming. Given today's and tomorrow's chips, design the best machine you can for that environment. It may not be able to run yesterday's programs without emulators, but it should permit application development which is much more automated and therefore faster and much more flexible. It should deal much more directly with end-user needs and may give no-fail service. It should be much easier to install with little or no demand for systems programmers.

Not surprisingly, perhaps, some of the best examples of new machines are coming from *new* companies such as Tandem Computers, Inc. IBM let its General Systems Division start with a clean sheet of paper rather than compatibility constraints, and it created the System 38, a machine architecture much more advanced than the 370 or 303x and *much* easier to install and create applications for.

THE NATURE OF ARCHITECTURE

The term *architecture* in the computer industry often implies a scheme which has not yet been fully implemented. It is a goal towards which the implementers strive. The term is used to describe data-base management systems, operating systems, and other highly complex software/hardware mechanisms. It is of particular importance in describing distributed processing and computer network systems because here so many potentially incompatible machines must fit together.

With much complex software there is an *architectural* definition stating the eventual requirements. For data-base systems, for example, CODASYL (the committee which developed COBOL) has defined a long-range data-base architecture and has specified some of the protocols involved in that architecture in great detail. As with network architectures, current implementations (at the time of writing) provide only some of the functions in the complete architecture.

A good architecture ought to relate primarily to the needs of the end users rather than to enthusiasms for particular techniques. A well-architected house is one which reflects the desired lifestyle of its owners rather than one which is designed to exploit a building technique which is currently in vogue. Fred Brooks defined architecture in a way which makes a clear distinction between architecture and engineering:

> Computer architecture, like other architecture, is the art of determining the needs of the user of a structure and then designing to meet those needs as effectively as possible within economic and technological constraints. Architecture must include engineering considerations, so that the design will be economical and feasible; but the emphasis in architecture is upon the needs of the user, whereas in engineering the emphasis is upon the needs of the fabricator. [1]

Some architectures have started life being well oriented to user needs and have evolved into forms excessively driven by hardware selection or software economics.

It is highly desirable that detailed conceptual thinking (i.e., an architecture) precede the mass of work needed in writing the software and developing associated hardware mechanisms. However, the arthictecture itself is not static but evolves as new requirements are perceived.

DISCIPLINE   Given the falling cost of microcomputers, there is little question about the correctness of using distributed intelligence. Most terminals other than the simplest, or else the terminal controllers, should have a microprocessor under the covers. The cost of a small microprocessor is less than 1% of the cost of a teletype machine.

Nevertheless, distributed intelligence, if not disciplined, could be a formula for chaos. Every terminal designer, and perhaps terminal users too, are likely, if unrestrained, to program "their own thing" under the covers of the terminal. There will then be little chance that the intelligent terminals of the world will be able to communicate—certainly little chance that they will jointly achieve the objectives listed in Chapter 9.

Similarly, minicomputers with terminals and files are being sold in large quantities, and it is desirable that they be interconnected in a disciplined fashion so that they can use one another's files. A wide variety of configurations is possible for an endless assortment of applications.

The full advantages of intelligent terminals, distributed processing, and computer networks can flower only with discipline, and the discipline must apply to a wide range of machines and software products. The protocols to which these products conform must relate to both the transport subsystem which moves data from one place to another and the higher-level functions which we will describe as session services.

In the mid-1970's major manufacturers began to announce "architectures" for distributed processing and computer networks. The first major ones were IBM's SNA (System Network Architecture), Sperry Univac's DCA (Distributed Communications Architecture), and DEC's DNA (Digital Network Architecture). Before long most mainframe and minicomputer vendors had announced an architecture for distributed processing. The architectures define, precisely, the interfaces and protocols to be used for computer networks and distributed processing.

The term "architecture" implies that SNA, DCA, DNA, and the others are long-range plans. The current software at any time may have implemented only a portion of the plan. The plan provides discipline for product developers in many locations and also gives them a goal to work towards. It is important to distinguish between the architecture and its current implementation.

The laboratories can be free to create many new products, providing they conform to the network architecture. These include file, data-base, language processor, and other products which the architecture does not define; it merely defines services which they use and how they interface with the networking facilities.

It is the objective that end users and programmers should be isolated from the complexities of the network and network services. As far as is reasonable, the programs should be independent of the technique for exchanging information.

Because SNA, DCA, DNA, and other manufacturers' equivalents are *architectures,* they are independent of any particular hardware or software products. Teleprocessing software products, such as IBM's VTAM, are current implementations which conform to and utilize the architecture. Manufacturer's network architectures are designed to serve the widest reasonable range of the manufacturer's products. They are not necessarily compatible with products of other manufacturers except for common carrier equipment.

The products which have to link into the network architecture are often themselves incompatible. They use different codes, formats, and control programs and have differing requirements. There is therefore need for conversion operations and for machines to agree before a session begins what resources, conversions, and protocols they will employ to make the session work.

TWO TYPES
OF APPROACH

There are two types of approach to distributed processing software. The first is to link together separate machines, each using conventional software, with straightforward data communications. The second is to use the new distributed processing architectures which are evolving, as described in the following chapters.

The first approach can be relatively simple. Each machine is a self-sufficient computer in its own right. It may be a large computer, minicomputer, or desk-top machine. It has a telecommunications adaptor and can send messages with a standard form of line control. The system designer plans what messages these machines will send to one another. The messages are designed and their format agreed upon and standardized for that installation. Each message will contain a header which indicates the message type and usually contains certain simple control information. Often a message from one machine requires a certain type of message in response. This must be specified in the design of the messages. All application programmers who are involved adhere to these specifications.

Often multiple messages are involved in the design of a transaction such as a car rental transaction, machine order, or invoice. The specification for the transaction must give details of these messages. Message and transaction design is discussed in Chapter 33.

The second approach is to use an architecture which hides the effects of distance, data formats, and incompatibility from the application programs. The application programs or end-user languages give commands as though the system were not distributed, and the software does all of the necessary conversions, data access, and networking.

LEVELS OF
INTERCONNECTION

The above approaches might be regarded as two extremes—complete transparency on the one hand, or design and handle your own messages on the other.

There are intermediate levels of interconnection representing a compromise between complete standardization and almost no standardization.

We will discuss several levels of interconnection in the following chapters. The architectures for distributed processing are built up in layers. The International Standards Organization (ISO) proposes seven layers. Many machines will have some but not all of these layers. Machines may be compatible at the lower layers but not the higher ones.

Before we explain the ISO layers in detail, let us note the possible levels of compatibility:

Layer 1 Compatibility: Physical Control

Layer 1 specifies the physical, electrical connection to a circuit. Machines interconnected at Layer 1 only may transmit and bit stream to one another with the network providing the bit timing. This is done on circuit-switched data networks like the Nordic network in Scandinavia and on point-to-point digital circuits.

Layer 2 Compatibility: Link Control

The machines use the same line-control protocol, such as HDLC (High Level Data Link Control), which specifies the header and trailer for each physical message that is transmitted, so that the receiving machine can recognize which is the first bit of the data, which is the last bit, and which the message is addressed to. Messages in error must be recognized and retransmitted in a failsafe manner.

Layer 3 Compatibility: Network Control

The machines use a common network—a packet-switching network or network which sends blocks of bits. The blocks cannot be greater than a certain size, so that long messages must be sliced into packets and reassembled after transmission. The user machines send both *data* packets and *control* packets for controlling the flow and use of the network. The Layer 3 description defines all of these types of packets and how they are used. Such networks can be private networks *within* corporations, national public networks used by multiple corporations, and worldwide networks spanning the national networks of industrial countries.

Layer 4 Compatibility: Transport End-to-End Control

Layer 3 provides a standard interface to a common network but does not apply *end-to-end* controls on data integrity. Furthermore, there are likely to be several different types of network, with different interfaces. Layer 4 provides a transport service interface standard which is independent of the type of common network used; it can work with packet-switched or circuit-switched networks, satellite networks, wideband office-of-the-future types of networks, and others, or combinations of these. Layer 4 provides end-to-end addressing, assurance of delivery, flow control, and in general end-to-end control of the transmission process.

Layer 6 Compatibility: Presentation Control

Terminals, computers, and other machines use different character sets, different control characters, different print page sizes or screen display areas, different editing controls and other means of presenting data. Some encipher the data; some compact the data. *Presentation control* refers to standard forms of transformation of information so that it can be edited, character-converted, adjusted to fit a screen, enciphered, compacted, etc. The application programmer codes for a standard *logical* unit, and his input/output is adjusted by software to fit a wide variety of *real* machines.

At this level of compatibility the communicating machines use compatible transport service mechanisms and compatible presentation services.

Layer 7 Compatibility: Process Control

At the highest level, remote machines may use compatible data-base management or application system techniques to support the information-processing function.

Layer 5 is not included in this list of compatibility levels because it is incomplete without the other layers. The following chapters explain the layers more fully.

COMPATIBILITY OF TODAY'S MACHINES　　Many of today's machines are compatible at Layer 2. They can send messages to one another if they are interconnected by a physical circuit. However, many machines are not compatible even at this low level, because there are many different link control protocols: telex, TWX, other start-stop line controls, airline system line control, IBM 2260 line control, binary synchronous, IBM's SDLC, and so on.

The telephone administrations (PTT's) and common carriers are building switched public data networks. Most of these use an international standard incorporating Layers 1, 2, and 3. This is the CCITT X.25 standard, primarily intended for packet-switched networks but used to enhance interconnectability on some other types of networks. Public X.25 networks are spreading around the world. Many manufacturers make equipment which interconnects to them.

At the high levels there is little compatibility between different manufacturers as yet. At the time of writing Layers 4 to 7 have not been agreed on in detail by the standards organizations. The need to be specified in detail to define every bit in the message headers and control messages and the protocols which employ these bits. There will be much argument before this is agreed upon and ratified standards are created. When these are created, it will cost large manufacturers tens of millions of dollars to change their product lines to conform to the new standards. This change will occur only slowly. Manufacturers with the largest established customer bases may be reluctant to make the change, partly because of cost, partly because they may believe that their own protocols are better, and partly because full use of the standards would allow competitors' equipment to be connected too easily to their equipment. They may find it a better marketing strategy to lock customers into their own product line.

Most major manufacturers have their own private standards for interconnecting machines at all seven layers. These standards form their DDP architecture. They constitute guidelines for future development of their products and software, so that the product line will tie together increasingly diverse machines at a high level. It is possible that the standards of a large manufacturer such as IBM or large common carrier such as AT&T (with its ACS network) will evolve into a *de facto* standard for a large class of machines.

Today the machines of one manufacturer cannot generally be linked to the machines of another except at a low level. Sometimes they can be linked at Layer 3. They can share a common packet-switching network. Sometimes only Layer 2 links are possible—a telephone line can interconnect them. At the time of writing there are very few links at Layer 4 or higher between machines of different manufacturers. Some manufacturers claim in their advertising to be compatible with IBM's System Network Architecture. When examined closely there is no high-level compatibility with the current version of SNA. The other manufactuer's machines may be connectable to SNA machines at Layer 2, SDLC (Synchronous Data Link Control), or may replace some specific SNA peripheral machine, such as a 3790 cluster controller.

A large manufactuer's protocols for connection at the higher levels are exceedingly complex and often difficult for a smaller vendor to copy because of incomplete information, and they are often changed as new versions come out.

Part of the strategic planning needed for DP in a corporation now is to decide what distributed architectures will be used and at what levels machines will communicate. Higher-level interconnection is extremely desirable but may lock the user into one vendor. We will discuss this strategic planning further in Chapter 35. First we must discuss more details of the layers in the objectives of DDP software.

27 THE ISO SEVEN LAYERS

Advanced computer systems have software which has grown up in layers rather like the skins of an onion. Different layers relate to different types of functions and services. This applies to operating systems, to data-base or storage software, and also to teleprocessing software.

INCREASING
USEFULNESS
Each layer that is added is an attempt to increase the usefulness or ease of use of the machines or to introduce modularity by dividing the complex set of functions into discrete layers. Figure 27.1 shows the growth of software layers around the central processing unit.

For distributed processing, in which distant machines are interconnected, layers of software (or hardware or microcode) are needed around the telecommunications links to make these more useful, to hide the complexity from the network users, and to separate the functions into more manageable slices.

Figure 27.2 illustrates types of layers which are fundamental to advanced teleprocessing systems.

The innermost layer is the *physical (electrical) connection* between the data machine and the telecommunications circuit.

The next layer is the *link control,* which relates to how data are transmitted over a physical line. Throughout the history of teleprocessing there have been many different forms of link control. Some were character-oriented, e.g., telex line control, start-stop line control with an ASCII character set. Some were oriented to blocks of characters, e.g., binary synchronous line control, line control for specific terminals such as the IBM 2260, line control for specific applications such as airline reservations. More recently the bit-oriented line-control procedures which we describe in this book (HDLC, SDLC, etc.) have emerged.

The third layer, *transmission control,* in conjunction with inner layers, pro-

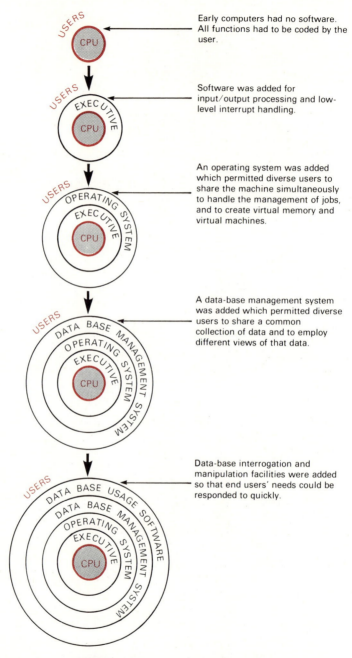

Early computers had no software. All functions had to be coded by the user.

Software was added for input/output processing and low-level interrupt handling.

An operating system was added which permitted diverse users to share the machine simultaneously to handle the management of jobs, and to create virtual memory and virtual machines.

A data-base management system was added which permitted diverse users to share a common collection of data and to employ different views of that data.

Data-base interrogation and manipulation facilities were added so that end users' needs could be responded to quickly.

Figure 27.1 Layers of software. Each layer that was added made the machine more capable and more useful.

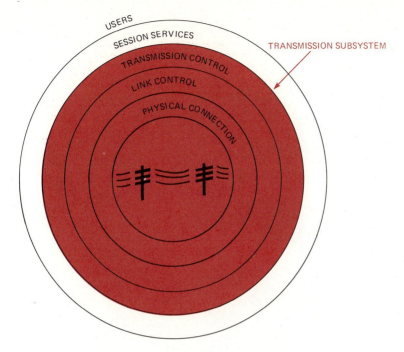

Figure 27.2   In a similar manner to Fig. 27.1 the layers of control for communications are intended to make the physical communications links more capable and more useful.

vides the transmission network—the transmission subsystem. The transmission network can be regarded as an entity which the higher levels employ for moving data from one user machine to another through multiple intermediate nodes such as concentrators, packet switches, and line controllers.

The layer external to the transmission subsystem in Fig. 27.2 provides a variety of services which are used to establish and operate sessions between the using machines. As we will see later, a rich array of such services is possible and desirable.

These four layers are fundamental to data networking and distributed systems. They are found in all of the computer manufacturers' architectures for distributed processing. Their detail differs somewhat from one manufacturer to another, especially in the outermost layer. The transmission control layer and the session services layer are themselves often split into sublayers.

ISO's SEVEN LAYERS   However the layers are defined, they form a standard with that manufacturer. Many different machines of one manufacturer incorporate the same standard layers. They form the basis for communication between machines which are otherwise diverse.

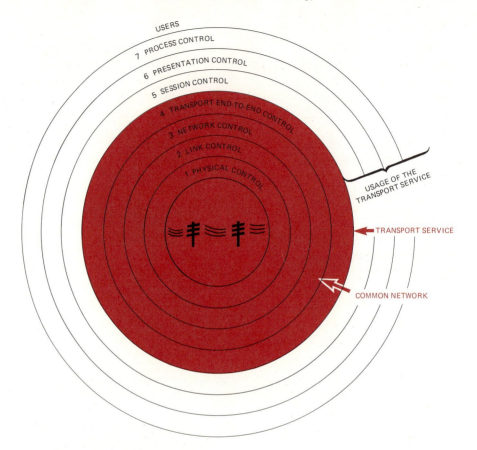

USERS

7 PROCESS CONTROL

6 PRESENTATION CONTROL

5 SESSION CONTROL

4 TRANSPORT END-TO-END CONTROL

3 NETWORK CONTROL

2 LINK CONTROL

1 PHYSICAL CONTROL

USAGE OF THE TRANSPORT SERVICE

TRANSPORT SERVICE

COMMON NETWORK

Figure 27.3. The International Standards Organization's seven layers of control for distributed processing.

It is highly desirable that machines of *different* manufacturers should be able to communicate. For this to be possible they have to use the same layers, and the formats of data and control messages which pass between the layers have to be compatible.

Given the immense proliferation of machines now occurring, one of the activities most important to the future of data processing is the setting of standards to enable machines of different manufacturers and different countries to communicate. As a start in the setting of such standards, ISO (the *International Standards Organization*) has defined seven layers, further subdividing the four layers of Fig. 27.2. These are shown in Fig. 27.3.

Their functions are as follows:

Layer 1: Physical Control

The innermost layer relates to setting up a physical circuit so that bits can be moved over it. It is concerned with the *physical, electrical, functional, and procedural characteristics to establish, maintain, and disconnect the physical link* [1]. If the user machine employs an analog circuit like a conventional telephone line, it will be connected to a modem. Its interface with the modem is a generally accepted standard, e.g., EIA RS 232-C and CCITT Recommendation V.24 [2]. If a digital circuit is used, a newer Recommendation for the physical interface, CCITT Recommendation X.21, can be used, or support for a V.24 interface can be achieved through the use of X.21 bis [3].

Layer 2: Link Control

This layer relates to the sending of blocks of data over a physical link. It is concerned with issues such as:

- *How does a machine know where a transmitted block starts and ends?*
- *How can transmission errors be detected?*
- *How can recovery from transmission errors be accomplished so as to give the appearance of an error-free link?*
- *When several machines share one physical circuit, how can they be controlled so that their transmissions do not overlap and become jumbled?*
- *How is a message addressed to one of several machines?*

The transmission of physical blocks of data requires a *physical link control* procedure which specifies the headers and trailers of blocks which are sent, and defines a protocol for the interchange of these blocks. Such procedures have been used since the earliest days of data communications. For distributed processing a more efficient line-control procedure than start-stop or binary synchronous is desirable, which permits continuous transmission in both directions, of data which can contain any bit pattern. The International Standards Organization, has specified such a line control procedure, HDLC (*Higher-level Data Link Control*). The American Standards Organization, the CCITT, and various computer manufacturers each have their own variants of this which differ slightly in subtle details.

Layer 3: Network Control

Prior to 1975, Layers 1 and 2 were all that were specified. These were adequate for communication between machines connected to the same physical line. The world of distributed processing and computer networks requires more layers, and these are substantially more complex.

Layer 3 relates to *virtual circuits,* sometimes called *logical circuits* or *logical links.* These are not actual circuits. They do not exist in physical reality, but Layer 3 pretends to the higher levels that they do exist.

The path between computers may at one instant be via a number of physical lines, as shown in Fig. 27.4. Each physical line spans two network machines which must use the Layer 1 and Layer 2 procedures to exchange data. The users do not wish to know what route the data travels or how many physical lines it travels over. The user machines want a simple interface with a virtual circuit. The Layer 3 layer of control creates the virtual circuit and provides the higher levels with an interface with it.

On some systems, the route on which data travel between two user machines varies from one instant to another. The network machines may require that users' messages be divided into slices called packets, no greater than a certain length. The packets must be reassembled into messages after transmission. On some networks the packets become out of sequence during transmission. The rules for Layer 3 state that the network must deliver the packets to the user machine in the same sequence as that in which they were sent by a user machine.

There are many such complications in the operation of a virtual circuit. Layer 3 provides a standard interface with the virtual circuit and, as far as possible, hides the complex mechanisms of its operation from the higher layers of software.

Layer 4: Transport End-to-End Control

The inner three layers of Fig. 27.3 represent a common network which many machines may share, independently of one another, just as many independent users may share the postal service. It is possible that a postal service might occasionally lose a letter. To ensure that this has not happened, two users might apply their own end-to-end controls, such as numbering their letters. Layer 4 is concerned with similar end-to-end controls of the transmission between two users having a session.

Figure 27.4 illustrates that whereas Layer 3 is concerned with the interface between the user machine and the network, Layer 4 (and the higher layers) is concerned with the end-to-end interaction between user processes. The functions executed in Layer 4 may include end-to-end integrity controls to prevent loss or double processing of transactions, flow control of transactions, and addressing of end-user machines or processes.

The lower four layers provide a *transport* service. They are concerned with the transport of blocks of bits from one user process to another, but not with the manipulation of those bits in any way. Some of the higher layers manipulate the bits.

The transport service in the future will take many different forms. Sometimes it will be a packet-switching network using the international standards from Layer 3 and below (CCITT Recommendation X.25, discussed later). Sometimes it will be quite different—wideband point-to-point circuits, the Xerox XTEN networks, satellite circuits, and so on. The interface from higher layers or from user machines

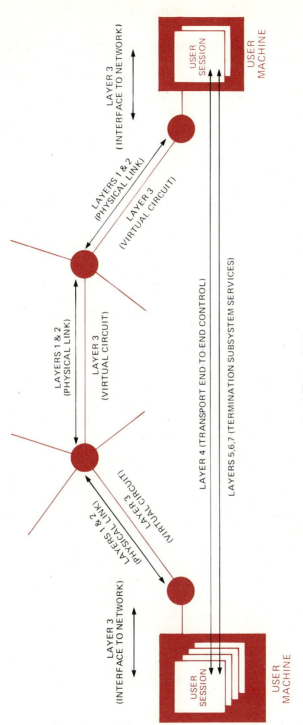

Figure 27.4

425

to Layer 4 is intended to provide a *standard interface to users of the transport service independent of what network type is used.*

Layer 5: Session Control

The task of setting up a session between user processes can be complex because there are so many different ways in which machines can cooperate. Like two businessmen agreeing to a joint venture, they must agree beforehand on the rules of the game. In effect they sign a contract stating the manner in which they will cooperate. We will describe this later in the book.

Layer 5 standardizes this process of establishing a session and of terminating it. If something goes wrong in mid-session, Layer 5 must restore the session without loss of data, or if this is not possible terminate the session in an orderly fashion. Checking and recovery are thus functions of Layer 5.

In some types of session a dialogue takes place between machines, and a protocol must regulate who speaks when and for how long. In some cases the two machines speak alternately. In others one machine may send many messages before the other replies. In some sessions one machine may interrupt the other, in other cases not. The rules for how the dialogue is conducted need to be agreed on when the session is set up.

Layer 6: Presentation Control

Layer 6 contains functions relating to the character set and data code which are used and to the way data are displayed on a screen or printer. A stream of characters reaching a terminal will result in certain actions to give an attractive display or printout. The character stream will contain characters which cause editing of the data, line skipping, tabbing to position the data in columns, adding fixed column headings, highlighting certain fields, use of color, and so on. Formats may be displayed into which an operator enters data, and then only the entered data are transmitted. A coded number sent to an intelligent terminal may cause it to select a panel for display and enter variable data into that display.

There are many possible functions concerned with the presentation of data. These are carried out by Layer 6. Many of them relate to the character stream, its codes, and the ways they are used.

In some cases application programmers perceive a *virtual terminal* or *virtual display space.* Input/output statements relate to this make-believe facility, and the Layer 6 software must do the conversion between the virtual facility and the real terminal.

It is desirable that devices with different character sets should be able to communicate. Conversion of character streams may therefore be a concern of Layer 6.

The character stream may be compacted into a smaller bit stream to save transmission costs. This may be a Layer 6 function.

Encryption and decryption for security reasons may also be a Layer 6 function.

Layer 7: Process Control

Layer 7 is concerned with higher-level functions which provide support to the application or system activities, for example, operator support, the use of remote data, file transfer control, distributed data-base activities, higher-level dialogue functions, and so on. The extent to which these are supported in the network architecture and in the software external to the network architecture, such as data-base software, will differ from one manufacturer to another.

When distributed files and data bases are used, various controls are needed to prevent integrity problems or deadlocks. Some of the types of controls for this are strongly related to networking, for example, the timestamping of transactions and delivery of transactions in timestamp sequence (sometimes called *pipelining*).

Pacing is necessary with some processes so that the transmitting machine can send records continuously without flooding the receiving machine or so that an application can keep a distant printer going at maximum speed.

SUBSYSTEMS   The lower four layers are all concerned with the transport of bits between one user process and another. We will refer to them collectively as *the transport subsystem*.

Layers 5, 6, and 7 provide a variety of services which are employed by the user sessions. We will refer to these layers collectively as the *session services subsystem*.

MANUFACTURERS'   The architectures for distributed processing from the
ARCHITECTURES   various computer and minicomputer manufacturers
contain all or part of the seven layers we have described. Layers 1, 2, and 3 are usually clearly distinguished, but the functions of Layers 4, 5, 6, and 7 may be intermixed and not broken into those layers recommended by the International Standards Organization. Increasingly, as distributed processing technology evolves, the clean separation of the layers will be necessary.

International standards exist, and are widely accepted, for Layers 1, 2, and 3. They are employed not only by the computer industry but by the telecommunications industry in creating public data networks. We described these standards and their use in Part III.

Partly because of the telecommunications industry use of Layers 1, 2, and 3, the computer industry is building hardware and software which employs these layers. Some computer vendors (notably IBM, Univac, and DEC) have created their own incompatible versions of Layer 3. Old versions of Layer 2 are in use and likely to remain so because old protocols take a long time to die.

At the higher layers different manufacturers are going their own way and creating their own in-house standards. These are perceived as extremely important by individual manufacturers because they make the many different machines in the product line interconnectable. But although machines of one manufacturer are interconnectable, those of different manufacturers cannot be interconnected at the higher layers. They can be interconnected only at Layers 1 and 2, and sometimes Layer 3.

The layers are being applied not only to computer and conventional terminal controllers but also to electronic "office of the future" equipment such as intelligent copying machines, word-processing equipment, electronic mail machines, document storage and retrieval equipment, process monitoring and control facilities, and security facilities. It is clear that these product lines are merging and need to be connected by networks.

DIFFERENT MACHINES In a distributed processing network the layers may be spread across a variety of different machines. Figure 27.5 shows several types of machines. A central processing unit may be designed to contain all seven layers, as with the computer on the left in Fig. 27.5, or, probably better, some of the layers may be removed to a separate front-end processor. A front-end processor may handle the lower three layers, or it may handle Layer 4 functions as well.

Terminals containing microprocessors may have enough power to handle all the layers, as the intelligent terminal in Fig. 27.5 does. This is less complex than the networking software at a computer site because the terminal supports only one session at a time, uses only one logical channel, and contains few management functions. In many cases the terminals are simpler machines connected to a terminal cluster controller, and it is this controller which contains the networking software, as shown at the bottom of Fig. 27.5. The terminals may be in the immediate vicinity of the controller, or they may be far away, connected by telecommunications, in which case the controller may be regarded as a concentrator. A concentrator may contain only the lower three layers.

Figure 27.5 does not show mid-network nodes such as packet-switching machines or concentrators. These may be part of the transport subsystem, with no Layer 5, 6, 7, or even Layer 4 functions.

FUNDAMENTAL LAYERS The concept of using separate layers of control is fundamental to all architectures for distributed processing. However, the layers used differ from one manufacturer to another.

Some of the layers are fundamental and widely accepted even in architectures which are otherwise entirely different. Layers 1, 2, and 3 are found in almost all architectures. They are fundamental: *the existence of an electrical interface with the transmission circuit* (Layer 1), *the existence of a link control procedure* (Layer 2), and *the separate existance of a common network to which many different machines can be connected* (Layer 3).

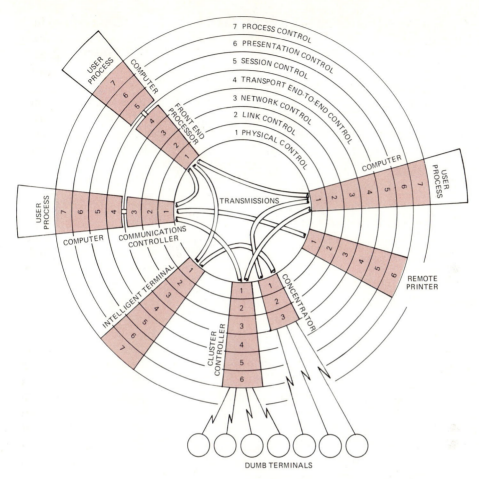

Figure 27.5 The layers of control are allocated between machines in different ways.

The common network may be a public network or may be private. Layers 1, 2, and 3 are vital to public networks. Private networks may use the same standards, and then they can be interconnected to public networks as well.

End-to-end control of the movement of data in a particular session is often (but not always) important. This is done by Layer 4. Where as one module of Layer 3 is needed in a machine which is connected to a network, one module of Layer 4 is needed *for each session* in that machine.

Session services are also needed for each session. The concept of a session services subsystem is fundamental. However, in software architectures it is not always broken into Layers 5, 6, and 7. The architecture may have one layer for providing session services.

Figure 27.6 illustrates the common network, the transport end-to-end control,

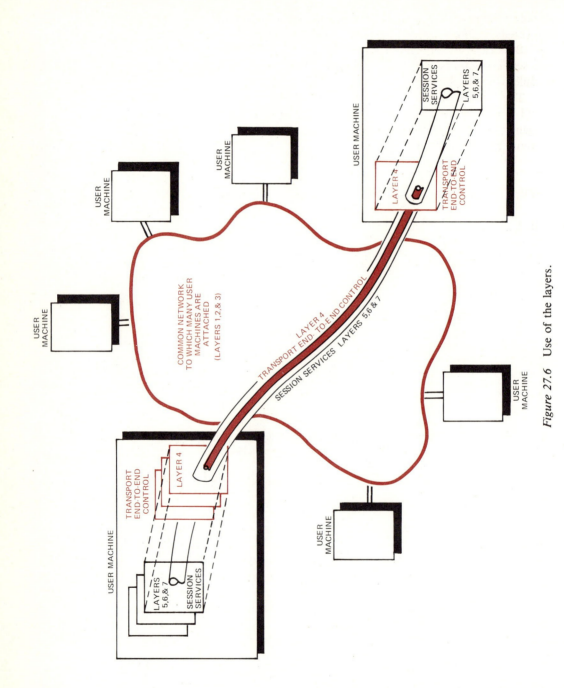

Figure 27.6 Use of the layers.

and the session services. These are three fundamental concepts, along with link control (Layer 2) and the electrical interface (Layer 1).

Because a session needs transport end-to-end control (Layer 4) as well as session services (Layers 5, 6, and 7), these are sometimes built into one module—the module which supports the session.

This separation of Layers 1, 2, 3, and (4 + 5 + 6 + 7) or Layers 1, 2, 3, 4, and (5 + 6 + 7) is found both in architectures for *vertical* networks connecting intelligent devices to computers and in architectures for *horizontal* networks which interconnect peer-related computers.

DIFFERENT NAMES   Different organizations use different names for the layers. Box 27.1 lists some of the alternative names used. Univac uses the term *Transport Network* and IBM *Transmission Subsystem*. IBM uses the term *Path Control* for Layer 3, DEC *Network Services Protocol* for Layers 3 and 4. The session services subsystem is called *Function Management* by

**BOX 27.1   Terms used for Layers 2, 3 and 4,
in different architectures.**

Terms Used In This Book	Terms Used By Common Carriers, Following CCITT Recommendation X.25	Terms Used In IBM's SNA Architecture	Terms Used In DEC's DECNET Architecture	Terms Used In Univac's DCA Architecture
Layer 4	—	Function Management	Dialogue Layer	Termination System
Layer 3	Level 3	Transmission Control and Path Control (Two layers)	Network Services Protocol (NSP layer)	Transport Network System
Layer 2	Level 2	SDLS (Synchronous Data Link Control)	DDCMP (Digital Data Communications Management Protocol)	UDLC (Universal Data Link Control)

IBM, *Dialogue Layer* by DEC, and *Termination System* by Univac; the session services provided differ in these three cases. Univac splits Layers 3 and 4, combined, into three sublayers.

SYMMETRY   In some cases, the networking layers are symmetrical. In other words, when a certain level of software exists at opposite ends of a link, both ends carry out the same functions. In Fig. 27.4 the outermost machines execute all seven layers; the inner machines (drawn as circles) execute only transport subsystem functions; but the layering is symmetrical. In a horizontal computer network all machines may contain the same networking software (with the exception of functions such as network monitoring and statistics gathering).

On the other hand, vertical networks are often asymmetrical. For reasons of economy the machines lower in the hierarchy have simpler software or control mechanisms than those at the top (at least at the higher-level layers). In Fig. 27.5 the computer and terminals at the left are in communication. However, the higher-level software may be designed to be much simpler in the terminal than in the computer or its front-end network machine.

In some networks the terms *primary* and *secondary* are used to describe asymmetrical relationships between machines. In some, the terms *master* and *slave* are used. In links between a computer and terminal controller, or a large computer and a minicomputer, a *primary/secondary* relationship is often employed. The management of the link is the responsibility of the *primary* machine. This machine takes most of the initiative. It sends messages, and the secondary machine responds. The primary machine is responsible for recovery when failures or problems occur.

We will see examples of symmetrical and asymmetrical relationships later in the book. Symmetry is generally appealing in horizontal networks. In vertical networks it may be unnecessarily expensive.

MESSAGES, PACKETS,   Different *units of data* are exchanged between the dif-
AND FRAMES   ferent layers. The lowest layer is concerned with the
                             transmission of *bits*. Layer 2, the physical link control
(such as HDLC, IBM's SDLC, and similar protocols), transmits *frames*. A frame is a group of bits which constitutes a single recoverable block transmitted over a physical line. It has a header and a trailer, which are necessary for controlling the physical transmission. They identify where it begins and ends. The header contains a physical link address and control information. The trailer contains redundant bits for detecting transmission errors.

Layer 3 passes blocks of data to Layer 2 for physical transmission. They are sometimes called *packets*. They do not contain the *frame* header and trailer, as this is of no concern to Layer 3. A packet may be defined as *a group of bits addressed to a network destination, which is routed to that destination as a composite whole; the packet may contain data and control signals, while some packets contain only control signals.* A block or packet is sometimes routed to its destination by means of packet switching, which we discuss later. However, it could be routed by concentrators or mechanisms different from those on today's packet-switched networks. The concept of a packet is of general value independently of whether packet switching is used. It is a grouping of data which travels to a destination over a virtual circuit. It must carry a network destination address like the address on a letter, which is different from the addresses of the physical nodes through which it passes on its way. Like a letter, it also contains an origination address so that it may be returned to its sender if something goes wrong and it cannot be delivered. Packets contain control information which regulates the end-to-end delivery.

Layer 4 communicates via the common network with Layer 4 at the other end in a session, as shown in Fig. 27.6. We will refer to the messages it sends as *session messages*. A session message may be too large to be transmitted as a single packet. Layer 4 may slice one such message up into multiple packets and reassemble the session message after transmission. In some cases the session messages may be very small, and for efficiency several of them could be (in theory) combined into one packet for Layer 3 transmission. On simpler systems there is no slicing or combining of session messages; the session message becomes the data portion of a packet.

The users of the communications system exchange *user messages*. A user message might be the same as a session message. Often it is not, however, because the Layer 6 software changes it by enciphering, code conversion, compaction, or editing.

We thus have five types of data units, transmitted by the different layers as shown in Fig. 27.7:

1. Bits

2. Frames

3. Packets

4. Session messages

5. User messages

Typical manipulation of a user message before transmission is shown in Fig. 27.8. Different systems use different names for the data units, as shown in Box 27.2, and may take somewhat different actions from those in Fig. 27.8 when handling them.

Figure 27.9 summarizes the main communication between the layers.

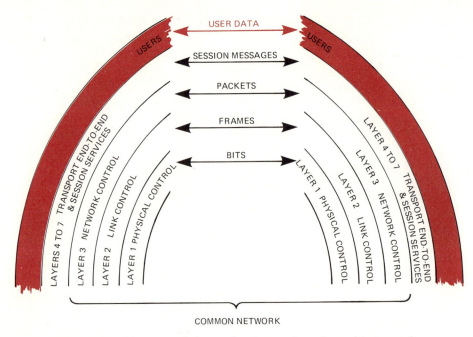

Figure 27.7 The types of data units that are interchanged between the layers. Different names are used for these in different networks architectures, as shown in Box 27.2.

BOX 27.2   Names used for different data units.

Data Units Interchanged Between:	Terms Used In This Book (see figs. 9.5 and 9.6)	Terms Used By CCITT Recommendations	Terms Used In IBM's SNA Architecture	Terms Used In DEC's DECNET Architecture	Terms Used In Univac's DCA Architecture
Users	User Data; User Messages	User Messages	User Data	User Data	User Data Set
Layer 4	Transmission Messages	—	Request/ Response Unit	DAP Message	Port Data Unit
Layer 3	Packets	Packet	Path Information Unit	NSP Message	Network Data Unit
Layer 2	Frames	Frame	Frame	DDCMP Message	Frame

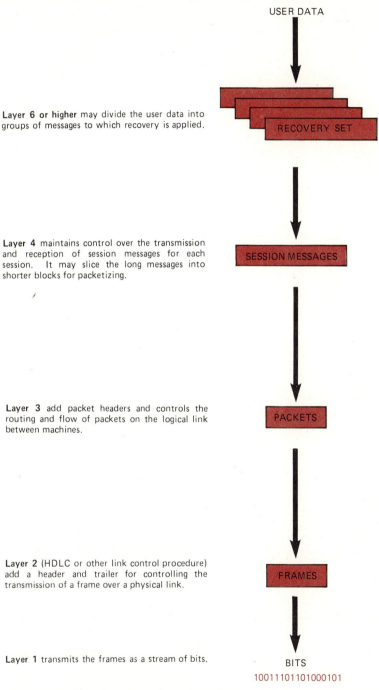

USER DATA

Layer 6 or higher may divide the user data into groups of messages to which recovery is applied.

RECOVERY SET

Layer 4 maintains control over the transmission and reception of session messages for each session. It may slice the long messages into shorter blocks for packetizing.

SESSION MESSAGES

Layer 3 add packet headers and controls the routing and flow of packets on the logical link between machines.

PACKETS

Layer 2 (HDLC or other link control procedure) add a header and trailer for controlling the transmission of a frame over a physical link.

FRAMES

Layer 1 transmits the frames as a stream of bits.

BITS

10011101101000101

Figure 27.8 User data may be manipulated as shown before transmission, after the conversion after transmission.

435

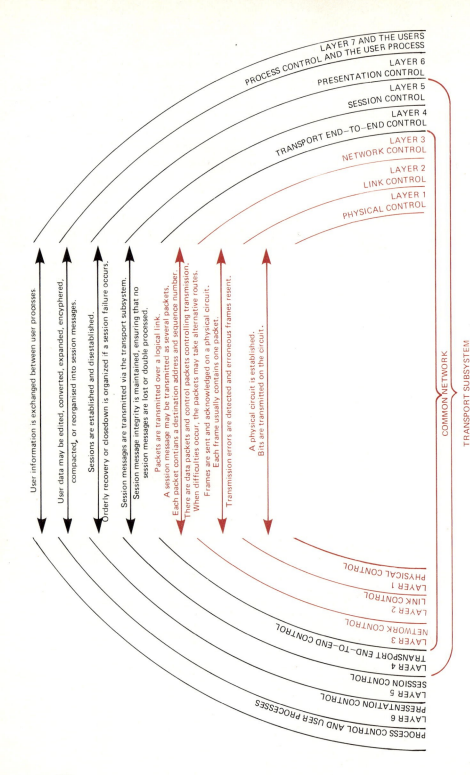

LAYER 7 AND THE USERS
PROCESS CONTROL AND THE USER PROCESS

LAYER 6
PRESENTATION CONTROL

LAYER 5
SESSION CONTROL

LAYER 4
TRANSPORT END—TO—END CONTROL

LAYER 3
NETWORK CONTROL

LAYER 2
LINK CONTROL

LAYER 1
PHYSICAL CONTROL

COMMON NETWORK

TRANSPORT SUBSYSTEM

User information is exchanged between user processes.

User data may be edited, converted, expanded, encyphered, compacted, or reorganised into session messages.

Sessions are established and disestablished.

Orderly recovery or closedown is organized if a session failure occurs.

Session messages are transmitted via the transport subsystem.

Session message integrity is maintained, ensuring that no session messages are lost or double processed.

Packets are transmitted over a logical link.
A session message may be transmitted as several packets.
Each packet contians a destination address and sequence number.
There are data packets and control packets controlling transmission.
When difficulties occur, the packets may take alternative routes.
Frames are sent and acknowledged on a physical circuit.
Each frame usually contains one packet.

Transmission errors are detected and erroneous frames resent.

A physical circuit is established.
Bits are transmitted on the circuit.

Figure 27.9 Each layer communicates with the equivalent layer in a distant machine and is concerned with the complexity of lower layers which make the communication possible.

436

When data is transmitted on a communication line, or stored on a storage unit, it becomes a serial stream of bits. In both cases layers of software exist between the user program and the physical storage or transmission. Conversion between the data the user perceives and what is physically transmitted or stored ranges from simple to complex, depending on the sophistication of the system. Figure 27.10 shows the layers used for data bases and networks. The layers closest to the user process provide user services and represent data in the form most useful to the user. As we move to the outer parts of Fig. 27.10, the data become more abstract. The bit streams stored or transmitted serve multiple applications and are manipulated to

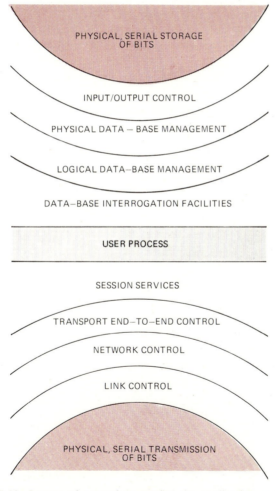

Figure 27.10   Layers of control separating the application programs or user process from (a) the physical, serial recording of bits and (b) the physical, serial transmission of bits.

437

suit the diverse mechanisms employed. The bit streams may be sliced or converted into different forms for reasons of economy, efficiency, reliability, or security.

INDEPENDENCE   A principle of a layered architecture is that the layers ought to be kept entirely independent.

Layer 1 (e.g., the standards EIA RS 232-C or CCITT V.24) is extensively used for all types of data transmission, many of which do not employ HDLC, SDLC, or related procedures, and most of which have no networking software.

Layer 2, the physical link control procedure (e.g., HDLC, SDLC) is also independent of the higher layers and is used for many data communications links which do not have higher-layer software.

The common network architecture should likewise be a self-contained set of procedures which can be employed by many different types of systems. It will be used by different types of Layer 4 and higher software and by systems with no higher-level software. Application programs, data-base software, or other types of software often plug directly into Layer 3 or Layer 2. The interfaces to Layers 2 and 3 should therefore be rigorously defined and preserved, independently of what goes on in the other layers.

Teleprocessing technology is changing rapidly and is likely to continue changing because new facilities are being installed or planned for data transmission. Satellites, microcomputers, value-added carriers, PCM transmission, data radio, and fast computerized switching create great opportunities as well as pressure for change [3]. It can be expected therefore that the mechanisms of the transport subsystem will change, in some cases beyond recognition. The interface to Layer 4 needs to remain constant to protect the users. As a system changes from using, say, a leased-line concentrator network to a common carrier virtual-circuit network, this change should be hidden inside the transmission subsystem. It should be transparent to higher-layer software, and especially to the application programs, so that these do not have to be rewritten.

The layers should thus be completely *separate and independent, and their interfaces rigorously defined.* In addition to facilitating change, this is a great aid to debugging and to the diagnosis of network faults.

There is often pressure during implementation to violate the separation of the layers or tamper with the interfaces between them to gain a performance advantage. It is important that this should not be done. To do so could make further development in the future extremely expensive, perhaps so expensive that it would prevent desirable improvements.

However, while the interfaces are preserved, some implementations may drop down to a lower interface to lessen the overhead.

DISADVANTAGE   The disadvantage of layered control is that it increases the total overhead required for communication. The Layer 2 frames, Layer 3 packets, and higher-layer session messages each need headers, and the total of these headers often adds up to more than 100 bits. Many of the bits would be required whether a layered architecture were used or not. However, when each layer is designed to be of general use independent of the other layers, the overhead is usually higher, and the number of processing instructions needed to control the transmission is higher.

When general-purpose layers are used, there may be some overlap of function. This may occur, for example, when the interfaces between the layers are standards adopted by a manufacturer or common carrier or by the standards organizations. We will see examples of this duplication of function later in the book. It is not a serious problem, merely an increase in overhead. In terms of processing cost it may be offset by placing Layer 2 and possibly Layer 3 in peripheral microprocessors—distributed systems within the machine room.

In all layered architectures there is a tradeoff between the advantages of layering and the increased overhead it incurs. The duplication of function is likely to be less if all the layers are designed by one design team to form part of a common architecture.

The overhead can be lessened by designing the mechanisms and message headers so that the more complex functions are *optional*. Simple networks should have simple mechanisms. Complex networks have more elaborate mechanisms and longer message headers. Both integration of the layers and variation in the degree of complexity and overhead are accomplished effectively, for example, in the Digital Equipment Corporation's architecture, DECNET. DECNET, being an architecture for minicomputers, needs to be especially careful about incurring avoidable overhead.

Layer 3 and Layer 4 and the session service layers are not needed for all communications. They may therefore be designed so that they can shrink to nothing or almost nothing when not needed. Simple communications should not be penalized by mechanisms designed for complex communications.

ADVANTAGES   The advantages of layering are immense. They are summarized in Box 27.3. There is no doubt that layered architectures and standard interfaces between the layers will lead to a much greater interconnectability of machines.

REFERENCES

1. The words in bold are taken from the description of the Layer 1 interface in the CCITT Recommendation X.25.

2. Described in Chapter 17 of James Martin, *Telecommunications and the Computer,* Second Edition, Prentice-Hall, Inc., Englewood Cliffs, N.J., 1976.

3. Described in James Martin, *Future Developments in Telecommuications,* Second Edition, Prentice-Hall, Inc., Englewood Cliffs, N.J., 1977.

BOX 27.3   Advantages and Disadvantages of Layering

ADVANTAGES OF LAYERED ARCHITECTURES

1. Any given layer can be modified or upgraded without affecting the other layers.
2. Modularization by means of layering simplifies the overall design.
3. Different layers can be assigned to different standards committees, or different design teams.
4. Fundamentally different mechanisms may be substituted without affecting more than one layer (e.g. packet switching vs. leased-line concentrators).
5. Different machines may plug in at different levels.
6. The relationships between the different control functions can be better understood when they are split into layers. This is especially true with the control actions which occur sequentially in time from layer to layer.
7. Common lower level services may be shared by different higher level users.
8. Functions, especially at the lower layers, may be removed from software and built into hardware or microcode.

DISADVANTAGES OF LAYERED ARCHITECTURES

1. The total overhead is somewhat higher.
2. The communicating machines may have to use certain functions which they could do without.
3. To make each layer usable by itself there is some small duplication of function between the layers.
4. As technology changes (e.g. as cryptography and compaction chips become available, or these functions can be built on to HDLC chips) the functions may not be in the most cost-effective layer.

IN GENERAL THE ADVANTAGES ARE GREAT, THE DISADVANTAGES SLIGHT.

28 ARCHITECTURE INTERFACES

Particularly important in a layered architecture are the interfaces between the layers. These must be precisely defined and adhered to rigorously. They are *candidates for standardization,* either in the international standards arena or in the architectural standards employed by a major common carrier or computer manufacturer. Intensive international standards activity has occurred relating to the Layer 1, 2, and 3 interfaces. Work is in progress on the higher layers. These are more difficult because their functions vary greatly from one system to another. Ideas are evolving rapidly about what session services should be provided.

The *mechanisms* of each layer will change as the technology develops. The interfaces between the layers are often designed to accommodate new mechanisms and, as far as possible, new functions when they may arise. As new mechanisms and network functions come into use, it is highly desirable that previously written programs continue to work. This is achieved by designing the interfaces appropriately and preserving them.

COMMUNICATION BETWEEN LAYERS

Each layer in an architecture for distributed processing communicates with an equivalent layer at the other end of a link. The reader might think of the communicating machines as layer cakes, as shown in Fig. 28.1. Each layer contains a different set of functions.

Sessions take place between user processes. The higher layers (4, 5, 6, and 7) relate to these sessions. The lower layers are not concerned with the sessions, but with the movement of data through a network shared by many machines. Figure 28.2 illustrates this. Layers 4, 5, 6, and 7 provide end-to-end communication between the sessions in user machines. Layers 1, 2, and 3 provide communication with the nodes of a shared network. These nodes may be packet switches, communica-

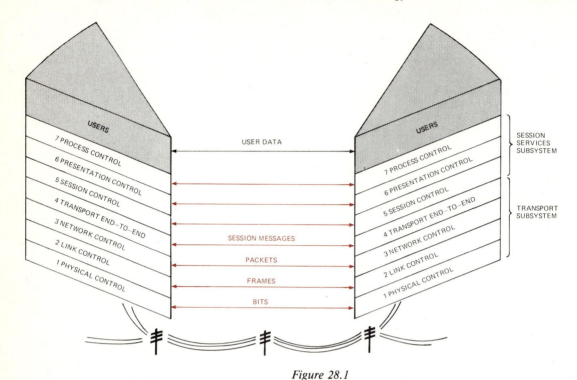

USER DATA

SESSION MESSAGES

PACKETS

FRAMES

BITS

USERS

7 PROCESS CONTROL

6 PRESENTATION CONTROL

5 SESSION CONTROL

4 TRANSPORT END–TO–END

3 NETWORK CONTROL

2 LINK CONTROL

1 PHYSICAL CONTROL

SESSION
SERVICES
SUBSYSTEM

TRANSPORT
SUBSYSTEM

Figure 28.1

tions controllers, concentrators, or other machines designed to make a data network operate.

There are two forms of communication between the layers in separate machines: *headers* and *control messages*. Figure 28.3 illustrates these.

HEADERS

Each layer of a layered architecture (except Layer 1) may add a header to the messages sent. This header is interpreted by the equivalent layer at the other end of the link.

Layer 2 frames contain a header to be used by the Layer 2 mechanisms at the other end of a physical link. They also contain a trailer which is used to indicate the end of the frame and to check whether the frame contains any transmission errors.

Layer 3 packets contain a header which directs the packet to its destination and is used by Layer 3 at that destination. Layer 4 messages may contain a header intended for use by the distant and complementary Layer 4. And so on.

In general, the Layer N header is not inspected by Layer $N - 1$. It appears like any other data being transmitted. Layer $N - 1$ then adds its own header. This is shown in Fig. 28.3.

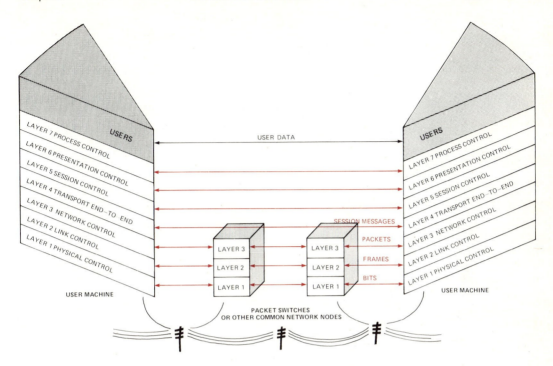

Figure 28.2 Layers 4 to 7 provide end-to-end communication between session software. Layers 1 to 3 provide an interface to a shared network.

Figure 28.2 shows transmission between two user machines via a network node which contains only transport subsystem software.

CONTROL MESSAGES   In addition, control messages are used which travel in the way data messages do but whose sole function is to carry control signals between the control layers. Separate types of control messages are exchanged by the different layers. They have functions such as setting up communication, dealing with errors or procedure violations, and regulating the rate of flow. In general, signals which occur frequently are carried in the message headers; signals which occur only infrequently or which require more than a few bytes are sent as separate control messages.

Control messages may be used when it is necessary to send a signal to the destination without delay. They travel with higher priority than data messages in most systems, bypassing the queues of data messages like ambulances screaming through the streets of a city.

The international standards define the control messages and the headers which each layer uses. This defines how the layers intercommunicate. Machines of

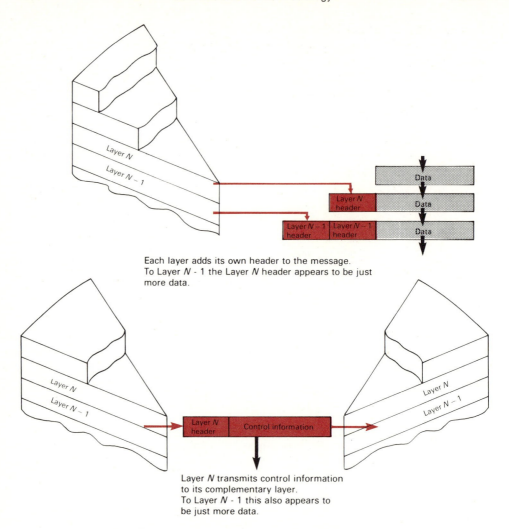

Each layer adds its own header to the message.
To Layer *N* - 1 the Layer *N* header appears to be just
more data.

Layer *N* transmits control information
to its complementary layer.
To Layer *N* - 1 this also appears to
be just more data.

Figure 28.3 There are two forms of communication between equivalent
layers: message headers for that layer, and control messages passed between the layers. These are, or will become the basis of international standards.

different manufacturers may communicate if they use the same headers and control
messages and interpret them in the same way.

INTRANODE
COMMUNICATION

Layers above and below each other in the same node
may communicate by means of parameters. These are
passed between the layers when the message is passed

from one layer to the next. They give information such as what address to send the message to, or what type of control is required. Figure 28.4 shows parameters being passed between layers in a node which is transmitting. The reverse direction of flow would be used when it is receiving.

The internal workings of a node, such as that in Fig. 28.4, does not need to be known in order for different nodes to communicate. For this purpose only the formats of the message headers and control messages are required. The international standards therefore avoid specifying the intranode communication. It is desirable to leave implementors as much freedom as possible in designing their nodes. This is especially true because of the rate of change of technology. Layer N in Fig. 28.4 might be in software today but in microcode or chips tomorrow. The layers might be in the same machine today but split between machines tomorrow. These changes should not affect the resulting messages perceived by a distant machine.

Although definition of the parameters in Fig. 28.4 should not be in the international standards, it may be part of a manufacturer's architecture definitions.

The behavior of each layer should be self-contained and not dependent on the operation of other layers. The other layers may change end users of a network. The protocols consist of controlled exchanges of precisely specified commands and responses.

In early data-transmission systems the protocols were relatively simple and related to sending data across a single link. Today, with distributed processing, multiple layers of control, and mesh-structured networks, the protocols become highly complex and must be thought out with meticulous care. Flaws in protocol

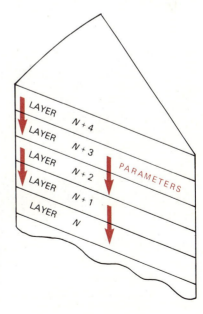

Figure 28.4 A manufacturer's architecture may define parameters which are passed from one layer to another in the same node. The interfaces between layers in a node are *not* defined in the international standards in order to leave the maximum freedom in architecture implementation.

design have occasionally led to subtle problems such as networks jamming with deadlocked traffic, or occasional messages being lost.

The protocols define the control information that is used for communicating between the layers as illustrated in Fig. 28.3, and how this control information is acted upon.

FOUR-LAYER ARCHITECTURES   Most manufacturers at the time of writing do not have the full seven layers of ISO. Many have four layers in which the session services and end-to-end integrity control are encompassed in one layer. The bottom three layers may follow the CCITT Recommendation X.25.

Figure 28.5 shows the use of headers in a four-layer architecture. Two user machines are communicating via a network node. The user machines have all four layers. The network node uses only the lower three layers needed for routing the data to their destination and controlling the physical transmission.

What is shown as a single Session Services Layer in Fig. 28.5 may be split into two or more layers. The exact layering at the higher levels differs from one manufacturer to another.

OVERHEAD   If all seven layers are used, then each of these except Layer 1 will create its own header, as shown in Fig. 28.6.

This appears to be a large overhead, in terms both of the extra bits transmitted and of the processing required to handle the layers. The former can be minimized by using a bit structure which permits optional fields to be omitted when not in use (including *all* of the fields for session services). More serious has been the machine cycles and memory needed to execute the software. As microminiature circuitry grows in power and the standards for architectures stabilize, so increasingly the functions will be built into cheap, mass-produced chips. This will occur both within one manufacturer's product line and in industrywide manufacturer-independent chips.

Already chips exists for executing the Layer 2 control (HDLC, SDLC, or nonstandard forms of Layer 2 such as the Digital Equipment Corporation's DDCMP) and for Layer 3 control (CCITT X.25 Layer 3). As chips increase in density, other functions will be moved outside computers so that they do not have to be executed in software.

HIGH-LEVEL LANGUAGES   An interface between machines needs to be defined in terms of the layers: the layer headers and control messages that are passed between layers as shown in Fig. 28.3. An application programmer may know nothing of these; he uses a higher-level language, and a compiler or interpreter creates the headers and control

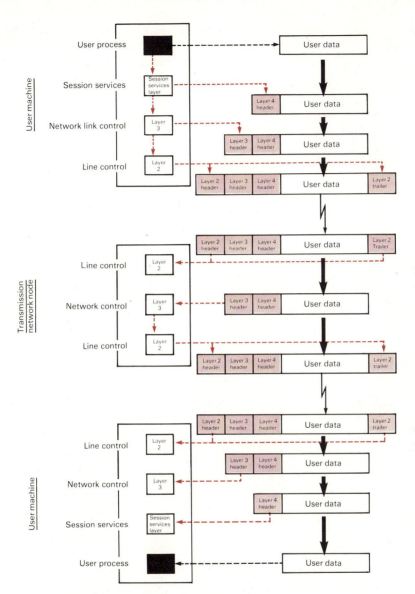

Figure 28.5 Use of headers as data is relayed through a network, for an architecture with four layers.

messages. The language may use commands such as GET, PUT, OPEN, and CLOSE, which refer to data or facilities in a distant machine.

This is shown in the first illustration in Fig. 28.7. The programmers perceive only the interface with the outermost layer and use a high-level language to communicate with this layer.

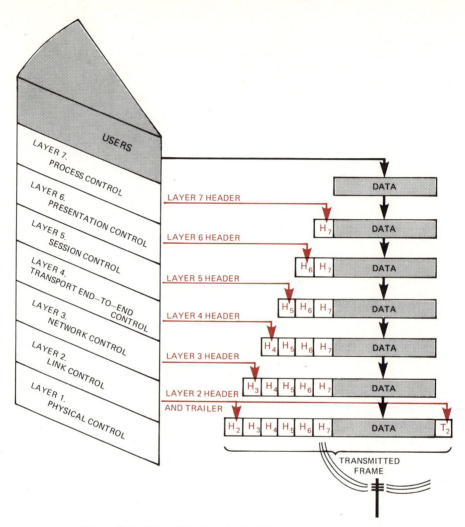

Figure 28.6   Use of headers in the ISO 7-layer architecture.

In some cases the programmers drop down to the Layer 4 interface, as shown in the second illustration in Fig. 28.7. This may be done for reasons of efficiency; the programmers can control the transport subsystem more directly. The interface to the transport subsystem is also defined in terms of control messages and message headers. Again, a high-level language may provide the programmer's means of communication with the transport subsystem.

The transport subsystem, looking out, perceives data messages (and in some cases, parameters) sent to it by those who employ it. It does not know whether they come from Layer 5 or 6 software or user processes, and it does not know whether a

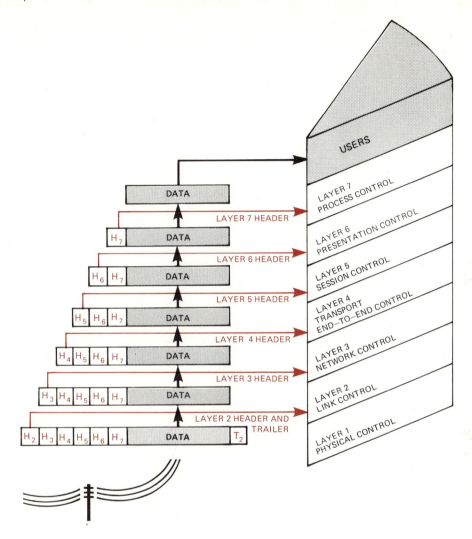

compiler or interpreter has been used. It knows only the precisely defined transmission subsystem interface.

In many cases the programmer uses Layer 3 rather than Layer 4; he uses the interface to a packet-switching (or other) network (third diagram in Fig. 28.7). He will usually employ input/output commands which generate the requisite packets and reassemble the input messages.

On older and simpler systems, there is no Layer 3 or 4—no logical links, only physical links. A program may use the Layer 2 software directly as in the fourth diagram in Fig. 28.7. It may use it by passing packets to Layer 2 ready for framing, or it may use a high-level language which employs commands such as SEND and

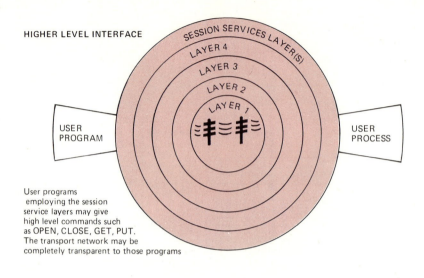

HIGHER LEVEL INTERFACE

SESSION SERVICES LAYER(S)
LAYER 4
LAYER 3
LAYER 2
LAYER 1

USER PROGRAM

USER PROCESS

User programs employing the session service layers may give high level commands such as OPEN, CLOSE, GET, PUT. The transport network may be completely transparent to those programs

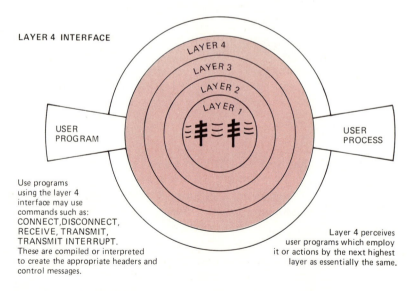

LAYER 4 INTERFACE

LAYER 4
LAYER 3
LAYER 2
LAYER 1

USER PROGRAM

USER PROCESS

Use programs using the layer 4 interface may use commands such as: CONNECT, DISCONNECT, RECEIVE, TRANSMIT, TRANSMIT INTERRUPT. These are compiled or interpreted to create the appropriate headers and control messages.

Layer 4 perceives user programs which employ it or actions by the next highest layer as essentially the same.

Figure 28.7   Different machines may interface to different layers.

LAYER 3 INTERFACE

Programs, software or chips using the Layer 3 interface directly create and accept the requisite data and control packets

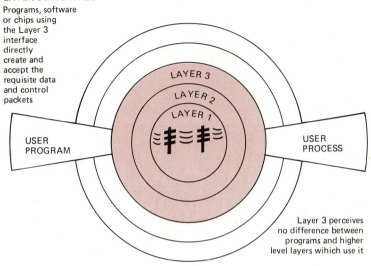

Layer 3 perceives no difference between programs and higher level layers wihich use it

LAYER 2 INTERFACE

Simple devices may use the layer 2 interface (HDLC, SDLC ,etc.) without using the higher layers. They employ the physical circuit directly, composing a suitable header and trailer for the frames that are sent.

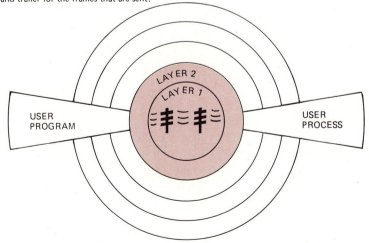

RECEIVE, in which case an operating system generates the control and data packets.

INTERFACE WITH OUTER LAYER

The user's or application programmer's interface with the outermost layer is designed to make the network and its complexities as transparent as possible.

There are two degrees of transparency. First, the network may be completely transparent. There is no difference between a program which uses the network and one which does not; both use the same commands. A remote file or printer is used in the same way as a local file or printer. This is sometimes called *local/remote transparency*.

Second, there may be partial transparency. The programmer uses high-level commands for setting up a connection and for disconnecting it and for sending and receiving messages.

Ideally, the application programmer should not have to know that a network exists. He writes input/output instructions into his programs, employing symbolic addresses as with any other input/output unit. The software must employ a table of network resources with which it can convert the symbolic references to network units into network addresses which can be used with the transport subsystem.

When a file record which is stored in a different location is requested, it will take some time to retrieve. The computer operating system will make the application program which made the request *wait* while other work continues. This happens with any storage unit operation; the difference is that the wait is longer. How long depends on the design of the transport subsystem.

In a transparent interface, commands such as OPEN, CLOSE, GET, PUT, and DELETE are used. For example, an application programmer's commands for the DECNET network employ them as shown in Box 28.1.

A somewhat less transparent interface would be one in which the application program sets up a connection and then uses that connection. Box 28.2 illustrates such use, also with commands from DECNET.

LAYER 3 INTERFACE

Layer 3 provides the interface to the common network. Sometimes this is a public packet switching network; sometimes it is a network structure and a manufacturer's architecture. The user packets transmitted and received are of two types:

1. Data messages

These contain user information to be relayed through the network. (The users of the transport subsystem could be higher-layer software modules, for example, interchanging messages which establish a user session.)

BOX 28.1 A high-level user program interface: an illustration of an interface to DECNET's session service subsystem

OPEN (5, 'FACTORY A', 'PAYROLL (50,100)')

> This command causes the file called PAYROLL stored under user account 50,100 on the computer system at location 'FAC-TORY = A' to be opened and referred to as logical unit 5 by the program that issued the command. A similar command is used for access to printers, card units, and other devices.

GET (5, BUFFER)

> This command causes data to be transferred from the remote file or device now known by this program as 5 into the user's buffer.

PUT (5, DATA)

> This command causes data to be transferred from the user's buffer to the remote file or device known as 5.

CLOSE (5)

> This command causes the remote file or device known as 5 to be closed and the link to the remote system terminated.

DELETE ('FACTORY A', 'OLD-CUST (90,70)')

> This command caused the file called OLD-DUST stored under user account 90,70 on the system at location 'FACTORY A' to be deleted (i.e., removed from the file directory for that account).

2. Control messages

These are used for actions such as requesting or terminating a virtual call, indicating when a called machine is busy or unavailable, regulating the rate of flow, maximizing the speed of a distant printer, controlling a distant file operation, dealing with failures, traffic jams, and breaches of protocol. The control messages are usually short—often only one byte of user information—and usually they need to reach their destination *fast*. Some control signals are not sent as separate messages but are "piggybacked" in data messages which are traveling to the same location.

Figure 28.5 illustrates a Layer 3 interface, showing typical control and data messages. The diagram is based on the CCITT Recommendation for a Layer 3 interface, which is used by many of the public packet-switching networks of the world and by many manufacturers' architectures. The headers and control messages

**BOX 28.2   A somewhat less transparent inter-
face than that in Box 28.1; also a
DECNET program**

CONNECT (3, 'FACTORY A', 'INVENTORY')

This causes a connection to be established between the issuing program and a program called 'INVENTORY' in a computer at a
location called 'FACTORY A'. In subsequent commands the program will refer to the connection with the number 3. The remote
program must agree to complete this connection.

SEND (3, DATA)

The program which set up connection 3 indicates that specified
data be sent to the program at the other end of that connection.

RECEIVE (3, BUFFER)

The program which set up connection 3 indicates its willingness to
receive data from the program at the other end of that connection.
No data will be transmitted until the program at one end of the
connection indicates that it has data to send and the other side indicates it has a buffer to receive it.

DISCONNECT (3)

The program which set up connection 3 indicates its desire to terminate it.

shown in black and white give complete instructions to the network software, and
no other parameters have to be passed. They are discussed in more detail later in the
book.

When user programs interface directly with the transport subsystem, they may
employ transmission-subsystem commands which are compiled or interpreted to
create messages such as those in Fig. 28.8. DEC software, for example, has five
transmission subsystem commands which users of DECNET can employ:

CONNECT

DISCONNECT

RECEIVE

TRANSMIT

TRANSMIT INTERRUPT (see Box 28.3).

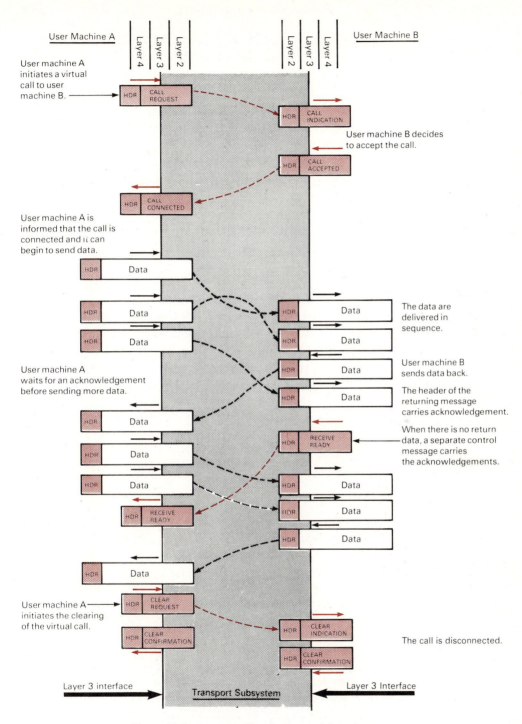

User Machine A

User machine A
initiates a virtual
call to user
machine B.

Layer 4 | Layer 3 | Layer 2

HDR CALL REQUEST

CALL INDICATION

User machine B decides
to accept the call.

CALL ACCEPTED

HDR CALL CONNECTED

User machine A is
informed that the call is
connected and it can
begin to send data.

HDR Data

HDR Data

HDR Data

User machine A
waits for an acknowledgement
before sending more data.

HDR Data

HDR Data

HDR Data

HDR RECEIVE READY

HDR Data

Layer 2 | Layer 3 | Layer 4

User Machine B

HDR Data

HDR Data

HDR Data

HDR Data

The data are
delivered in
sequence.

User machine B
sends data back.

The header of the
returning message
carries acknowledgement.

HDR RECEIVE READY

When there is no return
data, a separate control
message carries
the acknowledgements.

HDR Data

HDR Data

HDR Data

HDR Data

User machine A
initiates the clearing
of the virtual call.

HDR CLEAR REQUEST

HDR CLEAR CONFIRMATION

HDR CLEAR INDICATION

HDR CLEAR CONFIRMATION

The call is disconnected.

Layer 3 interface   Transport Subsystem   Layer 3 Interface

Figure 28.8 An example of a Layer 3 interface.

BOX 28.3   **Commands for a Layer 3 interface employed by DECNET**

CONNECT

Establishes a logical link to a distant user machine. The distant machine acknowledges its participation in the link.

DISCONNECT

Disestablishes the logical link, freeing the buffers and other facilities that were employed.

RECEIVE

This indicates that a machine is in RECEIVE status, i.e., is ready to receive a message, and has a buffer allocated to its reception.

TRANSMIT

This requests that data be sent over the link. Data can only be sent to a node in RECEIVE status which has allocated the necessary buffers. The burden of buffering is thus put on the users, which is not usually the case when Layer 4 software is employed.

TRANSMIT INTERRUPT

This is used to send a small message forcefully to a destination which is not necessarily in RECEIVE status. The message is small enough that no special buffer allocation is needed for it. It bypasses any queues in the network and goes directly to its destination.

The reason why small machines may interface directly with the transport subsystem is that more efficient operation may be achieved and the overhead or complexity associated with higher layers can be avoided.

LAYER 2 INTERFACE   In some cases machines drop down to the Layer 2 interface, physical data link control, as shown in Fig. 28.9, i.e., they have no Layer 3 or higher layer. Layer 2 control is often built into a terminal.

Terminals are often connected to a computer via a network interface machine, as shown in Fig. 28.9. They may be remote from this network node, connected to it via a physical link such as a leased or dialed telephone line. On this circuit Layer 2 link control is used. However, it might be different from the Layer 2 link control used by the network. Most networks employ an advanced data link control pro-

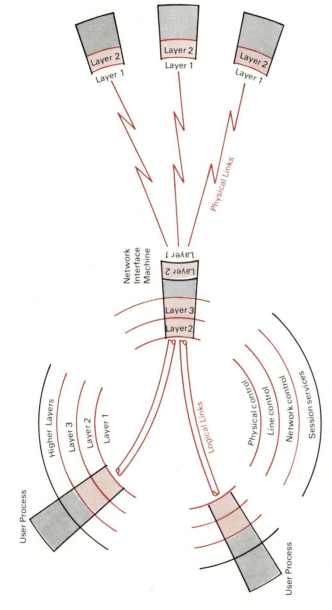

Figure 28.9 Terminals without Layer 3 software (or hardware) are connected to physical circuits going to a network interface machine.

457

cedure (such as HDLC, SDLC, or UDLC). Terminals may use simpler or older procedures. They may be *binary synchronous* or *start-stop* terminals. In this case the Layer 2 procedure on the network of Fig. 28.9 would be different from that used by the terminals on the right. The network interface machine handles the links to terminals with one link control procedure and the links which comprise the network with another.

LAYER 1 INTERFACE   The innermost interface, Layer 1, is usually the well-established 25-pin plug connection to a modem or other transmission equipment. Any data machine, with or without software, can send bits over it. A simple terminal may use start-stop transmission. If this terminal is connected to a computer network, it will be via a concentrator or gateway processor such as that in Fig. 28.10, and this machine will use the higher software layers.

The conventional connection between a data machine and a modem is the CCITT V.24 interface or the EIA RS 232-C interface in the United States. For a data machine with automatic dialing these are extended and become the CCITT V.25 and EIA RS 366 interfaces. New standards, EIA RS 422 and EIA RS 423, are coming into use to replace the EIA RS 232-C interface. They use an electrical connector interface, EIA RS 449.

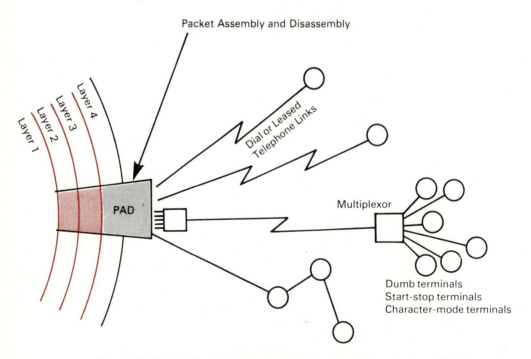

Figure 28.10 Dumb terminals connected to the network via a PAD (Packet Assembly and Disassembly) interface.

The above standards are for *analog* transmission. Increasingly, lines are being used which transmit end-to-end in a *digital,* not analog, fashion. No modems are used; an interface is needed with a digital line driver. The CCITT X.21 and X.21 BIS standards specify such interfaces.

It is desirable to have a miniature version of such an interface so that every pocket calculator, television set, and cheap terminal can have a cheap chip inside it which enables it to be connected to the conventional four-pin telephone outlet in the wall. Such an interface is sometimes referred to as a *mini-interface.*

BYPASSING THE INNER LAYERS   Lastly, a channel of a distributed processing system may bypass all or some of the inner layers when components can be connected more directly. Two machines in the same building may be connected by a high-capacity channel rather than a virtual circuit. Figure 28.11 shows user processes which employ the session services

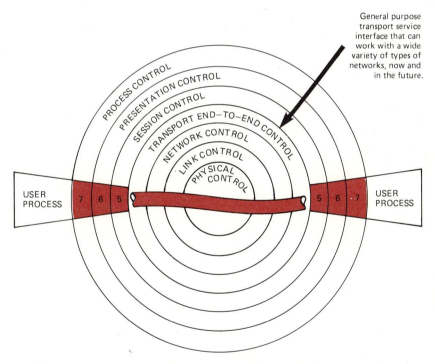

Figure 28.11 A system which uses the session services layers but not the transmission subsystem layers. It employs the *standard interface to Layer 4,* but transmission does not use CCITT X. 25 mechanisms or similar. It may be a wideband point-to-point channel, CATV, communication satellite network, office-of-the-future network, Ethernet, or merely a computer channel connecting machines in a building.

layers, but the modules are directly interconnected, bypassing the normal transmission subsystem layers. The session services subsystem uses the standard interface to Layer 4.

The transmission media used in Fig. 28.11 might be a point-to-point connection or a circuit-switched connection which does not need messages to be sliced into packets and which avoids the complications of Layer 3. It might be a communications satellite channel, an office-of-the-future network like Xerox's XTEN, a local wideband network, cable television, or merely a conventional computer channel connecting machines in a building. Some digital circuit-switched facilities use CCITT X.21 physical control. The interface to Layer 4 is intended to be a general-purpose transport service interface which can work with a wide variety of different types of networks.

To the user processes it may make no difference whether or not Layers 4, 3, 2, or 1 are used. The user processes may be kept waiting less if the inner layers are bypassed, but the code they use is unchanged. A well-designed architecture for distributed processing should make the details of how distribution is accomplished transparent to the users.

29 PHYSICAL LINK CONTROL

This chapter and the next two describe the three main layering subdivisions, first link control (Layer 2), then the transmission subsystem (Layers 1 to 4), and then the termination subsystem (Layers 5, 6, and 7). Boxes 29.1, 30.1, and 31.1 summarize the functions of these subdivisions.

The purpose of a physical link protocol is to transfer blocks of data without error between two devices connected to the same physical circuit. The reader might imagine the physical circuit to be a pair of copper telephone wires, although in reality the circuit could be more complex and include different transmission media.

In many cases the two devices will be at opposite ends of the physical circuit and no other device will transmit on that circuit. Sometimes, however, there will be multiple devices attached to the single physical circuit. The former is called a *point-to-point* circuit and the latter a *multidrop* circuit. With a multidrop circuit a device will receive, electrically, all transmissions including those not addressed to it. It must recognize those which *are* addressed to it and reject the others.

The bits transmitted are sometimes changed by transmission errors. A telephone line has far more noise and errors than the circuits within a computer room. The physical link protocol must be able to detect transmission errors and react to them by having the transmitting device resend the faulty packets.

The receiving machine must be able to detect when a message begins and when it ends. Some form of demarcation is needed because messages are of variable length.

When failures occur or problems are detected, such as a receiving machine not being ready, the machines must send control messages to initiate corrective action. Such messages are defined in the physical link protocol.

INTELLIGENT MACHINES

None of the foregoing is new. These processes have been carried out in some form or other since the dawn of data communications. In the mid-1970's, however,

BOX 29.1   Functions of Layer 1 and 2
control mechanisms

Layer 1

- Provide an electrical interface between the data machine (computer, terminal, concentrator, controller, etc.) and the data communication equipment (modem, line driver, etc.).

- Establish and disconnect a physical transmission path.

- Transmit bits over that path.

- Make the data machine aware of path failures.

Layer 2

- Transmit frames over a physical transmission path.

- Indicate which are the first and last bits of the frame.

- Detect transmission errors.

- Retransmit frames which were damaged by transmission errors.

- Permit frames to be of any length, up to a given maximum, and to contain any pattern of bits.

- Ensure that no frames are lost.

- If more than two data machines are connected to the physical path:

  1. address the frames to the correct machine;

  2. maintain discipline over the time when each machine transmits;

  3. the controlling machine should detect a failure to respond in any of the other machines.

- Where necessary, permit data to be transmitted in both directions at once.

- Where desirable, maximize the throughput of the line with techniques such as continuous ARQ or selective repeat ARQ.

one factor was new. Mass-produced microminiature circuitry made it reasonable to assume that communicating devices would have a buffer and a limited logic capability. In other words, in a world of *distributed intelligence,* communicating machines would have a certain amount of intelligence, perhaps on one microelectronic chip.

Given this assumption, it was possible to design physical link protocols which were more efficient than the earlier ones. They would make a higher transmission throughput possible on a given physical link and would permit data to be sent in both directions at once on a full duplex link.

Several organizations specified protocols for this environment which are similar in essentials but have had minor differences in detail. These are listed in Box 29.2.

The three standards organizations listed in Box 29.2 have stated that they intend to agree on one protocol. We will use the ISO name for it: HDLC, *Higher-level Data Link Control.*

Meanwhile, IBM has made extensive use of its protocol, SDLC, *Synchronous Data Link Control.* Much of IBM's data communications software and hardware since 1974 has employed SDLC. However, there are many IBM terminals still in existence using the older *binary synchronous* protocol, and so some of the new software must still accommodate this protocol.

The principles of HDLC and SDLC are essentially the same. SDLC is an allowed subset of HDLC. We will describe HDLC and then indicate how SDLC differs from it. Other manufacturers use other subsets.

BOX 29.2   Physical link control protocols similar to the International Standards Organization HDLC

PROTOCOL	ORGANIZATION WHICH SPECIFIED IT
HDLC Higher-level Data Link Control	ISO International Standards Organization
ADCCP Advanced Data Communication Control Procedures	ASA American Standards Association
Recommendation X.25 Layer 2 of this Recommendation (now identical to HDLC)	CCITT Comité Consultatif International Téléphonique et Télégraphique
SDLC Synchronous Data Link Control	IBM
UDLC Universal Data Link Control	Sperry Univac
CDLC (replaced by HDLC)	CDC
BDLC (replaced by HDLC)	Burroughs

Several other computer manufacturers have their own protocols similar to HDLC, but sometimes with minor differences in detail.

Another entirely different physical link protocol is used by the Digital Equipment Corporation for minicomputer networks—DDCMP, Digital Data Communications Management Protocol.

DATA TRANSPARENCY The data which are transmitted can be of any length and any pattern of bits. The data may not have any characteristics which are designed to assist the transmission protocol, and transmission must not interfere with any pattern of data. This property is referred to as *data transparency*.

How, in this case, is the end of a variable-length packet to be recognized? There are three possible ways:

1. A count

The header of the packet could contain a count of bits or bytes saying how long the packet is. This method is used in the Digital Equipment Corporation's protocol, DDCMP.

2. Character stuffing

The data, although transparent, could be divided into character lengths of, say 7-bits each. Certain bit patterns could be designated as *control characters* as they are in the ASCII code. Any of these control characters may occur by chance in the data. The data may, for example, contain the bit combination 1110100, which in the ASCII code is an ETB character meaning END OF TRANSMITTED BLOCK. The receiving machine must not interpret this as the end of transmission.

The bit sequence 1110100 cannot be used by itself to mean end of transmission. Consequently each control signal is composed of two characters, the first of which is DLE (DATA LINK ESCAPE, 00001000 in ASCII code). DLE ETB (0000100 1110100) is then interpreted as END OF TRANSMITTED BLOCK, and similarly with other control characters. DLE (0000100) could occur by chance in the *data* stream. In this case it must be sent as DLE DLE (0000100 0000100). This is referred to as *character stuffing* and permits any combination of data bits to be sent without being confused with control signals.

Character stuffing with DLE characters is used in IBM's *binary synchronous* line-control protocol.

3. Bit stuffing

HDLC and SDLC use a special bit combination called *flag,* 01111110, to indicate both the start of a packet and the end of a packet. Again, 01111110 might crop up by chance in the data stream. To prevent this causing problems, the data is

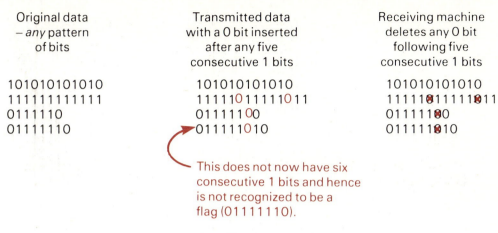

Original data – *any* pattern of bits	Transmitted data with a 0 bit inserted after any five consecutive 1 bits	Receiving machine deletes any 0 bit following five consecutive 1 bits
101010101010	101010101010	101010101010
111111111111	111110111110 11	111110111110 11
0111110	01111100	01111100
01111110	011111010	011111010

This does not now have six consecutive 1 bits and hence is not recognized to be a flag (01111110).

Figure 29.1   Bit stuffing in HDLC, SDLC etc.

scanned by the transmitting and receiving machines. Whenever five consecutive 1 bits are detected in the data stream the transmitting machine inserts an extra 0 bit. Whenever five consecutive 1 bits are detected by the receiving machine, it examines the next bit to see whether it is a 0 or 1 bit. If it is a 0 bit, the machine deletes it. If not, the receiving machine looks for the flag, 01111110. This procedure is illustrated in Fig. 29.1. It enables the receiving machine to detect the flag no matter what data bits were sent. This insertion of 0 bits is called *bit stuffing*.

MANY CONFIGURATIONS   When the devices connected to a line have some logic and buffering capability, a wide variety of configurations is possible (Fig. 29.2). It is desirable to have a physical link protocol which can handle all, or almost all, of these.

It should handle point-to-point and multipoint lines. On multipoint lines it should handle roll-call and hub polling [1] (with polling a "go-ahead" signal is passed from device to device on the line; with the more usual roll-call polling only the controlling master station sends "go-ahead" signals). It should handle loops of devices and other forms of multiple access line.

It should be efficient on both slow and fast lines and on lines with a long turn-around time or propagation delay. It should be efficient on both half duplex and full duplex lines. In a full duplex line, data messages should be able to flow in both directions at once, and if it is a multidrop line, data from different terminals should be able to be interleaved. Half duplex and full duplex devices should be able to operate simultaneously on the same physical link.

On some systems the terminals are constantly in an active condition. On others they can be dormant or off-line some of the time. The protocol needs to be able to handle a terminal which is not constantly being polled or one which changes from a dormant to an active condition.

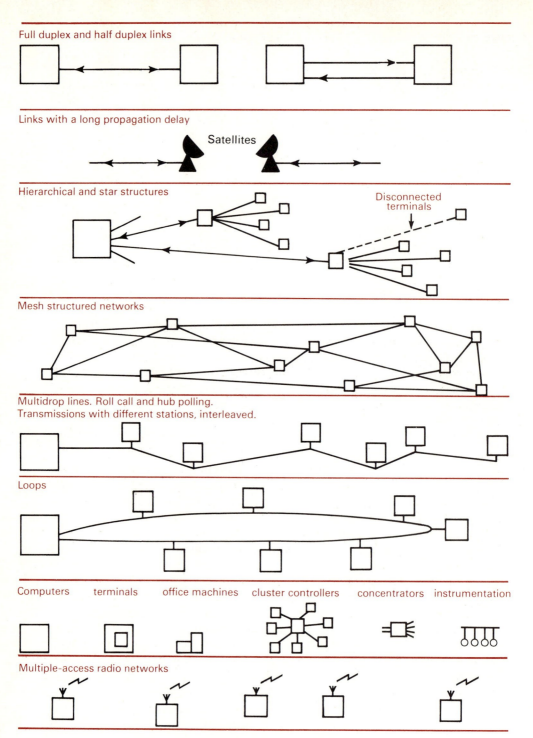

Figure 29.2 The physical link protocol ought to handle a wide variety of different configurations.

Some overhead is unavoidable in achieving this degree of generality. The protocol should handle all configurations as efficiently as possible, permitting high line throughputs. There is a case to be made for specialized protocols also handling specialized types of physical links (e.g., very high-speed satellite channels).

HIGH RELIABILITY

The physical link control mechanism should be able to deal with errors or temporary busy conditions without involving higher authority or higher layers of control.

Polynomial codes for error detection can be powerful. A 16-bit code is used in most cases, and with this the rate of undetected errors on telephone lines is typically about 1 bit in 10^{12}. A telephone line transmitting 4800 bits per second for 8 hours every day would have one undetected bit error every 20 years on the average. A typical interactive dialogue uses a much lower *average* bit rate, and if it had been used from the time of Christ until today, there is a good chance that no undetected error would have occurred in it!

Bit errors can occur not only in data fields but also in control bytes, address bytes, the flag pattern 01111110, and in any supervisory message. All of these should be protected with the error detecting code. The recovery procedures should be foolproof so that, when any of these errors occur, they do not cause user messages to be accidentally lost or delivered twice. (Double delivery may be serious in some systems, for example, with financial transactions.)

PHYSICAL BLOCK LENGTHS

On a given physical link there is a certain optimum length for the blocks of data, which will maximize the throughput possible on that link. If a block is very long, the probability of its containing an error and having to be retransmitted will be high. If the blocks are very short, the overhead and time taken in line turnarounds will be high. The optimum length can be calculated for a given link and is often a few thousand bits. Other network considerations often lead to a much shorter block length.

Switched data networks usually have their own maximum packet size. This is based on factors such as users' message lengths and buffering costs. Agreements exist between common carriers concerning packet sizes in packet-switching networks. CCITT Recommendation X.25 recommendations that the maximum data field length in a packet should be 128 8-bit bytes. It states that 16, 32, 64, 256, 512, or 1024 bytes, or, exceptionally, 255 bytes, may be used by some organizations.

When user messages exceed the maximum packet size, they must be sent a piece at a time and joined together after transmission. This is not the concern of the *physical link* protocol, however. The physical link protocol merely sends the pieces. The physical link protocol may take into consideration that packets are sent in groups and may require an acknowledgement of correct receipt when the last packet in the group is sent, rather than when every packet is sent.

SEQUENCING   It may or may not be a requirement of the physical link protocol that it always delivers messages in the same sequence as that in which they were sent. Most physical links do deliver the messages in sequence. However, where there is a long propagation delay, as on a satellite link, the most efficient form of recovery from errors is *selective repeat* error control. This retransmits the packet that was in error and does not retransmit the correct packets·which followed it. The result is packets being delivered in a different sequence from that in which they were sent.

Selective repeat error control is often avoided because of the delivery sequence problem.

PARALLEL CIRCUITS   Normally a physical link consists of one transmission circuit connecting the data machines. Occasionally two or more circuits are used in parallel. This is usually done to achieve a higher throughput. It can also improve reliability; if one circuit fails another is still usable. It may be done to handle peak loads; an extra dial-up circuit is added when the traffic exceeds a certain volume.

In most systems each parallel circuit requires its own physical link control. *How* the traffic is distributed to use the circuits is the concern of a higher-level layer of control. It is also possible to regard the pair or group of circuits as one physical link between two machines. In this case the physical link protocol will distribute the traffic among the circuits. It will make the group of parallel circuits *appear* as though they were *one* higher-speed circuit. Most physical line-control mechanisms do not do this. One which does is the Digital Equipment Corporation's physical line protocol, DDCMP (Digital Data Communications Management Protocol).

WHAT THE PHYSICAL LINK PROTOCOL DOES *NOT* DO   The physical link protocol is merely a means of delivering packets over a single physical link. It has no concern with what happens beyond that link, for example, how packets are routed through a multilink network, concentration techniques, device status and device control, end-to-end control functions, security techniques, how long messages are sliced into packets, or how short messages are gathered into blocks for transmission. It is not concerned with the establishment, maintenance, or disconnection of a switched path between stations.

REFERENCE

1. Roll-call and hub polling are explained in James Martin, *Systems Analysis for Data Transmission,* Prentice-Hall, Inc., Englewood Cliffs, N.J., 1972.

30 THE TRANSPORT SUBSYSTEM

The purpose of the transport subsystem is to permit many users to share the same transmission facilities. The mechanisms which permit this sharing may be complex, so the transport subsystem presents an interface to each user which makes it *appear* that it is using a simple point-to-point link.

In some cases a transport network is an entity in its own right, entirely separate from the machines which employ it. In other cases it is a subsystem of a computer communications architecture which also incorporates higher-level facilities and services.

Transport subsystems range from simple to highly complex. At one extreme is a system with leased lines for connecting a few terminals to a computer. At the other extreme is a multinational packet-switching network using different types of lines to interconnect many incompatible computers and terminals. All such transport subsystems should be transparent, giving users the appearance of a point-to-point link. The same higher-level software (Layers 4 to 7) may be used on both, so, ideally, both should present the same transport subsystem interface.

Transport subsystems are provided by computer manufacturers, by common carriers offering a switched data network, and, in countries where the law permits it, by independent organizations offering value-added or time-sharing networks. Some of these different organizations use different mechanisms and provide entirely different interfaces from the transmission subsystem. The CCITT X.25 Recommendation for a standard network interface is doing much to encourage compatibility between at least some networks. Box 30.1 lists the functions of transmission subsystem software.

HIGHER-SPEED BURSTS

Table 7.1 made apparent the need for line sharing in interactive systems. An interactive terminal has periods of silence which are much longer than its bursts of transmission. The *average* transmission rate during an interactive session is usually

BOX 30.1   Functions of transmission subsystem software

- Establish a logical link to a remote machine. The logical link may employ multiple physical links.

- Disconnect the logical link after use.

- Deliver messages over the logical link.

- Provide a precisely defined interface to higher layers of software (or application programs).

- Select a route through the network which is efficient.

- Ensure that no message is lost. If a message or part of a message is undeliverable, notify the sender or return the message to the sender.

- Deliver the messages in the sequence in which they were sent (first-in, first-out).

- Avoid delivering any message twice (e.g., after a failure has occurred).

- If necessary divide long messages into multiple packets to shorten the delivery time or to lessen the buffering needs of intermediate nodes.

- If messages are sent as multiple packets, reassemble the messages correctly.

- Avoid links or nodes which have failed, by means of *alternate routing*.

- *Dynamic alternate routing* may be used (i.e., different packets in the same session could travel by different routes) to minimize congestion and balance the traffic load.

- Permit the receiving machine to regulate the rate at which it receives messages so as to avoid overloading.

less than 20 bits per second for both directions of transmission combined. Even a simple voice line is less than 0.5% utilized when employed for one interactive session. Yet we would like to employ line speeds higher than those of a voice line for delivering to a user a screen full of information quickly, or for delivering a program routine, a piece of a data base, or a facsimile image or copy of a document.

A very attractive feature of a high level of sharing is that it makes economical the use of high-speed lines, and these permit faster response times. Fast delivery makes possible the transmission of program routines when needed for interactive use, fast interchange of portions of a data base, remote display of facsimile documents, and use of more attractive screen displays in man-computer dialogues.

In general, as computer technology evolves into distributed processing, computer networks, and better services for end users, so the need for transmission of high-speed bursts rather than low-speed bursts increases. To make this economical,

BOX 30.1 *continued*

- Permit the network to regulate the flow of traffic so as to avoid problems caused by congestion, buffer shortage, or message reassembly.

- Prevent any one user machine from overloading the transmission resources so that other users are excluded.

- If necessary, use parallel routes between user machines or parallel physical links between nodes, to increase the throughput.

- Short interrupt messages may be sent which bypass the queues and do not need buffer reservation.

- Messages may be sent with different priorities, e.g.,

    HIGHEST PRIORITY: Control messages

    PRIORITY 2:   Real-time or fast interactive messages

    PRIORITY 3:   Slow interactive messages

    PRIORITY 4:   Batch-processing traffic

    PRIORITY 5:   Traffic which can be deferred, e.g., mail

- Address conversions may be performed when user machines do not employ full or absolute network addresses.

- Access to a user machine may be restricted to a specified group of users for reasons of security or cost control.

- Traffic statistics may be accumulated for network monitoring.

- Information may be collected for billing users for transport subsystem usage.

- The mechanisms should be designed to avoid deadlocks.

a high level of line sharing is needed. This may come from common carrier services such as value-added networks or communications satellite systems. It may come from the design of private systems employing leased lines to provide corporations or government departments with networks serving many computers in many locations.

**BURST MULTIPLEXING
AND SWITCHING**
All telecommunications operations are characterized by major economies of scale. The greater the sharing, the lower the potential cost per user channel. This is true both of the telephone network and of data transmission. They are fundamentally different, as we stressed before, in that telephone users want continuous channels whereas most computer users want burst transmission. Figure 30.1 illustrates the difference between continuous-channel sharing and burst sharing.

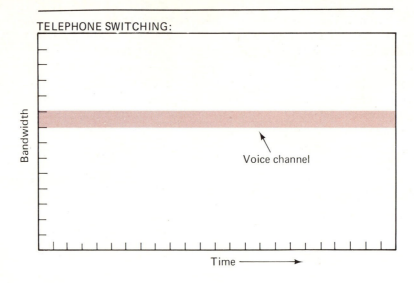

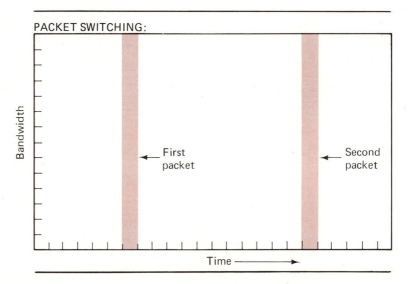

Figure 30.1   The circuit-switched telephone network slices up the available information-carrying capacity in a different way from a packet-switched network. The shaded blocks show the allocation to one user.

The outside rectangle in Fig. 30.1 represents a total communicating capability: channel capacity x time. The channel capacity of physical trunk circuits is much greater than that required by a telephone call. The mechanisms of the telephone system therefore allocate a portion of the capacity, which is continuous in time, to a telephone call. This is illustrated by the horizontal band in Fig. 30.1.

For computer networks we would like to be able to use the entire capacity for a brief instant in time to transmit a burst of data. Then, some time later, we would transmit another burst. This is illustrated by the vertical bands in Fig. 30.1. Bursts from many different users would be interleaved, as on a computer's burst multiplexer channel. To interconnect users at scattered locations a communications network needs both transmission and switching capability. The argument about continuous channels and bursts applies to both the transmission and the switching.

Transmission on telephone channels employs continuous-channel *multiplexing*—traditionally, frequency-division multiplexing. For computer operations a different form of multiplexing, which interleaves high-speed bursts, is needed.

Similarly, the *switches* on the telephone network connect continuous telephone channels. A data network needs switches which route bursts of data to their destination.

STORE-AND-FORWARD ROUTING AND CIRCUIT SWITCHING
Burst switching can be done in two ways.

First the switch can connect together transmission circuits, as do telephone switches, *but for a very brief time*—the time that it takes the burst to flow and no longer. This is called *fast-connect circuit switching*.

Second, the switch can have memory. It reads the burst of data into its memory, examines its address, and then transmits it on the appropriate channel. This is called *store-and-forward* operation.

There are several types of store-and-forward devices:

• **A concentrator**

This is usually used in a vertical network or subnetwork to connect multiple lines from lower-level machines to one line going to higher level machines.

• **A message switch**

This reads in messages, examines their address, and forwards them down an appropriate outgoing line. Traditional message switching is used for relaying administrative traffic, and the switching machine files the messages so that they can be retrieved later if necessary.

• **A packet switch**

Packet-switching networks slice messages into packets of a given maximum length (typically 128 bytes). They relay the packets individually through store-and-forward nodes to a destination node where the original message must be reassembled from the packets.

Any of these devices could be a small high-speed computer. With circuit switching, an end-to-end path is set up through computerized switches before the data are sent, as on the telephone system, though the time to connect the path is several milliseconds rather than several seconds. The path is disconnected as soon as the burst is transmitted, and the switching capacity can then be allocated to other bursts. With store-and-forward switching each message or packet carries information which enables the switch to determine how to route the packet. There is no setting up a path before transmission. After transmission the storage in the switch can be allocated to other traffic.

**TREE AND MESH
STRUCTURES**

As we have noted, transport networks may vary from very simple to extremely complex. It is desirable that control procedures should be devised which work well with complex networks but which can be subsetted for use with simple networks so that simple networks do not have unnecessary overhead.

Computer manufacturers with architectures for computer networks sometimes install systems in which only two computers are connected. Often they will install tree-structured networks in which all transmission paths go up or down the tree. There is no alternative routing.

Figure 30.2 shows a tree. A tree is composed of a hierarchy of nodes. The uppermost level of the hierarchy has only one node, called the *root*. With the exception of the root, every node has one node related to it at a higher level, and this is called the *parent*. No node has more than one parent. Each node can have one or more nodes related to it at a lower level. The top node is often the large computer center. The lowest nodes are often terminals. Nodes in between may be computers, concentrators, or terminal controllers, as in the vertical networks illustrated in Chapter 6.

A large tree-structured network is shown in Fig. 30.3. Such a network often

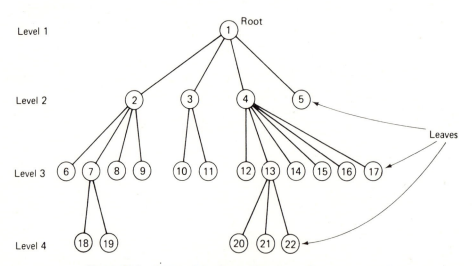

Figure 30.2   A tree. (No element has more than one parent.)

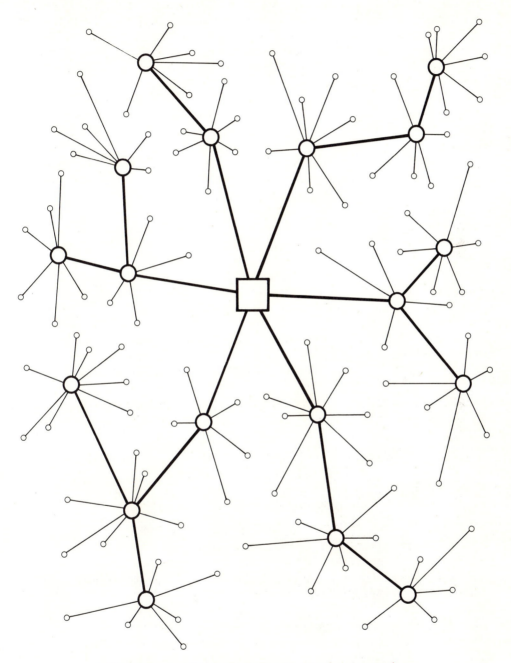

Figure 30.3 A tree-structured network. No alternate routing.

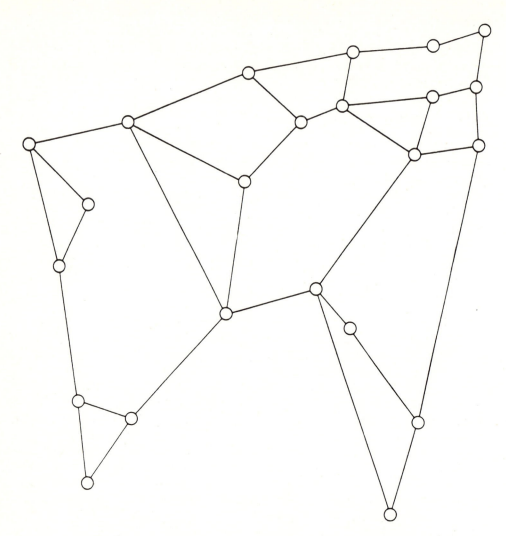

Figure 30.4 A mesh-structured network interconnecting computer centers.

uses store-and-forward concentrators. Sometimes a tree-structured network built with leased lines can use public switched circuits for backup when a leased line or node fails.

Figure 30.4 shows a large mesh-structured network. Here there is no hierarchical relationship. The term *peer-coupled* network is sometimes used because it connects computers which are peers, i.e., of equal status (although possibly differing greatly in size and importance).

VARIABLE ROUTING   Between any two nodes in Fig. 30.4 there are many possible routes, although one may be more direct than others. The route that a message takes may vary from one time to another, depending on the degree of congestion on different routes and on whether any lines or nodes are inoperative.

Variable routing introduces a variety of complications which we discuss later in the book. It is necessary to have an algorithm which decides which route a message or packet should take. That algorithm needs information about the conditions in the network which affect what would be the best route. Different slices of a message (packets) may be sent by different routes, and so might arrive at their destination out of order. It is necessary to reassemble them before they are delivered to the message user. The reassembly process needs buffer storage. There is a danger that a receiving node may run out of such storage when the traffic converging on it is exceptionally great. Some networks have encountered deadlocks caused by traffic overloads. When failures occur, message recovery is more difficult if variable routing is used, especially if different slices of the same message can travel by different routes.

FLOW CONTROL   To lessen the problems with deadlocks and traffic jams, it is desirable to regulate the flow of traffic. A high-speed computer is capable of pouring messages into the network at a speed which far exceeds the capacity of the lines, concentrators, or switching nodes. The input needs to be regulated so that sudden traffic floods do not jam the network. Even if no one machine sends an exceptional volume of traffic, a traffic overload could still occur when by chance many messages converge on the same network node or destination.

The mechanisms needed for traffic regulation can be simple or complex, depending on the overall structure of the network. It is desirable to make them straightforward; on some of the early networks they were not entirely successful, and serious traffic jams would occasionally lock up the network.

QUEUES AND PRIORITIES   Because of the fluctuating load on networks, queues build up. With a circuit-switching network the queues can be held at the outside of the network, possibly in transport/subsystem buffers, possibly external to the transport subsystem. With a store-and-forward network there are queues in the switching nodes and concentrators.

Different types of traffic have different timing requirements. Some messages need to be delivered rapidly to their destination, but with others speed does not matter. If a queuing system handles traffic in a first-in, first-out fashion, and the traffic is originated at random as in most data networks, then the utilization of queue "servers" such as lines and nodes cannot exceed a certain amount without the queues becoming lengthy. To maximize the utilization of the servers, the traffic may be divided into different priorities. High-priority traffic passes through the network as quickly as possible. Low-priority traffic is not sent until there is idle capacity.

If a network is to handle a variety of traffic types, as most networks do, then the needs of the users are best met by multipriority mechanisms. Today's mix of traffic can employ five levels of priority, shown in Box 30.2.

NETWORK ADDRESSES　　　　Networks need *addresses* for the various devices or user modules which they interconnect. A network address is analogous to a telephone number. A user wishing to contact another user states that user's address in the session initiation procedure, like dialing a telephone number, and the network makes the connection. The

BOX 30.2　Desirable priority levels

HIGHEST PRIORITY: Critical network control messages

These are not *data* messages. They are messages which affect the functioning of the network itself or the devices connected to it. They are needed for regulating the flow, pacing, sending urgent control signals, avoiding traffic jams, and breaking up deadlocks if they occur. They must jump the queues of user messages because they are needed to break up these queues when they are excessive. Like ambulances in city streets, they should scream through the traffic to where they are needed. They are generally short and do not have the buffering requirements that user messages have. Small buffers can be permanently allocated for them.

PRIORITY 2: Interactive or real-time traffic

This is user traffic which must be delivered quickly, often in a fraction of a second so that a total response time of less than, say, two seconds can be achieved. This traffic often dominates the design of the queuing mechanisms and buffers. The need for the fast response time has dominated the topology of many packet-switching networks and mandated their use of wideband circuits. A typical design criterion is that the majority of this class of messages (say, 99%) will be delivered in 200 milliseconds or less. To calculate the total response time it is necessary to add together the times for all the packets constituting a

BOX 30.2 *continued*

message and the response to it, and various other times such as compute time, file access time, and terminal editing time.

The wider the bandwidth of the times, the shorter the delivery time. But networks with high bandwidth lines need a high volume of traffic to be justifiable.

PRIORITY 3: Slow interactive traffic

Psychological studies of user behavior when operating with different response times shows that some responses ought to be less than two seconds. Others can take substantially longer. Priority 3 is for these messages which are interactive but which do not need a two-second response time. Five seconds, ten seconds, or even longer, is appropriate. For Priority 3 the design criterion might be that 99% of the packets are delivered within two seconds. (Again, two or more such one-way delivery times are included in the overall response time.)

PRIORITY 4: Batch and noninteractive traffic

This waits in the queues until higher-priority traffic has been sent. When all the resources are needed for Priority 3 and higher, it can be kept out of the network until capacity is available. In extreme circumstances, to make way for higher-priority traffic or to unlock traffic jams, it can be eliminated from the network queues and then resent later. Checkpoint restart mechanisms are designed to permit safe recovery from loss of such traffic.

LOWEST PRIORITY: Deferrable traffic

If any network (including a corporate telephone network) is designed solely for traffic which must be sent fairly quickly (at least in an hour or two), then the network is likely to be idle for much of the day. Figure 30.5 illustrates this. The network must be designed to carry the peak traffic of the peak day. The shaded portion of Fig. 30.5 is the time-critical traffic of an average day. The white area surrounding it represents unused network capacity. Traffic which can be deferred until the start of the following day can be sent in the white area. This can include electronic mail, non-time-critical batch traffic, file dumps, logs for auditors, and so on.

This deferrable traffic fills in the idle time. Higher-priority traffic can blast its way through the deferred traffic if necessary. In the future, *mail* will be the largest class of non-time-critical traffic on networks.

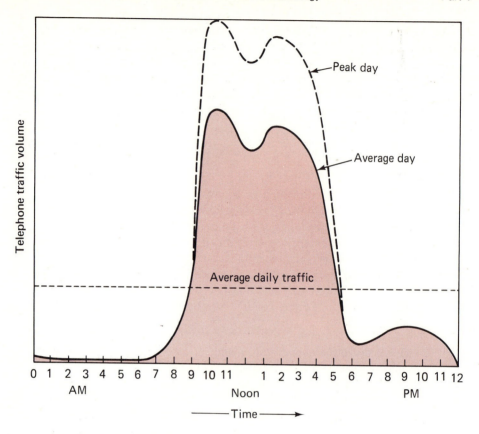

Figure 30.5 Telephone traffic. The unshaded part of the chart represents idle channel capacity.

simplest form of address is a single unique number in a large enough range of numbers to encompass all possible users. IBM's SNA (System Network Architecture) uses 16-bit addresses, presumably hoping that no SNA system will have more than 2^{16} (= 65,536) separate addresses. A *datagram* network proposed by a group of common carriers in Canada used 32-bit addresses, not because they expected 2^{32} (4 billion—slightly less than the world's population) users, but because 32 bits can represent any 10-digit North American telephone number (the second digit of the area code is 1 or 0), and a datagram machine could be connected to any telephone outlet. The Digital Equipment Corporation uses network addresses which can be any number of 8-bit bytes. Each byte contains seven bits of the address. The eighth bit is set to 1 if the following bit contains more of the address. Other systems use variable-length addresses and employ a count field to indicate the number of bits in the address. Variable-length addresses allow small networks to be handled with low address overhead but permit large addresses for large networks.

AREAS AND SUBAREAS

Large networks are usually divided into *areas* of smaller size, and these may be divided into *subareas*. A user may employ an area or subarea address rather than the complete address when contacting another user in the same area or subarea. For example, we dial a seven-digit telephone number when contacting a telephone in the same area. To dial a telephone a thousand miles away we have to preface the seven-digit number with a three-digit area code. To call a number on the same exchange it may be possible to use four digits. Similarly, on some computer networks an abbreviated address is used within a localized area. When a packet with a full network address reaches a localized area, it must go to a node in that area which has the task of converting the full network address to the area address and passing it onwards. This is sometimes called a *boundary* node. The function of converting from full network protocols to localized area protocols is called the bounary function (Fig. 30.6).

Some terminals are manufactured with a short, fixed address. A cluster controller, line controller, or concentrator converts between this terminal address and the full network address.

In some networks, user machines address each other *symbolically*. Each network *user* has a unique name, and the users refer to each other with these names. The machine which sets up the session converts these names into binary addresses which are employed during the session.

The binary address of the destination is carried by each transmitted packet so that it can be routed correctly to that destination. The packet also carries the address of the sender so that undelivered messages can be returned and so that recovery from failures can be accomplished without loss of messages.

NONEXPLICIT ADDRESSING

In some networks the messages do not carry the explicit addresses of the users. Instead, they carry some form of *session identification* and the address of a network node near to the destination, such as a network interface machine, a concentrator, or a terminal cluster controller. This network node uses the session identification to pass on the message either to the destination user or to a machine in contact with the destination user.

Nonexplicit addressing has two advantages. First, the address carried by the packets can be shorter. Second, it enhances security. An unauthorized person obtaining a data packet by wiretapping or other illicit means could not identify the destination or the originating user.

Often a user machine has multiple *ports*. In other terminology, it has multiple *logical channels* allocated to it. When it places a call, it selects a logical channel. Each logical channel has a number. The responding machine does not need to know the number of the logical channel. Instead the machine which sets up the session allocates an address to the session. Communicating user machines may then address each other with the session number, and the nodes of the transport subsystem use this number to select the transmission path and the port of the receiving machine.

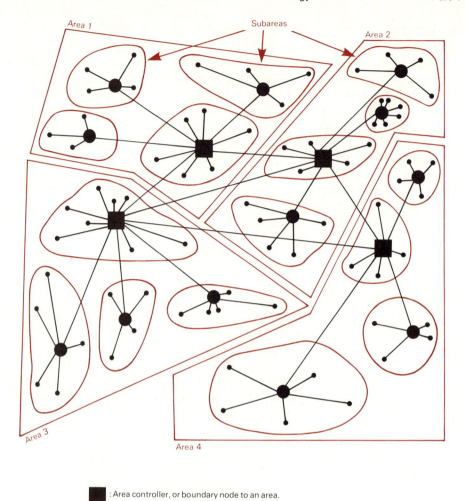

Figure 30.6   Areas and subareas.

TRANSPORT HEADERS   When a packet or message sets off on its journey
                          through a transport network, it must carry with it
certain information like the paperwork which accompanies a freight shipment. This
information is carried in Layer 3 and Layer 4 headers.

It must carry a *destination address* so that the various network machines can
route it to that destination. This is different from the address in the Layer 2 header,
which gives merely the next stop on the journey rather than the ultimate destination. It should also carry an *origination address* so that if it becomes undeliverable
for some reason it can be returned to its sender, or at least its sender can be

notified. It should carry a *serial number* so that it can be traced or referred to, if lost as a result of a machine malfunction.

Many virtual circuits share the same physical circuits, and so the packet or message should carry the *virtual circuit number* to which it relates, or a *session number*. On that virtual circuit there may be a means of regulating the rate of flow so that the receiving devices do not become overloaded. The flow control mechanisms commonly use two serial numbers, which we will discuss later—a *Send Sequence Number N_S* and a *Receive Sequence Number N_R*.

When long messages are sent on the virtual circuit, they are cut into slices and sent in multiple packets. The packets must contain information which enables the receiving node to join the slices together in the right sequence to form the original message. The Send Sequence Number may be sufficient for this when used in conjunction with a bit in a packet which indicates that *more data* are to follow.

The transport subsystem should use a priority scheme so that some messages have higher priority than others. A packet or message, then, may contain a *priority indicator,* and higher-priority items jump the queues of lower-priority items.

Different types of messages or packets may have different formats. A data message may be different from a control message. Again, different types of messages or packets may be routed to different software modules for handling. The item may therefore carry an indication of what *type of item* it is or what *format* is used.

TWO TRANSMISSION HEADERS   As we have indicated, two layers of transmission control are desirable:

- Layer 3: This relates to the mechanisms of a common shared network and is unconcerned with the problems of individual sessions in the machines which use the network.

- Layer 4: This relates to specific sessions, is concerned with the end-to-end control of transmission for these sessions, and is unconcerned with the mechanisms of the common network.

Box 30.3 lists the types of information desirable in the Layer 3 header. The bits which carry this information travel with each packet that is transmitted. In addition other control packets are needed to establish the virtual circuit indicating the addresses of the sending and receiving machines, disestablish the circuit, and deal with any failures.

The international standard for Layer 3, CCITT Recommendation X.25, is strongly oriented to packet-switching networks (Figure 30.7). It can function with other types of networks, such as leased-line concentrator networks, but is not appropriate for all networks. Circuit-switched or digital leased line networks, possibly using the CCITT Recommendation X.21, do not require the complexity of X.25. X.25 would be very inefficient with digital facsimile applications, which

BOX 30.3   Types of information desirable
in the Layer 3 header

- Identification of virtual circuit (logical channel) to which this packet relates.

  NOTE: To deliver the packet the network must know the *destination address*. In case the packet is undeliverable, the network must know the *origination address*. Neither of these relatively lengthy fields need be carried in a data packet. The network can deduce them from the number of the virtual circuit (logical channel or session). They must be sent in the packet which originally sets up the virtual circuit. Not including them in every packet shortens the packet headers and improves security.

- Packet type (so that the network knows whether merely to transmit the packet or to take some special action).

- Header format (so that the network knows which bits are which in the packet header; this might be deduced from the packet type).

- Send sequence number $\Big\}$ To control the flow on the virtual circuit and ensure that
- Receive sequence number no packets are lost.

- More-data bit. To indicate that this packet is not the last packet of a message which is being sent.

- Priority indicator. To indicate whether the packet should jump the queues (or possibly be stored for off-peak transmission).

- Diagnostic indicator. To indicate that this packet should be returned to its sender or traced (i.e., its journey logged for diagnostic purposes).

will assume greater importance as office of the future technology and electronic mail spread and converge with data processing.

The sessions using Layer 4 require a standard interface to a transport service. The formats and protocols used should work with different forms of transport service and should not be oriented to one particular form such as packet-switching. A given session may at one time operate via a packet-switching network and at another via a leased line, X.21 circuit, satellite circuit, or non-packet-switching network. Network technology is changing fast. Layer 4 should work with the many different network technologies of the future, including some which do not use Layer 3 (such as digital circuit-switched networks); see Fig. 30.8.

The communication within Layer 4 sends and receives messages, not packets

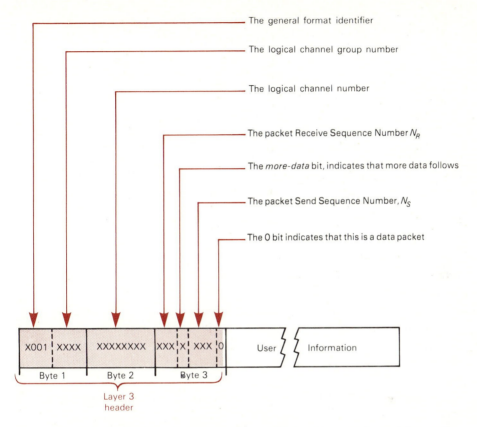

The general format identifier

The logical channel group number

The logical channel number

The packet Receive Sequence Number N_R

The *more-data* bit, indicates that more data follows

The packet Send Sequence Number, N_S

The 0 bit indicates that this is a data packet

| X001 | XXXX | XXXXXXXX | XXX | X | XXX | 0 | User | Information |

Byte 1   Byte 2   Byte 3

Layer 3 header

Figure 30.7 The Layer 3 header in the CCITT X. 25 protocol containing most of the functions listed in Box 5.3.

(i.e., the messages are not chopped up into slices). It applies end-to-end controls to the messages to ensure that none are lost or received twice. These controls may require that messages be serial-numbered separately for each session. The serial numbers are used to control restart and recovery after failures. The messages must contain an indication of which session is sending and receiving them. They may be directed to software other than *user* sessions, for example, the software which sets up and controls sessions or performs overall network control. Bits in the header would indicate this routing.

Layer 3 (at least in the X.25 Recommendation) does not allow data messages of different priorities. It allows short control messages to be transmitted with higher priority than the data messages. The levels of priority listed in Box 30.2 are desirable and may be a Layer 4 function if Layer 3 does not handle them. Layer 4 may store the low-priority items until transmission capacity is available.

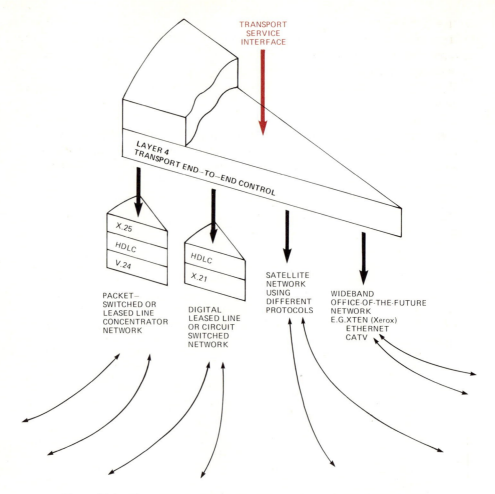

Figure 30.8   The transport Service Interface (to Layer 4) is independent of the network technology and will work with a diversity of future networks including some which do not employ a Layer 3.

ADDITIONAL OVERHEAD

To some extent the functions placed in Layer 4 in manufacturers' architectures result from the deficiencies in Layer 3. If an X.25 virtual circuit could be trusted *never* to lose a message, then end-to-end integrity control could be dispensed with in Layer 4. If Layer 3 handled priorities, Layer 4 would not need to. (It would be better to handle priorities in Layer 3 because the common network should enable high-priority items to jump the queues.)

The X.25 Layer 3 has been criticized from both sides. It has been attacked because it duplicates some of the functions in Layer 2 (HDLC) [1]. It has been attacked because it omits functions which cause additional controls to be necessary in

Layer 4 [2]. The problem arises because the different layers have been defined by different organizations with slightly different perceptions of the requirements. The main perception of the designers of X.25 was the building of public packet-switching networks which would handle the types of computer usage common in the late 1970's (e.g., *not* digital facsimile, mail, voice, teleconferencing, or high-bandwidth office of the future applications).

We have stressed that the building of widespread X.25 networks will be of great value to the future of computing. It is extremely beneficial that a standard exists and is coming into widespread use. That use of the standard involves somewhat higher overhead will be offset by the mass production of microelectronic circuitry to handle that overhead.

Some manufacturers may choose not to use X.25 and possibly to integrate Layers 3 and 4 into one transmission subsystem layer. As part of their integrated design they may subdivide this layer into their own sublayers.

SUBLAYERS   Univac's DCA (Distributed Communications Architecture), for example, divides its integrated equivalent of Layers 3 and 4 into three sublayers called *Trunk Control, Route Control,* and *Data Unit Control* (Fig. 30.9). *Data Unit Control,* the highest layer, chops the session

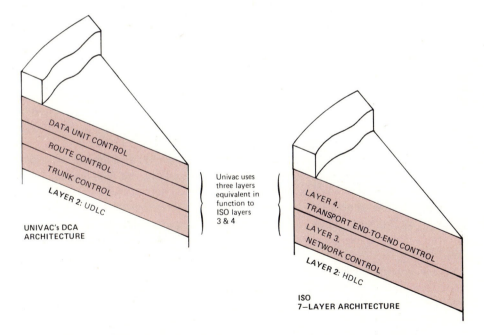

DATA UNIT CONTROL
ROUTE CONTROL
TRUNK CONTROL
LAYER 2: UDLC

UNIVAC's DCA
ARCHITECTURE

Univac uses three layers equivalent in function to ISO layers 3 & 4

LAYER 4.
TRANSPORT END-TO-END CONTROL
LAYER 3.
NETWORK CONTROL
LAYER 2: HDLC

ISO
7–LAYER ARCHITECTURE

Figure 30.9 Some manufacturers integrate 1SO layers 3 and 4 into one layer. This layer may be split into sublayers for implementation. Univac's DCA architecture uses three sublayers as shown here.

messages into packets, performs flow control on the packets (like X.25), and converts machine addresses to logical channel numbers and back again. *Route Control* determines the route through the network and sometimes joins small messages together to travel over the same route as one packet. *Trunk Control* queues packets to and from the communications links, performs initialization and recovery, and manages the communications resources.

NETWORK TRANSPARENCY

One of the reasons for a layered architecture is that the design of the transport system will probably change, and it is desirable that the user programs should not have to change with it.

The most common change is that the network configuration changes but uses the same techniques. On some systems this happens every few weeks. With more potentially disruptive alterations, the techniques themselves change. Variable routing is introduced into a system which previously had fixed routing. Use of public telephone links is replaced by leased lines and concentrators. A concentrator network is repaced by a packet-switching network. The change, especially if it occurs within the network architecture of one manufacturer, may be done in such a way that the external interface to Layer 4 remains the same.

One change in which the network transparency is less easily preserved is when new common carrier protocols, such as those in the CCITT X.25 Recommendation, are substituted for previously used network protocols of a different form. The change from a private leased line network to a public packet-switching network is likely to bring a different external interface to Layer 3. It is the task of Layer 4 to preserve the network transparency when this happens.

NETWORK CONVERSION

In the future there are likely to be multiple types of transport networks. There will be public packet-switching networks with a CCITT X.25 interface. There will be economic reasons still to use leased circuits, both digital and analog, with concentrators. There will be circuit-switched networks—both the telephone network and some circuit-switched data networks. Value-added networks like TYMNET will continue. A new generation of satellites offers interesting possibilities for new forms of networking. These different networks require different protocols, and also the various manufacturers' network architectures use fundamentally different protocols.

The software will sometimes have to convert from one type of transport network to another. It may have the function of *selecting* which type of network is employed for a session to a given destination. Is it cheaper to go via a public packet-switched network, a leased line facility, or a satellite network? These will have fundamentally different pricing structures, and *least-cost routing* may be a feature of the software. This might all take place within the transmission subsystem.

Unfortunately, networks have properties which have an effect external to the transmission subsystem. For example, satellites have a long propagation delay which affects the *pacing* control. Different networks permit different maximum message sizes. Some networks can provide a high bandwidth; others cannot.

Layer 4 software, then, may be involved in network interconnection and minimum-cost routing and may have to vary its end-to-end control from one network to another.

PAYMENT FUNCTIONS   Network users must be billed for their use of network resources. Transport subsystem software may record details of what each user has employed and pass this information to a billing program (which is itself a user program).

Some users may request that the party they want to communicate with pay, as with a telephone call on which the charges are reversed. The transport software may issue requests for reverse charging, and respond to such requests from distant nodes.

SUMMARY OF   To summarize, there are some basic types of mechan-
MECHANISMS   isms which a transmission subsystem for computer networking needs. They are listed in Box 30.4. These
mechanisms are found in the network architectures of both computer manufacturers and common carriers.

BOX 30.4   **Basic mechanisms required in transport subsystems**

- Physical link control
- Switching
- Traffic routing
- Message slicing and reassembly
- Flow control
- Queing

- Priorities
- Network management
- Error control
- Recovery
- Security
- Billing

REFERENCES

1. L. Pouzin, "A Restructuring of X.25 into HDLC," *Computer Communication Review,* ACM 7, No. 1, January 1977, pp. 9–28.

2. "Further Study of Packet Mode Operation on Public Data Networks," CCITT Study Group VII Contribution No. 60-E, January 1977.

31 THE SESSION SERVICES SUBSYSTEM

Whereas Layers 1, 2, 3, and 4 have an overall objective which can be consciously stated, the session services subsystem is a collection of diverse activities. Just what services are provided external to the transport subsystem differs greatly from one system to another. While the standards organizations can specify complete standards for Layers 1, 2, 3, and probably 4, they will have a more difficult time with the higher layers. However, these higher-layer standards are extremely desirable and important. When they exist and are widely accepted, they will greatly enhance the usefulness and value of networks.

The session services provided differ from one type of network to another. Different types of distributed processing need different types of services. So do different types of user software, such as data-base software. The session services subsystem differs widely from one computer manufacturer's architecture to another. If different transport subsystems were to become similar in the future, solving a common problem, the personality of different manufacturers' network software would reside largely in the session services subsystem. The main sales arguments of the future will probably relate to Layers 5, 6, and 7.

Box 31.1 lists the possible functions of the higher layers. We can divide them into three groups:

1. Functions required when setting up or disconnecting a session

2. Functions used during the normal running of a session

3. Functions employed when something goes wrong, such as a node failure or a protocol violation

Box 31.1 is a lengthy list (not necessarily complete), and no manufacturer's networking software comes close yet to providing the whole list. In the development of networking there is a long road ahead. We can perceive what is needed, but the protocols will be complex. As new protocols become accepted, new machines which

490

BOX 31.1 Possible functions of the session services subsystem

(A few of these functions are also listed as transport subsystems, because some transport subsystems perform them and some do not.)

1. Assistance in Establishing a Session

   - Determine where a requested function is performed or where requested data reside.

   - Establish communications with the node which owns or controls the requested function or data. Obtain its agreement to establish a session.

   - Check that the communicating nodes have the resources, such as buffering, necessary for the communication.

   - Check that the communicating nodes have the software necessary for the communication.

   - Exchange information about protocols to be used in the communication.

2. Basic Networking Functions

   - Convert the high-level statements or requests of the user programs into the protocols of the transport subsystem.

   - Correlate the requests and responses to those requests.

   - Queue the messages.

   - Prioritize the messages.

   - Divide messages into slices when they are too long for the transport subsystem and reassemble them after transmission.

   - Use serial numbers to maintain the correct sequence of messages, if this is not guaranteed by the transport subsystem.

   - Perform flow control to prevent overloading the user programs.

   - Control the timing of when messages are sent in order to make efficient use of distant mechanical devices with their own timing, such as printers and storage units. This is referred to as "pacing."

3. Application Macroinstructions

   - Process macroinstructions of programs written in conventional languages, e.g., GET, PUT, OPEN, and CLOSE in COBOL programs, which now refer to distant facilities.

   - Provide remote/local independence (i.e., the same program is used whether the facility it refers to is local or remote).

continued

BOX 31.1 *continued*

- Process application program instructions referring to virtual terminals, virtual presentation space, etc.

- Process macroinstructions which are more network-oriented, e.g., CONNECT, DISCONNECT, TRANSMIT, and INTERRUPT.

- Process commands from user processes which do not employ conventional programming, e.g., report generators, data-base interrogation languages, graphics dialogues, and special-purpose machines such as bank customer terminals.

4. Program Control Facilities

   - Down-line loading and execution of programs.

   - Up-line dumping.

   - Portability of programs.

   - Job control commands for network machines.

   - Interface to job control languages of operating systems.

5. File Access Functions

   - Provide access to single records (read, modify, delete, or insert new records).

   - Transfer whole files or portions of files. The node which has the file accepts one command to transmit the file and then sends it in a sequence of messages with appropriate control of pacing.

   - Insert the interpret indicators in the messages.

   - Search a file or multiple dispersed files to find information specified with secondary keys.

   - Facilitate distributed data-base operations (e.g., determine what physical records are needed to provide the logical data a user needs; determine where these data are located; access the data via the transport subsystem).

   - Find the physical location of data which are referred to symbolically.

6. Recovery and Error Control

   - Perform end-to-end acknowledgments and sequence-number checking, if it is felt necessary to have an additional check external to the transport subsystem.

   - Operate batch controls (e.g., both ends of the link take hash totals of the records transmitted and compare them).

BOX 31.1 *continued*

- Recover from a *reset* or *restart* condition in the transport subsystem. Layer 4 attempts to recover, retransmitting what is necessary, Without breaking the session.

- Provide orderly session closedown if that becomes necessary, and preserve data integrity when the session restarts.

- Checkpoint restart. The messages are divided into recoverable groups. If something goes wrong, the transmission is restarted at the beginning of the group—a checkpoint.

- Provide operator controls which bridge periods of a failure, e.g., a cash count in a banking terminal.

7. Editing and Translation

- Perform code conversion.

- Format the data for preprinted stationery.

- Format the data to fill a screen, print tables, etc.

- Add user appendages to data, such as page headers, dates, page numbers, and repetitive information.

- Format the data for maximum clarity and attractiveness.

- Use graphics to create graphs or charts.

- Format the data to meet the record specifications of an application program.

8. Dialogue Software

- Store frequently used wording and panels and display these upon receipt of an identifying code.

- Insert variable data into stored panels and display them.

- Facilitate and control data collection.

- Facilitate and control data entry by a terminal operator.

- Operate menu selection, command-and-response, or other forms of application-independent dialogue in which only the results of the dialogue are transmitted.

- Conduct data-base interrogation dialogue which assists a terminal operator in formulating data-base queries or operations.

continued

BOX 31.1 *continued*

9. Virtual Operations and Transparency

- Permit users to refer to virtual terminals. The Layer 4 software does the conversion between the virtual and real terminal formats and control signals.

- Permit the use of virtual machines other than terminals.

- Permit programmers to use *logical* input/output or display spaces, and map these to the characteristics of specific machines.

- Possibly provide user access to more than one transport subsystem (e.g., a leased line system with Layer 3 software, and a value-added carrier network).

- Select the network end protocol to use on the basis of least-cost routing.

- Make the operation of the transport subsystem or subsystems invisible to the users.

10. Compaction

- Perform code conversion to reduce the number of bits transmitted (e.g., compaction of ASCII code characters, zero and blank suppression, Huffman encoding).

- Use editing to reduce message lengths.

- Substitute coded identification numbers for repetitively used screens, formats, messages, or segments of text.

11. Payment Functions

- Record resource usage for billing purposes.

- Record usage of copyright programs, data, or text for the establishment of royalties.

- Issue or respond to requests for reverse charging.

12. Security and Audit Functions

- Screen incoming calls, permitting only those from authorized users.

- Control access, i.e., one machine or user can have a session only with certain specified machines or users.

- Issue with certain specified machines or users.

- Use cryptography to encipher and decipher messages transmitted where high transmission security is needed (e.g., with electronic fund transfer).

- Maintain journals or audit trails.

use them, will come into existence, and it will become steadily easier and cheaper to implement computer networks and distributed processing. This applies both within one manufacturer with a diverse assortment of machines and within the computer and telecommunications community in general.

SETTING UP A SESSION

The process of setting up a session differs widely from one type of usage to another. At its simplest it is merely a matter of sending a connection request to a distant node and accepting its confirmation. The Layer 5 software may generate messages for this purpose such as the CALL REQUEST and CALL ACCEPTED packets shown in Fig. 10.5. After the session it sends messages such as the CLEAR REQUEST and CLEAR CONFIRMATION packets of Fig. 10.5.

In networks other than the simplest, an authorization procedure is needed to determine whether an incoming request for a session is from an authorized user. This may be done simply, or it may be an elaborate security procedure.

Particularly important with intelligent machines is the process of *binding* to make sure that machines have the capability and correct protocols for communication.

BINDING

The term *bind* refers to the agreement which two parties make saying that they will work together with certain protocols to achieve a particular result. One party may send a BIND instruction to another; the other either agrees and sends a BIND instruction back or else disagrees and sends a negative response back. It is rather like the signing of a contract between the two parties. Before the contract is signed, some details of what is in it have to be agreed on.

In order to BIND a coffee machine you press a button or put a coin in it. The machine gives a positive response to the BIND by switching on a light or making a buzzing noise. Before that you may have had to establish certain parameters to govern its work, such as CREAM, SUGAR, EXTRA SUGAR, LARGE, etc. The machine may respond negatively, possibly because of lack of authorization (foreign coin), possibly because your parameters were invalid (CHICKEN SOUP with EXTRA CREAM and SUGAR), possibly because of lack of resources (no cream left), and possibly because of breakdown.

A beverage machine has a limited range of resources and parameters. A computer may have a vast range. The computer can enter into communication with many different users which may require different resources, different Layer 6 or 7 protocols, or different parameters within one protocol. A BIND command, or statements which pass between machines prior to that command for the purposes of setting up a session, contain details of the parameters and resources to be used in the session.

A response to the BIND agrees, disagrees, or possibly modifies the request.

The *resources* may include buffer storage, logging file space, a suitable communications path, software modules, cryptography, etc. The *protocols* agreed on may be protocols for end-to-end error control, end-to-end flow control, editing, specified virtual terminal operations, conversion, etc. The *parameters* may include timing parameters or may specify whether data interchange proceeds in a full duplex or half duplex fashion, what formats are to be used for editing, etc.

Once both parties have signed the contract in this way, communication between the applications environments begins.

We have described binding which takes place when a session is initiated. Binding *could* take place at the following times:

1. In the factory. In other words, the machines always communicate in the same way.

2. When the system software is generated.

3. When a network is started up or a machine or software ("logical unit," "virtual terminal," "application environment") is initiated.

4. When a session is established.

5. In mid-session when a particular interaction is initiated.

BASIC NETWORKING FUNCTIONS

Part of session services subsystem may execute functions which are necessary in order to utilize the transport subsystem.

If Layer 4 reassembles long messages, it must have some form of *message numbering* to control this. The sequential numbering will also be used to ensure that messages are not lost or duplicated. Sequential numbering may also be needed at Layer 6 to correlate session messages with the responses to those messages. In some manufacturer's architectures the Layer 4 functions are integrated with Layer 6 functions.

PACING

We mentioned the importance of regulating the flow in the transport network to prevent congestion and traffic jams. Control of timing is also needed in the session services subsystem to make efficient use of the machines and processes which are connected to the network. For example a line printer has a cycle time—the time to print one line. If the data are not ready at the start of the print cycle, it misses a complete cycle. On the other hand, it has a limited buffer. Suppose that the buffer on a remote printer can hold three lines of print. If data are sent to it too fast, the buffer capacity will be exceeded; data will be lost and have to be retransmitted. So sending data too fast or too slowly causes a drop in performance. Furthermore, the timing varies because the printer skips blank lines and skips from one page to another. To use the remote printer efficiently, there must be an end-to-end exchange of timing signals. This is called "pacing."

Pacing control is needed when any continuous electromechanical process is used remotely. A storage unit has variable access times, and if a file is being written, the sending machine must know when to send records. This control of timing is quite separate from the Layer 3 control of flow. In an integrated architecture common timing mechanisms could be used. More often the transport network has *its* flow control mechanism, and the higher-layer pacing mechanism is separate. We discuss this in Chapter 28.

HIGH-LEVEL MACROINSTRUCTIONS

As we commented in Chapter 28, applications programs should employ high-level macroinstructions for using the network, such as OPEN, CLOSE, GET, and PUT. In general, it is desirable that the macroinstructions for using a local peripheral device should be the same as those for using a remote device. There should be *local/remote transparency*. The programmer need not necessarily know the location of the file or printer that his program employs. This may be regarded as a Layer 4 function; it may be a function of layers external to Layer 4, or it may be a function of application software. If the interface to the transport network is that in the CCITT X.25 Recommendation, then Layer 4 must translate whatever high-level commands it receives into X.25 packets such as those shown in Fig. 28.8. The outer layers must correlate the responses with the commands and deliver the data in whatever form the user process requires.

There is a rapidly increasing number of user processes which do not use conventional programming languages with instructions like GET and PUT. Instead there are report generators, data-base interrogation languages, information retrieval dialogues, graphics dialogues, and machines for special purposes such as bank customer terminals, teaching machines and home television sets connected to a Viewdata-like network. A layer of software (hardware or firmware) is needed which will connect the mechanisms or programs of these to the transport network interface.

DOWN-LINE LOADING

Intelligent terminals, cluster controllers, and minicomputers connected to networks often have their programs loaded from a larger, distant machine. A data-processing center in charge of a network may manage, store, test, and maintain the programs used throughout the network. Session services software has the capability to transmit a program to a distant machine and initialize its use: transmit, load, and go.

UP-LINE DUMPING

Conversely, a dump may be taken of a distant program for testing or security purposes. The program is transmitted to a parent computer which prints it, stores it, or displays it.

These functions are called *down-line loading* and *up-line dumping*.

PROGRAM PORTABILITY   It is often desirable that a program can be moved easily from one machine to another or distributed from a parent machine to many others. If the machines are exactly compatible, this merely requires facilities for down-line loading and up-line dumping. If the machines have different instruction sets, the programs will have to be recompiled for the different machines and the network software must manage the separate copies, down-line loading them as required.

JOB CONTROL STATEMENTS   A conventional computer with no network is controlled with a set of commands and statements sometimes known collectively as a job control language. A broadly equivalent set of commands and responses is used on some networks to link the job control interfaces of major operating systems. These control both batch jobs and single-transaction processing. On Sperry Univac's Distributed Communications Architecture, for example, these job control commands and responses are part of the Port Presentation Services for each logical port on the network (equivalent to ISO Layer 6).

The future of network architectures will be related to the future of operating systems. Rather than having an operating system in one room controlling jobs, we need distributed control with the operating systems of many machines cooperating. Now that major network architectures have been defined, operating systems and other software will evolve to encompass the distributed environment. A logical link on a network is similar to a channel in a machine room, only slower. Distributed network-wide operating systems are theoretically possible. However, it may be better to have disjoint autonomous operating systems in separate machines with protocols linking them. It would be possible to build future operating systems to employ networking primitives.

FILE ACCESS   A particularly important function of networks is to provide access to remote storage units.

This requires a command set for reading or writing complete files and for reading, writing, deleting and inserting single records. It needs the ability to communicate end-of-file and exception conditions. Where data bases are used, it needs the various data-base commands and exception conditions to be handled on a network basis.

When more than one machine or user can update the same file (or data base), controls must be devised to prevent them from interfering with one another. While one user is making a change, the others must be briefly locked out, but in locking them out the possibility of deadlocks must be avoided.

Data-base management systems are complex. It is much more complex to ex-

498

tend them to a distributed environment. Much of the complexity comes from the need to preserve data integrity when multiple users may be updating the same data and when a variety of types of failures can occur. Because of this there will always be strong arguments for centralizing certain types of data.

In some networks a machine may make a reference to data, addressed symbolically, without knowing where those data reside. A function of the network software is then to find the data, using a directory.

RECOVERY AND ERROR CONTROL

The transport subsystem, as we have commented, has its own error and recovery control. This usually has to be supplemented with *end-to-end* control external to the transport subsystem.

Error control is built into Layer 2 protocols for physical link control, such as HDLC or SDLC. It is also built into Layer 3 logical link control, such as the CCITT X.25 standard. Most major architectures also have end-to-end error control in Layer 4. The session services subsystem may also have forms of error control. Why all of these? It is a principle of layered architectures that errors of failures should be handled at the lowest level possible. If a physical link control mechanism can deal with a transmission error. It should not allow the error to cause problems at higher levels. The types of failure that the different layers can cope with are different. Layer 2 deals with bit errors in transmission. Layer 3 deals with failures of circuits or switching nodes, bypassing them if possible. Layer 4 deals with higher-level problems such as failures which cause sessions to be terminated. In addition the session services subsystem may deal with errors in protocol usage which disrupt communication between two uses, printers running out of paper, invalid requests, and so on.

EDITING

In the days of punched-card installations, the clanking machines had changeable panels which the operators wired with masses of plug wires rather like colored spaghetti. These were used for editing. The relatively small number of characters compressed into a punched card were distributed onto preprinted stationery, constant fields were added, and totals were taken as directed by the panel wiring.

In networks the data is not squeezed into a punched card; it is squeezed into a *packet*. As with punched cards, the data in packets can be edited to produce attractive printouts, invoices, statements, and screen displays. The editing is not done by a plug-wired panel but by an intelligent terminal, controller, or minicomputer; a coded format is used to control the operation. The machine which does the editing can store many such formats. The format to be used may be selected when a session is set up, or it may be selected dynamically in mid-session. A data entry operation or a dialogue with a screen can employ many different formats. The session service message headers may contain a code saying which format is to be used with that message.

One sometimes sees printouts from terminals which are unattractive or confusing because of attempts to minimize the number of characters transmitted (including blank characters). I receive terminal-printed statements from a stockbroker which are barely intelligible. There is no longer any excuse for unattractive printouts or displays. Peripheral intelligence should be used to format the data with clarity.

For some uses of data, graphs and charts are a particularly informative type of display. Although they are slow to transmit over telephone-speed lines, they may be created rapidly at a peripheral machine.

COMPACTION   Processing costs are dropping much more rapidly than transmission costs. Increasingly it will be economically advantageous to compress data so as to lower the number of bits transmitted. The editing of messages for printing or display helps to reduce the number of bits transmitted. There is also a variety of compaction techniques.

In addition to saving transmission cost on some networks, compaction can reduce response times significantly when the data are long enough to take many seconds to transmit.

DIALOGUE   The primary consideration in dialogue design should be to make the system as easy to use and as psychologically effective as possible. To do so requires fast responses at times and sometimes a large number of characters displayed. Some of these characters are standard verbiage or display panels which can be stored peripherally. Instead of transmitting them, the network transmits a coded reference to them—five characters, perhaps, instead of five hundred.

The panels which are displayed in a screen dialogue may be standard panels but with some variable information in them. The message transmitted contains the variable information and identification of the panel. Associated with the panel are some instructions or an editing format saying how the variable information is to be inserted into the panel. The panel filing and editing capability may be part of the Layer 6 software.

The terminal software may control basic definable operations such as data collection, job entry, menu selection dialogues, file searching, or data-base inquiry. These can each form the basis of a predefined Layer 6 protocol. The Layer 6 software may be able to employ many such protocols. The ones to be used are selected when the session is established.

In some network architectures, users can either use standard presentation service or else define their own, to be invoked when a session is set up.

VIRTUAL TERMINALS   It would be useful if a person at *any* terminal could connect to the facilities of a network. The problem is that a great diversity of terminals exist. They employ different control procedures, different-size screens, and different mechanisms. The computer the person wishes to use may not know what control procedures to use to communicate with his terminal. It is therefore desirable that there be some standardization of the terminals in use (or at least the interfaces to them).

As the cost of electronics drops, the diversity of terminals will increase. Standardization should not inhibit the introduction of better terminal mechanisms and designs. Therefore network authorities refer to a make-believe terminal—a *virtual network terminal*. This has defined control procedures and display areas. A programmer can be told exactly how to communicate with the virtual terminal. The real terminal at which an end user is sitting may be different, so that Layer 6 software converts the control signals and data for the virtual terminal into those for the real terminal, and vice versa. A wide variety of different terminals can then communicate with the same application program.

Figure 31.1 illustrates this. The application process communicates using the virtual terminal protocols. The Layer 6 software (or firmware) at the terminal converts these to whatever local conventions are used. Unfortunately, host computers from different manufacturers use different virtual terminal protocols. The terminal controller may therefore store more than one conversion procedure. At one time it communicates with Manufacturer A using his protocol. At another time it communicates with Manufacturer B using a protocol defined by a standards committee.

In some cases the terminals may be simple, unintelligent machines connected by telephone lines to a controller with a buffer and software which makes them appear like a defined virtual terminal.

Terminals differ greatly in their basic characteristics. There is not much resemblance between a credit checking terminal with a bank-card reader and a visual display unit with a light pen. Furthermore, there may be not one but many widely accepted standards for terminals in the future—telex machines, ASCII visual display units, electronic fund transfer terminals, home Viewdata-like television sets, and so on. Because of this, host computers may have multiple standards for virtual terminal interfaces. The agreement about which to use must be made when a session is established.

Part of the conversion process is sometimes the conversion from one character set to another, e.g., telex to ASCII.

SECURITY   Several techniques are used for making a network secure. These are discussed in Chapter 36. They include the enciphering of messages, controlling access to the network, allowing one machine to have sessions only with certain specified machines, and thoroughly checking the authorization of network users. Audit trails or logs may be maintained

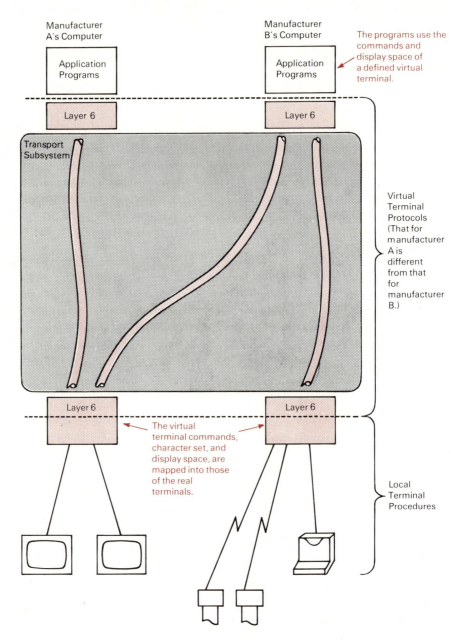

Manufacturer A's Computer

Manufacturer B's Computer

Application Programs

Application Programs

The programs use the commands and display space of a defined virtual terminal.

Layer 6

Layer 6

Transport Subsystem

Virtual Terminal Protocols (That for manufacturer A is different from that for manufacturer B.)

Layer 6

Layer 6

The virtual terminal commands, character set, and display space, are mapped into those of the real terminals.

Local Terminal Procedures

Figure 31.1   The principle of virtual terminals.

for security purposes. Tightly controlled communication with security officers' consoles may be provided.

TRANSPARENT AND NONTRANSPARENT SERVICES

Many of the functions listed in Box 31.1 can be invisible to the application programmer. He does not need to know whether compaction or cryptography is being used, or how it is used. He does not need to know that long messages are cut into slices before transmission. Some of the functions cannot be visible. For example, if repetitive phrases, headers, or panels are stored remotely from the program and referred to by brief identifiers, then the programmer must understand this and have a list of the formats and identifiers that are used. If dialogue software is used at a remote terminal location and only the results of the dialogue transmitted to the application program, then the application programmer must have specifications of the resulting messages which his program will receive.

One way of subdividing the session services software could be to split it into transparent and nontransparent layers, as shown in Fig. 31.2. The nontransparent outmost layer contains services which need a special interface to the application program, which must be specified in detail. The transparent layer is invisible to the application program.

Exactly how the diverse functions of Box 31.1 are allocated to the ISO layers or the layers of manufacturers' architectures will be the subject of many years of debate and systems evolution.

PUTTING IT ALL TOGETHER

To summarize, Fig. 31.3 shows the modules of software (or microcode or chips) which would exist in a full-function node following the ISO 7-layer proposed standards.

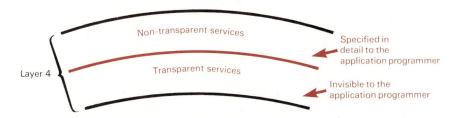

Figure 31.2 Session Services software divided into transparent non-transparent sublayers.

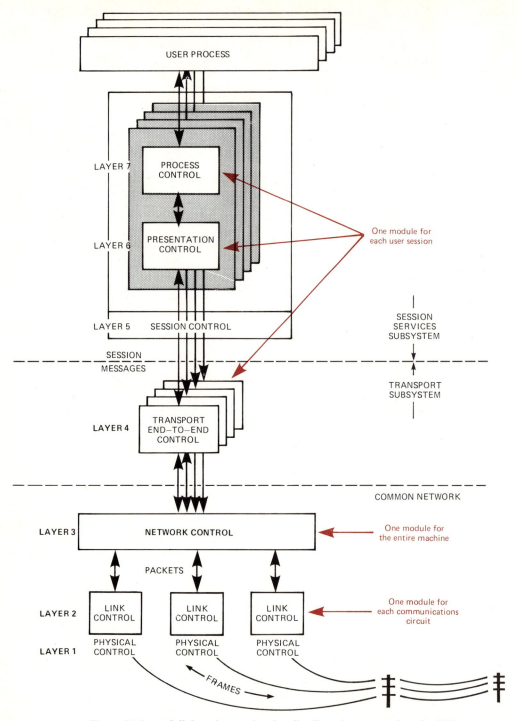

Figure 31.3 A full-function node of a distributed system using the ISO 7-layer architecture.

504

There is one module of Layer 1 and 2 control for each circuit. Layer 2 is HDLC. In most systems today Layer 1 is CCITT V.24, but as common carriers and PTTs provide digital circuits or digital interfaces to their circuits, it will increasingly be the cleaner, simpler interface of CCITT X.21 (with no modems).

Layer 3 is the interface to a common network shared by all the machines in a system or all the machines in many systems. This may be a packet-switching network, or a leased-line concentrator or other network with a CCITT X.25 interface to it. One module of Layer 4 exists for the entire machine handling the transmission and reception.

The higher layers are session-oriented. Layer 4, 6, and 7 have one module for each session using common code but maintaining separate data, registers, etc. The interface between the higher layers and Layer 4 is the interface to a transport service, which would be same with a wide variety of types of transmission resources. In particular, it might use an X.21 digital leased line or circuit-switched network with no packet interface and possibly no Layer 3.

Layer 5 manages the establishment and disestablishment of each user session, then manages restart and recovery after failures. Layer 5 information is maintained for each session.

Exactly how the diverse functions in Box 31.1 are allocated to the ISO layers or the layers of manufacturers' architectures will be the subject of many years of debate and systems evolution.

At the time of writing the manufacturers' architectures do not map exactly into the breakdown of function in Fig. 31.3, although there is some similarity. Figure 31.4 shows a full-function node of IBM's SNA (Systems Network Architecture).

Layer 1 is identical. Layer 2 uses SDLC a permissible subset of HDLC. Layer 3, *Path Control,* is broadly equivalent to Layer 3 of X.25 but bears no resemblance in detail.

SNA's *Transmission Control* contains more functions than those in the ISO Layer 4. It contains functions which relate to more than merely the transport service and which ISO would place in Layer 6. For example, the *Transmission Header* (TH) contains bits for session *pacing* control, agreements about who speaks when (must every message have a user response, or can several messages be transmitted before there is a response?), grouping of separate messages into *chains, bracketing* of dialogue messages and responses which represent one transaction, and an indication of whether there is a higher-level header. The reason so much has been included in the *Transmission Header* is that many messages do not have a higher-level header.

The major activity of SNA's *Function Management* is called *Presentation Services,* which corresponds to ISO's *Presentation Control.* Layer 7 functions may be in software, such as distributed data-base software, external to SNA.

ISO Layer 5 has its equivalent in SNA: *Logical Unit Services* and *Physical Unit Services,* which set up and serve the SNA sessions.

All manufacturers who want to market an advanced product line for

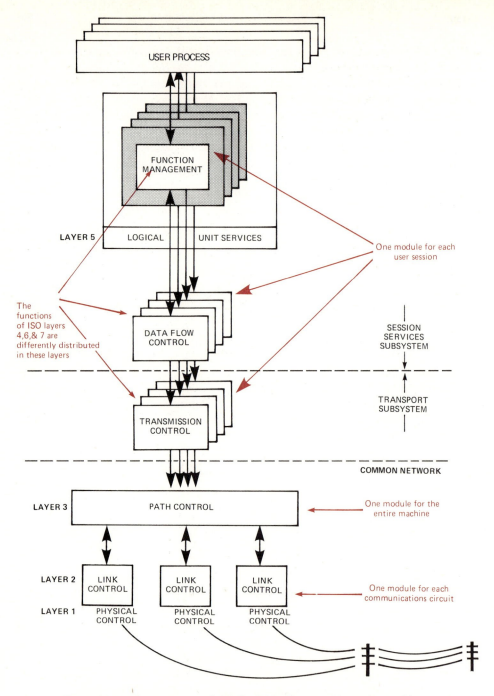

Figure 31.4 The structure of IBM's SNA (Systems Network, Architecture) compares broadly with the ISO 7-layer module (Fig. 31.3). The functions of Layers 4, 6 and 7 are differently distributed, and above Layer 2 the formats and protocols are entirely different.

distributed processing must create components (software, microcode, or chips) broadly equivalent to those shown in Fig. 31.3.

The problem at the time of writing is they are creating different ones. Instead of manufacturer-independent standardization at the higher layers, there are IBM standards, DEC standards, Univac standards, and so on. This creates a severe dilemma for DP management. Which standards should they select? How can machines of different manufacturers be linked? What should be the corporate strategy for distributed systems?

32 NETWORK MANAGEMENT

An office needs a variety of control and management functions to make it operate with the correct flow of paperwork. The same is true of a computer network. Some are low-level, repetitive functions performed by a worker each minute he is at his desk. Others are slightly less repetitive and are needed to initiate the handling of a new customer, terminate the handling of an old customer, or deal with simple problems in a mechanical, predefined manner. Others need intelligence and are not predefined. These fall into two categories: those concerned with operation and maintenance, i.e., keeping the existing system working, and those concerned with modifying, auditing, or overseeing the existing system.

In discussing computer networks the following four terms are used: *control, management, maintenance,* and *administration.* These words are sometimes used rather loosely. For clarity we will define them as follows:

- *Control* refers to the second-by-second operation of hardware or software functions that are repeated continuously for an extensive time (for example, the normal flow of data through the transport subsystem or the normal operation of a session which is already established).

- *Management* refers to software functions which are not part of the second-by-second repetitive control of operations. These functions could cease and the *control* mechanisms would continue to work, at least for a time. Management functions include the setting up of sessions, the termination of sessions, accounting and charging for sessions, programmed recovery, automatic switchover, and checkpoint-restart.

- *Maintenance* refers to the mainly human activity of keeping the network running—diagnosing failures, making and testing repairs, routine maintenance. To assist this human function a variety of machine facilities are needed, including diagnostics, error logging, and terminals and programs which enable the service engineers to check the network, run the diagnostics, and correct problems.

- *Administration* refers to the *human* work associated with operating the network. A network administrator starts up the network, shuts it down, monitors its performance, brings up new circuits or reconfigures the network when necessary, brings new user machines on-line, and is concerned with potential security violations. The network administrator requires a terminal and computer programs and is a special type of network end user. Software is needed throughout the network to assist in network administration.

NETWORK OWNERS AND USERS

The distinction between owners and users is important.

The owners operate the network as a service for the users. They are not interested in how the users employ it providing that they obey the rules. The owners bill the users for their employment of the network resources.

The owners employ different management facilities from the users. The owners are concerned with billing, network performance, reliability, and fast correction of problems. The users are concerned with end-to-end protocols and file usage, end-to-end session control and services, accuracy control, availability, end-to-end pacing, and security.

The management and administrative functions may be divided into modules serving these two groups.

DISTRIBUTION OF MANAGEMENT

Individual networks differ in the extent to which they distribute or centralize the above functions.

Control decisions, such as which way to route the packets, can be entirely centralized, partially centralized, made by multiple centers, or completely distributed.

Management decisions may be centralized to a greater extent. Some, such as changing the routing when failures occur, could be decentralized. Networks other than simple ones often have multiple management modules which intercommunicate for purposes of setting up and disconnecting sessions, dealing with failures, maintaining accounts for billing, and so on.

Maintenance engineers like to access the network from any user node and run tests or diagnostics. The diagnostic programs may reside only in certain computers but can be invoked from anywhere on the network. Network information which the engineers need, such as failure reports and error statistics, may be transmitted to a central location.

Administration of the network as a whole may take place at one location. This center maintains statistics on network use, congestion and performance. The staff there may start up and close down the network (although some networks never close). They reconfigure the network, possibly run simulations of it, deal with failures, sometimes telephoning a remote location to have a failure fixed, bring new devices, circuits, and end-users on-line, and are generally aware of the operational status of the network as a whole.

In complex networks there may be multiple administration centers, each dealing with a portion of the network. When a network is a vertical and horizontal combination as in Fig. 6.2, the computer at the top of each vertical portion may perform management and administration functions for that portion. In IBM's Systems Network Architecture (SNA) the vertical groupings are called *domains*. A host computer at the top of each domain carries out management functions for its domain and communicates horizontally with management modules at the top of other domains. Administration for each domain may be done at the top of that domain; administration for the horizontal links or the entire network could be done at one specific computer center. There may be multiple administrator terminals, each at any point in the network, and each having jurisdiction over a defined set of links and devices in its own domain or in other domains. The administrator terminals report to a parent (VTAM or TCAM) at the top of their domain.

Security is handled in different ways by different organizations. Sometimes the security officer is different from the network administrator. He or she needs a terminal from which to monitor the network and be provided with reports on network problems, misuse, and violations of security procedures whether they are accidental or possibly deliberate. Sometimes different security officers are concerned with different portions of a network.

Box 32.1 summarizes the various features for management and administration that a network might employ.

CONTROL MECHANISMS

It is necessary to have error control, flow control, and routing control as data passes through a transport subsystem, and pacing control and control of protocol usage in the session services subsystem.

MANAGEMENT MODULES

Network management often resides in several different places in modules which communicate across the network.

There needs to be some form of manager in or close to the end-user environment. It may have to make a request to central management for a session to be set up. If we were concerned only with the transmission subsystem, the user management would have the task of setting up and disconnecting the calls. It would be like saying to a secretary, "Get me a call to Fred in Hong Kong." With a CCITT X.25 network this could mean sending the packets which set up and disconnect a virtual call, as shown in Fig. 28.8. Usually, however, we are also concerned with higher-layer functions, and these need various resources allocating and protocol agreements establishing when a session is set up.

As we commented earlier, in setting up a session the management must ensure that the communicating parties

- are authorized to communicate,
- have the facilities they need to communicate, and
- agree on the manner in which they shall communicate.

Buffer space must be allocated, control of timing (pacing or flow control) must be agreed on, security authorizations must be checked, use of virtual network terminal protocols or file transfer protocols must be agreed on, procedures for editing, compaction, conversion, or encryption may have to be agreed on, and so on—in fact, any of the functions listed in the previous chapter.

CENTRALIZED vs. DECENTRALIZED MANAGEMENT   Where should the above management functions take place?

In some architectures the setting up and management of a session is done by the machine which participates in the session. In others it is done by a third party—centralized management.

In general there are four types of approaches to control or management; these are shown in Figs. 32.1 and 32.2.

First, there may be no separate manager. The communicating machines take care of their own problems. This situation is shown in the top two diagrams in Fig. 32.2.

In this situation there may be a *primary-secondary* (*master-slave*) relationship. One of the two machines is designated the primary (master) and the other the secondary (slave). The primary initiates the exchange, and when something goes wrong, the primary is responsible for the recovering action.

Alternatively, the two communicating machines may be equal with no primary-secondary relationship between them (second diagram in Fig. 32.2). They are *peer-coupled,* i.e., of equal status. Either machine can initiate the exchange. When a failure occurs, the machine which initiated the exchange (or initiated the transaction that is affected) is responsible for recovery.

Until the mid-1970's most teleprocessing used a primary-secondary relationship between the communicating machines. This was because one of the two machines was usually rather dumb. It was a terminal or secondary (slave) device designed to respond in a fairly simple fashion to the commands from the primary (master), which was usually a computer. By the late 1970's intelligent terminals, intelligent controllers, and computer-to-computer communication were common, and so peer-coupled protocols were practical.

A peer-coupled protocol is usually a *balanced* or *symmetrical* protocol in which both machines have the same algorithms. The advantage of this is that any such machine can communicate with any other and hence there is greater flexibility. With primary-secondary systems one secondary station usually cannot communicate with another secondary, except via a primary. A computer may have to behave as a primary for some communications and a secondary for others.

BOX 32.1 Facilities which may exist in network management and administration software

1. Sessions Services
   - Requests to have sessions are received.
   - The session requests are validated.
   - Resources are allocated to sessions.
   - Subchannels, table entries, session identifiers, etc., are assigned.
   - The route for the session is selected. Alternative routes in case of failure may also be selected. (This is for systems without dynamic routing of packets.)
   - The communicating parties are *bound* and their session initiated.
   - When the session is over, the communicating parties are *unbound* and their session terminated.
   - When failures occur, session recovery is initiated.
   - Accounting information is gathered for billing purposes.
   - Requests for network sessions with devices of foreign architecture are handled.

2. Handling of Physical Resources
   - A directory of physical resources (processors, terminals, cluster controllers, peripherals, channels, circuits, line groups, etc.) is maintained.
   - The management software permits these physical resources to be activated and deactivated.
   - Dynamic reconfiguration may take place when failures occur.
   - Recovery action may be initiated.
   - Information is provided to the network operators to enable them to deal with the physical resources.
   - Information is provided to the maintenance engineers about the physical resources.
   - Resources are monitored for performance measurement.

3. Maintenance
   - Terminal facilities are provided for maintenance engineers to access the network.
   - Errors and failures are logged.

BOX 32.1 *continued*

- Reports and analyses of the errors and failures are done and made available at the engineers terminals.

- Problems are automatically reported to a network operator.

- Diagnostics and confidence tests are run, possibly triggered automatically, possibly by an operator or engineer.

- Decisions to take down network components or circuits are made, on the basis of the severity or frequency of errors.

4. Security

- A surveillance log is maintained of all security procedure violations.

- The surveillance log is analyzed for the security officer, highlighting occurrences that need immediate attention.

- Triggering of alarms on detection of certain types of procedural violations.

- Files of passwords, cryptography keys, or other security information are securely managed.

- Terminals are provided for security officer functions.

5. Administration

- Terminals are provided for network operators.

- The operators can display details of the network and its various resources.

- The operator can start and stop the network.

- An operator can activate and deactivate network components.

- An operator can start and stop application programs.

- An operator can reconfigure the network dynamically (i.e., without shutting it down).

- An operator can change specifications of network control mechanisms.

- An operator can down-line load programs.

- An operator can initiate a dump of programs in peripheral machines, possibly transmitting the dump to a larger machine for printing.

- An operator can initiate trace programs or statistics-gathering programs.

- An operator can initiate performance measurement aids.

- Network performance can be measured, analyzed, and possibly experimented with.

- Information is collected for billing users, and bills are prepared.

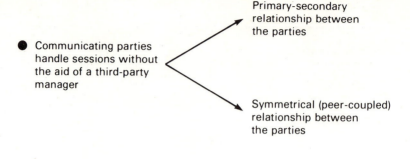

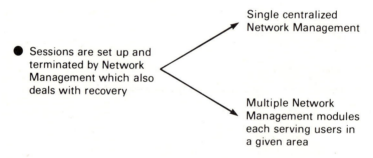

Figure 32.1   Four approaches to Network Management.

It is neater, and not necessarily more complicated, to avoid primary-secondary relationships and give each computer and terminal controller the same set of protocols.

Second, there are architectures in which a separate manager is employed. These are shown in the second two diagrams in Fig. 32.2. These fall into two categories: centralized systems with one network manager, and systems with multiple network managers as in the bottom diagram in Fig. 32.2.

If using machines are dumb, they need the help of network managers to set up their sessions. If they are intelligent, they could set up their own sessions without the help of a network manager. As microprocessors gain more power and machines gain more intelligence, there becomes less reason for having a separate network manager to set up sessions and handle recovery. Networks interconnecting com-

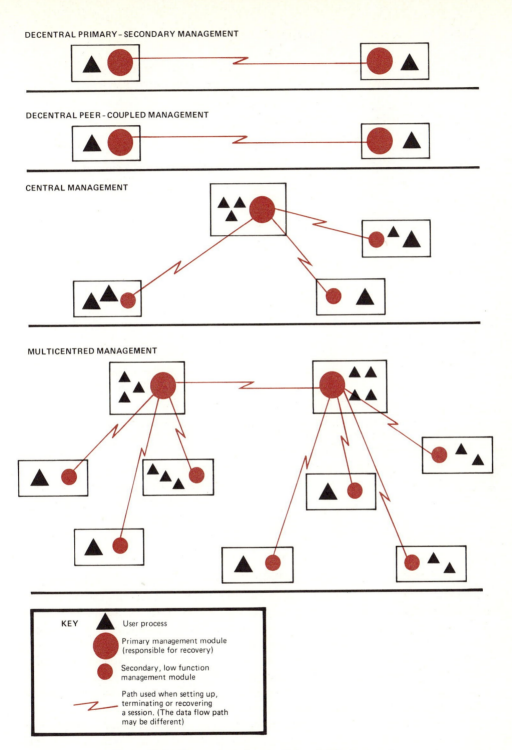

Figure 32.2 Four approaches to Network Management.

515

puters, such as ARPANET, do not have separate machines for session management. Nor do most network architectures for minicomputers. Some large computer manufacturers, such as IBM and Univac, *do* have centralized or multicentered session management. Powerful host computers manage the interconnection of peripheral, less powerful machines.

An argument for centralized session management is that the network manager can allocate the network resources in an optimal manner. The manager can make sure that there are enough trunks and buffers for the session. It may select the route that the session traffic will use. If there are more session requests than can be handled, it may give priority to the important ones. However, routing, trunk and buffer control, and priority can also be handled in a distributed fashion. Centralized session management can greatly assist in achieving an orderly recovery from failure. However, it has the disadvantage that when the central machine fails or has a software crash, a large number of sessions may be affected. Centralized session management can control security, allowing processing to communicate only if they are authorized and possibly allocating the cryptography keys.

The use of a session manager separate from the communicating parties can increase the *complexity* of setting up and terminating sessions and session recovery. Similarly, primary-secondary relationships can increase the complexity. The achievement of high availability is more complex with primary-secondary centralized management. Some of the architectures for distributed, peer-coupled networks are relatively simple.

There are furious arguments among network architectures about whether centralized or decentralized session management is the best. In practice both are working well. Decentralized session management appears cleaner and more flexible. Any machine can set up a session with any other. But it needs more capability in the communicating parties. The need for primary-secondary relationships and centralized or multicenter management stems from the need to handle nodes of limited power. As the power of microprocessors grows, distributed, symmetrical protocols look more attractive.

SYMMETRICAL SESSION MANAGEMENT

As the chips improve, session management may increasingly be done in a symmetrical fashion with no need for a third-party manager. The type of configuration shown in Fig. 32.3 is attractive. All machines have a standard interface to a common network. Any machine can initiate a session to any other machine which has the requisite attributes. Each pair of communicating machines is responsible for its own session security and recovery.

Small, simple machines may have a parent which does session management for them, as at the bottom left in Fig. 32.3.

The management functions of the network *owners* are quite separate from those of the network *users*. The owner functions of network maintenance and administration may be centralized or bicentralized.

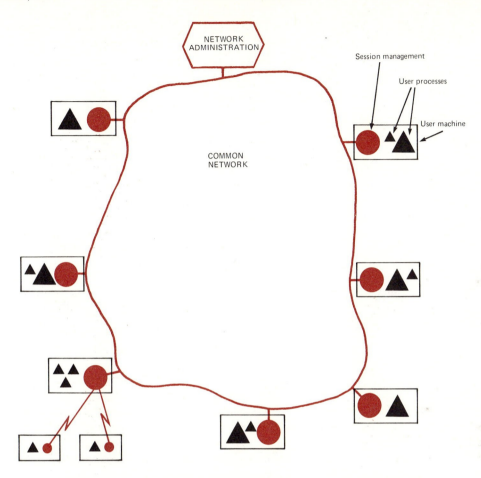

Figure 32.3 As chips and networks improve this form of management appears increasingly attractive. Any machine has the capability to have a session with any other machine without third-party management. All are connected to a common network which has its own network administration. Small simple machines, as in the bottom left hand corner may have a parent machine set up and manage their sessions.

PERMANENT SESSIONS

If a management module in a user machine has to contact a centralized management module in order to set up sessions, there is usually a permanent session in effect between these two management modules. Every decentral management module is permanently in session with the requisite central management module. This is illustrated in Fig. 32.4. The purpose of this is so that a user can request a session at any time and it will be set up quickly.

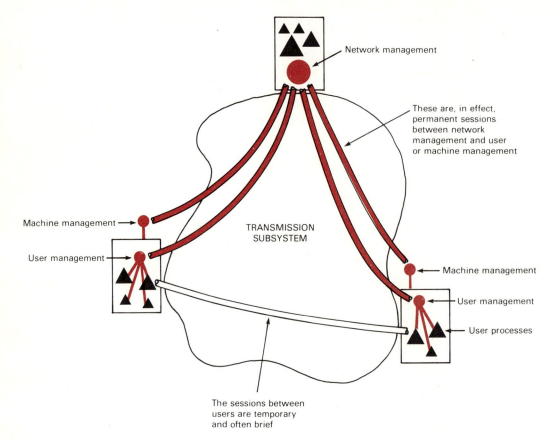

Figure 32.4   Permanent sessions for network management communication.

The fact that there is a permanent session does not mean that transmission capacity or buffer space is being used. That will only be the case when communication takes place over the session path. It does mean that requisite registers, pointers, or table entries are set up, to enable the two management modules to communicate without delay.

The central management, in addition to communicating with decentral session management, may also have links to the modules which manage *machines*. The purpose of this is to deal with problems such as printers running out of paper, machines not ready, or storage units having long, unpredictable access times. Some architectures have pemanent sessions in effect between machine management and network management modules.

If the network administrator module is separate from the network management, there may also be a permanent session between the network management module and network administrator module. Sperry Univac's architecture has three types of network management module: *local, area,* and *global* network management services. The *local* module is used to serve each major group of *machines.* The *area* module serves the *user* management (AMS Application Management Services) with which it is permanently in session. The *global* module serves the network *administrator* for the entire network. The user management and local management modules are permanently in session with the area network management, and the area network management modules are permanently in session with the one global network management module.

Figure 32.5 shows a session being set up between two users which report to different network managers. The request for the session is passed on between the network managers, and the agreement travels back by the same route. The user management allocates the necessary resources in the user environment. The network management allocates the necessary network resources and may establish the route through the network that the session traffic uses.

Different architectures use different words for this process. In IBM the network management modules are the SSCP (System Services Control Point) of TCAM (Tele-Communications Access Method) or VTAM (Virtual Telecommunica-

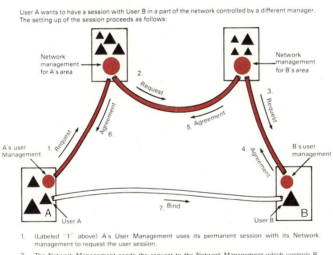

User A wants to have a session with User B in a part of the network controlled by a different manager. The setting up of the session proceeds as follows:

1. (Labeled "1" above) A's User Management uses its permanent session with its Network management to request the user session.

2. The Network Management sends the request to the Network Management which controls B. (There is a permanent session between the Network Management modules).

3. The request is passed on to B's User Management.

4. B's User Management agrees that B can enter into the session with A. It allocates the appropriate resources and sends a message to its Network Management saying that it agrees.

5 & The Network Management modules pass the agreement message to A's User Management,
6. allocating any network resources that are necessary.

7. A's User Management allocates the session resources and issues a BIND command. The session can begin.

Figure 32.5 Managing the establishment of a session with multicentered network management. (Different network architectures use different words for software modules which accomplish this).

tions Access Method) residing in the host computers. The modules which act for the users are called Logical Units (LU). In Sperry Univac the network management modules are the area NMS (Network Management Services), and the modules in the user environment are the AMS (Application Management Services).

In a completely distributed system there are no centralized or higher-level facilities for setting up sessions. Establishing a session may still be a complex process in which protocols have to be agreed on and resources allocated. This is the case in the Digital Equipment Corporation's DECNET architecture for interlinking minicomputers.

In a network which provides *only* the transport function (for example, a common carrier X.25 network or a corporate data network) it is necessary to set up Layer 3 sessions (transport sessions). An exchange of commands such as that shown at the top and bottom of Fig. 28.8 might be sent from the user machines to request a *virtual call* or *logical circuit*. This operation could be managed in a centralized, multiple-centered, or distributed fashion.

In an integrated architecture both Layer 3 and higher aspects of the session may be established by the same machines. If the transport network is architecturally separate from the session services subsystem, it may be separately managed. This might be the case where the transport network is a separate X.25 facility which users plug into. The management of the X.25 virtual calls and permanent virtual circuits might be in a separate module from the session management. The former could be decentralized and the latter centralized.

SESSION FAILURE   An important function of the management modules is to deal with failures.

Bit errors in transmission are dealt with automatically by the Layer 2 mechanism—physical link control (HDLC, SDLC, BISYNCH, etc.). Higher-level mechanisms must deal with problems such as lost packets, irretrievably damaged messages, node failures, line failures, security breaches, and harmful errors in protocol.

It is desirable that a management module be responsible for initiating the recovery action. This module will attempt to recover without terminating the session if possible. Failing this, it should attempt to close down the session in an orderly fashion without losing or damaging data, if possible.

THE NETWORK   A network operator has many functions to perform.
OPERATORS   He watches over the network with a console rather like the operator of an on-line computer. The console is often a terminal and can be located anywhere. There may be several network operators in different places, each with jurisdiction over a different set of nodes and facilities. This is often the case where a network serves several divisions of a

corporation. Each division has its own computers and terminals, and these are administered separately from any other division.

The operator console is connected to network administration software which is in one or multiple centers. This software permits the network to be controlled in two types of ways. First, it may allow an administrator to *define* a network and *generate* the systems programs which control and manage the network. This tailors the network and places an upper bound on its facilities such as numbers of trunks, terminals, and buffers. Second, the software permits a network operator to monitor or control the network or part of the network. The operator can display the status of the various facilities, activate and deactivate nodes, start and stop various facilities, may be able to adjust priorities, and so on.

NETWORK OPERATOR COMMANDS   The operator uses a set of *network operator commands*. These are provided by the network administration software, for example, IBM's VTAM. The commands enable the operator to take actions such as the following:

- **Display the status of categories of network entities.**

    In this way all terminals, all lines, all major nodes, all application programs, or all of the above within a given portion of the network could be checked.

    The display for all terminals might be a list of the names, addresses, and types of all terminals, whether they are active, and for logical units or virtual terminals the name of the associated physical unit and whether it is active, the names of the major node to which the terminal is connected, the name of the line or channel to which it is connected, or entities on the path to an associated host computer.

    The display for all lines might include a list of the lines in each portion (area, domain) of a network, whether they are active, line type, which nodes they are connected to, which node manages them, and possibly summary figures for their load, failures, and transmission errors.

    The display for applications programs might include the names of all applications programs, which node(s) they reside in, and whether they are active. Another display might show all nodes which can contain application programs and list the programs in them.

    From these summary listings an operator could display more detail or individual entities, as follows:

- **Display the status of individual network entities.**

    The condition of a particular terminal, a terminal cluster controller, a line, a trunk group, a part, switching equipment, a network control program, an application program, a session, and possibly files could be verified.

The display for a terminal might show whether it is active, whether it has power, the name of the application program (if any) to which it is connected, the name of the node to which it is connected, the name of associated physical units, the name of the line or line group to which it is assigned, details of the path which connects it to a host computer, the identification of the session it is participating in, and possibly a count of its activity.

The display for a line might show its type, whether it is active, what nodes it is connected to, whether it is switched or nonswitched, name of a line group to which it is assigned, which machine controls it, statistics of its traffic load, error retransmissions, and failures, whether its traffic is currently being counted or monitored, and parameters relating to its control such as specifications for polling delay, time-outs, and maximum number of errors retransmissions.

The display for an application program might include whether it is currently connected to the network software, its job and step names, the terminals connected to it, the terminals with requests for connection queued to it, and statistics of its usage.

- **Activate and deactivate network entities.**

Before a node can be used in a network it must be declared to the control program as "active." The same may be true with lines, logical or virtual units, and so on. The operator can activate and deactivate these.

- **Start and stop application programs.**

Sometimes an application program is started by a user at a terminal with a command such as LOG ON. Other users employ the terminal for a given application without logging on. A bank customer uses a cash-dispensing terminal, for example, without logging on. A network operator must start and stop programs which are not activated by their users.

- **Load programs into remote nodes.**

In a vertical network, programs are often maintained and stored in a central node. From there some of them are transmitted and loaded into peripheral machines. In a horizontal network, programs may be passed from one node to another. An operator may control the down-line loading of programs.

- **Activate a remote network control program.**

The network control programs in peripheral nodes may be activated, and possibly loaded, by a network operator. A peripheral node may be switched from one host computer to another when failures occur, and it may then need a modified control program.

- **Activate and deactivate files.**

Where the network management encompasses distributed files, the operator may be able to activate and deactivate files, and possibly create files. This is often in the province of *user* management rather than *network* management.

- **Activate and deactivate links to foreign equipment.**

It is usually desirable to connect foreign devices to a network, i.e., devices which do not conform to the network architecture. Sometimes these are older terminals or machines with protocols which predate those of the network architecture. The network software may permit these to be linked to the network, and the operator can activate and deactivate them.

- **Reconfigure the network.**

Additional circuits may be added to a network, additional machines connected, and the connections between machines modified. A peripheral node may be switched from one host to another. In practice many networks grow and change substantially. Within the limits of a given system generation which determines the scope of the software in use, the software changes for these reconfigurations can be made by the operators.

- **Enter messages for users.**

The operator may be able to enter messages which will be displayed to users when they log on.

- **Change transmission parameters.**

Adjustments may be made to parameters on-line, such as the polling delay, limit on negative responses to polling, time-outs, maximum number of retries when an error occurs.

- **Start and stop traffic monitors or testing aids.**

The operator may initiate the recording of traffic statistics or performance measurement data, and may initiate on-line testing or traces.

- **Initiate a dump.**

A program can be *down-line loaded* from a host computer to a smaller machine. The smaller machine can be *up-line dumped,* i.e., the contents of its memory at a given time transmitted to the larger machine and printed or stored. The operator may initiate a dump—either an up-line dump or a dump on a printer attached to the machine being dumped.

MAINTENANCE   For maintenance purposes the network software should log all errors and failures. The logs should be analyzed and summarized and prepared for the maintenance engineers. The management software may make decisions to automatically close down certain components or circuits when the severity or frequency of the errors or failure exceeds a certain threshold. It may automatically run diagnostics and confidence tests.

The maintenance engineer needs to be able to inspect the network, examine the error and failure logs, and run diagnostics. This would be done from terminals and so would require some of the facilities listed above for operators.

SECURITY   For security reasons the network may be monitored for procedural violations made by the users. Violations of more than a certain level may trigger alarms at the location of a security officer. All security procedure violations will be logged, and the logs should be analyzed for patterns or unusual frequencies of violations. The security officer should be able to inspect the violation logs and analyses at any time from a terminal.

Users may have to key in passwords or secret numbers to gain access to programs or network facilities. These should be maintained with maximum security by the security officer. Similarly, if keys are used for cryptography, these need to be maintained with maximum security. This is discussed in Chapter 36.

There may be one security officer or several. There may be one for the network as a whole and other persons with security responsibility in the various user environments. These persons need terminals with secure access to the facilities the network employs for security.

OTHER ADMINISTRATIVE FUNCTIONS   In addition to the functions mentioned, the network should have facilities for billing its users.

Some networks have a center where network measurements are made and performance is studied. Tools may exist in this center for analyzing the performance and summarizing and charting the network measurements. In some cases experiments are carried out during the quieter periods, on weekends, and at night to test the capacity of the network configuration. Tools may exist for simulating the network and evaluating how to reconfigure it for optimal performance.

33 LAYER 2 INTERCONNECTION MESSAGE AND TRANSACTION DESIGN

It is often desirable to interconnect machines with incompatible DDP software. A low-level interchange can usually be accomplished at Layer 2. The messages so interchanged can be designed to achieve some of the functions of the higher layers. This chapter discusses the design of messages for this low-level interchange.

When distant processors send messages to one another, they must carry two types of information: information which relates to the applications in question and information for control purposes.

When network architecture software is used, most (but possibly not all) of the control information is contained in the message headers created by that software. It is present in the headers of DEC's DECNET messages and IBM's SNA messages, for example. Often system designers do not use such an architecture but instead connect the distant processors by telephone lines with simple, conventional data transmission. An advantage of doing so is that they can interconnect machines from different manufacturers. In this case they must think out carefully what procedures are needed for controlling the interchange of messages.

ADVISABILITY OF THE DO-IT-YOURSELF APPROACH

It is generally inadvisable to create your own network software. The job inevitably seems to take much more programming time than anticipated. A do-it-yourself approach may be reasonable for simple point-to-point or dial telephone lines between processors. More complex forms of transport network need complex software—especially mesh-structured networks with alternate routing. These are sufficiently complex that a do-it-yourself approach is not advisable for most corporations.

Many of the header fields and control messages mentioned in this chapter are required, not for the control of the network but for the machines and programs which intercommunicate via it. Therefore if the designer purchases software which solves the transport network problem only, he may still have to specify message headers in order for processors to be able to use it.

A full-function architecture for distributed processing from a given manufacturer should do everything listed in this chapter.

MESSAGES,
TRANSACTIONS,
AND BATCHES

First let us distinguish between messages, transactions, and batches.

A *message* is a group of bits sent as a single communication between two machines. It is possible that for technical reasons, such as buffer storage use, a message may be divided into separate blocks for transmission (sometimes called *packets* or other terms). If that happens, the message will be reassembled before it is given to the process which uses it. We would therefore be more accurate to say *a message is a group of bits forming a single communication between user processes.*

A *transaction* consists of the data which form a basic unit of work for the application in question, for example, an order for a machine tool, a theater booking, an invoice, or a sum of money transferred between banks. To complete one transaction, several messages may have to go back and forth. For example, an interchange of several messages is used when making an airline booking, and the resulting booking is one transaction.

A group of transactions is sometimes sent together in one transmission, for example, from a peripheral processor used for data entry. This is referred to as a *batch*. It may be sent as multiple transmitted blocks, depending on what block size gives the most efficient transmission.

LINE CONTROL

Teleprocessing needs a *line-control procedure,* as we have discussed, to perform the following functions:

- Indicate the start and end of a message.
- Send an address with the message so that it goes to the requisite device.
- Detect transmission errors.
- Initiate retransmission of messages in error, or messages which failed to arrive.
- Maintain line discipline to ensure that two devices do not transmit at once and garble each other's messages.

The designer selecting processors to be interlinked must ensure that they use exactly compatible line-control procedures. Some line-control procedures, such as start-stop control with the CCITT Alphabet No. 5 (ASCII)[1] and binary synchronous line control [2], are used by machines of almost all manufactures.

The International Standards Organization (ISO) has standardized a line-control procedure called HDLC (Higher-Level Data Link Control) [3, 4]. This is designed for communication between buffered machines with a little more logic than the dumb terminals of the early 1970's. IBM's SDLC [5] is a subset of HDLC. Most other manufacturers have their own version of HDLC, sometimes with the first letter of the acronym changed (e.g., Univac's UDLC, CDC's CDLC). Unfortunately, multiple versions are permitted by the standard, and some of the separate versions cannot themselves intercommunicate.

HDLC, SDLC, etc., are more efficient than many of the earlier line-control procedures, especially for fast, full duplex, processor-to-processor communication, and also especially on communications satellite links [6].

Many machines are not equipped to use HDLC, SDLC, etc. It does not necessarily matter what line-control procedure the designer selects provided that the machines can communicate at a fast enough rate for the applications in question. An important early decision is to standardize on one line-control procedure, and it would be better to have an efficient one. If satellite links may be used in the future (and in some countries they will be cheaper), HDLC or a variant of it may be desirable. The Digital Equipment Corporation has a unique line-control procedure, DDCMP (Digital Data Communications Management Protocol), which is also efficient over satellite links [7].

CODE SELECTION

To communicate, the processors selected must be able to use not only the same line-control procedure but also the same character set, possibly the U.S. ASCII code or CCITT Alphabet No. 5.

MESSAGE HEADER

A variety of control information may be carried in the header of each message. The system designer who has elected to use conventional teleprocessing rather than a network architecture must determine what information is needed in the message headers. The following are some of the types of header information that might be necessary:

- **Type of message**

    Often a machine will receive more than one type of message. The header should indicate the type, possibly with one byte.

- **Destination address**

    If a single physical line connects the processors, there is no need for a destination address. However, many networks use concentrators or switches, so that the message travels over more than physical links. A destination address is needed to tell the concentrator or switch where to route the message.

- **Source address**

    The receiving processor needs to know where a message has come from. If it has traveled over more than one link via a concentrator switch, it must carry the address of its source. This address is placed in any response messages.

- **Message serial number**

    The messages may be given a sequential number. This may be used for the following purposes:

    - For ensuring that no message is lost
    - For associating a response with the message triggering that response
    - If a long message is split into blocks or packets, for reassembling that message
    - For identifying a message for audit purposes

- **Transaction serial number**

    When several messages are involved in one transaction, the transaction may be given a serial number rather than individual messages. This enables the transaction to be traced and referred to later for audit, testing, or retrieval purposes. If it is possible for one message within a transaction to be missing (for example, one line of an invoice), the message within a transaction may be numbered.

- **Chaining indicator**

    If a transaction can be split into multiple messages, a chaining indicator may indicate that more messages will follow in that transaction. Two bits are sometimes used in the chaining indicator, having the following meanings:

    - First message in transaction
    - Middle message (not the first or last)
    - Last message in transaction
    - Only message in transaction

- **Message reassembly indicator**

    If a long message is chopped up into blocks or packets, sufficient information must be included to reassemble the message and detect whether any packet is lost. This is usually done with a chaining indicator and sequential number.

- **Blocking indicator**

    Sometimes many short messages are grouped together into a block that is transmitted as a whole in order to improve transmission efficiency. Indicators are needed within the block to show the start and end of each message. If the messages are composed of characters, a special character (e.g., from the ASCII character set) can be used. If the messages contain bit patterns, a special character cannot be used by itself because it might occur by chance in the message. Instead a count may be used to indicate the length of each message within the block. Each message may begin with, say, an 8-bit start-of-message pattern followed by an 8-bit count. The start-of-message pattern is used as a check that the count has given the correct demarcation.

- **Response indicator**

Sometimes when a processor sends a message, it requires a response; it may be programmed to wait until it receives a response. In this case it should send an indication in the message saying that it is waiting. Again a 2-bit indicator is sometimes used having the following meanings:

- No response expected.
- A response *must* be sent to this message.
- A response *must* be sent to this chain of messages (or transaction) after the last message in the chain is indicated.
- A response may or may not be sent.

- **Time and data stamp**

For some types of application the messages are marked to indicate the time and date they were sent. This is used for reference and audit purposes.

- **Pacing**

When one processor sends traffic to another, it is possible that it could send it too fast for the receiving machine to handle. This is especially so when the receiving machine is carrying out a mechanical operation such as printing or filing the messages or using them to update a data base. Some mechanism is then needed for regulating the rate at which the transmitting machine sends messages.

The receiving machine usually sends a signal to the transmitting machine saying that it is ready to receive. The transmitting machine must neither send too fast nor send too slowly. If it is too slow, efficiency is impaired, so it may send not one message when it receives a go-ahead but a specified number. The number should be larger if the transmission delays are greater, for example, in transmission via a communications satellite.

In many systems a pair of numbers are used in the messages to regulate the rate of flow. The sending machine places a number, N_S, in the messages it sends. The receiving machine places a number, N_R, in its responses which says, in effect, "The next message I expect to receive is N_R." This indicates that the messages prior to N_R have been received correctly. These numbers are cyclic counts. A modulo 8 count may be sufficient. This requires 3 bits. After number 7 the count recycles to 0. When transmission delays are long, a larger count is used—often a modulo 128 count requiring 7 bits.

The sending and receiving of messages may be overlapped. In other words, processor A may be sending messages to and receiving messages from processor B, asynchronously. In this case the messages will carry both a send count, N_S, and a receive count, N_R. Using these two counts, the machines regulate the rate of flow from one another. The response counts, N_R, may be carried either in data messages or, if no data messages are ready to be sent, in special control messages.

This control of the rate of flow between user machines is sometimes called "pacing."

- **Batch controls**

Some distributed processors send a *batch* of traffic rather than individual transactions, sometimes the result of a data collection process. Demarcation controls are needed in the batch to indicate the start and end of individual records or transactions and the end of the batch. At the end of the batch a control record should be sent so that the receiving machine can check that the transactions received are complete and accurate. This control record may contain a count of the transactions and a *hash total,* i.e., an otherwise meaningless total of the values of given fields, such as account number or cash total.

The receiving machine adds up this total and ensures that it agrees with the total written by the transmitting machine in the control record.

CONTROL MESSAGES   To regulate the transfer of information and deal with exception conditions, certain messages are needed which do not carry application data but which are control signals. The following types of control messages are used:

- **Ready to receive**

One machine signals to another that it is ready to receive transmission.

- **Not ready**

A machine indicates that it is not at the moment ready to receive.

- **Request permission to transmit**

One machine contacts another, requesting permission to transmit.

- **Reject**

One machine rejects the transmission from another, indicating the reason. The rejection will not normally be due to a transmission error, because these are detected and dealt with by the line-control procedure (binary synchronous line control, HDLC, etc.). It will be a validity error or failure message of some type.

- **Retransmission request**

   The receiving machine requests that a message with a given number be resent; or possibly all messages after a given number. This may be necessitated by a machine or line failure of some type.

- **Interrupt**

   One processor may send an urgent message to interrupt another processor.

- **Initiate session**

   Various types of message may be interchanged to initiate a session between two machines or to check that the machines have permission and have the resources to communicate. Security checks may be necessary before the session can commence.

CRYPTOGRAPHY   To achieve protection against wiretapping or tampering with the transmission in a concentrator or switch, messages on some systems are enciphered before transmission, as spies would formerly encipher secret messages. The difference from the old spy stories is that now a computer does the enciphering. Today a microcomputer (or software in a large computer) can scramble the data so formidably that they are likely to be safe from persons who would attempt to crack the code. A microcomputer or software at the other end of the link deciphers it, ready for use.

   Cryptography is discussed in Chapter 36.

   The designer needs to decide whether or not this type of protection of the messages is necessary. For most transmission it is not. But for closely guarded corporate secrets, for information of high value such as oil-prospecting data, for sensitive personal information such as police records, and particularly for financial transactions such as electronic funds transfer between banks, enciphered transmission is desirable.

   Enciphered transmission is used between incompatible processors by means of separate units at each end of the link to do the enciphering and deciphering.

COMPACTION   If transmission efficiency is a major concern, data may be compressed before transmission. This can reduce the number of bits by one third or one half [8]. The compressed message will be restored to its original form at the other end of the link before use. The compression and expansion may be done by software in the using computers. Like cryptography, it may also be done by intelligent hardware external to the computers.

REFERENCES

1. Described in James Martin, *Systems Analysis for Data Transmission,* Prentice-Hall, Inc., Englewood Cliffs, N.J., 1974.

2. *IBM General Information Manual on Binary Synchronous Line Control,* Poughkeepsie, N.Y.

3. ISO documents.

4. HDLC is described in James Martin, *Computer Networks and Distributed Processing,* Prentice-Hall, Inc., Englewood Cliffs, N.J., 1981.

5. *IBM General Information Manual on SDLC,* Poughkeepsie, N.Y.

6. Efficiency of data transmission protocols on satellite links is described in James Martin, *Communications Satellite Systems,* Prentice-Hall, Inc., Englewood Cliffs, N.J., 1978.

7. Digital Equipment Corporation manual on DDCMP. DDCMP is described in Reference 4, above.

8. Message compaction is discussed in Reference 4, above.

34 FUTURE SOFTWARE REQUIREMENTS

The environment described in this book creates some fundamental changes in software requirements.

ISOLATION NO LONGER   First, prior to the DDP era, software operated in one computer, independently of any other computer. The software for different machines could be entirely different, developed by teams which did not talk to one another. The operating systems of the separate computer families of one manufacturer, such as DEC, could be entirely different. Now they have to intercommunicate.

From now on no machine can be developed in isolation, at least not if its developers want to maximize their market. All computer and office-of-the-future products are candidates for interconnection to a diversity of other machines. A data-base management system will be needed to operate with distributed data bases. A minicomputer will be needed to be part of a network and to run programs from elsewhere on the network.

It is difficult enough to develop software for one machine. To develop it as though all machines were one big family would be impossible. Too tight a coupling of machines would severely inhibit the development of new ideas in computer architecture. Therefore what is needed is a precise definition of interfaces and interface machine. The interfaces necessarily become complex if most of the features listed in Chapters 30 and 31 are to be included. What is needed is rigid adherence to these interfaces, but beyond that complete freedom for the creation of new ideas and architectures.

The ISO seven layers are an attempt to create the requisite interface standards. Other standards are needed in addition to these to permit program transfer between machines, freedom in distributing data bases, interconnection of office administration products using noncoded data (such as digital facsimile), and other types of interconnection. As networks like ACS, Prestel, and SBS develop, these will probably create their own standards as well.

The standards must be manufacturer-independent and truly international, although in some cases they might be created by one large manufacturer or country. As the international standards for DDP grow, *no* manufacturer or country is large enough to ignore them. To do so would damage it financially.

The creation of the requisite standards is exceedingly complex. All organizations in computing, telecommunications, and office products will benefit in the long run by supporting, encouraging, and contributing to the emerging standards, and above all by using them.

CONNECTION AT DIFFERENT LAYERS

Because of complexity and the unpredictable growth of new ideas, it is desirable that machines be interconnected at several levels, as discussed earlier. Simple Layer 2 interconnection can be used employing HDLC or related link control procedures. Layer 3 interconnection can be used to a packet-switching or other form of network. Layer 4 end-to-end transmission control can provide transport service access to fundamentally different types of networks. Layer 6 interconnection can occur between machines with no resemblance but which employ compatible presentation services.

SPLIT BETWEEN MACHINES

Because of the complexity, it is desirable to split functions so that they are done in different machines. This would not have been desirable before the mid-1970's, when small machines dropped in cost so much. The low cost of microcomputers and chips makes it desirable now. It is one form of distributed processing—the distribution of function between channel-connected machines. Done with appropriate configurations, it can lessen the complex entanglements between machines (as discussed in Chapter 11) and greatly increase functional availability.

The network management in most systems should be removed from the computer which runs the application code. The application processor should have a standard to the network machine. For high availability there should be more than one network machine and more than one application processor.

Similarly there is a strong argument for having a separate back-end processor which manages the data base or files. The application processor does not necessarily know whether data bases or files are in use. It sends across its channel commands which relate to *logical* records. The back-end machine derives these. Again, for high availability there may be two back-end machines. A configuration with duplicate processors is illustrated in Fig. 34.1.

The application processor gives input/output commands and references to

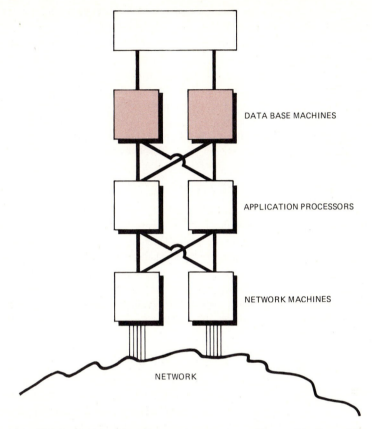

Figure 34.1 Separate data-base and network machines, with all machines
duplexed for high availability.

files or logical records. It ought to do this without network considerations. It
should not need to know where the data reside. The interface between the application processor and an attached data-base machine ought to be the same as the interface between the application processor and a machine which accesses the data via a
network. This remote/local independence is illustrated in Fig. 34.2.

The future of data processing lies to a large extent with on-line, network,
data-base machines which must serve their end users without disruptive failures.
Usage of such systems will often grow unpredictably. To accommodate both the unpredictable growth and the need for dependability, a building-block approach to
system design is needed. Figure 34.3 illustrates one such architecture. Additional
processors can be added to one system without disrupting any existing programs or
data. The input/output controllers, storage controllers, and network controllers
can be duplicated for reliability. When an application program reads or writes data,

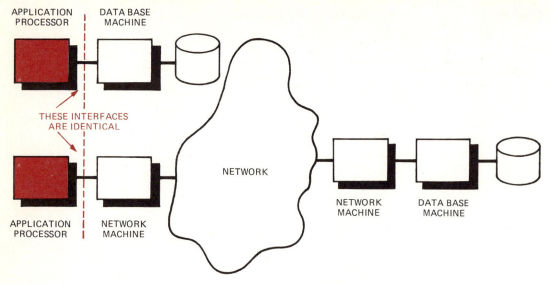

Figure 34.2 Remote/Local Data Base Independence.

it does not know where those data reside. It does not know whether they are stored with file management or data-base management. Automatic alternate routing is used to bypass any network failures.

A disk may fail, so when access to data needs high availability, duplicate copies must be stored on two separate disks. In this case the storage control software must have carefully designed recovery procedures. When the failed disk is restored, its data must be quickly brought to the level of update of that on the non-failed disk. This must be done while transactions are still being processed, and preservation of integrity is tricky because another failure could occur in the middle of the recovery process.

Suppose that the entire system in Fig. 34.4 became unavailable because of a power failure, strike, or some catastrophe. Other systems on the network would not be able to access the data. Lack of access is sometimes caused by failure of local loop telephone cables. A bulldozer might have torn up the cable. Such failures will be much less common than disk failures and *may* be discounted in system planning if individual sites have duplicated data, as in Fig. 34.4. The principles of recovery of mirrored volumes necessary for the Fig. 34.4 configuration can be extended to data duplicated at different sites. This is certainly desirable in some systems, and the protocols needed for control of integrity when remote duplicate data are maintained in a synchronized fashion need to become part of distributed processing software.

The configurations in Figs. 34.3 and 34.4 are supported by the products of Tandem Computers, Inc. It is significant that clearly planned and relatively simple software for no-fail, on-line, network systems came first from new organizations that did not have the millstone of old software around their necks.

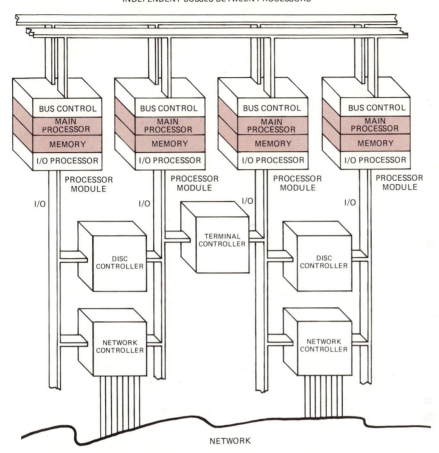

INDEPENDENT BUSSES BETWEEN PROCESSORS

Figure 34.3 The architecture of the future? Designed for non-stop network-data-base processing. All critical components are duplicated. There is automatic alternate routing through the network. The processing power can be upgraded a module at a time. The application programs do not know whether their input/output requests relate to local or distant units. This architecture is used by Tandem Computers, Inc.

SEPARATE TRANSPORT NETWORK

We can contrast systems in which transport network software is in the host computers which use the network, and systems in which the transport network is separate from the host computers. The transport network ought to be a separate entity, separately managed.

The latter is desirable for several reasons:

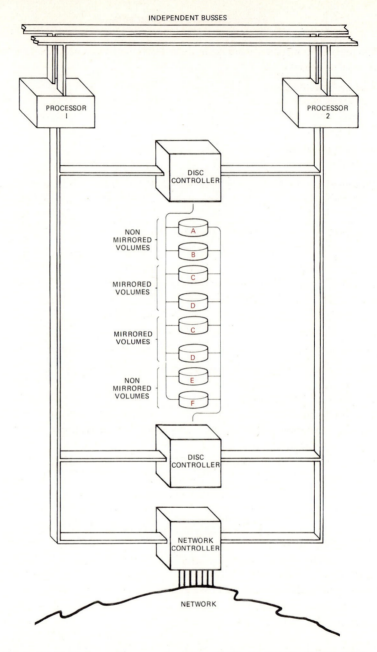

Figure 34.4 Data needing non-stop accessibility needs to be duplicated on two disks with separate controllers and access paths. Data C and D above is duplicated (mirrored). Data A, B, E, and F is not. Carefully designed recovery software is needed to restore a failed copy from the non-failed copy, while transactions are still being processed. Such configurations are used by the Tandem Computers architecture shown in Fig. 34.3.

- The network controllers which form the network entity can be small machines, small enough to be economical on small networks.

- When a host computer crashes, it does not disable the network. Often the large host computers which control a network are the least reliable part of the network. The network should be designed to be resilient and to remain usable when multiple machines fail.

- The common network should have a clean, simple structure. It should present a simple interface to its using machines.

- The interface to the using machines should be standard, preferably the ISO Layer 3 (or possibly Layer 4 in the future) standard, so that *machines of all manufacturers* can employ it.

- The network should be used not only for computing but for mail and other office automation applications.

- Perhaps most important, the network should be capable of connecting any machine to any other, in a fully flexible fashion. This is usually not the case when a host computer is responsible for setting up the logical paths through the network.

- The network should be adaptable so that it can assume any topology and serve any pattern of usage, without concern in the using machines.

- The network should have its own flexible alternate routing to bypass failed links or nodes. This should be independent of the using machines.

In Chapter 11 we contrasted a "bowl of spaghetti" image of DDP with an image of separate machines, separately developed, plugging with a standard plug into a common communication system. The transport mechanisms should not be entangled like spaghetti in the host software.

CHIPS AND MICROCODE

Another major change in software engineering relates to today's chips and microcode. Every year we have the capability to put more and more logic on a silicon chip. This dramatically changes the mix of what ought to be in hardware and software. It is unnecessarily expensive in machine cycles to put highly repetitive functions, such as scanning an incoming bit stream for an end-of-frame flag or secondary key searches, into software. We are beginning to find operating systems and data-base management systems built into the machine in microcode and chips [1].

Candidates for chip design are functions with the following characteristics:

- There is a mass market for them. The economics favor complex chips with very large sales.

- The function is well understood and not likely to be changed. Software can be changed; chips are very expensive to redesign.

- The function is executed repetitively, so that software would consume many processor cycles.

Clearly, the standardized interface mechanisms for distributed processing are candidates for chip design. There are chips which execute HDLC, X.25, encryption, and data compaction. More complex functions of DDP architectures will be built into chips. Eventually, perhaps, there will be a standard interface between application processors and DDP architecture machines which carry out all seven ISO layers.

OFFICE AUTOMATION SOFTWARE   One of the largest areas of sales for computers and distributed processing will be for the office-of-the-future uses described in Chapter 4. Fortunately, most of these applications are suitable to offices everywhere and do not need application programs unique to a specific department. Vendors can create application software with parameters that enable it to be tailored to a particular user without special programming for that user.

A major and lucrative thrust of software development is not these office-of-the-future uses.

APPLICATION BACKLOG   The application load in corporations and government is likely to continue to grow rapidly. The demand for applications grows as users become more aware of what computers could do to assist them and as machines drop in cost. Many corporations have a larger application backlog now than five years ago, in spite of working the data-processing departments hard for the last five years. A typical corporation has a three- or four-year backlog of applications identified as economical but not yet implemented.

As machines drop in cost, programmer productivity will become more and more important. There will be increasing numbers of machines, each capable of executing greater numbers of instructions per second, but only a limited supply of programmers. At the time of writing the millions of instructions per second (MIPS) of large mainframe machines *on order* from IBM is four times greater than the total number of millions of instructions per second *delivered* by IBM in its history. This figure says nothing about minicomputers and the very high sales of IBM's 4300 series and other small machines. Spokesmen for the minicomputer industry say that far more minicomputer MIPS will be delivered than mainframe MIPS during the next three years. Where are all the programmers going to come from?

To take advantage of the proliferating machines it is essential that *much* higher levels of productivity be achieved in application development.

APPLICATION DEVELOPMENT PRODUCTIVITY   Five years from the time of writing the number of MIPS installed per year in the United States, of machines with a mainframe instruction set, will be one hundred times greater than at present. This figure takes into account the increase in speed of machines as well as the increased sales volume due to decreasing cost and increasing awareness. If they were programmed with to-day's programmer productivity, this would require more than 30 million program-mers in the United States alone. Before long the entire population would need to be programmers if programming productivity did not change. It is not a small change needed, such as that resulting from structured techniques, but drastically new methods of creating what end users need.

This is perhaps the most fundamental problem that the computer industry must solve in the next ten years. If it is not solved, it will not only cause the growth of computing to be far less than its potential; it may put large computer manufac-turers out of business, because the cost of computers will inevitably fall rapidly. The application growth without increased productivity would not be enough to maintain the manufacturers' revenue. On the other hand the manufacturers can af-ford to use more software and more machine cycles to speed up application development.

There are many approaches to this problem. One of the most powerful is to provide end-user facilities which enable users (or analysts who work with them) to create their own information and transaction processing from existing data bases. In this view, data-base user languages become vitally important [2]. Most end-user dialogues will run in machines at the user's location. They may employ data at that location or elsewhere. Data will be distributed for the reasons discussed in Part IV.

In the user modules the emphasis should be mainly on generating information or applications without programming. The end-user interface should be as friendly and easy to use as possible. The user modules should have standard means of ac-cessing data in either local or remote data bases. The user module should perceive no difference (except access time) between local and distant data bases.

FUTURE DP PATTERN   A picture thus emerges of future data processing.

There are data-base systems, often data-base machines, in different parts of a corporation, plugged into a corporate data net-work. The network is fully flexible and accessible from all locations. It may or may not use a public switched data network. User machines can plug into the network, can access the data, and can communicate with one another. Many of them com-bine data processing and office administration functions.

The primary concern of software design for the end-user machines is to allow the users *to obtain the information they need for themselves,* preferably without programming. For this they have high-level data-base languages and dialogue struc-tures for information retrieval. The end users can create and maintain their own files, often deriving them from existing data bases. Most of the data in the systems are entered by end users. End-user managers or analysts can create, on-line, the screen panels or dialogues which other end users employ to enter or process data. They no longer design a purchase requisition *form;* they design a purchase requisi-tion *panel for a screen* with a dialogue for filling it in. The same screen is used for mail and messages, for handling employees' work queues, for a manager to place items on other persons' work queues, for work followup, project tracking, and office-of-the-future applications in general, using prepackaged software.

The aim of software development should be that most of the above can take place without necessarily employing professional application programmers. Languages of higher level than COBOL, FORTRAN, PL/I, and BASIC should be used, which end users can handle. Different types of users need different types of languages. Some use APL; some use simple data-base languages like NOMAD and QUERY-BY-EXAMPLE; some use more complex data-base languages; some use report generators; some use graphics dialogues; some use information retrieval dialogues like those of STAIRS or Viewdata.

Professional application programmers will still be needed for programming complex functions and elaborate applications such as financial modeling, simulation, and production scheduling. They will be needed to modify and maintain the existing application programs, until new methods make it cheaper to recreate these applications instead of to keep changing old programs.

SUMMARY OF OBJECTIVES OF DDP SOFTWARE

When we summarize all the objectives of DDP software, we have a formidable list. This is done in Box 34.1.

It is clear from this list that the computer industry has a long way to go yet in creating DDP software.

REFERENCES

1. The Microdata Reality system and the IBM System 38 were two of the first machines with operating systems and data-base management in microcode and hardware.

2. See the companion book to this, James Martin, *Software for Distributed Processing,* Prentice-Hall, Inc., Englewood Cliffs, N.J., 1981.

BOX 34.1 Objectives of distributed processing software

END USERS: Power to End Users

- Bring computing resources to the maximum number and diversity of end users.

Friendly User Interface

- Make the end-user facilities as psychologically powerful and easy to use as possible. Hide the complexities behind friendly end-user interfaces.

Diversity of Resources

- Enable end users to access a wide diversity of information and processing sources.

Diversity of Dialogues

- Provide end users with powerful dialogue and language facilities which enable them to obtain, understand, and process data from remote sources. Fundamentally different dialogues and languages will be needed for different types of users.

Maximum Application Development Productivity

- Provide resources which give the *maximum productivity of application development,* in many cases allowing users to develop their own requirements without programming in languages of the level of COBOL.

Good Cost-Performance Ratio

- Achieve a low cost/performance ratio, in the broadest sense of providing the maximum value to end users.

Location Independence

- Provide access to files, data bases, and processing power in such a way that the user does not necessarily know where they reside geographically or in system terms.

Configuration Independence

- Make usage of the system independent of system configuration.

Subset by Skill Level

- Subset the user dialogues and interfaces so that they are appropriate for users of different skill levels.

Help and Prompt Functions

- Provide the users with HELP functions, and prompt them when necessary.

continued

BOX 34.1 *continued*

Network Resource Directory

- Provide an easy-to-use directory of network resources (like a telephone directory Yellow Pages) so that certain users can find out what is available to them.

END-USER MECHANISMS

Cheap, Ubiquitous Terminals

- Provide cheap terminals, which may be derivatives of pocket calculators or television sets and cost little more than those. Give these cheap terminals access to resources everywhere by means of cheap, standard network connections.

Integrated Product Line

- Integrate office-of-the-future product lines with data-processing product lines. Office-of-the-future machines include word-processing facilities, devices for handling mail, intelligent copiers, voicegram devices, document storage and retrieval facilities, administrative office terminals, Viewdata-like services, graphics terminals, facsimile machines, security systems, displays for use in meetings and teleconferencing, video tape and video disk.

Human/Computer Synergy

- Use graphics and other media to combine human skills and perceptions with computer processing so as to achieve results that neither could achieve alone.

Standards for the Future

- Develop standards, protocols, logical units, and mechanisms that will be appropriate with future microelectronics, which will have a much higher chip density than today.

Increase in Distributed Function

- Employ the dropping cost of logic and storage to provide a major increase in distributed function, and recognize that this can change the fundamental nature of end-user mechanisms.

Diversity of Transmission Media

- Permit exploitation of a wide diversity of transmission media and network types.

Fast Response Times

- Achieve suitably fast response times (recognizing when a very fast response is needed and when it is not).

BOX 34.1 *continued*

Standard Access to Diverse Machines

- Mask the peculiarities and unique character of the end-user mechanisms from the application programmers so that they employ standard input/output commands, character sets, and display spaces.

Second-Level Building Blocks

- Permit the maximum diversity of terminals and mechanisms to be built with a small number of building blocks of hardware, microcode, and software.

PROGRAMS

Highest Development Productivity

- Provide the highest productivity of application development.

Conventional Program Commands

- Enable programs to use conventional macroinstructions such as GET, PUT, and CALL, as they would in a nondistributed environment, but now these commands can refer to remote programs, data, or resources.

Data Dictionaries

- Employ data dictionaries, which automatically generate the programmers' data descriptions, for the distributed data.

Virtual Terminals

- The programs should refer to *virtual* terminals and *virtual* display space, so that they can use multiple different terminals without being changed, and so that the terminals can be changed without the programs being changed.

Logical Records

- The programs should usually refer to logical records rather than real ones so that changes to data can be made without causing program rewriting (database technology).

Network Independence

- The programs should be entirely independent of the network or communications systems which are used and their mechanisms.

Portable Programs

- Make programs portable, as far as possible, from one network machine to another.

continued

BOX 34.1 *continued*

Facilities for Debugging

- Provide facilities for remote debugging of distributed programs, including, where necessary, the ability to transmit automatically a dump of a remote program.

Down-Line Loading

- Provide facilities for down-line loading programs into remote machines.

DISTRIBUTED ARCHITECTURE

Standard Formats, Protocols, and Interfaces

- Provide standard interfaces, message formats, and protocols which permit the maximum diversity of computer and user mechanisms to be interconnected, now and in the future.

Manufacturer-Independent Standards

- Create and conform to international, manufacturer-independent standards for the interfaces, message formats, and protocols, to permit worldwide interconnectability of different product lines, and hence maximize the market for new products.

ISO Layers

- Divide the architecture into the layered structure described by the International Standards Organization.

Separation of Layers

- Make each layer independent of the other layers so that different versions of the layers can be used without disrupting other layers.

Building-Block Approach

- Design a small number of building blocks (chip sets, microcode, and software modules) which can operate with the maximum diversity of network types, machines, and user services.

Option Subsets

- To avoid large overheads in the headers and protocol processing, design for optional subsets of the protocols and header fields, so that a layer can shrink almost to zero if its function is not used.

Standard Profiles

- Employ standard node and network profiles to control the choice of function subsets.

BOX 34.1 *continued*

Independent Box Architectures

- Make the communications function and protocols independent of the architecture of the using machines, as far as is practical, to permit maximum freedom and inventiveness in machine design.

Independent Communications Protocols

- Make the communications function and protocols independent of the user interfaces to permit maximum freedom and inventiveness in designing user facilities.

Hide the Complexity

- Hide the complexity under the covers to minimize the knowledge of the protocols and internal mechanisms that an operator, system programmer, manager, or user needs.

Easy Growth and Change

- Design the layers to make growth and change as easy as possible.

SESSION SERVICES

Rich Set of Services

- Provide a rich set of session services which user machines and processes can employ when they communicate.

Optional Selection of Services

- Make the session services optionally selectable, so that machines and processes can agree when they open a session which session services and service protocols they will use.

Distributed Intelligence

- Employ distributed intelligence in many ways to enhance the services given to end users or to lower their cost.

Standard Binding Procedure

- Provide a standard means of establishing sessions between diverse machines and user processes so that they can agree what session services they will employ, what resources they need, and what formats and protocols they will use to communicate.

Flow Control

- Perform flow control to prevent one user facility or machine from overloading another.

continued

BOX 34.1 *continued*

Pacing

- Send timing signals rapidly between remote machines so that they can control each other's timing (pacing) when necessary for efficient operation.

Command Interpretation

- Interpret commands from user programs or dialogues so that they employ the distributed resources as required.

Remote/Local Independence

- Provide remote/local independence so that facilities are employed by users or programs in the same way whether they are local or remote.

Standard Character Set Translation

- Provide the capability to translate from the standard character set used by the network to whatever character set is used by the local machines, and vice versa.

Editing

- Edit received character streams to lay out information attractively on reports, screens, or preprinted stationery.

Merge Transmitted and Fixed Data

- Merge variable data which are transmitted with fixed data or panels which are not transmitted, to create reports, forms, or displays.

Application-Independent Dialogue Structures

- Provide application-independent dialogue structures, often transmitting only the results of a dialogue, not its detailed to-and-fro operation.

Graphics

- Employ graphics characters or bit streams to create graphs and charts.

Standards Out of Diversity

- Map the functions of different types of user machines and processes in standard protocols, headers, and character sets.

Compaction

- Compress the messages sent so that they can be transmitted with a smaller number of bits, and expand them to their original form after transmission.

Encryption

- Encipher and decipher the messages sent, if necessary, in order to ensure transmission privacy.

BOX 34.1 *continued*

Virtual Display Space and Operation

• Enable application programs to be written for virtual terminals and virtual display space; provide mapping between the real and virtual facilities so that one program can be used with different types of facilities and new facilities can be introduced without forcing programs to have to be rewritten.

Data Entry

• Facilitate and control data entry by a terminal operator.

Data-Base Dialogues

• Provide dialogues which enable users to employ distant data bases, making inquiries, searching the data, generating reports, and, where desirable, updating and creating the data.

Billing

• Record all resource usage for billing purposes, allocate charges, and create bills.

Interarchitecture Conversion

• Provide conversion functions so that nodes with different processing architectures can be interconnected.

FILE AND DATA-BASE FACILITIES

Remote Data Appears Like Local

• Permit remote files and data bases to be used as though they were local. Application programs should be the same whether they use local or remote data.

Best Choice of Location

• Permit data to be stored at the most advantageous location geographically (recognizing that there are different arguments on different systems for centralization and decentralization of data).

Data Replication

• Permit data to be replicated at more than one location where this is advantageous, without causing data integrity problems.

Data Integrity

• Prevent integrity problems when multiple distributed processes update or read the same data.

continued

BOX 34.1 *continued*

Deadlock Avoidance

• Avoid rarely occurring deadlocks caused by procedures for locking data.

Clean Logical Structures

• Use simple, clean, logical data-base structures (relational, canonical third normal form) which are referred to in data dictionaries and directories, which can be used at multiple nodes.

Data Directory

• Employ a table or directory to locate and retrieve data automatically when a program or user dialogue refers to data not in its node.

High-Level Data-Base User Languages

• Permit the widespread use of high-level data-base user languages for retrieving data, formating reports, searching, and updating the data.

Separate Data Systems

• Permit separation of data for performance reasons with replication where necessary, e.g., separation of information systems and production systems.

Incompatible DBMS's

• Permit different and possibly incompatible file and data-base management systems in different machines to be interlinked.

Specialized Information Systems

• Permit the deployment of cheap, specialized, easy-to-use, functional information systems, free from the entanglements of large data-base complexity.

Local User Files

• Enable users to create their own local files or data bases for their own purposes, from the system files and data bases (which are tightly controlled).

COMMON DATA NETWORK

Separate Network Entity

• Regard the common network as an entity unto itself which many machines employ. It should be separately managed.

Standard Network Interface

• The common network should be designed with a standard interface into which many types of user machines (host computers, terminals, controllers, office-of-the-future machines) will plug.

BOX 34.1 *continued*

Flexibility and Reliability

- The common network should be extremely flexible and reliable, with alternate paths and a routing technique which automatically bypasses areas of failure and congestion.

Expandability

- The common network should have no limits (within reason) to its upward growth.

International Network Standards

- The common network should use international standards where possible, which permit direct interconnection to public networks.

User-Machine Independence

- The common network should be entirely independent of the user machines which plug into it.

Complexity Hidden

- Users, operators, systems programmers, and network administrators should need to know as little about the network mechanisms as possible. Its complexity should be hidden.

Control Signals

- Transmit brief control messages such as machine interrupts and timing signals very quickly through the network.

FIFO

- Ensure that the data on each logical circuit are delivered in the same sequence as that in which they are transmitted.

Transmission Billing

- Record network usage for billing purposes, and prepare bills.

Like Public Telephone Network

- The above characteristics all apply to the public telephone network, which serves as an excellent model of what a data network should be like.

TRANSPORT SUBSYSTEM

Diversity of Transmission Resources

- The transport subsystem may be designed to employ entirely different types of transmission facilities and networks, for example:

continued

BOX 34.1 *continued*

1. A common data network as described above.

2. A public packet-switching network (CCITT X.25)

3. A public circuit-switching data network (CCITT X.21)

4. The public telephone network

5. Leased lines, analog or digital

6. The telex network

7. Satellite channels

8. Conventional in-house wiring or an in-house network

9. Wideband in-house wiring

10. A wideband network (XTEN, CATV)

11. Computer channels

12. Channels, networks, satellites, etc., with demand-assigned multiple-access control

13. Mobile radio channels (e.g., packet radio)

Network Independence

- The interface to the transport subsystem should be independent of the type of network being used.

User-System Independence

- The external interface to the transmission subsystem should be independent of the machines and software connected to it.

End-to-End Integrity

- The transport subsystem should provide an end-to-end check on the correct delivery of messages.

Minimum Cost Routing

- The transport subsystem should select the lowest-cost means of transmission that is appropriate for the messages.

Local Area Addressing

- Local area networks may have their own type of transmission and their own addressing scheme, different from the form of addressing elsewhere. The transport subsystem must provide a boundary function to connect such local networks to the main transport facilities.

Connection for Dumb Terminals

- Old machines, cheap machines, and dumb terminals will use a different

BOX 34.1 *continued*

transmission protocol from the main transport facilities. The transmission subsystem should provide a conversion function for connecting these to the main
networks.

Transmission between Incompatible Machines

- The above facility should allow transmission between incompatible terminals
  and machines.

Priorities

- The transport subsystem should interleave transmissions of different priorities,
  for example, real-time control or data signals (delivered in a fraction of a second), interactive dialogue messages (delivered with the next highest priority),
  batch traffic (no urgency), and mail (can be saved for later delivery when there
  is capacity free).

Intermix Diverse Traffic

- The transport subsystem (using priorities) should be able to intermix traffic of
  quite different characteristics—real-time, control signals, process control,
  dialogues, batch, mail, facsimile, intermittent and continuous signals, and
  possibly speech.

DEPENDABILITY

Disruption-Free Service

- Give a very low probability of disruptions in the function of the system as
  perceived by the end users.

Alternate Routing

- Provide alternate paths which bypass network failures.

No-Fail Architectures

- Where desirable, provide no-fail computer architectures (such as that provided
  by Tandem Computers, Inc.)

Replicated Data

- Where desirable, duplicate critical data as a protection against storage-unit access failure. When this is done, provide safeguards against loss of integrity
  which can otherwise occur in duplicated data.

Recovery at the Lowest Layer

- Recover autonomously from failures at the lowest layer possible in a layered
  architecture (without higher layers being aware of the problem). Where

continued

BOX 34.1 *continued*

recovery is not possible at the layer responsible for it, pass error and status information to an appropriate higher layer.

End-to-End Checking

- Provide end-to-end checks on recovery and data integrity.

Failsafe Design

- Operate in a failsafe fashion so that failures and recovery from failures do not result in damage to data.

Deadlock-Free Protocols

- Use proven protocols which avoid rarely occurring network and data-base deadlocks.

Avoid Scheduling Problems

- Configure the system so as to avoid scheduling problems as end-user acceptance grows, terminals proliferate, certain uses become fashionable, and volumes exceed expectations.

Design for Quick Growth

- Design so that the system can be quickly expanded as certain types of usage grow unpredictably.

Avoid Restrictive Structures

- Avoid sole reliance on access methods or system structures which will cause severe scheduling or performance problems as usage becomes greater than expected.

Remote Diagnostics and Testing

- Provide remote diagnostic and program testing capabilities to facilitate debugging in a distributed environment; make diagnostics automatic where possible.

SECURITY AND PRIVACY

Positive Identification

- Users must be positively identifiable by password, secret code, identification number, magnetic encoded card, voiceprint, hand geometry, or other means.

Authorization

- Authorization tables will be used to determine whether a user, machine, or program is authorized to access the requested machine, program, or data.

BOX 34.1 *continued*

Alarms

- The systems will have alarm mechanisms so that a security officer can be immediately alerted to any suspected security violations or attempted violations.

Closed User Groups

- Closed user groups will be established on a shared network so that only members of the group can intercommunicate.

Cryptography

- Transmission will be made secure, where necessary, by cryptography. Enciphered data may also be stored on the files. Cryptography key management then becomes a major function of the session services.

Automatic Monitoring

- Usage of the system will be automatically recorded where this is desirable for security or auditability; all violations of security procedures should be recorded.

Data Logging

- All changes made to critical data should be logged for auditing purposes.

Reconstructability

- Critical data must be reconstructable if accidentally destroyed. The log of changes which is recorded for auditing purposes should also be designed to facilitate reconstruction.

Locks

- Data will be locked at the field, record, subschema, and data-base levels where necessary.

Auditing Facilities

- Facilities needed by auditors for thorough system auditing will be built into the software; facilities will be auditable by auditors at remote locations.

Tamperproofing

- The security controls will be designed to be tamperproof; this is often best accomplished by designing them into hardware, not software.

Physical Security

- Physical security safeguards (physical locks, alarms, chip protection, radiation avoidance, etc.) will be used where needed.

continued

BOX 34.1   *continued*

PERFORMANCE

Centralization/Decentralization

- Permit whatever mix of centralization and decentralization gives a good cost/performance ratio.

Integrate Transmission Services

- Combine as many transmission services as possible into one common network (data of all types: mail, facsimile, voice, video, and possibly videoconferencing).

Control Mechanisms

- Use control mechanisms which permit remote printers and other devices to function at maximum speed.

Self-Optimized Routing

- Provide network routing strategies which are self-optimizing.

Efficient Local Subnets

- Permit efficient local subnetworks and subsystems to operate with high performance, without interference or entanglements from centralized systems or long-distance networks.

Modular Structure

- Design with efficient, local, modular subsystems rather than all-embracing, convoluted structures which multiply the interactions and hence the software path lengths.

Separate Secondary-Key Usage

- Separate elaborate secondary-key data usage from high-volume primary-key usage, putting these in separate machines so as to avoid severe scheduling problems.

Function Separation

- Separate the processing and data into distributed machines where necessary to achieve good response times and avoid scheduling problems.

Module Expansion

- Design so that if usage of certain functions expands greatly, modules can be added which will absorb the increase, rather than the increase playing havoc with overall system performance.

BOX 34.1 *continued*

Monitoring

- Automatically monitor the usage of the network and subsystems and provide statistics needed for assessing and anticipating demand and reconfiguring the systems.

Design Tools

- Provide tools which assist in designing appropriate configurations.

GROWTH, CHANGE, MIGRATION

International Standards

- Conform as fully as possible to international and industry standards to minimize the difficulty of connecting other machines and networks in the future.

Easy Growth

- Recognize that growth and change will be constant and make this as easy as possible.

Conversion Modules

- Provide standard conversion modules so that older-style terminals, link control procedures, networks, and teleprocessing computers can be connected to the networks and systems with new architectures.

Dynamic Reconfiguration

- Permit changes in system configuration and network structure to be made with easy-to-use operator commands at a terminal, thus permitting dynamic rebuilding of the system.

Separate Systems

- Permit separate small or specialized systems to be implemented and linked into a larger network later.

Separate Network Interlinks

- Permit networks that have been implemented by different departments or divisions of a corporation to be merged later.

Interconnection of Diverse Communications

- Permit diverse communications facilities to be interconnected.

continued

BOX 34.1 *continued*

Migration Path

• Provide a planned migration path so that existing installed systems can evolve into distributed and network systems while preserving existing application programs.

SIMPLICITY

Hide the Complexity

• Hide the complexities under the covers so that they are not (and need not) be visible to users, applications programmers, systems programmers, system configurators, or managers.

Simple Modules

• Construct with simple, local, modular subsystems, rather than all-embracing convoluted designs in which the interactions needed for control purposes become exceedingly complex.

Separate Common Network

• Use a clearly structured common network which is managed separately from the user machines which plug into it.

Standard Network Interface

• Provide a simple, standard, mass-produced interface between the user machines and the common network.

Interactive Reconfigurability

• Make the network and user subsystems dynamically reconfigurable, the configuration being done with an easy-to-use dialogue at operator terminals.

Growth from Simple Subnets

• Design the interfaces and protocols so that small simple subnetworks can be developed and later integrated.

Friendly Dialogues

• Pay great attention to the dialogues employed in using, operating, and configuring the system, so that these dialogues are as psychologically effective and friendly as possible.

35 STRATEGY AND MANAGEMENT FOR CORPORATE NETWORKS

The corporation of the future will be laced with networks which handle not only its data processing but also its mail, word processing, and office-of-the-future requirements. Large computers, minicomputers, microcomputers, and intelligent terminals are becoming interconnected in all manner of configurations.

Unfortunately, the technology of distributed networks is very complicated. It is easy to perceive the idea of networks, but very complicated to understand the technical subtleties. The subtleties can and must be hidden from the end user. The user perceives merely the dialogue or simple procedure that is provided for him. But that requires network architectures.

Network architectures specify protocols or sets of rules which are needed to interconnect computers. These protocols are highly complex because there must be precise cooperation between distant intelligent machines.

The dilemma for management is that, as we have discussed, *the various architectures are incompatible.*

A most important function of a corporate strategy for networks is to prevent the incompatibilities from doing serious harm.

The end users are clamoring for distributed processing. They have the minicomputer salesman beating at the door. DP management knows that the scattered minicomputers must be hooked together, because much of the data stored in one location will be needed in other locations. Sometimes they ignore the problem and hope that new software will emerge to tie the fragments together. They hear that ARPANET connected incompatible machines. They hear that new standards are emerging, such as HDLC and X.25, which surely everyone will conform to.

The new standards will help, but not completely and not quickly. There is no resemblance between the major architectures from manufacturers and X.25. Neither ARPANET nor the current standards solve the most important of the incompatibility problems: the mechanisms external to the transport subsystem. The best that can be hoped for is a clumsy bridge at the transport subsystem level, but many of the worst problems are in the higher-level layers of the architecture.

What should a DP manager do?

He might close his eyes and do nothing. In this case he may deny his organization the very considerable advantages of the new machines. The end users may rebel, as they are doing in many places, and get their own machines. Distributed processing is happening by default in many corporations, unplanned and uncontrolled.

He may allow a proliferation of incompatibility without counting the future cost.

He could select one manufacturer's distributed architecture and stick with it. There is much to be said for this if the product line in question is sufficiently diverse. The manufacturers with major distributed processing architectures have planned a "migration path" into the future in which many new products will conform to the architecture and can be installed with the minimum disruption to existing application programs. But the DP manager may fear being locked into one manufacturer.

He could insist that the computer network conform to the new standards, especially X.25, but this would lock out most of the products of those major manufacturers which are not compatible with X.25.

He may plan a judicious mixture of these approaches, deciding where compatibility is vital, where it can be dispensed with, and where it is possible to build a bridge between different incompatible systems.

Whatever course is taken, it should be planned, and planned at a corporation-wide level with an understanding of the future implications of the choice.

The financial implications of making the right choice are great. Some corporations appear to the author to be taking the wrong course. He has attempted to estimate the eventual cost of this. There can be little doubt that it will cost millions of dollars in some corporations, in abandoned approaches, redesign, and program rewriting. And this does not count the lost opportunities and inability to obtain information needed by management because of the incompatibility and nonconnectability of separate systems, minicomputers, intelligent terminals, office-of-the-future products, etc.

CORPORATE COMMUNICATIONS STRATEGY

A corporate strategy for communications should include more than merely the computer networks. It should include a consideration of electronic mail, the telephone network, and possibly teleconferencing facilities.

It is useful to consider a corporate telecommunications strategy in two parts. One part evaluates the raw communications capacity needed and decides how it should be obtained: High bandwidth trunks? Satellite channels? Corporate earth stations? Specialized carriers? Local wideband networks? The other part considers what architectures will be used for data and mail. It attempts to prevent the spread of incompatible machines and software and to capitalize on the advantages of higher-level interconnections wherever possible. The *higher-level* protocols of a computer manufacturer's network architecture ought to be applicable, regardless of the type of channels used for physical transmission.

While a computer manufacturer's architecture may permit its user to employ different types of physical channels, independently, this is not true of a common carrier's data network architecture. Here the user buys a package—the common carrier provides both the physical transmission links and the value-added capability that provides virtual calls, virtual circuits, and possibly ACS-like message storage, data entry functions, and other facilities.

The objectives of the corporate communications strategy ought to be:

1. To ensure the maximum interconnectability between machines.

2. To provide the communications resources the corporation needs at the minimum cost.

3. To ensure a maximal level of flexibility in making future interconnections.

The strategy and plans for the *networks* in a corporation have certain characteristics which differ from the strategy and plans for *data*. The data will exist independently of the technology to some extent. It is possible to design the *logical* data resources without knowing exactly what machines and software will exist. The logical data structures are intended to be a machine-independent foundation stone on which future application development is built.

In planning networks and the strategy for networks, we are very dependent both on the common carrier facilities and the machines and software which exist for networking. The strategy is strongly concerned with questions such as whether good hardware will exist for integrating voice and data transmission, and to what extent the networking software of one manufacturer will be compatible with that of another or compatible with international standards.

On the other hand, network structures are often easier to change than data structures. Many man-years of application programming may reside on top of data structures, making them expensive to change except within the degree of flexibility permitted by a data-base management system. The expense and time needed for changing data structures is often such that the change is never made. Old programs never die; they just hang around. And so do the data structures they use. A change may be possible from one network structure to another without major application reprogramming, although the system programming will usually be complex.

Today there is a high degree of incompatibility, as we have stressed. Many machines are not interconnectable. A network strategy has a major effect on the present and near future, whereas a data-base strategy has more effect on the long-range future.

We have indicated that machines are interconnectable at several layers.

Layer 2: The capability to transmit bits or characters between the machines using a common line-control procedure, e.g., start-stop line control, binary synchronous line control, or HDLC.

Layer 3: Protocols for connection to a common data network. The most important such protocol which is manufacturer-independent is the CCITT X.25 recommendation.

Layer 4: Protocols giving end-to-end control of the transmission through a network. The interface to a manufacturer's transmission subsystem.

Higher Layers: Protocols for session control, dialogue control, and control of processors.

Layer 2 compatibility exists between many machines. Most computers can transmit to other computers using start-stop or binary synchronous line control. Machines of different manufacturers can sometimes transmit using HDLC or IBM's SDLC.

Layer 3 compatibility exists between a smaller number of machines. A growing number of machines can use the CCITT X.25 protocol for sending packets to one another. Unfortunately, there are several incompatible implementations of X.25 designed for different, slightly incompatible, national networks.

Layer 4 end-to-end control of virtual connections exists *within* most manufacturers' product lines, but the machines of one manufacturer often cannot communicate at Layer 4 with the machines of another manufacturer. The transport subsystems of some of the major manufacturers are completely incompatible.

It is at the layers above the transport network that interconnection of machines is most useful, in order to set up sessions, use logical units, use remote files and intelligent terminal facilities, and so on. But it is here that the incompatibility problems are worst. There is almost no compatibility between the product lines of different manufacturers.

At the time of writing no other manufacturers can plug fully into IBM's SNA and achieve *higher-level* communication. The case is similar with Univac's DCA, Digital Equipment Corporation's DECNET, and the architectures of several other manufacturers.

ZONES OF
COMPATIBILITY Because of the incompatibility of different manufacturers' distributed architectures, a corporation could decide that it will standardize on one manufacturer. Some corporations have done this. For example, some have standardized on IBM's SNA. Some have selected DECNET.

It certainly simplifies matters to have one architecture for all machines. However, many organizations do not want to be totally committed to one manufacturer. Some fear the future inflexibility of locking themselves into one supplier. In this case it may be decided that there will be certain zones of chosen architectures.

Within these zones there will be compatibility at the higher layers. Between the zones traffic will have to be sent as Layer 2 transactions or messages, or at Layer 3 with X.25

A standard may be enforced for all other computers in the corporation, saying that they can only use X.25, and in such a way ensuring that they are interconnectable at Layer 3.

Figure 35.1 illustrates zones of different networking architectures. The machines shown interconnected in the first diagram in Fig. 35.1 might be IBM machines using IBM's SNA (Systems Network Architecture), or Univac machines using DCA (Distributed Communications Architecture). The machines in the second diagram use a different and incompatible architecture, possibly from one of the minicomputer vendors. The corporation in question has a networking standard saying that all machines must employ a version of X.25 which makes them interconnectable at Layer 3 via private or public packet-switching networks. Unfortunately, this rule would lock the organization out of manufacturer *A,* which has a good high-level architecture, so an exception is made for the zone in which manufacturer *A*'s machines are used (third diagram in Fig. 35.1). In addition, a number of low-level connections between machines are used, possibly using binary synchronous transmission (fourth diagram in Fig. 35.1).

Figures 10.2 and 10.3 indicated how different management patterns and different distributed system architectures may be used in a large, complexly structured corporation. Figure 35.2 repeats those figures, emphasizing the network architectures. The locations using the network architecture type 1 can intercommunicate at the higher-level layers. Network architecture type 1 machines can communicate with other machines only at Layer 2 (start-stop or binary synchronous links). The factory machines using network architecture type 3 are X.25 compatible and can interchange packets with other X.25 machines.

In the effect it has on data processing, there is not much difference between Layer 2 and Layer 3 communications. Both send transmission messages to one another. There is a substantial difference, however, between these layers and the higher layers which provide session services. This difference will become more important as more functions are built into the higher-layer software, such as distributed data-base functions, intelligent data-base dialogue functions, message switching, more valuable uses of distributed intelligence, auditing functions, cryptography, and in general the use of remote facilities as though they were not remote.

A Layer 2 machine can often use a packet-switching network almost as though it were a Layer 3 machine by means of an intelligent concentrator or *packet assembly/disassembly* (PAD) facility.

Figure 35.1 The network strategy identifies certain zones in which the machines must use high level network architectures. All machines except those connected with architecture A must be interconnectable at Layer 3 using X.25. Some plain binary synchronous connections are also used, especially for linking the architecture A machines to other machines.

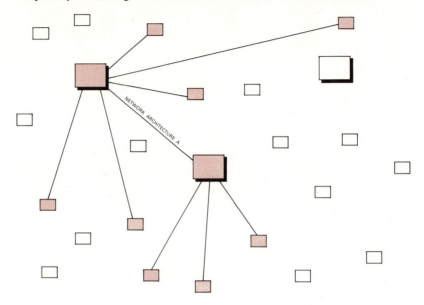

Figure 35.1a Machines from one manufacturer use high level communications with network architecture A.

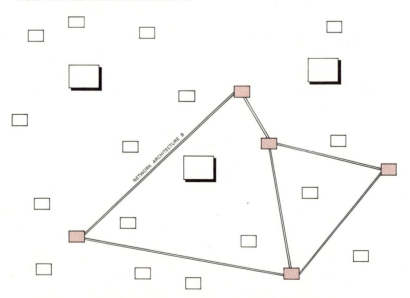

Figure 35.1b Machines from another manufacturer also use high level communications: network architecture B. But this is incompatible with network architecture A.

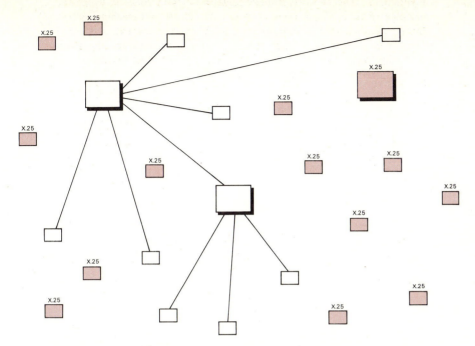

Figure 35.1c   A corporate standard says that all machines except those of network architecture A must be X.25 compatible so that Layer 3 communication can take place between them.

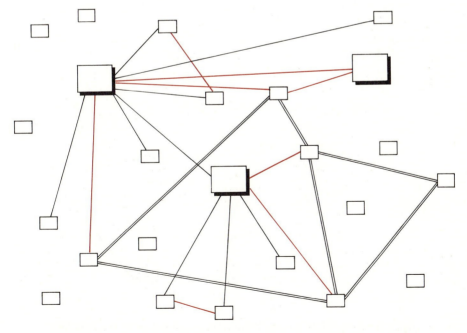

Figure 35.1d   In addition to the higher level communications, Layer 2 links interconnect some of the machines using, for example, binary synchronous transmission.

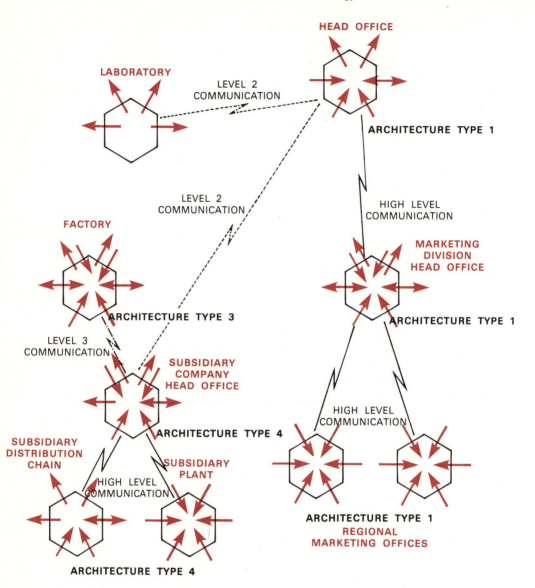

Figure 35.2   Levels of communication between different strategic zones.

PROLIFERATION OF NETWORKS

The major objective of a network strategy should be to have one network, or at least a tightly integrated set of networks, rather than a proliferation of incompatible networks and machines.

As we commented earlier, large corporations, especially in the United States, built up many separate data networks for different DP applications in the 1970's.

Having multiple data networks has the following disadvantages:

1. *Cost.* The separate networks often run roughly parallel to one another. To have multiple parallel networks is unnecessarily expensive. Each carries relatively little traffic and cannot take advantage of economies of scale (which are substantial).

2. *Incompatibility.* The different data networks often use different line-control procedures. They cannot be shared or interconnected without expensive conversion. In practice they are not shared. Each attaches to its own terminals and carries its own traffic.

3. *Inflexibility.* It would often be advantageous for a terminal at one location to be connected to different computers at different times, but they cannot; they can only use the network which is designed for them.

4. *Increased terminal costs.* Because each terminal cannot be connected to multiple computers, there must be more terminals. Different networks cannot share terminals. One U.S. automobile manufacturer has six incompatible data networks connected to its head office and six categories of terminals which cannot share networks.

5. *Availability.* Most networks designed for one system are tree-structured. If one leased link somewhere between a terminal and its host computer fails, the computer is inaccessible. There is no alternate routing. A network designed to serve multiple systems usually has alternate routing, and so this gives the user a higher availability.

6. *Response time.* A network serving one system might use lines which transmit at 4800 bits per second. A network serving a dozen such systems might use lines which transmit at 56,000 bits per second. With the faster lines the message would travel to its destination more quickly, giving a faster response time.

7. *Network management.* The administration of networks is complex and needs talents which are hard to find. With multiple networks the problems of network management are multiplied.

Many corporations with multiple data networks have attempted to replace them with a common network, but this has proved surprisingly expensive and difficult—so much so that the attempt has sometimes been abandoned.

INCOMPATIBILITIES WITH CARRIER ARCHITECTURE   The data network architecture of the common carrier is sometimes incompatible with that of a chosen computer manufacturer. IBM's SNA at the time of writing is entirely different from the X.25 networks of the world. An interlinking mechanism exists so that SNA facilities can use or be connected to X.25 facilities, but basically SNA and X.25 use fundamentally different forms of transport network.

Transport network incompatibilities are likely to be solved eventually, although they will create problems for some years. A more fundamental form of incompatibility exists external to the transport network. The higher-level functions of AT&T's ACS (Advanced Communications Service) are different from those of IBM's SNA, DEC's DECNET, and other manufacturers.

Both ACS and manufacturers' architectures have very useful features. Many corporations will want to use the features of both.

Features of ACS that are likely to remain particularly attractive in the future are:

- Its ubiquitous switching capability
- The low cost of obtaining connections to distant computers from a single, isolated terminal
- Distributed intelligence functions that a single, isolated terminal can use
- The interface to ACS will probably become a *de facto* standard accepted throughout the United States
- The message-switching and on-demand message delivery capability
- The network monitoring and management features

Features of computer manufacturers' architectures that are unlikely to be replicated by common carrier architectures are:

- Distributed storage and data-base control
- Pacing between remote machines to maximize machine utilization or speed
- Network directories which relate to resources within host machines
- End-to-end security features
- Establishment of complex sessions between computers
- Certain distributed intelligence dialogue features
- Interconnection between data-base management systems
- Remote use of higher-level data-base languages
- Interconnection of remote operating systems
- The creation of virtual computing and storage operations on a networkwide basis. For example, a programmer does not know where the data he uses reside or where a processing routine is executed; and end user does not know the location of data he displays or updates
- In general, complex forms of cooperation between machines or tight coupling between computers

Higher-level networking architectures are here to stay from both the computer and the telecommunications industry. Because of their different appeals a corporation will often want to use both. It might want to use both ACS and SNA, for example, although they are incompatible.

Future computers will be designed with telecommunications controllers which can employ both. They may be separate machines as illustrated in Fig. 35.3, one for public networks such as X.25 networks or ACS, one for private networks such as

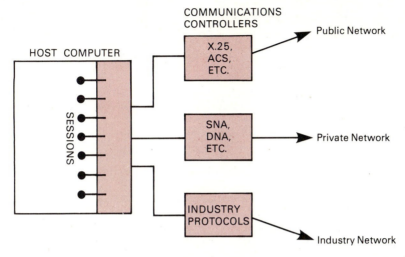

Figure 35.3 In future systems communications controllers for different transport network architectures may be connected to the same host computer.

IBM's SNA or DEC's DECNET, and one for specialized industry networks such as SWIFT (an interbank electronic funds transfer network) and SITA (a network interconnecting airline systems). The lower two controllers in Fig. 35.3 may themselves use X.25 and ACS in future systems.

Specialized industry networks will increasingly use X.25 and other standard protocols in the future. Many computers will require the functions of the top two communications controllers of Fig. 35.3. In some designs these two functions will reside in the same front-end machine.

ELEMENTS OF NETWORK STRATEGY

Figure 35.4 suggests steps in forming a corporate network strategy. Like Fig. 25.10, it is an expansion of the strategy diagram in Fig. 10.4.

In many corporations the mail, the telephone service, and the data networks fall under entirely different management. This made sense with earlier technology. Now the facilities for mail, data, telephone, and teleconferencing should be planned by one management on a corporationwide basis.

A common data network should be planned for all data transmission, including mail. The question whether or not telephone and data traffic should share the same trunks needs careful evaluation. If *public* data networks form the backbone of the data transmission facility, e.g., Bell's ACS or the X.25 packet networks, then the telephone facilities will be entirely separate. If leased data circuits are used, high-capacity trunks may carry both voice and data traffic. The SBS

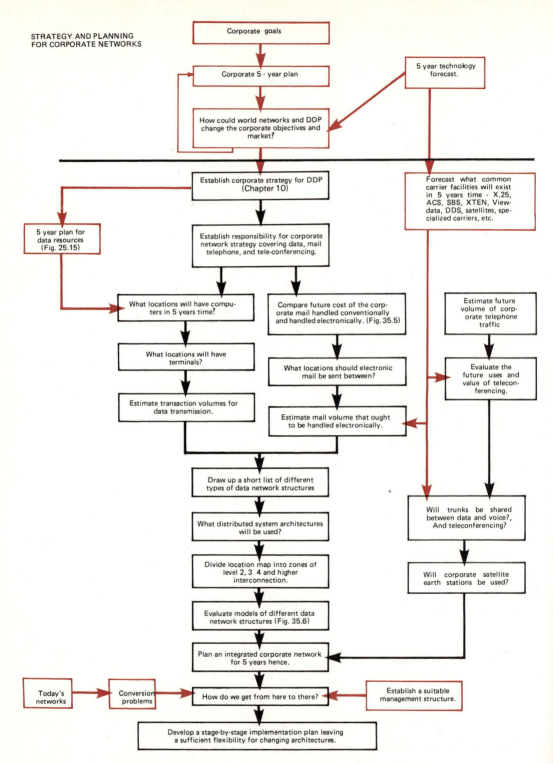

Figure 35.4 Strategy and planning for corporate networks.

facility (Satellite Business Systems, a subsidiary of IBM, Comsat, and Aetna) carries voice, data, image, and teleconferencing traffic in an integrated fashion, the speech and any other signals being digitized.

ELECTRONIC MAIL   The mail services of the world are steadily becoming more expensive, slower, and less reliable. The long delivery time and occasional loss of mail are becoming increasingly annoying to corporate users. At the same time the cost of sending mail electronically is plunging down. Electronic mail can be sent over the same network as computer data and may from the network point of view appear indistinguishable. If appropriately designed, the cost of electronic mail is already lower than conventional mail in many corporations. When a data network is designed for both mail and computer data, higher-bandwidth channels are used. This can give a faster response time for the computer data if an appropriate priority system is used.

Figure 35.5 plotted cost estimates made in a large U.S. corporation for their internal mail. It compares sending their mail manually and electronically. The cost projections assume no increase in mail volume but assume an inflation rate of 6% for postage and operating costs. The electronic mail would share the corporate data network. The operational costs include the following procedures:

- Sorting by geographical location
- Sorting by city
- Primary batching
- Secondary batching
- Weighing and adding postage
- Door-to-door mailroom operations
- Pickup and delivery
- Handling at field offices

Figure 35.5 was plotted from estimates in a top management communications strategy document. All corporations should include such an estimate in their network strategy.

**FASTER-THAN-MAIL
TRAFFIC**   The estimates behind Fig. 35.5 assume that the same mail as today will be sent, that it will be printed, and that most of it will originate from word-processing machines or computers. In fact, electronics will change the nature of mail and message sending for two reasons.

First, electronic mail is fast. It could be delivered in seconds if desirable. As we indicated in Chapter 4, when mail is this fast, people will use it in entirely dif-

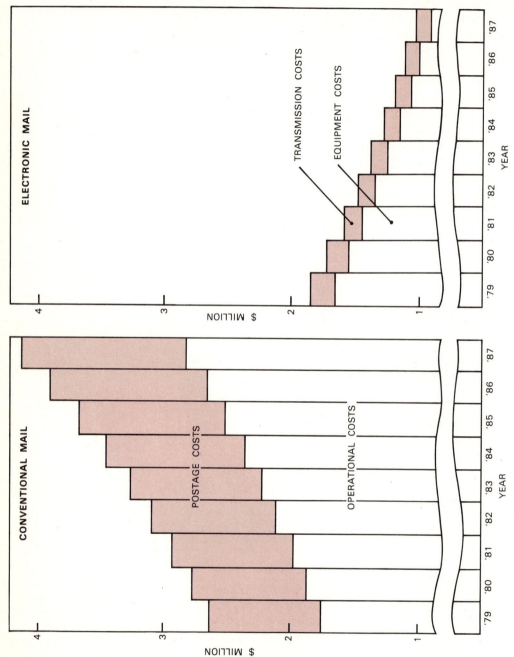

Figure 35.5 The estimated future costs of conventional internal mail versus electronic mail in a large U.S. corporation.

ferent ways. For some purposes it becomes equivalent to a telephone message. Three quarters of long distance business telephone calls in the United States fail to reach the person who was called. Thirty-two percent are not connected because of busy signals, no answers, and occasional failures [1]. Of the business calls which are completed, only 35% reach the called party [1]. Electronic systems can provide a means to send a fast one-way message which will be delivered despite busy conditions and be rerouted to the party at another location if necessary. Persons could inspect their message queue from many different locations. Sending an electronic message will be cheaper than the cost of a long distance telephone call.

Second, some messages need never be printed if sent electronically. They can be displayed on the office terminals. Many corporate memos can be filed in the system and displayed when needed. Acknowledgments to them can also be filed in the system.

Many individuals who use them have found electronic message-sending facilities very convenient. It is appealing to be able to use them from one's office terminal.

EXTERNAL MAIL   While it is difficult to place a dollar value on an improvement in people's ability to communicate, tangible figures *can* be quoted for the replacement of existing mail facilities, as in Fig. 35.5. Figure 35.5 relates to *internal* mail. Similar cost benefits can accrue from the automation of *external* mail. However, with intercorporate mail an agreement is needed between corporations as to how the traffic should be addressed, coded, and delivered. It is desirable that international standards for this should be created and widely accepted. One possibility is that intercorporate mail should be transmitted in the form of X.25 packets using the CCITT Alphabet No. 5 (U.S. ASCII code), with the first line of content being the machine address to which the receiving corporation's internal network should deliver the mail. Users would then give correspondents their machine address just as they might give them a telex number. This may happen with networks like Bell's ACS.

It should be noted that some powerful organizations are opposed to this form of electronic mail. The world's mail unions oppose it because it would put letter carriers out of work. The world's telex and cable authorities oppose it because it would undercut their market (it would murder their market if free competition existed).

Figure 35.5 related to alphanumeric traffic originated by word-processing machines and computers. There are a variety of forms of transmission sometimes described as electronic mail, which we listed in Box 4.4. These should be incorporated when appropriate.

TYPES OF DATA   There are many different mechanisms for building
NETWORKS   economical data networks. They include those listed in
                     Box 35.1.

**BOX 35.1   Some of the mechanisms that may
be evaluated when designing
data networks**

Polling on multidrop lines

Single multiplexors

Intelligent multiplexors

Concentrators

Concentrators with storage

Intelligent concentrators

Message switching

Circuit switching

Datagram packet switching

Virtual-circuit packet switching

Packet switching with distributed intelligence and storage (like ACS)

Communications satellite trunks

Communications satellites with time-division multiple access (TDMA)

Wideband circuits (DDS, CATV, XTEN)

Wideband circuits with time-division multiple access

The designer can employ leased lines with one, or combinations, of the above mechanisms. He can also employ public networks. There are fundamentally different types of public facilities:

- Switched telephone circuits
- Virtual calls and permanent virtual circuits on packet-switching services
- Satellite channels
- Telex
- TWX
- Wideband facilities like Xerox's planned XTEN service
- Fast-connect circuit-switched data networks in a few countries
- In the United States, Bell's Advanced Communications Service (ACS).

The designer has a rich array of choices, more in some countries than others. Which should he use?

A few of the above facilities may be incompatible with the software architecture that is chosen. IBM's SNA and most other such network architectures cannot use all of the above.

To evaluate the alternatives, approximate estimates should be made of the cost of different forms of network that can handle the anticipated traffic with appropriate response times. Using these estimates, a short list of network types can be drawn up and these may be modeled in detail. Some corporate network planning groups have created a dozen or more such models and optimized each to find out which network type is capable of giving the lowest cost. Figure 35.6 suggests a procedure for evaluating networks. Sometimes this requires the expertise of outside specialists.

Often the most potent way to minimize network cost is by making appropriate use of distributed processing and storage to lessen the amount of data transmitted, and to smooth out the peaks.

Network technology and tariffs are changing so fast that whatever gives the cheapest network structure today, the cheapest in five years time is likely to be a quite different type of structure. Therefore the network design and software should not be rigid. The network plan must be able to accommodate the rapid changes that are occurring.

COMBINED SPEECH AND DATA

Should the data and mail network be designed to be separate from the telephone network, or should speech and data be combined?

Some corporations digitize speech for transmission over long distances on their data network. With today's tariffs this is cheaper than conventional speech transmission only for long distances and *only* if some voice distortion is permissible. The words are recognizable, but the speaker may be less recognizable. This may be tolerated for internal corporate conversation, especially for international traffic where it can substantially reduce costs.

Speech is digitized with high quality on many telephone company trunks. This requires far more bits per second and is not economical for a telephone company *customer* to do over a leased data circuit. There is much talk about packetized voice, but equipment for this is not yet generally available.

What *is* economical in many countries is to lease high-capacity trunks and send both analog voice and data over them. Figure 35.7 illustrates this approach. It shows the corporate network of the British Steel Corporation. The trunks shown are supergroups with a bandwidth of 240 KHz, enough to carry 60 simultaneous telephone calls but costing substantially less than 60 telephone circuits. Using simple analog multiplexing equipment, British Steel derives from the trunks as many circuits as are necessary for voice and document transmission. This leaves a

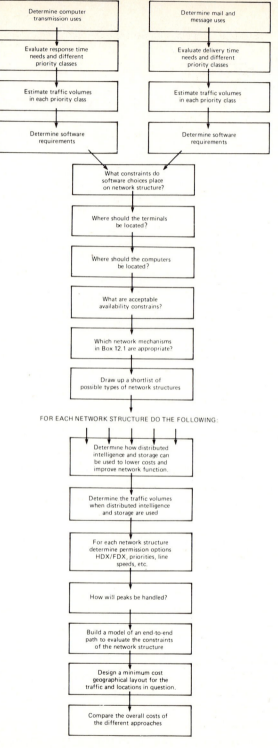

Figure 35.6 A suggested approach to network design. For network options in the future several years ahead need to be compared.

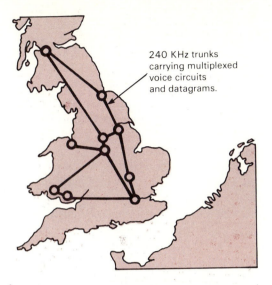

240 KHz trunks
carrying multiplexed
voice circuits
and datagrams.

Figure 35.7 The corporate network for British Steel. The links are 240 KHz supergroups (having the capacity of 60 voice channels). Most of this bandwidth is used for telephone traffic, with a little document transmission. 48 KHz is used to provide a corporate data network interconnecting host computers. Distant terminals are attached via concentrators. The host computer uses front-end protocol converters which emulate local terminals. The network has permitted specialization in the use of computer centers.

substantial bandwidth for data transmission: 48 KHz. A computer network using a simple form of packet switching (datagrams [2]) employs this bandwidth, interlinking computers. Distant terminals are connected to the network via concentrators.

Many corporations can save money by combining voice and data traffic in this fashion. In the United States the wideband circuits in question are sometimes obtained from the communications satellite or specialized common carriers.

IDLE CAPACITY   Links designed for *real-time* traffic alone always have idle capacity. Requests for their usage occur at random, and if the links are too heavily utilized, there will be large queues, long delays, or many busy signals. Queuing theory and probability calculations are used to determine how much idle capacity is needed to provide a given grade of service [3].

Telephone traffic has to be transmitted in *real-time,* i.e., when a person speaks his speech must be transmitted almost immediately. Idle capacity must be available for immediate use.

The transmission capacity must be designed for *peak* telephone traffic. The traffic during the peak hour of the day is several times higher than the average traffic. The peak hour of the peak day is substantially higher than that of the average day. The unshaded part of Fig. 30.5 represented idle capacity.

The most efficient way to utilize communication channels is to organize them so that real-time and non-real-time traffic can be intermixed and so that real-time traffic has absolute priority over non-real-time traffic. Non-real-time traffic should never delay the real-time traffic for more than a small fraction of a second, say, 50 milliseconds. Most corporate telephone networks do not carry interruptible non-real-time traffic, and consequently 75% to 85% of their total daily capacity is unused. With appropriate control mechanisms the mail or other non-real-time traffic could be sent over the telephone tie-line circuits with no increase in circuit capacity. The average corporate telephone (and sometimes data) network has a remarkably large capacity for absorbing such traffic. Even if a sophisticated mechanism is not employed, the mail can be sent over the telephone circuits at night or at off-peak hours.

FORECAST OF CARRIER FACILITIES   In attempting to make the best decisions about corporate networks it is desirable to forecast what new facilities will become available from the common carriers and telephone administrations. An attempt can be made to do this for several years ahead because, as we commented earlier, there is a long time between requesting and obtaining government permission and a substantial deployment of the service.

The new facilities will be different in different parts of the world. A knowledge of worldwide facilities is necessary when making plans for a worldwide corporation. In the United States there is a diversity of new plans by carriers (and would-be carriers) for new networks.

In forming a corporate strategy it would be desirable to check the latest plans for the Bell DDS network, the SBS satellite facilities, other satellite carriers, Tymnet, GTE-Telenet and other value-added carriers, GT&E's plans, Xerox's plans for its wideband XTEN network, ITT's plans, the plans of the specialized carriers, Bell's ACS service (most important), and so on. In stark contrast many countries have no plans other than the plain old telephone network. Most European countries are expanding a switching data network, usually conforming to the CCITT X.25 and related recommendations. Linking European countries is the Euronet X.25 network.

Worldwide, the various national X.25 networks are becoming interlinked. A node of an American or European X.25 network exists in several countries which do not have a data network of their own. Telex is still growing worldwide, and the international record carriers have various plans, notably the Japanese Venus network.

Further discussion of these is beyond the scope of this book and is found in the author's other books and reports.

PLANNED GOAL   In addition to data communications, mail and messages, and telephone traffic, other forms of communication will grow in popularity. Chapter 4 discussed video transmission, freeze-frame video, facsimile, and teleconferencing. SBS, the communications satellite subsidiary of IBM, Comsat, and Aetna, regards video conferencing as a future market, and Xerox stated in its FCC filing for its XTEN that much of its traffic would be image transmission for documents, projector foils, and video conferences.

A number of corporations use videoconferencing profitably even with the high cost of TV links. As the cost drops, and the links become those used for other purposes, videoconferencing and phone conversation with diagrams and document images will appear more attractive.

Such communication will have two main justifications. First, there is a cost justification. It replaces the cost of physical travel and the time executives spend in travel. Many corporations spend a large amount on airfares, some of it avoidable with better telecommunications. Dow Chemical has used a TV link for several years between its head office in Midland, Michigan, and its manufacturing division in Houston, Texas. Prior to using it, airfares between these two locations exceeded $1 million a year. An executive traveling between the two locations spent a minimum of 15 hours traveling time. This was too valuable to lose, and in addition most executives experienced much wear and tear from the trips [4].

Second, there are some communications that could otherwise take place only by telephone, and telephone is inadequate. Citibank uses video conferencing for certain critical financial decisions for this reason. The decisions can be made more satisfactorily, and this pays for the link. There would be much more communication between locations if they were linked for conversations or meetings with pictures. But it is difficult to estimate how much more or to put a figure on it. Again, you cannot tangibly justify the value of most business communications.

The office of the future will contain many devices which use telecommunications (Fig. 4.2). The strategy should estimate what channels will be used in five years' time.

Given a forecast of the networks needed in the future, the strategy then needs to ask, How do we get from here to there?

It is usually desirable to plan a succession of steps towards the networks of the future rather than one great leap forward. Data transmission may be moved from binary synchronous to HDLC, SDLC, etc. Computerized PBX's (private branch telephone exchanges) may be installed. Use of XTEN or SBS circuits may be introduced on a small scale to begin with. Experience may be gained with computer networking.

In some cases the conversion from existing networks is slow and expensive because software has to be modified, dialogues have to be changed, and that may mean rewriting application code. Sometimes bridges between the existing facilities and the new networks must be planned.

Working towards a planned goal will (as with data planning) in the long run be greatly more beneficial than *ad hoc* installation of new machine and facilities. That goal will probably look very different if future technology is considered rather than today's technology.

REFERENCES

1. Harry Newton, "Communications Lines," *Business Communications Review,* September 1976.

2. "Datagrams," Chapter 7 of James Martin, *Distributed Processing Network Mechanisms, Standards and Recovery,* Technical Report 5, Savant Research Studies, Carnforth, England, 1979.

3. Queuing and grade of service calculations are described in James Martin, *Systems Analysis for Data Transmission,* Prentice-Hall, Inc., Englewood Cliffs, N.J., 1973.

4. Charles E. Lathay, *Telecommunications Substitution for Travel: An Energy Conservation Potential,* Washington, D.C., Office of Telecommunications Policy, 1975.

PART **VI**   SECURITY AND AUDITABILITY

36 SECURITY AND PRIVACY

In spite of all their friends could say,
On a winter's morn, on a stormy day,
In a sieve they went to sea.
                    —Edward Lear

Security and privacy are important because many people in many places have access to a distributed system. The information stored in some of the distributed machines may be of great value to a corporation. It must not be lost, stolen, or damaged. It is important to protect the data and programs from hardware and software failures, from catastrophies, and from criminals, vandals, incompetents, and people who would misuse it.

A network is often shared by users for whom security is of little or no importance and other users for whom it is vital. It may be shared by users who are highly responsible with urgent business and others who are irresponsible and likely to try anything.

Security refers to *the protection of resources from damage and the protection of data against accidental or intentional disclosure to unauthorized persons or unauthorized modifications or destruction.*

Privacy refers to *the rights of individuals and organizations to determine for themselves when, how, and to what extent information about them is to be transmitted to others.*

Although the technology of privacy is closely related to that of security, privacy is an issue which goes far beyond computer centers and networks. To a large extent it is a problem of society. To preserve the privacy of data about individuals, solutions are needed beyond technical solutions. Future society, dependent on a massive use of networks and data banks, will need new legal and social controls if the degree of privacy of personal information that is cherished today is to be maintained.

Data can be locked up in computers as securely as they can be locked up in a bank vault. Nevertheless, the data on many systems cannot be regarded as being highly secure because insufficient attention has been paid to the design or implementation of the security procedures.

Security is a highly complex subject because there are so many different aspects to it. A systems analyst responsible for the design of security needs to be familiar with all features of the system because the system can be attacked or security breached in highly diverse ways. Sometimes a great amount of effort is put into one aspect of security and other aspects are neglected.

If a moat is seen as the way to make a castle secure, a great amount of security engineering could be applied to the moat. It could be very wide, and full of hungry piranha fish, and could have a fiercely guarded drawbridge. However, this alone would not make the castle secure. A determined intruder could tunnel under the moat. A security designer sometimes becomes so involved with one aspect of security design that he fails to see other ways of breaking into the system. It takes much knowledge and ingenuity to see all the possible ways.

TWELVE ESSENTIALS   Box 36.1 lists twelve essentials of distributed system security:

1 . The users of a network must be positively *identifiable* before they use it.

2. The systems and possibly also the network management must be able to check that their actions are *authorized*.

3. Their actions should be *monitored* so that if they do something wrong, they are likely to be found out.

4. Data, hardware, and software should be *protected* from fire, theft, or other forms of destruction.

5. They should be *locked* from unauthorized use.

6. The data should be *reconstructible* because, however good the precautions, accidents sometimes happen.

7. The data should be *auditable*. Failure to audit computer systems adequately has permitted some of the world's largest crimes.

8. The network and systems should be *tamperproof*. Ingenious programmers should not be able to bypass the control.

9. Transmission should be *failsafe* so that when errors or failures occur messages are not lost, double-processed, or unrecoverably garbled.

10. Transmissions should be *private* with some being protected from eavesdropping and tampering by cryptography.

BOX 36.1   The essence of network security

System users should be

- IDENTIFIABLE

Their actions should be

- AUTHORIZED

- MONITORED

Data, hardware and software should be

- PROTECTED

- LOCKED

Data should be

- RECONSTRUCTIBLE

- TAMPERPROOF

Transmission should be

- FAILSAFE

- PRIVATE

Vital computer centers should be

- CATASTROPHEPROOF

- REPLICATED

11. Computer centers should as far as possible be *catastropheproof.*

12. The system should not depend on one exceptionally vital center because it might be destroyed by fire, bombs, etc. Such a computer center should be *replicated.* Many corporations have recently planned a second computer center.

LAYERS OF PROTECTION
The nucleus of security control lies in the technical design of the network and computer systems. Without tight controls in the hardware and software, no other precautions can make the system secure.

However, design of tightly controlled systems is not enough by itself. Several types of protection are needed. Security can be represented by another layer diagram, as shown in Fig. 36.1. The layer of technical controls is surrounded by that of physical security. This refers to locks on the doors, guards, alarms, and other means of preventing unauthorized access, fire precautions, protection of

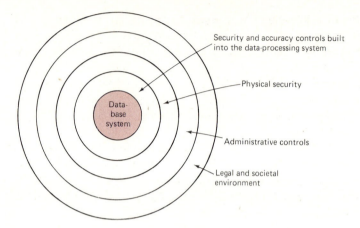

Figure 36.1   Four layers of control needed for data-base security and privacy.

stored data files, and so forth. It is not enough to have good hardware and software if disks can be stolen or the tape library destroyed by fire.

The next layer is that of administrative controls to ensure that the system is used correctly. The programmers and data-processing staff must be controlled so that they do not misuse the system. Controlled computer-room and program-testing procedures must be enforced. The administrative controls extend beyond the data-processing section to the user departments, scattered far across the network, the auditors, and general management.

The layers in Fig. 36.1 are not entirely separate. Physical security is not irrelevant when designing system techniques. The question of physical security affects what transmission and system safeguards are used. The administrative procedures are very much related to the system design, especially with a real-time or terminal-based system. The auditors need to be involved in the system design, and the views of general management concerning security very much affect the system design.

The outermost layer of Fig. 36.1 is by far the most problematical. When the network revolution has run its course, society will be very different. Many controls will no doubt have evolved, seeking to maximize the benefits and minimize the dangers of a technology of which George Orwell never dreamed. A legal framework is beginning to emerge in some countries which will relate to computers and networks.

TYPES OF SECURITY EXPOSURE   There is a wide diversity of different types of security exposure, most of them relating to the computer center, independent of networks [1]. Catastrophes such as major embezzlements have resulted in dramatic headlines, but by far the most common cause of computer calamities is human carelessness and accidents. One company reported "a $2.8 million deficiency" caused by an error in cutover. Usually failures are less spectacular and more frequent.

Distributed systems, if they are poorly designed or loosely managed, could increase the probability of accidents through carelessness. Data, instead of residing in one highly secure center, may be distributed among locations with less protection. The greater complexity of a distributed system has sometimes increased the frequency of problems. Control, instead of residing in one location with one management, may be scattered.

A major exposure introduced by networks is the ease with which persons and machines can gain access to a computer center. It is necessary to prevent unauthorized access and unauthorized communication between machines.

Another exposure is that data transmitted may be seen by unauthorized persons, recorded, diverted, or even modified by tampering with the lines or switching nodes.

THREE-LEVEL ATTACK   Each security exposure must be attacked in three ways:

1. *Minimize the probability of it happening at all.* A major part of fire precautions should be preventive, and this is just as important with all other security breaches. Would-be embezzlers should be discouraged from ever beginning.

2. *Minimize the damage if it does happen.* An intruder who succeeds in bypassing the physical or programmed controls that were intended to keep him out should still be very restricted in what he can accomplish. A fire, once started, should be prevented from spreading. If the security procedures are compromised, it must be possible to limit the harm that could result. Some security designers have made the grave error of supposing that their preventive measures will always work.

3. *Design a method of recovering from the damage.* It must be possible to reconstruct vital records or whole files if they become accidentally or willfully damaged or lost. It *must* be possible to recover from a fire sufficiently quickly to keep the business running. If an unauthorized person obtains a security code or a file of network passwords, it must be possible to change these quickly so that they are of no use to him. It is important to attack the security problem *in depth,* and recovery procedures are vital to the overall plan. The designers of the preventive mechanisms must not be allowed to become so infatuated with their schemes that they neglect recovery techniques.

PRIVACY LOCKS   The question of *who* is authorized to do *what* on a network is very important. Before each operation a computer should check that it is an authorized operation.

Authorization schemes vary from being very simple to highly complex. One of the simplest schemes requires the user to enter a *password* which only he should know. If it is an acceptable password for the program or file in question, he is allowed to proceed. The CODASYL Data Description Languages uses *privacy locks* appended to the data. The privacy lock is a single value which is specified in the data description. Data locked in this way cannot be used by a program unless the program provides a value which matches the privacy lock. It is rather like the user of a bank safe needing to know the combination which will open the safe. Unlike a bank safe, however, different combinations can be used for all different data types. The locking mechanism can be much more intricate than with a bank safe.

Figure 36.2 shows a possible sequence of events when a terminal is used, showing the variety of locks that could be applied. No one link through a network is likely to have all of these locks, but it should have several.

AUTHORIZATION SCHEMES

The locks which are built into systems and networks are related to authorization schemes and tables saying who is authorized to do what or what interconnections are permitted.

The authorization tables can relate to:

1. Individual users
2. Groups or categories of users
3. Security levels (top-secret, corporate confidential, etc.)
4. Application programs
5. Time of day (like a time lock on a bank vault)
6. Terminal or terminal location
7. Network node (e.g., host computer, cluster controllers, concentrator)
8. Transaction types
9. Combinations of these

Restrictions can be placed on the relationships between six different entities on a network—the users, the terminals or input/output devices that are used, the network nodes such as host computers or terminal cluster controllers, the application programs, the data sets or elements or data, and the volumes such as tapes or disks on which the data are recorded. Locks may exist on any of these relationships, and alarms may be used to bring attention to any suspected violation.

Figure 36.3 summarizes the relationships that may be locked:

1. The user himself may be identified and locked out of the terminal, or out of the node, program, data, or volume he requests.
2. A specific terminal may be considered in an insecure area and locked out of certain nodes, programs, data, or volumes.
3. A node such as a computer or terminal cluster controller may be locked out of other nodes, programs, data, or volumes.

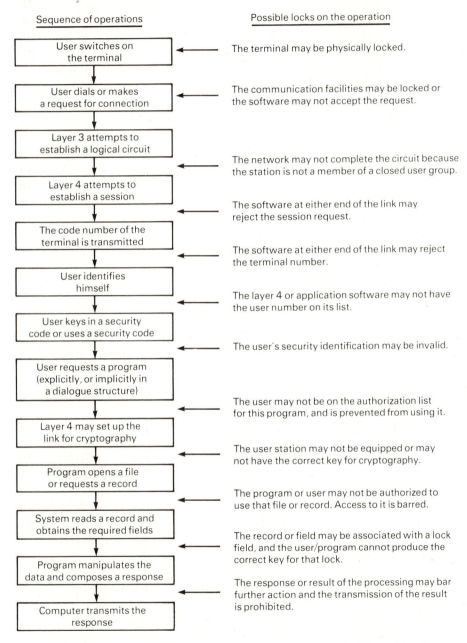

Sequence of operations   Possible locks on the operation

User switches on the terminal	The terminal may be physically locked.
User dials or makes a request for connection	The communication facilities may be locked or the software may not accept the request.
Layer 3 attempts to establish a logical circuit	
Layer 4 attempts to establish a session	The network may not complete the circuit because the station is not a member of a closed user group.
The code number of the terminal is transmitted	The software at either end of the link may reject the session request.
User identifies himself	The software at either end of the link may reject the terminal number.
User keys in a security code or uses a security code	The layer 4 or application software may not have the user number on its list.
User requests a program (explicitly, or implicitly in a dialogue structure)	The user's security identification may be invalid.
Layer 4 may set up the link for cryptography	The user may not be on the authorization list for this program, and is prevented from using it.
Program opens a file or requests a record	The user station may not be equipped or may not have the correct key for cryptography.
System reads a record and obtains the required fields	The program or user may not be authorized to use that file or record. Access to it is barred.
Program manipulates the data and composes a response	The record or field may be associated with a lock field, and the user/program cannot produce the correct key for that lock.
Computer transmits the response	The response or result of the processing may bar further action and the transmission of the result is prohibited.

Figure 36.2 A possible sequence of events when a terminal is used, and locks which could be applied at each stage.

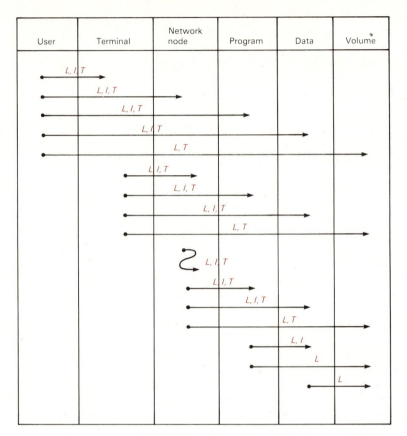

L = based on security *levels* (top secret, secret, corporate confidential).
I = based on *individual* items or persons, or groupings of these.
T = based on *time* of day (like a time lock on a bank vault).

Figure 36.3 Relationships covered by locks, alarms, and authorization tables.

4. A program may be prevented from accessing certain data or volumes.

5. Certain data may have a high security classification and so be prevented from being stored on any volume that has a lower classification.

   The locks may be based on security classification *levels,* on the *individual* entities or groups of entities, or on *time.* These are indicated by the letters L, I, and T, respectively, in Fig. 36.3.

   If security classification levels are used, the types of entities may each be assigned a classification, such as CONFIDENTIAL, SECRET, and so on. If a user is not security-cleared for SECRET information, he will not be permitted to use a terminal classified for SECRET work or permitted to use any program data or volume classified SECRET; SECRET data may not be transmitted to an unclassified terminal. If a volume is not labeled SECRET, SECRET data may not be written on it. And so on. As indicated in Fig. 36.3, any of the relationships may be based on such classification levels. There may be any number of levels.

Much greater precision is obtained by basing the relationships on individual users or entities. User A is only permitted to use program B, data C, and volumes D and E. Program X is only permitted to access data Y and Z. Or a certain file, volume, or program is labeled so that it can only be used by the person who created it. Some such schemes result in the need for large authorization tables. To lessen the size of the tables, the individual persons, items, or data entities can be arranged into groups and the locks based on groupings.

Last, the system may have time locks. Like a bank vault door, access may be permitted only at certain times of day. A *nocturnal* intruder will not be able to access data even if he knows the necessary passwords or security codes. A terminal in a secure area on the prime shift may be classified as insecure on other shifts. If a person is detected trying to use a magnetic-stripe card key on a terminal out of hours, he will immediately trigger an alarm.

ALARMS

To keep burglars out of a building or vault the locks on the windows and doors will be backed up by burglar alarms. The locks on networks, and surveillance methods designed to detect unauthorized entry, can sound alarms. Some systems send an immediate alarm message to a security officer's terminal, and possibly ring a bell there. Some systems inform a suitable authority at the user's location. Some do both. The potential intruder may be locked out of the system or may be kept talking harmlessly while the local security officer investigates.

The existence of alarms, but not the details of how they work or what triggers them, should be well publicized to act as a psychological deterrent.

IDENTIFYING THE TERMINAL USER

With some users of networks it is necessary to identify positively the person at the terminal. Until he is identified he should not be permitted to have access to any sensitive data or to make any modifications to the files. On other systems, it is not necessary to identify the terminal user, provided that the computer knows which terminal it is, because only security-cleared personnel can use that particular terminal.

There are three ways in which a person can be identified:

1. *By personal physical characteristics:* For example, a device can be used for reading and transmitting a person's fingerprints or thumbprint, and the computer can have a program for identifying this. Less expensive, his telephone voice, speaking certain prearranged digits or words, can be transmitted to the computer; the computer will have a program for

recognizing his voice by comparing his speech against a stored *voice print*. Some systems have a device which measures the lengths of a person's fingers on one hand (this being a set of variables which differs from one person to another like fingerprints and is not too expensive to measure and encode). Physical identification schemes are likely to be the most expensive of the three ways to recognize a person.

2. *By something carried:* A terminal user can carry a badge, card, or key. He inserts the badge into a terminal badge reader or the key into the terminal itself. Magnetically encoded cards like credit cards are used for this purpose.

3. *By something known or memorized:* He can memorize a password or answer a prearranged set of questions. Techniques of this type require no special hardware. They are the least expensive of the three, and under most circumstances they can be made reasonably secure if applied intelligently. The user's identification number, however, must not be a number that might be guessed, such as his birth date or car license number.

Keys, locks, machine-readable badges, and plastic cards all have one disadvantage: They can be lost. The user may fail to remove them from the terminal after the transaction is complete. If a sign-on action is used along with a badge or card, the user may forget to sign off. It may be possible to duplicate the key or badge. For these reasons, the use of the key, card, or badge is not necessarily more secure than identification of a terminal operator by a memorized security code or a sequence of questions. Keys on banking system terminals and badges in certain airline systems have been in operation for years, although nobody pretends that they would keep out an ingenious and persistent imposter, any more than an apartment lock would keep out an ingenious and determined burglar. They are better than no lock at all.

On some military systems the terminal has a small fence around it, and the operator cannot leave the area without opening a gate with the same badge or key that he uses on the terminal.

A password has been used on a number of systems to identify the user. In its simplest form, all the terminal users, or users of a given category or at a given location, know the same password; until this is typed in, the system will take no action. For any reasonable measure of security, however, it is desirabe to provide each of the individual terminal users with a different security code. He must type this code into the terminal. The computer will then check what the individual using that code is permitted to do. On some systems, the user keys in his own personal identification number, followed by a security code which has been issued to him. The computer checks that he has entered the correct security code and checks that the transactions he enters are authorized for that individual. A table such as that in Fig. 36.4 may be used. As a result of this check, categories of authorization may be established indicating what types of action the individual is permitted to take.

The security code must be changed periodically. On some systems, it is changed once per month. Each terminal user must take care not to let anyone else know his code. For example, the code for a user may be mailed in such a way that

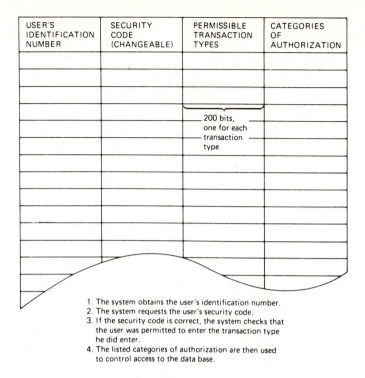

USER'S IDENTIFICATION NUMBER	SECURITY CODE (CHANGEABLE)	PERMISSIBLE TRANSACTION TYPES	CATEGORIES OF AUTHORIZATION

200 bits, one for each transaction type

1. The system obtains the user's identification number.
2. The system requests the user's security code.
3. If the security code is correct, the system checks that the user was permitted to enter the transaction type he did enter.
4. The listed categories of authorization are then used to control access to the data base.

Figure 36.4   Use of a simple authorization table.

the code is on a detachable piece of card with nothing else written on it. The receiver is instructed to detach this piece of card immediately. If the card with the security code on it is lost, anybody finding it is unlikely to associate it with the correct personnel number. It must be possible to issue a user with a new security code whenever he wants it. If he feels that security has been compromised in any way (for example, by someone looking over his shoulder and seeing his security code as he types it in the terminal), then he should be able to ask immediately for a new security code. On some terminals, the security code is automatically prevented from being printed or displayed as it is keyed in.

The disadvantage of the password or security code technique is that the code can be given to another person without any physical loss by the giver and without anything having to be duplicated. There is no physical evidence of the other person's possession of it. This technique must, therefore, be accompanied by rigorous controls and a serious attempt to catch, quickly and automatically, any person who is using another person's code. If the terminal users think that there is a high probability that they will be caught if they attempt to enter the system with another person's code, then they may be deterred psychologically from making an invalid entry.

MESSAGE AUTHENTICATION

Message authentication refers to steps taken to ensure that a message came from a legitimate source or goes to a legitimate destination. It is possible in a network that data might be accidentally misrouted. There have been cases of highly sensitive data being printed at the wrong location. Even the telephone network occasionally gets wrong numbers. It is possible that the misrouting could be deliberate or that an active wiretap is being used by an intruder who wants to gain access to files.

In one message authentication scheme, the sender and receiver put unique pseudorandom numbers on the messages. Both use the same set of numbers. They may both have these numbers stored or may generate them. The receiving software compares the number on the received message with what it expects and takes action if it is not identical.

CLOSED USER GROUPS

Some transport networks, including those using the CCITT X.25 standard, employ the concept of *closed user groups*. A closed user group is a defined set of user machines or processes; they can communicate with one another but can have no communication with machines or processes outside the group. A person at a terminal outside the group cannot use the network to contact a machine or process in the group. On one network there may be many closed user groups and many users who are freely interconnectable because they are not members of such a group.

CRYPTOGRAPHY

The safest way to have reasonable assurance that transmitted data have not been read, copied, or tampered with, is to use cryptography. This means that the data are enciphered before they are transmitted and deciphered after transmission. The enciphering process scrambles the bits so thoroughly that a person wanting the information is unlikely to be able to unscramble them.

Cryptography has been used since the time of the ancient Chinese by spies, lovers, and political schemers. Much has been written about it since the advent of radio and data transmission, and there has been a massive expenditure on it in military and intelligence circles. There are spectacular stories from World War II about enemy codes being broken. Japanese messages planning the bombing of Pearl Harbor were deciphered and then not acted upon.

Cryptography is a fight between the person who enciphers and the person who tries to crack the code. The subject has drastically changed its nature with the advent of computers. The enemy will use a computer to work on cracking the code, searching at high speed through very large numbers of possible transformations. However, the enciphering will also be done by a computer, and an inexpensive algorithm can scramble the data in a truly formidable way. On balance, if both sides act prudently, the sender is better off than the code cracker.

Microelectronics has further changed the applicability of cryptography. Now it can be done with a microprocessor or a special cryptography chip. With this the transmission from a terminal can be enciphered without great expense.

594

On networks, cryptography should be an *end-to-end* process, independent of the transport subsystem. It should thus be considered a function of the control layers external to the transport subsystem.

It is generally desirable for networks to interconnect many different machines from different manufacturers. To use cryptography, two communications machines must employ the same algorithm. One machine may need to contact many different machines on the network. It would help if all cryptography on the network used the same algorithm. If the same algorithm were used by large numbers of machines, it could be implemented in the form of a cheap, mass-produced chip.

Would this be safe? If a mass-produced crypto chip were employed, the enemy also could use it in attempts to break the code. To make such a scheme safe the enciphering must employ not only a suitably complex algorithm but also a *crypto key*. The key is a random collection of bits or characters which the transmitting and receiving stations use in conjunction with the algorithm for enciphering and deciphering (Fig. 36.5). If the enemy knows the crypto algorithm but not the key, it would take a large amount of work for him to break the code.

Many crypto devices use a key of 64 bits. If a code breaker attempted to decipher a message by using a computer to try out keys in a trial-and-error fashion, there would be 2^{64} possible keys to try. If an ultrafast special-purpose computer were used for code breaking which could try out one key every microsecond, the average time taken to find the right key would be

$$\frac{2^{64}}{2} \text{ microseconds} = \frac{2^{64}}{2 \times 1,000,000 \times 3600 \times 24 \times 356.25} \text{ years}$$

That is, 292,271 years.

A key of 80 bits would require a time longer than the age of the universe.

Data to be transmitted is enciphered with a crypto key and encipher algorithm:

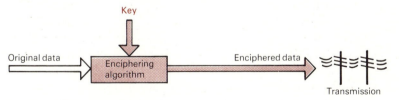

The data received is deciphered with the same crypto key and a decipher algorithm:

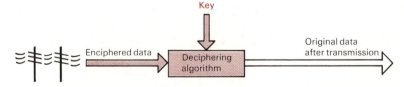

Figure 36.5 Crytography. Both the enciphering/deciphering algorithm and the key must be sufficiently complex.

With such keys complete trial and error will not succeed in breaking cryptography codes. The cryptanalyst is therefore forced to find shortcuts which avoid full trial and error. Consequently the encoding technique must do everything possible to prevent shortcuts from working; the data must be scrambled in a sufficiently complex fashion.

Most of the ciphers used prior to the development of computers can be broken by using computers. Today, however, a microelectronic chip can execute exceedingly complex unscrambling.

There are two ways to make codes uncrackable. One is sufficiently complex key usage; the other is sufficiently complex algorithms. Before computers the safest systems used a key that was used only once. Sometimes the key was very long. Some Army Signal Corps systems used a key which occupied an entire paper roll 8 inches in diameter. Every tenth character was numbered so that the tape could be set up at any designated starting position.

With computer-to-computer transmission, such a technique could employ disks containing keys of many millions of random bits. The sending and receiving installations must both have the same key disk. The enciphering can be simple, quick, and virtually uncrackable if the contents of the key disk are changed frequently. However, this change may be time-consuming.

KEY LEVERAGE   If a cryptographic system is to be secure, it is necessary to *manage* the use of keys securely, and on some networks it is desirable to transmit the keys. This is easier to accomplish if the keys are relatively small. A given quantity of key can be made to encode a larger quantity of data by utilizing it with a more complex algorithm. This is referred to as *key leverage*.

Modern cryptography hardware uses a relatively small key and scrambles it in association with the data in formidable ways. Figure 36.6 shows an enciphering technique employed by an IBM device called Lucifer [2], which was used in conjunction with terminals and computers requiring highly secure transmission. A very broadly similar algorithm from IBM formed the basis of an American federal standard for cryptography.

DATA ENCRYPTION   A national (and international) standard for cryp-
STANDARD   tography is needed in order to permit the machines of
                             many different manufacturers to be interconnected.
Such a standard is likely to be secure and practical if:

1. It scrambles the data sufficiently thoroughly.

2. It uses a long enough key to prohibit trial-and-error methods of code breaking.

3. It does not add significantly to transmission overhead.

4. It can be implemented on a single, mass-produced LSI chip.

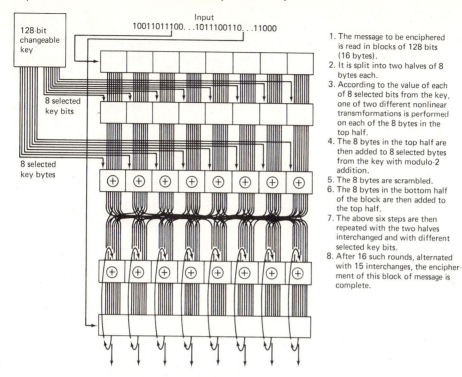

Input
10011011100...1011100110...11000

128-bit changeable key

8 selected key bits

8 selected key bytes

1. The message to be enciphered is read in blocks of 128 bits (16 bytes).
2. It is split into two halves of 8 bytes each.
3. According to the value of each of 8 selected bits from the key, one of two different nonlinear transmformations is performed on each of the 8 bytes in the top half.
4. The 8 bytes in the top half are then added to 8 selected bytes from the key with modulo-2 addition.
5. The 8 bytes are scrambled.
6. The 8 bytes in the bottom half of the block are then added to the top half.
7. The above six steps are then repeated with the two halves interchanged and with different selected key bits.
8. After 16 such rounds, alternated with 15 interchanges, the encipherment of this block of message is complete.

Figure 36.6   The operation of the cryptography module.

The U.S. National Bureau of Standards created a Data Encryption Standard (DES) [3] in 1977. It is now implemented on chips costing less than $50, although the extra equipment needed to employ them is much more expensive.

The data Encryption Standard has two modes of operation, called KAK (Key Auto Key) and CTAK (Cipher Text Auto Key). They are illustrated in Figs. 36.7 and 36.8.

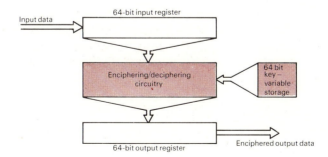

Input data

64-bit input register

Enciphering/deciphering circuitry

64 bit key – variable storage

64-bit output register

Enciphered output data

Figure 36.7

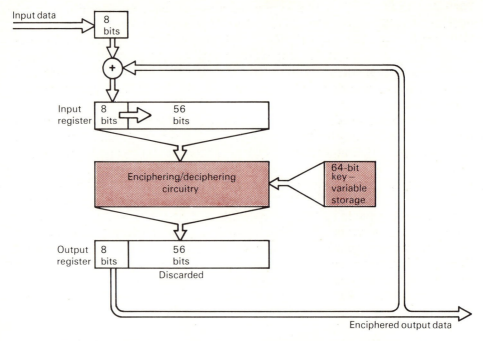

Figure 36.8 The U.S. Data Encryption Standard (DES) operating in Cipher Text Auto Key (CTAK) mode; 64 dummy bits are needed at start up and this degrades throughput especially when the message lengths are short.

In KAK mode the input data are read into a buffer 64 bits at a time. The 64 bits are then scrambled with a 64-bit key (somewhat similarly to Fig. 36.6) to produce 64 bits of output. The encoding operation starts with a START ENCIPHER command and then proceeds without further synchronization until the end of the data. The receiving machine knows when the data start. If a bit is lost in transmission, synchronization is lost and the data will have to be retransmitted.

CTAK mode is more complex and proceeds 8 bits at a time. It is thus convenient for transmitting a stream of 8-bit characters. The input stream enters a 64-bit register in groups of 8 bits until the register is full. Enciphering then occurs using a 64-bit key to produce bits of output. Only the left-hand 8 bits of this are used. They are both transmitted and fed back to be combined with 8 bits of input, as shown in Fig. 36.8. This technique is referred to as cipher-text feedback. It increases the difficulty of attempted code breaking, but it needs a dummy 64 bits entering into the circuit to start up the operation before live data are used. It adds this much overhead to the messages sent. The KAK mode adds no extra bits to the messages.

TIME AVAILABLE FOR BREAKING THE CODE   If a cryptanalyst has a very long time available for breaking a code, he is more likely to succeed. Again, he is more likely to succeed if he has a very large amount of text to work on. The computer system should be designed so that whenever possible it minimizes the time available to the code breaker. This can be done by designing the key so that it can be changed at suitably frequent intervals.

On some systems the time available for cracking the code can be made very short. The intruder may be trying to break into a computer system. However, the key is changed sufficiently frequently that if he takes a day to break the code, the result will still not enable him to gain access to the system.

On the other hand, some commercial data are kept on disk or tape and retain their value for a very long time. Data concerning oil drillings or mineral prospecting, for example, could be of great value to a thief, and in some cases they may retain their value for years. The thief has plenty of time to break the code. In such cases an especially complex algorithm and long key may be used. If a standard algorithm must be employed, many keys may be used for different portions of the data, or the data may be enciphered more than once using different keys.

There are three ways in which the keys used for transmission can be changed frequently enough to be sufficient:

1. They may be changed manually. Some enciphering devices have a small keyboard for the entry of keys.

2. The key may be changed at intervals by a computer which controls a session. The new keys are transmitted to the session participants and automatically loaded.

3. The key may be automatically selected and transmitted to the participants when a session is set up. It would be loaded and the crypto operation checked as part of the function of setting up the session.

In all three methods the new key is transmitted to one or both communicating parties. *That transmission must itself be enciphered.*

Which method is used may depend on the application and the properties of the network software. In an electronic fund transfer application with the machines permanently in session, the keys may be changed automatically. In some banking systems a new key is inserted manually when the system is started up each day. For the once-only transmission of a sensitive file, manual key insertion may be used.

The most satisfactory and trouble-free scheme for many networks is the automatic allocation of keys when a session is established—this being part of the binding process. When a session is set up, a decision is made whether cryptography is necessary or not, and if it is, the keys are allocated. The session management software must be designed to control this process with a suitably high level of security. The fact that cryptography is used in the session can be made completely transparent to the session user.

TIGHT DISCIPLINE   A chip which executes the DES algorithm can be bought at low cost. Unfortunately, much more than the chip is needed to achieve disciplined, secure transmission. The algorithm must be interfaced to the current network equipment and procedures. The message headers *and* trailers must still work correctly. The keys must be generated and managed in a secure fashion. The transmission must recover from failures without giving information to a would-be code breaker.

A wiretapper attempting to break a cipher may deliberately cause failures on the communication line and observe the recovery action that takes place. To stop this technique from being of any value, when an erroneous block is retransmitted it should be enciphered in the same way as the previous block, *using the same key*. This may happen automatically if it is merely a Level 2 error. If the intruder causes a higher-level failure, however, he might be able to cause retransmission of the same message with a different key. Comparing the two could assist him in cryptanalysis, especially if he could do it many times. The protocols should be designed to prevent this.

Synchronization between the transmitting and receiving machines is important with cryptography. Recovery from a loss of synchronization needs carefully thought-out protocols. Everything that can possibly go wrong needs to be carefully tested with the enciphering and deciphering mechanisms.

Cryptography + Loose discipline = Chaos

KEY MANAGEMENT   When a new key is selected at one end of the link, the same key must also be used at the other end. It could be sent by courier. Both systems could have a file of keys and select the next one in the file. More often the key is *transmitted* to the other end.

If a key is transmitted, this must be done securely, so the key is itself enciphered for transmission. What key is used to encipher the key? It could be the previous key used by that machine. This would work if machine A always communicates with machine B. However, if machine A communicates with machine B and then with machine C, how would machine C know what key to use? In some networks a terminal always communicates with the same host. In others there can be diverse interconnections between multiple machines. In the latter case *the machines may have to communicate with a management node to set up a session*. They have a permanent session with this management node, as discussed earlier, and transmission on this session may be enciphered.

Figure 36.9 shows this situation. Machine A contacts its manager and requests a session with Machine B. The manager sets up a session, binding the user processes, and transmits the key to be used to both A and B. This transmission is enciphered with a key stored in both A and the manager, and another key in B and the manager.

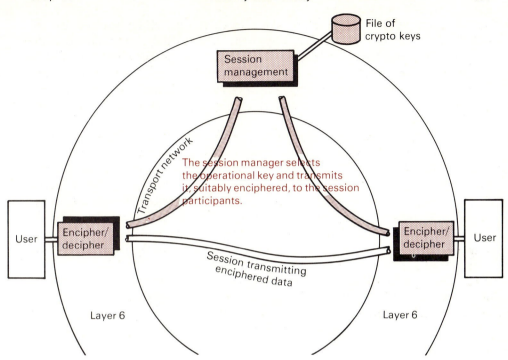

Figure 36.9   The cryptography key to be used in a session is selected at the start of the session by the session manager. The enciphering is completely transparent to the users.

The key which enciphers the data is sometimes called an *operational key*. The key which enciphers the transmission of the operational keys to machines which use them is sometimes called a *second-level key*.

The management node may store many keys, both operational keys and second level keys. This file of keys must be kept very securely, so it is also enciphered, using a *third-level key*.

In IBM systems, software is available for the management of cryptographic keys—the Programmed Cryptograhic Facility [4]. This generates keys using a pseudorandom number generator. It generates and stores operational keys, second-level keys, and third-level keys. The operational keys are employed for enciphering transmitted data or enciphering data stored on disks or tape. The second-level keys (called secondary keys) encipher the operational keys. The third-level keys (called primary keys) encipher the file of keys in which all levels of key are stored. Figure 36.10 illustrates these layers of protection.

All the keys must be generated automatically from a single *master key,* which is entered into the system manually. The set of keys may be changed as often as re-

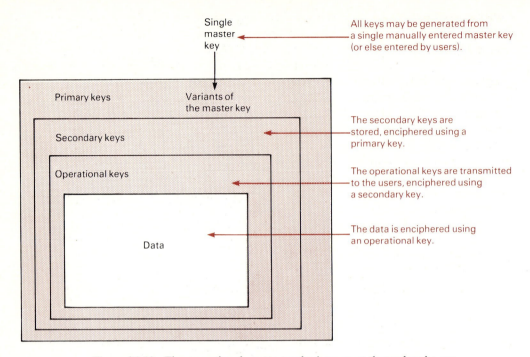

Single
master
key

All keys may be generated from
a single manually entered master key
(or else entered by users).

Primary keys

Variants of
the master key

Secondary keys

The secondary keys are
stored, enciphered using a
primary key.

Operational keys

The operational keys are transmitted
to the users, enciphered using
a secondary key.

The data is enciphered using
an operational key.

Data

Figure 36.10   The operational cryptography keys must themselves be protected by further cryptography.

quired by entering a new master key. When this is done, some of the old keys must
be kept because there are data on the files which are enciphered with them. Alternatively some or all of the keys may be entered manually. There are three types of
second-level key: those for communication between a host and a terminal, those for
communication between two hosts, and those used for enciphering data stored on
disks or tape.

Along with these cryptographic safeguards, it is necessary to have good
physical security with physical locks to prevent the stealing of key files, and good
administrative security to control who has knowledge of the master key or other
keys.

VALIDATION   When keys have been established at each end of a link,
                         the machines may exchange a brief test message to
ensure that the cryptography is synchronized and working correctly. With some
systems, validation can be done with a live message rather than a test message. It
may be sufficient to check that valid characters rather than a jumble of bits are
being received.

WHEN SHOULD CRYPTOGRAPHY BE USED?

Given the right software and hardware, cryptography can be trouble-free and automatic. All of the keys can be generated from a single master key at a major computer center. No overhead *need* be added to the messages except that involved in setting up the session.

Only a small fraction of network transmission needs enciphering, and most terminals and controllers will not have crypto hardware. Wiretapping or tampering with network switching nodes is rare, although it is remarkably easy to accomplish. Most telephone junction boxes in office buildings are unlocked and unprotected. It is easy to connect a tap, via a small isolation transformer out of sight behind the terminal panel, which connects to another line at the end of which the wiretapper can operate in comfort. He may even be able to dial a connection to his tap from his own premises.

Examples of types of transmission which need protecting are

1. Electronic fund transfer. Money transfers of millions of dollars are transmitted between banks in electronic form.

2. Cash-dispensing machines. In some banks these are remote terminals and a customer can withdraw a large sum if it is in his account.

3. Military and intelligence information.

4. Work relating to military contractors.

5. Diplomatic communication.

6. Valuable commercial data, such as oil or mineral prospecting results.

7. Data of value to competition, such as lists of customers, invoices, development plans, details of unannounced products, classified research.

8. Sensitive police or personnel information; payrolls; payroll checks transmitted to a bank.

9. Communication with a system security officer.

A distributed system may be divided into portions which are secure and portions which are not (Fig. 36.11). Certain portions, such as where valuable data are stored, where the crypto keys are stored, and the security officer's area, need to be extremely secure. Physical and administrative security will be maintained in these areas. The transmission links between them should be regarded as nonsecure unless cryptography is used. Certain data should be entered and certain types of interactive usage should occur only at the secure terminals.

Cryptography may be used to make sure that an intruder cannot gain access to the system via the network with a terminal of his own and a false use of passwords.

INDIRECT ADDRESSING

Some networks are designed so that if an eavesdropper records part of a (nonenciphered) session he cannot tell what machines are participating in the session because

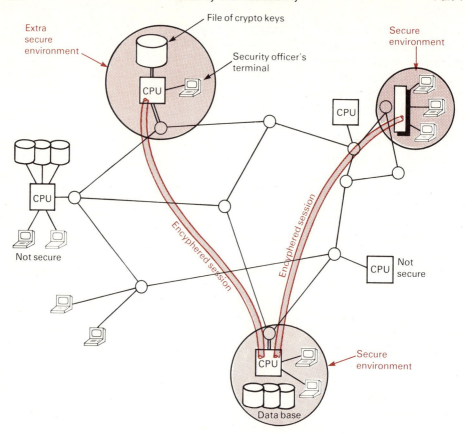

Figure 36.11 Some network facilities are secure and some are not.

the addresses carried by the messages are indirect addresses rather than machine addresses. Two sessions between the same two machines carry different session identifiers which are allocated when the session is set up. Only the nodes which set up the session can convert these identifiers into machine identifications.

THE SYSTEM'S POLICE

To maintain high security in any building or organization, police officers are needed. A secure computer system needs a staff responsible for the security of the data files and the control of the authorization to use these files. A security officer should be appointed as the sole person able to change the authorization tables or file lockword tables in the system. He will have details of what each individual is authorized to read or change on the files. He is responsible for issuing passwords or security codes and for ensuring that they are used correctly.

In a network environment there may be multiple security officers, possibly one associated with each host computer, or one associated with each corporate division or function. In a system with terminals in scattered locations, there should be a person responsible for security in each of these locations, where sensitive data are handled. A suitable person with another job, such as an office manager, can be a local security officer. He takes instructions from the main security officer. The system sends him listings of all detected violations of correct procedure that occur in his location.

When the system detects a violation of correct security procedures, it should immediately take some action. Most terminal users can be expected to make occasional mistakes. When a user's first violation is detected, the computer should ask him to reenter the data and log the fact that the violation occurred. However, if an operator who made a mistake immediately makes a second, again attempting to enter an invalid code or access an unauthorized file, this may be an indication that he is attempting to do something illegal on the terminal. The system may then immediately inform the local security officer in the hope that the culprit will be caught red-handed. This miscreant may be "kept talking" by the system, but locked out of any sensitive files, until he is caught.

A more common approach is to lock the terminal completely the moment the second violation occurs. The application programs are written in such a way that no more information is accepted from that terminal until the condition has been cleared. The only person who can clear it is the security officer for that location.

AUDIT AND CONTROL PROCEDURES

Any persons contemplating an invasion of the files either through curiosity or malicious intent should be deterred by the thought that there is a high probability that the system will detect them and inform the appropriate security officer.

A log should be kept of all violations of correct procedure, for example, when a terminal user types in a security code that is not the one allocated to him or attempts to access a file for which he has no authorization. Details of these violations are printed and sent to the security officers. A branch security officer will receive a listing of all the violations that have occurred within his branch. A file owner will be sent details of all unauthorized attempts to read or change records in his file. This log of violations should be analyzed to detect any unusual activity. Most violations are accidental and caused by a genuine mistake on the part of the terminal operator. The sudden departure from the norm in this activity, however, may indicate that some user is tampering with the system, possibly exploring and trying to find a method of gaining unauthorized access. The list of violations may be printed out once a week; on the other hand, it may pay to do it more frequently on a system containing highly secure and sensitive information. The location security officers may be sent a list of any violations that occur each night. Then a would-be intruder will have little time to practice.

It is particularly important to maintain extremely tight security over the authorization records, passwords, and file lock words, etc. If an imposter can change them, then most of his problems are solved. No one should be given the authority to read or change these records except the file owners or the security officers. If any change is made, then the appropriate file owner or security officer will be sent details of that change the following day. Such changes may be detected on a nightly run by comparing last night's authorization records and file lock tables with those of tonight. If an unauthorized person has managed to make changes in them, it will be detected quickly.

It is recommended that a history be kept in which all changes that are made to these security records are logged, indicating who made the change and where it was made.

A SOLVABLE PROBLEM

There is much more to security than we have described in this chapter, and the reader who would like to read further on the subject should obtain Reference 1.

In general, distributed system security should be regarded as a solvable problem. It needs to be solved at an appropriate cost for the systems in question. The systems analyst responsible for security needs the broadest possible view. Overemphasis on narrow security measures should be avoided.

REFERENCES

1. Computer security techniques in general are described in James Martin, *Security, Accuracy, and Privacy in Computer Systems,* Prentice-Hall, Inc., Englewood Cliffs, N.J., 1973.

2. IBM's Lucifer system is described in IBM Research Reports, Vol. 7, No. 4. Published by IBM Research, Yorktown Heights, NY.

3. Data Encryption Standard (DES), Federal Information Processing Standard #46, National Bureau of Standards, 1977. Available from national Technical Service, U.S. Department of Commerce, 5285 Port Royal Road, Springfield, Va. 22161.

4. *Programmed Cryptographic Facility, OS/VS1 and OS/VS2 MVS. General Information Manual.* IBM Manual No. GC28–0942, Program No. 5740–XY5, IBM, Poughkeepsie, N.Y.

A bibliography on cryptography:

• B. Tuckerman, *A Study of the Vigenere-Vernam Single and Multiple Loop Enciphering Systems,* IBM Report No. RC 2879, Thomas J. Watson Research

Center, Yorktown Heights, N.Y., 1970. (A study of the use of APL for code breaking.)

- B. D. Morgan and W. E. Smith, "Data Encryption: The High Cost of Installing a $50 Chip," *Data Communications,* February 1977.

- *IBM Cryptographic Subsystem: Concepts and Facilities,* IBM Manual No. GC 22-9063, Poughkeepsie, N.Y.

37 AUDITABILITY

Some distributed processing systems have been unauditable. The needs of auditors were forgotten in the enthusiasm of the overall design.

Are distributed systems normally likely to be a problem from the auditing point of view? No. In fact, as we will see, there are certain characteristics of distributed systems which make them attractive to auditors if they are designed appropriately. However, inappropriate DDP design can be a nightmare for the auditor.

An auditor requires a system to have the following properties: *predictability, controllability,* and *ease of examination and verification of what happened.*

PREDICTABILITY   *Predictability* means that for every stimulus to the system one can predict its response. Inputs which would cause unpredictable responses are rejected by the system. To achieve predictability the programs must obey their specifications and the specifications must be complete.

The more complex a system is, the more careful the design must be in order to achieve predictability. Excessively convoluted programs are not predictable, nor are excessively convoluted DDP systems. Instead, the complex system must be split into subsystems each of which is simple enough to be predictable itself, and the subsystems must be interlinked in a simple, precisely defined fashion.

Very complex systems run the danger of being neither predictable nor controllable unless they are divided into subsystems which are themselves predictable and controllable.

A jumbo jet is probably a more complex piece of engineering than a DDP system, but it is remarkably predictable and controllable. It can tolerate many component failures. You can have the failure of an engine or even two, a landing gear control, a navigational computer, radio equipment, the oven, and the movie projector, and it will still land safely.

Similarly, a DDP system can have many failures and problems but still maintain integrity of vital data. Like the jumbo's movie projector, some (in fact much) of a DDP system does not need the tight controls that are applied to the most vital data.

SUBSYSTEMS

Not all applications need auditing. Some distributed facilities are used for obtaining nonsensitive information or for carrying out relatively isolated applications such as shop-floor planning, engineering design, or market research. Auditing controls are necessary on any systems handling financial information, inventory data, personal data, or data which could be used for embezzlement or theft.

To make a complex system auditable it needs to be split into auditable subsystems. Each such subsystem needs to be small or elemental enough to be predictable. The subsystems must communicate only across predefined interfaces and only with a form and content which is precisely specified. The security controls must be such that there is no means of bypassing these predefined communication paths. The capability must exist to record the communication across the interfaces. The time, content, origination, and response must be recordable.

FEATURES WHICH HELP AUDITABILITY

A distributed processing system has certain features which can help auditability. First, by its nature it is compartmental. Peripheral processors are much simpler than mainframes and easier to make predictable and controllable. The great software complexity which has grown up in large mainframes and is now filtering down to small mainframes may be avoided in peripheral processors. Second, the communication paths between the processors are of narrow bandwidth. Cryptography can be used where needed to make them secure. Batches of transmission can be tightly controlled. Critical transmissions can be logged for auditing purposes.

Distributed intelligence can be employed for controlling access to systems. Distributed storage can be used for recording information which an auditor needs.

A trend in minicomputer design is to put operating system functions, storage control functions, and transmission control functions into hardware or microcode. This is very appealing from the auditor's point of view because it means that these functions are standard, predictable, and tamperproof. Such systems are designed to prevent ingenious bypassing of storage access controls, which is always possible with *software* mechanisms. Only by putting such controls in hardware can we be sure that ingenious programmers cannot tamper with them.

An auditable DDP system, then, is one with simple, secure nodes and simple, precisely defined controls. Tight controls prevent unauthorized access to or use

BOX 37.1   What makes systems unauditable

- Lack of audit trails. It is not possible to tell who did what.
- Controls which can be bypassed by ingenious techniques.
- Excessive complexity, so that the auditor cannot tell what happened.
- Data volumes which can be removed and tampered with elsewhere.
- Unauthorized access to a system via a network.
- Higher-level languages giving end users access to files or data bases without adequate controls or journals.
- Distributed data-base operations gathering or associate data from multiple nodes without adequate controls.
- Poor authorization control; unauthorized persons can gain access to the system.
- Integrity problems caused by poor software or inadequate restart-recovery control.
- Unpredictable or uncertain actions taken by programs of excessive complexity. A monolithic program of 50,000 instructions is unauditable.
- Complex and unpredictable patterns of communication between the nodes.

of the nodes. Journals of all critical actions and transmissions are kept. The auditor has the capability to inspect the journals, data, and programs easily.

An *unauditable* DDP system is one in which excessive complexity exists, complex patterns of intercommunication can take place, and appropriate journals are not kept recording who does what. In some DDP systems convoluted, uncontrolled interactions build up. As the software for distribution becomes more flexible and as end user software becomes more powerful, the capability and temptation to build unauditable systems will increase. Box 37.1 lists aspects of systems which can make them unauditable.

AUDITING SOFTWARE AND HARDWARE FEATURES   To render a distributed system auditable and controllable, hardware and software features are desirable which enable the auditor to take the following actions:

1. From one location, often a centralized location, the auditor can investigate what took place at distributed locations.

2. The auditor can establish what transactions were entered and by whom.

3. The auditor can follow the effects of a given transaction. This may involve tracing a transaction as it passes to other machines or subsystems or generates subsidiary transactions which affect other machines or subsystems.

4. As well as sampling routine data for routine checks, the auditor's attention should be drawn to data or transactions which are exceptional for some reason, so that the circumstances surrounding these cases can be investigated.

5. When reversals of processing or corrections of previous processing are made, the auditor must be able to check these and their accuracy.

6. The auditor must be able to check that programs at distributed locations have not been tampered with. The processing must be a reliable, repeatable process which conforms to specifications.

7. The auditor should be able to know what failures have occurred, how frequently, and what action was taken. He must ensure that the effects of failures not cause lasting damage.

8. The auditor should check the accuracy of the data input operations, which are often taking place on distributed machines.

9. The security and privacy controls should be as automatic as possible, with the auditor able to check their effectiveness.

10. The integrity controls and protection from the effects of machine, software, and line failures should be as automatic as possible, and the auditor should be able to check their effectiveness.

Box 37.2 lists hardware and software features to facilitate auditing control of distributed systems. This is a formidable list, and it is desirable that as much of it as possible should be purchased in the form of standard, fully debugged products.

The best manufacturers' architectures for distributed processing contain much that facilitate auditing and control. If a system consists of diverse machines not from an architected family, then either many auditing features have to be dispensed with, or much auditing software has to be specially written. Usually the geographically separate machines have to be audited separately rather than an auditor at one location having access to the distributed machines.

END-USER POWER   To some extent there is a conflict between the desire in distributed systems to allow the users to "do their own thing" and the need for tight controls and good auditing. The auditor must ensure that users are prevented from taking certain types of action, because if they did the auditor would lose control and not be able to ensure system integrity.

Some of the high-level dialogues and languages, designed to give as much power as possible to end users unskilled in computing, are anathema to the auditor. Their use needs to be carefully controlled with appropriate locks, logs, authorization controls, and security controls.

On some distributed systems that have been installed, it is not possible to tell

BOX 37.2 Software and hardware features to assist in the auditing of distributed systems

1. Software enables the auditor to examine all files from a central location. The files are protected so that the user of such a facility cannot damage the files.

2. Software enables the auditor to perform all terminal functions from a central location, as though he were at a remote location.

3. All end-user actions which modify data can be logged automatically with a time, date, and end-user identification. End-user *reading* of sensitive data may also be logged.

4. All file changes are automatically logged. These logs are designed to be used for reconstructing the data as well as for auditing it.

5. When one input affects several nodes or subsystems, the flow of information across nodes or subsystem boundaries should be traceable.

6. When data are updated incorrectly and corrections are subsequently made, these should be separately logged and brought to the auditor's attention.

7. Software permits the auditor to inspect all of the above logs from a central location.

8. Documentation at a central location shows what data and programs reside at distributed locations.

9. The auditor is able to examine programs in distributed machines from a central location. The software may permit him to transmit the programs to a central machine and compare them with locked and separately stored master copies.

10. The auditor has access to stored copies of source code, compilation listings, and symbol cross references.

11. A flag is automatically set if the system software or executives are modified. Any such modifications are automatically brought to the auditor's attention.

12. A list of all software modifications is automatically maintained at the auditor's location.

13. Highly sensitive portions of software may be in tamperproof microcode. Microcoding the file-access routines could prevent the automatic logs and safeguards from being bypassed.

14. All distributed processors have locks to prevent tampering with software.

15. Software enables the auditor to send his own programs to remote machines for testing purposes.

16. The auditor has his own securely locked files in the distributed machines. He

BOX 37.2 *continued*

can run transactions against these files to ensure that they are processed as executed. He can enter such transactions from the center as though they were external from peripheral machines and can follow the results where more than one computer is affected.

17. Every user is positively identified when signing on to the system, and each user has a unique number.

18. Authorization tables control the users' access to data, software, application programs, and machine resources, and also control which programs can access which data.

19. The authorization tables are securely locked and accessible only by appropriate security officers and auditors. The auditor can check these tables and all changes to them from the central location.

20. End-user data manipulation software, report generators, etc., are tightly controlled with user authorization controls. Users are restricted to a certain limited view of the overall system data. Logs are kept of all changes made to data. With sensitive data a log is kept of all accesses. Accesses to all data may be logged for billing purposes.

21. There should be an automatic log of all processor operator actions.

22. All violations of security procedures should be automatically logged.

23. All system failures, machine checks, line failures, etc., should be automatically logged, with date/time stamps. Statistical summaries of numbers of failures and transmission errors should be recorded.

24. The auditor should have access to all such logs from a central location. He may be able to inspect them in a last-in-first-out sequence (the most recent ones first). He should be able to correlate the failures with operator actions taken.

25. Units with removable media should be locked.

26. All removable media must have a volume and serial identification number, and their use should be automatically logged.

27. Because there is often little physical security at the distributed locations, and various employees can approach the processor, the range of operator actions at the processor may be restricted.

28. The distributed processors should be locked to prevent tampering or change of programs.

29. A thorough set of integrity controls should be applied to all data entry. Responsibility for accuracy of data entry should be clearly established. The auditor should have a means of checking the degree of accuracy.

continued

BOX 37.2   *continued*

30. All data entry and changes to data are regarded as temporary until a process *commitment* is made. If the process does not complete, the system automatically backs out and resets any data which have been changed.

31. When two processors attempt to update the same data, one of them is automatically locked from the data until the other has finished.

32. Exception codes are returned to programs when errors, security violations, failures, etc., occur. The auditor should check what actions the application programs take when these codes are returned.

33. When new records are entered, the system should check that their key is unique.

34. Teleprocessing controls should ensure that transmitted data are not damaged, lost, or accidentally double-entered. The controls require tight line-control procedures and end-to-end controls on critical data involving serial numbers and batch hash totals. The auditor should ensure that the controls are adequate. They are likely to be adequate if good end-to-end network architectures are used.

35. Counts of messages transmitted, amount totals, and hash totals may be automatically recorded for audit checking.

how a powerful end-user language was employed, what transactions passed from one machine to another, or what exactly transpired at the various minicomputer locations.

Nevertheless, the need to put more powerful resources into the users' hands is paramount. It is highly desirable to employ some of the end-user data-base software *even though it has inadequate controls from an auditor's point of view.* How can this dilemma be resolved?

First, the end-user software can be isolated in the end-user machine. Often it is permitted to access *only* the data in that machine.

Second, if such software *can* access data in a remote machine, it may be confined to reading those data and not permitted to modify them in any way. Appropriate security controls will be applied to the remote data, and audit trails will be maintained on all transmitted requests.

Third, the files or data bases which are used by end-user software may be created especially for that user. The end users are permitted to do whatever they want with their own data but not to invade anybody else's data. This principle is a particularly important one and can apply to both use of remote data and of data in the user's machine. Some languages, such as IBM's Query-by-Example, do not work with a traditional data base but with a specialized one that is created from the traditional data base (or files).

Fourth, it is necessary to divide computer usage into that which must be audited because money and goods are at risk and that which need not. The former needs tight, rigorous control. That latter needs control sufficient only to prevent system harm. Many end-user systems which are extremely valuable fall into the latter category: information systems showing what types of customers are ordering what products, graphics systems for planning equipment layout, financial modeling systems, systems for scheduling work through the factory, portfolio management systems, cash flow and budget planning systems, and so on. Such systems can employ high-level software, and provided it is restricted in its domain of use, it needs to be of only limited concern to the auditors.

PHYSICAL OPERATING ENVIRONMENT　Many distributed processors are quite different from centralized facilities in this physical environment. They are located in conventional office space without the controlled access to the machine room that major computers have. Anyone can walk up to the machine. It is desirable that stray personnel not be able to tamper with the distributed processors in a way that can do harm, modify programs, or damage the data.

The operating staff are likely to be less skilled and also less controlled. The distributed processors should therefore be designed to run with as little operator intervention as possible and as little scope as possible for operators taking actions which cause problems. There is unlikely to be the separation of duties of DP personnel used to aid security in big systems, or the machine scheduling, input/output control section, tape and disk library controls, and so on. Sometimes the auditors want to avoid having removable disks and disk libraries at the distributed sites. If removeable media *are* used, they want the disk or other media units to be lockable.

Some distributed processors have no operator's console like that on central or stand-alone systems. They are operated from a terminal. The IBM 8100 processor has a key lock with three positions: ENABLE, POWER-ONLY, and SECURE. When set to the ENABLE position, all switches on the processor are active. When set to POWER-ONLY, only the power ON and OFF switches are active, When set to SECURE, the processor may be powered down but only the key holder can turn it on. The desire to make operating procedures as simple as possible can coincide with the auditor's desire to control the actions of the distributed operators.

Many distributed processors are designed so that they can be left unattended. Some can be switched off from a central location or by an instruction in a jobstream following the last job.

The operating systems of peripheral processors may be designed so that all difficult operator actions are taken at the central machine to which they are attached. At this location there will be skilled operating staff. With this consideration there may be a substantial difference between a minicomputer designed for conventional stand-alone operation and one designed as a peripheral node of a distributed system.

It will greatly add to the security of a peripheral system if the local staff are locked out of its control programs so that no ingenious tampering can take place. They cannot bypass the auditing and security controls. This is especially true with the file or data-base management subsystem. The controls must not be circumventable so that records can be illicitly read or modified.

GOOD AND BAD DESIGN

We can return to the theme of good and bad design of distributed processing.

As we have said before, good design simplifies rather than complicates the overall structure of the system. A good DP system has relatively simple nodes at end-user locations. They are easy to install and easy to operate but cannot easily be tampered with. They have tightly controlled transmission links via a standardized flexibility network. They avoid the excessive software complexity that has grown up over the years in highly generalized mainframes.

It is said that if you open a can of worms it takes a larger container to recan them. The software of generalized mainframes has been recanned many times. Distributed processors ought to avoid this complexity and use new, simply structured software.

There is much to be said for having nonremovable disks for the data storage of peripheral processors. They are large enough for many locations, simplify the system operation, and improve its security.

Programs for many on-line peripheral systems may be down-line loaded from a central host. Again, this improves security. The programs should reside in the peripheral system so that it can carry out useful functions when cut off from the host by failures. But the programs should be controlled and maintained centrally.

Some minicomputers now have part of their control mechanisms in hardware or microcode rather than in software. Storage management and data-base management functions are also in hardware and microcode. This improves machine efficiency and can also improve security. Putting critical controls into hardware or microcode ensures that they cannot be bypassed by ingenious software experts.

Transmissions of *critical* data are safeguarded by cryptography. The cryptography mechanisms are better implemented in hardware (crypto chips) than software. All critical transmissions are logged for recovery and auditing purposes.

High-level inquiry, report generation and data manipulation languages are provided to users to put as much capability into their hands as possible. But their use is rigorously controlled and audited where necessary. They must be prevented from accessing unauthorized data, tampering with data, or obtaining data by accident. Any modification of data should be restricted to data which they own, and preferably this should reside in their own machine.

The searching of data, or information system activities in general, should usually be designed to take place on separate systems which are designed for this purpose. Data with a high level of secondary-key or inverted-file activities should usually be created separately from data for production runs, for reasons of improving performance, avoiding scheduling problems, and lessening the complexity of individual system nodes.

Again, data with which the end users "do their own thing" should be created separately for this purpose. The users should be given powerful software and a large amount of freedom with data created for them. They should be locked out of other users' data, master files, and data for production runs.

Although it is *possible* to build distributed data systems of great flexibility (such as SDD-1), caution should be used about employing this flexibility. It can result in highly convoluted, unauditable patterns of activity. Queries resulting in distributed activities like those in Fig. 22.10 are not a good idea for most commercial systems. For commercial distributed data systems, secondary key or searching activities should take place *within one node*. Primary key queries may employ remote machines, as they are relatively simple.

Nodes may be destroyed or damaged. A system should be designed so that it can be replaced and its data reconstructed. This is usually easy with peripheral processing but may be difficult with a large, central data-processing center. The concept of having *one* large, centralized location should be questioned. Some DP centers are now becoming too difficult to reconstruct after a catastrophe such as fire or bombs. A bicentral or decentralized system may be preferable. Many large corporations in recent years have split a central DP location and created a second version of the facilities with appropriate network connections.

Good DDP design, then, consists of discrete systems with secure interconnections between them. The subsystems are either auditable or rigorously confined to work which does not need to be audited in detail. The configuration is not vulnerable to the destruction of any one node. The subsystems avoid excessive complexity, and the overall configuration avoids convoluted interrelations between the subsystems. The end-user facilities are made as powerful and easy to use as possible. Tight security controls prevent unauthorized access, and the systems are designed to prevent the controls from being bypassed. Auditing of subsystems can be carried out remotely from central locations. The transport network is a discrete subsystem standardized and flexible in its interconnections. All communications across it are auditable and adhere exactly to specified format and content.

The designer should have in mind an image of separate autonomous nodes, each appearing to be simple to its users—the complexities hidden under the covers. The network interconnecting them is standard, flexible, and also appears to be simple, like the telephone network (again, its complexities are hidden under the covers). The decision of what happens on end-user processors and what happens on centralized processors is carefully thought out. The pattern of transmissions between the nodes is simple. The transmissions are secure, rigorously specified, and auditable. Each autonomous node is completely auditable except where it has been decided that this is not necessary.

INDEX

624   Index

U

Unauditable systems, 608
Uncontrolled distributed processing, 79
UNIVAC, 517
Unprofessional implementation, 78
Up-line loading, 495
U.S. Bureau of Standards, 595
User groups, 78
User requirements understanding, 22

V

Vertical distribution, 92, 124
Video communications, 68
Vietnam war, 220-23
Virtual terminals, 425

W

Word processing, 51-53
    speech-input, 53-54
Work queue management, 57
Working from home, 57-58

X

XTEN, 90, 423

Z

Zones of compatability, 560-67

BOOKS ABOUT DATA-BASE SYSTEMS:

PRINCIPLES OF DATA-BASE MANAGEMENT

An introduction to data-base systems and their use in corporations; management information systems; a survey of the principles likely to make such systems succeed.

COMPUTER DATA-BASE ORGANIZATION Second Edition

A guide to data base design, desig objectives; principles of data bas software; a survey of the alterna logical and physical structures an their trade-offs.

BOOKS ABOUT TELEPROCESSING:

INTRODUCTION TO TELEPROCESSING

Intended to provide the easiest possible means of learning the essential facts about data transmission. Contains detailed summary tables of all aspects of the subject.

TELEPROCESSING NETWORK ORGANIZATION

An explanation of the many typ of devices and procedures for co trolling and organizing the flow data on today's telecommunicatic lines.

BOOKS ABOUT TELECOMMUNICATIONS:

TELECOMMUNICATIONS AND THE COMPUTER Second Edition

A description of the working of t world's telecommunication links a their uses for data transmissio

COMMUNICATIONS SATELLITE SYSTEMS

An explanation of communicatio satellites and how they affect syster design: technology, tradeoffs, desi strategies.

BOOKS ABOUT INTERACTIVE SYSTEMS:

DESIGN OF REAL-TIME COMPUTER SYSTEMS

An overall review of technical co siderations and calculations in t design and implementation of re time systems.

KEY:

INTRODUCTORY BOOKS
These books are an easy-to-read introduction to the subjects.

DETAIL BOOKS

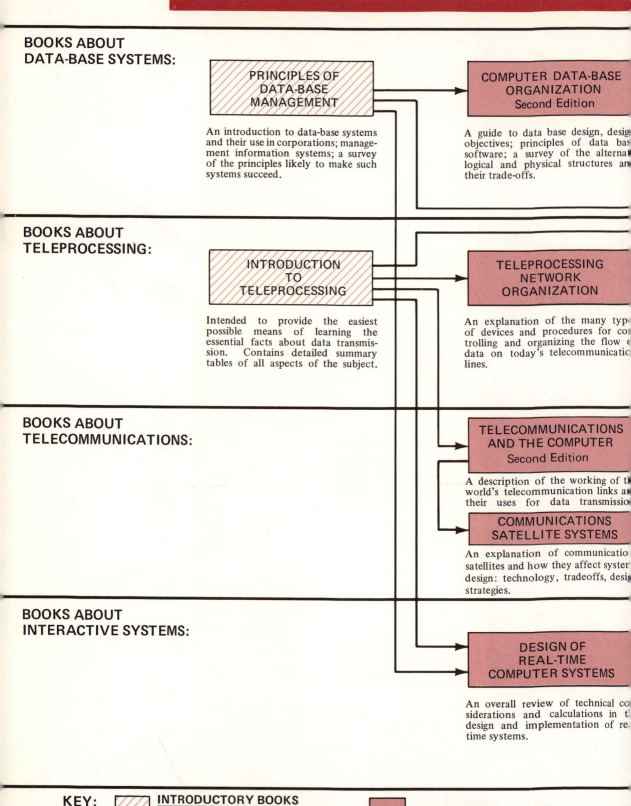